A History of the Canadian Economy

A HISTORY OF THE CANADIAN ECONOMY

Kenneth Norrie

Douglas Owram

Harcourt Brace Jovanovich, Canada

Toronto Orlando San Diego London Sydney

Canadian Cataloguing in Publication Data

Norrie, K. H. (Kenneth Harold), 1946–
A history of the Canadian economy

Includes bibliographical references.
ISBN 0-7747-3087-0

1. Canada - Economic conditions. I. Owram, Douglas, 1947– . II. Title.

HC113.N67 1991 330.971 C90-093474-3

Acquisitions Editor: Heather McWhinney
Developmental Editor: Iris Coupe
Managing Editor: Liz Radojkovic
Editorial Assistant: Robert Gordon
Copy Editor: Beverley Beetham Endersby
Cover and Interior Design: Leslie Smart & Associates Limited
Typesetting and Assembly: True to Type Inc.
Printing and Binding: The Alger Press Limited

Cover: *Lights of a City Street*, 1894, by F.M. Bell-Smith. Reproduced by permission of Simpsons Limited.

♾ This book was printed in Canada on acid-free paper.

1 2 3 4 5 95 94 93 92 91

To Paul and Erika, and to Kristine

Preface

Canada has a rich economic history for a nation that is, in the scheme of things, rather young. Endowed with an abundance of resources, vast territory, and varied climate, this nation has gone through many stages in its economic development. Native hunting and agricultural economies had evolved for centuries before European contact. Once that contact occurred, there was a complex mingling of the transatlantic economies as Europeans and natives looked to each other for trade and betterment. Gradually, though not for a surprisingly long time, the native economy gave way to the European-based one. Within both native and European systems, however, the essence of the Canadian economy has been primary resources through much of our history. Fur, fish, timber, agriculture, and minerals are the seemingly unromantic forces that have shaped not only the trade patterns but the social, governmental, and material realities of Canadian development. For a long time, these resources were practically the whole story. Even in the complex industrial and postindustrial structures of the twentieth century, they remain extremely important. Recent research has also shown, however, how any emphasis on resource activities must be mitigated by attention to the numerous other forces that shaped Canadian economic development over the years if a full understanding of the complexities of the subject is to be achieved.

This rich history has attracted considerable attention from scholars, and our purpose in writing this book was to structure and synthesize the vast array of research that has taken place on the elements which make up the Canadian economy. We wanted to put the pieces together to try to give the reader an overview of what has occurred over the past four centuries or more. Moreover, we very much wanted to present this story as one that, amid the tables, charts, and trade issues, was related to real lives and real places. Economic activity is a central human preoccupation and always has a political, a social, and a human context. Thus, to the degree that it was possible, we wanted to maintain a flavour of the times and of the progress of time. Thus, this is a story, as well as an analysis, of that very central theme in Canadian history — the search for material betterment.

This book was co-authored by a historian and an economist. Obviously, economic history is at the transition point between two disciplines. Historians and economists both have, through the years, written and taught in the field while eyeing their rivals, their demeanours part supportive and enthusiastic, part suspicious and critical. The result has been two streams of literature that have often been surprisingly divergent in method and readership. This fact seemed to rob the field of one of its greatest strengths — its multidisciplinary nature. We hoped that, by working together, we might bring the strengths of both disciplines to bear in a book that would draw upon the substantial work that has been done in recent years in both history and economics; the two disciplinary approaches could thus reinforce each other and act as a check on the excessively extravagant claims of each. This is what we have tried to do. It was an instructive experience, and, at times, we found it to be a revealing one — both about the limitations in our own knowledge and for what it said about the unnecessary divisions between our disciplines. Any frustrations (and there are always some) were, however, far outweighed by the positive outcomes. This was a challenging project, but it was educational for us and ultimately rewarding. Of course, it is our hope that the reader will have the same response.

In a project as wide-ranging as this one, we were, of course, very much dependent not only on the vast extant secondary literature but also on the advice and wisdom of our colleagues in both history and economics. Paul Voisey, David Mills, John Foster, and Gerhard Ens of the Department of History, and Mike Percy of the Department of Economics, at the University of Alberta read parts of the manuscript and were kind enough to comment upon it. At the University of Manitoba's Department of History, Barry Ferguson did the same. As well, the three anonymous readers gave many helpful suggestions. Many other colleagues, in Canadian and European history, were infinitely helpful in discussions on the literature and with ideas for substance and organization. We sometimes underrate the importance of these coffee sessions to the success of our work.

Our thanks, as well, to the very patient secretarial assistance we received. While we may have tried to bring the disciplines together, we never did manage to do the same with our computer preferences or equipment. Thus, it was left to Vanessa Radke and Charlene Hill to bring the distinct first drafts together and, later, to merge the final draft into a single and consistent form. They did an admirable job of making order out of the chaos of computer files and drafts.

At Harcourt Brace Jovanovich, Canada, two people deserve special mention. First, Heather McWhinney must take much of the credit or blame for this book. When we first broached an idea that still seemed rather daunting to us both, she reacted with enthusiasm and support. Before we knew it, her enthusiasm had converted our idea into a project (with a contract and a deadline!). She continued to be supportive even as the original deadline had to be moved back. Later, when the project turned into something approaching its final form, it was left to Iris Coupe to make our manuscript complete, ordered, coherent, and pleasing to work with. She did an admirable job and showed patience in the face of pressing deadlines and authors who never seemed to be available when needed. Our thanks as well to two people who were instrumental in the final stages of the long process from manuscript to book. Liz Radojkovic, managing editor, and Beverley Endersby, the copy editor, did an excellent job of refining the text and ensuring that all the pieces fit together. Altogether Harcourt Brace Jovanovich, Canada has been crucial to the success of this large and complex endeavour.

Kenneth Norrie and Doug Owram
University of Alberta
January 1990

Publisher's Note to Instructors and Students

This textbook is a key component of your course. If you are the instructor of this course, you undoubtedly considered a number of texts carefully before choosing this as the one that will work best for your students and you. The authors and publishers of this book spent considerable time and money to ensure its high quality, and we appreciate your recognition of this effort and accomplishment.

If you are a student, we are confident that this text will help you to meet the objectives of your course. You will also find it helpful after the course is finished, as a valuable addition to your personal library. So hold on to it.

As well, please don't forget that photocopying copyright work means the authors lose royalties that are rightfully theirs. This loss will discourage them from writing another edition of this text or other books, because doing so will simply not be worth their time and effort. If this happens, we all lose — students, instructors, authors, and publishers.

And since we want to hear what you think about this book, please be sure to send us the stamped reply card at the end of the text. This will help us to continue publishing high-quality books for your courses.

Contents

Introduction

The structure of this book very much reflects the fact that it is a synthesis, written by two authors, from two disciplines. Preparing a survey of more than five centuries of Canadian economic history means making choices about what to cover and how to cover it. Having two authors rather than one, from two disciplines rather than one, complicates the process of choice (although, one hopes, it enriches the outcome). Our approach to the challenge was to try to define from the outset what we were attempting to do in a work such as this one. To this end, we found it useful to ask ourselves three specific questions: What do readers expect of an economic-history text? What are the strengths and the limitations of the existing literature — the tradition, if you will? How does our work add to or alter that tradition? The structure of this book followed naturally once these issues were resolved.

From all the individual reasons that people read an overview of Canadian economic history, two general perspectives are discernible. Interestingly, the perspectives are at least loosely affiliated with the two disciplines involved. The first emphasizes the past. Readers with this perspective want to know why events unfolded as they did, and what life was like in times and circumstances removed from their own. How did the native population live prior to European contact? Why were France and Britain the main colonial powers over this land? Why did Canadians resist the entreaties of their counterparts in the American colonies to join the revolution? Did living standards rise as Canadian farmers gained preferential access to the U.K. market in the first half of the nineteenth century, or fall when they lost it at midcentury? Why did Confederation come when it did, in the form it did? What was the impact of the wheat boom? Are the origins of the Great Depression more directly traceable to external or to domestic factors? To what extent did the economic dislocation of World War II change the economic fortunes of women?

For other readers, knowledge of the past is sought as a key to understanding the present and to forming some impressions of the future. This perspective creates its own set of questions. Why is Canada among the richest and most economically advanced nations in the world today? What connections are there between this fact and the observations that we are a relatively small nation, that we depend disproportionately on natural-resource production, and that we are among the most trade-dependent economies in the industrial world? Is the economy more cyclically stable today than in the past? How did we come to be as regionally diverse as we obviously are? Has economic opportunity become more equal over time, whether viewed across regions, across groups, or among individuals?

In both general perspectives, interest extends beyond mere description to explanation, and even to evaluation. Readers want to know not just what happened but also why events turned out as they did. They want, as well, to be able to assess the developments. Did we Canadians do as well as we might have, given our endowments and the international environment we faced? Specifically, did we make the best use of the economic opportunities we had, given what we as a society were trying to achieve? Were the benefits and the costs of economic change shared fairly, however we may define that term?

There is a rich tradition of economic-history writing in Canada. Formal study of the subject dates from shortly before World War I, when new academic creatures known as social scientists or political economists began to make their appearance in Canadian universities. Adam Shortt at Queen's (appointed in 1888), James Mavor at the University of Toronto (appointed in 1892), and Stephen Leacock at McGill (appointed in 1903) were among the first generation of Canadian economists, and each saw economic history as a means of comprehending economic development in a nation such as ours. The tradition they established has influenced Canadian economic writing for many decades.

In spite of their rather small and humble presence at the end of the nineteenth century, economic historians were soon an important part of the academic community. Canada was undergoing rapid urbanization and industrialization, and explanations of what was happening were increasingly in demand. Indeed, it is possible to talk about the initiation of a "golden age" in Canadian economic history, beginning about the time of World War I. In a multivolume series entitled *Canada and Its Provinces*, published in 1914, economic history was very much present, notably in essays by Shortt and his younger colleague O.D. Skelton. From that point through to World War II, Canadian economic history was central to both of the disciplines from which it was derived. The economics profession was dominated by such figures as H.A. Innis of Toronto and W.A. Mackintosh of Queen's. Both were historical in their approaches to research and the analysis of problems. History, which previously had been oriented toward constitutional issues, increasingly fell under the spell of the exciting themes developed by the economists. Thus, Donald Creighton, Arthur Lower, J.B. Brebner, and others wrote books that drew upon the themes developed by the political economists.

For much of the first half of the century, then, economic history was seen as crucial to an understanding of Canada. Books such as Harold Innis's *History of the Canadian Pacific Railway* (1923) or Donald Creighton's *Commercial Empire of the St. Lawrence* (1937) were central both to history and to economics. Later, sociologists, such as Carl Dawson of McGill and S.D. Clark of Toronto, carried the historical tradition into their disciplines. Syntheses and college texts in economic history also abounded, including such works as Mary Quayle Innis's *An Economic History of Canada* (1935) and A.W. Currie's *Canadian Economic Development* (1942). Perhaps the most impressive example of this sort of work, and certainly the most massive, came in the late 1930s. The Royal Commission on Dominion-Provincial Relations (the Rowell-Sirois Commission), which was appointed in 1937, and reported in 1941, continued the tradition with masterful historical studies. Works developed for this commission, such as Donald Creighton's *British North America at Confederation* and W.A. Mackintosh's *Economic Background to Dominion-Provincial Relations*, remain important research sources to the present day.

The core of this historical tradition lay in what may justly be regarded as Canada's major contribution to economic theory during these years. The staples thesis, pioneered in Canada by Mackintosh in his 1923 article "Economic Factors in Canadian History,"[1] and

Innis in his *The Fur Trade in Canada: An Introduction to Canadian Economic History*, published in 1930, drew upon and further developed an idea expounded by American economic historian G.S. Callender. The thesis, as developed in this country, argued that the various stages in colonial development depended on the exploitation of a succession of key primary resources. The characteristics of the staples, from the technology of their production to the social infrastructures needed to support them, set the pattern of economic and political development of the colony. Canada, from the period of the fur trade of New France through that of the vast wheat exports in the early twentieth century, seemed an especially good example of the staples thesis at work in history.

The theory was reinforced by Canada's strength in another discipline, historical geography. Innis was familiar with the geopolitical theories of such leading geographers as Marion Newbigin, and saw them as particularly relevant to a nation like Canada, with such a vast landmass.[2] W.A. Mackintosh made his contribution to the massive series on prairie settlement in a work that combined geography and economics, *Prairie Settlement: The Geographical Setting* (1934). The course of rivers, the extent of agricultural and timber land, the forbidding Canadian Shield, the inhospitable Arctic, and especially distance and climate were obvious elements in Canadian history and fit in with the emphasis on resources inherent in staples theory. The land and its resources thus dominated the attempt by social scientists to understand Canadian development in the first half of the twentieth century.

The nature of the staples thesis and its strengths and weaknesses show up clearly in one of the latest and one of the best of the staples-tradition textbooks. W.T. Easterbrook and H.G.J. Aitken's *Canadian Economic History*, first published in 1956, used the themes developed over the previous 30 years to analyze Canadian development in the staples tradition. The fish of the Grand Banks, the fur trade of New France, the timber trade of the Canadas and New Brunswick, the wheat trades of central Canada and then the west provided the series of successful staples that allowed Canada to develop. Canals and railways followed in their wake, as governments assisted in economic development. Finally, the authors were acutely sensitive to how dependent Canada was on the international situation.

Excellent though Easterbrook and Aitken's work is, by today's standards it has at least three limitations. First, and most obviously, the book is more than 30 years out of date. We now have better data for the historical period and, thanks to the efforts of countless scholars in several disciplines, we know much more about the course of economic and social development. Many of the generalizations they were forced to make have since been abandoned, or at least modified.

The other two limitations are more fundamental. Easterbrook and Aitken's text loses much of its momentum as it moves beyond the agricultural economy of the pre–World War I era and tries to come to grips with modern industrial Canada. The authors abandon historical evolution and settle, instead, on a series of theme chapters, looking at some of the key sectors of the twentieth century. This approach was necessary, in part because the transformation was still quite recent at the time they wrote and in part because the organizing principle of the work, staples, had less and less relevance as the story of Canadian development moved toward the present.

The third limitation is related to the second. Critics of the staples school have commented on the way important sectors, or even whole regions, disappear from history once they no longer fit within the staples argument. Thus, the Maritimes are important during the great days of cod fishery, but are not easily comprehended (and, thus, not dealt with to any degree) once attention has turned to new staples. Central Canadian agriculture is crucial during the pre-Confederation era, but, as net exports disappear shortly thereafter, the sector sinks from sight. Likewise for the timber trade: it virtually disappears from the narrative with the abolition of preferential British duties in the mid-nineteenth century, reappearing again after 1900 as a new staple pulp and paper.

In sum, traditional Canadian economic-history writing appeals because it is eclectic. Economic developments are described in considerable detail, and political and social factors are woven in as a necessary part of the narrative. That very breadth is, at the same time, the main limitation of the approach. Connections between events are not always drawn explicitly, correlation is sometimes taken to imply causality, and qualitative conclusions are often given when quantitative ones are called for. Nor do accounts often move beyond description and explanation, to evaluation. Events are set out in detail, but there is little attempt to assess them by comparing what was to what might have been.

Even as Easterbrook and Aitken wrote, different approaches were beginning to dominate economics, in Canada as elsewhere. New specialties had emerged in the graduate schools, and a new emphasis on quantification and theory had severed economics from its political-economy roots. It was not long before economic historians, seeking to keep pace with modern techniques, abandoned the historical approach in favour of model-building, quantification, and hypothesis-testing. Historians, for their part, increasingly turned their backs on economics and were rarely comfortable with the esoteric symbolism of the "new" economic history. The two disciplines increasingly went their own ways.

The new economic history in Canada eventually produced its own textbooks. They updated our knowledge of recent research and introduced the findings of the new economic-history research to a more general audience. To do so, however, they had to move from a chronological to a thematic approach. As the first of the new texts — that by William L. Marr and Donald G. Paterson, *Canada: An Economic History* (1980) — states, "Such an ordering of historical material permits a clearer identification of the forces of economic change." Richard Pomfret's volume *The Economic Development of Canada* (1981) largely, but not completely, abandons the chronological approach as well.

The literature of the new economic history overcame some of the limitations of the traditional literature. The work is rigorous. Models describe interrelations (or at least the author's perception of them) precisely, causality is sought explicitly, quantitative answers are prized, and counterfactual exercises are standard fare. Yet, this rigour comes at the expense of simplification and narrowness. Too often, a historical experience becomes just another data set with which to test conjectures in economic theory. Elegance and cleverness are often sought as ends in themselves. The stress on quantification can mean that topics are taken up as much because data exist as because they are inherently interesting or important.

A fuller understanding of Canadian economic development will come only with a successful weaving of these two approaches. The richness of the one must be melded with the rigour of the other. The account must be chronological rather than thematic. It must, in other words, be a "story" of Canada's economic development from the earliest times to the present. This story must be guided by theory, but not subverted by it. It must stop at times to ask "why" or "what if," but not so obtrusively as to make it read like an economic-policy handbook. It must always remember that history involves real lives, in a real social setting, with the disparate elements of humanity, as messily complex as that is, engaging in daily activities.

We have sought this integration in a framework that is sufficiently formal to structure the presentation of the historical material, yet sufficiently general not to distort the presentation of events. We present, first, an accounting framework, designed to capture the various interdependencies of the economy and to relate them to economy-wide aggregates such as gross national product. Here, we do nothing more than make more of the formal links and interdependencies that are very much the stuff of traditional economic history. The second addition is a set of simple behavioural relationships for economic agents, customized to represent a small open economy. Put simply, we introduce the general notion that economic decisions represent the outcome of conscious maximizing calculations by consumers, firms, exporters, migrants, and international investors, subject to all the political, social, and economic constraints they face. This approach represents the spirit, if not the specific techniques, of the new economic history.

Ever since the Nobel Prize–winning work of the American economist W. Leontief, it has been standard practice to represent an economy by means of a simple input-output framework such as that depicted in Figure I.1 below. The figure is best understood by looking first at the individual blocks numbered I through III and then at the figure as a whole. Block I is known as the interindustry matrix and, as the name suggests, is intended to represent the transactions among producers in an economy. Individual industries are listed both across the top and down the side. Where such information is tabulated at a highly aggregate level, these entries would be agriculture, forestry, mining, manufacturing, and a few service activities, such as transportation and wholesale and retail trade. A more detailed figure would further divide these industries, breaking manufacturing into its several components, for example.

Block I contains two useful types of information. When read across a row, the entries record for this economy, at this time, the value of the outputs of each industry as intermediate inputs to all industries, including itself. If Industry 1 were agriculture; Industry

FIGURE I.1
The Structure of a Simple Economy

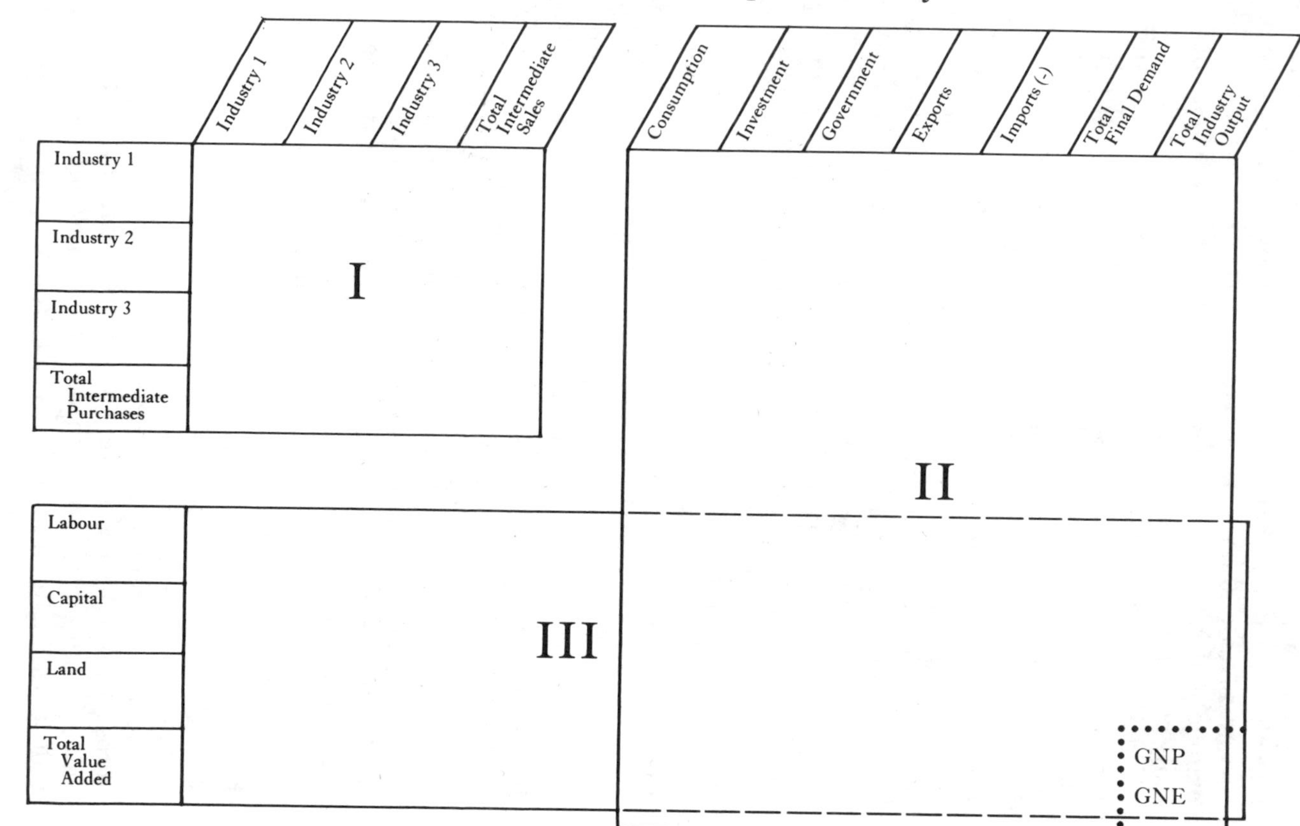

2, manufacturing; and Industry 3, services, to take an example, the first row would be the value of grain produced by the farm sector and retained for its own use (seed), the value of grain sold to manufacturers (flour mills), and the value of grain going to the service sector (which might well be zero). The sum of these three items is the total value of the output of Industry 1 sold as intermediate inputs. In dollar terms, it is the receipts of an industry from interindustry sales.

When read down a column, the entries record for each industry the values of purchases from other industries. Using the same example, the first column would list the purchases of agriculture from itself (seed), from manufacturing (machinery), and from the service sector (insurance). The sum of these items is the total expenditure of an industry on intermediate inputs. In dollar terms, it is the outlay of an industry on interindustry purchases.

Now, consider Block II. The headings indicate the purchases of goods and services in final or finished form, broken down into spending by consumers, investors, and governments, and allowing for exports and imports. Reading across the rows in this block gives the spending by final-demand category on what might be termed "industry product" (to be distinguished from the output of a domestic industry, since imports are involved). If Industry 1 is agriculture, as in the example used for Block I, the first row in Block II would be direct sales by farmers to consumers (milk), sales to businesses for investment purposes (likely zero), purchases from farmers by governments, and purchases by foreigners.

Assume the figure has been constructed to represent a country that exports Industry 1 product, but does not import it. For this product, the sum of entries in a row is the total final (as distinct from intermediate) demand and also the total domestic output. Domestic production is greater than domestic use, with the surplus sold abroad. Assume further that the country produces some Industry 2 product and imports the remainder. In this case, total domestic output of this product is obtained by subtracting the value of imports from the value of consumption plus investment, plus government spending. Total use of this product is greater than domestic production, with the difference made up of imports. Industry 3 is assumed to produce a nontradable product (no exports or imports), so total domestic output is identical to domestic usage.

Reading down a column of Block II gives the composition of spending by each category of final demand. For consumption, for example, the information contained in the column is what one would obtain by asking consumers to list the content of their spending by product. The sum of these entries is total or aggregate consumption spending. *I* is total investment, *E* is total exports, and *M* is total imports. The item denoted *GNE* is gross national expenditure. It can be calculated equally well by summing the value of final goods and services produced, or the value purchased.

Consider, finally, Block III, which records the contributions of the primary factors of production — labour, capital, and land. Reading across the first row in Block III gives the allocation of labour (or at least of wage and salary payments) across the various sectors of the economy. The sum of the row is total labour income in the economy. The subsequent two rows present the identical information for capital and land inputs.

Reading down a column in Block III gives the expenditure by each industry on primary factors of production. Thus, the first column gives the payments of Industry 1 for labour services, for capital services, and for land. The sum of this column represents the total payments by Industry 1 to primary factors or, more formally, value added, in that industry. The item denoted *GNP* is gross national product. It can be computed equally by summing income earned by factors or value added by industry. In principle, GNP is identical to GNE. In practice, they differ by a residual error of estimate.

There are two further items of interest to be gleaned from the figure. Summing total intermediate demand for any industry from Block I and total final demand from Block II gives the value of the total output of that industry. Adding together total intermediate purchases from Block I and value added from Block III gives the total outlays of an industry. Since, by definition, the value of output must equal the value of expenditures on inputs, these two sums are identical.

The other point to note concerns the distinction made above between the amount of a specific product produced in an economy in any time period and the amount of it actually used by residents. As noted, these values can be different to the extent that there are imports or exports. Thus, we produce more wheat than we use ourselves, but we use more computer equipment than we produce. The question is whether what is true for an individual product, such as wheat or computers, is also true for the economy as a whole. The answer is yes, and understanding how this can be so is the key to understanding the role of foreign investment in economic growth.

Consider the equation $GNE = C + I + G + X - M$, which is drawn from Block II of the figure. GNE is total domestic output, C is consumption expenditure, I is investment spending, G is spending by governments, X is the value of exports, and M is the value of imports. These terms can be rearranged as $(C + I + G) - GNE = M - X$. The term in brackets, $C + I + G$, represents the total value of final goods and services used by Canadians in a given period. GNE is the total value of final goods and services produced by Canadians in the same period. In a purely self-sufficient economy, total usage must be identical to total production (allowing for adding to or subtracting from inventories, which is covered, in an accounting sense, by the definition of the investment term). In an open economy, however, this identity need not hold. Canadians can use up ("absorb" in technical terms) more goods and services than they produce, to the extent that total imports in any period exceed total exports. A deficit on current account, as a trade imbalance of this type is known, is possible only if foreigners lend us foreign exchange to pay for the excess of imports. Thus, any imbalance in this one account must be matched by one of the opposite sign in the financial-flows account.

This figure, useful as it is as a schematic representation of an economy, is only an accounting framework. It tells us what the structure of the economy is at any moment, but it tells us nothing about how that structure came about or how it would alter as underlying circumstances changed. The next step, then, is to give this system of accounting identities an analytical basis. This is done by making three assumptions. The first is that the set of transactions among businesses, between businesses and individuals, and between Canadians and foreigners recorded in the rows and columns of the figure are, in fact, the outcomes of systematic decisions taken by individuals, governments, and businesses. The second is that these decisions to purchase or to supply goods and services interact through a system of interdependent markets. The third is that these markets adjust to changes in circumstances in a systematic and predictable fashion.

Consider, first, the decisions underlying the sales of the output of any one industry. Demand for the output comes from purchases by other industries for use as intermediate inputs, and from consumers, investors, governments, or foreigners as final products. Each of these decisions has its own rationale. The demand for a product as an intermediate input can logically be thought of as the outcome of firms facing a menu of ways to produce a given output (the menu given to them by their engineers) and choosing that combination that minimizes their costs. Entries in Block I capture the results of these decisions at a particular time. As prices of intermediate inputs change over time, firms will substitute cheaper for more expensive items to the extent that the menu allows. As technology changes over time, production decisions will similarly be altered. In either instance, the value of the coefficients in Block I will change.

The demand by consumers for any particular industry output is normally held to depend on total personal income and on the price of the product relative to those for all others, including imports. Investment demand is more complex, but generally can be thought of as the outcome of businesses' deciding whether additions to capital stock will generate sufficient profits in the future to compensate them for the cost of borrowing in the present. Government spending decisions represent political factors, which gives us considerable leeway as to how to represent them. The demand for a nation's exports depends on foreign incomes, domestic prices relative to foreign ones, and the exchange rate. The demand for imports by Canadians depends on local incomes, foreign prices relative to domestic ones, and the exchange rate. In all cases, as in Block I, the coefficients represent the outcomes of these decisions at one particular time and will change as circumstances do.

Firms make supply decisions to maximize expected profits, equal to total revenue minus total cost. Revenue is the product of price per unit of output and the number of units sold. Costs depend on the technology available to the firm and on the prices they face for primary and intermediate inputs. For each potential output level, firms are assumed to combine inputs so as to minimize total costs, which is another way of saying that there are well-defined cost curves. In general, production proceeds to the point where the expected return from producing one more unit of output equals the cost incurred in doing so.

The other set of markets in an economy is for the services of labour, capital, and land. Like that for intermediate inputs, the demand for these is a derived one, coming from businesses that have set their profit-maximizing level of output and, with it, the cost-minimizing employment of each factor per unit of that output. Owners of the various factors are assumed to provide supplies commensurate with their perception of the expected returns from doing so. Workers decide between income from employment and leisure or nonmarket activities. Potential emigrants assess the expected comparative economic rewards from moving to various locations. Suppliers of capital equipment, domestic and foreign, weigh the return from filling these orders relative to those for other products. Land is supplied as the rental payment exceeds the cost of bringing the land into production.

Overall, an idealized economy of this type is really a collection of numerous separate but interconnected markets. Individuals make purchases in one market with an eye to what might be obtained elsewhere, and firms hire an input only after considering what substitutes are available. Sellers of goods or of factors of production look at conditions in their current markets, considering all the while whether it might be profitable to shift production or labour services or investment elsewhere. Changes in demand or in supply in one market spill over into others, and these induced effects, in turn, flow back into the first one. Nor are the interdependencies limited to product markets. Output decisions in product markets depend on the remuneration that primary factors expect, yet these very rates depend on the demand for the factors, which depends on conditions in the product markets.

Much effort has been expended by theorists to show, first, that, if certain technical conditions are met, there is, for this idealized economy, a set of prices at which all markets are simultaneously in equilibrium; and, second, that the economy will move toward this set of values, if it is not at them already. Essentially the adjustment relies on the assertions that prices will change to remove excess demands or excess supplies in individual markets; that adjustments in one sector feed into all others, and that these adjustments, in turn, feed back on the original sector; and that this sequence of adjustments is stable.

The framework described thus far is of a general, idealized economy. To be of use in the study of Canadian economic history, it must be customized. One characteristic of the Canadian economy

— that of openness — is of particular importance in this respect. Canada's population has, on a world scale, remained small throughout its history. That small population has been exaggerated in its economic implications by our geographical position. Situated on the North American continent and within the North Atlantic trading zone, we have been, throughout our history, linked to countries more powerful than us — first France, then Britain, and currently the United States. As a small nation surrounded by larger ones, we are unusually dependent on international events.

This historical fact means we have to modify the general model to make it represent the structure of a small open economy. For product markets, this requirement can be met by asserting that, for all intents and purposes, Canada can take the international economic environment as given. This assumption means, first, that world markets set the conditions of sale for Canadian products going abroad; foreign govenments or chartered monopolies may regulate these sales, as in colonial times. Or, it may simply mean that Canada is a price-taker in these markets, as in more recent times. The point is that domestic producers cannot affect the terms.

The same assumption applies to imports. The world sets the conditions under which foreign products are available to Canadians. Again, this can be a result of explicit colonial policy or can come about via the existence of an infinitely elastic supply of output at the international price.

The assumption extends to factor supplies as well. Capital markets are most directly affected. Foreign investors set the terms by which a small open economy such as Canada's can add to its stock of capital equipment, by explicit policy, as in colonial times, or by virtue of being willing to invest as much as needed at some risk-adjusted interest rate. It is normal, as well, to assume that there is an infinitely elastic supply of foreign workers available to the economy at some price that reflects potential earnings in the next-best destination. The supply of land is given by nature, but foreign investment is available at some set price to improve and develop it.

The main implication of these features of a small open economy is that the adjustment process is constrained to operate in a particular fashion. Changes in prices account for less of an adjustment in markets for traded goods and services; changes in quantities, for more. Likewise, excess demands or supplies for capital are more likely to be resolved by changes in the quantity of transfers from abroad, and less likely, by a response in domestic savings rates. The internal adjustment that does result is centred more obviously in the nontraded sectors, meaning that swings in prices and incomes in these activities are more pronounced. Vague as these observations may be at this point, they will figure prominently in much of the political-economy discussion below.

It is important to note that this framework does not ignore government policies or other interventions into markets. On the contrary, it provides a framework for understanding them more fully. The conditions whereby Canadian products can enter foreign markets — or foreign products, the Canadian market — can equally well be set by a mercantilist imperial government or the international marketplace. The economic adjustment forced on the Canadian economy comes from the nature of the constraint and not its origins. Likewise, domestic policies can be introduced explicitly. Canadian governments can affect the profitability of supplying exports into world markets through varying taxes or subsidies or access to natural resources. They can affect the relative attractiveness of domestic products, as opposed to imports, via tariffs, quotas, and other nontariff barriers. They can control the amount of foreign investment or the flow of immigration.

Government policies, rather than being ignored, will, in fact, figure prominently in the narrative to follow. The specifics vary enormously, of course, but they fall into one of three broad categories. The first involves government effort, through edict or law, to regulate business with a view sometimes to shaping and sometimes to promoting economic development. From the time New France issued licences for the fur trade in the seventeenth century, regulation has been a part of Canadian economic life. The whole concept of mercantilism, which is important to a large part of our work, reflects this belief in the importance of the state to economic activity. Governments and their agencies regularly sought to spur development by direct and indirect means, from subsidies to ironworks in New France to canals and railways in the nineteenth century, to the massive efforts of today.

The second policy area involves government in large-scale macroeconomic manipulation. This is really a product of the twentieth century, mercantilism notwithstanding. At its base is the belief that the monetary and fiscal powers of the modern state make possible control not just of a particular activity but of the performance of the economy as a whole. The third area, nearly parallel in time to macro-economic co-ordination, was the growing tendency of governments to be involved not just in the creation of wealth but also in its distribution. Social welfare, small-scale and rudimentary as late as 1914, became an increasingly important aspect of government policy as time went on.

The structure of the narrative to follow derives from this broad framework. To understand what we attempt to do, assume for the moment that it is possible at any point in Canadian history to draw up a representation of the economy along the lines of the figure above. Each such figure would provide a snapshot of the economy at that moment, showing the relative importance of the various activities and all their interdependencies. New figures would look quite different from their predecessors. Additional sectors would emerge, and existing ones would disappear, or at least wither in relative importance. Interindustry links would change as technology and tastes did, as trading patterns altered, and so forth. Together, the sequence of figures would record the growth and development of the economy over time.

Of course, in attempting to re-create the historical reality, with all the limitations of the data, and with massively complex interactions among sectors, it is not possible to build a pure snapshot, nor, certainly, is it possible to link a series of snapshots together into some sort of moving or dynamic input-output figure. Even if we could, such a figure would not be history, for it would underplay the human, the random, and the interesting. Rather, therefore, the framework is a guideline for us. It provides a structure to order and, thus, to help understand the myriad shifts of people, wealth, and activity that shaped Canadian history.

It is interesting to note just how this approach compares to that traditionally employed in Canadian economic history — the venerable staples theory. It is easily seen that the staples theory is really only a special case of the more general framework outlined above. Staples are export products of one particular type — one row in the figure, so to speak. The backward, forward, and final-demand linkages associated with staples are, again, one particular set of interdependencies. The impulses to aggregate growth coming from staples trade are but one type of shock that can set the general adjustment process into motion.

The implication is that, in historical periods when natural-resource exports did truly dominate the Canadian economy, the framework employed here will add little to what the staples theory can reveal about the process of economic growth and change. As the economy becomes more complex, however, the usefulness of the more general approach becomes evident. Exports need not be natural-resource-based. Interdependencies can run equally from other sectors of the economy to natural-resource sectors and vice versa. Impulses to growth (or decline) can originate equally well in import-competing or nontraded sectors and in export sectors, and they can originate from government policies as much as from exogenous disturbances.

Once the methodology was decided, and the length of the book set, the structure fell naturally into a two-tiered system. The first tier comprises six sections that were seen by us to define major stages in Canadian economic development. Within each era, however, various subdivisions quickly became apparent. Depending on the literature and the issues, the precise decision as to the nature of the division varied. In the colonial era, the most appropriate divisions were usually based on political-constitutional entities (e.g., New France). After Confederation, however, that changed. Subdivisions of time (e.g., World War I) or, alternatively, sectoral themes tended to dominate (e.g., the rise of new staples in Chapter 13). Whatever the specific decision as to the nature of the new delineation, these subdivisions became the main chapters within the parts. In each part, however, there is an introductory section that draws together the major connections within the period and, in particular, emphasizes the international context upon which, as we have noted, Canada's small open economy is so dependent.

Finally, as a body, the themes we emphasize naturally led us to combine an examination of economics with a belief in the importance both of human decision making, especially when backed with the force of government, and of time, in understanding what really occurred. We would, therefore, place our work within the broad tradition of economics in Canada known as the political-economy school.

In recent years, political economy has taken on many connotations, many of them ideological. Our definition is somewhat more traditional. For us, it means an emphasis on the broad institutional and social framework that affects economic development. Agriculture cannot be separated from farmers' attempts to influence government, and the development of shipping cannot be understood without at least some reference to the policies of canal-building. Government policies during World War I are a part of the psychology of crisis that dominated those terrible years.

Political economy has a long and honourable presence in Canadian writing on the nation. Whatever modifications of theory or data the writings of the last generation have required, and however new social perspectives have altered our view of such groups as native persons or women, we have written this work in a manner that reflects our belief in the value of political economy as a means of understanding the complex interplay of forces that have shaped Canadian economic development.

Notes

1. *Canadian Historical Review* 4 (March 1923): 12–25.
2. On Harold Innis, see Carl Berger, *The Writing of Canadian History: Aspects of English Canadian Historical Writing Since 1900*, 2nd ed. (Toronto: University of Toronto Press, 1986).

I

The Early Colonial Era, 1600–1763

I

For centuries, two separate economies and societies had evolved on the two sides of the Atlantic Ocean. Though there was intermittent contact, such as the Vikings' landing at Newfoundland around A.D. 1000, the reality was that neither the small-scale hunting, trapping, and trading economies of the North American native population nor the relatively impoverished European feudal system had either the means or the will to take the necessary steps to bridge the ocean. Over time, that changed, however. European commerce recovered, and European technology, borrowing from the Middle East and Asia as well as relying on indigenous innovation, increasingly developed and improved the means for trade and travel. Europeans ventured eastward to the riches of Asia, southward around the Cape of Good Hope, and eventually westward to the New World. Columbus brought the two societies together on his famed 1492 voyage. Thereafter, there was regular contact and trade between the Americas and Europe, though it would be a long time before such trade led to settlement in what is now Canada. Finally, in 1608, Champlain founded Quebec, and the period of uninterrupted European settlement in Canada began. Over the next centuries, the two distinct economies of natives and Europeans would come to co-operate, and later compete, until one gave way and embraced the other.

Canadian economic development in the century and a half after 1608 was, to a large extent, a product of the imperial rivalries of that time. The land that is now Canada was colonized by two major European powers as parts of much larger empires extending around the globe. Colonies were held for economic, military, and religious reasons. The weight attached to each motive varied from one imperial power to another, and the vigour with which each pursued its interests changed with domestic and international circumstances. As imperial interests changed, so, too, did specific policies, often with dramatic implications for the colonies. Thus, any comprehensible account of this period in Canada's economic history must begin with a brief overview of how North America was divided among the main European powers, and of the doctrines that lay at the heart of policies toward the colonies.

At the beginning of the eighteenth century, France had clear claim to what are now the Maritime provinces of Prince Edward Island, Nova Scotia, and New Brunswick. Inland, its empire extended, by means of alliances with various native tribes, from its early bases along the St. Lawrence River, through the Great Lakes, into the heart of the continent. Explorers, fur traders, and missionaries had gone north of the Great Lakes into the Canadian Shield, and south along the Ohio and Mississippi river systems, reaching the Gulf of Mexico by 1682. French fishermen were active off Newfoundland, but here there was no clear jurisdiction. Like the other powers of the time, France also occupied islands in the Caribbean when advances in sugar cultivation after 1620 made them economically valuable (see Map I.1).

The other imperial power with an interest in Canada was England. The activities of the West Country fishermen drew attention to Newfoundland, which England claimed jointly with France. Throughout the seventeenth century, the fur trade drew the British farther and farther inland. A royal charter in 1670 granted to the Hudson's Bay Company the sole right to trade and commerce on "all those seas, straits, bays, rivers, lakes, creeks and sounds . . . that lie within the entrance of Hudson's Straits, together with all the lands, countries and territories upon the coasts and confines of the seas, straits, bays, lakes, rivers, creeks and sounds aforesaid." This area remained in dispute with France until the Treaty of Utrecht in 1713, under which Britain gained definite control of the Hudson Bay area and of Acadia (Nova Scotia). In the Caribbean, the British colonized some of the smaller sugar islands not held firmly by Spain, and, in 1655, they seized Jamaica.

The major British colonial thrust in North America occurred on what is now the eastern seaboard of the United States. Settlement of Jamestown in 1607 preceded, by one year, that at Quebec. Living conditions were primitive at first, but, when the first tobacco plants

MAP I.1
North American Empires, *c.* 1713

Source: D.G. Kerr, *Historical Atlas of Canada* (Toronto: Nelson, 1975), 23.

were introduced in 1613, the economic future of the colony was assured. Religious dissidents landed at Plymouth in 1619. Boston was founded in 1629 by the Puritans, followed by further settlements in Rhode Island, New Haven, and along the Connecticut River valley. Colonists survived, and ultimately prospered, by developing lumber, fish, whale oil, potash, meat, butter, and cheese, and developing shipping and shipbuilding. Dutch settlements in Manhattan and along the Hudson River, established in the years after 1612, were surrendered in 1674, adding to the area of British influence. Maryland and areas farther south, settlements based largely on the cultivation of tobacco, were occupied from the 1630s on. By 1670, halfway through the colonial period, there were about 100 000 residents in the area stretching from southern Maine to North Carolina.

The American colonies grew rapidly after 1670. The established areas of New England continued to develop, but their progress was slow compared to that of more recent settlements in Connecticut and Rhode Island, and especially compared to the middle and southern colonies. The rich farmlands of New York, New Jersey, and Pennsylvania, with their seemingly limitless bounty of fruits and grains and potential for the raising of livestock, attracted thousands of immigrants. Philadelphia, and then New York, grew to rival, and then surpass, Boston as centres of shipping and commerce. Rice and indigo were added to tobacco as important staple crops of the south. Population stood at about 470 000 in 1720 (compared to slightly more than 25 000 in New France); on the eve of the American Revolution, population figures had increased more than sixfold.

Military and religious motives figured in imperial strategies in relation to the colonies, but the main interest was economic, and the guiding doctrine was a set of policies that later writers were to label "mercantilist." Mercantilism was never a conscious strategy of any government, and the set of measures attibuted to it varied greatly from country to country. As one text explains, "mercantilism is the name given to that group of ideas and practices particularly characteristic of the period 1500 to 1800 by which the national state acting in the economic sphere sought by methods of control to secure its own unity and power."[1] Many aspects of mercantilism had little to do with colonies, but some did, and it is these that we must briefly mention here.

A basic tenet of mercantilism was bullionism — the accumulation of precious metals. Such metals were valuable for purchasing arms, ships, and soldiers. If gold and silver could not be obtained directly, as the Spanish did from their South American colonies, it had to come indirectly, through a favourable balance of trade, which allowed them to accumulate gold. This goal was achievable through the promotion of agricultural and industrial self-sufficiency and the restriction of trade and commerce to vessels from their nation. Colonies contributed to a positive payments balance by providing raw materials not available in the home country, by absorbing its processed products, and by acting as a training ground for its navy and merchant marine. In all these instances, the colonies reduced the need to pay out specie to competing powers.

French mercantilism reached its full development in the age of Intendant Jean Colbert (1661–83), chief minister of Louis XIV. There had been earlier efforts to regulate national economic life, particularly after 1600, but these had been "sporadic, uncoordinated and ill-enforced."[2] Under Louis XIII, Cardinal Richelieu had built up the French navy; encouraged and regulated industry and agriculture; and established commercial companies, including some in New France and the West Indies. Colbert, with the support of a powerful monarchy, worked these beginnings into a centralized, well-rounded mercantilist system. Colonies were of particular importance in this scheme, and Colbert strove to make the French possessions valuable sources of raw materials and destinations for French manufactured goods. In the New World, he did succeed in diverting the trade of the French West Indies from the Dutch, but neither he nor his successors were able to link this area economically with New France.

Great Britain's colonial policy was shaped by ruling landed- and business-class interests. The main goals were the classic mercantilist ones: support of the merchant marine at the expense of foreign competition, and promotion of self-sufficiency in resources and manufactured products. Key to the support of domestic shipping were the Navigation Acts, implemented first in 1651 and revised several times thereafter. Under the initial formulation, goods produced in Asia, Africa, and America could be imported into England only in British or colonial vessels. European exporters could use British ships or those of their own country, although, after 1661, goods brought in in this way faced higher duties. Foreigners were barred completely from the English coastal trade. Amendments in 1661 added the provision that all goods imported from or exported to English colonies must be transported in English or colonial ships. The Staples Act of 1663 stipulated that no European goods could be imported into the colonies that were not put on board in Great Britain. A provision ten years later placed duties on trade among the colonies, with the aim of making Great Britain the entrepôt of all colonial commerce.

The Navigation Acts affected the colonies in a number of ways. Shipowners benefited, at least early on, as they were given the same privileges as British vessels in the lucrative British trade. Indeed, much of their early success was predicated on fitting into colonial shipping patterns. Exporters and importers located in the colonies were unaffected if the prescribed shipping was the cheapest available, but found the restrictions constraining whenever they were denied access to cheaper non-British sources of supplies. The attempts to route all trade through Great Britain came to be constraining to New England merchants, in particular, leading to extensive smuggling and eventually becoming a contributing cause of the American Revolution.

The goal of self-sufficiency took various forms under British mercantilism. Domestic agriculture and industry were to be developed as much as possible to lessen reliance on imports and to promote sales abroad. Grain exports earned bounties in years of low prices, while imports faced sliding-scale tariffs (i.e., the duty increased as the foreign price fell). Manufacturers benefited from high tariffs and outright prohibitions on the import of some products. Colonies were to serve as markets for manufactured products, meaning that no goods were to be imported from other nations, nor were the colonies to develop industrial expertise of their own. When manufacturing did develop anyway, specific measures were enacted to discourage it. New England woollens, hats, and iron were particular examples of products that received special legislative attention.

A related tenet was that Britain's empire should, as much as possible, be able to draw its needed raw materials from within its own territories. The 1661 amendments noted above included a clause that enumerated articles — sugar, tobacco, cotton, indigo, ginger, dye woods — not to be exported from an English colony save to England or another colony. The list of enumerated articles was extended over time to include naval stores, rice and molasses, copper ore and furs, hides, potash, lumber, and pig and bar iron. This provision cut both ways for colonies: it could mean preferential access to the lucrative British market, but it could also deny access to trade that was otherwise profitable.

Britain was able to integrate its colonies in the New World somewhat better than was France. The North Atlantic fisheries supplied salted cod to Europe and to the West Indies plantations, and took foodstuffs and manufactured goods in return. Sugar, molasses, and rum from the Caribbean went to Britain for consumption, to continental Europe as trade goods, and to the fur trade as inputs. The islands, in turn, had to be provided with simple foodstuffs for the slave populations, and with lumber for buildings and barrel staves.

The American colonies fit into the British mercantile system from the beginning. Merchants were able to draw on local supplies to put together cargoes of lumber, fish, and agricultural products. As colonies, they were entitled to build their own ships and use them to transport approved goods along prescribed routes. Boston, in particular, benefited from this opportunity. It had an excellent harbour, and the mix of products produced in the area was ideally suited to the requirements of the plantation economies. By 1720, it was a "busy, crowded, complex, world port city," the largest in America at about 12 000 residents.[3] Other ports grew more rapidly after 1720 as a result of new products and new markets, but the West Indies trade remained important to New England and Boston until the American Revolution, and even after.

The success of the American colonies within the British mercantile system provides an important theme for the economic history of Canada in this period. New England's growth touched each of the colonies to the north, although it did so in quite different ways. For Newfoundland, New England represented a source of cheap inputs for the fisheries and an additional buyer for its codfish exports, so the net effect on settlement and development was positive. The opposite was true for the Maritime provinces. Their economic base (potential economic base, really, before 1750) was directly competitive with that of New England. As long as the colonies to the south were part of the British mercantile system, the Maritimes were relegated to being a minor tributary to them.

The success of the American colonies was most ominous for New France. The French military presence to the north alarmed New England, while French fur-trading activities down the valleys of the Ohio and Mississippi were increasingly resented by colonies intent on expansion across the Appalachians. Conflict between the two was inevitable. War between Britain and France broke out formally in 1756; skirmishes in North America had begun two years earlier. The outcome was predictable, even if delayed somewhat by the skill of French defence efforts. By the Treaty of Paris in 1763, France relinquished its 150-year-old colonial presence in North America. The era of competing mercantile claims ended, and Canada's future now rested on how the British would reorganize their much-expanded North American empire.

Notes

1. S.B. Clough and C.W. Cole, *Economic History of Europe* (Boston: D.C. Heath, 1966), 197.
2. Clough and Cole, *Economic History of Europe*, 215.
3. Gerald Gunderson, *A New Economic History of America* (New York: McGraw-Hill, 1976).

Further Reading

Clough, S.B., and C.W. Cole. *Economic History of Europe*. Boston: D.C. Heath, 1966.

Gunderson, Gerald. *A New Economic History of America*. New York: McGraw-Hill, 1976.

CHAPTER

1

The European Background to Colonization

"Like it or not," wrote historian K.G. Davies, "the Atlantic Ocean north of the equator was transformed in the course of the seventeenth century into a European lake."[1] The great barrier that had limited European expansion to the west was dissolved, and the way was opened for the spread of European military, economic, political, and religious influence. Two cultures and economies were dramatically and irrevocably affected by this western expansion. The Europeans found the New World sufficiently attractive economically to bring back with them elements of culture and economy and, eventually, to adopt these permanently. The native population of Canada, though dominant in the New World long after European settlement had begun, found themselves drawn to the seemingly irresistible forces of the European economy until their own economy had been subsumed by the latter.

The first phase of the story of Canadian economic development thus takes place in Europe. The question must be answered as to why Europe took its technology, its trade, and its people overseas at this time. It is also necessary to look at the economy and people that the Europeans came into contact with in North America. For, at the beginning of its written history, Canadian economic development is that of a vulnerable localized economy affected by an international, technologically superior, and expanding one. The "North Atlantic lake" and its implications for North America are the focus of this chapter.

In looking at exploration and settlement, there is a danger that one will telescope the process — land is discovered; settlers come over. Yet, it was more than a century after Cabot discovered Newfoundland in 1497, and nearly 75 years after Cartier went up the St. Lawrence in 1535, that a permanent European presence was established in Canada. These delays emphasize, first, the difference between isolated exploring expeditions and the development of regular trade between new and old lands and, second, the fact that trade does not necessarily mean that settlement will take place. The story of the North Atlantic lake is, therefore, also an assessment of the forces that, during the fifteenth and sixteenth centuries, led successively to exploration and trade and, ultimately, to settlement in northern North America.

An Expanding Europe

Europe, as historian Fernand Braudel has said, was a small world through much of the Middle Ages. It was limited on the west by the Atlantic barrier; on the south and north, by forbidding climates; and, on the east, by the powerful and hostile Islamic empire. Europe's geographical and commercial horizons had shrunk significantly from what they were in the days of the great Roman Empire. There may have been, as the fables and legends would have it, Irish monks or other intrepid travellers who crossed the Atlantic to discover new lands. If so, it hardly mattered, for nothing came of the contact. Even the more substantial, and easily substantiated, expansion of the Norse from Scandinavia to Iceland (A.D. 870) and Greenland (*c.* A.D. 985), and to Newfoundland (*c.* A.D. 1025), had little long-term effect.[2] The extended network of settlements could not be maintained, and Newfoundland, and then Greenland, was abandoned. The technological and economic conditions necessary for sustained European expansion did not yet exist. Even as the Greenland colony crumbled, however, forces were gathering that would once again send Europeans across the Atlantic. This time they would not retreat.

The prerequisites for successful European expansion to North America were many, but three stand out. First, a commercial system with sufficient speculative capital and expectations of reward was necessary in order for the desire and the capability to expand influence to new areas to exist. Second, there had to be the technology to exploit the sought resources. In the Atlantic, a voyage had to be, if not entirely safe, at least feasible, to be profitable. Third, there had to be something to draw the expanding trade in the direction of the Americas.

The European Commercial Revolution

The first precondition for expansion was perhaps the most important one: Europe had to have the economic wherewithal to move beyond its limited horizons. There was some long-distance trade in the fourteenth century. Extraordinary opportunities were always there for those who would transport goods of high value over long distances. Even in the absence of a banking system, credit arrangements were developed between individuals at long distance. Coastal shipping plied its way along the Baltic and Atlantic seaboards, carrying goods from port to port, while, in the Mediterranean, an important trade existed between the ports of Italy and Spain, on the one hand, and those of the Middle East and the North African coast, on the other. Most valuable and difficult of all was the trade between Europe and Asia, which developed during the thirteenth century (discussed below).

Nevertheless, the characteristics of medieval European trade, in relative terms, were localism, small volume, and an absence of financial services. There were various reasons for this. First, since the specie was limited, trade was limited to what could be sustained through the relatively inefficient barter system. Equally important was the miserable state of transportation, especially over land. Roads were bad, axle and wheel designs were inefficient, and there was a scarcity of good horses. The fragmented political state of the Continent exacerbated these transportation problems, tolls, tariffs, and the lack of personal safety further hindering the hauling of goods over long distances.

Moreover, the financial structures of Europe in this period were not designed to handle long-distance trade. Banking, in any modern sense of the word, was effectively nonexistent for most of the population. Cheques, lines of credit, currency exchange, and other such facilitators of trade were unavailable. For these reasons, therefore, most trade in Europe operated in a series of regional and local markets rather than in continental, much less intercontinental, ones.

The nature of trade began to change in the fifteenth century. However, the transformation did not occur overnight. Indeed, most historians talk of a commercial revolution encompassing the years from 1450 to 1750 or so. Its cumulative effect was dramatic, for it was as a part of this revolution that transatlantic trade was begun, colonies established, and the assertion of European commercial hegemony in much of the world accomplished.

The various forces that created the commercial revolution are complex. In the most basic terms, European trade began to expand, partly in response to a growing market for goods. In the Middle Ages, only the very top rungs of society would have been affected by long-distance trade. The vast majority of people depended on goods grown or manufactured in the local community. Through the fifteenth and sixteenth centuries, standards of living improved and more and more people were able to purchase at least some of their goods outside of the local economy. Traders responded to these potential profits by going farther afield, and the quantities of trade goods being transported around Europe increased.

The king of the emerging system was the merchant-entrepreneur, who profited not by manufacturing but by buying, transporting, and selling goods. As the range and volume of trade grew, so, too, did the capital involved. Successful merchants banded together to pool capital and resources to spread the risk. Business began to operate on a larger and more complex scale than it had previously. Improved banking and credit facilities were an important part of this growing economy. As merchants undertook longer-distance commitments, they increasingly needed agencies to handle credit and the transfer of funds and to fund large-scale ventures. The latter need, however, presented a problem. The doctrines of the medieval church saw usury, the lending of money for profit, as a sin. Restrictions on the amount that could be charged for borrowing money inhibited financial expansion and the development of credit facilities. That these restrictions diminished from the fifteenth through the seventeenth centuries was both a product and a cause of the commercial revolution. Gradually, banking houses began to develop throughout Europe. Many eventually had several regional offices and could serve to provide the credit arrangements, financial transfers, and other financial services for a dynamic merchant sector.

Within this expanding commercial system, there was no doubt which trade was the richest, and often the riskiest. Such trade was also at the longest distance, for it was with Asia. The Asian trade was also directly related to the European expansion to the Americas, for it was the lure of profits from Asia that drew Europe beyond its own boundaries and gave it reason to go, albeit unintentionally, to North America.

The Asian trade of the fifteenth and sixteenth centuries was very one-sided in terms of merchandise (see Map 1.1). The great Asian civilizations, such as China's, wanted little from Europe, except perhaps some muskets and ammunition. In contrast, Europe wanted several things from Asia — namely, jewellery, calico, jade, silks, and spices for the luxury market. Most important of these items were the spices. In the centuries before refrigeration, spice was essential, not just to enhance the flavour of foods, but to disguise the smell and taste of decay. Of all the spices, pepper was the most important. Estimates indicate that between 2 million and 3 million pounds of pepper annually were being shipped to Europe by the end of the fifteenth century.[3] Its crucial role in food preparation made pepper something more than a luxury good and gave it some of the aspects of a mass-consumption item. Certainly, it was the most important and most widely demanded of all goods imported into Europe before 1500.

The Asian trade was fraught with difficulties. Between the Asian sources and the European market lay the powerful Islamic regions. Europe could not penetrate these regions militarily, and thus had to depend on Islamic self-interest and good will to allow the trade to continue. Except in time of war, it was usually profitable for Muslims to allow the European trade to continue through the region. Pepper caravans regularly made their way from the Persian Gulf overland to Tripoli, or from the Red Sea to Cairo and Alexandria.[4] However, these routes were not without problems. Dependence on the Muslims was unfortunate, from the European point of view, given the long-standing religious and military animosity between the two groups. Disruptions such as war or disease in the Middle East could interrupt trade for considerable periods of time. When trade was not interrupted, there was a natural tendency for the Islamic nations to use their strategic position to extract certain tolls and tariffs from the traders. Finally, as was the case elsewhere, trade by land was much less efficient than that by sea, making travel on the Asian routes long and expensive.

One further objection made by much of Europe to the structure of the Asian trade had nothing to do with Muslim or Asian circumstances, and everything to do with European economic rivalry. The Asian trade was dominated, from the thirteenth century on,

MAP 1.1
Italian City-States, Eurasian Trade Routes, and the Islamic World, Mid-Fifteenth Century

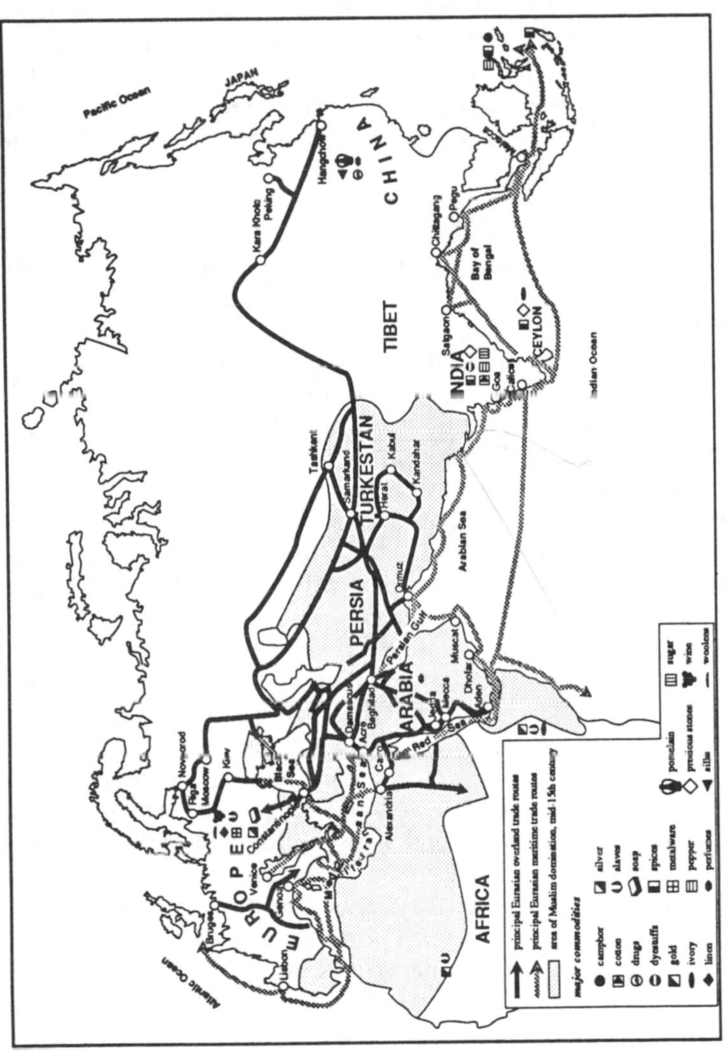

Source: Adapted from Geoffrey Barraclough, *The Times Atlas of World History* (London: Times Books, 1984), 146–47.

by a few Italian city-states. Pisa, Genoa, and, above all, Venice had become major centres of European commerce because they dominated the routes to the East. There was, as a result, a growing desire by merchants from other parts of the Continent to break the dominance of the Italian city-states and to reap greater rewards from the growing Asian trade. The desire to find a safer and cheaper route to Asia, together with the incentive to circumvent the Venetians, would lead Europeans to major new overseas ventures, including those that resulted in their discovery of the Americas (see Map 1.2).

Improvements in Technology

Before the Europeans could venture overseas with any regularity, however, they needed the means to get there. "A fanatic like Columbus," wrote K.G. Davies, "would probably have tried to cross the Atlantic in anything that floated, but working seamen with families needed reasonably safe and versatile ships which would stand up to Atlantic gales and sail approximately the course the navigator intended."[5] The second precondition for European expansion, the means to exploit the resources European traders sought, evolved in the fifteenth century. Even as the European economy expanded, and the Asian trade gave it reason to look outward, considerable improvements in vessel design and navigation techniques were achieved that made the voyages possible.

The state of navigation at the time was such that, until the fifteenth century, the sailor had no means, once out of sight of land, of determining where he was. All shipping took place along routes close to landfall. Voyages across open seas and out of sight of land were undertaken, but these were kept as brief as possible, and were limited to routes between known points. Certainly, the absence of navigational aids discouraged those who would head off into the unknown for long distances.

During the fifteenth century, this situation changed. By the middle of that century, it became possible for a trained captain to determine latitude (that is, the ship's position along a north-south axis). Longitude (position on an east-west axis) would remain impossible to know with accuracy for another three centuries, but the principle of "dead reckoning," when combined with the new ability to know latitude, gave the sailor at least a reasonable idea of where he was at any given time. This development, in turn, led to improvements in chart-making. Overall, these changes revolu-

MAP 1.2
The Beginnings of European Expansion

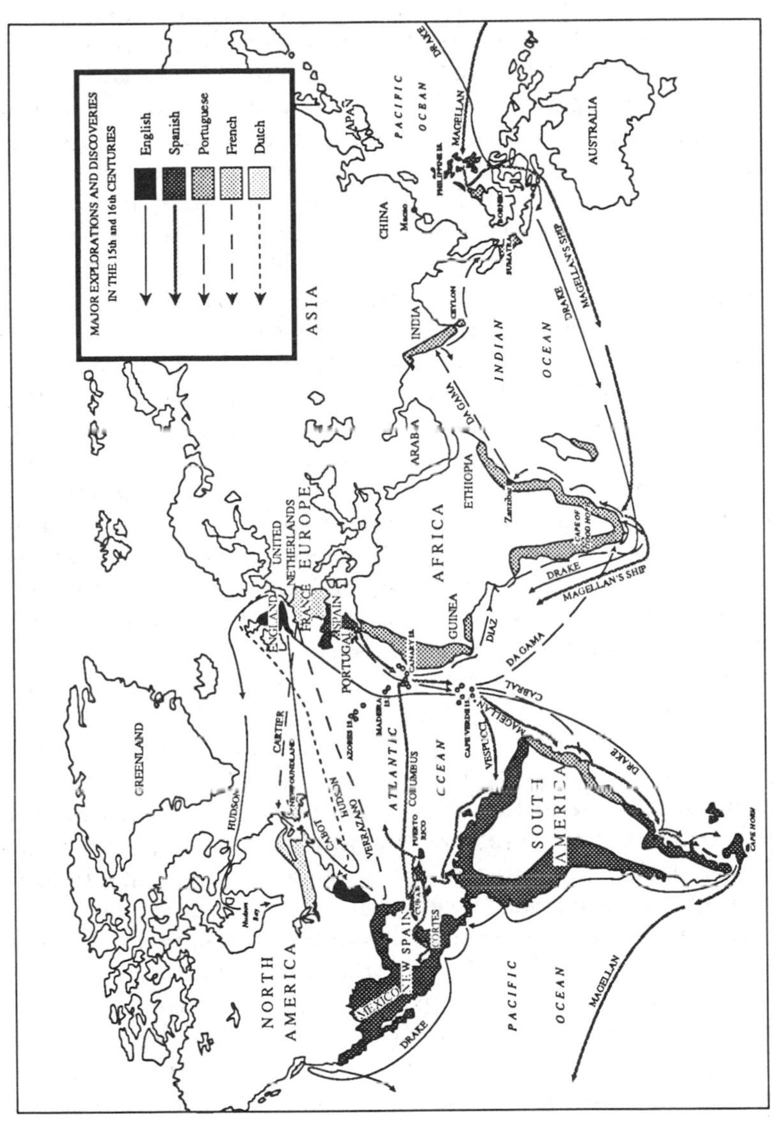

Source: E.M. Burns, *World Civilizations*, 7th ed. (New York: Norton, 1987), 512.

tionized the sailor's attitude to the ocean. By the end of the fifteenth century, captains and crew routinely headed off into the open ocean. The medieval sailor's "horror of the open sea," as one historian has described it, had dissipated.[6]

Improvements in navigation were paralleled by changes in ship design. For a long time, European technology, as was the case for European society generally, had been been backward, relative to that of the great Islamic and Asian civilizations. By the fifteenth century, however, the Europeans were gaining ground, both by borrowing from other civilizations and by developing innovations of their own. Overlapping planking on the hull was increasingly being replaced by carvel (smooth) planking. The latter, though a more difficult form of construction, had several advantages: it was easier to clean of barnacles, held up better under the stress of heavy seas, and allowed for greater cargo space without loss of stability.

A second area of change was the move from the single- to the triple-masted ship. The former had been in almost universal use at the beginning of the century; however, by the end of it, practically all larger ships had three masts. Most important was the combination of sails hoisted on these masts. The first two masts used a combination of square sails. The third mast used a lateen or triangular sail. This type of sail had been adopted from those in use on Islamic ships in the Mediterranean, and probably had its origins in India. The combination of a triangular mizzenmast sail and square sails on the other masts provided a level of power, manoeuvrability, and stability that neither the triangular nor the square sails alone could have done. In particular, the mizzenmast permitted the ship to tack with much greater efficiency against the wind. As the prevailing winds of the North Atlantic blew west to east much of the time, efficient tacking was of obvious importance on transatlantic voyages.[7]

Improvements were also made in the sails themselves — flax or cotton rather than wool was used, making sails lighter, especially when wet — and in rigging. These innovations and others increased efficiency, allowing a reduction in crew size, with all the implications such a reduction had for the cost of provisions and wages. Changing relationships between keel length and beam produced greater cargo space, further improving the cost-efficiency of shipping.

These technological improvements did two crucial things. First, they made the transatlantic ocean voyage less likely to be a suicidal act. By the early sixteenth century, even small ships were routinely making the voyage across the Atlantic on a seasonal basis; a round trip was possible (though far from assured) within about six weeks. Second, the improvements made the trip more efficient and thus less costly. The cost of transporting whatever might be found in the New World steadily decreased as ship design improved. The North Atlantic, which had for so long hemmed Europe in, was about to become a major commercial highway.

Early European Expansion: The Portuguese and Spanish

The early commercial revolution created the expanding economy that allowed Europe to look beyond its own borders. The changes in ship technology made it possible to attempt to circumvent the land routes dominated by Islamic powers and the Venetians. It was not long before Western European nations began to seek a means of tapping the wealthy Asian trade for themselves.

The first to do so were the Portuguese. Throughout the fifteenth century, they extended their trade and knowledge southward, along the coast of Africa. By 1488, they had rounded the Cape of Good Hope and landed in eastern Africa. They had discovered the way into the Indian Ocean, and thereby opened up the possibility of direct sea contact with rich Asian lands. Within a few more years, that contact was established. The economic implications of this development were enormous. The first shipments of Asian goods via Portugal arrived in northern Europe in 1501.[8] The monopoly of the Italian city-states had been broken and, though it would take time, power was beginning to shift northwestward from the Mediterranean basin. Portugal, for its part, was about to reap the rewards of its seafaring adventures with an overseas empire.

In the meantime, the lure of Asia led to a voyage that is much better known to most North Americans. For Christopher Columbus, the logical route to Asia was not around the Cape of Good Hope, but due westward, where, with a little luck, clear sailing would take one directly to Asia. In the 1480s, he petitioned the King of Portugal to fund such a trip. Portugal was not interested, but its neighbour, Spain, was convinced, and in 1492 Columbus proceeded westward, toward Asia. As was true for the Portuguese in Africa, economic opportunity provided a motive force, both for the explorers and for those who backed them.

Columbus did not find Asia, of course, but he did find a region that was quickly recognized to be important in its own right. After a few exploratory voyages, the Spanish discovered the vast wealth of the Aztec and Incan civilizations. This wealth provided the impetus for return visits, as military expeditions invaded these American civilizations and plundered their large holdings of gold and silver. Soon after, Spanish colonies were founded and transatlantic commerce was developed to service them. By the 1520s, both Spain and Portugal had converted the central Atlantic into a regularly travelled shipping lane. Gold and silver, plundered from the natives of Central and South America, headed eastward. Soldiers, and then slaves for the growing plantation system, headed west.

The record of Spanish and Portuguese development of the New World is beyond the scope of this book. It is important, however, to note the influence this chain of discoveries and plunders had on the North Atlantic region. The rapid influx of gold and silver into Europe increased the supply of money on the Continent. The result was a steady, though moderate, inflation. Prices doubled between 1550 and 1600, for example. There has been some debate as to whether this inflation undermined or assisted the European economy, but, on balance, the belief seems to be that the influx of new money was helpful to the ongoing commercial revolution. Trade had expanded tremendously over the past century but, until the plundering of the New World, the supply of money had not. The fact that the balance of trade with Asia was so one-sided made matters all that much worse. The influx of specie from America allowed Europe to continue to finance the imbalance in the Asian trade; provided additional money supplies, which spurred economic activity; and, perhaps most important, made it easier to fund later voyages.

The long-term impact of the inflow of American gold was uneven, however. Portugal and Spain experienced a century or more of tremendous power, prestige, and wealth from their American exploits. For the most part, however, these nations did not hold on to the specie from overseas. There were few linkages developed within their economies, and many of the items they sought had to be bought abroad. Much of the bullion from the New World, for example, stayed in Spain only long enough to be readdressed and sent on to China or other Asian destinations. Much also went northward, along the western coast of Europe, to rising trading nations such as England and Holland. Wars further depleted gold and silver reserves.

The movement of Iberian gold and silver paralleled what was happening in the European economy as a whole. Power was slipping northward. The Mediterranean had begun a decline that, by the end of the seventeenth century, would see it reduced from the most economically powerful part of Europe to a relatively poor region. Spain (which absorbed Portugal in 1580) found its fortunes in decline by the late sixteenth century, in spite of its vast overseas empire.

The emergent centres of economic power were in the north. Paris, Amsterdam, and London would dominate the next centuries. So far as the future North Atlantic trade is concerned, two things stand out. First, wealth was accumulating rapidly among the merchants of the major northern commercial centres. Such wealth would make speculative ventures more likely, including the extremely high-risk ones across the Atlantic. Second, these emergent nations were major sea powers. In each, a maritime tradition and access to numerous ships and experienced sailors made transatlantic commerce a natural step. When these nations did venture across the Atlantic, such advantages would make them important presences in the Americas.

Spain's presence there forced these nations to act."The Spanish King vexeth all the Princes of Europe," complained Sir Walter Raleigh, "and is become in a fewe years from a poore King of Castile the greatest monark of this part of the worlde."[9] Other nations, including England and France, sent expeditions, hoping to emulate Columbus by discovering new lands somewhere to the north of existing Spanish possessions. The lands were discovered, but when the Europeans found there was no quick plunder, they returned their attention to Spanish lands to the south, raiding Spanish commerce across the sea lanes. In a way, this dramatic saga of piracy, warfare, and adventure was an economic stage in the development of the New World. It gave other nations reason to go back to the New World — to plunder the Spanish, who had plundered the Indians. In the process, such people as Sir Francis Drake expanded the British knowledge of seamanship, in general, and of the Atlantic world, in particular.

In the meantime, there was activity in the north. In 1497, the British sent a Venetian captain, John Cabot, across the Atlantic. Like that of Columbus, his stated purpose was to find a route to the rich Asian market. The British hoped that the landmass the Spanish had run into would not extend as far north as the North Atlantic, and that he would discover a northwest passage to Asia. Cabot proceeded more or less due west from Bristol. Like Columbus, he found his way blocked. However, he brought back information that gave Europeans reason to return. This information also marks the beginning of a European economic presence in the vicinity of Canada. The third precondition for a European presence in the northern part of the continent was about to be met.

Products of North America

The Spanish had found near-mythical abundance of gold and silver in South America. What Cabot found was less dramatic, but almost as valuable. "The sea there," it was noted on his return,

> is swarming with fish, which can be taken not only with the net but in baskets let down with a stone, so that it sinks in the water. . . . These same English, his [Cabot's] companions, say that they could bring so many fish that this kingdom would have no further need of Iceland, from which place there comes a very great quantity of the fish called stockfish.[10]

The fish was the cod, and the discovery of the Grand Banks, the coves and bays of Newfoundland, and later, the Gulf of St. Lawrence, was to provide Europe with very good reason to cross the North Atlantic again and again.

Cod was valued because, even more than pepper, it was a mass-consumption item. There was a desperate need for a cheap source of protein in a time when beef was a luxury. Also, demand was enhanced considerably by contemporary religious doctrine. Various religious holidays were marked by the Roman Catholic church as meatless. As holy observances multiplied, so, too, did the number of meatless days. With Lent, the feast days associated with various saints, Fridays, and other "fish days," these numbers could be considerable. Altogether, in the sixteenth century, about one in three days was declared to be "meatless." The result was a tremendous demand for fish. Hundreds of British ships departed each year, in the late fifteenth century, for Iceland. Hundreds more British and French ships fished the Irish Sea and the Channel. In France, the port of Dieppe alone received some 530 tons of herring in 1475.[11] Thus, when the cod-rich waters of Newfoundland were discovered, there was a ready market. Moreover, cod was a fish that could be caught and preserved with relative ease. It is not surprising, given these facts, that Cabot's discovery soon opened up new transatlantic commerce.

Precise statistics on the early cod trade are impossible to come by. It is feasible, however, to map with some accuracy the general patterns of the trade and its economic importance through the sixteenth and early seventeenth centuries. The first notable thing about the cod fishery is the rapidity with which Bristol fishermen followed up on Cabot's discovery. Cabot arrived back in Bristol in August 1497. Fishermen accompanied him on his return trip to Newfoundland the next year, and by 1502 there were reports of loads of Newfoundland cod arriving in England. Obviously, the techniques and technology for the Atlantic trade were already in place. All that was needed was a location in which they could be put to use. Indeed, there has been speculation that Bristol fishermen may have been aware of the Newfoundland fisheries before Cabot's voyage.[12] While such is unprovable, there is no doubt that, by the early 1500s, the nations of Europe were moving to take advantage of this new resource.

Even though Cabot may have discovered the fishing grounds on behalf of the King of England, in the early years the English presence in Newfoundland was second to that of Portugal and France. Both nations had plentiful supplies of salt and, as is detailed in Chapter 2, salt facilitated the curing process. Economist Harold Innis discovered the records of some 128 ships that ventured to Newfoundland before 1550. Of these, 11 were English, 3 English-Portuguese, 9 Spanish, and 93 French.[13] Although, as the lack of a strong Portuguese presence in this listing indicates, records are not always reliable, it is clear that the French were present in overwhelming numbers.

The French fishery was based in western seaports such as La Rochelle, Rouen, St.-Malo, Nantes, Le Havre, and other areas of Normandy and Brittany, where a long tradition of Atlantic fishing existed. As one historian has noted, for the French "the switch from European waters to the northwestern Atlantic was the extension of a well-established industry and the application of familiar techniques."[14] Their market initially was France, the centre of that market being Paris; as one of the largest cities in Europe, Paris had a tremendous demand for cheap, protein-rich food.

In the longer term, however, the English were well situated to take advantage of the North American fishery. The West Country fishermen and merchants who dominated the North Atlantic trade were closer to the region than were their French and Spanish counterparts. They had the experience and equipment for the Atlantic fishery, as their regular voyages to Icelandic waters showed. Until the latter half of the sixteenth century, however, most British fishermen were content to fish in the vicinity of Iceland rather than face the competitive and often dangerous rivalries in the waters around Newfoundland.

By the latter part of the century, this situation changed. The Royal Navy's presence and power were growing ever stronger, especially with the defeat of the Spanish Armada in 1588. Further, the Danish government began to enforce stricter rules concerning Icelandic waters. Finally, though statistics are far from complete, the growing imports into the United Kingdom of Newfoundland fish from France may indicate the inadequacy of existing British fishing practices in meeting domestic demand. Whatever the reasons, by the end of the century, the British were increasingly turning their attention to the Newfoundland fishery.

The fishermen of France, England, Spain, and Portugal increased their efforts off Newfoundland after 1550. For many years, the precise strength of the fleets varied, depending on wars, resources committed, and luck. The Spanish fishery was very strong from approximately 1560 through the 1580s, and the French would long be a major presence in the region. Overall, however, it was the English who increased their presence most dramatically. By 1600, fishermen operating out of Dartmouth and other southern and western ports had supplanted the French as the dominant fishing nation in the Newfoundland area. Spain (which now included Portugal) had become a minor player.

As the number of ships involved in the Newfoundland trade mounted, a system of finance evolved that would remain more or less constant over the next century. This system nicely illustrates the way in which an adaptive commerce could take advantage of opportunities such as the Newfoundland fishery. Also, it applies, with some minor variations, to both the French and the English fisheries.[15]

First, financing was shaped by the speculative nature of the trade, and by the costs involved in outfitting an expedition. A ship could cost £200 to build, and chartering was also expensive. Victualling a crew, according to one contemporary, cost some £450. Nor was there any certainty of return. The Atlantic trade was a risky one. Ships could be lost in storms, captured by pirates, or seized during one of the many wars of the period. Marine insurance evolved slowly; thus, shipowners and investors often bore the better part of the risk of failure. However, the potential profits were great. The same contemporary who estimated the costs of victualling a ship also estimated that his return on the investment would, if all went well, be some £750 — a return of 79 percent on a four- to six-month investment. Such profits made the high risks worth bearing for many an investor.

Few ships' captains could afford to bear the costs or the risks alone, however. Indeed, many did not own their ships, but chartered them from others. In order to raise capital and spread risk, therefore, a standard response of fishing captains was to sell "shares" in their venture. Shares were often given to crews in lieu of wages, the standard in the English fishery being one-third, with fixed bonuses to those in key positions, such as the second mate or carpenter. Even without wages to the crew, the cost of provisioning a ship for the season was great, and arrangements had to be made with suppliers. Victuallers were also given a one-third share. The final third usually went to the ship's captain. Of course, shares could be further divided, and such division seems to have been common among individuals who invested small amounts in several shipping ventures rather than large amounts in one. One-sixth, one-eighth, and one-sixteenth shares were common in both the French and the English fisheries. Risk was spread out accordingly.

In many instances, those who were involved in the voyage did not themselves have the funds to invest. There was thus a secondary aspect to financing, involving the lending of money to those with shares in voyages. Normally, the loan was uninsured, and the lender was entitled to nothing should the ship sink or be captured. The loans were high-risk, and interest rates were commensurate. Those rates varied, depending on the lender, the time, and the ship, but 25 percent rates seem to have been common, although figures showing a 40 percent rate have been discovered.

The system says much about the successful development of European commerce. For one thing, it reveals the degree to which the commercial revolution had allowed the formation of risk capital.

Merchants and lenders knew they were investing in a risky business activity. The fact that they were willing to do so with regularity reflects both the funds available and the potential profits to be made. Second, the system was a flexible one, well adapted to the nature of the enterprise. Ships' captains could raise in small lots what might have been impossible to raise had only one source of funds been available. Also, as has been mentioned, the share system meant that, when losses did occur, they were more likely to be manageable for investors.

The Native Economy and European Contact

Once Europeans began to plant settlements in Canada, incidental contact with the native tribes of North America would become much more direct. Economic interaction between the newcomers and the original settlers of North America became the fundamental fact that shaped the economy and society of early colonial settlement. Initially, the native population, knowledgeable in its own habitat and aware of its own economic interests, was to dominate these relationships. Over time, however, the superior technology and greater numbers that the Europeans could bring to bear would transform the economy of North America. It is, thus, worthwhile to look at the nature of the native economy that was about to receive the Europeans, as it is to look at the economy that was being received.

Some preliminary points must be made before any description of the economy of the North American native population is undertaken. First, it is extremely difficult to discuss any single "native economy" before contact. For one thing, there were several native economies, varying from the harsh hunting/fishing economy of the Inuit to the agriculturally based economy of the Huron. Second, the term "before contact" presents problems. Contact occurred over an extended period. The impact of the Europeans on the Micmac of Nova Scotia or the Iroquois of the St. Lawrence came two centuries before European contact with the Blackfoot of the interior plains. Further, the absence of written records makes it all the more difficult to come to any full comprehension of the precontact native economy, even if the other problems could be resolved.

A final problem is pointed out by recent anthropological studies that demonstrate how native tribes were affected by Europe long before they had any direct contact with Europeans. Trade goods filtered inland through intermediary tribes and altered the technology of a society that had never seen a European. For example, archaeological digs in Southern Ontario have dated a good many European items in the region from the late sixteenth century, decades before European settlement began. For all these reasons, Bruce Trigger's concept of "proto-history" is an extremely useful one. This term refers to the period during which European influence altered the economy, technology, or society of a native group, even though no European had been to the region.[16] These qualifications made, it is still possible to give a general description of the economic structure of native society on the eve of European contact. Of immediate interest are the tribes east of Lake Huron, with whom the Europeans would first come into contact.

In most general terms, the tribes of eastern Canada can be divided into two groups. The first group populated the woodlands of Northern Ontario, northern and central Quebec, and much of the Maritimes and included such tribes as the Ottawa, Algonquians, and Micmac. They were hunter-gatherers whose food supplies came from the game of the vast forests and from fishing. This reliance made them nomadic, as they followed game resources and adapted to the demands of the various seasons. It also meant that they usually lived in fairly small bands or in individual family units. Any large concentration of the tribe would have quickly outstripped the game resources of an area.

A more complex economy had been developed sometime in the millennium before European arrival by the Iroquois and Huron tribes of Southern Ontario and upstate New York. Corn, beans, and squash had been introduced by tribes to the south, beginning around A.D. 500. By the time Cabot reached Newfoundland, these tribes had become primarily agricultural. This agricultural base affected their social and tribal structures. Larger groups could, and did, live together in villages of up to a thousand people. Hunting took place but, as it was secondary to agriculture, it placed less strain on the game resources. This fact meant that a given area of land was able to support a larger number of people than was the case in a society totally dependent on hunting. The population of the Huronia area (roughly between Lake Simcoe and Georgian Bay) has been estimated at about 10 000 at the end of the sixteenth century. To the south of the Great Lakes, the Iroquois confederacy is estimated to have had a population of 10 000 at the time of contact (see Map 1.3).

Until recently, it has been common to assume that economic rivalry and the genocidal warfare observed during the first phase of European settlement were by-products of that European presence. European trade goods, the argument went, created new rivalries, based on economic competition, in traditional warfare. Wars thus escalated from minor skirmishes to all-out assaults. Now, though there is still debate, two things seem apparent. First, since there was considerable trade between tribes, trade rivalries existed long before European contact. Copper from the Lake Superior region had been traded into the lower Great Lakes area for centuries, for example. Likewise, seashells from the east coast of the United States had found their way inland. The filtering of European goods only added to this trade. Second, there is evidence to suggest that economic rivalries had led to extremely destructive wars before initial contact took place with Europeans.

When the European goods appeared on the scene, therefore, neither the concept of trade nor that of economic rivalry — including warfare — was strange to the native population. What was strange and difficult to comprehend was European technological society. Beads and metal initially had associations with magic, and were used by native peoples in a religious rather than a utilitarian manner. Such religious overtones meant that, at first, tribes would accept in trade almost anything from the Europeans who dabbled in furs along the coasts. As goods filtered inland, traded by the Micmac or other tribes along the coast, they were accepted in the same way.

Sometime about 1580, this pattern began to change. It appears that, after this date, many more European goods penetrated inland. Further, tribes involved in trading had by now passed beyond their initial willingness to accept anything, and were looking for more practical goods. At the same time, Europeans along the coasts seem to have been doing more and more fur trading. The invasion of European goods into Canada, if not yet of Europeans, was well under way. Indications are that a whole sector of the native economy now revolved around the acquisition and disposal of European goods. Regular trade routes existed, and tribes were already jockeying for a better position to take advantage of this new economic role. Wars and large-scale population movements occurred around such questions. There is even a possibility that European diseases

MAP 1.3
Huronia and Iroquois Territories, Sixteenth Century

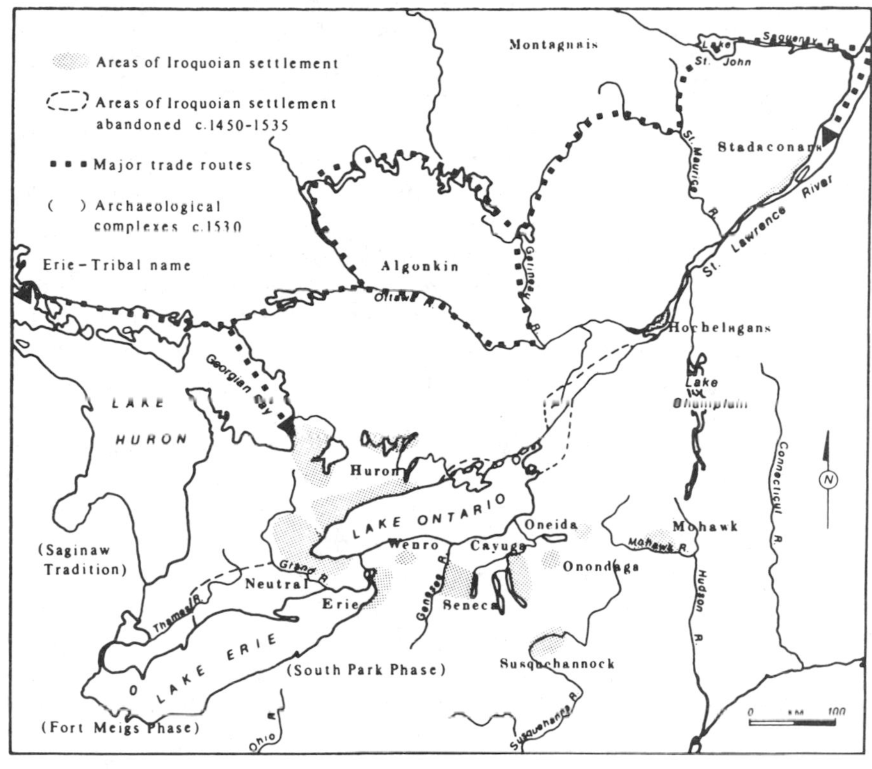

Source: Bruce Trigger, *Natives and Newcomers: Canada's "Heroic Age" Reconsidered* (Montreal and Kingston: McGill-Queen's University Press, 1985), 150.

ravaged Nova Scotian tribes as early as the late sixteenth century, before European settlement had begun.

On the eve of colonization, therefore, certain key facts stand out about the native economy. First, though that economy remained primarily dependent on hunting and agriculture, commerce, including commerce in European goods, was an important feature. Second, the impact of European goods had already significantly altered the economies, not just of the coast, but of the interior. Anthropologist Bruce Trigger has concluded that, by the end of the sixteenth century, "Tadoussac [at the confluence of the Saguenay and the St. Lawrence rivers] was clearly the most important fur trading centre in North America. It stood at the head of a large number of native trade routes leading into the interior of North America."[17] Finally, a population shift of considerable importance had taken place sometime during the proto-historic period. When Jacques Cartier sailed up the St. Lawrence in 1535, he found the region occupied by Iroquoian tribes. Between that time and Champlain's arrival in 1608, those tribes disappeared from the area. Whether this displacement was the result of the rivalry for European goods or of other events is unknown. It did mean that, when the Europeans came to settle, they had available to them a largely empty stretch of land along the St. Lawrence.

For more than a century, Europeans had crossed to the New World in the vicinity of Canada. For decades, that European presence had affected the native economies of much of the eastern portion of the continent. Now, at the beginning of the seventeenth century, the third stage in the expansion of Europe to Canada was about to begin, with the establishment of a permanent settlement at Quebec.

Conclusion

In summary, colonization in North America was preceded by three important events. The first was the development of an aggressive European economy. The second was the development of the improved technologies necessary to expand to new areas. The third was the discovery that the fishery was a resource that made transatlantic commerce worthwhile; this ensured that the major nations of Europe remained active in the North Atlantic, even if North America was at first little more than a dry-dock facility. The value of the fishery meant that, from the very outset, nations would contend for dominance in the region during the colonial period. Spain and Portugal had yielded to the North Atlantic nations of France and Britain. Now, early in the seventeenth century, these two nations were about to plant themselves in North America. On the North American side, a number of native tribes, already affected by European goods and attuned to trading possibilities, would see their trade routes, their warfare, and their way of life affected by the arrival of the Europeans.

Notes

1. K.G. Davies, *The North Atlantic World in the Seventeenth Century* (Minneapolis: University of Minnesota Press, 1974), xi.
2. On the Greenland and Vinland (Newfoundland) experiences of the Norse, see Samuel Eliot Morison, *The European Discovery of America: The Northern Voyages* (New York: Oxford University Press, 1971), 32–62.
3. Kristoff Glamann, "European Trade 1500–1740," in *The Sixteenth and Seventeenth Centuries: The Fontana Economic History of Europe*, edited by Carlo M. Cipolla (Glasgow: Fontana, 1974), 477.
4. Glamann, "European Trade," 476.
5. Davies, *The North Atlantic World*, 31.
6. J.H. Parry, *The Establishment of European Hegemony, 1415–1715* (New York: Harper and Row, 1961), 18.
7. The best description of the changes in ship technology is in Morison, *The European Discovery of America*, 112–27.
8. Glamann, "European Trade," 479.
9. Cited in Davies, *The North Atlantic World*, 22.
10. Cited in H.A. Innis, *The Cod Fisheries: The History of an International Economy*, rev. ed. (Toronto: University of Toronto Press, 1954), 11.
11. Davies, *The North Atlantic World*, 14.
12. D.B. Quinn, "The Argument for the English Discovery of America Between 1480 and 1494," *Geographical Journal* 112 (1961): 277–85.
13. Innis, *The Cod Fisheries*, 11.
14. Davies, *The North Atlantic World*, 14.
15. The best description of financing is found in Gillian Cell, *English Enterprise in Newfoundland, 1577–1660* (Toronto: McClelland and Stewart, 1969), 6–18. Innis, *The Cod Fisheries*, 18–23, also has useful information on the organization of the French trade. The following paragraphs are taken primarily from these two sources.
16. Bruce Trigger, *Natives and Newcomers: Canada's "Heroic Age" Reconsidered* (Montreal and Kingston: McGill-Queen's University Press, 1985), 116. Much of the discussion below on the proto-historic period is derived from Trigger's excellent study.
17. Trigger, *Natives and Newcomers*, 141.

Further Reading

Cell, Gillian. *English Enterprise in Newfoundland, 1577–1660.* Toronto: McClelland and Stewart, 1969.

Davies, K.G. *The North Atlantic World in the Seventeenth Century.* Minneapolis: University of Minnesota Press, 1974.

Glamann, Kristoff. "European Trade 1500–1750." In *The Sixteenth and Seventeenth Centuries: The Fontana Economic History of Europe*, edited by Carlo M. Cipolla. Glasgow: Fontana, 1974.

Trigger, Bruce. *Natives and Newcomers: Canada's "Heroic Age" Reconsidered.* Montreal and Kingston: McGill-Queen's University Press, 1985.

CHAPTER

2

The Atlantic Colonies

The central theme in the economic history of Atlantic Canada for the century and a half after 1600 is the evolution of the area from its status as a fishery to that of a collection of colonies capable of supporting permanent populations. At the start of the period, only the rich fishing banks of the continental shelf were of any economic consequence to the European powers. The landmasses served merely as places to stop temporarily to dry fish and repair boats and fishing gear. The region was still basically a fishery in 1713, when control over most of the area shifted from France to Britain. The only European settlers were a handful of transient fishermen in Newfoundland and a slightly larger group of Acadian subsistence farmers scattered along the shores of the Bay of Fundy.

Settlements that can, in any real sense, be called permanent did not begin until the eighteenth century, more than 200 years after Cabot's first voyage. While mercantilist doctrine figured in the establishment of both Newfoundland and the Maritimes, it did so in quite different ways. In Newfoundland's case, the economics of the fishing industry dictated a transition from a migratory to a residentiary trade, and with this shift came the impetus for permanent settlement of the island. British mercantile interests opposed this development and, for a considerable time, were able to influence policy accordingly. Economic reality won out, however, and the mid-eighteenth century marks the transition of the island from fishery to colony.

The same transition in the fisheries occurred in the Maritime provinces, and here, too, it contributed to the establishment of permanent settlement. More important in explaining settlement and economic development in this region, though, were the attempts by the British government after 1745 to defend its political and economic interests in North America against the French. Soldiers were sent to Nova Scotia, followed by merchants, land developers, and other commercial interests intent on making British presence in the area felt. Like that of Newfoundland, the economic history of the Maritime provinces really does not begin before the mid-eighteenth century, nearly two centuries after the area was discovered by Europeans. Unlike that of the island, however, settlement proceeded because of British mercantile policy and not in spite of it.

The Cod Fishery

The development of the cod fishery was shaped, to a very large degree, by the habits of the codfish. The cod breeds and survives best in the particular ocean temperatures and currents of the continental shelf and Grand Banks (see Map 2.1). It is a migratory fish. In the fall and winter, it concentrates out on the continental shelf. After spawning in spring, it moves toward the bays and coastal areas of Newfoundland, returning to the deeper water in the fall.

The habits of the cod determined the habits of the cod fishermen. As the trade developed throughout the sixteenth and seventeenth centuries, two cycles appeared. One cycle (the first in the season but the second to develop) involved fishing for cod in the open oceans of the continental shelf. Fishermen left their European ports in late January or February. Making the cold Atlantic crossing, they would arrive off the Grand Banks in late winter, fish through May, and return home as the cod headed in toward shore.

The second cycle involved fishing for cod in its summer habitat along the coastal areas. Leaving Europe from March through May, ships headed toward Newfoundland, landed, and set up stations on shore. Fishermen would then go out into the coastal waters in small fishing boats, such as shallops, manned by a crew of five. They fished, as weather permitted, through to September. A good fisherman, on a good day, could land as many as 300 cod, using hook and line. A 100-ton boat could, in a good season, return with 20 000 to 25 000 cod. There are several recorded instances of ships that made two trips in a season, presumably taking advantage of both fishing cycles.

Each cycle was associated with a particular preservation method. The deeper-sea or bank fishing used the so-called green method

MAP 2.1
Fishing and Fish, Seventeenth-Century Newfoundland

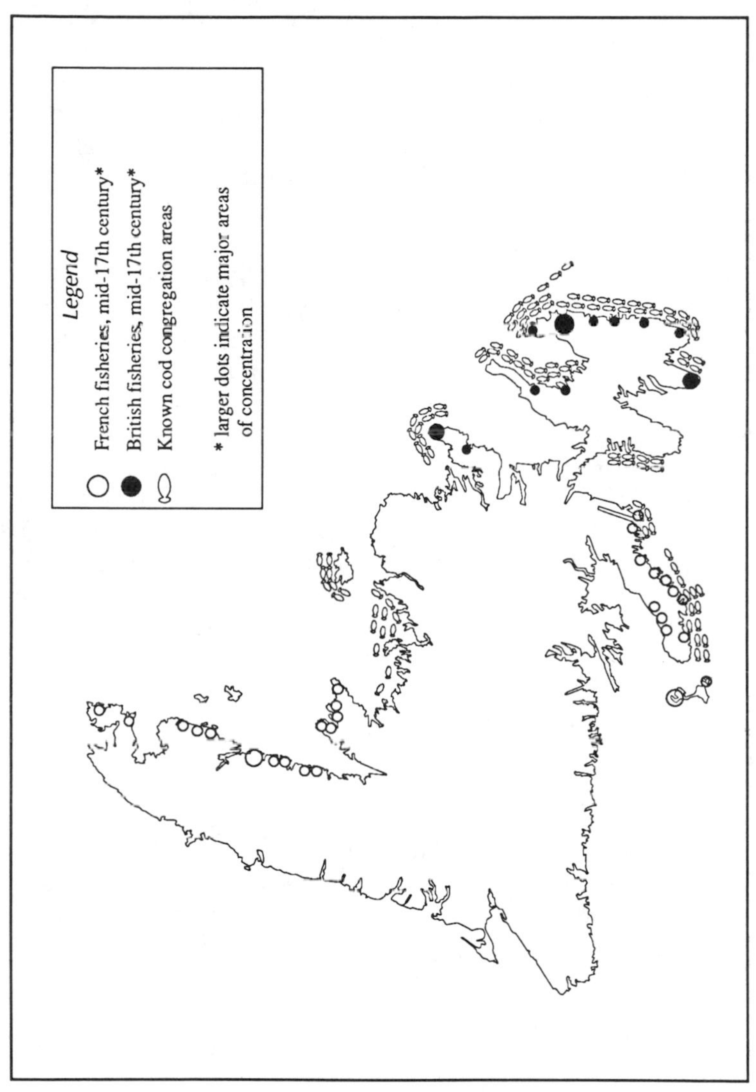

Source: Adapted from Grant Head, *Eighteenth Century Newfoundland* (Toronto: McClelland and Stewart, 1976), 24.

most commonly. The day's fish were gutted, heavily salted, and, after three days, resalted. Thus preserved, they could last long periods of time in reasonable condition. The ship could deliver a load that was, by the standards of the day, reasonably edible and thus claim a fairly high price on the market.

The main drawback of the green-cure method was that it required enormous amounts of salt. Salt not only was an expense in its own right, but was in restricted supply. The only part of Europe that possessed sufficient quantities of salt to meet the demands of the fishery was a stretch of the coast running from La Rochelle, in France, down to Portugal, a fact that explains why these nations are associated with the technique. Other countries wanting to use the green-cure method would have to import large quantities of salt before setting off. Profits would diminish accordingly and, in times of war, when salt imports were jeopardized, essential food supplies could be endangered.

The implications of green cure for the subsequent history of the region are important. The method meant that fishing boats could operate independently of land. Barring storms or other problems, it was possible for the ship to act as a self-contained unit, fishing off the Grand Banks, preserving the fish, and returning home without even seeing shore. As the fishery was independent of land, it led to little or no exploration or development of the region. In a sense, North America was irrelevant to the green fishermen, except as a refuge in bad weather and as a source of fresh wood and water.

The alternative technique for preservation was the so-called dry fishery, associated with the second of the two cycles. Fishermen came over for the summer season, set up temporary headquarters on the shore, and fished from small boats along the bays and coasts. Fish were cleaned on shore and dried in the sun. Once dried, they were salted and packed aboard ocean-going vessels for the return trip. The great advantage of the dry fishery was that it used considerably less salt. This fact was particularly important for nations that, like England, were chronically short of salt.

By the end of the sixteenth century, England and France had, as noted in Chapter 1, assumed a dominant position in the Newfoundland trade. The French were kept out of much of the Avalon Peninsula by the strong English presence there. They were represented, instead, off the shores of Nova Scotia and in the Gulf

"A Fishing Station" by Gerard Edema. (c. *1652*–c. *1700) The Painting shows a harbour in Placentia Bay, Newfoundland, about 1690. Such a station would provide British and French fishermen with a temporary haven where they could dry fish or repair boats and fishing gear. Permanent settlements were not established until the eighteenth century.*

of St. Lawrence. In Newfoundland, they were concentrated along the southern coast, including the islands of St. Pierre and Miquelon, and along the northeastern coasts. By the seventeenth century, their presence in the south would be anchored by a small garrison at Placentia, just as the British would establish a fort in St. John's harbour. Relying, as they did, on the green-cure technique, they made infrequent and brief contact with the land and no permanent settlement resulted. In 1750, after two and a half centuries of activity in Canada's Atlantic fisheries, there were no French settlements that can be linked directly to this industry.

The British fishery relied almost exclusively on the dry-cure method, and centred on St. John's harbour and along the Avalon

Peninsula, supplanting previous Spanish and Portuguese presences. Southward, along the peninsula, a series of smaller bays and harbours also provided good bases. Northward, Harbour Grace and Trinity were major gathering points, with several smaller sites scattered between them.[1] All the sites of the English were centred around the giant schools of cod in the area, as Map 2.1 indicates.

Unlike the French, with their green-cure technique, the British made frequent and ongoing contact with the land, as such was an essential feature of the dry-cure method. The dry fishery brought a European presence to the landmass of North America, albeit seasonally and only on the easternmost reaches. By the late seventeenth century, up to 1200 men would congegrate in St. John's harbour and along the Avalon Peninsula each summer to work the fishery. Such places as Harbour Grace and Trinity saw 200 or 300 men gathered; smaller areas saw anything from a handful to several score.[2]

Newfoundland

The contact of the British dry fishers with the land led eventually to permanent settlement in Newfoundland, although the transition from a migratory to a residentiary fishery was very gradual. Wintering over was the first step. Ships brought extra crew to the island to construct and maintain the harbours and stages necessary for the dry-cure fishery. As competition became more intense, these men were often left through the winter to stake a claim to the best drying sites for the following season. Most returned to Britain eventually, and some continued on to New England, but a few remained in Newfoundland on a more or less permanent basis.

The link between fishing technology and the tendency to settlement is more noticeable as the fishery developed. Ships arriving from the West Country ports could catch more in a season than they could transport to market. This surplus, together with what the tiny resident population could contribute, was available for someone else to take to market. Beginning in the early years of the seventeenth century, British merchants began sending vessels, called sack ships, to Newfoundland to purchase the surplus, whence they sailed to the markets in Portugal and Spain, and then back to Britain. They duplicated the activities of the West Country merchants, in effect, except that they did not fish themselves.

The sack ships initially were a response to the appearance of a surplus catch in Newfoundland, but, once established, they also allowed this output to grow. By providing a market for the output of the tiny resident population, they afforded that population the possibility of more permanence. With the sack ships came another group of fishermen, the byeboat keepers, who were neither purely resident nor purely migratory. Byeboat keepers operated in the inshore fisheries during the summer season, selling their catch to the sack ships. When winter came, they would return to Britain in the vessels of the West Country fishermen, leaving their own boats in Newfoundland until the following season, when they would seek return passage on the same fishing vessels, to begin all over. The fact that the West Country ships travelled to Newfoundland in ballast gave the captains an incentive to offer cheap passage to this group of fishermen. Byeboat keepers were a cross between the migratory fishermen, who used the island only to dry their catch, and the residents, who lived there more or less year-round.

The richness of the Newfoundland fisheries drew other interests into the trade. Chartered companies were formed with the object of operating the fishery in much the same manner as plantation interests did the sugar islands to the south. Permanent residents were to do the actual fishing. Ships would be sent to Newfoundland to pick up the catch, transport it to market, and bring the trade goods back to Britain. The first settlement plan was instituted in 1578, with six more attempts made between 1603 and 1625. All failed, in part because of the hostile conditions on the island and in part as a result of the active opposition of the West Country interests. Some individuals remained, however, and they and their descendants joined the winter crews from the ship fishery as the beginnings of a permanent population.

Eventually, those wintering over did not return or move on and byeboat keepers stayed on the island rather than returning at the end of each season. Population figures fluctuated wildly, depending on conditions in the industry and on international political developments. Population jumped from 2400 in 1710 to more than 4000 in 1715, and back to 2500 in 1720, for example. The long-term trend was upwards. There were between 1500 and 2000 residents in 1650, slightly more than 4000 in 1715, and about 5000 by the middle of the eighteenth century. The island was given its first resident governor and magistrates' court in 1729, an acknowledgement of the growing permanent population.

Residents and byeboat keepers were opposed at every turn by the West Country merchants. These interlopers, as they were viewed, competed for the best fishing spots, harbours, and drying areas, and their demands for some sort of resident government challenged the authority of the ships' captains. For a time, West Country interests prevailed. Regulations drawn up to govern the island discouraged settlement in every way possible. One measure made it illegal for fishing vessels to transport persons to the island who were not crew members. Another forbade the levy of a tax on codfish, a move designed to deprive any local government of revenue. Another prohibited residents from cutting wood that might be useful for erecting drying stages and from building houses near the shore. These regulations were relaxed somewhat toward the end of the seventeenth century as the population became more firmly established, but the political conflict remained for nearly another century.

There was little economic life on the island outside the cod fishery. Boats and fishing equipment were imported from Europe, and, other than drying, no further processing of the export product was required. Most of the food was imported as well, mainly because it was cheaper to do so than to attempt to tame Newfoundland's rugged environment. St. John's did develop as an entrepôt after 1713, establishing a dominance in Newfoundland that has lasted to the present day. Ships brought supplies for the fishing industry to the port, and picked up cod for transport to New England, the West Indies, or Europe. In this sense, Newfoundland's early development is a classic example of what might be termed "staple determinism." It is essential to consider the characteristics of the main resource export in order to understand the extent and pattern of economic development more generally, and, by and large, that is all that is really required to do so.

The defeat of France in the Seven Years' War at midcentury had relatively little impact on Newfoundland. The residentiary fishery prospered during the war, as it had whenever conflicts in Europe interrupted the migratory trade. France had ceded all its claims to Newfoundland by the Treaty of Utrecht in 1713, but retained the right to catch and dry fish on the shore from Cape Bonavista west to the northern point, and from there south to Point Rich.

Article 5 of the Treaty of Paris in 1763 reaffirmed the shore provisions agreed to in 1713, while Article 6 granted France control over the islands of St. Pierre and Miquelon. The French remained as competitors in the fishing industry, as they have until this day, but Newfoundland was now undisputably part of the British colonial and mercantile system.

The Maritimes

Besides the fishermen of Newfoundland, the only other permanent presence in Atlantic Canada in 1713 was that of the Acadians in what is now Nova Scotia and New Brunswick. Descendants of early French attempts to establish a colony at Port Royal in the early seventeenth century, the Acadians had gradually spread northwards along the Bay of Fundy, crossing over to the valley of the Petitcodiac by the turn of the eighteenth century. From a handful of households in 1650, population grew to an estimated 5000 in 1713 through immigration from France and through a very high natural rate of increase. They were mainly farmers, building dikes to keep the sea from the rich marshland soil. Wheat, rye, peas, and livestock were the principal outputs. Any surplus production went, illicitly, to New England in exchange for British manufactured goods. Fishing and hunting were other economic activities.

The Treaty of Utrecht in 1713 brought a major political change to Nova Scotia, and a minor economic one. France ceded control over most of this area to Britain, but retained Cape Breton and Prince Edward Island (then Île St.-Jean) and promptly constructed a large fort at Louisbourg on Cape Breton to defend its remaining interests in North America. The area that is modern-day New Brunswick remained under dispute.

The transfer of Nova Scotia to the British in 1713 had little immediate effect on the region. A dry fishery developed at Canso, by New Englanders, at first, and then by sack ships from Britain. The port was too close to French territory to grow much, however, and by the 1740s was in relative decline. There were a couple of half-hearted attempts to settle western Nova Scotia to produce pine masts for the British navy, but they came to nothing. Some settlement came from the south, as New Englanders moved north along the coast of Maine and into the valley of the Kennebeck, but this migration was still quite limited.

The British gained control over the Acadians in 1713. An initial offer was made to move them to areas of French control, but, thereafter, British authorities felt they were less of a security threat, isolated as they were along the Bay of Fundy, and they were largely ignored. Immigration to Acadia from France ceased after 1713, but fertility was sufficiently high that the population increased nonetheless. From around 5000 souls in 1712, the number of Acadians grew to 10 000 by 1750, and to 13 000 by 1755.

Unlike those of Newfoundland, the fortunes of the Maritimes changed markedly with the European wars at midcentury. The reasons were political more than economic. British neglect of Acadia ended in 1745, when the War of the Austrian Succession spilled over to North America. Nova Scotia had to be secured for New England as a barrier against the French. Three thousand settlers were established at the newly founded port of Halifax in 1749 to provide a military and administrative presence, and this figure rose to 5000 the following year. Fifteen hundred German and Swiss settlers were brought to Halifax, settling eventually in Lunenburg in 1753.

With the war, the Acadians scattered along the Bay of Fundy were once again seen as a military threat, given their refusal to swear allegiance to the British crown and the supplies they managed to send to the fort at Louisbourg. There was an economic interest in their lands as well. The movement of New Englanders northward after 1713 had generated pressure to expel the Acadian farmers from the rich marshlands. British authorities finally succumbed to the demands, and, in 1755, the settlers were forcibly expelled from their lands and scattered among the American colonies, whence many went to Quebec or to France.

The immediate impact of the Seven Years' War (1756–63) on Nova Scotia was the influx of some 7000 New Englanders into the region. Some were fishermen who had long worked in the area and were simply moving closer to their sources of supply. Others were farmers, occupying, among other areas, land taken from the Acadians. Still others were merchants and traders, coming very quickly to dominate the economic life of Halifax and the other larger centres. Population was further augmented after 1764, when the Acadians returned to the Chaleur Bay region, and as New England settlement continued to move into the region.

In a few short years, war had accomplished what two centuries of fishing activity had not; it had created the basis for permanent settlement of what are now Canada's Maritime provinces. The contrast with Newfoundland in this respect is striking, and provides an early warning of the limits of the more naïve version of the staples theory. Neither the largely subsistent economy of the Acadians nor the garrison economy of Halifax fits neatly into that framework. Political factors, first those stranding the Acadians and then those establishing Nova Scotia as an outpost of the British Empire, figure at least as prominently in the early economic history of the region as do the characteristics of the cod fisheries.

Nova Scotia emerged from these political and military realignments with two distinct economies. The garrison town of Halifax looked to the British fleet, and to the mercantile and outfitting duties that connection promised. Their view was across the Atlantic and to the West Indies. They were imperial in perspective, and the powerful merchant fleets of Massachusetts were their main rivals. The outports and farms, however, were largely isolated from imperial economic development. Massachusetts was not so much their rival as it was their metropolis, a primary source of supplies and the home of their families. This position of simultaneously competing with and relying on the more advanced economies to the south is an important theme of Maritime economic history through to today, and one it has shared with Newfoundland.

Notes

1. Grant Head, *Eighteenth Century Newfoundland: A Geographer's Perspective* (Toronto: McClelland and Stewart, 1976), 8–15.
2. Head, *Newfoundland*, Chapter 1.

Further Reading

Buckner, P.A., and David Frank, eds. *Atlantic Canada Before Confederation*. The Acadiensis Reader, Vol. 1. Fredericton: Acadiensis Press, 1985.

Head, Grant. *Eighteenth Century Newfoundland: A Geographer's Perspective*. Toronto: McClelland and Stewart, 1976.

Innis, H.A. *The Cod Fisheries: The History of an International Economy*. Rev. ed. Toronto: University of Toronto Press, 1954.

C H A P T E R

3

New France

Newfoundland's transient settlers notwithstanding, Samuel de Champlain's arrival at Quebec in 1608 marked the beginning of permanent and officially recognized European settlement in what would become Canada. It also marked the beginning of the transition of the continent's economy from one based on the native population's tradition of communal landholding and egalitarian tribal government to one based on private property and the concept of the state — from a Stone Age culture to an emerging technological society. By the time New France fell to the British a century and a half later, the eastern half of the continent would be dominated by the Europeans, and by European economic practices.

Before beginning a detailed discussion of New France, it is worth commenting on two of its key characteristics. First, it was a colony. That may seem an unremarkable statement, but, as J.F. Bosher has noted, there is a tendency among historians to look to New France as "an early chapter in the history of Canada."[1] This temptation is understandable but, taken too far, leads to an underrating of the interrelationships of the colony with the mother country. New France was a small centre of settlement throughout its existence and, for the first 50 years, was little more than a trading post — a tiny extension of the Old World's commercial and religious interests to the New. Over time, it evolved a more complex society and economy, but even at the time of the conquest by the British in 1759, the European population was just over 70 000. Specie was scarce, capital accumulation was limited, and the range of production, though much expanded in recent years, still fell far short of that of the English colonies to the south.

Instead, New France was a colony that, throughout its existence, was dependent on the staples trade. This dependence is the second crucial characteristic of the economy. The fur trade — and especially the beaver trade — dominated commercial transactions from the colony's beginning to its end. Initially, furs were its only export product. Later, efforts were made to diversify exports, and a rising population did allow some economic diversification, with limited exports in foodstuffs, and with a growing range of locally produced goods to meet domestic demand. However, furs provided the initial reason for the colony's establishment and dominated its trade.

The Early Fur Trade and Early New France, 1608–1663

The fur trade was dependent on European fashion. The more exotic furs were used for luxury items of clothing or trim. Most important, however, was the beaver. Its inner coat was used for the making of felt hats. Before 1600, most of the European demand was met internally. Between Cartier's visits in the 1530s and that of Champlain in 1608, though, two things had happened to make a trade in North American supplies viable. First, fashion dictated that the brims on hats be larger than had previously been the case; thus, the overall amount of beaver required to meet the demand of the hat trade had increased. Second, the European supply of beaver was nearly exhausted. An item of trade that, in North America, had been a sideline to the fisheries over the past century was on the verge of becoming a major item of trade in its own right.

The hat trade, once established, would continue to be of considerable importance to Canadian economic development through to the middle of the nineteenth century. As a product of fashion, however, the demand for beaver pelts varied considerably from year to year. Fashions changed; brims widened and narrowed. Since supplies could not be varied easily in the short run, prices swung in response to changes in demand. At other times, prices fluctuated according to erratic shifts in supply, with demand being relatively unresponsive. Expansion of trade networks, or severe competition between parties, companies, or nations, could quickly glut the market.

For these reasons, those engaged in the fur trade attempted to secure a monopoly position. A monopoly over sales in Europe could better weather the changing demand and, most important, control of the trade in North America could regulate the supply of the resource. Thus, throughout the trade's history, officials in France and New France sought to establish a monopoly of one form or another — the settlement of Quebec in 1608 was, in part, one attempt at monopoly. All the while, there were those, subjects of New France or of other countries, who had reasons to try to subvert that monopoly control.

Another important characteristic of the trade is that furs are what are known as "high value, low bulk"; that is, a relatively small quantity of furs is worth a great deal. Transport costs were thus a relatively low factor in the overall cost of doing business, and even the long times and vast distances involved in regular seventeenth-century crossings between Quebec and France were worthwhile. Within North America, this meant that such practical local forms of transportation as the birchbark canoe, used by, and adopted from, the natives, were efficient means of carrying on the trade.

Also shaping the colony of New France was the peculiar nature of the way its territory evolved — an evolution determined, in large part, by its staples trade. W.J. Eccles has accurately noted that New France possessed a frontier configuration that was unique and differed radically from the one in British settlement colonies to the south.[2] For the British, the line of agricultural settlement and the colony's boundaries were more or less the same; however, such was not the case for New France. Instead, New France evolved as what has been termed a "river empire," with long tentacles of economic, political, and military influence stretching thousands of miles beyond the area of settlement. As Map 3.1 indicates, even by 1750 the settled portion of New France was confined to a stretch of land running from just below Quebec City to Montreal. The population was a mere 50 000. Yet, this same colony's influence extended through the Great Lakes to the Prairie west, southward into the Mississippi and Ohio river basins, and all the way to the Gulf of Mexico.

This unusual expansion was made possible by the river systems. Champlain had established his settlement on the waterway that provided the best access into the interior of the continent. The St. Lawrence–Great Lakes system provided a natural transportation route, extending thousands of miles west, northwest, and, with relatively short portages, south as well. In contrast, access was much more restricted for the English colonies to the south. Only New

MAP 3.1

New France as a "River Empire," *c.* 1750

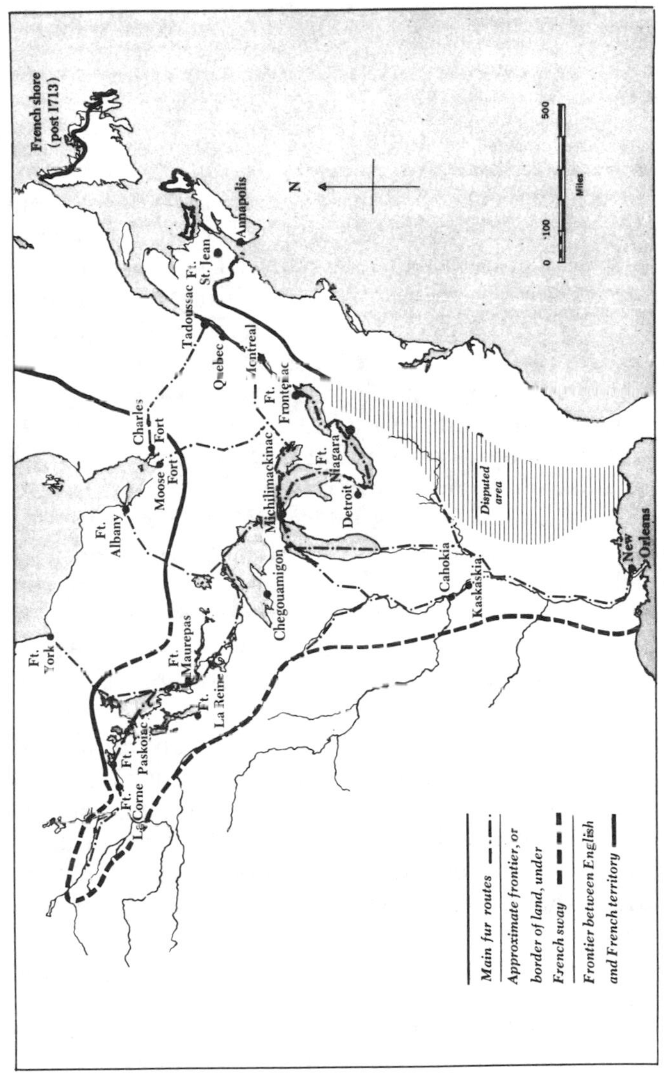

Source: W.J. Eccles, *The Canadian Frontier, 1534–1760* (Toronto: Holt, Rinehart and Winston, 1969), 169.

York's Hudson-Mohawk system provided anything like the easy transportation the French enjoyed. The other colonies not only lacked good river access to the interior but faced the barrier of the Allegheny mountains. Nothing blocked the French, however, and it was indicative of the future of New France that, within a few years of their arrival, the French routinely travelled more than 300 miles inland from Quebec, visiting their allies, the powerful Huron tribe, located between Georgian Bay and Lake Simcoe.

The French presence in the interior was thus marked by rapid movement and influence over vast distances. It was also much more dependent on native good will than was agricultural settlement. The natives vastly outnumbered the French, for one thing; for another, the fur trade could not have been carried on without them. From the beginning, the natives trapped the furs and transported them to the French. The alliances with these tribes also gave the French whatever power they had in the interior. For their part, the tribes wanted access to French trade goods and were not immediately threatened with displacement by the French agricultural frontier.

There were still conflicts. The Europeans were eminently capable of high-handed tactics and could easily alienate potential allies. In this, however, Champlain was lucky. When he settled at Quebec, the previously powerful Iroquois tribes of the region had been pushed back, south of the Great Lakes. The St. Lawrence valley below Montreal was thus a largely empty land, and the Europeans were more easily able to establish their presence. At no time in the history of New France did French settlement seriously encroach on occupied tribal lands.

In effect, the French inserted their settlement among three main tribal groups. To the north were the Montagnais and Algonquian peoples. They were nomadic, depending on the hunt. They were also excellent trappers and would be important to the French fur trade. To the west were the Huron. When Champlain arrived, they were probably the most powerful tribe in the region, with a population of perhaps 30 000. Champlain's early alliance with the Huron put them in the enviable position of being middlemen in the fur trade. They were the tribe that had direct access to French technology, and they had the power to prevent tribes farther west from equivalent access. They could act as intermediaries, passing along French goods (with suitable profit) to interior tribes, while returning furs from those tribes (with suitable profit) to the French.

The alliance meant one other very important thing. In order to cement the Huron alliance, Champlain had, in 1609, taken part in a raid on an Iroquois village, and by so doing had stepped into a long-standing war between the two powerful tribes. Thus, New France was, from the beginning, the enemy of the Iroquois. Moreover, the intertribal war gained intensity in relation to the desire to control access to European goods. The Iroquois had good reason to wish to deny their Huron enemies access to the French. These reasons were reinforced when, in 1613, the Dutch established a colony at the mouth of the Hudson River (present-day New York) and, soon after, a trading post upriver, at Albany. The Iroquois assumed the same role for the Dutch fur trade as that of the Huron in trade with the French. Both wished to displace their rivals and to gain a monopoly of access to European goods. For the next 30 years, the Huron and Iroquois battled for supremacy in the region.

The importance of the native tribes to the economic structure of New France cannot be overemphasized. In the first half-century after the Europeans landed, the French colony was, in many ways, an insignificant thing. Fifteen years after Champlain established his settlement, there were still fewer than 70 settlers in New France. There was no agriculture other than a few plots to feed the garrison, and there were practically no families. It was, in the words of W.J. Eccles, not really a settlement at all, but a mere "commercial outpost" to facilitate the gathering of furs. The fur trade was, in effect, an international trade. The French Empire extended as far as Quebec, where it dealt with the independent native tribes. Only because the native tribes supplied the skill and labour to exploit the beaver trade was there any trade at all.

State policy also helps explain the slow growth of New France in the early years. The King of France may have wanted a flourishing settlement in North America, but, as was the case with other governments, he was loath to commit his nation to large expenditures for risky overseas ventures. As a substitute, therefore, the state turned over the responsibility for settlement to private companies. The idea was that the state could limit the drain on its revenues if it gave special trading privileges in the New World to some company. In return, the company would underwrite and manage the costs of exploration and subsequent settlement. This was the technique under which Champlain had settled Quebec and, indeed, though the companies would change, it was to be the technique used to underwrite the Quebec venture until 1663. New France was, then, legally as well as figuratively, a commercial outpost.

The problem was that company and crown interests did not always coincide. Critics argued that the companies allowed settlement to languish while they pursued profits. Defenders of the company pointed to arbitrary court interventions, uncertain jurisdictional lines, and frequent changes of government policy. The fact was that the sustenance and growth of an agricultural colony in a relatively harsh climatic environment such as the St. Lawrence required significant subsidies on an ongoing basis. Such subsidies were more than most companies could afford. Company monopoly was certainly not the optimum means to promote settlement, but its use was a symptom rather than a cause of the lack of growth.

The real problem was that there was no economic reason for the colony to grow beyond a rather minimal size without massive subsidization. The fur trade did not require a large French population. The small population, together with the arduous task of clearing the lands, the repeated clashes with the Iroquois, and the unlikelihood that any crop grown in New France could find an export market, prohibited much agricultural development. As late as 1660, the European population of all of New France was only about 3000 people. The three communities of Quebec City, Three Rivers, and Montreal were little more than villages. Most of the land along the St. Lawrence remained wilderness, and only around Quebec was there sufficient cultivation for it to be called an agricultural community. As Marcel Trudel has so aptly put it, "there was the constant feeling that at any moment everyone might pack up and go back to France."[3]

The Royal Colony

Quebec was, however, on the eve of momentous change. Two major developments brought about these changes and would finally allow the colony to be established on a firm footing. The economy would, in the process, become more complex. Furs would remain the staple, but a growing population would create meaningful agricultural settlement and even more ambitious schemes for growth.

One major change came from the French taking an increasingly active role in the fur trade. For some decades, individuals (known as coureurs de bois) had ventured out into the wilderness to explore; to establish contacts with more distant tribes; and, as entrepreneurs, to undertake a little trade and transport of furs themselves. The governments of the day had often condemned these independents. They were, it was said, engaging in immoral practices and, even more important, making regulation of supply difficult. Still, the system continued, and even flourished, as the same river networks that had made the colony dominant in the fur trade allowed people easy access to the interior.

In 1649, a major shift took place in the local balance of power. The Iroquois launched a successful assault upon the Huron nation, dispersing its people and thereby ending Huron dominance of the fur trade. The Iroquois then turned on the French, and on such tribes as the Ottawa, who threatened to replace the Huron. The Iroquois ultimately failed to gain a dominant position themselves, but they did cause chaos in the transportation system over the next fifteen years. In the process, the middleman role of the native tribes was considerably weakened. The Ottawa, Algonquian, and Montagnais tribes would all have liked to assume the role taken by the Huron — as, for that matter, would the Iroquois — but none was able to. Instead, the French took over the role themselves. Over the next 30 years, as we will see, tremendous expansion of the French presence and influence took place. All of this meant greater manpower requirements and greater opportunities for those who would emigrate to the struggling colony.[4]

A second major change occurred in 1663, when the French government finally abandoned the concept of the company monopoly and made New France a royal colony. The government of the colony became, in theory at least, like that of any other French province, responsible, in this case, to the Ministry of Marine. Decision making was increasingly centralized (though distance always imposed limits), and the French government took a much more serious interest in the colony at long last. In the immediate sense, what this meant was an infusion of military support (the Carignan-Salières Regiment) to suppress the Iroquois threat, increased financial aid, and energetic though relatively short-term support for immigration. Members of the Carignan-Salières Regiment were encouraged to settle, and some 400 did. Immigrants were subsidized to come across, and groups of artisans, women (known as *filles du roi*), were given additional incentives. Within a decade, the population increased from 2600 to 7000. For the first time, the population was big enough that the colony was secure, and activities other than the fur trade began to take on importance.

The newly established royal colony of New France was put under the energetic direction of Jean Colbert, Minister of Marine, one of Louis XIV's main advisers. For Colbert, and for the king he served, two key principles seemed operative in the formation of policy. The first was theological: for reasons that had much to do with recent French history, Louis XIV wanted to ensure that the powerful and influential religious presence in New France was kept under control. Second, and most relevant to New France's economy, Colbert and the king wanted to integrate New France more closely into the overall economy of the French Empire. This integration was to proceed along the lines of the favoured French economic policy of mercantilism.

The challenge for Colbert was to use mercantile policy to develop New France (and the lucrative West Indies) by encouraging more fruitful trade within the Empire. The New World should be more of a buttress to the Old and, along the way, the New World's economy would become more developed. The fur trade would continue, of course, but it should be joined and strengthened by other activities. It was with these principles in mind that Colbert created a new official for New France, the intendant. The intendant was Colbert's personal representative in the colony and was the individual in charge of economic development.

What Colbert and his initial appointee to this new post, Jean Talon, wanted to do, in specific terms, was reasonably straightforward. First, they wanted to diversify the economy. Far too many basic resources had to be brought over from France. The colony could not even feed itself, much less provide surpluses that might help meet imperial needs elsewhere. All too often, ships returning from New France did so in ballast because there were no cargoes to bring out. All too often, as well, those same ships had been in New France, supplying grains or artisanal products that, seemingly, the colony itself should have been able to produce. The result was a severe trade imbalance and costly shipping system that retarded the growth of the colony and cost the mother country dearly.

The model to emulate existed to the south. Rapidly growing English colonies such as Massachusetts (under the Massachusetts Bay Company, founded in 1629) had established a successful series of

Confederation Life Collection

A shipyard in New France. *The first appointee to the post of Intendant of New France, Jean Talon (shown on the left in this romanticized picture), embarked upon a number of ventures intended to diversify the economy of the colony. One was the foundation of the first Canadian shipyard.*

trade connections both with the mother country and with the British West Indies. The British system seemed to Colbert an ideal to which the French colonial system could aspire. New France, while exporting furs to France, might send wheat, fish, or timber to the West Indies. Sugar from the West Indies could go either to France or to New France. Of course, France would continue to export manufactured and luxury goods to the colonies, but colonial prosperity and a larger colonial population would considerably increase the French market there. All of this trade would also, in good mercantilist fashion, be restricted to French shipping and thereby encourage the growth of the French merchant marine.

In an effort to achieve the development of these potential export industries, the French crown, through Colbert and Talon, put considerable effort and funds into various schemes.[5] It has been estimated that, in its first years, the considerable annual sum of 200 000 livres was invested in the colony.[6] None of the ventures was very successful. Agriculture did develop to a degree, as will be discussed below, but an export market was not achieved until much later. The fisheries remained marginal and could never really compete in outside markets with the Grand Banks fleets. Colonial shipbuilding (and ancillary activities such as rope and sail production) was never able to compete with production in France itself.

By the early 1670s, the enthusiasm of the French crown for its North American colony had waned. The problems had proved more intractable than expected, and the costs higher. The failure of the various subsidized activities makes it tempting to conclude that Colbert's mercantilism was at fault. Certainly, Talon's recall to France in 1672 would seem to indicate that the French government thought this to be the case. Yet, there is a danger of dwelling too much on the failure of shipbuilding or other industries. Most important to the colony of New France was the influx of military support, capital, and civilian population that occurred in these years. Though the real impetus lasted only a decade, it allowed the colony to become something more than a fur-trade outpost, though it was always in the shadow of that export-oriented trade. The fur trade itself was on the verge of tremendous expansion and, with it, the frontiers of New France. Neither of these developments would have been possible without the strengthened economic and population base.

What distinguished the post-1663 colony was the emergence of landholding and farming as increasingly important activities. More and more people moved out onto the land, especially after the Iroquois threat was lessened. Thus, the system of landholding and its implications, largely irrelevant up to that point, began to take on added significance.

Agricultural Expansion, 1663–1713

As was the case in most colonies, the system of land title used was derived from the mother country. For New France, this meant that the seigneurial system, based upon the Coutume de Paris, was the standard from the time that agricultural land-granting began.[7] It was a feudally based system in which the crown granted land to certain nobles or seigneurs who, in return, swore allegiance to the crown. The seigneurs then allotted portions of their land to those who farmed it, known as censitaires or, as became common in New France, habitants. In contrast to practice under the British

FIGURE 3.1
Seigneurial "Ranges"

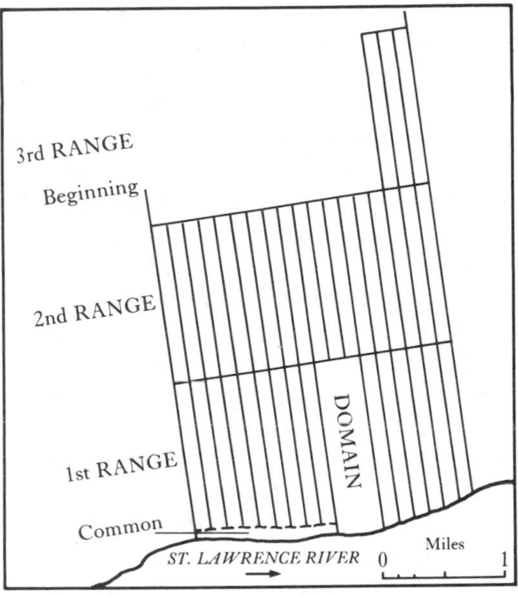

Source: R. Cole Harris, *The Seigneurial System in Early Canada: A Geographical Study*, 2nd ed. (Montreal and Kingston: McGill-Queen's University Press, 1984), 175.

freehold system, the censitaire did not own the land outright but had it as part of a feudal relationship in which he owed allegiance and certain duties to the seigneur, just as the seigneur owed certain responsibilities to the censitaires.

In New France, the landholding system of the seigneury also took on special characteristics. The first of these was the result of geography. The St. Lawrence was the natural (and, for decades, the only) highway in the colony. Access to the river was thus crucial, and the design of landholdings reflected that. In order to maximize the number of individuals with this important access to the river, the allocations to censitaires tended to be narrow but deep (see Figure 3.1). Eventually, as the population grew and the seigneury filled up, a second row would be settled. In the early years of the royal colony, however, this scheme was largely hypothetical, as most seigneuries had yet to open even a significant portion of their prime waterfront lands. Many had no cleared land at all.

The river gave the landholding patterns of New France yet another characteristic. As the population settled along the riverbank, there developed a long, thin ribbon of population that stretched intermittently along the St. Lawrence. There were no villages in any traditional sense, in that there were no real dividing points that distinguished the "centre" of a community from its periphery or from the countryside. Only the forest at the back of a settlement gave it definition. Thus, the importation of a European system of landholding led, under different geographical circumstances, to a radically modified dispersion of population and of activities.

The slow growth in population meant that the seigneurial system was slow to overlay the forested lands. As Map 3.2 indicates, the number of seigneuries granted by 1663 was relatively small. Large gaps appeared between them. Even these gaps, however, seriously understate the amount of wilderness that still existed in the St. Lawrence valley. Very little of the granted seigneurial land was actually cleared. Indeed, many seigneuries were completely empty and reflected only the dreams of some individual with the connections or position to obtain a grant. As late as 1700, after considerable additional population growth, one estimate concludes that perhaps only 5 percent of seigneurial land was actually cleared. Only well into the eighteenth century is it possible, therefore, to talk of the St. Lawrence valley as a settled agricultural community.

A more realistic idea of the progress of agricultural development is given by Map 3.3, which shows the distribution of people along the St. Lawrence valley some 30 years after the establishment of the royal colony. Even then, as can be seen, wilderness dominated much of the St. Lawrence valley. The only really extensive continuous settlements occurred near Quebec City (downriver for approximately twenty miles, and on the Île d'Orléans) and near Montreal (primarily on the south shore). Huge stretches — especially on the south shore — remained unsettled. The whole settlement clung to the river's edge.

This slow growth, even after the establishment of a royal colony, says much about the difficulties that faced would-be seigneurs and censitaires. Land, such a valuable commodity in Europe, assumed a much more uncertain worth in the New World. Only when converted into a productive farm did it acquire value, and such conversion was not an easy task. The St. Lawrence valley was heavily

MAP 3.2
The Seigneurial System in Early Canada

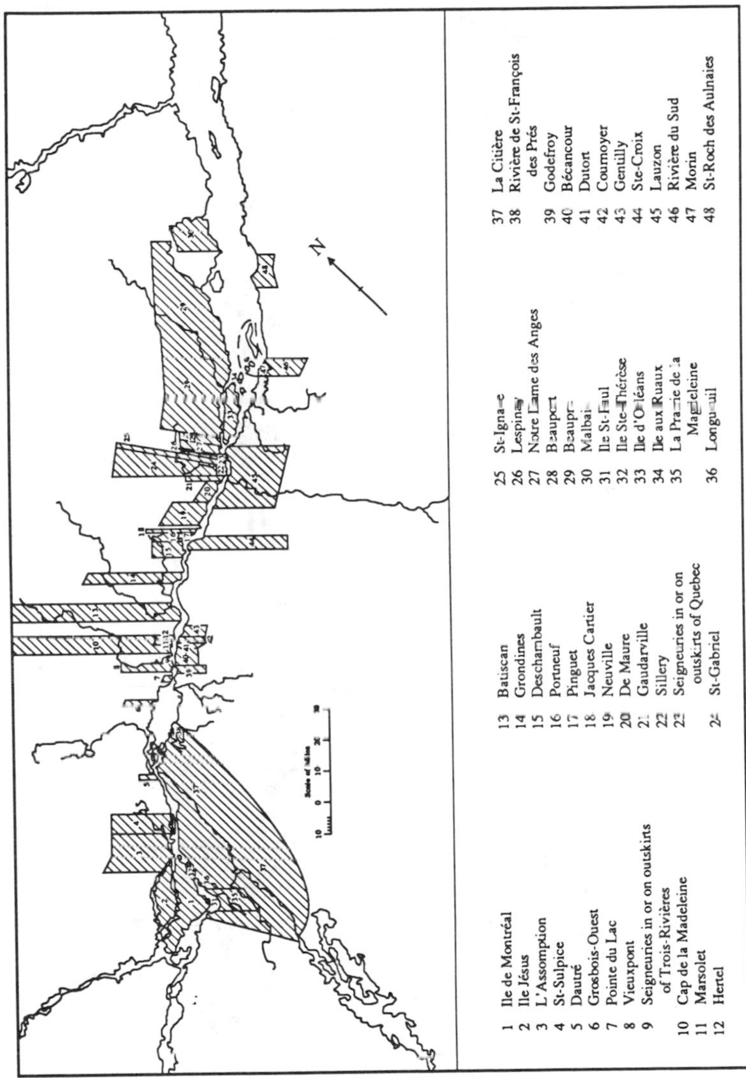

Source: R. Cole Harris, *The Seigneurial System in Early Canada*, 1st ed. (Montreal and Kingston: McGill-Queen's University Press, 1966), inside front cover.

MAP 3.3
Canadian Settlement, 1692 and at the End of the French Regime

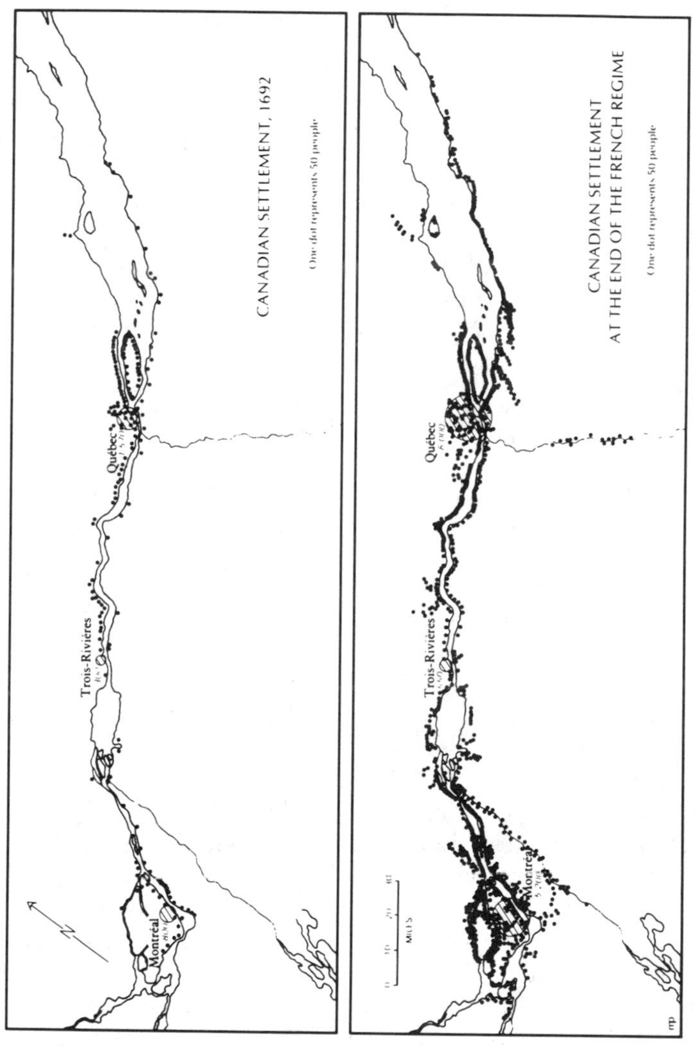

Source: R. Cole Harris and John Warkentin, *Canada Before Confederation: A Study in Historical Geography* (Toronto: Oxford University Press, 1974), 35.

treed and, in this preindustrial age, the process of clearing the land was extremely time-consuming and expensive. The costs and the time involved depended, of course, on the availability of labour and on the nature of the forest the settler faced. One estimate, however, concludes that, on average, a farmer could clear only about two arpents (1 arpent = 5/6 acre) a year! It was, thus, several years before a farmer could clear sufficient land to feed a family, much less provide any sort of potential cash surplus.

Also, given the agricultural techniques and the crops of the era, the St. Lawrence valley was a far from ideal agricultural region. Its growing season was shorter than France's, the soil was relatively sandy, and the lowland character of much of the region made drainage a problem. Along much of the north shore, the rocky surface of the Laurentian Shield reached almost to the river. "All in all," as Cole Harris concluded, "the soil sources of early Canada were scanty."[8]

One of the questions that has been discussed by historians is whether the seigneurial system itself retarded settlement. The system was encumbered by certain economic obligations for both parties. The seigneur was expected to provide a grist mill and a modicum of protection, in addition to other administrative responsibilities. The censitaire, or habitant, had to pay rent to the seigneur (*cens et rentes*), undertake labour for a fixed number of days on the roads or bridges in the seigneury (the *corvée*), grind his grain at the seigneur's mill (the *banalités*), and pay a fee to the seigneur upon the sale of his property (*lods et ventes*).[9]

The impact of these encumbrances should not be overstated, for, though New France's was a hierarchical society, it was much less so than that of France itself. The availability of cheap land and the seigneur's desperate need to attract people to that land to make it productive contrasted sharply with the situation in the mother country. The net effect was a levelling of incomes and social status relative to those in France. As visitors to New France repeatedly noted, seigneurs were poorer and had less power than did their counterparts in France, while the habitants had more relative wealth and a greater ability to influence events. New France in the seventeenth century provides a classic example of what can happen to social and economic structures when the relative values of various commodities — in this case, land and labour — change.

Nonetheless, the years after the establishment of royal government did bring serious agricultural settlement to New France. The influx of population and capital also allowed a degree of diversification and urban development. Neither Montreal nor Quebec was exactly a rival to Paris. As late as 1744, Quebec City's population was only 4600, and that of Montreal (founded in 1642) only about 3500. Three Rivers, the other "urban" community, had reached only 400. Still, the colony of New France was now firmly established as more than a commercial outpost. The native population would no longer be able to challenge the French for control of the St. Lawrence valley.

The Expansion of the Fur Trade, 1663–1713

In spite of this agricultural expansion and the other developments, the fur trade remained, throughout these years, the central economic activity of the colony, so far as the international trading system was concerned. Animal pelts in one form or another accounted for more than 90 percent of the exports of New France well into the eighteenth century.[10] For all the plans of Talon and Colbert, furs remained the one really valuable resource in which New France (and the native lands around it) had a distinct economic advantage. Thus, the establishment of a royal colony, far from marking a policy shift away from furs, was to see a tremendous expansion of the fur trade.

It is interesting that this expansion of the fur trade came as much in spite of government policy as because of it. As mentioned earlier, the displacement of the Huron brought an increasing number of French into the interior, acting the role of middlemen themselves. For the would-be farmer who still had much land to clear, or for the town labourer with only intermittent work, the fur trade offered a rare opportunity for quick profit. By the 1660s, a growing number of men were operating as independent entrepreneurs. This small-scale entrepreneurship contrasted sharply with the official policy of monopoly, which was thought to be the most effective means of carrying on the fur trade.

Some accommodation had to be reached, and Colbert thought he had a reasonable solution when he allowed free trading in the interior to continue but decreed that all beaver pelts and moose hides must be sold to officials of the Compagnie de l'Occident — the crown's corporate agent in New France. There were two problems with this solution. First, the presence of the English posts to the south provided an alternative destination for furs. Even the Iroquois could act as a suitable middleman when the occasion arose. Second, and more important, the price set for pelts by the company (which actually sublet its rights) proved too attractive. The interior trade expanded, business opportunism being reinforced by the abatement of the wars with the Iroquois. Furs flowed into the official warehouses at a growing rate, yet the government failed to lower the price sufficiently to reduce the oversupply. In effect, the costs — the result partly of policy, and partly of errors in price setting — were absorbed by the state.

Not only did this expansion create problems for the fur merchants, but it drew valuable manpower away from the colony. Colbert argued that, if New France were to develop, it had to begin by truly settling the St. Lawrence valley and not by spreading itself over thousands of square miles of forest in search of beaver pelts. A "compact colony," he argued, was the solution. Thus, the French government tried, throughout the 1670s, to restrict the number of traders in the interior. Such restrictions proved useless. Reduced (but still guaranteed) prices, official decrees banning the trade, and a system of licences (*congés*) had no long-term effect. The trade not only continued, but expanded, and an increasing number of French found themselves drawn westward.

In part, the failure of trade restrictions to limit trade may have been related to the fact that Colbert and the crown were not completely supported by the government of New France. In particular, Comte de Frontenac (governor from 1672 to 1682, and from 1689 to 1698) supported a policy of expansion. Of course, this was not the expansion of settlement or of agriculture — New France had not even developed the St. Lawrence valley. Rather, Frontenac was extending the colony on the same principles that had governed it from the beginning. The small settled region could influence a much larger area through key posts, and especially through alliances with the native population. The rivers could provide the means of access; the fur trade, the economic incentive.[11]

The 1670s and 1680s saw the most dramatic territorial expansion of the fur trade that was to take place in the history of New France. In 1673, Frontenac established Fort Frontenac on the site of present-day Kingston, while René-Robert Cavelier de La Salle explored southward, reaching the mouth of the Mississippi within a few years. Exploration was followed or accompanied by new alliances, the opening of new fur regions, and a tremendous inflow of furs to the warehouses in New France, greatly increasing the personal gain of La Salle and Frontenac. There was also expansion to the northwest, albeit on a less dramatic scale, as coureurs de bois made new contacts and broadened their trade areas to the west of Lake Superior. By the 1680s, the French "river empire" had expanded over thousands of square miles and extended over much of the eastern half of the continent.

Such expansion had several effects. First, it altered the nature of the fur trade. Initially, the role of trader and transporter had belonged either to the Indians or to the highly independent entrepreneurs, the coureurs de bois. As the trade expanded westward, however, the journeys grew longer, and, therefore, the time between the purchase of trade goods and the ultimate return on that investment increased. In this way, capital and credit became increasingly important. Those larger-scale merchants with access to both began to dominate the trade. There was still a place for the habitant who wished to make a living in the trade, but it was more often as a hired paddler and agent, a voyageur, than as an independent small businessman.

The second effect of expansion was oversupply. W.J. Eccles has estimated that, between 1675 and 1685, given the prices that existed, "twice as much beaver was shipped to France as the French market could absorb."[12] Between 1675 and 1685, exports of furs doubled. By the late 1690s, they doubled again. Inevitably, the price declined. Instead of fewer furs coming in in response, however, there were more. This result could be explained in part by the effort of traders to maintain income by increasing quantity, and in part by government decisions to maintain a relatively high price for furs. It also reflects, however, a particular response of some native tribes. Many of them were nomadic, and accumulation of goods presented real difficulties. Extra pots, pans, or whatever, could be burdensome during the journeys from place to place. There was, in other words, a fixed number of goods desired by many Indian bands. The higher the price for their furs, the fewer the furs that would be necessary to supply their wants. In times of lower prices, however, more would be needed and more would be supplied.

Thus, a decline in prices actually brought an increase in the number of furs. From an average annual output, between 1675 and 1685, of some 89 599 pounds, production rose to an amazing peak of 296 000 pounds by the end of the century. The glut continued to grow so that, by the late 1690s, there was some ten years' worth of beaver pelts stocked in warehouses. The situation was so desperate that the French government ordered the west closed to the fur trade, and the majority of posts abandoned. The trade would, henceforth, occur only when the natives brought pelts to the French along the St. Lawrence or at Fort Frontenac. Even that did not resolve the problem, however; over the next few years, there were several reorganizations of the fur-trading monopoly, new restrictions of the trade, several bankruptcies, and considerable overall economic hardship for the colony. By 1705, one report indicated that every pelt brought to France was being sold at a loss.[13] Not until 1714 did the restrictions finally have the desired effect, creating demand for new supplies of beaver in France.

The third consequence of the expansion of the trade was to intensify old rivalries. Neither the English nor the Iroquois were willing to stand by and watch the French expansion. The Iroquois faced the danger of being outflanked by the French in the fur trade and thus having their source of supplies for trade to the English cut off. By 1680, the Iroquois launched attacks on the Illinois tribes to the west. Over the next several years, they expanded their attacks on the Indian allies of the French. By 1689, the French themselves were coming under attack. In August of that year, for example, the Iroquois virtually destroyed the village of Lachine, burning it to the ground and taking numerous prisoners. Not until 1700 was any sort of longer-term peace achieved between the Iroquois, on the one hand, and the French and their Indian allies, on the other.

The Iroquois were acting independently, but the disruption of French alliances in the west was welcome to the English colonies. For the English, the French presence in the interior meant two things. First, as the Iroquois had, English fur-trade merchants became concerned about future sources of supply. If ever-more tribes were connected to the French alliance system, it became doubtful whether the English would be able to maintain adequate supplies for themselves. Such concerns, however, affected only a small number of English colonists, largely in New York.

French expansion seemed even more threatening to the Americans for what it implied in terms of geographical control. The dominance of the French in the interior seemed to endanger the future expansion of British colonies. As of the late seventeenth century, the need to settle the trans-Appalachian west was not a pressing matter, but the giant crescent of French influence that now surrounded the English colonies seemed a very real threat. Map 3.1, though depicting a somewhat later state, indicates the pattern that was developing.

The French also had cause to fear the English. The primary reason was the establishment, in 1670, of the Company of Adventurers Trading into Hudson's Bay (the Hudson's Bay Company). If the English feared an encirclement by the French, the French began to fear a pincer movement by the English. This English presence was especially important for the fur trade, as posts on the bay could draw native tribes northward and thus divert furs from the French system. The New York traders were already enough of a threat in this regard, and it was with some concern, therefore, that the French watched this English attempt to gain access to the tribes that, so far, had been most removed from English competition. Over the next 40 years, French and English would try combinations of competition, diplomacy, and armed assault as a means of resolving control of the bay.

Ultimately, the French lost. In 1713, in the Treaty of Utrecht, they recognized English claims over Hudson Bay. This was a case of military victory following economic victory. The English were successful in developing an integrated system between the bay posts and the British metropolitan fur market. The French, however, seemed to view their activities around the bay merely as counters to the English and as a buffer for more important trade activities occurring elsewhere. Their system in the bay area was never fully integrated and never very efficient.

The conflict over the bay was only part of the growing clash in North America between the two great imperial powers. By 1690, the French were convinced that the English were actively supporting the Iroquois in their wars. In response, New France raided a series of smaller English settlements in the northern English colonies. The English colonists, predictably, retaliated. This marked the beginning of an on-again, off-again war for dominance in North America. In fact, the next 80 years would see almost as many years of war (1690–97, 1701–13, 1744–48, 1755–63) as years of peace. Before this period was over, the conflicts between the colonies began to take on a life of their own, overshadowing and eventually precipitating conflict between the parent countries.

The details of the conflicts are beyond the scope of this study. As a general proposition, however, it is worth noting that the continual wars had a significant effect on the economy of New France. Indeed, many historians have argued that the warfare was as important as the fur trade in shaping both the society and the economy of the colony. The payroll for troops (regular or militia), the policies of the French government, the alliances with the native tribes, and a host of other factors that emerged from war affected the economy.

Overall, the effect of war on the economy of New France was probably negative rather than positive, despite the addition of the military payroll. In part, this effect resulted because, to the degree it was oriented toward war, the French government did not put its resources into peaceful economic development. Such was especially the case during the War of the Spanish Succession (1701–13). France simply could not afford to put any resources into its North American colony, while, in the meantime, enemy shipping reduced the attractiveness of trade with the colony. Given the already depressed state of the fur trade, the result was a decline of almost 50 percent in the number of ships moving into and out of the colony.[14]

The war also exacerbated the colony's existing fiscal and monetary problems. This was an age in which the supply of money more or less depended on the supply of gold and silver bullion. As was mentioned earlier, throughout much of the seventeenth century, Europe had insufficient bullion to meet the demands of a growing population and economy. In other words, an inadequate money supply acted as a retardant on economic growth throughout Europe. By the eighteenth century, this situation eased in Europe but not in the colonies. Imbalanced trade flows, exacerbated by mercantilist discouragement of colonial manufacturing, created a chronic monetary shortage, whether in peace or war.

The early eighteenth century was, however, an especially bad time in this regard. Beaver prices were the main source of export revenue and, as mentioned above, those prices were depressed throughout this period. Second, the costs of the war for France and its colony strained fiscal resources to the breaking point. Each year, governments were spending far more than their income, and each year, as well, the insufficiency of the bullion supply became more and more apparent. The result was a series of expedients. The most famous of these was "card money," so called because it involved the issue of playing cards, stamped and signed by government officials, as paper money. First used in the late seventeenth century, this method became an increasingly common way of dealing with lack of specie through the simple expedient of an alternative medium of exchange. Officials back in France alternately tolerated and condemned the practice, but the reality was that the French government itself was using similar expedients, and besides, French officials knew that the only alternative to monetizing the debt was bankruptcy of its colonial government. Throughout the rest of the war, New France thus limped along with a barely solvent government, depressed trade, and a monetary system that was flimsy at best.

Yet, the colony was important to France and becoming ever more so. It was increasingly being seen as an integral part of imperial strategy. France's overall desire for hegemony in Europe was to have effects on its small colony across the Atlantic. In particular, the French government had abandoned Colbert's idea of consolidation of the colony and had more or less accepted the more grandiose visions of officials in New France. In a despatch of 1701, Louis XIV favoured using the extension and consolidation of the French river empire as a means of hemming in the growing British colonies to the south. This vision gave the colony a purpose beyond the fur trade and gave the French government reason to put increased effort (when it could afford to) into the strengthening of New France. It also reversed priorities along the frontier. As W.J. Eccles has noted in his classic study on the Canadian frontier, a colony that previously had rested on the economic cornerstone of the fur trade now found the fur trade was often used as an instrument of imperial strategy.[15] The logic was simple. Alliances with western tribes became valuable as part of the consolidation of the frontier against English expansion. Good prices for furs would help cement those alliances.

The logic was simple, but there were several things that made success difficult. First, and foremost, was the fact that the British traders out of New York were able to provide a more attractive range of goods and to do so more cheaply. Only the barrier of the Iroquois had prevented the western tribes from turning to the English with increasing frequency. This points to the second problem: by 1700, the Iroquois were considerably weakened. The long war with the French and their allies had taken its toll. They were unlikely to act as a barrier much longer and, indeed, they made various moves in the first years of the eighteenth century that indicated they might be willing to facilitate rather than hamper the trade between the English and other tribes. This the French could not allow, for reasons of state. In response, therefore, the government began to offer increasingly valuable gifts and to subsidize the price of furs with key allied tribes. The vast frontier to the west, opened for the sake of the trade, had now become an end in itself, and the fur trade, though still very much profit-oriented in general, was now a subject of state policy. Part of the reason the fur-trade glut mentioned earlier took so long to clear up was that, after 1700, furs became a matter of state and thus prices were maintained at artificial levels.

Growth, Diversification, and Conflict, 1713–1750

In 1713, the War of the Spanish Succession came to an end. The French achieved their main aim in the war, which was to put a relative of Louis XIV on the throne of Spain, but had to make concessions elsewhere. In North America, France lost Acadia and its claim on the Hudson Bay regions. The future of the French Empire in North America had suffered a severe blow. Yet, New France itself was, after a long period of stagnation, about to enter an era of unprecedented growth and prosperity.

There are several reasons for the growth after 1713. The first was the extended period of peace, lasting some 30 years. Second, the already-mentioned rising demand for beaver in European markets coincided with the end of the war. With peace, shipping increased, financial circumstances stabilized (though not immediately), and attention could be turned from war to development. The revival of the fur trade, as might be expected, created a new optimism among both the average citizens and the merchants who hired them. Increases in the value of fur exports improved trade balances and brought more consumption goods into the colony.

Some of the forces encouraging prosperity had little to do with New France. Most importantly, Europe was emerging from a long period of economic stagnation. In what Miquelon calls the "metamorphosis of the seventeenth century into the eighteenth,"[16] inflows of gold and silver, in the generation after 1680, eased the monetary shortage, and trade revived. For its part, France, after running large deficits in the war and after a postwar financial and speculative scandal, acted to put its own financial house in order. Together, these changes yielded impressive results. From the depressed years immediately after Utrecht through to the early 1740s, French trade with its colonies increased sevenfold.

The bulk of that increase was not with New France but with the West Indies. Nevertheless, there were events in the North Atlantic that benefited New France. Foremost of these was that, in response to the loss of Acadia, the French government constructed the fortress town of Louisbourg on what is now Cape Breton Island. This town reached a population of more than 2000 by the 1730s. This might not seem to be a significant addition to the economy of the region until one remembers that Quebec City had a population of only about 5000 — and that was after one and a third centuries. Louisbourg provided a significant new market for the agricultural and forest products of New France. In addition, the growing market in the West Indies meant that shipments of grains, fish, timber, and other products did begin to go, though less regularly, from New France to the West Indies. New France finally achieved a diversified, if still limited, export market (see Table 3.1).

Such export trade was reflected in the domestic growth of the colony's economy. The fur trade was and would remain the primary activity of the colony, but the revival of trade and the demand for local products encouraged new land settlement, new immigration, and new ventures. In part, this diversification was brought about by local population growth. By the 1740s, a high birth rate and increased immigration had pushed the population to 50 000 and, by the 1750s, to something over 60 000, a tremendous rate of growth compared to that of earlier decades. Moreover, as the colony developed, work became more specialized. There was now a meaningful urban population. By 1740, Quebec City had a population of 5000, Montreal 3500; by 1760, population in these settlements had reached 8000 and 5000, respectively. Much of the population was engaged in commerce, finance, or education and did not grow their own food. They, therefore, provided a market for agricultural surpluses on the land.

The growing population encouraged more than merely agriculture. In 1734, a small forge at St. Maurice began production of stoves and iron. It was natural that the production of such goods would be undertaken locally, given their weight and the consequent costs of transportation from France. However, the plant required to undertake such production involved an expensive outlay. Thus, in perhaps the first of several instances in Canadian history, capital

TABLE 3.1
Exports from Quebec, 1736

	France	*Île Royale*	*West Indies*
Total value (livres)	954 000	123 900	97 400
Percentage of total trade	81%	11%	8%
Fish and other	6%	—	19%
Victuals	—	99%	71%
Furs	32%	—	—
Beaver	43%	—	—
Hides	19%	—	—
Timber	—	—	10%

Source: Derived from R. Cole Harris, ed., *Historical Atlas of Canada* (Toronto: University of Toronto Press, 1987), Plate 48.

costs seemed to prevent the development of an enterprise deemed essential to the community. That, at least, was how energetic promoters presented their case for government support. They succeeded, and were able to obtain ever-larger loans and grants from the government of New France. In the end, the forges produced some million pounds of iron, and then, in 1741, promptly went bankrupt.[17]

The St. Maurice ironworks is an index of both the growth of the economy by the later stages of the regime and the limitations to that growth. These major areas of diversification were matched in dozens of smaller ventures — new grist mills on the seigneuries, new artisan shops in the towns, greater activity by merchants, sealing along the north shore. There were even revivals of plans for shipbuilding, and other grandiose attempts to create major new economic activities.

New France on the Eve of Conquest

These developments raise two basic questions about the economy of New France in the years between the Treaty of Utrecht and the fall of the colony. The first concerns the agricultural sector. Were the patterns of mature settlement different from those of the seventeenth century, and did these differences affect the relationship between seigneur and habitant?

Certainly, by the mid-eighteenth century, the agricultural landscape of the St. Lawrence had changed. By now, there were some 250 seigneuries, ranging from the well-established to the largely uncleared ones on the edge of agricultural settlement. Also, in distinct contrast to the earlier period, the St. Lawrence valley had been more or less continuously settled by Europeans from below Quebec City to above Montreal. Along the south shore, that settlement stretched considerably east of Quebec. It was also beginning to spread southward along the Richelieu River system. The shape of settlement had not changed, however. The combination of a narrow band of fertile soil with the continued desirability of access to the St. Lawrence had created an agricultural New France that was a long narrow strip of settlement, straggling along the banks of the rivers. As one eighteenth-century observer commented, "it could really be called a village, beginning at Montreal and ending at Quebec, which is a distance of more than one hundred and eighty miles."[18]

The question, however, is whether economic and social relationships had changed, even though the shape of settlement had remained the same. Some have argued that class distinctions were widening and that, if there ever had been a frontier egalitarianism, it was now passing.[19] Others have emphasized the permanency of the earlier situation. What had been done could not be undone, according to this argument. The eighteenth-century habitant was wealthier and more independent that was his peasant counterpart in France. The seigneur was not the equivalent of an old-country aristocrat.

These viewpoints are not mutually exclusive, and it is likely that both contain elements of truth. Land was still less valuable relative to that in France, but it was more valuable than it had been a half-century before. Especially in wealthier and more productive seigneuries, there was an increased surplus to be taken off the land and, therefore, an increased advantage to the seigneur. For some seigneurs, the income derived from the various dues would have been meaningful by this time. One estimate is that one-half to two-thirds of the seigneurs were wealthy enough that much of the manual work on their farms would have been done by employees.[20] On other seigneuries, subsistence farming or pioneer conditions left little for the seigneur to extract.

It is also important to take time into account. Both yield and prices varied considerably from year to year, and crop failures were far from unknown. Thus, for example, in the later 1720s and early 1730s, when times were good, it is likely that seigneurial rents were considerable. When the crop failed in 1735 and 1736, however, only the most productive seigneuries were likely to produce much revenue for their owners. Alternative sources of income as well as personal capital could, thus, be of great importance to the seigneur. Large institutions, such as the church, or wealthy individuals were better able to weather the downturns and to maintain themselves as their aristocratic status demanded than were those who depended on the yearly income of the seigneury.

The other, and even more contentious, question surrounding the economy of New France in the eighteenth century concerns commerce. There has been considerable debate as to the extent and nature of the bourgeois class in New France. The debate has been particularly contentious because it has strong political overtones. Traditional anglophone interpretations have argued that New France, however heroic and interesting, was a backward colony of a backward system. Only after the British conquest, this argument continues, was there significant growth of a commercial class, and this class was British. Recent years have brought variations on this argument from both francophone and anglophone historians, but the argument remains essentially the same. New France was never sufficiently developed to have a meaningful merchant class, nor was the outlook of this preindustrial colony designed to encourage one.

In contrast, the Quebec nationalist school of historians began, in the 1940s, to argue that the extent of the bourgeoisie in New France had been underestimated. The colony was moving toward a more complex and more complete economy when the conquest by the British in 1760 stunted the development. In an argument known as the decapitation theory, this school concluded that the conquest caused the wealthiest and most educated in the colony to return to France, thus "decapitating" the social structure of the colony by removing its most powerful and innovative members. A vacuum was created, into which English and Scottish merchants moved. It is a politically evocative image of a "proto-nation" whose destiny was forever and tragically altered by military conquest.

The political controversy surrounding these two schools has ensured that, over the last generation, a great deal of attention has been paid to the question of the bourgeoisie and of business in New France, especially in its later days. It is thus impossible to come up with a more detailed reconstruction of commerce under the old regime than otherwise would have been the case.

The trade with New France was shaped by certain characteristics that were the result of the age and the distances involved.[21] First, trade was dependent on credit, and the duration of that credit could be quite long. In the autumn, a fur trader in New France might purchase a cargo of trade goods on credit. The next spring those goods would be parcelled out and sent inland in the care of the various groups of voyageurs and traders. After a summer of trading, they would return in the fall to sell their furs and repay their debt. A year had passed, and frequent problems in timing meant that a two-year delay was not uncommon. Second, the transatlantic trade was a risky one. Voyages could take from somewhat fewer than 30 to more than 120 days, and ships were regularly lost at sea. The frequent wars of the age added to the risks — though, of course, they also tended to add to the profits of those ships that survived the hazards.

Considerable resources were needed to engage in the transatlantic trade with any success, and, for that reason, among others, the control of the transatlantic trade remained in France. The colonial merchants simply did not have the financial strength or the connections to take it over themselves. In particular, as Figure 3.2 shows, the trade was dominated by merchants in one or two ports. Most important was La Rochelle, which had the longest and steadiest connections to New France. Bordeaux provided competition, and other ports, such as Rouen and Nantes, entered the picture on occasion. Overall, however, it was a concentrated trade, with one or two ports receiving the furs and providing the merchandise to the colony. Indeed, through much of the period, trade was more concentrated than that, as in many decades two or three families controlled the great bulk of the transatlantic trade with New France. Two other features of the shipping patterns should be noted. First, there is the tremendous increase in shipping during the years from 1720 to the conquest. Second, though La Rochelle may have dominated the trade through much of the colony's history, that was not the

FIGURE 3.2

Origins of Shipping to New France, 1680s to 1744

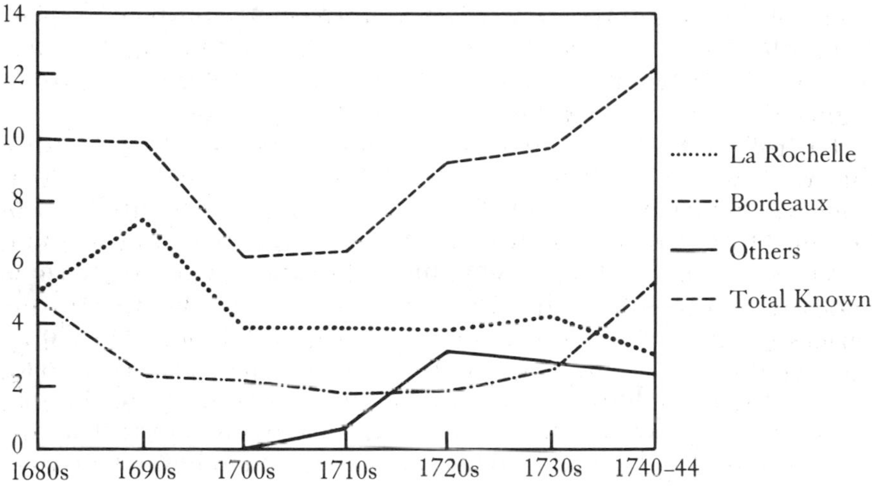

Source: J.S. Pritchard, "Ships, Men and Commerce: A Study of Maritime Activity in New France," Ph.D. thesis, University of Toronto, 1971, cited in Dale Miquelon, *New France, 1701–1744* (Toronto: McClelland and Stewart, 1987), 128.

case by the final years. Bordeaux and others had now become important in the transatlantic trade.

The merchants from La Rochelle and elsewhere carried out their trade in various ways. In many instances, they had an agent or factor living in Quebec. This person would act as a middleman, taking orders from smaller retailers, fur traders, and others, and then dispensing the goods that arrived on the ships from France. Sometimes these orders were handled strictly on a commission basis. The merchant obtained and shipped the good for a fee. Other times, the merchant sent the good over on his own behalf, and his agent in Quebec sold it. There was also a third variant, used by less-established companies, in which no permanent agent existed; instead, a cargo would arrive and be sold on the spot by itinerant merchants, often the captain of the ship that transported the goods in the first place.

There was some local wealth: some had accumulated considerable fortunes in trade; others had had success in the local carrying trade with Louisbourg, or in seal fisheries and other enterprises. Most important, however, was the fur trade. By the mid-eighteenth century, some twenty outfitters, almost all Canadian-born, dominated the trade.[22] Even for these, however, the transport of furs to France, and their sale once there, depended on those same La Rochelle and Bordeaux merchants. The size of their fortunes, moreover, while important in a small colony, was usually quite small compared to those of the French merchants with whom they dealt.

Overall, this situation can be characterized as a classic metropolitan-colonial relationship. The bourgeoisie was divided between France and New France, both by wealth and by function. The powerful and wealthy export-import business remained in metropolitan hands, as did credit facilities and capital. The lesser commercial enterprises, those of storekeeper and merchant, were in local control. However, the business in the interior belonged to citizens of New France. Metropolitan control could not penetrate that far inland, and considerable business activity thus concentrated in the rising city of Montreal, foreshadowing its eventual dominance over Quebec City.

This picture has implications for the way in which the conquest is depicted. When the British captured Quebec City in 1759 and gained the whole of New France by treaty in 1763, they did disrupt the normal business, but the way in which they did so was affected by the dualism in the nature of the bourgeoisie. The Canadian-born fur traders were not likely to head to France. Montreal, after all, was their home, and their business depended on the fur trade. Likewise, the average storekeeper or trader had neither the means nor the will to leave. In other words, to the extent that there was a local bourgeoisie, it remained more or less intact. If there was a decapitation, it was a transatlantic one. It was the merchant class of La Rochelle and elsewhere, along with their agents, who found the trade of New France cut off. Before long, local merchants found alternative suppliers in merchants from New England or Scotland, and thus the internal (as opposed to external) business structure of the colony was not severely disrupted.

What is most important, however, is that the exact size or nature of the bourgeois class was not what determined the fate of New France — it was population. New France's orientation toward the fur trade as well as the limits imposed on agriculture by soil and climate had kept the population small, however vast the territory held. In contrast, to the south, the English colonies had grown steadily, both in number and in population. By 1756, when the Seven Years' War broke out, the English population was more than two million, compared to New France's 55 000 or 60 000. With each passing year, the disparity of populations had grown, and by the mid-eighteenth century, the British colonies had reached a size that threatened to overwhelm that of any combination of the French and the native tribes. Ultimately, the French could not be defeated in the wilderness, and their alliances with the native tribes remained intact to the end. It didn't matter, however. The one settled portion of New France fell to the British, and in 1763 the whole territory was ceded to the English. A new era in the society and economy of North America was about to begin. The French river empire, with its fur-trade staple, was now joined with the British settlement empire and its agricultural staples.

Notes

1. J.F. Bosher, *The Canada Merchants, 1713-1763* (Oxford: Oxford University Press, 1987), 3.
2. W.J. Eccles, *The Canadian Frontier, 1534-1760* (New York: Holt, Rinehart and Winston, 1969).
3. Marcel Trudel, *The Beginnings of New France, 1524-1663* (Toronto: McClelland and Stewart, 1973), 270.
4. Brian Young and John Dickinson, *A Short History of Quebec: A Socio-Economic Perspective* (Toronto: Copp Clark Pitman, 1988), 29-30.
5. On these various schemes, see W.J. Eccles, *Canada Under Louis XIV, 1663-1701* (Toronto: McClelland and Stewart, 1964), 46-58.
6. Eccles, *Canada Under Louis XIV*, 52.
7. The standard work on the seigneurial system remains Richard Cole Harris, *The Seigneurial System in Early Canada: A Geographical Study*, 2nd ed. (Montreal and Kingston: McGill-Queen's University Press, 1984).
8. Harris, *The Seigneurial System in Early Canada*, 17.
9. The *banalités* could include other seigneurial revenues but the grist mill was the only one to achieve widespread effect in New France.
10. R. Cole Harris, ed., *Historical Atlas of Canada*, Vol. 1 (Toronto: University of Toronto Press, 1987), Plate 48.
11. On Frontenac, see Eccles, *Canada Under Louis XIV*.
12. Eccles, *Canada Under Louis XIV*, 110-11.
13. Dale Miquelon, *New France, 1701-1744* (Toronto: McClelland and Stewart, 1987),16-17, 58, 67.
14. Miquelon, *New France 1701-1744*, 72.

15. Eccles, *The Canadian Frontier, 1534–1760*, 131–33.
16. Miquelon, *New France, 1701–1744*, 83.
17. Michael Bliss, *Northern Enterprise: Five Centuries of Canadian Business* (Toronto: McClelland and Stewart, 1987), 65–66.
18. The traveller was Peter Kalm, a Swedish botanist; this quote is from Miquelon, *New France, 1701–1744*, 190.
19. Allan Greer, *Peasant, Lord and Merchant: Rural Society in Three Quebec Parishes 1740–1840* (Toronto: University of Toronto Press, 1985).
20. Miquelon, *New France, 1701–1744*, 196–97.
21. The following paragraphs are drawn from Bosher, *The Canada Merchants*; Dale Miquelon, *Dugard of Rouen: French Trade to Canada and the West Indies* (Montreal and Kingston: McGill-Queen's University Press, 1978); and Miquelon, *New France, 1701–1744.*
22. Miquelon, *New France, 1701–1744*, 157.

Further Reading

Crean, J.F. "Hats and the Fur Trade." *Canadian Journal of Economics and Political Science* 28 (1962): 373–86.

Dechêne, Louise. *Habitants et marchands de Montréal au xviie siècle*. Paris: Plan, 1974.

Eccles, W.J. *The Canadian Frontier, 1534–1760*. New York: Holt, Rinehart and Winston, 1969.

Harris, R. Cole. *The Seigneurial System in Early Canada: A Geographical Study*. Montreal and Kingston: McGill-Queen's University Press, 1984.

Innis, Harold. *The Fur Trade in Canada*. New Haven: Yale University Press, 1962.

Miquelon, Dale. *New France, 1701–1744*. Toronto: McClelland and Stewart, 1987.

II

British North America in the Mercantile Era, 1763–1846

II

In 1763, when France ceded its North American possessions to England, there was great rejoicing, both in England itself and in the American colonies. The great struggle for a continent had ended, and a threat to existence had been removed from north of the American colonies. The economic future of these new possessions was not a matter of high priority, however. Fishing was an important business, it was true, but much of that had long been carried on by the Grand Bank fleets with Newfoundland. Quebec added relatively little to the value of this important British trade item. As for the interior, the newly acquired Province of Quebec was noted for its presence in the fur trade and little else.

Politics, not economics, dominated British considerations in the first years. Specifically, the British government faced three challenges. First, it had to placate the existing French population. British rule had to be relatively stable, economically and politically. After years of war and a period marked by corruption among French officials, there was an opportunity to win the loyalty of a population that had traditionally been an enemy of the British Empire. Second, and equally important, the British had to convince the many native tribes allied with the French that there was no reason to resist the British presence. This task would be especially difficult since the French policy in past years had been to subsidize the fur trade for the sake of native support. If the British cut back on such subsidies, and on outright grants, too quickly, the existing restiveness would only be made worse. This possibility was demonstrated clearly in 1763, when Chief Pontiac and a coalition of tribes led a widespread revolt against new British rule. It would take two years before peace was restored along the frontier.

Finally, the British had to try to incorporate their new possessions into their already diverse American empire. Some economic means had to be found to give form and purpose to an economy that ranged from the sugar plantations of the West Indies to the far-flung fur trade of the French, from the frontier settlements of the Western Carolinas and of the trans-Appalachian regions to the highly complex and wealthy New England area and the fishing outports of the Maritimes.

The British had earned a measure of success in the first two of these tasks by the time of the American Revolution (1775–83). The Quebec Act of 1774 meant that British rule was at least tolerated. By restoring much of its traditional hinterland and by establishing a structure of government and religion supported by Quebec elites, the act did much to give the colony a sense of security within the empire. Certainly there was no particular reason for the French to look to the rebellious American colonists. In the west, the native tribes not only had accepted the British presence but fought as their allies against the American colonists.

In the third task, the integration and development of the economy, the British had little or no success. The home government and the American colonies could not agree on the principles of economic policy, much less on its details. As for what was to become British North America, little or nothing had been done in terms of policy except to reunite the old fur-trade hinterland under the Quebec Act. There had been considerable movement of opportunistic Scottish and American colonial merchants into the niches and vacancies of Quebec commercial society. They had begun to be a presence in the fur trade and had always been involved in the provisioning of local garrisons. In general terms, however, the structure of Quebec society — and, for that matter, that of the Maritimes — was much the same in 1775 as it had been at the time of the conquest. Before any significant changes could take place in Britain's northernmost colonies, full-scale rebellion was to dismember Britain's American possessions.

The uprising in the American colonies that began in 1775 would take eight years to resolve. The conflict was, in many ways, a civil war, as Americans fought to decide whether their future lay in independence or in the British Empire. In some colonies, such as Massachusetts and Virginia, the leadership and populace were overwhelmingly rebels, while in others, such as New York, up to half the people actively supported the British. It was a fierce struggle, with families divided and with the basic principles of nationhood and human rights at stake. In the end, of course, the Americans won their independence. The British could not sustain a war at such distance, especially as the English people were themselves increasingly war-weary. Thus, in 1783, thirteen of Britain's colonies became independent.

With the end of the American Revolution, Britain was left with a remnant of its once massive North American empire. Composed of a naval garrison at Halifax, numerous fishing villages scattered along the Atlantic shoreline of Nova Scotia, the small settlements of Newfoundland, the French-Catholic regions of the St. Lawrence, and the thinly populated wilderness beyond, it was a diverse and largely empty region that had been of little consequence to overall British economic planning before 1776. An earlier Board of Trade report had neatly summarized the importance of this part of British North America by noting that "the Newfoundland fishery as a means of wealth and power" was worth more than Quebec.[1] So, too, were the important sugar islands of the West Indies. The remaining colonies in British North America were thought largely irrelevant to Britain's own economic prosperity, though both Quebec City and Halifax had a certain military significance in the minds of British strategists.

However marginal they might be to the British, the colonies would nevertheless be shaped by overall British economic thinking. The development of Quebec (after 1791, Upper and Lower Canada), Nova Scotia (divided into Nova Scotia and New Brunswick in 1784), and the valuable Newfoundland fishery were profoundly affected by the currents emanating from British merchant and government circles.

The first of these currents came in the form of an economic policy — or, for those who find "policy" connotes too much organization for such a diverse doctrine, an outlook. This outlook continued firmly in the mercantilist framework, which, as we have seen, influenced policy during earlier British experiences in North America and French ones in New France. The British still believed in state aggrandizement, while recognizing the importance of commerce as its key. These colonies would develop over the next 60 years in the shadow of this grand imperial policy framework.

As befitted the general principles of this creed, Great Britain's

MAP II.1
Boundaries of British North America, *c.* 1860, Showing the Colonies

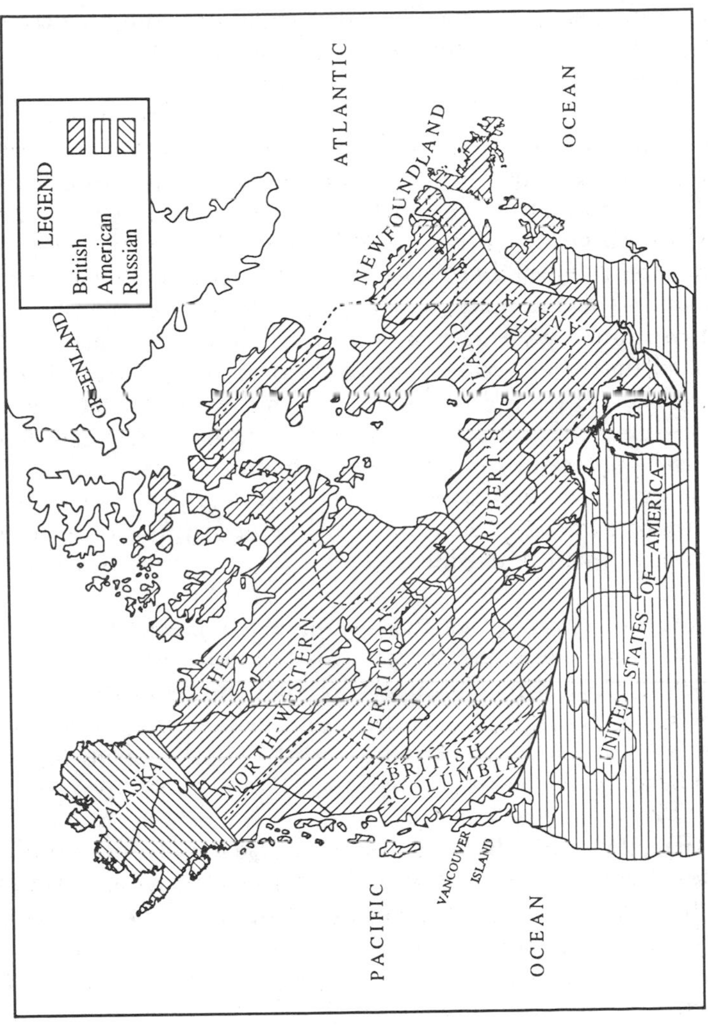

Source: Based on information taken from *The National Atlas of Canada* (Toronto: Macmillan, 1974), 84: *Canada 1862*. Her Majesty the Queen in Right of Canada with permission of Energy, Mines and Resources Canada.

mercantilist policy emphasized two related themes. The first was a continuation of the Navigation Acts, which put a series of prohibitions and restrictions on any foreign ship carrying merchandise into England. The details were complex, but the net effect was to reserve to British ships the entrepôt trade into the wealthy and increasingly large English market while restricting those who could carry goods within the colonial network. One of the complaints of New England seamen had been that the acts operated against colonial interests. One of the great hopes of Nova Scotians at the end of the American Revolution was that those same acts would now allow Halifax to supplant Boston in the West Indies trade.

The second general strategy of mercantilism rested on the long-standing belief in self-sufficiency and encouraged the Empire to draw its needed raw materials from within its own territories. That general principle was no more absolute after 1763 than it had been previously, however, and there were continuing shifts in the details of the policy. In some instances, it would work on a truly imperial basis, and in British North America's favour. Thus, as we will see, Britain set out, in the early nineteenth century, to encourage a timber industry in Canada, even though it was possible to buy from Baltic sources more cheaply. On other occasions, there were contradictions. Not all members of the Empire were created equal, as the Americans had long complained, and the developing British North American colonies would have to compete with favoured home interests that often sought protection and regulation at the expense of fellow British subjects in the colonies.

The Navigation Acts and the general policy of self-sufficiency have been seen in action before. Both would continue to be important, especially to the Maritime colonies. Newly important to British North America in the nineteenth century, however, was a series of tariffs, trade barriers, and outright prohibitions known as the Corn Laws ("corn" is the British term for wheat). These laws varied tremendously over the period of their existence (1660–1846), but their principles remained sufficiently constant that it is possible to generalize.

Their purpose was, first, to protect home agricultural interests from overseas competition and, second, within the limits of this first condition, to give colonial wheat an advantage over foreign wheat. Throughout much of their operation, the Corn Laws prescribed behaviour under three market conditions. One condition was that of an abundant harvest at home. In this case, the law was designed to reserve a glutted market for British wheat farmers. All offshore wheat, colonial or foreign, was prohibited. The second, and opposite, condition presumed a failure or severe shortage at home. In such a case, the British market was thrown open to all comers. The third condition was related to a middle range, whereby some wheat was necessary from abroad. In such a case, a sliding tariff was often used: British agriculture would be given first preference; colonial agriculture, the second; and foreign agriculture, the last. The greater the shortage of wheat (as reflected in rising prices), the lower the restrictions on offshore wheat — but with colonial wheat holding an advantage.

There is another important factor to take into account in looking at mercantilism, one that distinguishes this period from the previous one. Mercantilism was a policy and a philosophy increasingly under challenge. New theories of trade, of the economy, and of the role of the state were already present. Adam Smith's anti-mercantilist *Wealth of Nations* had been published in 1776. Though Smith's economic thinking was not adopted immediately, his impact on the shape of the future empire was to be almost as great as that of the American Declaration of Independence, which was signed the same year. Smith, and those who followed in his footsteps, mounted a widespread assault on the principles of state involvement and protectionism so prevalent in mercantilist thought.

It was to be nearly three-quarters of a century before the principles inherent in Smith's 1776 work were to be fully developed in British policy. When that time came, in the 1840s, it would be one of the events that closed this second era of British North American development. Long before the final collapse of mercantilism, however, the effect of free-trade thinking began to show up in policy. To understand British North American development in this period, therefore, it is important to remember that it was a product not just of British mercantilism but of the erosion over time of that mercantilist policy.

Mercantilism continued to provide the policy framework for these years, but it is only part of the story. It is all too easy to discuss both the policies of the mother country and the economic development of the colonies as if the mother country was nothing more than the issuer of regulations. It was much more than that, of course; it was the major market for colonial goods. Indeed, through this entire period, Britain was effectively the only significant market for colonial goods. Only toward the 1840s did the United States begin to provide an alternative.

Given this fact, it is significant that this period of colonial development took place parallel to one of the greatest events in economic history — the British industrial revolution. Britain was going through one of the most tumultuous periods of change and growth in its history. Both population and wealth were increasing rapidly. In the decade after the American Revolution, Britain's population would increase by 10 percent, and that was nothing compared to what would happen in the next decades. The colonies were, thus, tied to a nation that had an abundance of sophisticated goods to export, savings to invest, and a rapidly growing population that could serve both as a market for colonial produce and as a source for colonial immigration. Obviously, then, the generally rapid development of British North America in these decades was affected by the industrialization taking place in Britain.

One final force that was coming into play throughout this phase of British North American development was the presence, to the south, of the new United States of America. From the beginning, there were close cross-border contacts in trade and immigration. Over the decades, such contacts would grow until they became a central fact in the Canadian economy. But rivalry was important too. British North America and the United States were heirs to the long-standing contests between New France and the American colonies for dominance of a continent, a situation unaffected by the changes in political allegiance or in the products being developed. Continental contact and continental rivalry, set against a background of political animosity and distrust, were yet another general theme running through the evolution of British North America. Indeed, the instability that marked North America between 1763 and 1815 indicates that, in many ways, the struggle for mastery of a continent that had dominated during the previous period continued. Only after the end of the War of 1812 did that unresolved struggle settle into anything like stability.

To summarize, three threads external to British North America itself affected its economy in the period between 1763 and the 1840s. The first of these was mercantilism and its gradual erosion. The second was the ongoing industrial revolution in Great Britain, a revolution that would make Britain, by the end of this period, the most powerful industrial, financial, and commercial nation on the face of the globe. Finally, there was the often annoying and often indispensable presence of the rising former American colonies. In this period, they were small in wealth and power compared to the mother country. However, they were growing rapidly in both population and wealth and would become an increasingly important market for Canadian products. All of these threads must be understood in relation to the particular circumstances of time and place that shaped each region. We must now turn, therefore, to the development of the various colonies.

Notes

1. Cited in Gerald Graham, *British Policy and Canada, 1774–1791* (London: Longmans, Green, 1930), 9.

CHAPTER

4

The Atlantic Colonies

The period from 1763 to 1850 is arguably the most dramatic in Atlantic Canada's economic history. At its outset, Newfoundland and Nova Scotia barely qualified as colonies. There were, perhaps, 5000 or 6000 individuals residing over the winter in Newfoundland in 1750. The numbers increased under the stimulus of war, as was generally the case, but declined again as the migratory fishing trade resumed. It can be said only that the settlement clung precariously to existence, without British sanction and with only the most rudimentary of governmental systems. Nova Scotia's position was not much firmer at the time. There were only a few thousand residents — fishermen, subsistence farmers, soldiers, and a few traders and merchants.

The position of the colonies was much different 90 years later. Newfoundland had a permanent population of 120 000. Fishing still dominated the economy, but now it was almost exclusively a residentiary activity. There was some diversification into the spring seal fishery, and into shipping and trading. Politically, the island had been granted colonial status in 1824, and representative government eight years later.

The change in status was even more pronounced in the case of Nova Scotia. Now there were three colonies, with a combined population of nearly 534 000 — 277 000 in Nova Scotia, 194 000 in New Brunswick, and 63 000 in Prince Edward Island. Fishing was still a key sector, but the economies had diversified considerably. Shipbuilding and shipping and trading were important activities in each colony. As well, Prince Edward Island produced a net agricultural surplus, New Brunswick was an important timber exporter, and Nova Scotia boasted some mineral production. Small-scale manufacturing activities had grown up in the larger centres. The economic development was matched by political evolution; all three colonies had attained responsible government by the 1850s.

These developments are readily explained as the products of the forces identified in the introduction to Part II — the application of British mercantile policy to the colonies, the rising American presence, and the changes wrought by the industrial revolution. As important as the fact of extensive economic development, however, was its nature. As small open economies, the economic structures the Atlantic colonies developed in these decades were to be profoundly affected by the political and economic changes coming in the mid-nineteenth century. It is at least arguable that, however much this period was a "Golden Age" for Atlantic Canada, it was also a precursor of problems that have plagued the region to the present day.

Newfoundland

The return of peace in 1763 brought predictable consequences for the Newfoundland economy. The migratory fishing trade regained some of its earlier importance, as markets in Europe opened up again and as the transatlantic voyage became safer. Population on the island fell at first from its wartime levels, but rose again in the ensuing decades. The introduction of the potato at this time provided a local substitute for imported flour and bread, easing one of the perennial difficulties of the residentiary fishery.

The American Revolution and the subsequent exclusion of the thirteen colonies from the British mercantile system had significant implications for Newfoundland's economic development. The effects were mixed, since New England was, at the same time, a competitor with Newfoundland and one of its most important suppliers. As a competitor, the island stood to gain from any British measure to exclude New England fishing ships from Newfoundland waters and New England fish from European markets. There was also some hope that St. John's might pick up some of the fish, molasses, and rum trade with the West Indies from New England. But the island relied on imports of foodstuffs and other supplies from New England, and any attempt to curtail this trade would affect the population adversely.

The immediate consequence of the revolution was prosperity, as

New England boats were excluded from the fisheries by the powerful Royal Navy. As Table 4.1 shows, the total catch of codfish rose from 250 000 quintals (1 quintal of cod = 112 pounds) in 1781 to nearly 950 000 quintals in 1788. Output by resident fishermen rose by 2.7 times in this period, yet their share of the total catch fell from two-thirds to less than one-half. In keeping with historical patterns, the migratory trade rebounded as hostilities ended.

Eventually, though, the adverse consequence of the American Revolution outweighed the positive ones for the island. The Navigation Acts forbade the importation of food and other supplies from New England. Substitutes from British colonies were inadequate and more expensive, putting a squeeze on the residentiary fishery. This pressure on settlement was compounded by renewed attempts by British officials to discourage the residentiary fishery, apparently as a means of interfering with the commercial activities of the newly independent Americans. Population, which had risen to nearly 20 000 in the late 1780s, fell to fewer than 12 000 by 1797. Total catch in the same year was only 375 000 quintals (see Table 4.1) or 40 percent of the 1788 level.

War broke out again in Europe in 1793, and ran, with some interruption, to 1815. These hostilities imposed great hardship on the Newfoundland fishery in the early years. The important Spanish market was closed in 1797, and remained so until 1809. This loss left Gibraltar and Portugal as the main European markets, and in these Newfoundland faced stiff competition from Norway and the United States. Prices for fish fell and remained low. In some years, the poor quality of the catch added to the woe; 1797 was judged by contemporaries as the worst year since the American Revolution. Fears of starvation led in 1803 to permission to import food from New England. Beginning in 1804, however, conditions turned around, and, by 1815, catches of more than 860 000 quintals were being recorded (see Table 4.1).

These disruptions were hard on the industry as a whole, but especially so on the migratory fishery. In the late 1780s and early 1790s, residents accounted for about one-half of the total codfish catch. By 1801, this proportion had risen to nearly three-quarters; by 1815, virtually the entire catch was local. This shift to a residentiary fishery was the final step in a process that had been going on since the first wintering over, in 1610. It had been stopped only temporarily by the prohibition on the importation of New England

TABLE 4.1

Codfish Caught by Inhabitants of Newfoundland and Total Catch, 1771–1791, 1796–1820

(totals in quintals)

Year	*Inhabitants*	*Total*	*Year*	*Inhabitants*	*Total*
1771	261 240	639 919	1798	*	485 764
1772	298 605	759 843	1799	*	466 332
1773	366 466	780 328	1800	*	517 348
1774	312 426	695 866	1801	195 400	255 740
1775	230 540	658 315	1802	*	461 144
1776	205 448	549 903	1803	410 188	536 188
1777	*	*	1804	531 084	609 684
1778	205 840	501 140	1805	662 800	706 314
1779	262 500	409 670	1806	*	772 809
1780	*	*	1807	462 250	520 552
1781	168 150	255 150	1808	468 185	478 735
1782	*	*	1809	625 941	677 761
1783	*	*	1810	299 515	317 415
1784	212 616	437 316	1811	601 894	618 494
1785	262 576	544 942	1812	674 611	709 163
1786	257 547	569 142	1813	819 250	869 750
1787	341 620	732 015	1814	797 762	865 132
1788	457 105	948 970	1815	802 668	866 580
1789	339 260	771 569	1816	739 977	819 200
1790	302 974	649 092	1817	712 487	778 227
1791	229 770	536 287	1818	559 183	606 733
1796	*	445 471	1819	588 149	717 909
1797	261 570	374 940	1820	736 524	810 074

* denotes data unavailable

Source: Shannon Ryan, "Fishery to Colony: A Newfoundland Watershed, 1793–1815," in *Atlantic Canada Before Confederation*, The Acadiensis Reader, Vol. I, edited by P.A. Buckner and David Frank (Fredericton: Acadiensis Press, 1985), 141. This source provides information on the derivation of particular estimates.

food and other supplies. These regulations were suspended in stages as the other British colonies proved unable to meet the needs of the island, and with the relaxation the residentiary fishery regained its competitive edge.

This period represents a critical stage in Newfoundland history. It has been described as a "watershed."[1] As historian Shannon Ryan put it, "Newfoundland, which had always been a fishery based around an island, would finally become a colony based on a fishery." Another Newfoundland scholar, economic historian David Alexander, adds to the point by noting that, while it is customary to claim a history for Newfoundland of several hundred years, it is more appropriate to view it as one of the countries of nineteenth-century European settlement. Even the British government finally yielded, as noted earlier, granting the island colonial status in 1824.[2]

The end of the Napoleonic Wars in 1815 forced the island fishery, strengthened by war after 1804, to adapt to peacetime conditions. French fishermen returned in force to the North Atlantic fishery, encouraged by a system of bounties introduced by the French government. St. Pierre was the centre of this resurgence. Pressure from the St. John's commercial elite forced the Newfoundland government to respond to this competition by attempting to restrict the supply of bait to the French, to lobby to prevent encroachment into British waters, and to keep to as narrow an interpretation of the eighteenth-century treaties as possible. None of these efforts was particularly successful, however, and the French presence grew. The population of the French islands rose tenfold between 1820 and 1870, from only 500 to more than 5000.

The residentiary fishery, which had grown so dramatically during the Napoleonic Wars, entered a long period of relative stagnation after 1815. The trend is shown in Table 4.2. Salt cod exports, which had averaged more than one million quintals between 1815 and 1819, declined to fewer than 800 000 in the 1830s, before recovering again to around 950 000 quintals in the 1840s. Prices declined as well; they averaged $3.90 per quintal in 1815–19 but did not rise above $3.00 again until 1865–69. Gross export value fell from about $3 million in 1815–19 to $2.5 million in 1845–49. Recognizing that population more than doubled over the same period, it is clear that per-capita output, in both physical and value terms, fell significantly.

TABLE 4.2

Quinquennial Averages in Salt Cod Exports for Newfoundland: Volumes, Prices, and Gross Export Values, 1815–19 to 1930–34

Period	*Volumes* (*000 quintals*)	*Prices* (*$ per quintal*)	*Gross export value* (*$000*)
1815–19	1 018	3.90	2 968
1820–24	883	2.46	2 175
1825–29	923	2.08	1 942
1830–34	763	2.42	1 840
1835–39	788	2.78	2 193
1840–44	944	2.79	2 637
1845–49	963	2.66	2 547
1850–54	955	2.61	2 454
1855–59	1 205	3.33	4 008
1860–64	1 172	2.65	4 218
1865–69	969	3.86	3 731
1870–74	1 273	3.93	5 026
1875–79	1 134	3.88	4 354
1880–84	1 460	3.82	5 582
1885–89	1 192	3.66	4 316
1890–94	1 101	3.60	3 957
1895–99	1 224	2.89	3 549
1900–04	1 302	4.19	5 562
1905–09	1 574	n/a	n/a
1910–14	1 346	5.66	7 583
1915–19	1 517	9.35	15 650
1920–24	1 499	8.67	13 265
1925–29	1 398	8.37	11 587
1930–34	1 179	5.90	7 010

Source: David Alexander, "Newfoundland's Traditional Economy and Development to 1934," in *Newfoundland in the Nineteenth and Twentieth Centuries*, edited by James Hiller and Peter Neary (Toronto: University of Toronto Press, 1980), 20.

The international trade in dried cod was growing. The problem was that Newfoundland did not maintain its share. Exports from the island to Portugal and Italy remained roughly constant in absolute terms, with other countries picking up most of the new demand in these countries. Exports to Spain actually fell substantially, mainly to the benefit of Norway, which had emerged as a major competitor after the Napoleonic Wars. There was little change in the absolute volumes sent to the West Indies. The only new market developed was Brazil, which had opened up after 1808 and by 1848 was taking over 100 000 quintals.

In part, Newfoundland's relative decline was unavoidable. Competitors such as Norway were certain to emerge in the nineteenth century as technology advanced and shipping costs fell. In part, though, the problems seem to have been self-imposed.[3] The highly fluctuating nature of the trade, and the secular decline after 1815, led Newfoundland fishermen to pay less attention to the curing of the fish, giving rise to problems of quality control and a reputation for inferior products that exacerbated the competition problem.

New fishing areas were opened up after 1815. East-coast fishermen, particularly those from Conception Bay, moved into the north-shore areas during the Napoleonic Wars, practising their own brand of migratory fishing. When the French returned in 1815, the Newfoundland fishermen moved farther north to exploit the Labrador fishery. This process was like the early history of Newfoundland in miniature, in effect. Some fishermen, called stationers, established themselves on shore, catching and curing the fish in one place. Others — floaters — operated from on board their ships and moved from one fishing area to another. The trade expanded during the early part of the century and then stabilized at these levels through to midcentury.

The Labrador fishery was not feasible by itself, given the great distances involved. It was profitable, however, when combined with a new staple activity, the spring seal fishery. Ships first sailed from Newfoundland after 1793 in search of seal herds. Exports of seal oil jumped during the Napoleonic War years and remained high to midcentury. In 1827, there were 290 ships and 5418 men involved in the industry; by 1857, these figures peaked at 370 ships and 13 600 men.[4]

Changes in the organization of the fishery in the nineteenth century reflected the shift from a migratory to a residentiary fishery. In the early days, British shipowners and captains from the West Country ports had left caretakers on the island. As the migratory trade declined, these caretakers evolved into agents and clerks, still located in the outports, purchasing output from residents and providing supplies in return. During the Napoleonic Wars, firms from St. John's became involved in this activity. They supplied local traders, who would in turn supply the outport fishermen. There was, in effect, a change from the old merchant-fishermen credit relationship to a St. John's merchant–small outport merchant or trader-fishermen one.[5] The process had proceeded so far by the mid-nineteenth century that a contemporary observer identified St. John's as the "emporium of the Island."

The Newfoundland economy relied heavily on shipping services — to harvest the cod and seal, to carry these products to market, and to distribute supplies to the outports. At first, the ships and the shipping services were obtained from Europe, primarily Britain. Gradually, however, Newfoundland began to produce and operate some of its own vessels, giving the island an important backward linkage from its main staple exports. This development was possible as the scope of the trade grew, and as local merchants developed the expertise and capital to invest in these activities. They concentrated on the fishing and coastal trades, building schooners and other smaller craft. Newfoundlanders owned and operated larger ships as well, but these were typically purchased offshore, in part from other British North American colonies.

In sum, Newfoundland had come a long way since 1763. It was firmly established as a new country by 1850, something it had not been even 50 years earlier. Its economy was still a highly specialized one, dominated by the codfish industry to an extent unrivalled in any of the other North American possessions. It continued to be, in words used in this book, a classic example of staple determinism. Virtually the entire life of the community revolved around the fortunes of the export trade — from the fishermen themselves to the boatbuilders scattered across the islands, to the traders in the outports, to the merchants in St. John's.

Newfoundland could fall by the residentiary cod fishery as it had risen from it. The question for the future was whether a settled traditional economy such as Newfoundland's in 1840 could adjust to the economic and political changes that were gathering, or whether, as David Alexander notes, it would just "expand to the point of impoverishing a country."[6]

The Maritimes

Nova Scotia developed very little economically between the end of the Seven Years' War and the American Revolution. The population of Halifax, for example, fell to about 1500 in 1755, from 5000 five years earlier, as military fears waned and as fishing bounties were reduced. Several hundred Ulster Irish arrived in the colony, some redirected from New England, and an advance guard of what was ultimately to be a large migration of Scots came in 1773. The newly acquired regions of Cape Breton and St. John's Island (Prince Edward Island separated from Nova Scotia in 1769) fared no better. There were but 271 inhabitants in the latter in 1768, rising to about 1000 by 1773, with just a few soldiers and fishermen in Cape Breton. With the defence motive gone, the colony possessed no real attraction beyond access to the fisheries and the availability of land for largely subsistence agriculture.

The region's economic problems lay partly with the inappropriate policies of the imperial government. Restrictions were placed on the export of coal from Cape Breton, and forests were reserved for the Royal Navy. Land policies were more controversial yet. Cape Breton and St. John's Island were divided into 20 000-acre lots in 1763. Four years later, the entire area of the latter colony was disposed of by lottery to British nobility in the form of 64 land grants. The object was to make the colony self-financing by having the landlords sponsor settlement and pay rents to cover administrative expenses. They met neither of these responsibilities with any regularity, and the resultant conflict between the resident elites and the absentee landowners, known as the "land question," dominated economic and political life in Prince Edward Island for the next century. Similar types of land grants were issued in Nova Scotia proper to a much lesser extent, but with the same lack of success.

The main problem, though, was that Nova Scotia's economic endowments put it in direct competition with New England for a place in the British mercantile system, and, in this contest, Nova Scotia simply could not compete with its more established neighbour. Nova Scotia did not have the requisite timber and agricultural surpluses to send to the West Indies, and lacked the expertise in shipping and shipbuilding to compete even in the carrying trade. New England was able to produce cheaper and better-quality supplies of timber and agricultural supplies. Only the fisheries were naturally competitive, as the long presence of New Englanders along the Nova Scotia coasts attested. As long as the colonies to the south were part of the British Empire, it seemed, the Maritimes were destined to be tributary to them.

When the American Revolution broke out, there was some sympathy with the revolutionaries but never any serious threat that the "neutral Yankees of Nova Scotia" would secede. The British naval presence is only part of the explanation. More fundamentally, unlike the thirteen colonies, Nova Scotia could look to the mercantile system as a source of support rather than constraint. With the American colonies on the other side of the Navigation Acts, Nova Scotia might be able to take up the role that natural competitive disadvantage had until then denied it.

There were three developments of particular importance that stemmed from the American Revolution. Most immediately, the British navy turned to the pine forests of Nova Scotia for the masts that it had been securing from New England. This was not a large-volume trade, but it was a high-value one, and it did set the stage for the developments in the timber industry that were to follow.

More important, at least potentially, was the decision by the British in 1783 to end what had been an effective exemption of New England from the terms of the Navigation Acts. With this step — one not taken lightly, given the importance of New England to the British mercantile system — the West Indies trade was reserved for the British North American colonies. The potential this development opened up was enormous. Fish from the region were already going to the sugar plantations; with New England excluded from this trade, the British North American colonies could expect their share of this market to grow. Agriculture could be developed to supply the foodstuffs previously coming from New England farms, and timber would be available for construction and barrels. Further, as these materials had to be shipped to the islands, and the sugar and molasses taken to Britain, a stimulus would be provided to the shipping interests in the port communities and to the shipbuilders who would supply them with vessels.

The revolution also provided an important influx of population into the region. Several thousand Loyalists came to the region during the war, although many of them subsequently left. The wave that came in 1783 consisted mainly of farmers. They took up land in the river valleys of what is now New Brunswick. Others settled in Nova Scotia proper, others in Cape Breton (another new colony), and a few in Prince Edward Island. Another wave came in 1784, when it became clear that the Navigation Acts were to be applied to New England. These were mainly merchants and traders, settling in Halifax, Saint John, and other coastal towns. In all, the population of the Maritimes approximately doubled in a short time with these arrivals.

Because many of these refugees settled on the western side of the Bay of Fundy, in what was very lightly populated territory, they had a significant impact. This newly bustling region around Saint John created a second centre of settlement in Nova Scotia, a rival to Halifax. Geographic distinctiveness as well as political differences led, in 1784, to the creation of New Brunswick, which became for many years thereafter a colony dominated by a Loyalist elite.

Like migrant groups throughout history, the Loyalists had a dual effect on the local economy. In the short term, they provided new markets for the produce of the population that was already there. Recent research has traced the development and subsequent specialization of agriculture on the Bay of Fundy — the old Acadian lands — to the arrival of the Loyalists and the markets they provided.[7] In the longer term, they added to the labour force, increasing the potential output of the economy. They were the farmers, fishermen, loggers, shippers, and sailors of the Maritimes' new economic status in the British mercantile system.

If the hopes for the region in these years were high, the reality was something less. Simply put, the Maritime colonies were unable to fill the role expected of them. Fishing progressed satisfactorily enough, and there was some development of shipbuilding and of the carrying trade. The main obstacles to supplanting New England in the mercantile system continued to be the lack of a surplus of timber and of cheap agricultural supplies. Sawmills were established near harbours soon after the revolution, and timber was produced for export. As the most accessible stands of timber were cut, however, costs rose dramatically. Nor did agriculture develop as planned. The Halifax area produced only a small surplus of beef and flour.

Settlers continued to come to Prince Edward Island — the population had grown to about 4400 by 1798 — but whatever surplus they provided was taken by the other colonies. New Brunswick and Cape Breton provided virtually no sustainable surpluses.

The consequences of these failures were predictable. Plantation interests in the West Indies began to lobby for the re-entry of New England suppliers, just as the fisheries of Newfoundland had. Partly in response to these pressures, and partly out of a desire to create good will with the United States in its war with France, the imperial government began to grant re-entry. American breadstuffs were made legal traffic in 1786. Jay's Treaty of 1794 effectively re-established New England as the main supplier of produce and shipping services to the British plantations. The British North American colonies were still involved in the trade, but now only as an offshoot of New England activity. All direct trade between Nova Scotia and the West Indies had virtually ceased by 1804. The lack of success in taking over New England's role, combined with an unfortunate decision in 1790 not to make further land grants (which was expected to be temporary but, in fact, lasted for seventeen years), led to substantial outmigration from the colonies.

The outbreak of war in 1793 brought a second chance to the region, and this time the inducements were enough to bring about a notable response. The threat to British shipping posed by Napoleon's blockade caused a tighter enforcement of the Navigation Acts, leading, in 1803, to a partial withdrawal of New England's West Indies privileges. This advantage was accentuated in 1807, when the United States passed the Embargo Act, prohibiting all commerce with Europe out of American ports. This measure was replaced in 1809 by the Non-intercourse Act, which freed Americans to trade with other countries, but imposed even tougher regulations on trade with Britain and France.

Colonial merchants jumped at the opportunities this embargo provided. Trade with the West Indies grew dramatically after 1807. Nova Scotia doubled its trade in the period between 1808 and 1811, compared to that of the previous four years; New Brunswick doubled its trade in one year, 1811, alone. Whatever local produce was available was sent directly to the islands. The remainder of the demand was met by picking up supplies from New England, obtained by smuggling or by open defiance of U.S. law. Cargoes from Europe were imported into Nova Scotia, for re-export to the Caribbean. Nova Scotia merchants seemed finally to have delivered on their earlier claim that, with the proper inducements, they could replace New England in the British mercantile system. The real test would come, however, when more normal times returned.

The economic repercussions of the Napoleonic Wars on the Maritimes extended well beyond the West Indies trade. The blockade of the Baltic ports interrupted the supply of timber to Britain. With its economic and military power thereby threatened, Britain turned to the colonies. Exports of squared timber (logs squared roughly with a broadaxe in the forest after felling) from British North America jumped tenfold between 1805 and 1809. This opening was only temporary, however, unless some form of preferential access to the British market could be negotiated. The low-value, high-bulk nature of squared timber meant that transport costs made it impossible for North American supplies to compete on equal terms with the more accessible Baltic supplies.

The British government agreed to requests for protection. A differential duty between foreign and colonial timber was already in effect, but it was less than the extra transportation charges from North America. Duties were raised as a wartime measure in 1809. One year later, all temporary and permanent tariffs were doubled, and they were raised another 25 percent in 1813. Since duties on foreign wood were much higher to begin with, these proportionate increases widened the advantage given colonial products significantly. Already, by 1811, the tariff preference clearly exceeded the transport-cost differential, and the 1813 increase just added to the advantage. Capital and labour were drawn to the industry, and British North America had another staple export.

Timber operations followed waterways closely. Nova Scotia lacked good river access to the interior, so once the most accessible coastal stands were cut, the potential for further expansion was limited. What production there was from the Atlantic-coast area went mainly to Britain, while that from the Bay of Fundy region went to the West Indies. Newfoundland and Prince Edward Island figured even less in the timber trade than did Nova Scotia, and the industry was even less important to the local economies. In all three colonies, once the most accessible stands were taken, wood was cut mainly as an input into shipbuilding.

In New Brunswick, timber quickly came to dominate the

economy. Vast reserves of pine and spruce were accessible via the several rivers that led into the interior. As the preferential duties were imposed, New Brunswick was transformed into a giant lumber camp. Figure 4.1 shows timber and lumber exports from New Brunswick from 1800 to 1850. Exports of squared timber rose twentyfold between 1805 and 1812, to reach nearly 100 000 tons. They fell off slightly for a year but, by 1815, had surpassed their 1812 level. As the Napoleonic Wars ended, the trade was firmly established in the colony.

The organization of the squared-timber trade was unique. Gangs of four to six men — usually local farmers and often from the same family — ventured into the woods in the fall. They selected and cut trees, squared them with a broadaxe, and dragged them to the river. There the timbers were made into rafts and floated to the port cities, where they were bought by one of the British timber firms that had set up subsidiary operations there, and sent to England. Sometimes these merchants owned the ships on which the timber was transported, but more often they contracted with "cargo seekers." In England, the timber was cut into planks for naval use or, after 1815, for general construction.

The effect of the timber trade on New Brunswick was immediate. The harvesting of timber was a relatively labour-intensive process, creating employment and thereby attracting immigrants. Population nearly trebled, from 25 000 in 1805 to 74 000 in 1824, at the time of the first official census. The timber trade also had linkages to other sectors of the economy. New businesses sprang up to service the timber industry and the attendant growing population. Shipping increased dramatically out of Saint John, and that city, in particular, saw considerable growth in businesses oriented both to staples export and to local consumption.

The combination of revolution, war, American retaliation, and mercantile policy with respect to the Navigation Acts and timber preferences gave the Maritimes a start in its economic life. Historically, the period from 1815 to the 1840s is one of attempts to parlay this hot-house beginning into a permanent economic base. Success or failure depended on several things. Would the fisheries be reserved for local fishermen, or would the Americans obtain renewed access to them? Would the Navigation Acts be applied consistently, or would New Englanders work their way back into the trade? Would timber preferences be maintained after the war?

FIGURE 4.1

New Brunswick Timber and Lumber Exports, 1800–1850

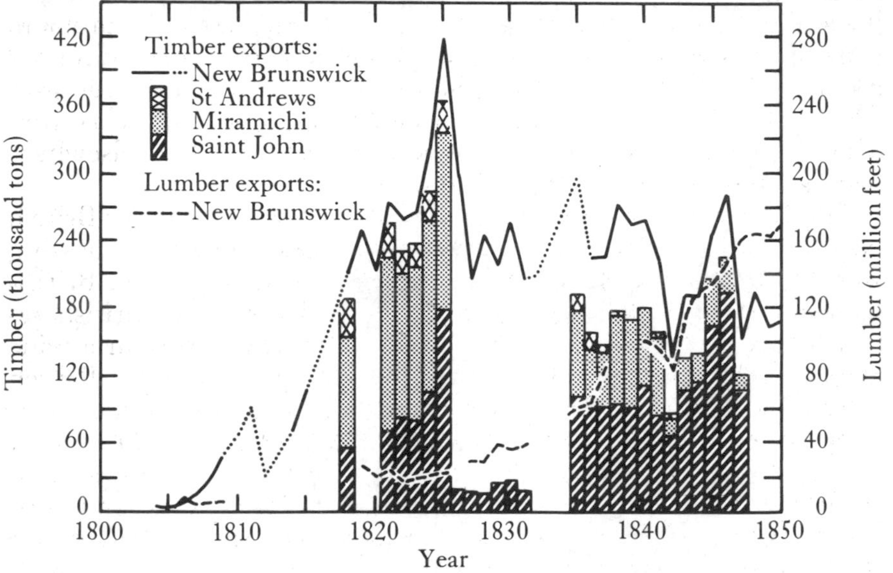

Source: Graeme Wynn, *Timber Colony* (Toronto: University of Toronto Press, 1981), 34.

In all cases, to what extent would these beginnings, however artificial their origins, lead to self-sustaining economic growth?

The first challenge came, as expected, in the fisheries. Britain responded to pressure from Nova Scotia and sent naval ships to keep the Americans outside the three-mile limit and away from ports and landing sites. Negotiations led eventually to the Convention of 1818, under the terms of which American fishermen renounced all rights to fish within three miles of any "coasts, bays, creeks or harbours" of the colonies. They could, however, land for shelter or repairs, as long as existing property rights were respected. In exchange, they were granted fishing rights on the south and west shores of Newfoundland and off Labrador. The provisions were sufficiently vague, however, that disputes were more or less continuous until a temporary resolution was reached with the Reciprocity Treaty of 1854.

The West Indies carrying trade was also at stake after 1815. The Maritimes had prospered greatly by the wars and the American Embargo Act of 1807, which essentially forbade trade out of American ports, but the area had not yet evolved to the point where it could be an effective replacement for New England. The problem continued to be the lack of a surplus of cheap agricultural and timber products. Predictably, New England sought access to this trade after 1815, plantation interests on the islands supported this relaxation of the Navigation Acts, and merchants in Nova Scotia and elsewhere had to lobby for their continuation.

The Navigation Acts were intended to reserve the trade for British North America. The United States responded to them by passing its own Navigation Act in 1818, closing American ports to British vessels coming from or going to the West Indies. The British retaliation was the Free Port Act of the same year, wherein a wide range of American products could be imported into the British North American colonies in either American or British ships, something not previously possible under the Navigation Acts. The intent was to reroute this produce to the West Indies, using the ships and trading facilities of the now free ports of Halifax, Saint John, and St. Andrews. This provision had its intended effect, causing the Americans to react with even stricter legislation, which, in turn, invited British retaliation, and so on; finally, a compromise "reciprocity agreement" was reached in 1830 wherein New England was given parity in regard to British vessels with the West Indies carrying trade. The Maritimes' position was protected, in part, by the imposition of a duty on products being brought into the islands from New England, which was waived for products from the colonies. Thus, while the merchants of the area were unable to retain the privileged position they had had during the Napoleonic Wars, they did manage to secure enough of it to keep themselves in relative prosperity.

Predictably, timber duties came under attack after the war. Pressure to remove them by consumers in Britain encountered the opposition of shipowners and colonists, who defended them, often using traditional mercantilist arguments to bolster their case. The latter groups won out, and the duties were made permanent in 1816, although the levy on colonial timber was increased slightly in 1821, and that on foreign timber lowered. Opposition to the duties never let up, and there was a nearly continuous succession of hearings and investigations that merged with the growing chorus of general anti-mercantilist sentiment. Not until the 1840s, however, did the first reduction come.

Timber dominated the New Brunswick economy after 1815, surpassing fishing and agriculture in importance. As British population increased, so, too, did the demand for construction materials. Exports of squared timber from New Brunswick alone rose from 100 000 tons in 1812 to 240 000 in 1819, and to their all-time peak of 417 000 tons in 1825 (see Figure 4.1). They fell thereafter, and averaged around 200 000 tons until the early 1840s. The industry was very volatile. Aside from that of 1812, there were recessions in 1821, 1826–27, and much of the 1830s. Part of the instability stemmed from the supply side, as the amount and quality of timber that ended up in the ports varied from season to season. More important, though, was the fact that lumber, being tied to the cyclically prone construction industry, was one of the first activities to suffer in a general recession.

As the industry became established, the production of deals (sawn planks) became increasingly important. In staples-theory terms, a forward linkage developed out of the timber trade. Logs were floated to sawmill sites, where they were cut into planks. Deals made better use of the logs than did squared timber, and they provided more value added to the resource prior to export. Most sawmills were located at waterpower sites, although a steam operation was in place in Saint John in 1821. Some of the output was used locally, and more went to Britain, where it overtook Baltic imports by 1835. American capital began to penetrate New Brunswick timber lands in the 1830s in search of supplies, but, in the main, that market would not be significant for another decade.

Perhaps the most interesting developments in the Maritime economies after 1815 were those in shipbuilding and shipping. Certainly, they were the most complex. Thanks to a major research effort (by the Atlantic Canada Shipping Project, based at Memorial University, in Newfoundland), it is now possible to provide some indication of developments in these two important activities, and of their impacts on the economic development of Atlantic Canada more generally. The detailed work is still incomplete, so we can do no more than summarize the broad picture that is developing.

Two main points emerge from the research. First, it is necessary to distinguish between shipbuilding and shipping. There was considerable overlap between these two activities, of course, but to wrap them together, as many traditional accounts do, is to miss some essential features of both. Second, it is important to distinguish among centres of activity. There was not one shipbuilding or shipping industry in Atlantic Canada, but rather several, generating different products and responding to different markets.

People in the Atlantic colonies were building three types of sailing vessels by the mid-nineteenth century. Coastal vessels were being used in the fishery and for coastal trading. All ports built such vessels, although they were especially important early on in Halifax and, as noted earlier, St. John's, where they were almost the sole output. They were intended mainly for local use. In staples-theory terms, they can be thought of as backward links from the fisheries.

As well, ships were being constructed for the transfer trade. Ocean-going vessels were built in British North America for marketing abroad — primarily, but not exclusively, in Britain. Again, most ports built such ships, but production was concentrated in Saint John and in Prince Edward Island, Yarmouth and Halifax being important centres as well. The industry in Saint John was linked closely to the timber trade, and thus conforms most closely to the traditional picture. Indeed, in that colony, the two trades often merged. Builders would construct a vessel, fill it with timber, and sell both cargo and ship in Britain.

Although the fact is most often overlooked in traditional accounts, a significant number of ocean-going vessels were constructed not for export but for use by local shippers and traders. The great boom in Atlantic Canada shipping occurred in the 1860s and 1870s, and will be discussed below. But research by the Memorial group has shown that the roots of this boom period stretch further back than was originally believed. There was a significant amount of tonnage registered in Atlantic ports well before 1860.

Figure 4.2 plots the tonnage built in British North America shipyards (Newfoundland excepted, but Quebec included) for the period from 1785 to 1905. Activity was quite limited until 1809, with construction consisting mainly of coastal vessels. Construction increased during the Napoleonic Wars, fell off again to around 1820, and then increased, albeit with great swings, to midcentury. The dominance of Saint John is apparent in the data, followed by the Nova Scotia ports and those on Prince Edward Island.

FIGURE 4.2

British-American Shipbuilding, by Province, 1785–1905

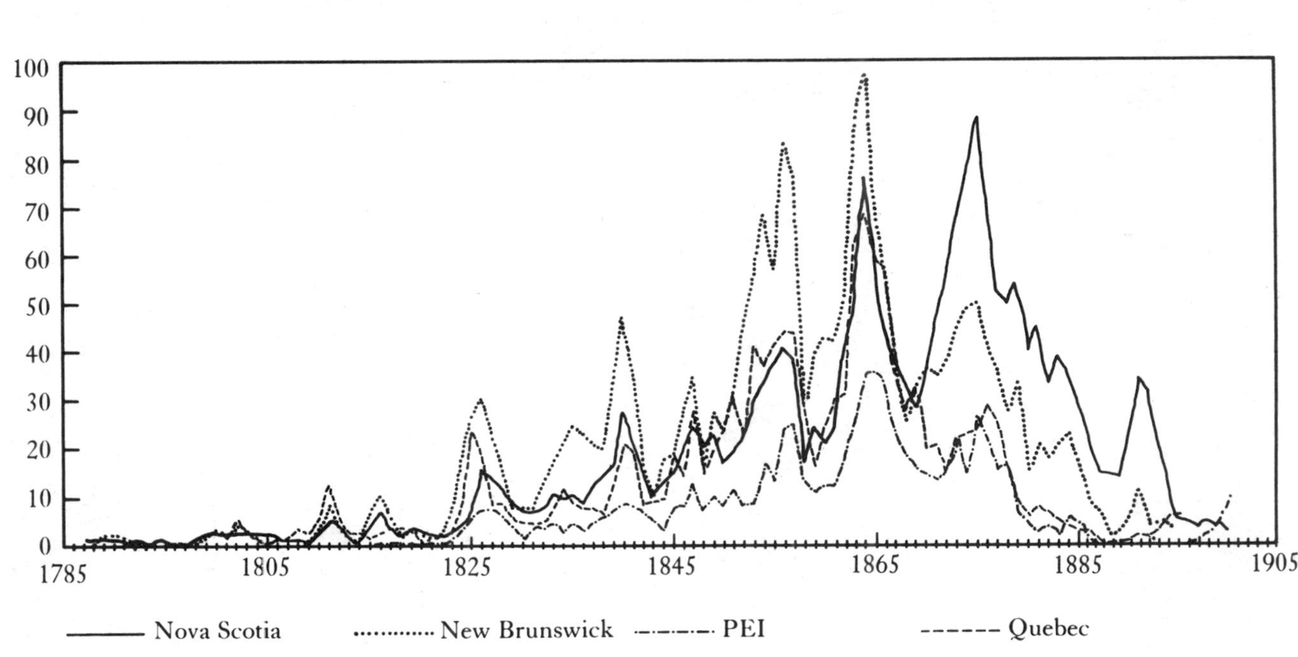

Source: Richard Rice, "Measuring British Dominance of Shipbuilding in the Maritimes, 1784–1890," in *Ships and Shipbuilding in the North Atlantic Region*, edited by Keith Matthews and Gerald Panting (St. John's: Memorial University Press, 1978), insert.

Table 4.3 shows the number and tonnage of ships on registry at Canadian ports in 1830, 1840, and 1849. Newfoundland accounts for between 21 percent and 24 percent of the ships registered, but for less than 20 percent of the tonnage, reflecting the preponderance of small coastal vessels. Around 60 percent of the vessels were registered in Nova Scotia, as was between 38 percent and 51 percent of the tonnage, showing again the importance of the coastal trade. Prince Edward Island accounts for 6 percent to 8 percent of both. The pattern in New Brunswick is opposite that of Nova Scotia and Newfoundland; its share of the tonnage exceeds that for the number of ships. The concentration on the transfer trade, with its linkages into timber, is evident.

Agriculture remained the weak point of the Maritime economies after 1815. Immigrants developed the rich soils of Prince Edward Island, the absentee-landlord situation notwithstanding, but its area was too small to support much export trade. About 85 percent of what was sent went in small ships to neighbouring colonies. Oats was the principal earner of credit, supplemented by shipments of potatoes, grains, and livestock. Many P.E.I. farmers added to their income by spending the winter cutting timber in New Brunswick and Maine. Nova Scotia developed little specialized agricultural activity. Farmers were also fishermen, and occasionally also shipbuilders and shippers. The small surpluses of beef, poultry, vegetables, and coarse grains that were produced went into the coastal trade, primarily to Newfoundland.

New Brunswick still imported most of its food requirements as late as the 1830s. The failure to develop an agricultural surplus is commonly attributed to the drawing power of the other staples, timber in particular. In an early version of a phenomenon that, in the 1970s, came to be labelled "the Dutch disease," New Brunswick's very success in one natural-resource product is said to have worked against the growth of a more diversified economy. Lumber drew capital and labour out of the more sedentary agriculture and into the more speculative but potentially more profitable trades. The parallel with the fur trade and agricultural development in New France is obvious.

This explanation is not entirely satisfactory, however. In principle, agriculture and timber were complementary activities. Indeed, they are usually portrayed as such in the Ottawa valley timber trade. Farmers could attend to their land in the spring and summer

TABLE 4.3

Number and Tonnage of Vessels on Canadian Registry, Various Years

	1830		*1840*		*1849*	
	No.	*% of Canada*	*No.*	*% of Canada*	*No.*	*% of Canada*
Newfoundland						
vessels	465	21	702	24	970	24
tons	28 846	17	43 949	16	59 501	16
Nova Scotia						
vessels	1 299	59	1 727	58	2 467	60
tons	83 981	51	103 871	38	153 051	42
P.E.I.						
vessels	135	6	195	7	301	7
tons	7 661	5	15 696	6	28 587	8
New Brunswick						
vessels	434	20	608	20	775	19
tons	43 532	26	109 003	40	117 475	32
CANADA						
vessels	2 210	100	2 973	100	11 108	100
tons	165 782	100	270 802	100	361 105	100

Source: Derived from Keith Matthews, "The Shipping Industry of Atlantic Canada: Themes and Problems," in *Ships and Shipbuilding in the North Atlantic Region*, edited by Keith Matthews and Gerald Panting (St. John's: Memorial University Press, 1978), Appendix I: 9.

going into the woods in the fall and winter to cut timber to supplement their income. In New Brunswick's case, however, it is alleged that the activities overlapped. There were often problems in getting the timber to market in the spring in time to return to the land; when schedules did permit, the prices were often so low that the farmer found himself in debt. Inevitably, agriculture lost out. Just why this should have been so in New Brunswick but not in Upper and Lower Canada has never been explained.

Nova Scotia developed a small mining industry in this period. The Duke of York's mineral rights for Cape Breton coal were taken over in 1826 by the General Mining Association of London, which began to develop the property as a source for exports to the other colonies, to the United States, and as a coaling station for North Atlantic steamships. Access to the United States was restricted by high duties, though, and, in the other British North American colonies, Cape Breton supplies had to compete with British coal that came in as ballast on timber ships. Thus, the activity remained small in scale.

Two types of manufacturing developed in the region. Sawmills, shipyards, and flour mills were direct spinoffs of the staples trades, either as backward linkages providing inputs to the export sectors, or as forward linkages further processing the output. As well, such relatively small enterprises as tanneries, iron foundries, furniture shops, carriage works, and breweries served the local market and were protected by transport costs from imports from Britain and the United States. Halifax and Saint John, the largest centres in the region, were the most important manufacturing locations. These cities also saw developments in financial and commercial services, usually by the same merchants engaged in the main staples trades. Like manufacturing, some business was directly involved with the staples trades, and some existed to provide services to the resident population.

Tables 4.4 and 4.5 provide an overview of the Maritime economy at midcentury. The data in Table 4.4 can be summarized a number of ways, but perhaps are most revealing when organized by province. Nova Scotia had the most geographically diversified trading pattern of the group. The bulk of its exports — nearly two-thirds — went to other North American colonies or the West Indies. The United States took another 21 percent, other foreign nations 11 percent, and Britain less than 5 percent. The United Kingdom was the dominant supplier, however, followed by the United States, other North American colonies, and other foreign nations.

Britain took more than three-quarters of New Brunswick's exports, in contrast to Nova Scotia's very limited shipments, reflecting the importance of the shipbuilding and timber sectors. The United States and other North American colonies were second, and about equally important, at around 10 percent; other sales were negligible. New Brunswick was the most dependent of the three

TABLE 4.4

Trade of the Maritime Colonies, 1851

(percentage of total)

	Nova Scotia		*New Brunswick*		*P.E.I.*	
	Imports	*Exports*	*Imports*	*Exports*	*Imports*	*Exports*
U.K.	38.9	4.3	46.8	75.4	38.0	18.7
British Possessions	19.2	63.8	16.7	11.5	49.1	50.8
North America	18.5	38.1	16.4	9.4	49.1	50.3
West Indies	0.7	25.7	0.1	1.6	—	0.5
Other	—	—	0.2	0.5	—	—
Foreign	41.9	31.9	36.5	13.1	12.9	30.5
U.S.	25.2	20.8	33.7	10.8	—	—
Other	16.7	11.1	2.8	2.3	12.9	30.5

Source: S.A. Saunders, *The Economic History of the Maritime Provinces* (Fredericton: Acadiensis Press, 1984), Appendix: Table I (p. 99).

Atlantic colonies on British suppliers, at nearly 50 percent, with the United States providing another 34 percent of its imports.

Prince Edward Island was the most linked by trade to the other North American colonies. Fully 50 percent of its total exports and the same percentage of imports were accounted for by intercolonial sales. The island relied most, in proportional terms, as well, on other foreign markets for sales (31 percent), although, in absolute terms, the volumes were not very large. The United Kingdom purchased less than 20 percent of exports, and other markets were negligible. Prince Edward Island depended to about the same extent as did Nova Scotia on Britain for imports, but apparently purchased little from the United States.

The composition of trade by region is given in Table 4.5. In 1853, Nova Scotia's largest export was fishery products, at 36 percent, followed by agricultural products, at 22 percent; forest products, at 16 percent; manufactures, at 11 percent; and mineral products, at 9 percent. Manufactures were the largest component of imports, at 45 percent; followed by agriculture products, at 36 percent. More than 82 percent of New Brunswick's exports were

TABLE 4.5

Trade of the Maritime Colonies by Product, 1853

(percentage of total)

	Nova Scotia		*New Brunswick*		*Prince Edward Island (Year 1852)*		*Province of Canada*	
	Imports	*Exports*	*Imports*	*Exports*	*Imports*	*Exports*	*Imports*	*Exports*
Agricultural	35.9	21.9	34.2	2.9	17.8	65.0	13.9	48.1
Fishery	8.0	35.9	2.3	5.3	3.0	10.1	1.2	1.8
Forest	0.7	16.2	2.8	82.1	0.2	18.1	0.3	48.2
Manufactures and miscellaneous	44.5	10.9	53.6	6.7	70.9	6.8	80.2	1.2
Mineral	1.7	9.4	2.6	2.0	1.2	—	1.9	0.6
Wines and liquors	9.2	5.7	4.5	1.0	6.9	—	2.5	0.1

Source: S.A. Saunders, *The Economic History of the Maritime Provinces* (Fredericton: Acadiensis Press, 1984), 103.

classed as forest products, with no other sector accounting for more than 7 percent. Manufactures made up 54 percent of imports; agricultural products, another 34 percent. Of Prince Edward Island's foreign sales, 65 percent were of agricultural products, 18 percent forest products, and 10 percent fishery products. Manufactures accounted for 71 percent of imports; agricultural products, 18 percent.

The ambiguity associated with applying staples theory to Maritime economic development in this period remains. In many ways, growth was predicated on the appearance of new staples, and the form it took followed from the nature of the export. New Brunswick, with its timber economy, is perhaps the clearest example. Yet, much is left unexplained by the approach, as the reference to the connection between timber and agricultural development in New Brunswick suggests. Other examples could be cited, but the point remains that, in contrast to the case of Newfoundland, reference to staples activities is a necessary but far from sufficient condition for understanding the economic histories of the three Maritime provinces.

One further point bears stressing here. As we have seen, the Maritime economies began life as a response to revolution, war, and British mercantile policy. After 1815, they were forced to deal with continuous pressure to remove whatever advantages they had secured, whether in the fisheries or with respect to the Navigation Acts and timber preferences. They also experienced some diversification of activity beyond these staples trades, most notably into shipping and shipbuilding. The question facing the region in the 1840s, then, as the mercantile provisions were ending and as industrialization was spreading to North America, was whether the economy had matured enough to survive and prosper from these changes.

Conclusion

In summary, by midcentury, the Maritimes looked vastly different from the way it had in 1760. From a few thousand fishermen, soldiers, suppliers, and subsistence farmers at the earlier date, population had grown to more than 533 000, or 22 percent of the total of all British North American colonies at the time (excluding Newfoundland). The economies were dominated by the production of a few products for sale abroad. Fishing was a key sector, especially in Nova Scotia. The main market was still the West Indies, followed by the United States, the Spanish West Indies, the Mediterranean countries, and South America. Timber was prominent in New Brunswick. Britain took the bulk of the exports in the form of square timber, with ancillary sales of sawn timber to the West Indies and the United States.

Prince Edward Island was the only region to have developed a small agricultural surplus for export. In the other economies, agriculture was ancillary to lumbering, fishing, and other activities, and food imports were common. There was some mineral production, mainly in Nova Scotia. Shipbuilding was the main processing activity, with output going to the local coastal trade, to offshore markets, and, increasingly, to local merchants and traders. The other processing activities produced for the local market, behind the natural protection of distance. Shipping and trade were the main service activities. The next decades would tell how robust this economic base was.

Notes

1. Shannon Ryan, "Fishery to Colony: A Newfoundland Watershed, 1793–1815," in *Atlantic Canada Before Confederation*. The Acadiensis Reader, Vol. 1, edited by P.A. Buckner and David Frank (Fredericton: Acadiensis Press, 1985), 130.
2. Ryan, "Fishery to Colony," 148. See also David Alexander, "Newfoundland's Traditional Economy and Development to 1934," in *Newfoundland in the Nineteenth and Twentieth Centuries*, edited by James Hiller and Peter Neary (Toronto: University of Toronto Press, 1980).
3. Shannon Ryan, "The Newfoundland Salt Cod Trade in the Nineteenth Century," in *Newfoundland*, 50.
4. Ryan, "The Newfoundland Salt Cod Trade in the Nineteenth Century," 45.
5. Ryan, "The Newfoundland Salt Cod Trade in the Nineteenth Century," 49.
6. Alexander, "Newfoundland's Traditional Economy," in *Newfoundland*, 19.
7. Graeme Wynn, "Late Eighteenth Century Agriculture in the Bay of Fundy Marshlands," in *Atlantic Canada Before Confederation*.

Further Reading

Acheson, T.W. *St. John: The Making of a Colonial Urban Community* Toronto: University of Toronto Press, 1985.

MacNutt, W.S. *The Atlantic Provinces: The Emergence of Colonial Society, 1712–1857.* Toronto: McClelland and Stewart, 1965.

Matthews, Keith, and Gerald Panting, eds. *Ships and Shipbuilding in the North Atlantic Region*. St. John's: Memorial University Press, 1978.

Ryan, Shannon. "Fishery to Colony: A Newfoundland Watershed, 1793–1815." In *Atlantic Canada Before Confederation*, The Acadiensis Reader, Vol. I. Edited by P.A. Buckner and David Frank. Fredericton: Acadiensis Press, 1985.

Saunders, S.A. *The Economic History of the Maritime Provinces*. Edited and with an introduction by T.W. Acheson. Fredericton: Acadiensis Press, 1984.

Wynn, Graeme. *Timber Colony*. Toronto: University of Toronto Press, 1981.

CHAPTER

5

Quebec and Lower Canada

In 1759, Quebec City fell to the British. Four years later, the end of the Seven Years' War confirmed by treaty what had occurred in conflict: New France was ceded to Great Britain. The people of the region were faced with new challenges and an uncertain future; not the least of these challenges was the political and economic place of this newest colony within the British Empire.

For their part, the British got at least three things when they gained possession of Quebec. First, and foremost, they removed a threat on their northern frontier. Second, they gained a monopoly on the North American fur trade. Finally, they acquired a colony that was predominantly rural, with a population primarily dependent upon subsistence agriculture. This population was also French and Catholic, with its own history, culture, laws, and institutions. The removal of the threat and control of the fur trade were important gains; however, the presence of a large population of French Catholics was problematic.

The British were well aware that they faced a major challenge if they were to successfully integrate the new colony into the existing empire. This task was especially difficult since the fabric of the whole North American empire seemed about to tear apart. The English colonies to the south had become increasingly restive under British rule, and the removal of the threat of New France made them feel they had no further need for British protection. Disputes over tax laws led to civil disobedience, violence, and, in 1775, the outbreak of the American Revolution. Before long, armies would once again be invading Quebec; this time the invaders would be American.

Because Britain's attempt to deal with its recent conquest took place in an era of upheaval and war, the political approach to the Quebec problem was dictated by the need to maintain some internal stability. The French Catholics had to be won over to the British crown, or, at the very least, brought to the point where they were unlikely to join their troublesome neighbours to the south. The result was a series of experimental and oft-changing laws and systems. English and French law competed for pride and place, as did English and French religious establishments.

Most fundamentally, the basic institutions of government were in flux. Initially, the British ran the colony by means of a military government. This temporary measure, expedient in the midst of war, was abolished when the colony was formally ceded to England and the British issued the Proclamation of 1763. Faced with contradictory pressures from the residents of Quebec, from native tribes to the west, and from the American colonies to the south, the British reduced the boundaries of Quebec to little more than the St. Lawrence valley. The vast river empire that had been so much a part of the French experience and economy in North America was excised. Then, only eleven years later, the British reversed themselves. In the Quebec Act of 1774, Quebec's boundaries were extended to include much of the old hinterland of New France. The unity of the fur trade was thus reasserted.

Finally, after the American rebellion, and with the southern part of the old territory lost to the newly formed United States of America, the British implemented the Constitutional Act of 1791. The St. Lawrence valley–Great Lakes region was split in two. The western portion became Upper Canada; the eastern portion — the settled portion of what had been New France — became Lower Canada. Also, for the first time, Lower Canada and the French Catholics who represented the vast majority of its population were granted a legislative assembly. However, that concession did not end the political turbulence. Divisions of class and language combined with tensions within the constitutional system of Lower Canada to exacerbate relations between French and English. By 1837, the colony was in a state of rebellion, and before long the constitution would be suspended and authoritarian rule once again in place, albeit temporarily.

These political approaches were paralleled by British attempts to integrate Quebec into the British imperial economy. Like the French before them, the British had shaped policy according to the principles of mercantilism. There were differences in the particulars, but this framework provided a constant point of reference in the transfer from the old to the new regime, and during the various constitutional alterations that ensued. The British adherence to the principles inherent in the Navigation Acts and Corn Laws reflected a framework of empire that had much in common with that of the French. Further, the presence of the American colonies to the south and, especially, the British West Indies seemed to provide opportunities for the sort of triangular trade that fit within the mercantile system. Policies thus emphasized the traditional hinterland-metropolis relationship and the importance of the primary commodity in the staples trade, furs. In addition, the British sought, again like the French before them, to diversify the Quebec trade network and to increase ties with the West Indies.

The combination of political demands (to avoid French resistance to British rule), economic policy (British mercantilism and imperial interests), and the internal forces that were developing within Quebec shaped the evolution of the colony's economy over the first 80 years of British rule. These are factors that pertain to the entire history of Lower Canada. Still, as will be shown, sufficiently important changes occur that it is possible to characterize the economic development of Quebec (and, after 1791, Lower Canada) as having three distinct phases.

The first phase, from the conquest to the early nineteenth century, was marked by considerable growth and potential opportunity. The traditional staple — furs — continued to be central to the economy, while new markets seemed to be opening up for agricultural products. As a result, the rapidly increasing population was accommodated by an economy that grew even more rapidly. The second era, beginning in the early nineteenth century and continuing through to the early 1830s, was more mixed. The importance and viability of staples shifted dramatically. New ones, such as timber, became important as old ones collapsed or experienced tremendous fluctuations from year to year. There was, thus, both growth and considerable dislocation. Finally, in the 1830s, dislocation and growth were replaced with stagnation and decline. No new area of growth had yet appeared, while existing staples were either effectively finished (furs), in a state of crisis (agriculture), or no longer experiencing growth (timber).

This depiction of events has, itself, created some controversy. The question has been raised as to whether emphasizing a few resource staples is a sufficient basis for understanding the nature of the economic circumstances in Lower Canada. Does overreliance on one theme lead to the exclusion or subordination of others? This warning must be kept in mind. Still, the dominant importance of staples cannot be set aside, even though alternative sources of growth must also be explored.

Adjustment to the New Regime, 1760–1802

The first era opened with economic upheaval that flowed from the constitutional disruption brought by the conquest. Metropolitan-hinterland relationships and practices built up over the past century were suddenly torn apart. The Rouen and Bordeaux merchants were gone. Local French businessmen and agents were cut off from their backers and suppliers. Many inhabitants found themselves holding worthless card money or IOUs from the former regime. Louisbourg, the one steady export market for agricultural products in previous years, was now destroyed. There was no certainty as to how the trade structure of the St. Lawrence valley, and of the fur trade beyond it, would fit into the imperial system of the new government of the region, that of the British Empire.

It was not long before British merchants, financiers, and investors moved in to fill the vacuum. Merchants from the American colonies had accompanied the army into Quebec in 1759, and many remained once the war was over, hoping to supply the garrisons and to sell to the population of Quebec. As was true during the French regime, however, it was not local merchants, French or English, who dominated trade. Rather, large London-based partnerships, such as those headed by Brook Watson and Gregory Rashleigh, emerged with the capital and connections necessary to assume control of this new market. Like their French predecessors, they used local agents to promote their interests and handle affairs on site.

Powerful individuals did emerge in Quebec itself. For example, George Allsop acted as an agent for such people as Brook Watson but was also active in his own right in both the merchandise and the fur trades. Other, less wealthy, merchants brought goods in by the shipload or worked with ship captains to carve out a niche for themselves. Still, until well after the end of the American Revolution, the bulk of the import-export trade and of the provisioning of army garrisons was controlled by those large-scale operators centred in London or, to a lesser degree, Boston or New York. As one historian has said of the transition from the old to the new regime, "the names changed but the structure remained intact."[1]

Local capital did develop, and, not surprisingly, one of the first places it did so was in the traditional staple area of the fur trade. After the conquest, the fur trade went through considerable adjustment. First, there was the disruption of financial and supply arrangements resulting from the conquest. Then, a two-year native resistance known as Pontiac's Rebellion swept much of the western frontier. Third, the American Revolution again disrupted trade to the southwest. By the 1780s, however, the trade out of Montreal had been renewed, as new groups of fur traders emerged. The actual trade in the west is discussed later in this volume, but it is important to note that, from Quebec's perspective, the fur trade remained an important staple, still accounting for more than three-quarters of the exports of Quebec in the late 1760s, and between two-thirds and three-quarters of those exports in most of the years before 1790.[2]

During these transitional years, French Canadians continued to control much of the trade. They were, after all, the experts, and through the 1760s, owned 80 percent of the canoes heading west. Finances matter, however, and there was not the savings in the colony to handle the large investments and the long-term gap between outlay and return. Thus, British capital became increasingly influential. By the 1780s, more and more of the furs from the west came through the businesses of Scottish merchants such as the McGills and the Frobishers. When the smaller partnerships began, in the 1780s, to come together under the large North West Company syndicate, control rested firmly in the hands of interconnected Scottish clans — the McTavishes, the McGillivrays, the Frobishers. The work force continued, as before, to be drawn from the French-Catholic habitant class, but now the line between management and worker was increasingly an ethnic and linguistic one as well.

The tremendous impact of the English and Scottish merchants on Quebec in these years implies that the historical emphasis should be on discontinuity brought about by an ascendant British presence in the region. Yet, in many areas, there were strong elements of continuity in spite of the changes that were taking place. For one thing, the British consciously sought to prop up many of the institutional and social characteristics of the *ancien régime*. The seigneurial system would remain intact until 1854, and, until 1791, the British routinely granted new lands in the colony on a seigneurial basis. Further, the nonrepresentative institutions that existed before 1791 enabled the British to look to the seigneurial class as the natural representatives of the French population, while tending to ignore the bumptious merchants. Thus, the French-Catholic elite was propped up by continued access to government power and patronage. Nor should the fact that Quebec was under an authoritarian form of government be overlooked. The failure of the British to give Quebec the representative government typical in other parts of the continent was anomalous, but it also meant that there was a degree of continuity between old and new regimes.

Economic and social continuity as well existed for the bulk of the population. Merchants and government officials might have found their careers and lives in flux, but more than 80 percent of the population of Quebec lived in rural areas, and for these small storekeepers and parish priests — and, especially, for the habitants — life did not change dramatically. New monetary stability was felt almost immediately, but the daily rhythms of life went on as before. Patterns that appeared in the final decades of New France continued without interruption in the postconquest years.

The most dramatic of these patterns was demographic. After a long period of slow population growth, New France had, in the final decades of its existence, begun to experience rapid population growth. This change was largely attributable to natural increase. Birth rates went up, and death rates, which had always been relatively low, declined. This pattern continued without interruption after the conquest and, indeed, accelerated. Very rarely in the late eighteenth and early nineteenth centuries did the birth rate fall below 50 per 1000. (In comparison, during the famous baby boom of the 1950s, Canadian birth rates were in the order of 24 to 28 per 1000). Aided by rising English immigration, population rose phenomenally[3] — from a little more than 60 000 people in the 1750s to approximately 165 000 by 1790, to more than 300 000 by 1815. In two generations, the population increased fivefold! By 1840, it would double again, to 600 000.

Intermittent bursts of significant immigration abetted this process and, more importantly, altered the linguistic and religious balances of the colony. During and after the American Revolution, thousands of Loyalist refugees headed northward toward British North America. Most of them settled in Nova Scotia or Upper Canada (they are discussed in chapters 4 and 6, which deal with those regions). However, some settled in what was to be Lower Canada. The area known as the Eastern Townships was largely opened and settled by Loyalists and later British immigrants. In the cities, there was also a steady influx of anglophones, so that, by the early nineteenth century, 40 percent of the population of Quebec City and 33 percent of that of Montreal was anglophone.[4] Still, the cities were small, and, by 1815, these inflows, rural and urban, had brought the anglophone population of Lower Canada to only about 15 percent.

This population growth transformed the countryside. The small straggling population of New France hugging the St. Lawrence was replaced by a population expanding quickly into new agricultural areas. Existing seigneuries were pushed back from the St. Lawrence, while new seigneuries were opened at a regular rate; after 1791, freehold tenure was established for new lands. The edge of settlement receded toward the Laurentian mountains to the north and up the Ottawa valley at the western edge of the colony. Though the rivers would long be at the centre of the colonial transportation system, their impact was lessened by the development of more extensive road systems.

The rapid rise in population also brought to an end the "one continuous village" that had characterized eighteenth-century New France. The number of villages and towns began to increase. Centred on the parish church, local stores, and artisans' shops, these villages were largely service centres for the surrounding agricultural community. Most had a population of fewer than 1000, however, and did little to change the overwhelming dominance of agriculture outside of Quebec City and Montreal. In fact, estimates of population indicate that Quebec was more rural in 1810 than it had been in 1760. From being more than one-quarter of the population in 1787, the urban population of Lower Canada fell to less than one-sixth of the total by the end of the War of 1812, and to perhaps one-tenth before the trend began to reverse itself.

A demographic shift of this magnitude raises the obvious question of how all of these new people were absorbed into the economy. Did the increase in population mean that resources were spread more thinly and, thus, that the standard of living declined, or did economic growth prove as enduring as that of population? The best evidence available to date indicates that, at least in the years before 1800, the standard of living in Quebec was not only maintained but improved and that, therefore, economic growth must have been faster than population growth.

Though there were undoubtedly numerous reasons for this demographic shift, two or three major changes in the Lower Canadian economy seem central. First, there were direct expenditures by the British government. The army brought with it considerable amounts of specie. As was noted in Chapter 3, shortage of specie had always acted as a retarding factor in the growth of that colony. The easing of such shortages allowed money to circulate more widely and, therefore, spurred development. Behind the specie lay new possibilities for work with the British garrisons. Though the largest suppliers of the garrisons were merchants from outside the colony, there were still numerous opportunities for local profits on a smaller scale. Troops were billeted in homes, for example, and although this imposition was not always welcome, it did provide cash to the homeowner. Likewise, contracts to supply local garrisons with firewood, fresh produce, and other such materials added to the opportunities for profit.

There were dramatic changes in farm production as well. Agricultural output grew sufficiently to feed all those new mouths and, in fact, generated surpluses. After experiencing some lean years in the 1760s, the agricultural sector produced increasing quantities of wheat, potatoes, peas, flax, and some animals.[5] Much of this production, of course, went to feed the expanding population, for the subsistence economy still largely affected the average habitant farm. Still, such was less the case in 1800 than it had been in 1750, as habitants in many parts of the province devoted an increased percentage of their efforts to commercial production and to exports of cereals.

These exports reflected the growth of Britain and the British West Indies as export markets for Lower Canadian wheat. Initially, this trade was sporadic and reasonably small-scale, although the amount could occasionally be significant. Thus, in 1774, nearly half a million bushels of wheat were exported. By the 1780s, exports had become established, and farmers geared production to the possibilities overseas. By the early 1790s, exports were between 400 000 and 600 000 bushels a year (see Table 5.1). In the better years, agricultural exports now rivalled those of the fur trade in importance. Certainly, given the high percentage of the Lower Canadian population that depended on agriculture, this growth in exports was, as Fernand Ouellet has noted, the central overall pattern of economic development in Lower Canada in these years.[6]

Though the precise figures are debatable, the trends indicated in Table 5.1 are clear enough. From at least the early 1790s through to the end of the first decade of the nineteenth century, wheat exports were a consistent part of the economy of Lower Canada. Further, studies of habitant life have concluded that this same period saw a more consistent appearance of cash in the countryside.

The growing population and the increased amount of cash in rural areas provided opportunities for ancillary activities. It was now possible for artisans and small merchants to expand their operations. Villages that developed with the rising population were logical locations for these merchants and artisans, who, in turn, were supplied by larger wholesalers and merchants (some English and some French) operating out of Montreal and Quebec. All in all, this meant several things. First, the domestic market for products was gaining in importance. Second, the links were thus drawn somewhat more closely between town and country than had been the case in the *ancien régime*. Finally, the market economy began to intrude upon subsistence agriculture; subsistence farming declined as farmers took advantage of the new export market.

It is important to realize, however, that participation in the emerging wheat economy was not uniform across the colony, for two main reasons. First, some lands were more suited for wheat than others, just as the size of some landholdings was better suited for efficient production. Second, there existed strong traditions of mixed farming in Lower Canada. Oats, potatoes, corn, and peas were standard crops, though none was as important as wheat, which, in 1815, accounted for roughly 75 percent of all field crops.[7] In addition, there was an increasing number of livestock in the colony by the end of the eighteenth century. Most farms had at least a few cattle, some sheep and poultry, and some hogs. Dairying was a growing industry.[8] Lower Canada never became a monoculture in which farmers specialized in wheat at the expense of all else — not even in the best wheat years.

Mixed farming was traditional in subsistence agriculture. The

TABLE 5.1

Wheat Exports from Lower Canada, 1793–1810

(000 minots, 1 minot = 1.07 bushels)

1793	542	1802	1151
1794	483	1803	438
1795	449	1804	273
1796	25	1805	115
1797	101	1806	152
1798	139	1807	334
1799	201	1808	399
1800	318	1809	—
1801	663	1810	—

Source: Figures from T.J. Le Goff, "Agricultural Crisis in Lower Canada," *Canadian Historical Review* 55, no. 1 (March 1974): 22.

tendency of peasant families to provide much (never all) of the goods to feed and clothe their families required an eclectic mixture of crops, livestock, and dairy animals. The type of farming that appeared in the late eighteenth and early nineteenth centuries, however, was not representative of a system in which wheat was uniformly supplanting an older tradition of peasant agriculture. Mixed farming was also becoming more market-oriented and, thus, represented a parallel or alternative strategy to a concentration in wheat. Local village and urban markets now existed for the products of mixed farming, and, though information is incomplete, there was a degree of specialization among farmers; one concentrating in, say, dairy products might supply another concentrating in something else. Here, as elsewhere, the cash economy was gradually eroding the isolation of the countryside.

Agriculture Adjustment and New Staples, 1815–1840

In the early nineteenth century, the forces that had been building up within the economy led to some dislocations and dramatic changes. The nature of the changes and the implications they have for the history of Quebec have resulted in some of the most detailed literature and intense controversy in Canadian economic history. However, the basic fact underlying the controversy is incontrovertible. In the late eighteenth century, Quebec seemed to be emerging as a significant exporter of grain. From a staples point of view, a new product thus seemed about to assume the role played by furs in colonial New France. By the 1830s, however, it was apparent that Quebec had not become a wheat exporter. The growing surpluses of earlier years had become erratic and then, in the 1830s, ceased, not recurring as even an occasional event. Lower Canada was, by then, a net importer of wheat. The problem for economists and historians, then, has been to discover what happened between the time of those rising exports at the turn of the century and the situation in the 1830s. As is often the case, these economic questions also have larger implications. In 1837, rebellion broke out in Lower Canada (as it did in Upper Canada). The economic position of the colony and the failure to maintain earlier patterns of growth have led many historians to link economic stagnation with rebellion.

The most important statement of this link came from Fernand Ouellet in 1966. Ouellet argued three basic points. First, he said, there was an agricultural crisis in the early part of the nineteenth century. Crop yields declined, and Quebec moved from surplus to subsistence, to deficiency in grains. Second, a self-serving group of professionals (mainly doctors and lawyers) sought to take advantage of French nationalism to gain support for their bid for political power by using the new British institution of the elected assembly. Third, the two events merged because the combination of declining economic circumstances and a patriotic appeal proved irresistible. The Patriote party of Louis-Joseph Papineau drew support from devastated farmers and, instead of responding constructively to circumstances, headed down the road that led to rebellion.[9]

In response to Ouellet, several alternative viewpoints and modifications have emerged. One of the best-known of these argued that there was no particular crisis in agriculture in the early nineteenth century, though it may not have been the rapid-growth sector it had been in previous years. Further, according to this position, agriculture should not be isolated from the broader economy. An absence of agricultural growth does not mean an absence of growth overall. New sectors of the economy opened, and the French-Canadian bourgeoisie as well as the average person adapted quite well to these altered circumstances. By the time the transition was complete, a new and modern market economy had emerged from the structures of the *ancien régime*. This interpretation, as its best-known supporters recently said, "suggests rather a dynamic and entrepreneurial view of Lower Canada at the turn of the nineteenth century."[10]

The debate has a tremendous number of complexities and reveals how ideology, interpretations of partial and incomplete data, and the greater or lesser powers of human reasoning affect interpretations. In a most general way, however, all of the figures and debates on the agricultural sector centre on one basic issue. Amid all this discussion, there is no doubt that the Lower Canadian export market in wheat did not develop. As the figures in Table 5.1 indicate, promising surpluses had become erratic by the end of the first decade of the century. They would recover periodically but were never consistent until, in the 1830s, the market collapsed altogether, and Lower Canada became a net importer of wheat.

This trend in the export markets was matched in the fields. Though wheat remained an important crop through to the 1830s, it did not increase as quickly as did total acreage under cultivation or population. Rather, mixed farming increased, and beef and dairy cattle, in particular, became more and more numerous, as did sheep. Cattle, for example, increased ninefold between 1784 and 1831, and sheep 6.5 times. In contrast, the number of horses increased more slowly, at a rate roughly comparable to population increase. In other words, more and more farmers were moving into new areas of specialization, while wheat declined in relative importance. Overall, it has been estimated that between 1800 and 1831 wheat fell from 60 percent to 21 percent of all agricultural produce.[11]

There has been much debate as to whether this shift marked a move on the part of the habitant to take advantage of emerging new opportunities or a forced adjustment to deteriorating circumstances. Connected with this debate is the question of whether the habitant's standard of living was improving or declining in these years. For the one side, this shift in orientation marks a new interest in the domestic market as well as a movement away from the risky international trade in wheat. For the other, the shift marks a return to subsistence agriculture, as cattle and sheep provided home products (milk, cheese, and wool) necessary for subsistence farming. This issue is difficult to resolve, but the one thing that can be said with certainty is that by the 1820s Quebec was no longer a significant wheat exporter. The question is whether it failed because farmers could not produce a marketable surplus (a failure of supply) or because they left the market voluntarily, responding to other opportunities (inadequate demand).

Those who feel the decline in exports reflects a failure of supply point, with varying degrees of emphasis, to several forces. First, and most controversial, there is the argument that the Lower Canadian habitant was simply a bad farmer. Initially, the new soils of frontier lands obscured this problem. As the farms grew older and as the demands of the marketplace grew more competitive, however, the weaknesses in farming practices became clearer. Yields declined and varied more from year to year. Ouellet estimates that wheat production per family declined from something between 100 and 200 minots in the 1760–1802 period to fewer than 50 minots by 1831.[12] The market pulled the habitant briefly into commercial farming toward the end of the eighteenth century; he could not respond to the requirements and opportunities, however, and sank back into subsistence.

A second argument in favour of a failure of supply focuses on the rising population of the colony. The filling up of good areas, the division of farms through inheritance until they were too small to be efficient, and the simple necessity of feeding his own family drove the farmer back toward subsistence agriculture with some side trade in the local communities. As one historian put it, "it was not so much that wheat production had declined after the record highs of 1801–2, it was simply that it stagnated after this date near its earlier levels while population continued to rise, steadily and inexorably."[13] Reinforcing this viewpoint is the argument that wheat was always a marginal crop for the St. Lawrence valley and that conditions (for example, farm size and soil) had to be optimal for it to be competitive. Some combination of a rising population, subdivision of farms, and soil exhaustion thus caused farmers to shift away from wheat production or to become less competitive at it. In their place, the wheat frontiers of the United States and of Upper Canada (as we will see in Chapter 6) became the major suppliers to the British market.

In one way or another, therefore, these viewpoints (and there are variants on them) see an economy in crisis. After a century or more of basic subsistence farming, the habitants and seigneurs of the St. Lawrence began to develop an export market — first, in Louisbourg, under the old regime, and then, under the British, in the West Indies and Britain itself. The exports could not be sustained, however, and Lower Canada entered a period of economic uncertainty and even crisis that would continue to the 1840s.

Those who look not to a collapse of supply but to a dwindling of demand often have quite a different perspective. They question whether wheat ever was a meaningful staple in the period before 1840 and whether the changes that took place in Lower Canadian agriculture can be seen, therefore, as any real crisis. For them, the key is the uncertainty of the Atlantic trading system, and of the British market for wheat, in particular. Demand was erratic and undependable. There were some good years, but, after a period of time, farmers found it not worth their while to continue growing for the British market. Instead, in a conservative but rational process, they returned their production to a more mixed type of agriculture to meet the needs of the local population. In this view, there was no agricultural crisis, and the standard of living in the agricultural sector may actually have improved in the first part of the nineteenth century.[14]

The debate is not yet resolved and, given the limitations of the data, it is unlikely that there ever will be a final definitive word. In general, however, certain things are apparent. First, the debate has been carried on with a certain intransigence on both sides, perhaps because of the political implications inherent in it. For those who assume a slightly more distant view of it, however, it is apparent that the extremes on both sides need modification. Second, although there was undoubtedly peasant conservatism in the habitant's farming habits, it is also true that European agriculture reformers were uniformly shocked at the "wasteful" habits of North American farmers, whether in Lower Canada, the United States, or, later, Upper Canada and the Prairie west. Indeed, recent research of the new economic-history type has argued that the French-Canadian farmer was no less efficient than his English-Canadian counterpart. Farming habits alone are thus unlikely to explain the precipitous decline in agricultural exports. Instead, the marginality of some of the lands, the division of farms (though not to as great an extent as originally surmised), and the quality of wheat affected the farmer's ability to make specialization in wheat profitable.

The failure of wheat as a staple meant that, whether there was an agricultural crisis or successful adaptation by farmers, wheat exports did not act as a primary force in driving the economy. The economic growth necessary to sustain an increasing population would have to come from another quarter.

That economic growth would not be supplied by the traditional staple of the region — the fur trade. For Montreal, the heyday of that trade was over. The merger in 1804 of the North West Company and XY Company, both based in Montreal, marked the realization that supply lines were becoming longer and that profits were more difficult to achieve in the face of fierce competition from the Hudson's Bay Company. It was still an important trade for those engaged in it, but it was a much smaller part of Lower Canada's economy than it had been a half-century before, if for no other reason than that the population was so much bigger. Even before the War of 1812, fur exports had shrunk to less than 10 percent of the Lower Canadian total.[15] In 1821, as noted in Chapter 4, the trade would effectively disappear from the St. Lawrence valley altogether. A tradition lasting two centuries was coming to an end.

A new staple developed in these years, however — timber cut from the vast forests of Upper and Lower Canada and exported to Great Britain. Within a few short years, the timber trade changed from being a minor and specialized activity to become Lower Canada's most important export. It would remain vital to the economy through much of the century. It is also perhaps the best example of the way in which an imperial policy had a direct and immediate effect on the British North American economy.

Local businessmen and colonial governments had, for years, tried to turn the vast resources of the North American forest into an exportable good. As far back as the 1660s, Colbert and Talon had included lumbering in their ambitious program for New France. That plan failed, but on various occasions thereafter the idea was revived. There were even some occasional exports, but generally it was difficult for local entrepreneurs to compete with European sources. Baltic suppliers were much closer to both France and Britain. Still, a minor trade had slowly developed, in the years after the conquest accounting for from 5 percent to as much as 20 percent of Quebec exports. Overall, however, British North American timber exports served only a small fraction of the vast British market, where Baltic sources still dominated.[16]

As was discussed in Chapter 2, the early nineteenth century saw the high politics of war and trade affect imperial timber policy.

During the Napoleonic Wars, the British moved to find new and more secure sources of supply. Thus, in 1805, they raised the tariff on foreign timber to 25 shillings a load, and in 1809, to more than 39 shillings. In Canada, as in New Brunswick, the timber trade exploded. By the end of the decade, Lower Canada alone accounted for more imports into Britain than did all Baltic sources. As early as 1810, timber was a more important export for Lower Canada than fur and wheat combined. By the 1820s, more than 100 000 tons of squared pine, 20 000 tons of squared oak, and millions of individual "deals" (softwood planks) and staves were exported annually from the St. Lawrence valley. This new trade was reflected in seaport traffic, as a tremendous increase in shipping into the St. Lawrence took place. From an average volume of less than 15 000 tons in the late eighteenth century, shipping rose to 137 000 tons by 1810.[17] As Figure 5.1 indicates for the Port of Quebec, there was a direct correlation between the dramatic rises in shipping and

FIGURE 5.1

Timber Exports and Total Shipping, Port of Quebec, 1808–12 to 1838–42

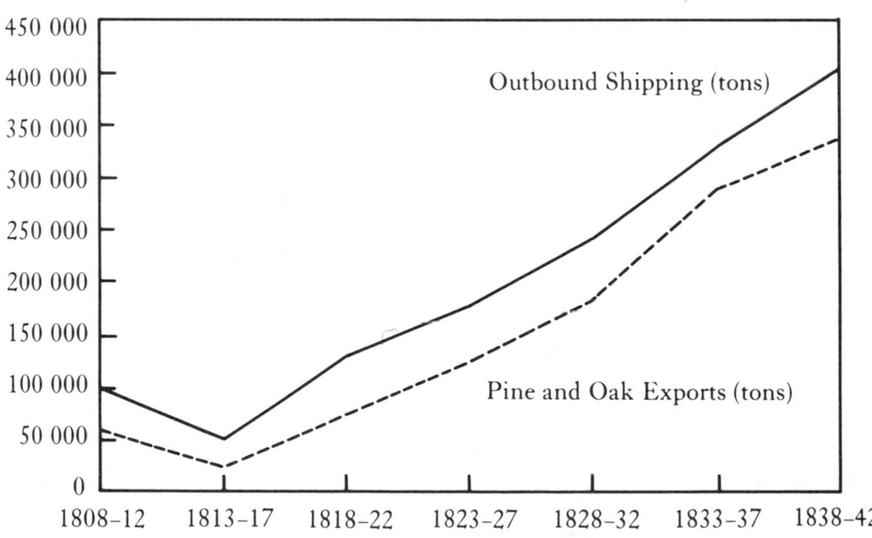

Source: Derived from Fernand Ouellet, *Lower Canada, 1791–1840: Social Change and Modernism*. (Toronto: McClelland and Stewart, 1980), 352.

National Archives of Canada/C-40326

Timber raft on the St. Lawrence, c. *1838. Unlike other staples, timber provided its own transportation. Squared-off timber, lashed together to form a makeshift raft and with a cabin or tent for the crew, was floated downstream to the St. Lawrence and, ultimately, to Quebec City.*

in the timber trade. Lower Canada had found its new staple.

The timber trade was quite different in its characteristics and requirements from both farming and the fur trade. Farming was carried on within the frontiers of settlement, and the fur trade well beyond it. The timber trade, however, was carried out on its edges. In particular, the trade thrived along the numerous rivers feeding into the St. Lawrence from the Shield — most importantly, the Saguenay and up the Ottawa valley, where huge stands of prime timber were available for the axe and where rivers acted as highways to carry the product to the ships that would transport it to Europe.

The rhythm of the trade was, as with so much else in preindustrial society, seasonal. In the winter, crews based in tumbledown shanty camps worked long, arduous days, cutting the timber and hauling it to the nearest body of water suitable for use as a means of transportation. Then, when spring breakup came, the interior camps became quiet as the crews either disbanded or moved downstream with the wood.

In the first years of the trade, the bulk of timber exports were in the form of squared timber (pine or oak). This primitive form of processing fitted the frontier conditions and also allowed the trade to develop one of its most characteristic features — the timber raft. Once on larger rivers, such as the Ottawa or Saguenay, the timbers could be lashed together to form a makeshift raft. The raft was then floated downstream to the St. Lawrence and, ultimately, to Quebec City. Tents or makeshift cabins erected on the rafts provided shelter for the crew that tended them. Unlike other staples, timber provided its own transportation. As the trade developed, the export of deals increased and, with it, the number of sawmills connected to the timber trade.

The hard life of winter in the camps and spring and summer on the move created an especially volatile lumbering society. As one historian noted, the "lumber trade was not one designed to produce the clean-cut, all-round, all-Canadian personality."[18] For one thing, the trade operated within a strictly hierarchical and authoritarian society. Lumber communities were divided, especially in their earlier years, between the lumber "barons" who dominated the region and the men who worked at a hard job for poor wages. The barons of the Ottawa region, for example, initially consisted of such Americans as Philemon Wright, Braddish Billings, and Ira Honeywell. Later, Scottish and English merchants joined them in the race to exploit the riches of the region.

In many cases, these men ruled over quite large concerns, involving hundreds, even thousands, of men. Through much of the period, the workers comprised a mixture of recent Irish immigrants and French Canadians. Cut off from the wider community during much of the year, they returned to settled areas often for a spree of heavy drinking and lavish spending. The ethnic mix was also a volatile one, as French and Irish often warred with each other for dominance of the labour market in the region. A drink too much, a hostile word: anything might set off dangerous and occasionally fatal clashes between the two groups. Canada's frontier society was not always, as myth would have it, all that peaceable.

It would be a mistake, however, to portray lumbering as the exclusive preserve of large groups of rough transients. Indeed, the seasonal nature of cutting and hauling meant that lumbering, especially hauling, was often a part-time activity for farmers in the vicinity of the trade. Like the fur trade before it, the timber trade provided them with an opportunity to obtain cash. This incentive was especially significant because the trade was carried out on the fringes of settlement, where farms were often not yet fully established; the winter activities of the timber trade carried families over the early years while their farms were being developed. Moreover, for some, the trade was more than a transitory activity. Much of the farmland of the Saguenay and of the Ottawa valley was less than ideal for farming. Thus, there developed a kind of symbiosis between the marginal farms of the region and the trade. The marginal farms provided labour to assist in the trade; the trade allowed the marginal farmer to survive on his land.

In communities such as Hull and Bytown, along certain parts of the Saguenay, and in other spots on the Shield, the timber trade was the lifeblood of the community. More difficult to evaluate, however, is the impact of the trade on the larger society of Lower Canada. How important was it? To what degree could a resource trade along the edges of civilization act as an alternative for continued agricultural growth or for the nascent industrial developments of the region?

First, the trade did generate a significant demand for labour. As we have indicated, lumbering required thousands of men at certain times of the year and thus provided work for new immigrants such as the Irish or for those French Canadians who could not make a living on the farm. It was not only the habitant who benefited. Many seigneurs suddenly found that all that unwanted forest was a more valuable asset than agricultural land. Later, as the trade moved from squared timber to deals, seigneurs or other entrepreneurs found that additional money could be made in the development and operation of sawmills.

Second, the trade also had an important impact on urban centres in Lower Canada, particularly Quebec City. Quebec was the financial and shipping and shipbuilding centre of the entire Canadian trade. In that sense, the colony of Upper Canada was tributary to its Lower Canadian counterpart. As Figure 5.1 indicates, the trade enlivened the port activities of Quebec to an unparalleled degree. Numerous "coves" sprang up, as local timber merchants and forwarders built wharves; employed clerks and labourers; and arranged for the buying, selling, and oceanic transportation of the timber.[19] Also a part of this metropolitan side of the trade were the fortunes made in it. Wealth accumulated not only to the barons on the Ottawa but also to the merchant traders of Quebec. Other business activities and a degree of economic diversification thus resulted, as it was supposed to, from the pursuit of this staple resource.[20] Much more work will be necessary, however, before we can say with precision just how much.

Overall, then, between the early nineteenth century and approximately 1830, elements of the Lower Canadian economy underwent significant transition. Not only, as many historians have argued, was the market economy more fully developed than previously but the staples trade changed. The fur trade, which had been central to the economy of New France, became peripheral to Lower Canada's. In the meantime, the agricultural sector, though perhaps not in crisis, did not assume the fur trade's old mantle as a staple economy. This would have been a serious problem for the overall trade balance of the colony as well as for any prospects of diversification had it not been for the fortuitous decision of the British to develop a colonial timber trade. While the trade did not always promote the most desirable social structures and its effects were unevenly distributed across the regions of Lower Canada, it did provide the colony with a major export, and the people in the colony with new jobs.

There is a danger in looking at Lower Canada in these years only in terms of commercial activities. Considerable change had undoubtedly taken place as the old fur staple collapsed, as the new staple of wheat was tried and abandoned, and as the population grew dramatically. Yet, the vast population of the colony were farmers, and, for them, daily life had hardly changed at all. Even the timber trade, important though it was, affected the work patterns of only certain parts of the colony — mainly the Ottawa valley. Those settled in that area were probably more tied in to the market economy than their grandparents had been and, depending on the region and whom you read, their standard of living may have been a little higher or a little lower: but overall, the patterns of daily work and the human relationship to the land and to the seasons had altered little.

Agricultural Crisis and Metropolitan Commerce

Between the grandfather who had farmed immediately after the conquest and the grandson who took up farming around 1830, one important thing had changed, in spite of all the continuities of habitant life. For the former, expectations had been high. British currency and a rising demand for wheat seemed to indicate prosperity for the future. This was not the case by 1830. To date, population pressure had been manageable, as new lands had been developed or as children had moved into new areas of endeavour, such as the timber trade or, to a lesser degree, the labouring jobs that came with the associated rise in shipping. Now, however, land pressure was becoming a problem. The good lands were largely taken, and population growth did not show any sign of abating. The promise of the export market in wheat had passed, and the agricultural frontier had moved into Upper Canada. The future did not seem as promising.

These problems were made much worse in the 1830s, when a series of blights hit the Lower Canadian wheat crop. Wheat midge, in particular, devastated crops in several years and, from at least 1833 on, there was a recurring agricultural crisis in the colony. Several regions reported widespread hunger, even starvation, and the agricultural population experienced a serious decline in its standard of living. The colony that had, in the late eighteenth century, hoped to become a major wheat exporter was, by the 1830s, dependent on imported crops to feed itself. The 1830s brought home the fact that agricultural production directly affected the majority of the population. Only so many could be absorbed into forest work or into the shipyards of Quebec. The problem was that the vastness of the rural agricultural population overwhelmed any employment possibilities in the timber trade.

The immediate crisis in Lower Canada's agricultural sector would pass, but the transformation was permanent. By the 1840s, two things were clear. First, there was no immediate likelihood of any significant expansion of agricultural opportunity. Second, farmers had abandoned wheat as a major crop in favour of the mixed agricultural style that had begun to emerge in the first decades of the century. In some instances, this new style of farming led to the development of an urban-oriented and successful agricultural strategy. In many other instances, however, the cash sales were small supplements to what was essentially subsistence farming. Moreover, with the good farm lands settled, future population would have to be accommodated elsewhere.

What choices did the offspring of the Lower Canadian farmer have? As was the case where other types of land were scarce, they had to decide whether to remain within the limited economic horizons offered by their own community or to move. Family and friendships vied with economic opportunity. For Lower Canadians, the choice was especially difficult because to leave the colony implied being absorbed in the sea of English Protestantism that surrounded them. Even the cities of Lower Canada seemed a threat, with their large English-speaking populations and their foreign world of commerce. Over the next decades, clergy and government would urge farmers to locate on the marginal lands of the Shield rather than see them lost to the traditions of their forefathers.

Ultimately, however, exodus was the choice of thousands. Interestingly, that exodus was not mainly to new agricultural frontiers, though some did head off to the frontier regions in the United States. Instead, the attraction was to the cities and towns. In particular, a long-term trend emerged that saw the population go southward, across the border to the United States. Beginning in the 1820s, French Canadians had moved off to New England and elsewhere to take advantage of the embryonic industrial economy developing to the south. As the agricultural crisis worsened and as the pace of New England's industrial developent quickened, the rate of emigration from Lower Canada increased. By the 1840s, New England was probably the primary frontier (albeit an industrial one) for the agricultural population of the St. Lawrence valley. It would remain so through much of the century.

This exodus raises the question of the urban alternatives within Lower Canada, for there is a danger that, in the emphasis on staples, the significance of the urban centres and their contribution to overall economic development will be overlooked. By midcentury, Montreal was clearly the dominant city in British North America and would be the centre of industry and commerce well into the twentieth century. Quebec City, as we have already seen, was the centre of the timber trade, and a local and very wealthy elite had sprung up in the region. What, then, was happening in these two urban centres in the first four decades of the nineteenth century and to what extent must they be taken into account in understanding the economic evolution of the colony?

Certainly their place in the overall economy was much less significant than it would become by the latter part of the century. As was mentioned earlier, Lower Canada actually became more rural in the late eighteenth and early nineteenth centuries. Only toward the end of this period, at the height of the agricultural crisis, did this tendency of Lower Canada to become more rural reverse itself. Montreal, with a population of between 15 000 and 20 000 around 1820, had just overtaken Quebec City and would, over the next decades, assume a dominant position. In these years, however, both cities still exhibited the standard characteristics of rather small preindustrial centres of population. Neighbourhoods were largely undifferentiated ethnically, and types of residence hardly at all. It is not possible to talk of residential, commercial, and institutional quarters of the city; they were intermixed.[21]

Of the two cities, Quebec had the less complex economy. Both its social and its economic structure remained reasonably constant between the War of 1812 and the 1850s. In particular, the economy centred on two forces. The first was the timber trade, with its linkages to shipping and shipbuilding. The second was the significant institutional presence of a large military garrison, several church institutions, and, until the Union of the Canadas in 1840, the seat of government for Lower Canada. In addition, it acted as a supply and service centre to the well-settled agricultural hinterland around it.

Montreal's economy was more dynamic and went through several complex changes in the period from 1800 to the beginnings of industrialization in the 1850s. In the late eighteenth century, the city's economy was dependent, as it had been for the previous century, on the fur trade. The richest merchants were those, such as the McGills, the Frobishers, and the McTavishes, who dominated that trade. For these merchants, the dominance of half a continent seemed the natural destiny of their city. They, like the French government before them, looked to the St. Lawrence system as a giant highway from which might be drawn the wealth of North America. Their ideal was, as Donald Creighton termed it, that of an empire of the St. Lawrence.[22]

With the new century came an important transition, and it was Montreal's success in making this transition that would eventually propel it to dominance. Specifically, Montreal was successful in becoming the metropolitan centre for the growing settlements of the Great Lakes region. Its geographical location on the natural transportation system and as the closest city to the new frontier meant that, as the region developed as a settlement frontier, Montreal was the natural metropolitan centre in which to locate government and business activities. Only gradually would new Upper Canadian metropolitan centres, particularly Toronto, assert their own influence. As one historian has noted, until about 1820, Upper Canada was in many ways a colony of Lower Canada.[23]

The role played by Montreal in Upper Canadian activities flowed naturally from the fur trade. The big fur traders had, after all, long supplied European manufactured goods to the interior in return for staples. As the native population of the interior was supplemented by a growing European and agricultural population, many of the fur-trade firms simply found themselves expanding their business. As Chapter 6 will indicate further, along with supplies to the native tribes would go those destined for new settlements at Niagara or Kingston. Along with furs from the interior would come supplies of potash, wheat, and other commodities. As the new staples grew in importance and as the fur trade declined, the emphasis could be shifted accordingly.

Of course, such a brief description underestimates the difficulties involved in such a transition. Such shifts involved dislocations of accustomed business practices and demanded a readiness to adapt to new circumstances. Networks of merchant storekeepers had to be established across Upper Canada (and in Lower Canada as well) to act as the distributors to the new population, while transportation facilities had to be improved to handle the much bulkier staples of the agricultural frontier. Along the way, a good many Montreal wholesalers and shippers failed. For the group as a whole, however, the advantage of having a growing frontier next door facilitated a transition away from the fur trade.

The movement into the commodity trade points out something else about the evolution of Montreal commerce — its diversification. In essence, the fur trade brought considerable wealth into the hands of a Montreal elite. That elite was successful in taking that wealth and moving into new ventures. The Upper Canada trade was a prime example of this type of activity, but there were others. Thus, for example, John Molson founded his fortune on the inevitable demands for beer. By the early nineteenth century, however, he was moving into shipping and was, in fact, the owner of the first steamship to be built in the Canadas, the *Accommodation*. Steamship construction soon developed, as the demand for the new technology increased. In a slightly later instance of the same investment of

Bank of Montreal Archives

Canada's first bank. *The oldest bank in the country, The Bank of Montreal, opened in 1817. In 1819, it moved into its first permanent home, on St. James Street, Montreal, site of the present-day bank headquarters.*

capital, the Redpath fortune, earned in construction, was turned to sugar-refining and other activities.[24]

The presence of a large and wealthy community of businessmen also meant that Montreal led the way in developing the financial infrastructure necessary for modern business. In 1817, the Bank of Montreal, which still exists, was founded, and over the next twenty years the now defunct Bank of Canada, City Bank, and Banque du Peuple followed. Likewise, the demands of the new staples trade led Montreal businessmen to form the first major canal company in the Canadas. In 1819, the Lachine Canal Company was created to overcome the rapids that had stopped Cartier back in 1534 and now added greatly to the costs of shipment in and out of Upper Canada. Eventually, as in so many other instances of Canadian development, the company was taken over by the government. Still, a rudimentary canal was finished in 1824.[25] Likewise, there were improvements to the harbour and city roads.

Other examples could be given, but the point is that the fur trade had, early on, made Montreal the centre of finance and wealth in British North America. The movement of that capital into new areas of endeavour — from wholesaling through shipping, and, eventually, manufacturing — reinforced Montreal's position in the economy, accumulated more capital for it, and allowed the city to emerge as the predominant business centre with a hinterland that would eventually be transcontinental in scope.

One other point needs to be made about both cities. As the stereotype would have it, the English were, indeed, concentrated in the cities. One estimate concludes that, in 1825, about 33 percent of all the English in Lower Canada lived in the three main centres of population, compared to about 5 percent of the French.[26] Likewise, what had drawn the English there, to a large extent, was the commerce. Still, it would be dangerous and simplistic to conclude from this that business was a purely English activity. The continuity of French bourgeois activities was strongest in the area of merchandising. Disadvantages of capital were outweighed here, in many instances, by a common language and by a network of ties through the smaller rural villages. The penetration of consumer goods into the countryside (discussed above) provided a new outlet for the wholesaler and retailer in the years after the American Revolution. Thus, in many instances, especially at the retail level, the chief businessmen were French Catholics.

This urban concentration had two implications. First, as recent studies have shown, wealth generated from business activities in the cities would increasingly be invested in diverse pursuits as the city's economic base broadened. French Canadians were active by the 1840s in such areas as banks, property, and insurance. Second, however, the orientation of French-Catholic businessmen toward the local retail trade meant that, as Montreal's influence expanded to become continental, they were less involved than were their English counterparts. The national business image of Montreal, well established by the later nineteenth century, was English-speaking in spite of a continuing francophone business community.

Conclusion

By the time of the union with Upper Canada in 1840–41, Lower Canada was on the eve of a new era. The preindustrial society, with its rural predisposition and traditional values, was about to be overtaken by industrialization. The dynamic sectors of the province would shift to the cities, especially Montreal, and there the roots developed in the early part of the century would soon explode in a series of new business ventures and industrial activity. None of this was apparent in the late 1830s, however. Open rebellion had torn the community apart, while the repeated recent failures of the wheat crop had lowered the standard of living for the agricultural community and, indeed, for much of the colony. The political unrest had frightened the English business community and discouraged immigration and new investment. The growth and economic optimism of the late eighteenth century seemed a long way off.

Notes

1. Linda Kerr, "Merchant Activity in Quebec: The Decade After the Conquest," unpublished paper presented at the North American Conference on British History, Coeur d'Alene, Idaho, October 1988, 3. For a good summary of merchant activity, see Jose Iguarta, "A Change in Climate: The Conquest and the Marchands of Montreal," *Canadian Historical Association Papers*, 1974, 115–34.
2. Fernand Ouellet, *Economic and Social History of Quebec, 1760–1850* (Toronto: McClelland and Stewart, 1980), 83.
3. These figures on French-Catholic population are from T.J.A. Le Goff, "The Agricultural Crisis in Lower Canada, 1802–1812: A Review of the Controversy," *Canadian Historical Review* 55, no. 1 (March 1974): 1–31.
4. Gilles Paquet and Jean-Pierre Wallot, *Lower Canada at the Turn of the Nineteenth Century: Restructuring and Modernization*, CHA Historical Booklet No. 45, 1988, 5.
5. Ouellet, *Economic and Social History*, 84–89.
6. Ouellet, *Economic and Social History*, 8.
7. Serge Courville and Normand Sequin, *Rural Life in Nineteenth Century Quebec*, CHA Historical Booklet No. 47, 1989, 10.
8. Fernand Ouellet, *Lower Canada, 1791–1840: Social Change and Nationalism* (Toronto: McClelland and Stewart, 1980), 4.
9. Ouellet, *Economic and Social History of Quebec*.
10. Paquet and Wallot, *Lower Canada at the Turn of the Nineteenth Century*, 3. For a flavour of the controversy, see Le Goff, "Agricultural Crisis"; Gilles Paquet and Jean-Pierre Wallot, "The Agricultural Crisis in Lower Canada: Mise au point — A Response to T.J.A. Le Goff," and T.J.A. Le Goff, "A Reply," both in *Canadian Historical Review* 56, no. 2 (June 1975); and R.M. McInnis, "A Reconsideration of the State of Agriculture in Lower Canada in the First Half of the Nineteenth Century," in *Canadian Papers in Rural History*, Vol. 3, edited by Donald Akenson (Gananoque: Langdale, 1983).

11. Ouellet, *Lower Canada*, 120.
12. Ouellet, *Lower Canada*, 120.
13. Le Goff, "Agricultural Crisis," 22.
14. Gilles Paquet and Jean-Pierre Wallot, "Crise agricole et tensions socio-ethniques dans le Bas Canada 1802–1812: éléments pour une réinterprétation," *Revue d'histoire de l'Amérique française* 26 (September 1972): 185–207.
15. Paquet and Wallot, "Crise agricole," 54.
16. The figures of 5 percent and 20 percent are from R. Cole Harris and John Warkentin, *Canada Before Confederation: A Study in Historical Geography* (Toronto: Oxford University Press, 1974), 86.
17. The standard work on the British timber trade is A.R.M. Lower, *Great Britain's Woodyard: British America and the Timber Trade, 1763–1867* (Montreal and Kingston: McGill-Queen's University Press, 1973).
18. Ouellet, *Economic and Social History*, 38. For export figures see Ouellet, *Lower Canada*, 352.
19. Michael Cross, "The Lumbering Community of Upper Canada, 1815–1867," in *Canadian History Before Confederation: Essays and Interpretations*, 2nd ed., edited by J.M. Bumsted (Toronto: Irwin-Dorsey, 1979). The general description of social life in the trade is drawn largely from this article.
20. Lower, *Great Britain's Woodyard*, Chapter 17.
21. For a good representation of this at a slightly earlier date, see R. Cole Harris, ed., *Historical Atlas of Canada* (Toronto: University of Toronto Press, 1987), Plate 50.
22. Donald Creighton, *Empire of the St. Lawrence* (Toronto: Macmillan, 1956).
23. Ouellet, *Economic and Social History*, 157.
24. The best discussion of the business community in Montreal at the end of the Lower Canadian era is in Gerald Tulchinsky, *The River Barons: Montreal Businessmen and the Growth of Industry and Transportation, 1837–1853* (Toronto: University of Toronto Press, 1977).
25. On the canal and the controversy surrounding it, see Creighton, *Empire of the St. Lawrence*, 197–211; see also Ouellet, *Lower Canada*, 133–35, on the Lachine and other early canals.
26. Harris and Warkentin, *Canada Before Confederation*, 97.

Further Reading

Greer, Allen. *Peasant, Lord and Merchant: Rural Society in Three Quebec Parishes 1740–1840*. Toronto: University of Toronto Press, 1985.

Lower, A.R.M. *Great Britain's Woodyard: British America and the Timber Trade, 1763–1867*. Montreal and Kingston: McGill-Queen's University Press, 1973.

McInnis, R.M. "A Reconsideration of the State of Agriculture in Lower Canada in the First Half of the Nineteenth Century." In *Canadian Pa-*

pers in Rural History, Vol. 3., edited by Donald Akenson. Gananoque: Langdale, 1983.

Ouellet, Fernand. *Lower Canada, 1791–1870: Social Change and Nationalism*. Toronto: McClelland and Stewart, 1980.

Paquet, Gilles, and Jean-Pierre Wallot. "The Agricultural Crisis in Lower Canada: Mise au point — A Response to T.J.A. Le Goff." *Canadian Historical Review* 56 (June 1975): 133–55.

CHAPTER 6

Upper Canada

Upper Canada, as the area would become in 1791, was initially very much on the periphery of the empire. It was the hinterland of a hinterland, and, even in the remnant of North America left to the British after the American Revolution, it initially played a marginal part. Newfoundland, with its valuable fish trade; Nova Scotia, with its strategic value; and the St. Lawrence valley, with its relatively large population, ranked ahead of this wilderness in importance to the British. Yet, within 50 years, it was to become the most important of all Britain's North American possessions. Strong economic development was crucial to this growing importance.

The economic development of Upper Canada/Canada West from the American Revolution to the abolition of the Corn Laws in 1846 can be divided into three general phases. The first phase, from 1783 to about 1820, involved the development of a generally simple pioneer economy, tributary to both Great Britain and Montreal. The second stage, from 1820 to the late 1830s, saw growth of output and population as well as considerable cyclical volatility. It also saw the increasingly active intervention of the government and of investors to facilitate commerce, in general, and staple exports to Great Britain, in particular. Considerable progress was made, but fiscal strain and the inadequacy of local savings and governmental institutions soon became apparent. The third stage, from the late 1830s through to the abolition of the Corn Laws in 1846, brought better economic times and a more secure fiscal base. Continuing immigration permitted the rapid development of a mature agricultural-commercial colony. As a whole, this final phase would also prepare the way for the beginnings of industrialization.

The Pioneer Economy, 1783–1820

The dominant feature of the Upper Canadian economy at the beginning of the American Revolution and the basic factor determining economic issues was its wilderness state. The lands west of Montreal, which represented the frontier of Quebec, were practically unsettled by Europeans by the outbreak of the American Revolution. In the normal course of events, it would have been another generation before significant European settlement intruded upon the area. The French, it was true, had established some fur-trading posts and defensive forts there during their regime. These, however, as with so much of the frontier of New France, were but a series of way stations in the wilderness. They were designed to encourage the trade and support of the real rulers of the territory, the native population. Even the small settlement that sprang up near the present-day city of Windsor did not change the fact that the economy of this region was much as it had been 50 years before.

The American Revolution changed all of this. Loyalists, threatened at home, sought a refuge during the conflict. Throughout the Revolution, groups from the frontier of New York State fled to the north to find a secure base for families and noncombatants, while military groups, such as Butler's Rangers, moved back and forth across the frontier as circumstances demanded. These concentrations of people thus had characteristics reminiscent of refugee camps, military encampments, and communities in their first years. During the war, few were certain they would not be returning to the south. Crops and farming remained secondary to military activities, and these communities could not have survived without the assistance of the British military, which supplied both the weapons of war and the necessary food.

As the Revolution neared its end, Loyalist units and communities realized that what had been a military base was now likely to become a permanent home. Two military groups, one under the leadership of Colonel William Butler at Niagara, and the other under the Johnsons at the eastern end of Lake Ontario, established communities based on what had previously been military groupings. There was a great deal of movement in and out in the first months and years. Loyalists drifted westward from the area around the Richelieu, while others, unsuited for the wilderness life, returned to the United States or left for England. There were no customs houses

National Archives of Canada/C-23633

Pioneer life in Upper Canada: one of the earliest Loyalist settlements. *Loyalist refugees from the American Revolution found a wilderness that was practically unsettled by Europeans. Yet, in 50 years, Upper Canada was to become the most important of all Britain's North American possessions.*

to contact or complicated forms to be filled out, and thus many came in unannounced and unnoticed by the officials. Generally, however, the best estimate is that the Loyalist population of what were still the western reaches of Quebec was somewhere around 6000 by the end of the American Revolution. A region that was still beyond the frontier of settlement and had come into existence for military reasons now had to try to develop some permanent existence and some means of livelihood for its newly arrived people. For most Loyalists, there was no returning home. They had no choice but to try to create a livelihood on the frontiers of settlement of North America.

There were certain disadvantages faced by those who hoped to see their new homeland prosper and grow. This was the first British colony without a seaport, which, in the period before the development of canals, could be a crucial handicap. In this early period, the cost of shipment from Montreal to Prescott, the head of navigation on Lake Ontario, was greater than the cost of shipment from Liverpool to Montreal.[1] In an age when commerce and military defence depended so much on the open seas, the absence of a seaport was a distinct problem.

That was not all: the colony was across the border from a new nation that regarded the British presence in North America as an unmistakable threat. Finally, it was initially a part of an even more distinctive British colony, French-Catholic Quebec. This status had an obvious effect on the region. In its founding years, government, financial influence, and goods emanated from Quebec, and especially from Montreal. Even after the region became a colony, Upper Canada remained tied for a long time to the merchants, forwarders, and bankers of Montreal. London was thus twice removed. It was Montreal that provided the route of transportation, the source of credit, and the access to goods and power needed by the infant colony. Subservience to and, later, rivalry with that metropolitan centre and that French-Catholic population would do much over the years to shape both the economics and politics of the lower Great Lakes communities.

Yet, for all these distinctive features, Upper Canada possessed many of the characteristics of other frontier economies. Most importantly, the land was unclaimed and undeveloped. This feature had two contradictory implications, which shape the history of most new areas of settlement. First, the empty land was the great asset of the region. Cheap, available land was a resource that could not be offered by Europe or even by the more settled regions of North America. Yet, land was relatively valueless, at least in the early period. Both settlers and speculators would find, to their dismay, that ownership of land meant nothing without ready access to developed centres. Second, population was scarce, as was true of other frontier areas. Estimates vary, but it is unlikely that the European population of Upper Canada was more than 12 000 when it became a colony in 1791 (see Table 6.1). The sparse settlements begun by the ex-Loyalist units had expanded somewhat with sporadic immigration. Occasionally, there were relatively large groups, such as the 520 Scots Catholics who settled in Glengarry in 1786.[2] More often, smaller numbers of people drifted in from Quebec, Nova Scotia, Scotland, and even the United States. Yet, much of the lakeshore remained empty and the back concessions were still untapped. However, transportation was, effectively, by water alone. To carve

TABLE 6.1

Upper Canadian Population, 1785–1840

1785	6 000	1824	150 000
1790	12 000	1826	166 379
1791	14 000	1830	213 000
1794	25 000	1832	263 000
1805	46 000	1834	321 000
1811	77 000	1840	432 000
1814	95 000		

Source: Douglas McCalla, "The 'Loyalist' Economy of Upper Canada," *Social History* 16, no. 32 (November 1983), 285.

roads through the wilderness would be a particular concern of the first governor of the colony, John Graves Simcoe, but it would be more than 60 years before there was more than the most rudimentary and limited access to the interior.

The abundance of land — and, conversely, the high value of labour — could attract immigrants and thus provide the means by which the colony could grow. This connection was crucial, for immigration was central to the development of all frontier colonies. People alone would not ensure prosperity and growth; but, without people, it was certain that Upper Canada would remain little more than a way station on the traditional fur-trade routes of North America.

The system of land settlement was obviously crucial to a territory as desperately dependent on immigration as was this one. From the beginning, however, there were contradictions in the approaches to land and settlement in what would become Upper Canada. In particular, two things would plague its government and people over the next few years. The first was simply a question of the nature of land ownership. As part of the province of Quebec, land in this new frontier was presumably to be held on a seigneurial system, something confirmed in instructions to Governor Haldimand in 1783.[3] Yet, for the Loyalists who flooded north during and after the American Revolution, the seigneurial system was foreign, mystifying, and unacceptable. To them, land ownership meant land ownership, and nothing else. Moreover, many colonial officials agreed, sensing that the land system would have to be altered if immigrants were to be attracted. Thus, over the next several years, the settlers acted, to all intents and purposes, as if they were operating under a freehold system. Land was exchanged, sold, and purchased as if it were freehold, even though, in fact, it was held under seigneurial tenure.

In 1791, the problems of uniting a new English-Protestant population and an existing French-Catholic system led to the division of Quebec into Upper Canada and Lower Canada. This division also meant that the seigneurial system was abolished in Upper Canada. Even then, however, problems continued. In fact, not until 1796 was the Upper Canadian government sufficiently organized to implement a straightforward system through which a would-be settler could progress, in a more or less orderly manner, from arrival to clear title. As one historian has noted, "the most telling evidence against the land-granting system in Upper Canada before 1796 is that in 1796 only a very small proportion of settlers of the province had patents or any other legally valid title to lands which had been granted to them in the past thirty-five years."[4]

The land system, as it had evolved by 1795, was really two systems, both based on freehold tenure. The first involved what were termed "official" settlers: those granted lands, without condition, on account of service or position. The great majority of such settlers were Loyalists and military officials who had served in the American Revolution. The precise size and distribution of grants varied over time, but generally they ranged from 5000 acres for field officers to 200 acres for privates and for civilian Loyalist males. These land grants were intended for settlement purposes but did not have to be occupied to be retained. In many cases, they became assets, held not for development but for speculation against the future worth of land in the colony.

The other class of settlers was the immigrants whose right to land came not from service to the crown but from their potential role in developing the colony. They also had the opportunity to acquire 200 acres of land, but only under certain conditions. Initially, they were given a location ticket to the land. In order to convert that location ticket into clear title, they had to fulfil certain requirements — to live on the land, clear the roadway allowance, build a home, and fence and clear a certain portion of the land. Once that was done (and it often took much longer than the optimistic twelve months that the government set down as the standard), a patent could be issued.

The existence of the two groups of settlers, "official" and "immigrant," created the second and much more persistent problem for the development of Upper Canada. The aims and interests of the two classes of settlers were often at odds. Many official grantees settled on the land and acted to improve it in the same way that settlers fulfilling requirements would. Others, however, saw land as a speculative asset to be held, but not occupied, until such time as increased population pushed the value up. The existence of speculative landholding contradicted the general government policy, set out by Simcoe and his successors, of encouraging agricultural development and population growth. Empty lands in prime locations sat vacant, while bona fide immigrants were forced on to more remote locations. Compounding this problem was the fact that the government did not open all lands for settlement. In each township, one-seventh of the land was set aside as a clergy reserve to support the Church of England, and another one-seventh as a crown reserve. Not only was the immigrant likely to find vacant speculative lands nearby, but vacant church and government lands as well. In a colony with a small, scattered population, this meant less likelihood of adequate schools within reasonable range and adequate roads anywhere but on the main routes set out by Simcoe.

Such problems would be persistent, but the initial questions were who would come and how many? Until the mid-1790s, settlers arrived only slowly. The problems of landholding outlined above were part of the problem, but so, too, was the simple fact that one of the most fertile sources of future immigration, New York's expanding frontier of settlement, had not yet reached Canada (see Map 6.1). The Eastern Townships of Quebec, not Upper Canada, attracted the majority of American immigrants. Nevertheless, by the time the government regularized the procedures for land titles, the population had reached between 20 000 and 25 000 individuals, and it was possible to talk of something approaching settled communities in the Niagara district, in the eastern counties of the colony, and around York, the new capital.

In the late 1790s, the American movement into Canada began in earnest. Niagara, which until that time had been a rather isolated community, separated from the natural frontier pushing westward from Quebec, now found itself at the edge of the aggressive, expanding American frontier. New York State still had, at the end of the American Revolution, many areas of undeveloped land along its northwestern frontier. The state's population grew rapidly, how-

MAP 6.1
Upper Canada and New York Frontier of Settlement, 1790

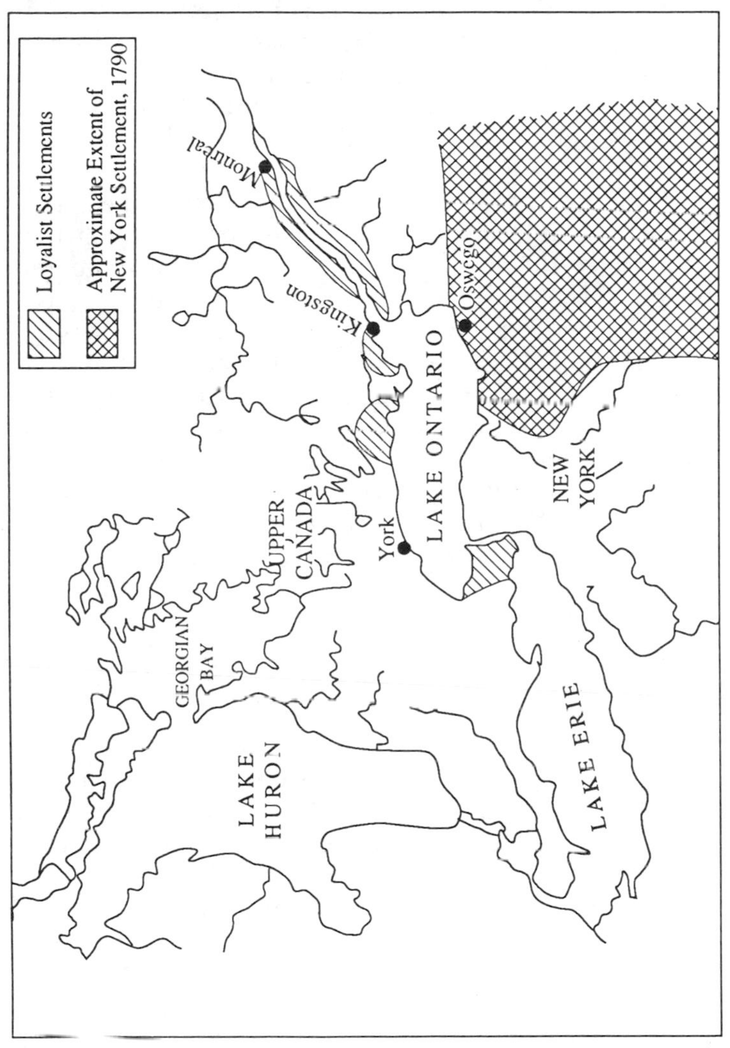

Source: Adapted from Sam B. Hillard, "A Robust New Nation, 1783–1820," in *North America: The Historical Geography of a Changing Continent*, edited by Robert D. Mitchell and Paul A. Groves (Totowa, NJ: Rowman and Littlefield, 1987), 168.

ever, from 340 000 in 1790 to 959 000 by 1810. Such growth pushed the western frontier outward until it reached the borders of British North America. The border proved a small deterrence and, given native restiveness along the American frontier, a positive incentive for many. The result was dramatic, particularly in the large unsettled areas that stretched inland from Niagara. Township after township opened up to meet the demand of American settlers. Upper Canada's population expanded accordingly, reaching approximately 50 000 by 1806.

People came to Upper Canada because they hoped to farm and because the land and climate seemed to promise them that opportunity. Moreover, the outbreak of war between England and France in 1793 spurred a rise in wheat prices in Britain and provided a favourable climate for a developing wheat economy, thereby encouraging immigration. Until recently, historical writing has tended to reflect this fact by concentrating on the period after sufficient settlement and land-clearing had taken place to allow significant farming to develop. Much of the economic literature on Upper Canada has focussed on the emergence of a farming frontier and, therefore, has jumped quickly from the arrival of the Loyalists in the early 1780s to the wheat economy, which was beginning to come into being by from 1805 to about 1810.

Recent literature has focussed increasingly on the problems of the intervening twenty years. It has recognized that commercial farming, while ultimately the basis of colonial development, was, before the War of 1812, peripheral to most individuals and to the colony. Establishing a farm took time. This was a heavily treed region, and clearing the land, first of trees and then of stumps, was not only back-breaking labour, but a slow task. Estimates are that a farmer could clear only about 1.5 to 3 acres a year. Thus, it would take a lifetime to establish a moderate-size farm unless the settler had sufficient capital to hire clearing crews. Most did not. Surplus, in other words, could come only over time. About three acres (or two to three years of labour) were needed just to feed the average-size family.[5]

Even if sufficient land were cleared to produce a surplus, other obstacles existed, especially in the first years of settlement. No outlets existed to transport grain to distant markets, nor were there local mills to produce flour. Until the later 1780s, there were only two flour mills in the entire colony, one on the Bay of Quinte and the other near Niagara. For most immigrants, milling was done by hand, and an evening's labour might produce only enough for the next day's needs. There was, in other words, a considerable lag between the time a family occupied a piece of wilderness land and the time that sufficient crops could be grown for any significant or regular sales to take place. Likewise, therefore, there was a considerable lag between the time of initial settlement and the time that Upper Canada was able to produce a staple for export. It was 1794 before the first wheat exports came from Upper Canada through Montreal, and 1800 before those exports became even sporadically significant.

Potash, it was true, was produced more quickly, as it was acquired as a by-product of the clearing process itself. There are two perspectives on the potash trade, however, and the significance of the trade will vary depending on the perspective taken. First, from a macro-economic perspective, it is unlikely that potash was ever very important to the foundation of the colony's economy. The trade was a transitory one for settlers and, as wheat cultivation replaced land-clearing, it invariably fell off. In any given year, therefore, only a certain percentage of settlers were involved in the trade, and the overall export figures were only rarely of overall significance to the colony. From the perspective of the individual settler, however, potash was very important, providing a cash return in the early years of settlement.

The slow development of agricultural surpluses means that it is necessary to look at other things to understand the economy of Upper Canada in its first years. Rather than look at the early economy as one dependent on a staple export, it is more appropriate to see it as an economic dependency, surviving because of various supports from external sources. Foreign exchange needed to purchase imports came into the colony in three ways: via the British government, money brought by immigrants, and trade. These inflows allowed a pioneer society without any significant export and without, as yet, the means of livelihood for people who were still attempting to become farmers to purchase the necessary goods to sustain itself.

Particularly important was the role of the British government. Relative to many other colonial ventures, the Upper Canadian economy received considerable support from the mother country. The British contribution to the region came in two main forms. First, the government in London recognized the claim of the Loyalists on it. They had fought for the Empire in a bloody civil war, and many had lost homes, businesses, and income in the effort. Aside from the land grants already mentioned, the Loyalists got assistance in a number of other ways, depending on time and locality. Food, clothing, implements, building materials, and seed were typical items of distribution. From 1783 through to 1788, Loyalist families thus depended on direct handouts from the British government. The importance of these grants is revealed by the fact that, when the subsidies ended in 1788–89, the year became known locally as "the hungry year" as unprepared families found it difficult to get by without British assistance.

In addition to these supports, there were the "Loyalist claims." Those Loyalists who had suffered losses of income or property as a result of their loyalty to the crown were able to submit a claim to the British government and to ask for compensation. At the very least, these claims were driven to their maximum figure by a sense of grievance for wrongs suffered. Most likely, they were rife with deliberate exaggeration. In either case, however, British payments of Loyalist claims averaged £178 per claim, an amount sufficient to live on for a year, and acted as a further transfer of British resources to the wilderness of Upper Canada.

In the short run, these direct payments and indirect subsidies were extremely important. In effect, the British government subsidized the initial stages of settlement in Upper Canada. It also meant that there was profit to be made by merchants who could supply these immigrants. The initial fortunes, whether large or small, of a new commercial class rested on the most readily available source of income — British reparations for a lost war.

The Loyalist grants were important, but they were temporary. The other major contribution of British government funds to the new colony was to last somewhat longer and was probably even more important than the subsidies. The end of the American Revolution in 1783 did not end the struggle between the United States and its old parent for supremacy in North America. In many ways, in fact, little beyond the independence of the actual thirteen colonies was resolved. In the west, the British remained in control of thousands of square miles of the old French hinterland, even though the land was now recognized by both as U.S. territory. In British North America, there was optimistic (and vain) talk of using this control as a means to gain additional territory. Along both borders, there was a fear of what might come, and, as a result, there was a need to reinforce the boundaries on the map with military force.

British garrisons, in the west and in the emergent Upper Canada, were important not only for whatever sense of security they gave but, even more so, for the income they created in a local economy. In the case of the Niagara region, for instance, or that of Kingston, the impact was considerable. Whether providing the British with materials from the local market or acting as the agent to import them from Montreal or England, local entrepreneurs, such as Niagara's Robert Hamilton, found British military contracts to be a key to success on the frontier. For the more modest citizen, the garrison provided a market to which one could sell (through such people as Hamilton) the first crops of wheat, vegetables, or even occasional fruit. The presence of the forts also provided work, as baking, brewing, hauling, carpentry, or whatever other need could not be handled internally.[6]

Unfortunately, it is impossible to be precise about the amount spent by garrisons in Upper Canada. Military accounts on the cost of the garrison, inexact in themselves, do not distinguish between money spent locally and that sent out for imported supplies. A recent estimate concludes that something between £54 000 and £77 000 was spent annually in Upper Canada in each of the years from 1795 through 1805.[7] Especially in the early years, when the population was small and before wheat exports became significant, the impact of the garrisons on the colony would seem crucial. In 1795, for example, such estimates would indicate that the British spent some £2 for every resident of Upper Canada. Even as late as 1805, the annual expenditure might very well have amounted to £1 per capita. Such estimates are very rough but, even so, it would seem that, for many settlers still struggling to move beyond subsistence, the expenditures by the British military in Canada were probably one of the few means of acquiring currency.

Relative to the garrisons and Loyalist claims, the old activity of the fur trade, still so important to Montreal, was not very significant to Upper Canada. When Upper Canada's first governor, John Graves Simcoe, proclaimed in 1792, "I consider the fur trade on its present foundation to be of no use whatever to Upper Canada," he was simply reflecting the reality about the marginal importance of that trade to Upper Canada.[8] True, considerable portaging took place to the southwest in the 1780s and early 1790s. For such people as Hamilton, the supply of the fur trade was yet another lucrative possibility for business on the frontier. Yet, two things stand out about this trade. First, it is unlikely that it had much impact beyond the immediate localities of the portages. Second, whatever impact it did have was lessening by the mid-1790s. The British had in 1794 agreed to hand over their western posts to the United States, and the southwest fur trade was unlikely to remain dominated by British capitalists for much longer. The northwest trade was still expanding, but many of the supplies for that went up the Ottawa River and not through the settled portion of Upper Canada at all. The fur trade was an activity in which Montreal was dominant, and Upper Canada was largely irrelevant, even in its early days.

If the fur trade was marginal to the economic well-being of the average settler, the settlers themselves were central to the economic well-being of the colony. Upper Canada sustained a very high rate of immigration through the entire period from the establishment of Upper Canada in 1791 to the War of 1812. These settlers were relatively common folk, but most, nevertheless, had some means. This was not the famine migration of later years. "Immigration," grumbled one Scot who was left behind, "is a glorious thing for them that have the money."[9] The average per-capita wealth of those coming from the United States was likely even greater than that of the Scots. Many of these, by the later 1790s, were established farmers who had sold previous holdings to move on.

Most settlers, therefore, had funds, and all had to spend a considerable amount for tools, provisions, clothing, and other items in order to establish a farm. One estimate is that it required about £100 to turn a wilderness homestead site into a productive farm. As that farm was being developed, there were also linkages to other sectors of the economy. Sawmills sprang into being to house the population and, given the similar technologies, often provided the basis for grist mills. Initially, the sawmill would help house the developing population. As settlement and construction moved beyond the region, flour milling would assume greater importance. Flour milling, further, was naturally linked to distilleries, given the latter's need for grain. There was also a growing market in key goods provided by an expanding population. For example, two men who founded a sawmill near York early in the nineteenth century soon found themselves milling flour and distilling grain into whisky.

Messrs. Gooderham and Worts thereby established a long-lasting business that rested directly on the demands of a growing population.

For the shopkeepers and forwarders, external spending gave them their livelihood at a time when the earnings of the local farmers were still relatively small. Expenditures by the garrisons, by Loyalists, and by incoming immigrants went through their hands and, to a degree, back out of the colony, to suppliers in Montreal and beyond. British exports to the Canadas between 1800 and 1812 amounted to an average of £376 671 between 1800 and 1812; so, at least a portion of the funds that came over from the home country went back to its growing industrial sector. Though exact figures are hard to come by, those that are available indicate that there was a large net flow of capital (primarily cash) from Britain to Canada through the entire period from the American Revolution to 1812.

Given the importance of the assistance to Loyalists, the economic importance of the British garrisons, and the amount of income flowing into the colony by means of immigration, it is possible to conclude tentatively that the economy of Upper Canada rested, in its earliest period, to a large degree on the expenditure of imported wealth. For political and economic reasons, people and governments were willing to invest in the future of Upper Canada long before it could pay its own way. Whatever shortages of specie did exist, and they did, Upper Canada was nevertheless fortunate in its early years compared to New France or the Maritime colonies during comparable stages of development. The steady influx of people and foreign exchange meant that the colony was sustained as it went through the process of moving from wilderness to farming frontier.

The end of this initial stage, sometime soon after the end of the War of 1812, left the colony with three economic characteristics. First, and most important, was the straightforward fact that the land, empty in 1783, was now much more populated. The 1814 population of 95 000 was hardly a large one, compared to Lower Canada's 300 000, but now there were sufficient people to allow a continuous line of settlement along the north shore of Lake Ontario, from Prescott to Niagara. Settlement was also pushing westward from the Niagara region, and Lake Erie was the destination of small but growing numbers of pioneers. To the north, in the Ottawa valley, lumbering had penetrated the region, but settlement in areas distant from the major water arteries was still largely in the future. The Niagara region, the Bay of Quinte, and the territory immediately around the capital of York were the only places where population was at all large.

The second characteristic of the economy at this time involved the emergent staples trades. Timber had been important from 1806, though less so to Upper than to Lower Canada. By the end of the War of 1812, nearly a quarter-million bushels of wheat were being sent out of the colony.[10] By 1826, the first year for which even remotely accurate figures are available, nearly 600 000 acres of land were under cultivation, and Upper Canada began to be seen as a region with great potential in wheat.[11] The dependence on primary resources was reflected in the third characteristic of the economy. Even more so than Lower Canada, Upper Canada was overwhelmingly rural. Urban centres were insignificant. The Town of York, the capital of the colony, had fewer than 1700 people as late as 1824; Kingston, the largest town in the colony, had a population of 2300 in 1820. The population was over 95 percent rural.[12] This pattern would continue well into the next stage of colonial development. Only in the 1840s would there develop any sort of rapid urban growth in this small agrarian colony.

By the end of the War of 1812 the colony was at a crossroads. Immigration and capital imports would continue to be important in the future but could no longer sustain the colony's development. The initial period of frontier settlement was over, and the growing population would increasingly have to generate its own wealth. Exports and fledgling business and commercial activities were increasingly important to the development of the colony.

Immigration and Settlement, 1815–1841

In the years after the War of 1812, immigration continued at a high rate and remained both a basic determinant and a reflection of economic growth. The source of the immigration was different, however. Before the War of 1812, it had been the expansion of the U.S. frontier of settlement that had accounted for the bulk of Upper Canadian immigrants. There had been immigration from the British Isles, but that had been secondary. After 1815, the proportions reversed. American immigration slowed, for two reasons. First, the frontier of open land in the United States had moved westward. Native resistance having been eliminated in the previous decades, the rapid expansion of American agriculture moved beyond the shores of Lake Erie and Lake Ontario to new lands in the Ohio region and beyond. Indiana became a state in 1816; Illinois, in 1818. Upper Canada was no longer in the direct path of those heading to the frontier of settlement.

There were also institutional impediments that were the result of the postwar suspicions, including various measures on the part of the Upper Canadian and British governments to make land ownership more difficult for American citizens. In 1815, for example, the colonial secretary issued instructions to refuse grants of lands to any American immigrant.[13] This regulation would later be modified, but other provisions and uncertainties, including uncertainties as to the rights of "aliens" to obtain lands, meant that, for the next several years, immigration from the United States was severely restricted.

Forces across the Atlantic meant that an ample supply of immigrants could offset the decline of American settlement. Most importantly, the population of Great Britain was growing at a tremendous rate. In 1700, England's population had been just over 5 million, representing a growth of approximately a million people in the previous century. By the time of the conquest in 1759, that population had grown another million; by the end of the American Revolution, by another million; and by the turn of the century, by another million and a half. By 1821 it would be nearly 3 million larger than it had been in 1801.[14] This accelerating growth was the result, to a large degree, of a decline in mortality rates, dating from the middle of the eighteenth century and reflecting greater agricultural productivity. The increase in population was also crucial to the continuation of an industrial revolution that made England the foremost economic power in the world.

To those who lived through this demographic explosion, the rapidly growing population seemed more of a burden than a spur. The growing population seemed to threaten the food surpluses that had existed with regularity for the first time in the past half-century. These fears were articulated and given the prestige of economic theory when, in 1798, Thomas Malthus published *An Essay on the Principle of Population* in Great Britain. Population, he warned, would always tend to increase more rapidly than food supply. Only famine, disease, and war could stem the tide. Any rise in the standard of living would soon be destroyed by the sheer increase in the number of mouths to be fed.

The end of the Napoleonic Wars in 1815 and the following recession helped change the attitude of the British government toward emigration. A concern about a rising population had existed previously but had been countered by the traditional view that the military strength of a nation rested on its people. The nation was weakened, it followed, if the people left. Mercantilist perspectives thus applied to human beings as well as to gold and commodities. After 1815, this attitude changed. Population figures continued to rise and, with them, unemployment and the costs of poor relief. The government came to two conclusions. First, emigration might be both necessary and desirable. Second, if something was not done to channel that outgoing human tide toward the British colonies, it would head to the recent enemy of the British, the United States. Then the people would truly be lost to the Empire.

In response to these concerns, the British government initiated measures to assist would-be emigrants to settle in British North America. The measures varied considerably, depending on time and place, but, over the years from 1815 to 1825, a series of schemes sought both to relieve the economic situation at home and to develop the colonies by means of state-assisted emigration. Typical was the 1815 scheme that provided some 700 emigrants with 100 acres of land, rations for eight months, and implements.

Over the next several years, other groups followed and, with government assistance, began to open up new districts of Upper Canada. Historians who have assessed these schemes have tended to see them as disappointing, if not outright failures. From the British government's point of view, the expense was greater than had been anticipated. Certainly, assisted emigration would provide no solution to overpopulation at home. From the point of view of overall level of emigration, moreover, assisted emigration was relatively unimportant. Even at the height of British support for migrants, unassisted emigration remained much more important. It was for these reasons and others that the British government abandoned the idea of assisted emigration in 1825.

Yet, assisted emigration did have positive aspects. First, though statistics are far from exact, there seems to have been a relatively high success rate among assisted emigrants. A good number did stay, at least long enough to clear their land and obtain the patent.

Second, the fact that the immigrants were under an arrangement with the government meant that they could, to a degree, be directed to lands that the government wanted to see opened. Many such groups were thus instrumental in opening up new townships away from Lake Ontario. For example, British military settlement schemes opened the Perth region to settlement between 1817 and 1822. By the latter date, some 4000 people had taken up land in this area, which otherwise would have remained empty. Also, all too typical was the fact that when immigrants arrived in Upper Canada, they were directed, as was the 1815 group, to some remote district to which, as one Canadian historian noted, "they had to cut their way through twenty miles of unbroken bush."[15]

When the assisted-emigration scheme was abandoned, in 1825, it was replaced by a plan based on private enterprise. John Galt had been one of a number of officials appointed by the British government to investigate civilian losses during the War of 1812. Along the way, he came up with a scheme to create a privately owned land company to assist in immigration and settlement. The proposal was timed perfectly, for the British were tired of their direct involvement in assisting emigration. This seemed like a suitable alternative, and, in 1826, the Canada Company, as it was known, began operations.

The basis of the company's plans was a million-acre tract of land stretching west from the present-day city of Guelph to Goderich. Known as the Huron Tract, this wedge-shaped parcel had been bought from the crown and was to be developed by the company as a means of attracting immigrants. Over the next years, development did take place, and numbers of immigrants were brought in. The land was, however, west of the current frontier of settlement, and the London-based directors found, as had the British government before them, that immigration was an expensive business.[16]

British assistance helped increase the flow of immigration. So, too, did the Canada Company. Far more important than either, however, were the thousands of immigrants who, propelled by a depressed economy at home, depended on their own financial resources to get to Canada and to carry them through the first years of settlement. The records do not exist that would allow any completely accurate figures as to the rate of immigration. Figure 6.1 does give a reasonable estimate, however, and shows how British

FIGURE 6.1

British Emigration to British North America, 1815–1840

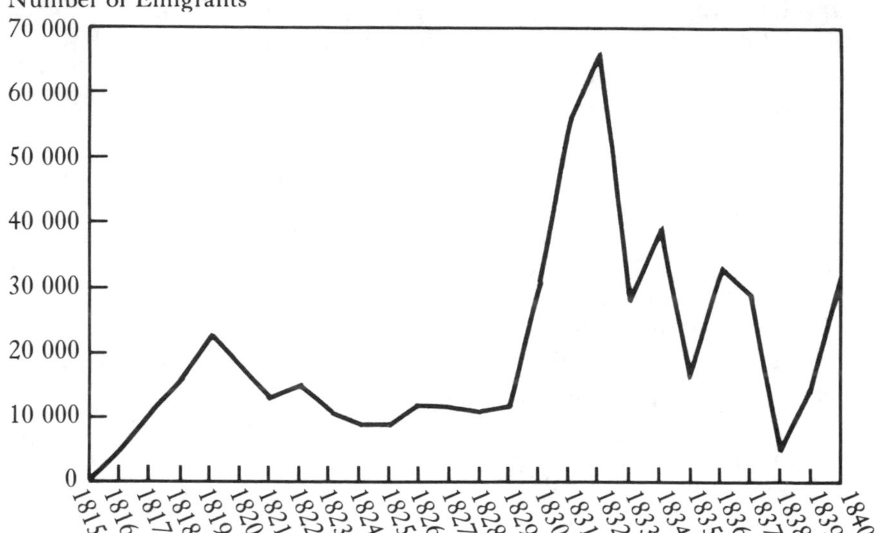

Source: Derived from Helen Cowan, *British Emigration to British North America* (Toronto: University of Toronto Press, 1961), Appendix.

immigration increased from practically nothing to some 23 000 by 1819, and to an average of more than 12 000 annually through the 1820s. Though the precise figures are open to debate, there is little doubt about the trend of settlement. Upper Canada was an increasingly popular destination after 1815. Economic cycles, political circumstances, and other factors might affect the actual immigration in any given year, but the trend was upward.[17]

The population of Upper Canada reflected this immigration, growing from 95 000 at the end of the War of 1812 to 197 000 by the end of the 1820s, and 432 000 by 1840. In a generation it had more than quadrupled (see Table 6.1 on page 164).

This population growth provides some continuities with the prewar period. Immigration was still a major economic spur for the colony. Moreover, for the new arrivals, life often differed little from that of their predecessors. Even government assistance and the Canada Company made little difference to the harsh routine of settlement. For most, it was still a matter of saving sufficient funds to take care of transportation, fees for land claims, and rations until crops could be grown. Their experience was not all that different from that of the earlier generation who had come out when Upper Canada was but an adjunct of Quebec.

There was a real opportunity to improve their social and material standing over time. The standard of living of an Upper Canadian farmer owning a piece of cleared, fertile land was considerably higher than most could have realized in anything like an analogous social position in England, Scotland, or Ireland. The degree to which that improvement could be realized depended, as always, on a combination of skill, luck, and hard work. It also depended on the savings that an immigrant could invest in his new piece of land. The well-off, for example, might avoid the wilderness site in the woods and buy an accessible piece of land from one of the numerous speculators. Others would be able to move to a productive position even more quickly by purchasing an improved farm from some pioneer who wished to sell out and move on.

Yet, for all the similarities in the experience of the pre- and post-1812 pioneer, the economy was changing. Before the War of 1812, agricultural produce may have been important to individual farmers, but agriculture was still in a rudimentary stage and, for most people, the return from cash crops was less important than the appreciation on farmsteads resulting from the clearing of land, the erection of buildings, and so on.[18] After the war, however, a rudimentary pioneer economy, based on land appreciation and the inflow of immigrants, ran parallel to an increasingly productive agricultural sector. Agricultural produce, and not just the potential of the future, was becoming central to the shape of the Upper Canadian economy after 1820.

The growth of agriculture as a staple after the War of 1812 was not without difficulties. The war had kept prices high for farmers who were fortunate enough not to have their farms in the line of marching armies or foraging raiders. After the war, prices remained high for a while, in part as a result of continued purchases by enlarged British garrisons and a high demand for wheat in Great Britain.

In the long term, however, markets depended on continued access to the United Kingdom. Under the complex mercantilist structure of the Corn Laws, the continued right of entry was not guaranteed. The Corn Laws, which have been discussed in general terms previously (see Figure 6.2), need further description, for it was in these years that they began to affect Canadian wheat exports. As was mentioned, these laws were designed to provide agricultural interests in the United Kingdom with protection from offshore competition. All offshore wheat was not created equal, however, as the Corn Laws were designed, first, to protect British agricultural interests and, when they were protected, to assist colonial agricultural interests over those of foreign exporters of wheat.

The principles were simple, but the details were excruciatingly complex, varying from year to year, depending on the vicissitudes of the market and the ever-shifting regulatory and legal details of the Corn Laws themselves. Yet, a fairly clear pattern can be discerned. Before 1815, the net effect of the laws was, in fact, quite minor. The regulations were not yet fully developed, and, most of the time, Canadian wheat entered the United Kingdom free of duty because of the high demand for wheat in the rapidly growing British market. It was only in 1820 that Canadian wheat was excluded, as British wheat yields were good and prices fell. The effect on Canadian agriculture in that year was disastrous, with Canadian wheat prices plummeting from $1.00 to $0.50 a bushel.[19]

Inroads were being made on protectionist thought in Britain, however, and the exclusion of colonial wheat only increased the force of the challenge. Over the next few years, British Corn Law regulations underwent a series of modifications that had the net effect, by 1827, of turning a strong protectionist and exclusionist system into a moderate tariff preference for British farmers (see Figure 6.2). Thereafter, the net effect of the Corn Laws was beneficial to Canada. The regulations usually did little to prohibit Canadian wheat from competing in the British market, while the harsher rules applying to foreign wheat benefited Canada in various ways. It is hard to derive any specific conclusion as to the effect on agriculture in British North America. At the very least, the changing nature of the Corn Laws gave the wheat farmers in Upper Canada some assurance they would not be banned from selling in their biggest potential market. In many years, when prices were in the right range, they provided Canadian wheat with a decided advantage over American competition.

There was one additional complication: American wheat coming through Canada or ground into flour in Canada counted as Canadian supplies. Until 1831, the effect of this was moderated by

FIGURE 6.2

Corn Law Tariff Structure, 1822–1825 and 1827–1842

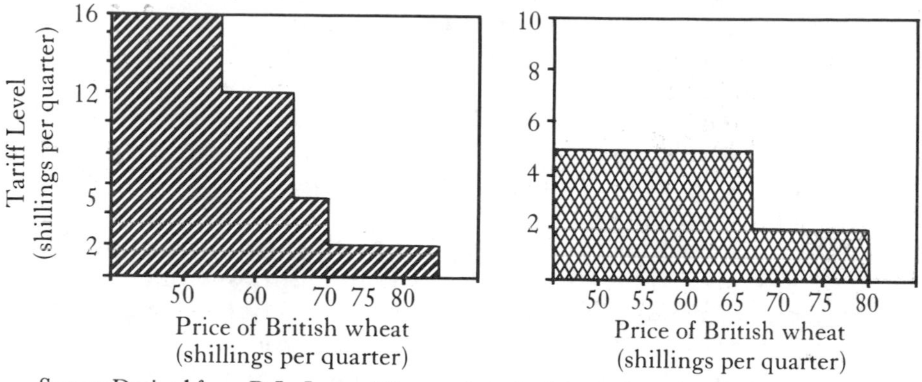

Source: Derived from R.L. Jones, *History of Agriculture in Ontario, 1613–1880* (Toronto: University of Toronto Press, 1946), 46–47.

a Canadian tariff on American wheat. In that year, however, the British government abolished all duties on American agricultural products entering Canada. Canadian farmers, therefore, no longer had an advantage over their American counterparts who chose to ship their produce via the St. Lawrence. Thereafter, the main benefit of the Corn Laws went not to the Canadian farmers but to Canadian merchants and forwarders. The merchants, after all, got to carry all of that American wheat as well as Canadian. Indeed, the shifts in attitudes toward imports of American flour and wheat reveal the rise of a merchant class whose views did not always coincide with those of farmers.

The modification of the Corn Laws and the generally high demand for Canadian wheat in Britain were factors encouraging the development of large-scale wheat exports. Another was closer to home. As is discussed elsewhere, Lower Canada was producing less wheat than it had in the past. Already by the 1830s, wheat coming from the west to Montreal accounted for nearly three-quarters of net exports from the Canadas.[20] By the period 1824–31, quantities of wheat coming into Montreal from the west were greater, on average, than the total exports from the St. Lawrence system. In other words, western wheat not only dominated the export trade but increasingly fed Lower Canada.

The combination of a more accessible British market and the

lessening of Lower Canadian wheat production allowed for recovery from the agricultural recession of the early 1820s. By the latter half of the decade, Upper Canadian agriculture was strong, and, by 1830–31, its success was central to the growing attractiveness of the region to British immigrants.

The growing importance of agricultural production can be demonstrated in a number of ways. First, there was the fact that, in 1826, some 599 000 acres of land were "under culture." By 1829, that figure had grown to more than 717 000 acres, and, by 1832, to 916 000 acres. Parts of the province, such as Niagara and the areas immediately adjacent to Kingston and to York, were, by the latter date, well-established agricultural communities with farms far removed from the pioneer stage.

The impact of this developing agricultural sector is shown as well by the export figures for wheat. As was mentioned above, wheat from the western United States and from Upper Canada flowed through Montreal in ever-larger amounts during the 1820s. As the records do not separate American from Upper Canadian produce, it is not possible to make any exact statement on the growth of wheat exports. Overall, however, the movement of western wheat through Montreal increased from an 1817–22 mean of 281 000 bushels to an 1824–31 mean of 534 000 bushels. In 1831, more than 1 million bushels of wheat from the west moved down the St. Lawrence (see Table 6.2). Given the opening of alternative outlets for western wheat in the Erie Canal (see below) and given the tariff that was imposed on American wheat and flour coming into Canada in the 1820s, there is nothing to indicate that this growth was disproportionately the result of American shipment through Canada.

Wheat was Upper Canada's most important agricultural product, but it was not the only one. The Upper Canadian frontier was still, in many respects, a pioneer economy where farmers provided themselves and their families with a range of foods, even as they concentrated the majority of their land on one or two key crops. Likewise, livestock of various sorts, from hogs through chickens and cattle, provided extra sources both of food for the family and of cash sales to local towns or to British garrisons. There was also an element of sexual specialization that showed up in these different farming activities. Many, though not all, of these nonwheat activities were the responsibility of women. The fact that only a relatively small portion of these activities found their way into the marketplace

MAP 6.2
Distribution of Population, Upper Canada, 1794, 1824, and 1840

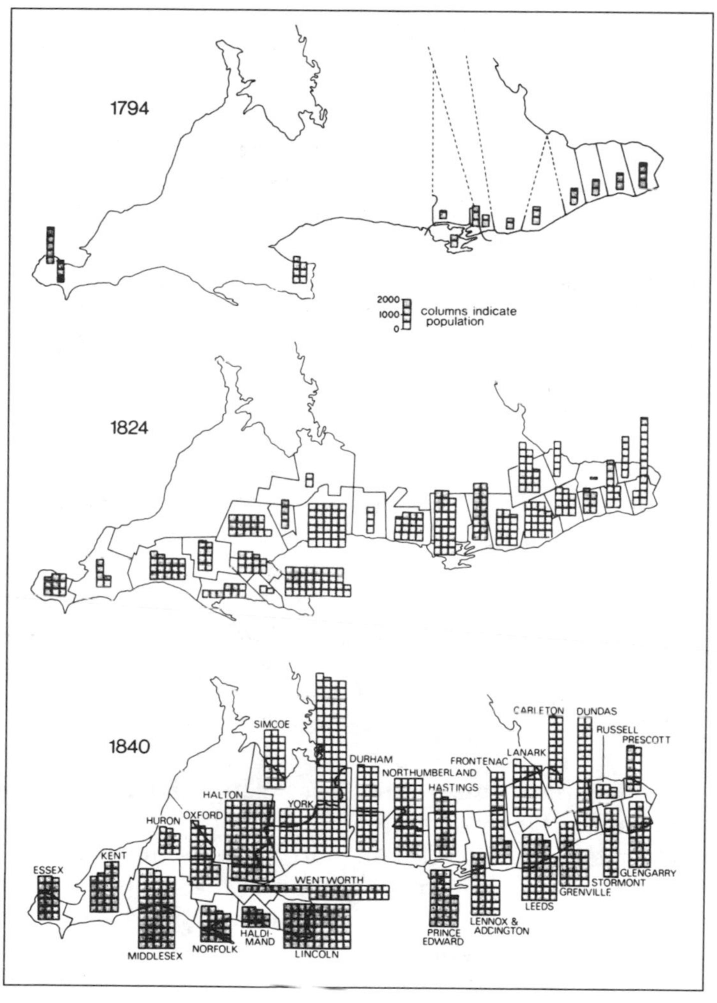

Source: J. David Wood, "The Population of Ontario," in *Patterns of the Past*, edited by Roger Hall et al. (Toronto: Dundurn Press, 1988), 57.

TABLE 6.2

Shipments of Wheat from West to Quebec and Overseas, 1817–1847

(thousands of tons)

1817	219	1833	1177
1818	229	1834	400
1819	78	1835	109
1820	416	1836	Unknown
1821	421	1837	Unknown
1822	326	1838	644
1823	Unknown	1839	1045
1824	240	1840	2943
1825	186	1841	3438
1826	371	1842	Unknown
1827	627	1843	Unknown
1828	517	1844	3271
1829	337	1845	3791
1830	931	1846	4593
1831	1069	1847	5757
1832	Unknown		

Source: John McCallum, *Unequal Beginnings: Agriculture and Economic Development in Quebec and Ontario to 1870* (Toronto: University of Toronto Press, 1980), Table S.1.

has often caused historians to underestimate their importance, and thereby, the importance of women's contributions. Yet, these activities were vital to the well-being of the farm operation. For one thing, a good part of the family's food and clothing on even the relatively commercialized nineteenth-century wheat farm was home-grown or -made. The kitchen garden was not a hobby but a vital source of food, as was the milk obtained from farm cows. Common, as well, was the mixing of these operations as a part cash, part self-provisioning activity. Thus, in many cases, milk or eggs would provide a small cash sale to the local village or town. As these operations could be started relatively rapidly, income from them often predated significant sales of wheat and, thus, like potash or work for the local garrisons, provided crucial funds during the first years. Even after the farm was established, these ancillary activities were vital to the farming operation.[21]

Particular parts of the province also concentrated on particular crops. One of the better examples was the decline in wheat prices in the period after 1820 that led a number of farmers in Essex and Kent counties to grow tobacco. It was a crop that required effort to grow but was also lucrative and, by the time wheat prices recovered, many in the region had become sufficiently specialized that they did not return to wheat.[22]

Nevertheless, in only a few regions were specialized crops such as tobacco important. Wheat created capital, brought in people, and allowed the development of commerce and manufacturing. Wheat was undoubtedly the dominant crop of Upper Canada. The growth of the wheat economy in the period from the early 1820s through the later 1830s has led some economists and historians to argue strongly that wheat provided the central impetus to growth in the sense that this was implied by traditional staples theory.[23] As one author put it, "a more classic case of staple production would be difficult to imagine."[24]

Others, while admitting the obvious importance of wheat, note that it is very difficult to relate wheat exports to overall economic prosperity and growth in the colony. High wheat exports are not easily matched with the attraction of immigrants or, at least in the short term, to commercial prosperity.[25] There is general consensus, however, both that wheat was the key to the agricultural sector in Canada and that agricultural production was central to the continued prosperity of the economy through the later 1820s and early 1830s.

Transportation, 1815–1848

Transportation in early Upper Canada was, as earlier, in New France, largely dependent on water. To move away from the waterfront was to encounter the vast forest, which acted as an obstacle both to farming and to movement. There were, it was true, a few roads from the beginning. Yonge Street, running north from York, and Dundas Street, which went west from the head of the lake, were opened by Governor Simcoe before 1800 for the dual purposes of defence and colonization. Both were but strips through the wilderness, however. Trees were cleared to the point where an axle could pass over the remaining stumps. These conditions would remain unchanged for many years to come, except for the ruts that passing traffic wore along the forest track. Gradually the regions were settled, and as farmers took up land, other local roads appeared, usually of the same primitive variety.

These realities imposed certain limitations and rhythms on the movements of the farmer in this period (see Figure 6.3). A great deal of travel took place immediately after harvest in the fall. Grain was moved to the mill, supplies bought for the winter, and a break taken to mark the completion of another growing season. This was the time to visit the town and to look to whatever purchases of clothing, materials, or other "luxuries" might be affordable. An even better time for movement was in the dead of winter. Travel by sleighs running over snow was invariably superior in this period to that over the best roads that Upper Canada had to offer. When the snow melted in some untimely winter thaw or with the coming of spring, the muddy tracks became impassable for a wagon, and movement of heavy goods ceased. By midsummer, roads had dried out enough that another round of purchases, movement of supplies, and visits could take place before the busy harvest season began.[26]

The primitive road system and the slowness with which a wagon could move goods meant that water continued to be the key method of transportation for bulk goods over long distances through to the coming of the railway at midcentury. This fact was both the great advantage of Upper Canada and, paradoxically, one of its great burdens. The advantage came from the fact that the St. Lawrence–lower Great Lakes system had provided this inland colony with access to the sea. People and goods were able to move back and forth with an ease that would have been impossible had there been no direct water route. The burden was that the natural state of the St. Lawrence–Great Lakes system was far from ideal. It was one thing for fur traders to portage their goods at several points. Furs were high value-to-bulk goods that could be shipped profitably in spite of transport costs. Wheat was a bulk good, however, and the costs of transshipment left very little profit for farmers, given the fixed prices they faced in export markets. To employ a rough illustration: a valuable load of furs could be transported relatively easily by canoe around the obstacles that existed in the natural system; however, should anyone be so obstinate as to insist on portaging a canoe-load of wheat down the St. Lawrence, very little

FIGURE 6.3

Cycle of Wheat Delivery to Yonge Mills, 1834

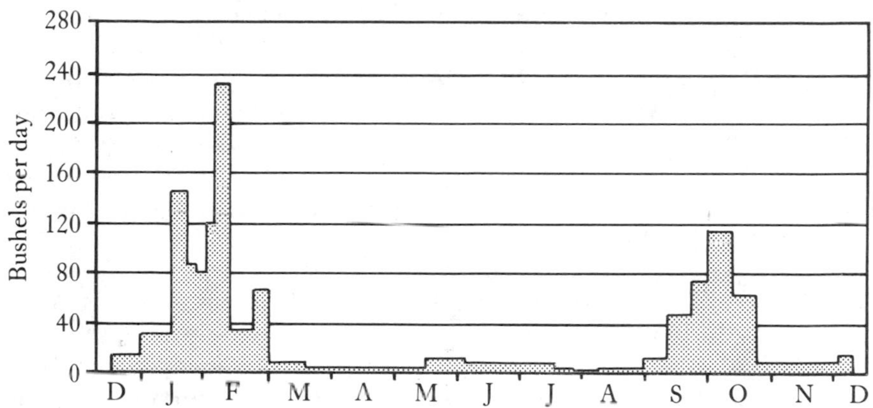

Source: Thomas McIlwraith, "The Adequacy of Rural Roads in the Era Before Railways: An Illustration from Upper Canada," *Canadian Geographer* 14, no. 4 (Winter 1970): 357.

return for the effort would be earned upon reaching Montreal.

If the new staple, wheat, were to develop, therefore, improvements in transport had to be made. Moreover, the merchants and forwarders of the Canadas were not interested just in Upper Canadian wheat but in the dominance of a vast hinterland stretching through Upper New York State, the Ohio country, and the new territories to the west.[27] Just as Robert Hamilton and his compatriots had done much of the supplying of fur traders in this region in the late eighteenth century, so those who succeeded Hamilton wanted to ensure that it was they who shipped American wheat to England and supplied the growing back-country population of both British North America and the United States with the latest luxuries and manufactures from the United Kingdom.

The problem was that there were also U.S. merchants, shippers, forwarders, and financiers with their eye on the growing produce of this transborder frontier region. The need for improved transportation facilities to supply the west led to a concrete step by New York to counter the natural advantages of the St. Lawrence waterway. In 1825, the Erie Canal was opened, connecting Lake Erie to the Hudson-Mohawk river system and thence to New York.

Three years later, the Oswego feeder connected the Erie system to Lake Ontario.

In the Canadas, improvements had also begun. In 1819, St. Catharines businessman William Merritt began work on the Welland Canal between Lakes Erie and Ontario. Developed in part because of Merritt's need for more abundant supplies of water for his milling operations, the Welland was an ambitious project that, once completed, would overcome one of the longer portages in the Great Lakes system. At the other end of the system, as mentioned in Chapter 5, a group of Montreal businessmen had begun work on the Lachine Canal near Montreal.

At this point, differences between the state of development in New York and that in the Canadas became apparent. New York was a heavily populated region with an increasingly diverse economy. It had a population of well over a million people and considerable wealth. Therefore, it had little trouble financing the Erie system. The Canadian economy was still in an early stage of development and did not possess any significant amount of savings. It is, therefore, not really surprising that both the Welland and the Lachine soon ran into financial trouble.

In Upper Canada, the importance of the grain trade and of the aspirations to commercial hegemony over the American West soon became apparent. Merritt went, cap in hand, to government, and, in 1826, the government purchased some £25 000 in stock. Once in, it could not easily get out, and other stock purchases and grants soon followed the first one. As H.G. Aitken noted in his study of the canal, by 1827, the "Welland Canal Company was already degenerating into a privately controlled institution for the disbursement of public funds." By 1834 the government recognized its irrevocable stake in the canal when, as part of another grant, it insisted on the right to appoint three of the seven directors of the canal company. By 1839, it was moving to take over the canal completely.[28]

In Lower Canada, the fate of the Lachine was much the same. The original investors could not make a go of it, and the Legislative Assembly of Lower Canada had to take over. There were two differences in the pattern, however. First, the collapse of the original company meant that, unlike Welland, the Lachine became a government operation by 1821. Second, political divisions between the predominantly English-Canadian merchant class and French-

Canadian professional and farm interests meant that the Legislative Assembly became hostile to further canal development. It was to be many years later, under different political circumstances, that canals were built to circumvent the other rapids on the upper St. Lawrence.

There was a third canal project. In 1826, the imperial government funded the construction of the Rideau Canal system in order to assure military supply movements in the event of another war with the United States. When completed in 1832, it ran from Kingston through the Rideau waterway to the Ottawa River at Bytown (now Ottawa) and provided a minimum depth of 4.5 feet for boats running from Montreal to Lake Ontario. Together with the Welland, this canal provided direct access from Montreal to the interior and marked a significant improvement upon the natural transportation system of the Great Lakes. It is thus fair to see the transportation infrastructure improving parallel and in response to the rise of a significant wheat-export sector.

Yet, the improvements to date were of limited use. The Rideau Canal was a circuitous way to get anything or anybody from Kingston to Montreal. The very thing that made it attractive to the military — its distance from the vulnerable upper St. Lawrence — hampered its effectiveness as a commercial supply system. Further, the depths in the system varied from the 4.5 feet of the Rideau to the 8 feet of the Welland. Ships plying the Great Lakes were unlikely to be able to proceed through the Rideau. Boats or barges with a shallow-enough draft to ply the Rideau were unlikely to venture out on the stormy Great Lakes. Transshipment was still necessary. Over the next twenty years, the development of the St. Lawrence canal system and its ongoing rivalry with American transportation routes was to be a central theme in the welfare of farmers, merchants, and governments. It would also prove a severe financial strain. As early as 1829, three-quarters of the government's debt to the Bank of Upper Canada was related to expenditures on the Welland Canal.[29]

Several years ago, Aitken coined the phrase "defensive expansionism" to sum up the policy of development represented by the Welland and other canals. In brief, Aitken argued that the development of the canal system was necessary because of the American moves to capture the grain trade. Yet, as Merritt quickly discovered, Upper Canada did not possess the savings to undertake such a project, and investors elsewhere were not likely to be enthusiastic about such a dubious scheme. In other words, the project was crucial to the aspirations of the colony but was not a viable private market venture. The only alternative was government involvement as an agent of development. It is a pattern that has been a characteristic of Canadian economic development ever since.

A transportation infrastructure was one of the necessary by-products of an agrarian export economy. It also raises the question of what linkages, if any, the export grain economy had with other facets of Upper Canadian economic development. Did agricultural requirements lead to other developments within the economy? Did it, in other words, have linkages that helped diversify and develop the Upper Canadian economy, as classical theories about a successful staple would have it? This is a difficult question to answer, at least for the period before 1840. There were some linkages, of course. The small metropolitan centres existed mainly to serve the attendant farm communities. The merchant community stocked its wares and planned its budget according to the rhythms of farm life. Equally, it has been argued that the presence of a viable farm hinterland was central in the 1830s to the assertion of pre-eminence by the city of Toronto. The existence of Yonge Street, stretching north to Holland Landing, and the presence of a fertile and accessible hinterland gave Toronto an opportunity for growth.[30] Between 1826 and 1841, the population of the city grew from 1719 to more than 14 000. It was not exactly a major urban centre yet, but it was, by 1841, significantly larger than any of its Upper Canadian rivals.

It is also possible to argue that the period before 1840 saw the beginnings of a distinct merchant-capitalist class and that such a class was directly or indirectly dependent on agricultural exports. More work needs to be done in this area of research before any final conclusions can be drawn, but various pieces of evidence point to the period between 1820 and 1840 as being crucial in this regard. First, it was in this period that the financial infrastructure necessary for regular merchant and financial activities came into being. In 1821, the first bank in the colony, the Bank of Upper Canada, was chartered by the legislature. Strongly interlinked with the governing clique known as the Family Compact, the bank was able to secure favour over rival interests in Kingston and to force a withdrawal of the Bank of Montreal from many parts of the province.

It is revealing to compare the state of the bank at the time of its formation with its state at the time of the 1841 union with Lower Canada. Such a comparison reveals much about the development of capital within Upper Canada. Initially the bank was required by the legislature to have £20 000 in deposits before it could begin business. Even with the backing of the Compact, and even though it was the only bank in the colony, it could not raise the money. The requirement was lowered to £10 000. That was still too much. One estimate is that it had only £8 000 on opening day. Only an illegal advance from the army chest allowed it to meet minimum requirements. To the degree that this reflects the resources in the provincial capital, it indicates the absence of any significant capitalist class.

The subsequent years stand in sharp contrast. As population poured into the province and as the grain trade developed, so, too, did savings. The bank paid regular dividends through the 1820s, and soon had branches in Niagara, Cobourg, Kingston, and Brockville. By 1840, in spite of the financial crisis that hit the colony in 1837–38, the bank remained a prosperous and viable institution — a fact reflected in the £38 000 in dividends that it had paid out over the years.[31]

Thus, there was, by the 1830s, an emerging class of entrepreneurs who, though tied to the political elite of the colony, were distinct forces in their own right. Such people as William Allen, the first president of the Bank of Upper Canada, were involved in a range of business activities running from life insurance to the Welland Canal. Along the way, Allen and others, such as grain forwarder Isaac Buchanan, or merchant James Newbigging, amassed considerable financial resources and developed intercolonial and even transatlantic connections. These resources would prove important when the colony moved to the expensive venture of railway development a few years later.[32]

The rise of a business class distinct from that of Montreal also had implications within the colony. More and more it was the grain distributors, the merchants, or the bankers in Toronto or Hamilton that stepped into the place of Montrealers. As they gained wealth and strength, they also gained autonomy from Montreal, often dealing directly with New York or London. At the same time, they asserted their dominance over the surrounding region. Small communities were increasingly oriented toward Toronto or Hamilton.

Metropolitan Toronto Reference Library, J. Ross Robertson Collection

The town of York in the early 1830s, looking east along King Street E. *Although the town itself was small, the population dependent on it increased rapidly. By the time of the union, one in five Upper Canadians lived within 75 miles of the city of Toronto, foreshadowing that city's importance within the colony.*

The process was not complete by 1840, but, however much other lakefront communities might spin dreams of their own glorious prospects, the future golden horseshoe was already beginning to take shape.

The rise of Toronto and Hamilton is clearly reflected in the patterns of settlement after 1820. The established districts around Kingston remained static or declined in terms of share of the provincial population. So, too, did the fertile Niagara region. This fact has been attributed to poor soil in the hinterland, in the case of Kingston, and to an absence of free land, in the case of Niagara. That may be the case, but it is revealing that the frontier London and western regions saw little or no relative population growth in the later 1820s. In the 1830s, this situation changed somewhat but, even by 1840, this whole frontier of open and available land had increased its portion of the provincial population by only a little more than 3 percent.

What grew, in relative terms, was the area immediately adjacent to the communities of Toronto and Hamilton. The Town of York, as Toronto was called before 1834, may have been small, but the population dependent on it was increasing rapidly. The Home District increased its population from 18 400 in 1826 to 78 900 by 1841. The District of Gore increased from 13 000 to 56 400 in the same period. Together, their share of the provincial population increased by more than 10 percent in this fifteen-year period. By the time of the union, one in five Upper Canadians lived within 75 miles of Toronto. This was a shift of some importance and, when combined with the rising Toronto merchant class, clearly foreshadowed that city's pre-eminence within the colony. By the time the provincial government left the city, in 1841, it was no longer crucial to Toronto's survival. It had been transformed from an administrative centre to a commercial city. It was not yet able to challenge Montreal's far-flung resources or to dream, as Montrealers had long done, of commercial supremacy over wide swaths of the continent. Such challenges and such dreams were only a few years away, however.

The Beginnings of a New Economic Order, 1840–1846

For all the progress and growth that had occurred in the 1820s and early 1830s, Upper Canada was in trouble by the middle of the decade. Wheat prices in Britain had collapsed, and many farmers found themselves facing an increasingly uncertain future. Immigration fell off by the middle of the decade, as the British ceased to leave their homeland in such great numbers. Certainly the absence of a significant demand for wheat made pioneer life in the colonies a less-attractive proposition.

Things were equally difficult for the government. Revenues for a colonial government in this period were always precarious. Some British grants could be counted on, as could some excise taxes. The largest single item of government revenue, however, was customs duties — tariffs on goods entering the country. The great majority of goods entering Upper Canada, however, cleared customs and paid the attendant duties not in the province but at Montreal. Throughout the years, this fact had been a source of controversy between Upper and Lower Canada and, though both the British and the Lower Canadian government accepted in principle the right of Upper Canada to have a share of these revenues, the difficulties remained.

Part of the problem with Lower Canada was political. The control of funds was a major focal point of the battle between reformers and conservatives in that province. There was also a natural desire to hold on to as much as possible. Upper Canada complained loudly and often that it never got its fair share. Part of the problem was the simple fact that Upper Canada contained the primary settlement frontier for British North America. It was this province, therefore, that had the most rapidly growing population. In 1814, for example, Upper Canada's population was only 28 percent of that of Lower Canada. By 1831, it was 43 percent, and, by the union of 1841, was probably approaching 70 percent, in spite of Lower Canada's high birth rate. Such rapid change meant that, by the time an agreement was made with Lower Canada on the basis of population, it was outdated. There was always a lag between the actual population of Upper Canada and the revenues it got to support that population.

The frontier position of Upper Canada created difficulties not only on the revenue but also on the expenditure side. The Family Compact and the rising merchant class of the colony were firm believers in the necessity of extensive growth. People had to be attracted, exports had to increase, and investments had to be made. To do this, financing was necessary and, as the Welland Canal experience illustrates, Upper Canada soon found itself directly involved in the heavy costs of development. Even if revenues had been more equitably distributed, and external depressions and financial crises had not intruded, it is likely the government would have found itself overextended by the later 1830s. As it was, it nearly went bankrupt. The crisis resulting from political division, government overexpenditure, and farm discontent climaxed in 1837. By that time, depression had settled over the province, and government and financial circles began to fear for the soundness of Upper Canada's young banking system. In the spring of 1837, a series of economic and political events in the United States caused the New York banks to suspend specie payments. The suspension soon spread to other American banks, and the panic reached across the boarder. In Lower Canada, the Bank of Montreal suspended specie payments in the spring, and, by June, the legislature allowed the banks in Upper Canada to follow suit.[33]

All of this was serious enough, but the rebellions in both Lower

Canada and Upper Canada at the end of the year created an image of political instability that threatened to prevent recovery. The government remained in a precarious financial state. Indeed, by 1839, Sir George Arthur, the lieutenant-governor of Upper Canada, noted with chagrin that "the public debt of this province . . . involves an expenditure in interest nearly equal to the whole revenues of the colony." Immigrants were naturally hesitant to come to a land plagued by depression, rebellion, and recurring postrebellion border incidents. Whereas some 12 000 immigrants landed at Quebec in 1836, only 990 did so in 1838, and 1586 in 1839.[34] External intervention would be necessary if the economic and fiscal soundness of the colony were to be restored within a reasonable time.

That external assistance came in two forms. First, the British government moved to unite Upper and Lower Canada. One motive was political. It was hoped that a growing English population would eventually dominate and assimilate the existing French-Catholic population. There was also an economic motive. The creation of the single Province of Canada was very much an attempt to create a rational economic unit with a strong fiscal base for future development.

The economic motivation of the British government was clearly reflected in the special report by Lord Durham, who had been sent in the wake of the rebellion to advise upon remedies for the future. For Durham, the key to happiness and loyalty, at least among the English colonials, was prosperity. Those measures that developed the economy were henceforth to be seen as a part of the great imperial effort to bring contentment to this part of the Empire. Charles Poulet Thomson (soon to be Lord Sydenham), the first governor general of the united Province of Canada, symbolized the new attitude of Britain. Unlike past governors, who had had professional military and diplomatic backgrounds, Thomson, a former president of the British Board of Trade and former MP from the industrial centre of Manchester, was a man focussed on economic growth. Outside assistance was also provided in order to promote development and to gain support for the efforts of Sydenham. The British government guaranteed a £1.5 million loan to the new province. Provincial loans raised under this guarantee would have all the prestige and financial security of the mother government. Canada would be able to raise money in Britain once again to undertake rapid development.

The British efforts as well as the return of political stability in Canada had the desired effect. Immigration picked up, population increased, and wheat exports rose to record levels. There was also a considerable infusion of spending directly from the government, as it used the British guarantee to develop a through canal system with a depth of nine feet, from Lake Erie to the Atlantic. With a reorganized Board of Works spending the £1.5 million and more, and with up to 6000 labourers employed on canal works, the colonial government became, for the first time, a significant-enough spender to have a direct effect on the economy.

The commercial possibilities of the new Province of Canada depended, as always, on the health of the primary-resource sector, in general, and on the export markets for timber and wheat, in particular. The state of the latter staple was potentially a problem. From the early 1830s, farmers had been unhappy with British policies — policies that seemed to favour commercial interests. Since the mid-1830s, farmers had faced uncertain wheat prices in Britain and had been frustrated by the protective remnants of the Corn Laws. To some degree, the rebellions of 1837 reflected the agrarian discontent with the trends of recent years.

The continuing erosion of mercantilism helped Canadian farmers in this instance. In the Canada Corn Act of 1843, the British government agreed to accept Canadian wheat in Britain, regardless of local prices, for the nominal duty of one shilling per quarter (1 quarter = 8 bushels). Canada, for its part, had responded to British and agricultural concerns the year before by levying a duty of three shillings per quarter on all American agricultural produce coming into Canada. It was a situation with something to please everyone. The duty was not high enough to prevent Americans from taking advantage of the Corn Act by shipping along the St. Lawrence, and the merchants could thus look forward to expanded business. At the same time, Canadian farmers finally had a concrete price advantage over their American competitors in dealing with wholesalers.

None of these policy decisions would have had any dramatic effect had there not been demand for Canadian products. Fortunately for Canada, there was. In timber and wheat, there was a generally strong demand in Britain and a still small but growing market in the United States. Wheat exports from Canada were, by 1840, higher than they had ever been before. By 1846 and 1847, even that record amount had almost tripled. In the latter two years, the total exports were greater than those of the entire period from 1817 to 1839. Over the next decade, such orders of magnitude were not at all uncommon. Prosperity was reflected in population growth and in urban development. The actual rates were remarkable, surpassing by far those of the mother country at the peak of its demographic explosion. Canada West increased from a total population of 432 000 in 1840 to 725 000 by 1848. The city of Toronto grew from a mere 14 000 people at the time of the union to 23 500 by 1848, and to nearly 31 000 by 1851. It was, by then, a city with a significant hinterland. Wholesalers now had the connections, the money, and the volume to import directly from New York or London. They, in turn, were the distributors for many smaller urban centres in Ontario.[35]

In Canada East, the population growth was encouraged not only by a healthy inflow of immigrants but also by a continuation of the high birth rate and low mortality rate. A population of around 600 000 at the time of the union grew to 890 000 by 1851. Montreal, which for all Toronto's growth was still the commercial and financial centre of the province, experienced the benefits of the commercial prosperity of the first half of the decade. Its population grew from approximately 40 000 at the time of the union to more than 57 000 by 1851. In spite of such a healthy growth rate, however, Canada East did not grow as quickly as did Canada West. There was simply not as much cheap fertile land as there was in Canada West, and the agricultural output, as has been discussed, was mixed at best. By 1851, Canada West had surpassed Canada East in population, an event that was to create considerable political upset over the next years.

Conclusion

The changes of the 1840s also brought Canada to the threshold of a new era. Once pioneer settlements were established, the growth of the colonies, and especially that of the fledgling Upper Canada, depended on a staple economy resting on wheat, timber, and a few other goods. Underlying this dependence on a few key staples was a belief that the British mercantile system, with its complex protective measures, dictated a certain type of economic growth. Rapid immigration had allowed the settlement of large tracts of land, so that, by midcentury, settlement was pretty much complete over large parts of southern Canada West. A population of a few thousand in 1783 had grown to almost a million in less than 70 years. Only on the northern fringes of settlement, where fertile land met the Canadian Shield, and in the area west of London, was there still any significant amount of homestead land. Before long, these too would be gone. The agricultural frontier was about to move beyond the Province of Canada.

The new era was also coming because of revolutions in the imperial system. The Canada Corn Act, which had been so praised, was but another manifestation of the British movement away from mercantilism. In 1846, as a result of famine in Ireland, the Corn Laws were suspended, and then abolished. Henceforth, an economic system that had grown up under assumptions predicated on mercantilism would have to adjust to the new world of open trade. For many Canadians, especially millers and forwarders, it was not a comforting thought.

Finally, a new economic era was about to begin because of changing technology, especially in the era of transportation. Steam power had come to the Great Lakes earlier in the century. Now, by the later 1840s, steam power was about to lessen the importance of the lakes as a transportation route. Canada was on the verge of the railway era, and this would have massive implications, not only for transportation but for the nature of finance, the distribution of wealth, the degree of capital accumulation, and the overall structure and diversity of the economy.

Transportation, the legislative framework within which the economy operated, and the impending passing of the agricultural frontier thus marked the end of one stage of Canadian development. The next stage would see Canada move to a much larger political base in order in part to facilitate further economic development. It would also see increasing diversity within the economy and the movement, at least in the central regions, away from a simple staple economy. In other words, Confederation and the beginnings of industrialization were key to the economic developments of the years after 1846.

Notes

1. T.W. Acheson, "The Nature and Structure of York Commerce in the 1820's," *Canadian Historical Review* 50, no. 4 (1969): 406–28.

2. J.M. Bumsted, *The People's Clearance, 1770–1815* (Edinburgh: University of Edinburgh Press, 1982), 73.
3. T. Regehr, "Land Ownership in Upper Canada, 1783–1796," *Ontario History* 55 (1963):37.
4. Regehr, "Land Ownership," 46.
5. Peter Russell, "Upper Canada: A Poor Man's Country? Some Statistical Evidence," *Canadian Papers in Rural History* III (Gananoque: Langdale, 1978). 136–37.
6. See John Philip, "The Economic and Social Effects of the British Garrisons on the Development of Western Upper Canada, *Ontario History* 41 (1949); Bruce Wilson, *The Enterprises of Robert Hamilton* (Toronto: University of Toronto Press, 1983).
7. Douglas McCalla, "The 'Loyalist' Economy of Upper Canada," *Social History* 16, no. 32 (November 1983): 291.
8. Simcoe to Henry Dundas, April 28, 1792; cited in E.A. Cruikshank, ed., *The Correspondence of Lt. Governor John Graves Simcoe*, Vol. I (Toronto: Ontario Historical Society, 1931), 141.
9. Cited in Helen Cowan, *British Emigration to British North America*, (Toronto: University of Toronto Press, 1961), 25. See also on the question of capital, Bumsted, *The People's Clearance*.
10. John McCallum, *Unequal Beginnings: Agriculture and Economic Development in Quebec and Ontario Until 1870* (Toronto: University of Toronto Press, 1980), Appendix S2.
11. *Census of Canada*, 1826.
12. McCalla, "The 'Loyalist' Economy."
13. M.L. Hansen and J.B. Brebner, *The Mingling of the Canadian and American Peoples* (New Haven: Yale University Press, 1940), 95.
14. From E.A. Wrigley and R.S. Schofield, *The Population History of England* (London: Edward Arnold, 1981), Table 7.8. Figures are less certain for Scotland and Ireland, but those that exist indicate that Scotland's growth rate was approximately that of England. Ireland's may have been even higher.
15. Cowan, *British Emigration*, 43.
16. On the Canada Company, see Clarence Karr, *The Canada Land Company: The Early Years* (Ottawa: Ontario Historical Society, 1974).
17. Cited in Cowan, *British Emigration*, Appendix B.
18. Russell, "Upper Canada."
19. Robert Leslie Jones, *History of Agriculture in Ontario, 1613–1880* (Toronto: University of Toronto Press, 1946), 39.
20. Some of that wheat was American. As figures are not consistent, it is impossible to separate wheat of U.S. origin from that of Upper Canadian origin. The irregular figures that do exist indicate, however, that Upper Canada was the supplier of the predominance of this wheat. See McCallum, *Unequal Beginnings*, Appendix S1.
21. See, on the earliest stages of farming in Upper Canada, Janice Potter, "Patriarchy and Paternalism: The Case of Eastern Ontario Loyalist Women," unpublished paper presented at the Canadian Historical Association Annual meeting, June 1988. See also Alison Prentice et al., *Canadian Women: A History* (Toronto: Harcourt Brace Jovanovich, 1988), 76–77.

22. Jones, *History of Agriculture*, 42.
23. The most straightforward case for the application of the staples theory to Upper Canadian wheat is seen in McCallum, *Unequal Beginnings*.
24. McCallum, *Unequal Beginnings*, 4.
25. Douglas McCalla, "The Wheat Staple," CHA *Historical Papers*, 1978, 34–46.
26. See Thomas McIlwraith, "The Adequacy of Rural Roads in the Era Before Railways: An Illustration from Upper Canada," *Canadian Geographer* 14, no. 4 (Winter 1970): 344–60; and T.W. Acheson, "The Nature and Structure of York Commerce in the 1820's," in *Historical Essays on Upper Canada*, edited by J.K. Johnson (Toronto: McClelland and Stewart, 1975).
27. The classic statement of this merchant outlook is Donald Creighton, *Empire of the St. Lawrence* (Toronto: Macmillan, 1956).
28. H.G. Aitken, *The Welland Canal Company: A Study in Canadian Enterprise* (Cambridge, MA: Harvard University Press, 1954), 41–42.
29. Acheson, "The Nature and Structure of York Commerce," 189.
30. Acheson, "The Nature and Structure of York Commerce."
31. Carol Vaughan, "The Bank of Upper Canada in Politics, 1817–1840," *Ontario History* 60 (December 1968): 185–204; and Peter Baskerville, ed., *The Bank of Upper Canada* (Ottawa: Carleton University Press, 1987).
32. See Peter Baskerville, "Entrepreneurship and the Family Compact, 1822–1855," *Urban History Review* 3 (February 1981): 15–34. For a good example of the rise of an Upper Canadian business in the 1830s and after, see Douglas McCalla, *The Upper Canada Trade, 1834–1872: A Study of the Buchanans' Business* (Toronto: University of Toronto Press, 1979).
33. Angela Redish, "The Economic Crisis of 1837–1839 in Upper Canada: Case Study of a Temporary Suspension of Specie Payments," *Explorations in Economic History* 20 (1983): 402–17.
34. Cited in Cowan, *British Emigration*, Appendix B.
35. D.C. Masters, *The Rise of Toronto* (Toronto: University of Toronto Press, 1987).

Further Reading

Craig, Gerald. *Upper Canada: The Formative Years, 1784–1841.* Toronto: McClelland and Stewart, 1963.

Johnson, Keith, ed. *Historical Essays on Upper Canada*. Toronto: McClelland and Stewart, 1975.

McCalla, Douglas. "The 'Loyalist' Economy of Upper Canada." *Social History* 16, no. 32 (November 1983): 279–304.

McCallum, John. *Unequal Beginnings: Agriculture and Economic Development in Quebec and Ontario Until 1870.* Toronto: University of Toronto Press, 1980.

Wilson, Bruce. *The Enterprises of Robert Hamilton*. Toronto: University of Toronto Press, 1983.

III

The End of Mercantilism and the Coming of Industrialization, 1846–1867

III

The middle of the nineteenth century is an important turning point in Canadian economic history. Development after 1840 would proceed along a different course from that which it had previously followed, for several reasons. Most obviously, the British mercantile system came to an end after more than 200 years of existence. Henceforth, the North American colonies would have to do without the shipping regulations, Corn Laws, and timber duties that, as we have previously seen, had variously stimulated, limited, and shaped their economic development from the very beginning.

A second and closely related departure involves the political counterpart of the abrogation of the mercantile system. The British made it clear at this time as well that they were willing to give up administrative responsibility for the domestic affairs of their North American colonies. The colonies had a measure of self-government already, but those powers had been sought, and exercised, mainly to consolidate the colonies' position under the British umbrella. Now, the North American colonies were to be given additional authority and responsibility, and were to use it in entirely new, if unspecified, ways.

A third major factor that affected Canada's development profoundly at this time was the U.S. progress toward becoming the world's leading industrial nation. The territorial dimensions of the United States were laid out in a 50-year period beginning with the Louisiana Purchase of 1803 and ending with the Gadsden Purchase (southern Arizona and New Mexico) in 1853. The northern border was established in its present form by 1850 through a series of agreements with Britain, although this fact did not entirely quell Canadian fears of further U.S. territorial expansion. Much of the central plain of the United States remained unsettled by Europeans in the 1850s, but robust expansion was under way. The territories of Kansas, Nebraska, and Minnesota experienced agricultural settlement in these years. On the west coast, California and Oregon both saw a considerable influx of American settlement.

The major features of American economic expansion to 1860 were a revolution in transportation, rapid industrialization, and growth and regional specialization in agriculture. The transport revolution was striking and, in many ways, was an essential forerunner of the other developments. Steamboats were developed and improved, reducing river rates, especially upstream ones, dramatically. A spate of canal construction followed the successful opening of the Erie Canal in 1825. Although these ventures proved to be the least successful of the transport improvements, canal rates did drop dramatically after 1830. The "turnpike era" after 1815 provided long-distance road links between areas not served otherwise, and local authorities filled in the connecting roads.

The most significant development by far, however, was railway construction. There were fewer than 100 miles of track in the United States in 1830, when working railways began to appear there and in the United Kingdom. This total would rise to more than 3000 miles a decade later, and to more than 30 000 miles by 1860. The bulk of the construction was in the densely settled northern states, with large areas of the south still unconnected to the national network. Railway freight rates fell by more than 50 percent between 1830 and 1860, as technological advances gradually brought down construction and operating costs. Rates were still well above those for canals and river steamboats, but railways provided quicker and more reliable service, and they quickly took over passenger traffic and the higher-value freight business.

American industry grew rapidly in the first half of the nineteenth century, increasing twelvefold in real terms between 1815 and 1860.[1] Manufacturing made up less than 5 percent of GNP in 1810, but more than 15 percent in 1860. Cotton textiles, concentrated in the New England states, were the leading sector. Factory production replaced handicraft methods, slowly at first, and then rapidly after about 1815. New England cotton-industry output stood at 2.4 million yards in 1815 and at 857.2 million yards in 1860 — an annual growth rate of nearly 15 percent — making it the largest manufacturing industry in the nation in 1860. Production of wool, silk, linen, and other textiles complemented this development. Iron production was another important sector, especially as it came to be linked with the great expansion in railway mileage.

The trends in agriculture were equally significant. Agriculture declined in relative terms, as it had to, given its preponderance at the turn of the nineteenth century, but its absolute output rose, and the pattern of production became regionally specialized. Essentially, the wheat frontier shifted westward with settlement, and older areas turned increasingly to more specialized products. This reallocation was partly forced on the established areas (western wheat had a lower cost), and partly it reflected the growth of demand for animal and dairy products in the rapidly developing industrial towns and cities. The demand for southern cotton grew apace with the revolution in cotton textiles in Britain and New England, although the market for tobacco was gradually lost after 1815 as a result of rising labour costs.

The Civil War (1861–65) was as dramatic an economic development as it was a political and military one. American historians have debated both the reasons for the war and the impacts it had on the subsequent life of the nation. The short-run economic impacts were obviously enormous, considering the loss of life and the destruction of property. The longer-run ones are more difficult to determine. Most analysts now agree that the Civil War was not the major impetus to industrialization it was once believed to be. There were already significant changes in that direction prior to the war, and presumably they would have continued apace. It seems clear as well that the economic retardation of the South relative to the North in terms of per-capita income dates from the war and the destruction it caused.

The British colonies that were to become Canada had been affected by developments in the United States from the outset of colonization, as previous chapters have shown, so American influence as a theme is not new. The connections just became more pervasive after midcentury. This shift was partly the result of the relative decline of the United Kingdom, and partly the result of the rising might of the United States. America became a market for some Canadian products, and a competitor in the production of others. Always it would be a destination for immigrants, but occasionally the number of Americans arriving was greater than that of Canadians leaving. The huge U.S. economy would look to Canada for investment opportunities and, at other times, would draw Canadian savings south. Sharing a language and cultural heritage with the majority of Canadians, Americans extended their influence beyond the purely economic into the political and cultural.

The final factor affecting the Canadian economy from midcentury on is really an extension of the third point. Like the United States, and, indeed, like all other Western nations, Canada was touched by the technological revolution that was taking place at this time, and by the international economic and political developments that accompanied it. About 1850, the world entered into a second phase of the industrial revolution, a phase that the noted historian David Landes described as "marked in essence by the working-out on the Continent of those innovations that constitute the heart of the Industrial Revolution and had been developed and diffused in Britain a generation or more earlier."[2] Steam power, railways, textiles, and iron production spread from Britain onto the European continent, mainly to regions (often cutting across national boundaries) that bore considerable similarity in terms of resource endowments to those of the host nation.

Political response followed economic developments, altering the international environment even more. Economic liberalization spread from Britain to the Continent, for a time at least. Napoleon III lowered French import duties on grain, cattle, coal, and iron in the 1850s and, in 1860, concluded a far-reaching commercial agreement with the United Kingdom. Both partners then made separate treaties, first with the Zollverein and Belgium, and then with other nations. As Sidney Pollard notes, "a free-trade world seemed to be in the making in capitalist Europe."[3]

The British North American colonies were on the fringe of these industrial and commercial developments. Railways were important to a region as vast as this one was, so it is not surprising that efforts in this direction took priority in the decades after 1840. Other aspects of this second phase of industrialization affected Canada as well, although much less so. Sparse population and limited energy sources precluded much development of textiles and iron products. As a trading nation, Canada benefited from the generally prosperous economic conditions on the Continent and from the liberalization of trade, but only in a general way, as none of these markets was particularly important compared to those of Britain and, increasingly, the United States.

The adjustments of the Canadian economy — indeed, of Canadian society — to these mid-nineteenth-century developments came over a very long time. Part III focusses on the immediate consequences, beginning in 1840, as the mercantile system was being dismantled, and running to Confederation in 1867. Here we emphasize four themes, each of which forms a chapter in what follows. The first is the short-term economic and political adjustment of the colonies to the withdrawal of mercantile preferences and imperial governance. The second is the steady underlying economic growth and change built on railway construction, technological change, and population increase. The third is Confederation and the British North America Act, a political transformation that we see as coming, in about equal measure, out of the first two developments. A fourth chapter looks at the west in the years from the Treaty of Utrecht to the eve of its transfer to Canada.

Notes

1. Gerald Gunderson, *A New Economic History of America* (New York: McGraw-Hill, 1976), 156.
2. David Landes, *The Unbound Prometheus: Technological Change and Industrial Development in Western Europe from 1750 to the Present* (Cambridge: Cambridge University Press, 1969), 193.
3. Sidney Pollard, *Peaceful Conquest: The Industrialization of Europe, 1760–1970* (London: Oxford University Press, 1981), 257.

CHAPTER

7

Adjustment to the End of Mercantilism

The British mercantile system unravelled quickly once the process began. Timber duties were the first to be affected, with the initial cuts coming in 1842 and the last of the differential duties gone by 1860. The Navigation Acts were repealed in two steps, in 1849 and 1854. Thereafter, British ports were open on equal terms to the vessels of all nations. Agricultural duties ended as well. The Irish famine of 1845–46 forced the British government to admit offshore wheat freely. Notice was given the following year that, effective as of 1849, grain could be imported into the United Kingdom upon payment of a nominal duty, and even this small levy was removed in 1869. Trade liberalization proceeded beyond agriculture. An estimated 1150 items carried duties in 1840, but fewer than 50 did by 1860. Britain was a free-trade nation in practice as well as in doctrine.

The Staples Trades

If the dismantlement of the British mercantile system created some unease in the British North American colonies, the reaction is understandable. To a great extent, the colonial economies owed their very beginnings to the Navigation Acts, the timber preferences, and the Corn Laws. Now, all were going, raising several questions in the minds of contemporaries. Would squared timber from New Brunswick and Quebec still find a market in the United Kingdom if forced to compete on equal terms with supplies from the Baltic? Could Canadian grains still find a market in Britain? Even if they could, would they and their American competitors continue to travel there via the Great Lakes–St. Lawrence forwarding system? To what extent did Atlantic Canada's carrying trade still depend on the Navigation Acts? Were there other products — ships or fish, perhaps — that owed some of their market penetration to mercantile preferences? Finally, would the supply of British products to the colonies be altered in any way, and, if so, with what consequences?

The altered tariff on squared timber in 1842 had immediate and adverse consequences on the British North American industry. Exports fell off by more than 25 percent in 1843, and signs of depression abounded. The decline proved temporary, however. Exports recovered the following year, as the British building cycle made an upswing and railway-building reached fever pitch. The all-time high for this trade was achieved in 1845, when 480 million board feet of squared timber reached Britain — nearly double the 1843 figure and 20 percent above what it had been in 1841, the final year of protection. Conditions held for another year after 1845 and then deteriorated, as Britain's building boom ended. In the short run, at least, whatever effect tariff reductions had on the squared-timber industry was dwarfed by cyclical swings in British demand.

Contrary to what is sometimes believed, the squared-timber trade survived, and even prospered, for a time after 1850. By 1852, Canadian shipments to Britain had regained their level of the early 1840s. Exports then fluctuated around a more or less constant trend until the mid-1860s, when they began to decline. Still, it was 1858 before Baltic supplies finally overtook colonial ones in the British market, and at Confederation, in 1867, exports of squared timber were larger in volume terms than at any time during the period in which preferences were in effect. In value terms, it was 1879 before exports fell below their levels of the early 1850s.

A full account of the success of the squared-timber trade for a period after the tariff cuts in 1842 has yet to be made. Several factors are clearly important, however.[1] First, as already noted, differential duties were reduced in 1842, but were not completely removed until 1860. Thus, North American timber enjoyed preferential treatment in Britain for nearly two decades after the initial cuts, albeit at a decreasing rate. Second, British timber demand was high in the

1850s as a result of booms in building and shipbuilding. These industries were able to absorb the increasing supplies from the Baltic without displacing those from British North America. In the 1860s, British demand for Canadian timber was flat. Exports in 1870 were at about the same level as in 1860 (see Figure 7.1). The incremental demand was made up entirely from Baltic supplies.

The other development of note in this period is the growing importance of an export trade in processed timber products. British North America had exported some deals (large-dimension planks) to Britain as far back as the 1790s, although the trade was minuscule until about 1820. It rose steadily thereafter, surpassing supplies from the Baltic in the early 1830s and remaining ahead of them until about 1860.[2] In value terms, exports of deals were equal to those of squared timber by 1850, when the first reliable data appear, and consistently dominate them thereafter. Unlike that of squared timber, the export of deals continued to grow over the 1860s, with the result that, in 1870, the latter exceeded the former by nearly 75 percent. Since deals went almost exclusively to Britain, it is probable that a part of the squared-timber trade was giving way to this higher-value export product.

The other processed wood product was planks and boards, and here a new market, the United States, was involved. Exports of sawn timber to the United States began in the 1830s. By 1850, the value of shipments of planks and boards, which is nearly identical to that of total shipments of wood products to the United States, was about 60 percent of that for deals and nearly 40 percent of that for squared timber. Put differently: Great Britain accounted for around 80 percent of Canadian wood exports in 1850, with the United States taking most of the remaining 20 percent (see Figure 7.2). Little wonder, then, that, as Britain began to move away from colonial preferences, timber producers in this country expressed an interest in furthering commercial ties with their American neighbours.

The wheat trade was the other activity most obviously linked to the British mercantile system. There were two separate interests involved here — the farmers who grew the wheat for export and the merchants who processed it and moved it to market in Britain — and they were not necessarily affected in the same manner or to the same extent. When Britain moved to abolish its Corn Laws in 1846, it ended the long-standing aspirations of the merchants

FIGURE 7.1
Wood Exports, 1850–1870

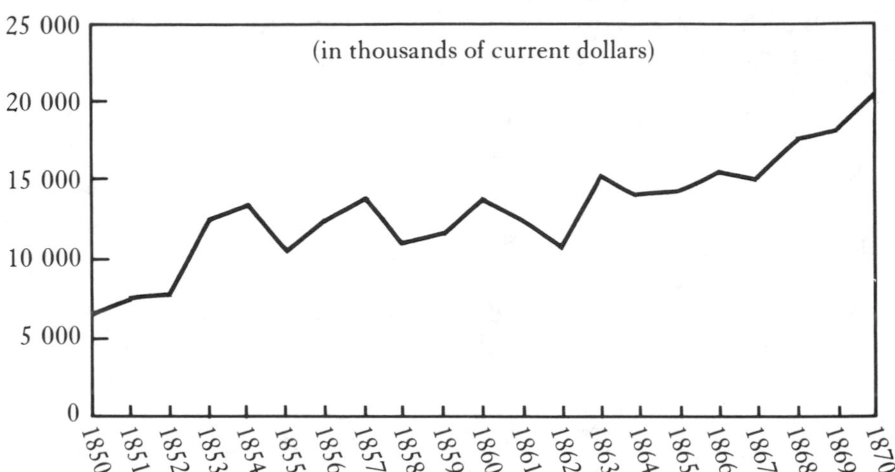

Source: Calculated from R.M. McInnis, "From Hewn Timber to Sawn Timber: The Canadian Forest Industry in the Latter Half of the Nineteenth Century," unpublished paper, Queen's University, 1988, 33–34.

of the Province of Canada to be the forwarders of a large hinterland draining into the Great Lakes. Huge investments had gone into canal-building as a means of competing with the United States, as entrepreneurs responded to the opportunities provided by the Canada Corn Act and other legislation.

The most obvious examples of business responding to imperial legislation were the investments in flour mills along the St. Lawrence in the 1840s. American wheat could come into Canada without significant duty, but American flour could not. Yet, all flour shipped out of the Canadas could benefit from the imperial system. It thus benefited Americans to ship their wheat to Canada and have it ground into flour, and Canadians were happy to oblige. With the opening of the British wheat market to all on an equal basis, Canada found itself with far too much flour-milling capacity, and bankruptcies were the inevitable result. From there, a ripple effect occurred, as workers were let go, banks declared loans to be in default, and carters and haulers found their business with the mills down drastically.

FIGURE 7.2

Exports to Great Britain as Percentage of Total of Canadian Wood Products, 1850–1870

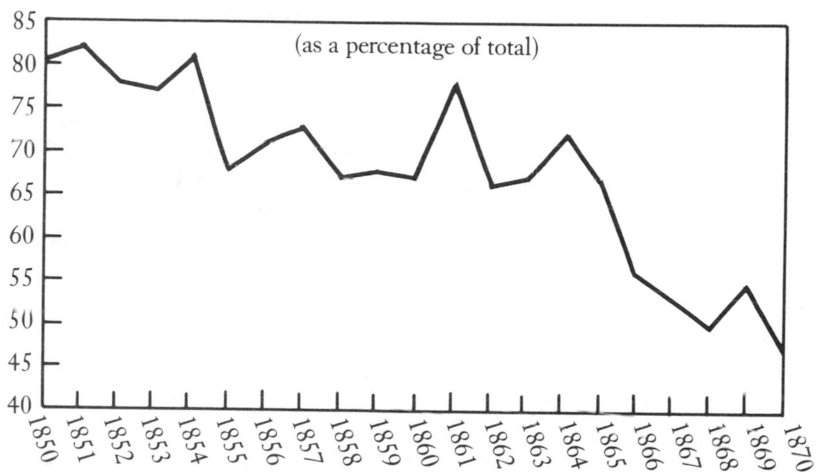

Source: Calculated from R.M. McInnis, "From Hewn Timber to Sawn Timber: The Canadian Forest Industry in the Latter Half of the Nineteenth Century," unpublished paper, Queen's University, 1988, 33–34.

Another group to be affected were the shippers and forwarders who depended on the carrying trade from the United States. Aside from contending with the abolition of the Corn Laws, they had to adjust to the passage of the Drawback Acts by the United States in 1845 and 1846. These acts permitted goods in transit through the United States to be carried in bond. Henceforth, Canadian wholesalers purchasing from Britain, and Canadian farmers exporting their product, could look to either the St. Lawrence or the American system for the best rates.

In such an open competition, the Americans had an advantage. Canadian shipping rates through the Great Lakes were lower than those along the American Erie Canal system. One optimistic report estimated that advantage to be as much as $4 per ton from Detroit. The problem was that the inland Canadian route led to Montreal, and the American one to New York. The former was a seasonal port far up a river noted for stretches of tricky navigation. The other was an ice-free port with ready access to the open ocean.

Lower rates from New York to Liverpool more than compensated for higher American rates inland. Canadian shippers could still compete, but it would henceforth be much more difficult to do so. Many feared the worst, and clamoured loudly that the mother country had betrayed imperial necessity and, not incidentally, Canadian pocketbooks.

Depression in trade along the St. Lawrence followed. Exports via the St. Lawrence fell from a figure of £2.7 million in 1845 to a low of £1.7 million in 1848. Government revenue from the expensive canal system also tumbled, the Welland's tolls falling some 60 percent between 1846 and 1848.[3] With its finances already overextended by the construction of the canal system, the government soon found itself facing yet another fiscal crisis. Fears of bankruptcy and difficulties on the British credit market added to the sense of panic and instability that existed.

Finally, adding to the woes was the vast immigration of 1846–48. The same famine that had acted as a catalyst for the suspension of the Corn Laws drove more than a million Irish out of their homeland between 1846 and 1851.[4] British North America received almost a quarter of a million of these refugees at the very time that the economy was adjusting to the dismantlement of the British mercantile system.[5] Normally, immigration responded to, and hence reflected, underlying economic growth in the receiving region. This wave, however, emanated from push factors in the sending area, and came to an economy ill-prepared to deal with it. Immigrants traditionally had been seen as the lifeblood of the colonies. As Canadians reacted to the arrival of a flood of poor and often diseased refugees, that view changed, at least temporarily. The Irish, the prejudices of the time would have it, were a benighted people who would never be anything but a drain on the land. The problems of Europe, it was feared, were being sent to North America.

Famine migration, financial ruin, imperial desertion, and government impecuniousness thus mark the traditional view of the period from 1846 through 1850. Yet, it is difficult to posit too gloomy a scenario. The panic of these years was, to a large degree, a reflection of human psychology rather than economic collapse. That psychology emanated from a sincere belief by a circle of businessmen and politicians (often the same individuals) who had consistently overestimated the importance of, and therefore the effect of the absence of, the imperial system to Canadian development. Their mood was made worse by the assertion of power by the Reform Party, and by the controversial 1849 Rebellion Losses Bill, which compensated certain rebels from 1837. It was climaxed by a short-lived but emotional campaign for annexation to the United States.

In fact, the years from 1846 to 1850 were ones of commercial readjustment rather than of any fundamental depression in the Canadian economy. In 1847, a record total of more than 5 million bushels of wheat went downriver from Canada West and 3.8 million bushels were sent overseas. Thus, the actual effects of the commercial upset were specific, in terms of both occupation and region. Farmers were not as hard hit as were merchants. The merchants of Canada West were seemingly not as hard hit as those Montrealers whose livelihood rested on the St. Lawrence trade. Canada West as a whole does not seem to have experienced the same sense of panic as the business community of Canada East.

Even among the commercial class of Montreal, the serious problems resulting from 1846 were short-lived. By 1850–51, there was a strong recovery under way, fuelled by international prosperity, and the Province of Canada entered a period of rapid economic growth that belied the pessimism both business and government had shown only a couple of years earlier. Such rapid growth underlines the fact that the basic strengths of the economy were not seriously undermined by the British movement away from a mercantile structure.

The commercial crisis was short-lived, mainly because the underlying staples trades, including that of wheat, were basically robust. A series of circumstances after 1850, including the generally prosperous state of the European economy, the Reciprocity Treaty (discussed below), war in the Crimea (1854–56) on the part of Britain, and the U.S. Civil War (1861–65), created a healthy demand for Canadian products. In 1845, the last full year of the Corn Laws, Canada West had exported some 4.5 million bushels of wheat. That figure rose to 12 million in 1856, slumped through the later 1850s, and rose again to more than 13 million bushels by 1863. The value of agricultural production in the province as a whole increased from $43.2 million to $101.8 million between 1851 and 1860.[6] Agriculture, in general, and wheat, in particular, sparked the boom of the 1850s, through other activities would expand and sustain it.

The agricultural boom was primarily dependent on international factors, over which Canada had no control. Yet, technological innovation was facilitated by the strong demand for wheat and, in turn, made farm production more efficient. The actual process of harvesting had changed little in the past century. It was slow, labour-intensive, and severely limiting to the size of farming operations. By the 1850s, however, mechanical reapers were beginning to make an appearance in the province. These implements reduced the time and labour necessary to undertake the actual cutting of the crop. With the development of the self-rake reaper by the 1860s, another tedious step in the harvesting process was made more efficient. Good grain prices in these years encouraged farmers to move to the reaper more quickly than otherwise might have been the case, and the adoption of the reaper made farmers able to respond to the opportunities for increased grain production. By 1871, there were nearly 37 000 mowers and reapers in operation in Ontario alone.[7]

Strong demand together with investment in new technology meant that wheat continued to be an important export product for at least a decade after the removal of Corn Law preferences. Marvin McInnis, for instance, identifies the mid-1850s as the peak years of this staple trade.[8] Clearly the removal of the Corn Laws had little effect on Canada's ability to compete in British markets. When the end to the export trade came, as it did by 1869, when Canada became a net importer of wheat and flour, it did so, not because farmers were forced out of wheat production because of a lack of markets but, rather, because they were drawn to more profitable ones for other products. As in the contiguous region south of the border, expanding urban markets together with declining transport costs created by railway construction increased the relative profitability of devoting agricultural land to mixed farming.

Atlantic Canada's fisheries were not directly affected by the end of the mercantile arrangements. Shipping and shipbuilding were more closely tied to the policy, as seen in earlier chapters, so their fates were less certain. As it turned out, shipbuilding boomed after 1842 (see Table 4.3); 262 vessels were built in the Maritime provinces in 1843, totalling more than 26 000 tons. In 1864, the historic peak of the industry, 586 vessels were built, more than 210 000 tons. The number of ships constructed more than doubled, and the tonnage they represented increased more than eightfold in two decades. Clearly, any initial advantage that had been derived from participation in the British mercantile system had long since been transformed into a natural competitive advantage, resting on the skills and resource endowments of the region.

The trend in shipping more or less paralleled that for shipbuilding. Tonnage on registry in Atlantic ports fell off slightly in the mid-1840s, but then climbed more or less continuously and peaked in the early 1880s. The main business was carrying American staple products — grain, cotton, and tobacco — to British and European markets. In 1863–64, this trade made up over 70 percent of the voyages of vessels on registry in four of the ports. The West Indies contributed another 10 percent, with the remaining trade distributed around the world.[9] As in the case of shipbuilding, whatever initial advantage the region had derived from the British mercantile system had been parlayed into a natural competitiveness.

The Reciprocity Treaty

The end of the British mercantile system may not have been the economic catastrophe for the staples trades that some had predicted in 1846. Nevertheless, a vision that had propelled ambitious merchants and shaped government policy had collapsed. There was much less certainty about the future of key exports, such as timber and wheat, to Britain. The British purchaser could now look to the world market without paying duties. Canadians thus looked for alternative places to send their products and, after 1846, politicians and businessmen increasingly focussed their enthusiasms south of the border. If Canada could not capture the American carrying trade, perhaps it could sell some of its produce to the Americans.

The attraction of the United States as a market was possible because of the tremendous changes that had taken place over the past couple of decades. When Upper Canada was created in 1791, the United States had a population of 4 million. By 1850, that population had increased to 23.4 million, much of it clustered along the British North American border. Moreover, recent years had seen the beginning of meaningful industrialization in New England and other areas. The demand for raw materials to build the factories and the houses of the growing cities, to feed the machines and the increasingly urban population, grew rapidly through the 1840s. By 1850, nearly $5 million worth of such goods as timber, sawn planks, fish, and other primary and semiprocessed resources were going south annually. American consumption of British North American products was still much smaller than was British consumption, but it was growing. Given such figures, it was natural that Canadians would look to the United States as an alternative export market.

Once Canada became interested in the American market, the idea of free trade followed naturally. A special arrangement with the United States might help restore some of the certainty about access to markets for staple products closed by the loss of favour in the British market. The reverse side of the coin was the fact that the United States had heretofore used tariff barriers to discourage key British North American products. For example, Canada's biggest export, timber, was taxed at an ad valorem rate of 20 percent. Other key products faced similar barriers. British North American exporters were thus at a disadvantage in trying to compete with American producers. Lowering American barriers might permit them to develop this new market.

The reciprocity movement had its origins in Canada West. For many years, the American market had been looked upon covetously by businessmen such William Hamilton Merritt of Welland Canal fame. Then, when the abolition of mercantilism led to the short but frightening annexation movement in Montreal, Canadian businessmen and politicians began to consider some sort of trade arrangement with the United States as an alternative. Such an arrangement would provide the benefits of commercial access to the neighbour to the south while avoiding the extreme action advocated by the annexationists. In other words, as Governor Elgin argued on behalf of his Canadian government, reciprocity was an alternative to annexation. It was also, from the more material point of view, seen as good business. Thus, from the late 1840s on, talk of reciprocity began to be heard more and more frequently in Canada.

The first formal move in the Atlantic region came in 1849, when New Brunswick organized a conference on the question. Prince Edward Island was the first colony to move explicitly, passing a bill in 1849 providing for free trade for a specified list of commodities if the United States reciprocated. Similar measures were enacted by Nova Scotia and New Brunswick in 1850. Only in Newfoundland was there little interest in the proposal. Opinions in the Atlantic region shifted, beginning in 1852. By then, it had become apparent that the Americans would demand access to the offshore fisheries of the Maritime colonies as part of any package. Such competition would seem to cut into the profitability of the Maritime fishery. Nova Scotia became the most outspoken critic of the idea of concessions, and found support in New Brunswick and Prince Edward Island. Interestingly, Newfoundland, which had been indifferent until this point, remained out of step with the other provinces by suddenly pressing for an agreement.

The result of this interest in North American trade liberalization was the Reciprocity Treaty of 1854. The negotiations for the treaty provide an almost casebook lesson concerning two North American realities. First, it was the smaller party — Canada — that was most interested in the treaty. American interest was confined to certain specialized sectors and was countered by suspicion or apathy on the part of most politicians and businessmen. Thus, it was up to Canada to find a means of gaining acceptance in the United States. (It is interesting that, more than 130 years later, a similar pattern developed during the Canadian-American free-trade negotiations of the 1980s.)

Second, the treaty illustrated both the regional differences that are so much a part of Canadian history and the realities of power when such regional differences clash. The one thing that the Americans were interested in was fish. Moreover, strict British enforcement of boundary regulations concerning fishing in Maritime waters led to a series of confrontations between American fishermen and British naval patrols. Diplomacy was now becoming enmeshed in trade policy. The Americans were apathetic about trade with the Province of Canada, but the dual desire to avoid diplomatic confrontation with Great Britain and to gain access to the Maritime fisheries began to alter their view.

There was one complication. Several of the Atlantic colonies, with Nova Scotia at the forefront, were nervous about opening their waters to the American fishermen, even in return for access to American waters. It mattered little, however. By this time both Canada and Great Britain were interested in pursuing the treaty for diplomatic and economic reasons. Nova Scotia was pressured into accepting the 1854 Reciprocity Treaty. The tactic was simple: Britain threatened to withdraw its patrol boats, thus making American encroachment likely, with or without a treaty. The Province of Canada was not to be denied in 1854; neither would it be denied in 1867, under a much more important economic and political arrangement.

The Reciprocity Treaty, signed in June 1854, reflected the orientation of the British North American economies toward primary resources. Articles I and II of the treaty provided for reciprocal access, with some exceptions, to the coastal fisheries. Article III provided for the free importation into each country of a range of products, from grains and breadstuffs through animals and animal products to fish, timber, and minerals. Altogether, the items covered accounted for approximately 90 percent of the existing trade across the British North American–U.S. border. The treaty was to last for ten years and, thereafter, for twelve months following an announcement by one party of intention to terminate it. This the Americans did in 1865; the treaty came to an end on March 17, 1866.

The traditional view of the Reciprocity Treaty stresses its contribution to the economic growth of the colonies in the 1850s and 1860s. Certainly, casual examination of the data suggests such a correlation. Trade between British North America and the United States increased in the period covered by the treaty, and the United States gained in relative importance as an export market. Total Canadian exports to the United States rose fourfold, from $8.6 million in 1854 to $34.8 million in 1866, or from 40.7 percent of total exports, at the beginning of the treaty, to 69.2 percent, at the end. The change in imports was less marked, rising from $15.5 million to $20.4 million over the same period, with the share remaining constant at 38 percent.

The problem, of course, is that there were many other important developments in this period in Canada, the United States, and abroad that might have affected trade between the two nations at least as much as did the treaty. To determine the effect the treaty actually had, two questions need to be posed and answered. First, what was the probable impact of the Reciprocity Treaty on the volume of trade between Canada and the United States? Second, whatever impact there was on volume, how did these changes in trade flows contribute to real economic gains?

The first question can be addressed with the aid of some data assembled by Officer and Smith for their influential study of the Reciprocity Treaty, presented in Table 7.1. The obvious place to start is with changes in trade patterns in the initial year of the treaty and in the year after its termination, since these can be more confidently ascribed to the treaty than can figures stretching over a decade and a half. Looking at exports first, Officer and Smith's data show that shipments of items covered by the treaty increased by more than $8 million in 1855 from what they were in 1854, or by 96 percent. They rose again in 1856, fell off to about 50 percent above their pretreaty level for three years, and then jumped again during the Civil War.

This result certainly suggests that the treaty was effective. To be certain, however, other possible explanations need to be ruled out. One possibility is that Canadian reciprocity items were more attractive (relatively cheaper) for reasons that had nothing to do with reciprocity — abundant harvests or transportation improvements coming on stream, for example. If so, however, exports of the same items to the rest of the world should have increased as well. In fact, they fell in value terms from 1854 to 1855 by $3.9 million, or 37 percent. The apparent conclusion is that the treaty did divert some primary products from offshore to American markets. Whatever effect there was, however, was temporary. By 1856, exports of reciprocity items to the rest of the world were back to their 1854 levels.

Another possible explanation for the 96 percent increase in the export of reciprocity items to the United States in 1855 is that American demand for Canadian products increased for reasons that had nothing to do with reciprocity — a relative inflation or a general disruption in production, such as that experienced later during the Civil War, for example. If so, however, all Canadian exports to the United States should have increased, not just reciprocity items. In fact, shipments of nonreciprocity items declined slightly, by $8000, or 3.4 percent, again suggesting that the treaty must have had some initial effect. However, as this decline in exports of nonreciprocity items to the United States is less than the $556 000 (26.6 percent) registered in the same category for the rest of the world, some change in the U.S. economy unrelated to reciprocity was possibly under way as well.

The situation with respect to imports is similar. Imports of reciprocity items from the United States increased nearly fourfold in 1855 over 1854 figures, or by $5.8 million. Sales from the rest of the world fell slightly at the same time, as did imports of nonreciprocity items from both the United States and abroad, so the explanation cannot be a general deterioration of Canadian competitiveness. Imports remained at the 1855 level until 1862, when they jumped significantly for two years before dropping back to 1855 values.

The figures for the termination of the treaty are less conclusive.

There was a large drop in exports of reciprocity items from Canada in 1867, although this drop is largely explained by the fact that the 1866 figure was abnormally high. There was a glut of shipments going ahead of the announced reimposition of tariffs. Imports of reciprocity items from the United States fell by 43 percent, while imports of nonreciprocity items rose by 21 percent, which is consistent with what abrogation of the treaty would imply. But imports of reciprocity goods from the rest of the world fell by 13 percent

TABLE 7.1

Canadian Trade Statistics, 1850–1868

(thousands of dollars)

	Imports into Canada of			
	Reciprocity Articles from		*Nonreciprocity Articles from*	
Year	*U.S.*	*Rest of World*	*U.S.*	*Rest of World*
1850	1 238	187	5 358	10 197
1851	1 039	355	7 325	12 713
1852	940	453	7 536	11 355
1853	1 281	657	10 499	19 543
1854	1 976	855	13 556	24 141
1855	7 726	649	13 102	14 608
1856	8 083	1 083	14 621	19 797
1857	8 642	1 025	11 582	18 183
1858	5 565	1 036	10 070	12 407
1859	7 106	1 424	10 487	14 538
1860	7 069	1 407	10 204	15 766
1861	9 981	1 316	11 088	20 670
1862	14 431	1 700	10 742	21 727
1863	12 339	1 667	10 770	21 188
1864[a]	4 876	657	5 551	12 799
1865	9 132	1 851	10 457	23 180
1866	8 752	2 213	11 672	31 165
1867	6 114	1 925	14 159	36 852
1868	5 461	1 451	16 993	33 343

Year	*Exports from Canada of* Reciprocity Articles from U.S.	Reciprocity Articles from Rest of World	Nonreciprocity Articles from U.S.	Nonreciprocity Articles from Rest of World
1850	4 756	5 684	196	1 324
1851	3 860	7 188	212	1 704
1852	6 048	6 672	236	1 100
1853	8 696	10 524	340	2 452
1854	8 412	10 508	236	2 092
1855	16 508	6 652	228	1 536
1856	17 776	10 400	204	1 428
1857	12 912	10 640	296	1 600
1858	11 656	9 190	274	909
1859	13 625	8 455	297	725
1860	18 096	12 787	332	1 146
1861	13 972	18 646	414	1 685
1862	14 566	15 289	498	1 326
1863	17 573	16 608	2 477	2 689
1864[a]	6 769	4 118	953	1 067
1865	20 567	13 994	2 372	2 675
1866	31 337	13 245	3 433	2 242
1867	22 051	16 108	3 533	3 278
1868	19 376	15 516	4 974	4 672

[a]Data available for January 1 to June 30 only; 1850–63 data for year ending December 31; 1865–68 data for year ending June 30.

Source: Lawrence Officer and Lawrence Smith, "The Canadian American Reciprocity Treaty of 1855 to 1868," *Journal of Economic History* 28 (December 1968): 600.

and those of nonreciprocity items rose by 18 percent as well; clearly, other factors were at work.

Officer and Smith go on to examine the impacts of the treaty on particular sectors.[10] They find little effect on the trade in timber, animals, wool, and barley, and some possible adverse consequences for the Canadian cheese industry. Wheat, oats, and flour probably benefited, which m on trade flows, then, pales in comparison to those of the U.S. Civil War, railway construction, and general income and population growth in the two countries.

The final issue is what impact even these small trade-flow effects had on economic welfare. Officer and Smith conclude that the trade that was affected — that in grains — was largely convenience trade, meaning that the way grain supplies were shipped to markets in the two countries was altered to save on transport costs. Since relative price differences were, therefore, likely small prior to the trade, the welfare effects would be minimal. Reciprocity added little to real income growth in Canada in this period.

Conclusion

Generally, the staples trades of the British North American colonies adjusted fairly well to the rather abrupt end of a system that had, for so long, shaped their economic and political development. Existing activities survived and even prospered for a time, and new products were developed and new markets found. The relative ease of the transition would have surprised those generations of colonial politicians and businessmen who had lobbied so hard and so long in London for retention and extension of imperial privileges.

Notes

1. R.M. McInnis, "Canada in the World Market for Forest Products, 1850–1895," unpublished ms., Queen's University, 1988.
2. A.R.M. Lower, *Great Britain's Woodyard: British America and the Timber Trade, 1763–1867* (Montreal and Kingston: McGill-Queen's University Press, 1973), 260.
3. Department of Public Works (Province of Canada), Annual Reports, 1846–1850.
4. D.H. Akenson, *The Irish in Ontario: A Study in Rural History* (Montreal and Kingston: McGill-Queen's University Press, 1984), 29.
5. Akenson, *The Irish in Ontario*, 32.
6. John McCallum, *Unequal Beginnings: Agriculture and Economic Development in Quebec and Ontario until 1870* (Toronto: University of Toronto Press, 1980), 124, 216, 127. These figures include exports to Canada East and the Maritimes.
7. Richard Pomfret, "The Mechanization of Reaping in Nineteenth Century Ontario," in *Perspectives on Canadian Economic History*, edited by D. McCalla (Toronto: Copp Clark Pitman, 1987), 81–95.

8. Marvin McInnis, "The Changing Structure of Canadian Agriculture, 1867–1897," *Journal of Economic History* 42, no. 1 (March 1982): 194.
9. Eric W. Sager and Lewis R. Fischer, "Atlantic Canada and the Age of Sail Revisited," *Canadian Historical Review* 63, no. 2 (1982): 125–50 (Figure 1).
10. Lawrence Officer and Lawrence Smith, "The Canadian American Reciprocity Treaty of 1855 to 1866," *Journal of Economic History* 28 (December 1968): 598–623.

Further Reading

Masters, D.C. *The Reciprocity Treaty of 1854*. Carleton Library #9. Toronto: McClelland and Stewart, 1963.

Officer, L., and L. Smith. "The Canadian American Reciprocity Treaty of 1855 to 1866." *Journal of Economic History* 28 (December 1968): 598–623.

Pomfret, Richard. "The Mechanization of Reaping in Nineteenth Century Ontario." In *Perspectives on Canadian Economic History*, edited by D. McCalla. Toronto: Copp Clark Pitman, 1987.

Sager, Eric W., and Lewis R. Fischer. "Atlantic Canada and the Age of Sail Revisited." *Canadian Historical Review* 63, no. 2 (1982): 125–50.

Tucker, G. *The Canadian Commercial Revolution, 1845–1851*. Carleton Library #19. Toronto: McClelland and Stewart, 1970.

C H A P T E R

8

Railways and Industrialization

As we have seen, the staples trades of the British North American colonies underwent profound change in the years from the union in 1841 to Confederation in 1867. The pioneer economy of Canada, with its heavy dependence on human and capital inflows, was replaced by a more mature agricultural and commercial system. Atlantic shipping and shipbuilding moved from being a small offshoot of the fishing industry and of the Navigation Acts to become a significant presence in their own right. Equally important to this era, though, and very much a portent of the future, was the development of more complex production techniques locally, including the beginnings of industrialization. As British North America grew in population, and wealth and skills, its economy was able to employ more advanced technologies derived from advanced industrial nations.

Railways

The impact of technology on the economy was demonstrated most clearly in the area of transportation. Railways, operational as practical vehicles of transportation in Europe since the 1830s, transformed the nature of business in the colonies, the structure of cities and villages, and the life of the average citizen. To enthusiasts, they were almost supernatural in their potential. "Poverty, indifference, the bigotry or jealousy of religious denominations, local dissensions or political demagogueism may stifle or neutralize the influence of the best intended efforts of an educational system but that invisible power [steam] . . . will assuredly overcome the prejudices of mental weakness or the design of mental tyrants."[1]

Railways were particularly important in British North America because of the long distances involved in moving people and goods, a factor relatively unknown in more compact European nations. As was true in the United States, transportation costs assumed enormous proportions as the frontier of settlement moved farther and farther inland. The expensive canals developed during the 1840s had been intended to meet this problem, but canals had their limitations. First, they could improve the movement of goods only along natural waterways; they could do nothing to assist inland settlements. Further, and this provided the second great attraction of railways, canals were subject to the tyranny of the Canadian winter. From late fall through spring each year, transport of goods ground to a near halt as the waterways froze over. Railways, in contrast, were relatively immune to the effects of winter and could reach beyond the waterways to wherever potential traffic justified their presence. Finally, they were faster than water transportation and, in comparison with any other type of land transport, much less likely to damage the goods in transit. For the settler who wished to break out of social and economic isolation, for the merchant who hoped to make his shipping system more efficient, for the promoter who wished to sell off lands, and for the nationalists and enthusiasts, the technology of the steam railway seemed the answer.

Yet, the vast distances and scattered population that made the railway so important to British North America also created problems. Railways were tremendously expensive, much more so than canals and much more so than any other project undertaken in British North America until this time. There was not sufficient speculative capital in the colonies to undertake such risky ventures. Thus, with the exception of a successful but short railway line along the Richelieu River, built in 1836, British North Americans continued to plan, dream, and promote, but not to build, railways through the 1830s and 1840s. Government-supported canals remained the focus of transportation planning through the 1840s, even as the United States expanded its railway network from about 100 miles in 1830 to 9000 miles by 1850, and approximately 30 000 by 1860.

By 1850, however, circumstances were becoming more favourable for would-be railway-builders. First, Great Britain's stock of private investment funds was growing rapidly and its domestic interest rates were falling. The success of the industrial revolution had generated tremendous amounts of income, and ever-greater percentages of it were available for investment. In the 1830s and 1840s, the great enthusiasm of British investors had been for domestic railways, but, by 1850, the initial boom of British railway construction was slowing and opportunities for domestic investment declined. To the evolving financier class in Great Britain, overseas investments were more attractive than they had been a decade or so earlier.

Even so, the small colonies of British North America were not all that attractive as a destination for British capital; speculative railway ventures by unknown Canadian promoters were even less so. Something would have to be done to encourage private investment, and the only body powerful enough to have any meaningful influence was the government itself. If railways were going to be built in British North America, governments would have to get involved, as they had earlier with canals. This time, however, authorities were determined to avoid direct public ownership and sought, instead, to make private-investment schemes more attractive.

The Province of Canada proceeded by throwing its credit behind railway ventures. In 1849, it passed the Railway Loan Guarantee Act. This act stipulated that, if railways met certain conditions, they could have the interest on their bond issues guaranteed by the Government of Canada. The Municipal Loan Act of 1852 provided an alternative channel to the same end. Provincial credit was made available to those municipalities that wished to get involved in the game of railway subsidization. Many did, and towns and villages soon joined the rush to spread the magic of the steel rail into their community. To a society both enthusiastic about and often directly involved in railway ventures, it made eminent sense. To the Canadian politician whose personal investment in railways often meshed conveniently with his enthusiasm for such legislation, a chance for personal profit was enhanced. Most important to the British investor, it reduced the risks sufficiently to make British North American railways a worthwhile venture.

As it turned out, the Canadian government was nearly driven to bankruptcy. Municipalities foundered on the rocks of ill-conceived investments, and British investors found their loans disappearing into the pockets of Canadian contractors and promoters. Nevertheless, it was fortunate for Canada's transportation system that such events were not foreseen. The commitments were made, the investment came in, and the railways were built.

From 1850 through 1857, the Province of Canada underwent a boom in railway construction. Financing came not only from British capitalists but from private Canadian sources, from the United States, and from municipalities. Major completions included the St. Lawrence and Atlantic, operating between Montreal and Portland, Maine, by 1853; the Great Western railway, from Niagara through Hamilton and London to Detroit, by 1855; and, in the same year, the Ontario, Simcoe and Lake Huron, from Toronto to Collingwood (see Map 8.1).

All of these were feeder lines, designed to tie the farming hinterlands of Canada to urban centres along the Great Lakes and St. Lawrence. More ambitious was the Grand Trunk Railway, which used British engineering skills and British capital to run from Quebec City in the east to Sarnia in the west by 1859. It tied together the major cities of the province and cost more than $67 million to complete.[2] Something of the enormous expense of railways can be comprehended when it is realized that this sum alone was greater than all the money spent on public works — canals, bridges, roads, buildings — by the Province of Canada between the Act of Union in 1841 and Confederation.

By 1857, the boom was over. Canada may have perceived that it needed railways, but that does not mean that the railways actually built were paying ventures. The province had gone from 66 miles of railway in 1849 to 1800 miles by the time the Grand Trunk reached Sarnia. The traffic generated often could not bear the costs of operating the railway, much less its capital investment. On occasion after occasion, the government had to step in to rescue collapsing railways, to pay interest on bond defaults, and to explain why politicians with large investments in railways always seemed to be willing to pour good government money after bad. Henceforth, at least until the annexation of the west provided new temptations, railway construction proceeded much more cautiously.

The economic impact of the railway was enormous in several ways. First, even more than the Reciprocity Treaty and perhaps as much as the increase in agricultural exports, the railway construction boom of the 1850s accounts for the prosperity of those

MAP 8.1
Rail Lines in the Province of Canada, 1860

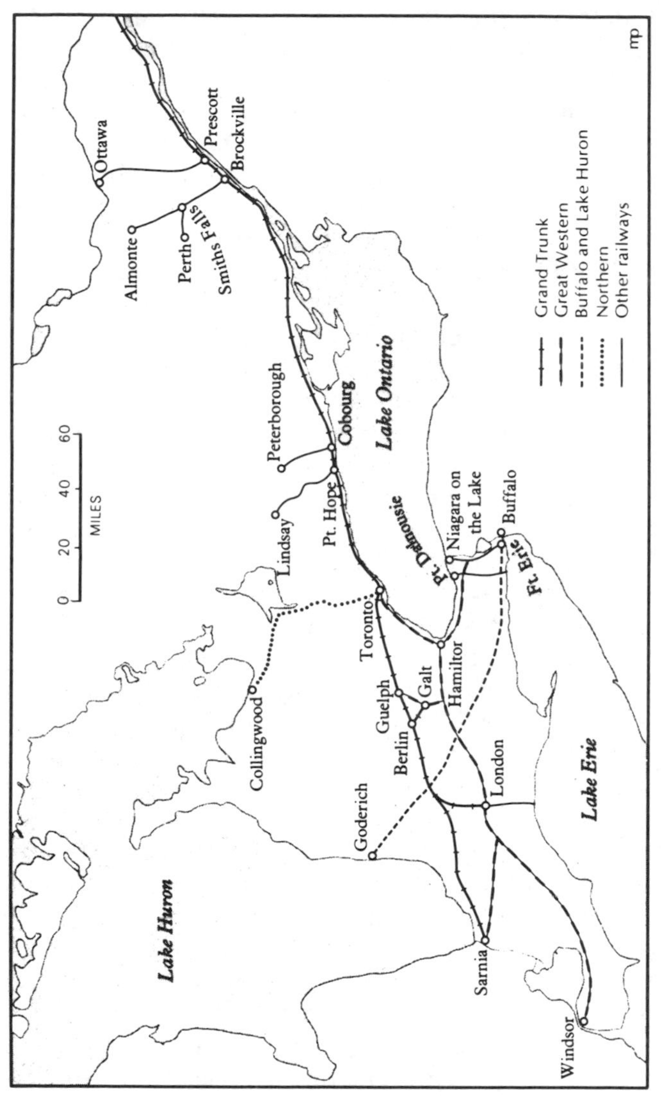

Source: R. Cole Harris and John Warkentin, *Canada Before Confederation: A Study in Historical Geography* (Toronto: Oxford University Press, 1974), 155.

years (see Table 8.1). Millions of dollars of foreign investment flowed into Canada, largely from Britain, generating employment for the huge work forces necessary for railway survey and construction.

The coming of the railway also had a major impact on the metropolis-hinterland relationship within the colony. Those urban centres that were at the terminus of key railways could expand their own hinterlands and increasingly tighten their economic control of the regions around them. Village artisans, small industries, and local wholesalers, previously protected by the costs of transport, now found themselves vulnerable to more cheaply made goods sent by train from the larger urban centres. Local newspapers began their long slide into obscurity as the larger, flashier, and more powerful newspapers of the cities could now penetrate the countryside by means of railway. The Toronto *Globe*, for example, was able to extend its range of influence over much of Canada West. Its political views, centred in Toronto, now helped shape the thinking of a large portion of the province.

The railway thus allowed Montreal, Toronto, Hamilton, and a few other centres increasingly to dominate smaller communities. The Great Western, which extended its line to Toronto in the later 1850s; the Grand Trunk; and the Ontario, Simcoe and Huron (later the Northern) meant that Toronto businesses now had easy access for their goods to all of what is now Southern Ontario. Likewise, the St. Lawrence and Atlantic and the Grand Trunk gave Montreal increased dominance over the other towns and villages of Canada East. The process would take a generation, but the configuration of railways meant that, by 1860, the trends were set.

There was a certain relentless logic to it all. It was because a few centres were larger than others that the railways gravitated toward them. That gravitation, in turn, confirmed the dominance of those centres and allowed them to increase the range and variety of their influence. Population movements then responded to new opportunities in these larger cities. Montreal grew from some 40 000 inhabitants at the time of the union to 115 000 by 1871; Toronto, from a mere 14 000 to 59 000. The former would almost double, and the latter almost triple, its 1871 population within another twenty years.

Railways also affected the nature of manufacturing and the structure and location of industries, and were instrumental in creating

TABLE 8.1

New Railway Miles in Operation and Net Capital Formation Resulting from Railway Transport and Telegraph, 1850–1862

Year	*Railway Miles Opened*	*Net Capital Formation ($ millions)*
1850	12	1.3
1851	63	2.5
1852	118	6.2
1853	444	13.7
1854	332	13.3
1855	335	16.7
1856	441	9.2
1857	103	7.3
1858	150	10.3
1859	520	4.5
1860	44	5.2
1861	9	1.8
1862	0	1.5

Source: Lawrence H. Officer and Lawrence B. Smith, "The Canadian American Reciprocity Treaty of 1855 to 1866," *Journal of Economic History* 28 (December 1968): 603, 609.

new industries. There was one thing railways did not do, however: they did not supplant canals or natural waterways as the primary transportation system for bulk goods. Water transport remained cheaper than rail, and the canal system of the Canadas continued to carry the majority of Canada's export goods for many years to come. One contemporary set of figures estimated that only 6.6 percent of grain reaching Montreal in 1862 came by rail and that only 5.3 percent going seaward from Montreal did so.[3] Railways supplemented the canal system, acted as feeders to it, and operated more quickly and without regard to season. For the farmer and merchant, what the railways did was to extend the reach of, and make more flexible, the existing transportation system of the Canadas. They did not replace it.

National Gallery of Canada/21303 (P72:001:18 RG)

A Grand Trunk locomotive, c. ***1860.*** *The Grand Trunk Railway, which tied together the major cities of the province, cost more than $67 million to build. The line from Toronto to Montreal opened in 1856; by 1859, it ran from Quebec City in the east to Sarnia in the west. The Grand Trunk Railway was later taken over by the government and was eventually absorbed into the Canadian National Railway system.*

In the Maritimes, railway fever caught hold as it had in the Province of Canada, but, as it turned out, the construction of such expensive projects was even more difficult for these smaller colonies. Those strongly in favour of railway construction in the Maritimes had two objectives in mind. The first was to consolidate the hold of the main urban centres — Saint John and Halifax, essentially — over their own hinterlands. The second was to establish the region as the entrepôt of trade between the continent and Europe, which meant constructing a trunk line to Quebec, or to Maine, or, in the most ambitious scheme, to both.

Plans to tap the trade of the continent, and the difficulties in doing so, are best illustrated by the main proposals vying for financing in the 1840s. The Halifax and Quebec line was to run from Halifax through eastern New Brunswick to Quebec. The European and North American project (one of the more grandiose titles ever bestowed upon a railway project) was intended to proceed from Halifax, through southern New Brunswick, to Portland, Maine, linking to Canada from there via the St. Lawrence and

Atlantic. The British government was unwilling to finance a line through U.S. territory, however, while the governments of Nova Scotia and New Brunswick fought over routing within the region. No resolution was found, and the problems were carried over to the post-Confederation era as the Intercolonial project.

In the meantime, construction of lines within the region proceeded, albeit slowly. The government of Nova Scotia built a line from Halifax to Truro, with a branch to Windsor, in the 1850s. In 1867, the line was extended to Pictou, giving Nova Scotia a total of 145 miles of railway by 1867. In New Brunswick, the old St. Andrews and Quebec project, dating back to the 1820s, was resurrected in 1847 as the New Brunswick and Canada, and, from that date in 1867, 126 miles of track were laid between Saint John and Woodstock. Another line of 108 miles was completed between Saint John and Shediac.

By Confederation, the Maritimes had fewer than 400 miles of track in operation, and no trunk lines to either Canada or the United States. They had managed to link Halifax to both the Bay of Fundy and the gulf region, and Saint John to the gulf. They had also, in the process, amassed a considerable debt burden that was weighing on the slim resources of the colonial governments. Both this debt and the desire to secure the links to the interior were instrumental in pushing the colonies toward Confederation.

Industrialization

The linkages to heavy industry promoted by railways point to an important but as yet open question in Canadian economic development. Was British North America moving toward industrialization during the 1850s? To pose this question is not to argue that it became a full-fledged industrial power before Confederation. Obviously, primary resources remained the source of livelihood for the great majority of Canadians. Rather, it is a question of whether the population growth, prosperity, and linkages resulting from railway construction in the 1850s prompted the Canadian economy to diversify into a range of manufacturing goods previously imported from outside of the colony and changed the nature of production, moving from smaller "cottage" operations to larger factory systems.

Before that issue can be addressed, two preliminary points have to be made. The first is that there was always a range of cottage industries and small ventures catering to the local market, finding niches in the trade network from the metropolitan centres. The development of such activities in Halifax and St. John's was noted earlier. New France had its share of ventures, and, by the 1780s, in Quebec, a considerable range of activity — commercial, financial, and industrial — was being carried on in the province. As the frontier expanded into what became Upper Canada, a range of activities soon followed. Sawmills and grist mills were there from the beginning. They would remain the largest employers in the manufacturing sector through to midcentury. Distilleries and breweries were not far behind. Tanneries, saltworks, and even ironworks had come into being before the War of 1812. As well, local service industries — such as the baker, blacksmith, and harness maker — could often grow from a one-person operation to a small industry as local population developed. Through the 1820s to 1840s, operations grew more complex. Paper-making put in an appearance by 1830. Shipbuilding grew apace with the increasing trade along the Great Lakes. By the 1851 census, a marine railway and shipyard in Toronto employed some 50 workers.[4] Agricultural-implement companies evolved to meet the needs of the still-dominant farming population and would, within another generation, develop into one of Canada's leading manufacturing exports.

None of these industries was very large. Even by midcentury, only a few employed more than a score of workers. Further, their presence does not change the fact that all of the British North American colonies depended on the sale of raw and semiprocessed primary resources. Nor were the basic trade patterns of a colonial society altered. The flow of goods from Britain was dominated by manufactured goods and by luxury items; that from Canada, by primary resources or semiprocessed goods. Such small industries, however, were a necessary prerequisite to more significant industrialization, for, in the successful merchandizing, forwarding, tanning, distilling, and myriad other operations, an entrepreneurial instinct was being developed, as were a skilled work force, the technology, and the pools of savings that could respond should the opportunity arise.

The second point is that, quite aside from these small industries, the colonies were capitalist and commercial long before they were industrial. From the shippers and traders in the Atlantic region through the Hamiltons, McTavishes, and Molsons in Canada, there was a strong orientation toward business from the beginning. By the time of the union, Halifax, Saint John, Toronto, and Montreal were, above all, cities of "merchants, tradesmen and artisans."[5]

In the years between the conquest and the beginning of the nineteenth century, Canadian merchants did, it was true, find themselves faced by a military-government elite that held the business of trade and profit making in disdain. The confrontation was short-lived, however, for there was not and could not be a strong-enough landed gentry to counter the power and pretensions of the businessmen. Indeed, the largest landowners were often active businessmen. By 1800, if not before, the values of commerce and growth had triumphed in Upper Canada. In Lower Canada, the complex relationships between language, religion, and occupation made the issue more difficult to resolve, but, as the early governors found, the business class of Montreal, French or English, did not accept a limited role in society. Certainly by 1840, if not before, the old aristocratic and anti-commercial social attitudes of Lower Canada were an anachronism. Profit, loss, extensive growth, efficiency, and a myth of individualism pervaded the Canadian economy and the Canadian political scene by the early nineteenth century. Values and political institutions were geared to the move to industrialism. When the opportunity came, there would be no great difficulties posed by either the social climate or the political structures. Indeed, when the British appointed a former president of the Board of Trade as governor general in 1841, they were, in a symbolic way, recognizing the hegemony of the capitalist system in the new Province of Canada.

The profits earned by the commercial class also prepared the way for industrialization. Success in commerce led to pools of savings that became available for entrepreneurial applications of technology to production. It was John Molson, using new wealth acquired from the thirst of Canadians, who, in 1809, built the first steamboat in the Canadas. It was John Frothingham of Montreal who first gained wealth as a hardware merchant and then used his income to begin his own industrial productions.[6] Peter McGill of Montreal began in the fur trade before the War of 1812 and moved from there into timber, shipping, sawmills, and the Marmora ironworks.[7] There was, thus, by the time of the union, a considerable business class with the outlook and the income to be ready when circumstances dictated changes in the Canadian economy. In this, as in so many other ways, the Canada of the union was quite different than it had been even a generation before. Diversification was a natural process, as successful merchants and manufacturers ventured into new areas.

Appropriate governmental policies, social institutions, entrepreneurial values, and available capital prepared the way for industrialization. Also necessary was a labour force. One of the most striking features of the New World had been the relative abundance of resources and the scarcity of people. Labour-intensive activity could, therefore, be hampered by high wage rates and an absence of suitable skills. Certainly travellers from Europe, throughout the nineteenth century, were struck by the affluence of Canadian workers and by the high wages they commanded.

Any discussion in labour history is fraught with debate. The role of class, the relationship between classes, and the degree of exploitation or benefit derived from class relationships are always contested issues, in the history of Canada no less so than elsewhere. There does seem to be agreement, however, that, sometime between 1840 and 1860, there developed in Canada a significant non-landowning working class. The presence of such a class both differentiated the Canada of Confederation from that of a half-century before and was central to the development of manufacturing.

Changing opportunities and options for immigrants were crucial to the evolution of the working class. On the one hand, it became increasingly expensive for new arrivals to homestead. Some have argued that there was a deliberate government policy designed to create a labour force. Others see the outcome as incidental to the increase in population and the receding of the frontier of settlement. Population increased dramatically with the high immigration of the 1840s. Moreover, the absence of savings on the part of many of the Irish famine immigrants meant that there was less opportunity to take up such settlement opportunities as existed.[8] Certainly, by Confederation, there existed a significant "class" of individuals who owned no agricultural land, and often no real property of any sort, but who followed opportunities to earn wages where they could.

Yet, it is simplistic to see the creation of a landless work force as something arising from the misery and desperation of famine immigration. Recent works have shown that a high percentage of the Irish did have some means and did settle on the land. Also important, therefore, were those forces attracting individuals away from the settlement process.

In this instance, both the 1840s and the 1850s were important.

The drive that began after the union to complete the canals required large numbers of labourers. There was little industrial technology applied to the construction of canals, and it was not uncommon in the 1840s to have upwards of 6000 people employed during peak seasons. As the canal boom ended in the late 1840s, the railway boom came along. Much work has yet to be done on whether the same workers moved from site to site and from canals, to, say, logging, to railway construction, or whether successions of workers moved through the labour camps to eventually settle on the land. Whichever case proves most correct, however, the fact is that, at least from the 1840s, a permanent work force existed. Government began to concern itself with such issues as unemployment and with civil disturbance from groups of workers on canal and railway sites, and other such matters. That is not to say that there was, as yet, a large number of factory wage-earners, in the modern sense. Such a development would not come until later. The development of a landless class, however, provided the possibilities for the evolution of a wage-earning factory class to come into being once it was required.

The presence of the necessary prerequisites to industry meant that, as opportunities developed, it was possible to take advantage of them. Initially, as might be expected, economic diversification in the Canadas was not designed to compete in the international marketplace with British, Continental, or American firms. Rather, as with the earlier grist mills, the industries of the 1840s and 1850s arose as adjuncts to other sectors of the economy. Once developed, however, the technology and expertise were in place. As firms developed, it was increasingly possible to supplant foreign suppliers.

Typical in its origins, though not in its tremendous success, was the Massey Company. Hart Massey had typified the Upper Canadian settler of the first phase of development. He made money as much, or more, by clearing land and reselling it as by any of the crops he grew. Then, on a trip to the United States, he saw one of the earliest mechanical threshers and began to assemble them for the Canadian market. Expertise and profits followed, and, by the later 1840s, he moved into the manufacture of the implement. An American import was replaced by a Canadian-made machine, both serving the dominant agricultural sector. As well, a firm began that was soon to be one of the world leaders in agricultural-implement production.[9]

Similar stories of assembly, repair, and then manufacturing could be recounted for steam engines, to meet the growing demand for steamers along the Great Lakes; for tanning, to meet local demands; or for the progress from sewing imported materials into clothes to the rise of a textile industry. Most dramatic of all, however, was the impact of the railway on Canadian industry. For, if companies were to operate the ultimate technology of the industrial revolution, they needed to import all those aspects of industrialism that supported such technology. A railway could not run without freight cars, locomotives, and the hundreds of parts and materials that were required to keep such complex machinery in operation.

Initially, these materials were imported, but repair facilities were necessary on site, and these facilities soon developed production capabilities. The result was that the larger railways, such as the Grand Trunk and the Great Western, soon developed their own industrial plants. These plants quickly became among the largest in British North America. By 1871, for example, the Grand Trunk operations at Pointe St-Charles, Quebec, employed some 790 employees, and those of the Great Western, at Hamilton, nearly 1000 (see Table 8.2). Rolling mills, steel foundry, and other related activities were either established directly by the companies or came into existence because of the opportunities that were available to supply the railways.[10] Several other plants operated that were owned separately from the railways but existed to supply railway needs. So impressive is the impact of the railway on manufacturing that it is tempting to argue that railways brought heavy industry to Canada.

With industry came cries for protection and support of that industry. This was a natural attitude for businessmen to take as they sought to maximize profits and reduce competition. The myth of free and open competition seems never to have blunted the drive for advantage. It was also natural that the cries would get a positive reception in Canada. It was a small colony, dependent on primary resources, and economic diversification had a great appeal. As early as 1847, Conservative politician Robert Baldwin Sullivan complained, "I do not like to see hatters importing hats, shoemakers selling foreign shoes; and tanners offering foreign leather as superior articles."[11] As manufacturing became a greater force, so, too, did the cries that foreign competition must be discouraged.

This changing attitude first showed up as policy in the Galt-

TABLE 8.2
Major Railway Establishments in Canada, 1871

(in order of size)

Firm	*No. of Employees*	*Annual Wages ($)*
Great Western: Hamilton	984	500 000
Grand Trunk: Pointe St-Charles shops	790	250 000
Northern: Toronto	561	215 818
Grand Trunk: Brantford car and locomotive shops	315	182 000
W.P. Bartley Engine Works and Foundry: Montreal	222	49 200
St. Lawrence Foundry Machine and Car Shop: Toronto	200	100 000

Source: Paul Craven and Tom Traves, "Canadian Railways as Manufactures, 1850–1880," in *Perspectives on Canadian Economic History*, edited by D. McCalla (Toronto: Copp Clark Pitman, 1987), 127–28.

Cayley Tariff of 1859. A range of manufacturers were given a significant degree of protection, and industrialists apparently responded. Recent research provides a convincing link between the imposition of duties and the subsequent expansion of manufacturing output.[12] This protection applied not only to foreign nations, such as the United States, but to the British as well. The mother country was not pleased but had to accept the fact that, having gone its own way over colonial protests in 1846, it could hardly turn around and insist that the colonies now act for the greater Empire. Canadian officials, sensitive to free traders in England and at home, did emphasize the need to raise revenue to cover the disastrous outlays to railways. Recent arguments, however, leave little doubt that protection and not just revenue was crucial in the minds of the policy makers.[13]

Industrial production was also a factor of growing importance in the Maritimes prior to Confederation. Wood-processing and ship-

Grand Trunk Railway erecting shops, Pointe St-Charles, 1860. *Larger railways required repair facilities on site, and these soon developed production capabilities. Grand Trunk developed its own industrial plant, which quickly became among the largest in British North America. By 1871, the Grand Trunk operations at Pointe St-Charles employed nearly 400 people.*

building industries dominated, understandably. Beyond these activities, there was the usual range of small concerns producing mainly for the domestic market behind the natural protection provided by transport costs. Saint John, for example, is described as an "important manufacturing centre" in 1850.[14] In addition to shipbuilding and sawmilling, the city hosted tanneries, flour mills, iron and brass foundries, furniture shops, carriage-makers, and breweries. These activities grew over the next two decades until, in 1871, manufacturing output in New Brunswick rivalled that of Ontario and Quebec in per-capita terms. The relative decline of the region came later (discussed below).

One contrast with the Province of Canada in this early period of industrialization is worth noting. As seen above, merchants in Canada moved into industrial pursuits as opportunities opened up. In the Maritimes, it has been argued,[15] the two pursuits were competitive rather than complementary. In Saint John, for example, the merchants played essentially no part in industrial developments before 1840. They remained free traders as the British mercantile system collapsed, stoutly opposing any attempts by local farmers and industrialists to secure a degree of protection from American and British imports. Industrialization did proceed after 1850, T.W. Acheson concedes, but the actions of the merchants delayed this development by two crucial decades.

Conclusion

The arrival of railways, the development of some industry, the rise of key urban centres, and protectionist policies such as those of Galt and Cayley raise the question of whether British North America, in general, and the Province of Canada, in particular, underwent a profound and crucial shift in the years between 1850 and 1867. Many historians and some economists have argued that the series of events mentioned above sowed the seeds for a fundamental reorientation both in Canadian economic thinking and in the direction of Canadian development.

According to this argument, three things came together. First, the railways created a need for a broader financial base for the government, as canals had a generation earlier. They also provided the transportation systems that allowed urban centres such as Montreal and Toronto to seek wider hinterlands. Second, the extensive growth of the prosperous and crucial agricultural frontier was threatened, even as wheat farming reached new levels of value. To put it simply: the agricultural frontier that had fuelled development in Upper Canada/Canada West from the beginning was coming to an end. In Canada East, the opportunities for new settlement had been limited from the 1830s. Overall, by the later 1850s, with Canada West filling up, there was little good crown land available for settlement left south of the Shield. Farming was also changing, and, by Confederation, wheat was no longer a dominant staple. Indeed, by 1869, Ontario was, as Quebec had long been, a net importer of wheat.

Third, and finally, the Province of Canada saw great possibilities for commercial, financial, and, most ambitious of all, industrial development. All of these things were seen as dependent on continued growth in the traditional sources of economic strength — the exploitation of primary resources and the immigration of people and

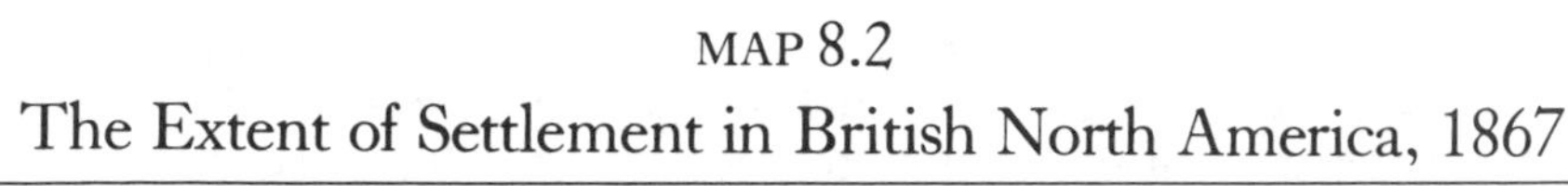

MAP 8.2
The Extent of Settlement in British North America, 1867

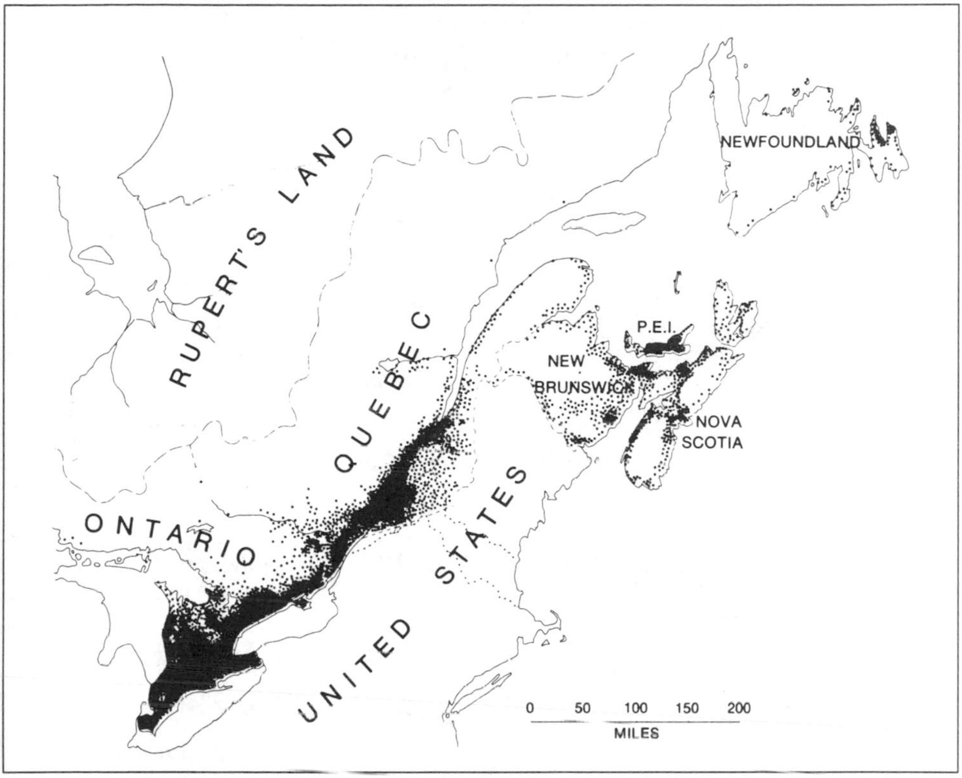

Source: John Warkentin, *Canada: A Geographical Interpretation* (Toronto: Methuen, 1970), 45.

capital. New minerals, new timber stands, and, most of all, a new agricultural frontier would be necessary if the growth of past decades was to continue.

From such concerns, the politician-businessmen, the nationalists, and the enthusiasts of the Province of Canada began to seek ways to break out of the confines of the St. Lawrence valley and to continue the extensive growth that had been so central to Canadian economic development. To the east lay the Maritime colonies, well settled and prosperous. To the west lay the vast untapped resources of the Hudson Bay territories. Only some new political arrangement, however, could allow the province to realize its economic ambitions. In this light, it is significant that one of the first to propose the idea of expansion to the west and of a federal system for all British North America was Alexander Galt, author of Canada's first protectionist tariff. The policies, purposes, and effects of Confederation on all of British North America thus cannot be divorced from the economic development that had taken place by 1867.

Notes

1. Thomas Keefer, *The Philosophy of Railroads* (Toronto: University of Toronto Press, 1972; original publication 1849), 11.
2. Michael Bliss, *Northern Enterprise: Five Centuries of Canadian Business* (Toronto: McClelland and Stewart, 1987), 184.
3. H.Y. Hind, T.C. Keefer, J.G. Hodgson, Charles Robb, M.H. Perley, and Rev. William Murray, *Eighty Years' Progress of British North America* (Toronto: L. Nichols, 1864), 207.
4. J. Spelt, *Urban Development in South-Central Ontario* (Toronto: McClelland and Stewart, 1972), 72.
5. Peter Goheen, *Victorian Toronto 1850 to 1900* (Chicago: University of Chicago Press, 1970), 50. Goheen's quote refers to Toronto, but the statement is equally correct for the other cities.
6. Bliss, *Northern Enterprise*, 161; Gerald Tulchinsky, *The River Barons: Montreal Businessmen and the Growth of Industry and Transportation, 1837–1853* (Toronto: University of Toronto Press, 1977), 12–13.
7. Tulchinsky, *The River Barons*, 21.
8. On the former view see Leo Johnson, "Land Policy, Population Growth and Social Structure in the Home District, 1793–1851," in *Historical Essays on Upper Canada*, edited by J.K. Johnson (Toronto: McClelland and Stewart, 1975), 32–57; Gary Teeple, "Land, Labour and Capital in Pre-Confederation Canada," in *Capitalism and the National Question in Canada*, edited by Gary Teeple (Toronto: University of Toronto Press, 1972), 43–46.
9. Details from Claude Bissell, *The Young Vincent Massey* (Toronto: University of Toronto Press, 1981), 8–9.
10. Paul Craven and Tom Traves, "Canadian Railways as Manufactures, 1850–1880," in *Perspectives on Canadian Economic History*, edited by D. McCalla (Toronto: Copp Clark Pitman, 1987), have done some excellent work in establishing the importance of such railway-related operations.
11. Cited in A. Den Otter, "Alexander Galt, the 1859 Tariff and Canadian Economic Nationalism," *Canadian Historical Review* 63, no. 2 (June 1982): 158.
12. D.F. Barnett, "The Galt Tariff: Incidental or Effective Protection?" *Canadian Journal of Economics* 9, no. 3 (August 1976): 389–407.
13. Den Otter, "Alexander Galt"; Barnett, "The Galt Tariff."

14. T.W. Acheson, "The Great Merchant and Economic Development in Saint John, 1820–1850," *Atlantic Canada Before Confederation*, The Acadiensis Reader, Vol. I, edited by P.A. Buckner and David Frank (Fredericton: Acadiensis Press, 1985), 177.
15. Acheson, "The Great Merchant and Economic Development," 177.

Further Reading

Barnett, D.F. "The Galt Tariff: Incidental or Effective Protection?" *Canadian Journal of Economics* 9, no. 3 (August 1976): 389–407.

Craven, Paul, and Tom Traves. "Canadian Railways as Manufactures, 1850–1880." In *Perspectives on Canadian Economic History*, edited by D. McCalla. Toronto: Copp Clark Pitman, 1987.

McCalla, Douglas. "An Introduction to the Nineteenth-Century Business World." In *Essays in Canadian Business History*, edited by T. Traves. Toronto: McClelland and Stewart, 1984.

CHAPTER

9

The Western Economy, 1713–1870

The Meeting of European and Native Economies

The economic history of western British North America before the transfer of the region to Canada has two characteristics that must be kept in mind. First, like that of so many other parts of Canada before Confederation, the commercial economy rested on the exchange of manufactured European trade goods for key primary resources of the region; in this case, the trade was such items as tools, clothing, blankets, weapons, and cooking utensils for various types of furs. These furs were used for two purposes in Europe: a luxury trade in fur coats and other apparel and the primary felt trade, which had been the same since the time of Champlain, and for which the fur of the beaver was the essential ingredient.[1]

The second characteristic distinguished the western region from other parts of North America. In those regions, this exchange was carried on primarily between an ocean-based or an agriculturally based community of European origin and the Europeans themselves. Settlement and development of the region accompanied the economic process. In the west, however, the years before 1870 saw the dominant exchange take place between indigenous non-European peoples and Europeans — who, throughout most of the period and most of the region, never controlled or even attempted to control the overall social and political or even economic structures of the region. Settlement and development came, but slowly, for it was not a necessary part of the economic activity of western Canada to either party involved.

Other subordinate themes must be traced in tandem with dominant ones. The first is that the nature of the fur trade (and of the accompanying provision trade) tended to encourage oligopolistic and even monopolistic behaviour on the part of suppliers of the European technology. Transportation costs, the delay between investment and return, the advantages of resource control, and the impact of governmental decisions: all helped shape this tendency.

There is also a point of some importance concerning the dual role of the natives in the fur-trade process. Until recently, the native population had tended to be seen as a passive part of the whole trade, perhaps exploited or perhaps treated fairly, but little able to control their own destiny. More recently, however, excellent works by historians, economists, and geographers have demonstrated that this was far from the case. The native participants had a very active role in the trade and were, especially in the years before 1850, often able to control the directions of the trade better than were their European suppliers. It was their own land and their own society; they knew how to exploit it better than did the interloper.

Finally, however, the system broke down. European interlopers were increasingly able to penetrate the region and to dictate the terms of trade. Further, by the final decades of the Hudson's Bay Company charter, the social and economic structure of the region was changing. Agriculture was appearing on the eastern periphery, and from the southern U.S. settlement hemmed in the tribes. The economy was in transition and, as is often the case in such instances, the economic power in the region shifted accordingly.

The Era of the Middleman: 1713–1770s

By the early to mid-eighteenth century, the pattern of the fur trade in the northwest had stabilized. As noted in Chapter 3, French incursions against Hudson's Bay Company posts had been resolved by the 1713 Treaty of Utrecht. Under this treaty, the French relinquished all claim to Hudson Bay. Therefore, until the fall of New France, the fur trade would be divided between the great North American powers on the basis of geography — the French operating out of Montreal, and the English from the bay.

The most important characteristic of the fur trade, the one that defines this era in the history of the western economy, was the effective control of the trade by key middlemen tribes. By the mid-eighteenth century, the Cree and Assiniboine were able, as were the Ottawa and Algonquian earlier, to dominate the exchange of goods between the Europeans and the native tribes of the interior. This control put them in a very powerful position, both economically and politically, as they could decide to what degree European technology would filter inland, and at what price. They could also determine what furs, and in what quantities, went to each of the European companies. It was a good position to be in, and the territories they controlled expanded accordingly.

Central to their power were the costs and difficulties of transportation to both Europeans and natives. The northwest was a vast territory with a small population. Population had to remain relatively scattered lest it exhaust game resources at any particular location. Transportation was difficult and, if the timing relative to seasons was wrong, highly dangerous. It was extremely unattractive for a tribe in the distant interior to make the trip thousands of miles to one of the bay forts — especially given the limited needs of a nomadic people. This was an area where the Cree and Assiniboine could perform a useful service.

These two tribes were located in a strategic position geographically. Scattered along forest and parkland to the south and west of the bay, they were the first native tribes with regular contact with the Hudson's Bay Company traders. They were also in a good position to take advantage as the French traders began to push west, past the Ottawa tribe, who had for so long in the past acted as middlemen. Located as they were between the forest and what is now mid-Saskatchewan, these tribes could make the trip to the bay in relative ease, if one can describe a 200- to 700-mile trip by canoe in those terms. They could also save more distant tribes the difficulties of transport by buying their furs and by selling them Hudson's Bay Company or French goods in return.

None of this is to imply a selfless service on the part of the middleman. The markup for such a service could be considerable. For example, a gun purchased at York by a Cree trading group would sell to the Blackfoot, a Cree enemy, for three and a half times the purchase price. Knives could jump ninefold in price.[2] Nor were these goods new. The traditional practice was for the middlemen to use the implement or weapon for a while and then to pass it off at high prices to tribes in the interior. Further, where the distances involved did not dissuade interior tribes from heading toward

MAP 9.1

Tribal Distribution in the West, *c.* 1750

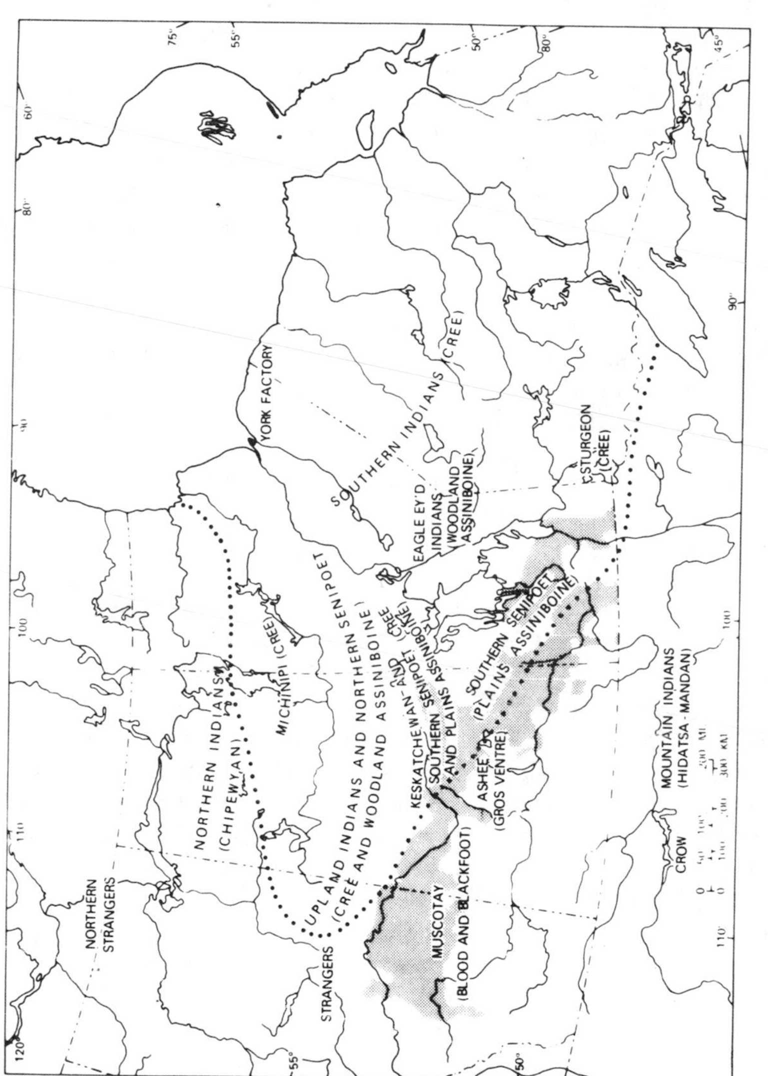

Source: A.J. Ray, *Indians in the Fur Trade: Their Role as Hunters, Trappers, and Middlemen in the Lands Southwest of Hudson Bay, 1660–1870* (Toronto: University of Toronto Press, 1974), 20.

the bay, a show of force might. The access to guns by the middleman made this show of force somewhat more persuasive.

By the early eighteenth century, the system was in place. The Cree and Assiniboine had interposed themselves between two valuable resources and, much like the merchants of Montreal themselves, profited by facilitating the exchange of these resources. This system lasted a long time; not until late in the century did anything disturb it. The French, it was true, did penetrate beyond the Great Lakes and on to the prairies by the 1730s. All that did, however, was to bring them into the lands of the Cree and Assiniboine and, thus, make it easier for the middlemen. These two tribes had what has been described as a "virtual monopoly" over much of the trade during most of the eighteenth century. Counts done at York Factory in the late 1750s indicate that practically "all the Indians coming to the post were either Cree or Assiniboine."[3]

There are two other striking things about the eighteenth-century fur trade. First, as the presence of the middlemen indicates, this trade was more controlled and dominated by the natives than by the Europeans. The latter sat, for the most part, on the coast of Hudson Bay, and, from their trade centres at such places as Fort Albany, Fort Churchill, and, most importantly, Fort York, acted as collecters of furs brought from the interior by native bands. The Europeans' knowledge of the inland territories and their control of economic events therein were scant. Even when the French began to push on to the prairies in the 1730s, they affected only the edge of the fur trade. The collection depots moved a little closer to the trading bands but the fundamental principles remained the same.

It was the Europeans who had to adapt to a large degree if they wished to succeed in the region. Trade practices had to alter to conform to the patterns of native life. For example, currency had little meaning or purpose for the interior tribes, and the Hudson's Bay Company and French traders could not really reckon their pricing system accordingly. Instead, a barter accounting system on the basis of MB (made beaver), which denoted the rate of exchange based on a prime beaver pelt, became the standard usage of the Hudson's Bay Company. The failure of a European currency system to penetrate the country indicates the degree to which the indigenous population retained economic dominance in the region.

Most peculiar to the fur trade, however, was the attitude of the native toward trade goods. In economic terms, native marginal utility for durable goods diminished rapidly. The Europeans found in the west, as they had earlier found in much of the east, that native traders wanted only so much in terms of kettles, axes, guns, and the like. Once they had these goods, better prices or more attractive durable goods would not produce a change in supplies. Indeed, at times when the demand for beaver was especially high, the European traders were often dismayed to find that the native traders would bring fewer rather than more furs to trade. The reason was simple: they could obtain their required trade goods (once estimated at about 70 MB a year) with fewer furs. Only when native traders were enticed with ephemeral goods, such as liquor, or easily transportable ones, such as beads, could the pattern be broken.

Such behaviour has occasioned much comment and judgement, then and since. For contemporary traders, it was often taken as a sign of the native's basically weak or lazy character. For writers since, those more sympathetic to the native, it has been seen as an indication of the tendency of the fur-trading companies to exploit the native population with worthless objects. Much of the judgement of both sides is based more on emotion than on substance, however. Such economic behaviour by the natives is entirely rational, given their mode of life.

The native tribes of the British North American interior were, without exception, nomadic. Theirs was a subsistence economy, based on the pursuit of food supplies in a land with a harsh climate and with food resources that fluctuated wildly, depending on the season. For example, the open prairie might prove abundant in summer if buffalo could be found, but was a desolate, gameless place in winter. Conversely, the forests of the north provided better shelter in winter, but had limited game. The native life was, thus, one of constant movement, determined by the search for buffalo, large forest game, or fish, depending on the tribe and the season.[4]

The simple reality was that the burden of transport made excess goods valueless, a fact that helps to explain the use and then resale of trade goods by the middlemen. An axe or two, a kettle and some pots, and perhaps a gun gave the native an advanced technology with which to face daily tasks. To have transported 50 or 100 pots, or to have possessed many fine suits of European cloth, would have created transport difficulties completely destructive to survival. Liquor was socially destructive to much of the native population, but, from an economic view, the native who obtained 70 MB worth of goods and then traded any excess credits for alcohol or beads, or anything else that was instantly consumable, was making a rational economic decision.

There was another native economic practice to which Europeans had to adjust. Indian traders routinely made ritual exchanges of goods between themselves. Band meeting band would give presents as a token of friendship and good will. When the Europeans arrived, they found it expedient to adopt this native practice. When a group of traders arrived at a Hudson's Bay Company fort, a ceremony occurred in which the leading officials at the fort would give welcome to the leading representatives of the natives, and gifts would be exchanged. Only after a due amount of ceremony could trading begin, usually the next day.

This institutionalized gift-giving has led to the argument that the native economy should not be seen in market terms at all. In preindustrial societies, the argument goes, security of person and of group became paramount. Exchanges of goods were, therefore, based not on expectations of profit or loss but on intergroup exchanges for reasons of alliance, or at least of noninterference. "The coming of the market system," according to this view, "had still to await the development of peaceful conditions, adequate and reliable policing, and a common legal framework."[5]

There is an element of truth in this assertion. There is no doubt that the ritual gift-giving was derived from such a diplomatic practice. It is one thing, however, to say that the native economy was different from that of the European in its precise behaviour. The loosely based system of kinship and alliances as well as the nomadic lifestyle ensured that would be the case. It is quite another to say that it was not a market economy. The native population was interested in using goods to secure friendship and security, of course. These were independent peoples, and there was no arbiter to turn to should peaceful understanding break down. Nothing in the practice contradicts the existence of a market economy, however, any more than the modern ledger entry under "good will" should imply a lack of interest in profit. Gift-giving was a natural outgrowth of the state of the country. For the Hudson's Bay Company and the native trader alike, it was just one more cost of doing business.

The pattern of trade that existed through much of the eighteenth century rested on three elements. The first was the Hudson's Bay Company. Forts Albany, Churchill, and York on the bay provided depots for European goods and collection points for the furs brought from the interior. Those bringing the furs, the Cree and Assiniboine, provided the second central element in the trade. Finally, to the south and the west, French interlopers began, by the 1740s, to attract native traders away from the bay, at least part of the time. These three elements carried on a competitive and continuous trade. Guns, hatchets, blankets, knives, chisels, tobacco, and liquor formed the staples of the trade. Determination of the precise value of the trade at any given time is difficult. It was a valuable one, however, and large enough to attract the massive capital and effort required to broach the interior of North America far ahead of the settlement frontier.

Yet, there is one important qualification to be made. For the European, the health of the western economy in the eighteenth century would be assessed in terms of the fur trade. A high demand for furs and a ready supply would mean economic prosperity. Still, it would be false to impose the fur-trade companies' concept of the trade cycle on the western interior. For the natives, the populace of the region, economic prosperity depended throughout this period less on the fur trade than on the state and movements of wild game. This was still a nonmonetary economy, dependent for its well-being on the hunt. European technology and European trade had an impact but did not alter this fact in any fundamental way until much later.

The Era of Competition

Beginning in the mid-eighteenth century, the dynamics of the economy of the interior underwent a series of changes. First, in the late 1750s, the French traders disappeared. New France was about to fall to the English, and their sources of supply, and soon of capital, were collapsing. For a few years, the Hudson's Bay Company once again had a monopoly in the region. The use of liquor was cut back, and the price given for furs was lowered, at least to a degree.

Then, within a decade, new traders began to spread westward from the Great Lakes. These were the so-called pedlars operating once again out of Montreal. In many cases, the canoemen and traders were men familiar with the business from before the fall of New France. This time, however, they were backed by English and Scottish capital, and the expeditions were headed by the representatives of the new British merchant class moving into Montreal. As the Hudson's Bay Company would quickly discover, the change of rulers at Quebec did not alter the fundamental rivalry between the two major routes to the west, the St. Lawrence River and the bay. Indeed, the two systems were about to enter into a period of especially fierce competition.

Initially, the pedlars out of Montreal were small outfitters. As has been discussed earlier, however, the nature of the fur trade encouraged combination. The formation, re-formation, and merging of outfits in the period from the 1760s through the 1790s is bewildering, given the sheer number of events that took place. There are really only two events that demand attention here. The first is that there did emerge, by the 1780s, a dominant syndicate out of Montreal, known as the North West Company.[6] Headed by the Scottish merchants of the McTavish and Frobisher clans and held together by a series of partnership arrangements, the North West Company had the resources and desire to challenge the Hudson's Bay Company head-on.

The second point to note is that, while the advantages of combination might be very clear, there was no easy way to ensure that some new interloper did not appear on the scene. Through this entire period, both the Hudson's Bay Company (which considered the North West Company an interloper) and the North West Company were harassed by the appearance of new fur-trade partnerships out of Montreal. If these new companies could be driven out of business, then all was well. If not, the best practice, at least as far as the North West Company was concerned, was to absorb them.

This characteristic of the trade was shown most clearly in the greatest challenge to the North West Company. In 1794, the British signed Jay's Treaty with the United States, handing over the thousands of miles of British-occupied territory south and west of the Great Lakes. The southwest fur trade was thereby reserved for American citizens. Various merchants and traders turned their eyes north and west of the Great Lakes. In 1798, two new Montreal firms emerged to challenge the supremacy of the North West Company. This challenge grew more serious when Sir Alexander Mackenzie, one of the most renowned of the fur traders, abandoned the North West Company and threw in his lot with a new company. The Sir Alexander Mackenzie Company, or the XY Company as it was popularly known, had both the resources and the determination to challenge the supremacy of the North West Company.

The rivalries that sprang up in the northwest after 1770 had a marked effect on the nature of the fur trade. The Montreal companies quickly expanded their operations to territories never visited by the French before the conquest. By 1778, Peter Pond of the North West Company had a post on Lake Athabasca, and, by 1793, Alexander Mackenzie, then still of the North West Company, had journeyed overland to the Pacific. By the early 1800s, as the three-cornered rivalry between the North West, XY, and Hudson's Bay companies reached new heights, scores of posts sprang up along the rivers of the parkland and forest belt.

This rapid penetration inland brought major changes in the economic activity of the interior. The first change was on the part of the Hudson's Bay Company. For more than a century, the company had maintained a strategic position on the bay. The native middlemen had made the trek to it. As the Montreal traders penetrated to the Saskatchewan system and then to the Athabasca, however, natives found it less and less necessary to make the arduous trip to the shores of Hudson Bay. The traders would come to them.

The result was that the company began to lose its share of the trade. York Factory, for example, saw a rapid decline as the central entrepôt of the fur trade. Whereas some 25 000 to 40 000 MB per annum went through the post in the first half of the eighteenth century, the number was down to 18 000 by 1768 and to a mere 8000 by 1773. Overall, one estimate is that, by the 1780s, the Hudson's Bay Company was doing only about £30 000 worth of trade, while, in contrast, the Montreal traders garnered somewhere between £165 000 and £245 000. The company that, only a few years before, had enjoyed a monopoly in the interior was, in other words, doing only about 15 percent of the fur-trade business.[7]

The company had to respond or face bankruptcy. When it became obvious that native traders were no longer making the trek to the bay, the company decided to move inland. In 1774, it established Fort Cumberland on the Saskatchewan River, about 250 miles southwest of York Factory. From there, it spread westward along the Saskatchewan system and its tributaries, until, in 1795, it established Fort Edmonton. In the early nineteenth century, the system would continue to expand, westward to the Rockies and northward into the Athabasca system.

To supply this growing network of posts, the company instituted another innovation. Increasingly, in the early nineteenth century, it hauled its goods not by the traditional *canot du nord* but by York boat. This 40-foot boat required the same number of crew as a *canot du nord* (six to eight), but carried twice the cargo. The efficiency of such loads more than made up for the difficulties in portaging and in loading and unloading. The use of the York boat, in combination with the efficiency of transporting goods to the interior via Hudson Bay, was the greatest strength of the Hudson's Bay Company. With every mile inland that the Montreal merchants extended their network, the transportation advantages of the bay became more obvious. The York boat only accentuated those advantages.

In contrast, one of the great disadvantages faced by the Hudson's Bay Company was of its own making. The North West Company rested on a series of partnerships and incentives that tied the success of the company to the income of senior personnel. Most important in this regard was the fact that a good portion of the company was owned by the wintering partners (so called because they wintered over in the territories). The experts in the actual day-to-day operations of the trade in the field thus had both incentive and involvement in policy. Their ideas made the North West Company innovative and tremendously expansionary. This setup also meant that knowledge of the interior was regularly conveyed to those back in Montreal, and new schemes resting on first-hand experience could be developed. Conversely, the Hudson's Bay Company was rigidly centralized. Wages were determined in London, and there was little flexibility for those acting in the territories. This policy of centralized authority and rigid personnel practices reflected the same caution that had led the company to sit on the bay for more than a century. Only when pushed by its competition did it begin to change policy.

In 1770, a system of bonuses was developed for Hudson's Bay Company employees. Over the years, these would be extended to the point where they could become a significant part of an individual's annual salary.[8] Salary was only a part of the problem, however, and the lack of consultation, centralized decision making, and rigid practices continued to plague the company well into the nineteenth century.

In spite of the move inland by the Hudson's Bay Company, and in spite of that company's growing transportation advantages, the

Montreal merchants remained dominant in the fur trade into the nineteenth century. The Montreal merchants, undaunted by the countermoves of their rivals, simply pushed their network farther afield, competing with each other as well as with the Hudson's Bay Company. Between 1789 and 1805, when the rivalry among companies was at its height, some 325 new posts were built in the thinly populated interior.[9] When, in 1804, the North West Company merged with the XY Company, that dominance seemed all the greater. So weak was the Hudson's Bay Company position that, in 1808, with problems accentuated by European wars, it suspended dividends. It seemed only a matter of time until the English-based company succumbed before the onslaught from Montreal.

The most dramatic aspect of this expansion was the movement of the North West Company into the transmountain west and what is now British Columbia. Alexander Mackenzie's trip to the Pacific had been a daring example of exploration, but competition within the fur trade led, over the first decade or so of the nineteenth century, to the addition of thousands of miles of rugged mountainous areas, valleys, and Pacific coastline to the already huge areas covered by the trade. The expansion also created particular problems and pointed to the limits faced by the North West Company in its drive for supremacy.

Initially, the trade developed slowly. The traders found that both the geography and the native population of British Columbia posed problems. The geographical difficulties are fairly obvious. In what was later termed "the sea of mountains," it was extremely difficult to find an easily travelled river route that would permit the ready transport of furs, trade goods, and supplies. Not until about 1811 was the Columbia River route sufficiently well known that it provided that link — a link that was, of course, but a thin ribbon travelling through a vast and segmented geography. Even so, by the War of 1812, the expansionary mood of the age had led to a series of posts throughout the interior. In 1813, the North West Company used the War of 1812 and a nearby British warship to coerce the American Fur Company into "selling" Fort Astoria on the Columbia River, and the network was complete.

A modification of native trade practices was also required. The North West Company was never able to develop a series of stable trade relationships with the tribes of the far west. The reasons may have been related to numbers, for this region was much more heavily populated than the plains, or to the different types of band and tribal relationships that had grown out of the geography and culture of the region. Various approaches were taken, including the use of members of eastern bands as trappers, but the solutions were never really satisfactory.[10] Even in the first stages of European contact, the economy of British Columbia proved to have a unique character that required considerable changes in technique.

The vast expansion of the Montreal trade network created problems not only for the Europeans, whether of the Hudson's Bay or the North West Company, but also for the native population. The extension of the European trading networks rapidly destroyed the privileged position of the Cree and Assiniboine tribes. Interior bands could now trade directly with any of two or three companies without making the arduous journey to the bay and without paying the high markup demanded by the middlemen tribes. "Henceforth, the trading post moved with the Indian trappers; access to it could no longer be controlled by native traders."[11] The European presence now extended over much of the western half of British North America.

The inland expansion of the fur companies also brought new opportunities for the natives. The ever-growing numbers of Europeans inland required food supplies for their extended network of forts. Thus, the exchange of European technology for local animal pelts became a more complex economic operation, involving support services rendered by the local community. From the various regions of the interior, but especially from the buffalo regions of parkland and prairie, a series of new trade patterns developed. Cree and Blackfoot groups sent provisions northward to fur-trade posts along the well-travelled Saskatchewan and Lake Winnipeg routes.

These supply movements were far from peripheral to the economy of the west. The requirements of each post were sizable. Arthur Ray has estimated that, at one medium-sized post on the Pembina River, nearly 150 buffalo were killed, more than 1000 fish caught, and 325 bushels of potatoes required to provide basic food supplies for one year. In 1813, the North West Company contracted for some 644 bags of pemmican meat, each bag weighing 90 pounds. This amount filled more than 200 canoes.[12] Before long, some of the largest posts in the interior, such as Fort Edmonton, would exist as bases for the exchange of food supplies rather than as fur-trade centres.

MAP 9.2

The Extent of the Fur Trade, 1820s

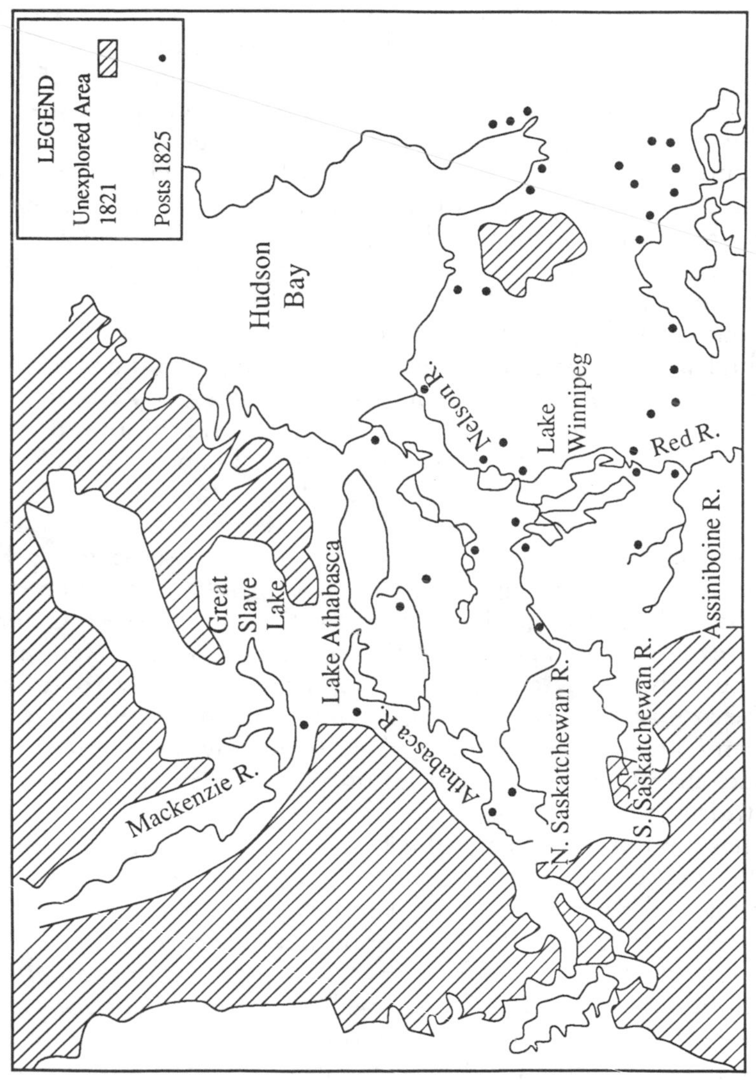

Source: Adapted from R. Cole Harris, *Historical Atlas of Canada* (Toronto: University of Toronto Press, 1987), plates 67 and 69.

The Cree situated in the parkland/prairie region of the west and the Assiniboine found a new role for themselves. As their middleman role disappeared, they moved quickly into the role of suppliers to the various fur-trade companies. As early as 1790, Alexander Mackenzie could comment of the Assiniboine that "they are not beaver hunters. . . . They confine themselves to hunting buffalo and trapping wolves, which cover the country."[13] This transition was aided by the adoption of the horse by the plains tribes over the past century, which made the buffalo hunt much more efficient and also made the transport of meat both easier and faster. The Cree, the Assiniboine, and, less regularly, the Blackfoot thus became the major suppliers of the new network of posts springing up in the interior. The same event that took one livelihood away quite fortuitously provided another.

There were also significant economic changes taking place among the Europeans in the west. The ailing Hudson's Bay Company had been vulnerable to a takeover for some time, and the Earl of Selkirk was able to take control of the company. Then, in 1811, he persuaded the company to grant him a large tract of land south of Lake Winnipeg, where he founded the Red River settlement. Selkirk's primary purpose was to assist the dispossessed Scottish Highlanders. Yet, his timing and his choice of site were bound to be viewed as less than philanthropic by the North West Company. The settlement, established at the confluence of the Red and Assiniboine rivers, lay along one of the primary supply routes to the northern posts. It also lay near the main transportation route from eastern Canada. To the North West Company, the settlement was but another move in the escalating competition between the bay and the river.

Over the next few years, the Red River colony inflamed the already intense competition between the two companies. The governor of Red River interrupted pemmican shipments to the interior, thus threatening starvation to a good many North West employees in the interior. The Nor'Westers tried to entice the settlers away and, when that effort failed, turned to the emergent *bois-brûlé* or Métis people, who saw their interests as allied with those of the North West Company. The climax came in 1816, when confrontation between settlers and Métis at Seven Oaks left 22 dead. Competition had turned to harassment, and harassment to something approaching open warfare.

The violence at Red River brought the chaos in the interior of North America to the attention of officials in London. Pressure was put on the two organizations to find a means of resolving their dispute. An incentive was also given: if a resolution could be achieved, the British government was prepared to guarantee the resulting organization an exclusive licence to trade in the region. In other words, if this battle could be resolved, the British government would pledge itself to see that no new competition arose.

The companies were surprisingly compliant. For all the enmity that had built up over the years, there was a recognition that competition had been ruinous to all involved. Overbuilding of posts and overmanning in the interior had led both to a glut of furs and to dangerous depletion of the resource in some areas. Increasing use of liquor had damaged the morale of the native trappers and, from the companies' point of view, had led to an unstable relationship with the native population.

Yet this raises an interesting question, one that cannot be fully answered. Only a decade or so earlier, the North West Company had been confident of its hold on the trade and equally confident of its ability to take over or destroy the Hudson's Bay Company within a few years. Yet, as the merger took shape, it was to be the Hudson's Bay Company that survived, albeit in somewhat altered form. What had happened to the dominance of the Montreal traders?

By 1821, the large and impressive North West Company was much weaker than it appeared. The reason most commonly offered for this depletion of strength is the vast cost of running a transcontinental transportation system from Montreal. Within a few decades, the company had added thousands of miles of new territory to its operations, had expanded over the mountains into British Columbia, and had undertaken its vast building program to undercut the Hudson's Bay Company. The distance from tidewater to the trapper in the field simply became too enormous. Indeed, by the end of the period, the coastal regions of British Columbia were being supplied by ship rather than overland. Even so, the interior of the region and the vast prairie and subarctic areas were still supplied by ship and canoe all the way from Montreal — a trip, in some instances, of more than 3000 miles.[14] There were other problems as well, including administrative ones in the accounting and capitalization system of the company. Specifically, no provision was made for capital renewal, and all profits were distributed to the partners. Reserves, therefore, did not exist, and costs had to be met out of operating revenues. Undercapitalization and tremendous costs thus came together to create what, in modern parlance, would be termed a liquidity crisis just as the competition reached its peak.

In these speculations as to the collapse of the North West Company, it is also worth considering the effects of sheer fatigue and profit taking on the part of the Montreal proprietors. The North West Company had always seen a degree of tension between its Montreal partners and those wintering in the interior. It is quite possible that, in later years, some of the aging senior partners were quite willing to take a cash settlement to leave the troublesome winterers behind and to turn to other pursuits. McTavish and Company, representing the Montreal partners, got a generous settlement, worth some 30 percent of the new company.[15] As we have seen, by the 1820s, the St. Lawrence and lower Great Lakes offered a good many opportunities for the diversification of business. The new staples trade and export-import businesses to supply the growing population of the Canadas would attract many ex-fur traders over the next years. Few of the great proprietors of the old North West Company would succeed, however, and many disposed of their stock to pay off debts or to make investments in other ventures. By the mid-1820s, the partnership of 1821 had effectively been dissolved. The winterers had been absorbed into the Hudson's Bay Company and the Montreal proprietors forced out.[16]

The new company created by the 1821 merger reflected the strengths of both of the former institutions. On the one hand, the bay, not the river, would be the future supply line to the northwest. Henceforth, the economy of the fur trade and the economy of the rest of British North America were to operate largely independently of each other. On the other hand, the new Hudson's Bay Company had to find some way of absorbing the wintering partners of the North West Company. The merger reflected the strength of a system that had integrated those with experience and skill in the interior into the management of the company. Thus, in 1821, the company adopted what was known as the deed poll. Some 85 shares (about 40 percent of the company's stock) were distributed among the wintering partners. Chief factors, the senior officials at major posts, each received two of these shares, and each chief trader (the level below factor) received one share. In good times, these shares could be worth a great deal. For example, in 1855, as the fur trade prospered, a chief factor's share of the profits amounted to well over £800, an amount comparable to that earned by the top rank of civil servants in the Province of Canada at the time.[17]

All in all, it was a restructuring that gave the new company the best of both worlds. It had the transportation advantages of the Hudson's Bay Company, some of the entrepreneurial drive of the North West Company, and a legal monopoly from Great Britain. The trick now was to take advantage of these operations in the field. Order had to be restored, redundant posts abandoned, excess personnel retired — all would take time and skill.

The Company Monopoly

The merger of 1821 and subsequent events altered the economic structure of the west as profoundly as had the earlier penetration of the North West Company. The fur companies of the eighteenth and early nineteenth centuries have been described accurately as "premodern" or, alternatively, as an "anachronism" in their structure and approach to the trade.[18] The North West Company was a loose syndicate of partnerships, unwieldy in size and bizarre in its accounting procedures. The Hudson's Bay Company rested, of course, on the concept of the chartered monopoly, a creature of the seventeenth century existing into the nineteenth.

The way in which the fur-trade companies waged competition in the interior also reflected an approach to commerce different from that of the modern era. As had been the case under Elizabeth I, when part-pirate, part-merchant, part-naval officers sailed the oceans for the Empire, the fur-trade companies freely mixed commerce with aspects of sovereign authority and with sheer theft. Thus, for example, both companies used an old law that gave Canadian justices of the peace jurisdiction in the northwest as a means of harassing and arresting opponents. Violence and semimilitary activities were adopted, as had been used in Seven Oaks or in Selkirk's subsequent employment of Swiss mercenaries to seize North West Company supplies and furs at Fort William.

These premodern approaches also extended into other areas. Inventory management was nonexistent, while family relationships and personal status often took precedence over the profitability of the firm. The makeup of new outfits rested more on tradition than on demand, as identical supplies were ordered year after year, even if certain items had been shown not to be in demand. Likewise, staffing policy rested on a combination of paternalism, tradition, and nepotism, once again indicating that profitability and efficiency took second place in the planning of the two organizations.

All this was in the process of change with the merger of 1821. Indeed, many of the changes had begun in the Hudson's Bay Company in the years immediately before the merger. Faced with the struggle for survival against the North West Company, the new Hudson's Bay Company owners, under the leadership of Selkirk, had introduced personnel reductions, stricter financial accountability, and other cost-reduction measures. Within two years, they turned the company annual operations from a loss to a profit.

It was with the merger that the real changes came, however. These were facilitated by two facts. The first was that the merger had left redundant posts, overstaffing, and redundant inventory. As one historian has commented,

> the sudden end of rivalry made nonsense of the trading structures which the two companies had built. There were surplus posts and personnel, and over-lavish trading practices. Prices paid to Indians had risen during the years of competition, and alcohol traded with irresponsible abandon. Trapping had been carried out at all seasons, of young as well as of adult animals, and many areas were now denuded of furs.[19]

Even under the most traditional management, change would have been necessary.

Traditional management was not what they got. George Simpson, the man appointed by London to oversee the reorganization of the company, was an individual who put the corporation ahead of kinship, and modern efficiency ahead of tradition. The "Little Emperor," as Simpson was known, moved, over the next few years, to reduce costs and personnel as quickly as possible. Within five years, staff was cut by almost two-thirds, the number of posts reduced to 45 (when some 325 had been built between 1789 and 1805), the use of liquor reduced tremendously. The power of the wintering partners declined while Simpson's increased. The faraway London board increasingly trusted his judgement and left the day-to-day operations in the field to their man on the spot. Within a very few years, the ungainly operation left by the merger of two companies had been reshaped into a well-organized unit.[20]

The merger also brought changes to the economy of the region as a whole. Most immediately, Red River became a natural spot both as a residence for redundant employees and as a centre for those who would attempt economic diversification in the region. There were various attempts at such diversification, including the Buffalo Wool Company, the Tallow Company, and experiments with flax and hemp. All were failures. With no local market and with the colony isolated from metropolitan centres, such results were not surprising.[21]

What Red River did become was a focal point for the surrounding territory. Fur traders and their families increasingly joined the original Scottish settlers — as, ironically, did the Métis, who had initially seen the colony as such a threat. Moreover, the settlement did have a distinct economic purpose: supplying provisions to the fur-trade posts throughout the interior. It was located on a major supply route and thus became a natural site for the collection and transshipment of such supplies as pemmican and buffalo meat. Further, as agriculture in the region developed, the surpluses could be used to vary the provisions sent out to the posts. Finally, the developing Métis community used Red River as a base from which to set out on the semiannual buffalo hunts that supplied both their own food and goods for the provisioning trade. Strange though it might seem to talk of a colony of 6000 people or so as a metropolitan centre, that is exactly what Red River became. It was the centre, moreover, for a vast area running from the Shield on the east to the Rockies on the west, and well into the parkland regions to the north. Of course, its influence was weaker than that of similar urban-rural relationships in more settled areas, but there was certainly no other metropolitan centre to challenge it.

The role of Red River has been much discussed in the histories of the region. There was a feeling, dating back to the Nor'Westers, that such an agricultural settlement in the midst of a fur-trading region was threatening. Agriculture and settlement, the argument went, were hostile to the fur trade. This argument was, in turn, picked up and expanded upon by later economic historians who, looking back at the rise of free trade in the 1840s and the development of the west as an extension of the Canadian agricultural frontier, saw the colony as "a vulnerable point in the defenses of the company."[22]

To a degree, this argument depends on the benefit of hindsight

As will be argued, the rise of free trade and the eventual agricultural settlement of the west had much more to do with forces external to the region than with the presence of Red River. Indeed, Red River was a natural, even essential, development. Once the Europeans began to assert a permanent presence inland, there was a need for a centre of settlement that reflected European social and economic practices, even if modified to meet the demands of the country. Red River provided such a place.

One of the most dramatic examples of the relationship between the settlement and the country came in the coalescence of the Métis community in the years after the founding of the colony. The Métis, or mixed bloods, were descendants of unions between French fur traders and native women. What gave them a distinct identity, however, and what brought them together as a community, was their sense of being indigenous to the country but distinct from the native communities of their mothers. Indeed, many of mixed parentage were never Métis in any meaningful sense, in that they adopted the economic and social practices of their native mothers.

The Métis' sense of distinctiveness was shaped by cultural factors (such as the use of French), by religion (Roman Catholicism), and by a distinct economic role in the northwest. In one sense, they were in an awkward position. Class and social barriers meant that it was extremely difficult for them to rise very far in the ranks of the fur trade. Most remained canoemen or casual labourers. Further, they were not routinely the actual trappers of furs, as were the natives. The Métis were far less nomadic than the natives and thus had both a greater interest in and a greater need for European goods on a larger scale. Somehow, they had to find a niche in the existing economy of the northwest.

As mentioned above, they found that niche in the nineteenth century by playing an important role in the provisioning trade. Even more than the Cree, the Métis depended for their well-being on the demands of the fur trade for buffalo meat. Every summer there were large and well-organized commercial hunts, followed by the preparation of pemmican and its transport to the outlying posts. The buffalo hunt, as a commercial operation, both gave the Métis their primary distinctiveness as a community and provided them with their main source of cash in the first half of the nineteenth century.

Yet, this depiction of the Métis as buffalo hunters must be qualified. The Métis were not a purely nomadic people, following the buffalo. Rather, at Red River and in other isolated sites around the region, they developed a mixed economy of small-scale farming, seasonal employment with the Hudson's Bay Company, and the provisioning of the trade. They were, thus, neither a purely peasant society rooted to a single spot nor a nomadic people dependent on the cycle of game; rather, they stood somewhere between the two. Later English observers would be critical of them for failing to follow agriculture more aggressively. In these years, however, the Métis' activities made sense both traditionally, in terms of their own culture, and economically. The combination of activities was their best means of taking advantage of the opportunities created by the Europeans' continued penetration of the interior.

A new period of stability thus developed in the west between 1821 and the 1840s, brought on initially by the absence of competition among European fur traders. Without competition, the Hudson's Bay Company could regularize its practices without sacrificing profitability. By the mid-1820s, dividends had reach 10 percent; they stayed at that level or higher over the next several years. A trader with one share in the deed poll would, it has been estimated, receive an average of £400 per annum in profits through the 1820s.[23]

The stability after 1821 also reflected the fact that other groups in the region had made the necessary economic transition to a world where the European fur traders were present throughout the interior. The Cree and Assiniboine found, as did the Métis, at least a partial substitute for their middleman role in the provisioning trade — as, to a lesser degree, did the Blackfoot confederacy. The Cree supplemented their provisioning with trapping and, of course, with a continued reliance on the hunt and fishing. The Métis supplemented their provisioning with hunting for personal consumption, small-scale agricultural production, and labour for the company. Red River, after a period of turbulence during its founding years, became a centre for both Europeans and Métis. The end of expansion and the development of monopoly seemed to have returned stability to the western economy.

The Hudson's Bay Company was very much aware of the advantages of monopoly and followed a policy of actively preserving it through a practice known as a "frontier policy." In this procedure, certain areas of the company's trading regions were designated both vulnerable and expendable. When outside competition ap peared in these areas, the company was willing to pursue ruthless competitive means to ensure that this competition did not expand into the heartland of company operations. For example, the company waged a price war with American fur traders in the territory west of Superior for several years in the 1820s and 1830s. The company traded at a loss in a deliberate attempt to drive the intruding companies into bankruptcy. In another case, also in the late 1820s, Peter Skene Ogden of the company headed south to the Snake River country. American trappers and traders had been pushing westward and appeared to endanger the fertile Oregon region. Ogden therefore "trapped out" the region, deliberately wiping out the fur-bearing animals. A trappers' desert was thus interposed between expanding American businessmen and the operations the company considered important.[24]

The Intrusion of New Forces

The stability was temporary. The absence of expansion on the part of the company did not alter longer-range trends brought on by the European presence in the region. In various ways, forces were gathering that would upset the balance in the region. The economy of exchange in the region rested largely on two natural resources, furs and buffalo. The balance in the region rested on the ability of both the Métis and the native population to enter into profitable trade with the Hudson's Bay Company without falling into too vulnerable a position. Both the resource base and the balance between groups were being undermined, even during the relatively calm period of the monopoly years. Within twenty years of the merger, new and fundamental shifts were taking place in the economy and society of the region. As Gerald Friesen has noted, "the 1840s can stand as a dividing line between one era and another."[25]

During the period of three-cornered competition, the endangered resource in the region had appeared to be the beaver. Indeed, Simpson and other officials made balanced trapping a priority after 1821. As it turned out, however, it was not the beaver but the buffalo that proved the more serious problem as time went on. In the early years of the Red River settlement, it was possible in some years to see buffalo from the Red River colony. By the 1840s, it was necessary to travel hundreds of miles westward to find the herds.

Throughout the region, reports accumulated that, though far from scientific, indicated that the great buffalo herds were in decline.

The exact reasons for the decline are still a matter of discussion among historians. Various forces seem to have played a part. First, and perhaps most important, was the long-term impact of the horse. By the end of the eighteenth century, buffalo hunting on foot had been replaced by the horseback raid that was so common in later European imagery of the west. What the horse did, however, was to make the native or Métis hunter more efficient. The chance of a kill was greater and, most significantly, the hunter had the speed and mobility to bypass the undesirable bull to kill the cow.

This increased efficiency in the hunt had a greater effect on the herds because of ancillary factors. First, though the statistics are necessarily absent, indications are that the native/Métis population of the west was increasing throughout the late eighteenth century and into the nineteenth. There were more mouths to feed, so more buffalo had to be hunted. Also, aside from the demands of band and family, there was the opportunity to supply the fur-trade companies with buffalo meat. Finally, it may also be that disease, possibly transmitted by European animals introduced into the region, affected the herds by the 1840s. The herds thus had an increasingly difficult time replenishing themselves.

The diminished herds may also have been brought about, in part, by an apparent increase in the demand for European goods on the part of the plains bands. Previously the great bulk of native purchases had been of metal-based implements, from pots and pans to weapons. By the 1840s, however, new goods were in great demand: cloth, flour, molasses. Basic food and clothing were now sought not from the land but from trade with the Europeans. The independence that had previously characterized native relations with the fur traders was being replaced by a new vulnerability. The rhythm of hunting and fishing, which, as was argued above, had been the real determinator of the western economy in the eighteenth century, was gradually being replaced by an economy dependent on the exchange of goods between the Europeans and the population of the region. In 1840, the process was sufficiently under way that it hinted of the transformation to a modern agricultural economy over the next generation.

The economic position of the Hudson's Bay Company was also being altered drastically in the 1840s. Until then, the company had been able to preserve its monopoly over the valuable fur trade by driving out competitors. The American frontier of settlement was drawing ever closer, however, and with it came an advance guard of fur traders determined to siphon off some of the business of the Hudson's Bay Company. Until the 1840s, the Hudson's Bay Company was protected to some extent by an arrangement with the large American Fur Company that prevented cross-border raiding by either company. In the early 1840s, however, the American Fur Company went into receivership, and the arrangement effectively terminated. Now the way was open for a direct challenge to the company.

Until this time, the Hudson's Bay Company had always relied on economic means to retain its monopoly. Distance, effective transportation systems, economies of scale, and the willingness to take a loss in one region to protect another had allowed the company to preserve control of the region. There had long been a group of free-lance trappers and traders among the Métis and others in the west. However, they, like the natives, had usually found it advantageous to trade at company stores. In effect, their activities differed little from the traditional business of the company. Then, a challenge appeared at Pembina, just south of the border. Norman Kittson, an American fur trader, established a post there and had sufficient capital backing to challenge the Hudson's Bay Company. Before long "free traders" from the Red River area were making the trek south to Kittson's post. The isolation of the region was coming to an end.

In response, the company abandoned its strongest weapon — the economic position it held — and resorted to its weakest — its legal position under the Charter and the Exclusive Licence to Trade. Various measures were attempted but, except for a brief period in 1846–48, when British troops were stationed in Red River, all failed. Although the company tried to assume many quasi-governmental functions in the territories, it was, ultimately, a commercial concern; it had no military power to back up its edicts, and its powers to imprison or fine people who considered themselves eligible for the full privileges accorded a British subject were of dubious legitimacy. Every action taken led to screams of tyranny, and when, at the famous Sayer trial in 1849, the Métis community at Red River made it apparent that they would no longer tolerate pretenses to monopoly, the whole legal strategy of the company collapsed. The period of monopoly was now over. Those who came into possession of furs, whether by trapping or trading, could now look to whomever they wished.

Overall, then, the 1840s brought the west into a state of transition once again. The collapse of the company's monopoly, the changing trade practices of the native and Métis communities, the receding buffalo herds, and the approach of the American frontier of settlement created new forces that signalled the erosion of a regional economy based on an important but small number of activities: the fur and provisioning trade, hunting and trapping. Continental and international events were impinging on the region now and would do so with ever-greater effect over the next generation. The west was about to be overtaken by the greatest force in colonial North American economic development, the agricultural frontier. The questions now were who would develop that frontier and what would happen to those whose economic livelihood rested on the old order?

Expansionism

Borders provide an interesting complication in the study of economic development. Economists and historians like to emphasize the transcendent reality of economic forces, whatever borders or artificial government creations may exist. Thus, for example, the Charter of the Hudson's Bay Company could not prevent the leakage of furs south of the border once the American presence at Pembina took hold. Equally, the early settlement of Upper Canada was to a large degree the result of its being in the path of the natural frontier of settlement westward from New York. The border had little effect on this movement, in spite of the enmity between Britain and the United States at the time.

Yet, borders can have an important effect. Tariff policies, import quotas, government projects, and other measures are obvious examples of this. In the case of the northwest, between 1850 and 1870, the presence of a border, even one represented on the northerly side only by a commercial concern, did make a difference. Red River was, by the 1850s, in the path of an expanding American frontier of settlement. The Minnesota territory, established in 1849, was becoming an influential presence in Red River and beyond. By 1860, it would have a population of 172 000, more than that of the entire Hudson's Bay territories. In 1859, the first steamboat on the Red River, the *Anson Northrup*, tied the major settlement of the region directly into the American commercial system. In a move that symbolized the changing commercial poles of the area, the Hudson's Bay Company decided to supply Red River from the United States rather than the bay. Politically, a group of enthusiasts in Minnesota looked with covetous eyes on the region as a natural place for future commercial and political development.[26]

For all this, the territory was not swallowed up, as was Oregon, in 1846, by American settlers. The ability of the border to withstand the pulls from the United States was increased first by the U.S. Civil War (1861–65), which slowed settlement, and second by a Sioux uprising in northern Minnesota in 1862, which drove back outlying settlers and further slowed settlement in that particular direction. In the meantime, the Province of Canada, its own agricultural expansion halted by the marginal lands of the Shield, could use the common British flag to its advantage. Enthusiastic expansionists pressed for the transfer of the region as a means of providing a new hinterland for development. When Confederation came in 1867, the political structure finally existed that could allow transcontinental development. In 1870, the northwest was transferred to Canada and, though the fur trade continued to exist, especially in more northerly regions, agriculture was to be the new staple resource of the region.

The transfer to Canada and the replacement of the fur trade with agriculture had profound effects on the economic relationships within the region. It is possible, indeed, to see the economic development of the region to the late nineteenth century in terms of the relationships between the major population groups. Successive stages were marked by a growing presence of the European population group, until, in the years after 1870, that group became the only significant economic power in the region. The native and Métis populations would be forced into a position of economic and social marginality that contrasted sharply with their dominant position through the first century of the fur trade and even with the combination of growing material dependence and cultural distinctiveness that marked the period after 1840.

The hegemony of the European economy would have come regardless of the response of the indigenous peoples. Once the wave of population of the agricultural frontier reached the west, it was inevitable that the small and scattered population of the region would either assimilate into the new system or be displaced economically. Ironically, however, the hegemony of the new economic order may have come more rapidly and with more devastating effect because of the particular economic response of the native and Métis peoples during the 1860s and 1870s.

For years, there had been a trade in buffalo robes carried on by the Hudson's Bay Company. Almost all the robes were sold in North America, and the great majority of these were used as sleigh blankets. Through the 1840s and 1860s, the robe trade had provided Métis and native provisioners with a useful sideline. It was generally a minor activity, however. The demand for robes was more or less constant, and the robe "worth only about as much as a common fox skin."[27] The trade may thus have contributed in a small way to the depletion of the herds through the 1840s and 1850s, but was not likely a crucial factor.

Then, beginning in the later 1860s, there was a sudden and sharp shift in the demand for furs. The average Hudson's Bay Company price for a robe rose from $4.82 in 1866 to $8.82 in 1870 and would remain near that level for several years thereafter.[28] The expansion of the American rail and steamboat network also meant that the costs of transporting the bulky robes declined. The robe trade was suddenly a very attractive proposition.

It was also a trade that, given the circumstances, invited destruction of the resource on which it was based. For one thing, the buffalo herds were already under severe pressure. For another, the Hudson's Bay Company was no longer, if it ever had been, in a position to control the farming of the resource. Indeed, the company's role in the trade had always been secondary to that of American frontiersmen operating out of such places as Fort Benton in Montana. Also, these American traders operated, to a degree, on a speculative basis. The prices offered and the supplies they acquired made economic sense only if the boom in robes continued for years to come. Perhaps, they even sensed how their own economic activity was creating an ever-scarcer resource and were stockpiling against the future. That is conjecture, but, whatever the reason, there is no doubt of the tremendous inventories acquired in a short period of time.

This trade had numerous effects. First, the use of whisky by some of the traders and some notorious incidents in the early 1870s caused the Canadian government to assert its control more quickly over the prairie region. This move would facilitate the development of new economic activity. Second, the Métis and native tribes, such as the Cree and Blackfoot, responded to the opportunity that existed by shifting much of their energy to the buffalo-robe trade. Finally, however, all of this meant that the basic staple of the plains tribes was being hunted in greater numbers than ever before. The herds had had trouble replenishing themselves since the 1840s. In the 1870s, increased hunting north and south of the border turned an ecological imbalance into a slaughter.

This destruction was the final in a series of steps that marked the end of the old economic order in the west, one that had rested on the game resources of the region. Game had been both the basis of independence from the Europeans and the basis of trade with them. Independence was tied to the ability of a native band to live off the land, by hunting or fishing. European technology was a source of convenience and comfort long before it was a necessity to the tribes of the northwest. It was the basis of trade, of course, in that both the fur and the provisioning trades rested on the continued demand for the furs of the region. Long before 1870, however, the balance was beginning to shift. The commercial ties to the Europeans were becoming closer, and the dependence on trade goods greater. The Europeans and the Métis, for their part, were increasingly present in the interior. Both the Métis buffalo hunt and the crops grown at Red River diminished the importance of the native provisioning trade. In the meantime, the buffalo on which the provisioning rested were becoming scarcer.

Then, in the 1870s, two things happened that destroyed the economic basis of the old order. First, the isolation of the region came to an end as first the American and then the Canadian frontier reached the area. Second, the already tenuous balance of economic power among the various groups in the region (Indian, Métis, European) was shattered. The European population of the region grew more in the 5 years after the transfer than it had in the previous 200! Much of this population was still resident in the eastern part of the region, but the direction was clear: henceforth, Canadian/Western European economic structures and practices would shape the region.

The third, and final, event was the destruction of the buffalo. Eventually, the native population and the Métis would have been forced to abandon the hunt anyway. The concept of the communal territory over which hunters might roam conflicted too sharply with the demands of agriculture for protection of crops and with the European concept of private property. The destruction of the herds, south as well as north of the border, however, left the native population with no economic basis with which to resist European hegemony. By the later 1870s, the buffalo was nearly extinct, and tribes of the region had no choice but to accept treaties offered by the Canadian government and to move on to reservations.

The great commonality of land and the dual use of game resources, for trade and subsistence, which had been the basis of the western economy prior to the arrival of the Hudson's Bay Company, were forever gone, to be replaced by the more complex structures of an agricultural/industrial society. Both the people and the activities of the old order became marginal to the existence of the new.

Notes

1. Gerald Friesen, *The Canadian Prairies: A History* (Toronto: University of Toronto Press, 1985), 46.
2. Arthur J. Ray, *Indians in the Fur Trade: Their Role as Hunters, Trappers, and Middlemen in the Lands Southwest of Hudson Bay* (Toronto: University of Toronto Press, 1974), 69.
3. Ray, *Indians in the Fur Trade*, 61.
4. For a detailed commentary on the native cycle, see Ray, *Indians in the Fur Trade*, 44–45.
5. Abraham Rotstein, "Trade and Politics: An Institutional Approach," *Western Canadian Journal of Anthropology* 3, no. 1 (1972): 1.
6. The North West Company emerged from a series of temporary partnerships between outfitters. Initially, these partnerships were short-lived. Thus, historians might choose different dates for the formation of the company. The first partnership was in 1776; a second, in 1779. In 1780, the first multi-year arrangement was made.
7. Friesen, *The Canadian Prairies*, 62.
8. Harold Innis, *The Fur Trade in Canada* (Toronto: University of Toronto Press, 1970), 157.
9. Graeme Wynn, "On the Margins of Empire," in *The Illustrated History of Canada*, edited by Craig Brown (Toronto: Lester and Orpen Dennys, 1987), 235.
10. R. Cole Harris and John Warkentin, *Canada Before Confederation* (Toronto: Oxford University Press, 1974), 290–91.
11. Friesen, *The Canadian Prairies*, 39.

12. Ray, *Indians in the Fur Trade*, 130–32.
13. Cited in Ray, *Indians in the Fur Trade*, 133.
14. Innis, *The Fur Trade in Canada*, Chapter 9; W.T. Easterbrook and H.G.J. Aitken, *Canadian Economic History* (Toronto: Macmillan, 1956), 173.
15. Innis, *The Fur Trade in Canada*, 280.
16. Gerald Tulchinsky, *The River Barons: Montreal Businessmen and the Growth of Industry and Transportation, 1837–1853* (Toronto: University of Toronto Press, 1977), 4, 108–10 refers to some of these new investments. See also "Edward Ellice," *Dictionary of Canadian Biography*, Vol. 9, 233–39.
17. Innis, *The Fur Trade in Canada*, 284–85.
18. Michael Bliss, *Northern Enterprise: Five Centuries of Canadian Business* (Toronto: McClelland and Stewart, 1987), 105; J. Foster and D. Richeson, *The Fur Trade in Canada Since 1867* (Ottawa: Museum of Man, 1986), 6.
19. Glyndwr Williams, "The Hudson's Bay Company and the Fur Trade: 1670–1870," *The Beaver: Magazine of the North*, Outfit 314.2 (Autumn 1983): 51.
20. J.S. Galbraith, *The Little Emperor: Governor Simpson of the Hudson's Bay Company* (Toronto: Macmillan, 1976).
21. On the various experiments, see E.E. Rich, *The Fur Trade and the Northwest to 1857* (Toronto: McClelland and Stewart, 1967), 250–52.
22. Innis, *The Fur Trade in Canada*, 330.
23. Innis, *The Fur Trade in Canada*, 337.
24. On the general policy of the company, see J.S. Galbraith, *The Hudson's Bay Company as an Imperial Factor, 1821–1869* (Berkeley: University of California Press, 1957), 88–96.
25. Friesen, *The Canadian Prairies*, 91.
26. Alvin Gluek, *Minnesota and the Manifest Destiny of the Canadian North-West* (Toronto: University of Toronto Press, 1965).
27. On the buffalo-robe trade, see Bob Beal, "The Buffalo Robe Trade," in *The Métis Hivernant Settlement at Buffalo Lake, 1872–1877: An Historical Report Prepared for the Department of Culture*, prepared by John Foster (Edmonton: Government of Alberta, 1987).
28. Beal, "The Buffalo Robe Trade," 88.

Further Reading

Galbraith, John S. *The Little Emperor: Governor Simpson of the Hudson's Bay Company*. Toronto: Macmillan, 1976.

Innis, Harold. *The Fur Trade in Canada*. Toronto: University of Toronto Press, 1970.

Ray, Arthur J. *Indians in the Fur Trade: Their Role as Hunters, Trappers and Middlemen in the Lands Southwest of Hudson Bay, 1660–1870*. Toronto: University of Toronto Press, 1974.

CHAPTER

10

Confederation and the British North America Act

For decades, British North Americans had discussed the desirability of greater autonomy within the British Empire and had, on occasion, even flirted with the idea of leaving the Empire altogether. For a time, the British had resisted this tendency, but the changing philosophies toward colonial possessions that accompanied the demise of mercantilism, as well as the growing stridence of colonial demands, led to a reversal of policy. In 1848, the British had granted the colonies responsible government, which effectively gave British North Americans control over their domestic affairs. Through the 1850s, colonial autonomy had been demonstrated in a number of bills, including those establishing a separate currency and creating tariffs against the mother country. Confederation was the next logical step in the process of devolving control over the colonies. It was also a response to particular concerns of the 1860s, including political stalemate in the Province of Canada and fear of the forces emanating from the Civil War in the United States.

Without denying the importance of these political motives, it is possible to argue that Confederation was equally, perhaps even primarily, the product of two separate economic forces. In part, its roots lay in the mercantile period and in the attempts in the 1850s and 1860s to re-create that environment (outlined in Chapter 7). The perception remained that commercial prosperity and industrial success were linked to an expanding resource frontier. By the mid-1860s, that resource hinterland had been extended to include the fertile plains of the Canadian west. Reaching that frontier, however, involved a commitment well beyond the means of the colonies in their present state. In this sense, then, as Vernon Fowke has written, "the national policy predated the creation of a national government in Canada and envisaged the establishment of such a government as one of its indispensable instruments."[1]

Confederation was not just a desperate reaction of a commercial elite unable to re-establish the old dependency or establish a new one, however, much popular history notwithstanding. It was also a product of the industrialization and urbanization outlined in Chapter 9, and of the confidence that came with those developments. Confederation may have been perceived as necessary because of the developments of the preceding three decades, but it was also possible because of them.

British North America at Confederation

The economic position of British North America on the eve of Confederation can be outlined briefly as follows. Population had grown from 2.4 million in 1851 to 3.2 million in 1861, and to 3.5 million in 1867. Table 10.1 shows the totals for Canada and the provinces for the census years 1851–71, the growth from period to period, and the share of each province in the total. The rapid growth to 1851 is apparent, especially in Upper Canada. Rates were slower everywhere but New Brunswick in the 1850s, and Upper Canada again led the way. Population growth slowed across the board in the 1860s and was more evenly spread; only Quebec was out of line, with an increase of about half that for the other provinces. The net result was that the share of the total population of British North America fell very slightly for each of the three Maritime provinces between 1851 and 1871, declined somewhat more for Quebec, and rose for Ontario.

The population was about 80 percent rural in 1867. Montreal was, by far, the largest city, with 100 000 inhabitants. Quebec City followed, with a population of 60 000, then Toronto, with about 50 000. Halifax had slightly fewer than 30 000 residents in 1867, and Saint John about 700 fewer than Halifax. The remainder of the 3.5 million Canadians lived in small villages and towns, in lumber camps, and on farms.

TABLE 10.1

Population of Canada and the Provinces to 1871:
Growth from Previous Decade and Percentage of Total, 1851–1871

	1851			*1861*			*1871*		
	Population (000)	*Growth (%)*	*% of Total*	*Population (000)*	*Growth (%)*	*% of Total*	*Population (000)*	*Growth (%)*	*% of Total*
Nova Scotia	276.9	36.7	11.4	330.9	19.5	10.2	378.8	17.2	10.5
New Brunswick	193.8	24.1	8.0	252.0	30.4	7.8	285.6	13.0	7.7
P.E.I.	62.7	33.2	2.6	80.9	29.0	2.5	94.0	16.3	2.5
Maritimes	533.3	31.4	22.0	664.4	24.6	20.6	767.4	15.5	20.8
U.C./Ont.	952.0	95.5	39.1	1396.1	46.6	43.2	1620.9	16.1	43.9
L.C./Que.	890.3	31.9	36.5	1111.6	24.9	34.4	1191.5	7.2	32.3
British Columbia	55.0	+	2.3	55.5	+	1.6	36.2	+	1.0
N.W.T.	5.7	+	—	6.7	+	0.2	48.0	+	1.3
Manitoba	—	+	—	—	+		25.2	+	0.7
Total	2436.3		100.0	3229.6		100.0	3689.3		100.0

+ not applicable — boundaries changed

Source: M.C. Urquhart and K.A.H. Buckley, eds., *Historical Statistics of Canada* (Toronto: Macmillan, 1965), Series A2–14; and S.A. Saunders, *The Economic History of the Maritime Provinces*, edited and with an introduction by T.W. Acheson (Fredericton: Acadiensis Press, 1984), 105.

In spite of the dominance of rural life, this was not the pioneer economy of earlier days. Except for struggling farms clinging to the Shield in Canada West and Canada East, there was little frontier left. The farms were established ones, often three generations so, and the more prosperous boasted comfortable brick houses, well-built barns, considerable equipment, and well-established service centres nearby.

There was also a greater diversity of occupation than would have been the case even a quarter-century earlier (see Table 10.2). Farmers, lumbermen, and fishermen accounted for 51 percent of the gainfully employed in 1871, a figure that was pretty much common to all four provinces. Manufacturing and handicrafts made up another 13 percent, and here Ontario had a slight edge. Another 18 percent classed themselves as construction and unskilled labourers. Of Nova Scotia's work force, 2 percent were miners, the only ones reported. The remaining shares — from 17 percent in Ontario to 21 percent in Nova Scotia and 18 percent overall — were in service occupations, such as wholesale and retail trade, transportation and communication, finance, the professions, and government.

The provinces appear quite similar by these broad occupational classes, but, when compared in more specific terms, differences become apparent. Agriculture dominated the economy of Prince Edward Island, but was relatively unimportant elsewhere in the Maritimes. Fishing, shipbuilding, shipping, and timber were the main pursuits of the other two Maritime provinces, with fishing relatively more important in Nova Scotia, and timber much more so in New Brunswick. As T.W. Acheson wrote: "The Maritime provinces of Canada in 1870 probably come the closest of any region to representing the classic ideal of the staple economy."[2] Agriculture was very important in the Province of Canada, as was timber.

These orientations are reflected in the trade statistics for each province (see Table 10.3). Nearly 40 percent of Nova Scotia's exports in 1865 were fishery products, followed by agricultural products at 18 percent and minerals at 16 percent. Manufactures made up only 12 percent of exports, but 58 percent of imports. Agricultural products accounted for another 30 percent of imports. Two-thirds of New Brunswick's export trade appears in the category forest products, followed by 13 percent in manufactures. Manufactured goods were the largest import (47 percent) for that colony in 1865,

TABLE 10.2

Occupations of the People, Percentage Distribution, 1871

	Ontario (%)	*Quebec* (%)	*New Brunswick* (%)	*Nova Scotia* (%)	*Total* (%)
Farmers, lumbermen, and fishermen	51	52	51	52	51
Manufacturing and handicrafts	14	11	12	10	13
Construction and unskilled labourers	18	17	18	15	18
Miners	—	—	—	2	—
Subtotal	83	80	81	79	82
Services*	17	20	19	21	18
Total	100	100	100	100	100

*Includes wholesale and retail trade, transportation and communication, government and education, finance, the professions, and personal services.

Source: Royal Commission on Dominion-Provincial Relations, *Report*, Book I: *Canada, 1867–1939* (Ottawa: King's Printer, 1940), 22.

followed by agricultural products at 40 percent. Three-quarters of Prince Edward Island's exports were classed as agricultural, with another 18 percent coming from the fisheries. Manufactures made up more than 50 percent of the island's imports; agricultural products, another 24 percent. Agricultural products were the leading export of the Province of Canada (52 percent), followed by forest products (40 percent). Manufactures (58 percent) and agricultural goods (31 percent) were the dominant imports.

The orientation of this trade is important, given the intent of Confederation to unite the colonies into a commercial union. The pattern for the Maritimes is shown in Table 10.4, and can be sum-

TABLE 10.3

Composition of Trade, the Maritimes and Can

Products	N.S. Imp.	N.S. Exp.	N.B. Imp.	N.B. Exp.	P.E.I. Imp.	P.E.I. Exp.	
Agricultural	29.6	18.4	39.5	6.8	24.2	73.0	3[illegible]
Fishery	2.7	39.3	1.5	2.5	[illegible]	17.6	1[illegible]
Forest	1.8	8.8	1.0	60.3	6.8	8.4	1[illegible]
Manuf. and misc	57.8	11.7	47.4	13.3	55.3	0.5	57.9
Mineral	1.3	15.5	3.6	5.1	3.5	0.3	5.5
Wines and liquors	6.4	6.3	7.0	1.0	5.6	0.2	3.[illegible]

Source: S.A. Saunders, *The Economic History of the Maritime Provinces*, edited with an introduction by T.W. Acheson (Fredericton: Acadiensis Press, 1984),

marized as follows: in terms of exports, as of 1865, Nova Scotia was the most dependent of the three Maritime colonies on the United States; the most dependent, by far, on the West Indies; and the least tied to the United Kingdom. New Brunswick was second to Nova Scotia in terms of its dependence on the United States, relied less on the West Indies, but was by far the most tied of the three to the United Kingdom. Prince Edward Island reported no exports to the United States and a minuscule amount to the West Indies. Foreign nations took nearly half of the island's exports, other North American colonies another third, and the United Kingdom 20 percent. The United States was the leading exporter to New Brunswick; the United Kingdom, second. The pattern was almost exactly reversed for Nova Scotia. Intercolonial trade was small, by comparison, for both colonies. Britain was Prince Edward Island's main source of supply in 1865, followed by other North American colonies. No U.S. products were reported. Unfortunately, similar data are not available for the other provinces.

Confederation and the BNA *Act*

The idea of linking the British North American colonies together in some governmental system had been around for some time. It was a natural sort of reorganization to undertake. Such schemes, however, had always been vague and had been met with profound

TABLE 10.4

Maritime Trade by Countries, 1865

(£ and Percentage)

	Nova Scotia		New Brunswick		Prince Edward Island	
	Imports	Exports	Imports	Exports	Imports	Exports
TOTAL	£2,876,332	£1,766,139	£1,476,374	£1,153,068	£381,015	£291,545
United Kingdom	43.9%	8.7%	32.2%	46.9%	42.0%	22.2%
British Possessions:						
North America	11.1	19.8	20.3	13.9	32.8	33.2
West Indies	4.6	22.3	1.7	0.7	1.3	1.9
Elsewhere	—	0.7	0.2	—	—	—
TOTAL BRITISH TRADE	59.6	51.5	54.4	61.5	76.1	57.3
United States	30.1	41.0	43.1	31.4	—	—
Foreign countries	10.3	7.5	2.5	7.1	23.9	42.7
TOTAL FOREIGN TRADE	40.4	48.5	45.6	38.5	23.9	42.7
	100.0	100.0	100.0	100.0	100.0	100.0

Source: S.A. Saunders, *The Economic History of the Maritime Provinces*, edited and with an introduction by T.W. Acheson (Fredericton: Acadiensis Press, 1984), 100.

indifference in Great Britain. Only with the American Civil War and the apparent success of the North in that war did the idea gain much currency. The British were interested in cutting back their commitment to the North American colonies, especially given the fact that the colonies already controlled domestic affairs. Yet, in the face of the rising power of the United States, both colonial and British statesmen were aware that the separate colonies would not survive the pull from the south if left on their own. Thus, the next time that Confederation was brought up the British responded with enthusiasm.

The idea itself emerged in an unusual manner. In the Maritimes, there had been long-standing discussions of Maritime union. In 1864, New Brunswick, Nova Scotia, and Prince Edward Island agreed to hold a conference at Charlottetown to discuss the idea. In the meantime, internal politics in the Province of Canada had led to the creation of a coalition government pledged to try to end a political deadlock that had created unstable ministries and fruitless elections. One way out of the deadlock was to abolish the legislative union of Canada East and Canada West in favour of some sort of federal system, perhaps including the other British North American colonies. Thus, when the Canadians heard about the Charlottetown conference, they asked for the right to present their own thoughts on the future of the British North American colonies. In the face of their enthusiasm, the original idea of Maritime union, which had never really generated much excitement, was swept aside, and the idea of Confederation came to the fore.

The Charlottetown conference had dealt only in principles. In September 1864, a follow-up conference at Quebec City hammered out the basic terms of what would become, with some modifications, the British North America Act. Now the various colonies could see more precisely what this grandiose idea implied. As it turned out, some were not as enthusiastic as others.

Newfoundland showed little interest, early on, in the idea of Confederation, or even of Maritime union. The colony was represented at the Quebec conference in 1864, and the delegates returned with some enthusiasm for the idea. Two major groups on the island opposed any such moves, however. Roman Catholics did so because they were predominantly Irish, and Confederation smacked of British conquest. Merchants opposed it because they saw it (correctly, it might be added) as leading to higher tariffs on supplies to the fisheries and a financial commitment to a government primarily obsessed with furthering the interests (defence and economic development) of the central provinces. Opposition waned some in the mid-1860s in the midst of recession, but economic conditions had improved somewhat in 1869, when an election on the issue was held. The anti-confederates won, and Confederation for Newfoundland had to await another 80 years and another set of circumstances.

Positions were not so clear-cut in the Maritimes. Proponents of Confederation in Nova Scotia and New Brunswick saw two main advantages to union. Ports such as Halifax and Saint John could serve as year-round, ice-free outlets for the products of the interior — Canadian, and perhaps even American — on their way to Europe. The large and growing central Canadian market beckoned as well, for everything from coal to manufactured goods. Both objectives required rail connection to Montreal and Toronto, an expanded branch-line network within the region, and free movement of goods among the colonies. All requirements were more easily met through co-ordinated action.

Opponents of Confederation in Nova Scotia and New Brunswick varied, depending on time and place. It was possible to trot out well-remembered tales of Upper Canadian betrayal, especially on earlier plans to build an intercolonial railway, and to point to the violence-prone nature of Canadian politics dating back to 1837. Most common, however, was the fear that Canada would threaten the Maritime economy with a high tariff structure and with a high debt charge from profligate canal and railway construction.

Prince Edward Island shared many of these fears, and was as well mired in local political rivalries that involved personality, old wounds left by absentee landlords, and, most genuinely, a realization of just what a small power this province would be in a Canadian federation. A sense of local pride, concern for the loss of identity, and internal politics caused them to turn their backs on the initial proposal. However, the island's politicians were not able to resist the temptation of railway politics, and, by 1873, the bills had become so high that federation with Canada was the only alternative to bankruptcy.

The main enthusiasm for political union lay in central Canada. Here, though, hope rested less on what integration promised from expanding economic contacts among existing economies than on what it seemed to make possible in the way of establishing new ones. Central Canadian business interests were as confident of capturing Maritime markets for primary and manufactured products as were their counterparts of the reverse, to be sure. The real prize, though, lay in establishing a transcontinental economy along the lines of the obviously successful one to the south. Development of the resource potential of the west, broadly defined, would provide the country with a new staple for export and a new frontier of investment. As W.L. Morton put it, central Canada wanted to "break out" of the confines of the St. Lawrence.[3] Canadians, as the Toronto *Globe* stated as early as December 10, 1856, were "looking for new worlds to conquer."

Transcontinental expansion was difficult, however. Most obviously, the plains area had to be made part of Canada. Then, a rail line had to be built in time to pre-empt American expansion into the area. That task required financing beyond the resources of the colonies. Political union would create a larger fiscal base with which to attract British investors. Confederation would also give the new Dominion greater control over tariff and immigration policies, the former to help finance rail expansion onto the plains and the latter to guide settlers to them. As Vernon Fowke argues, settlement was the goal; railways, tariffs, and land and immigration policies were the means; and Confederation was the major constitutional instrument.[4]

A quick look at the terms of the British North America Act of 1867 illustrates the force of Fowke's interpretation. The federal government is given clear authority over defence and national economic development. The preamble to Section 91 empowers Ottawa to make laws for the "Peace, Order and Good Government of Canada," in all matters not specifically assigned to the provinces. A list of specific responsibilities is then included, "for greater certainty." Of particular interest for economic development are the regulation of trade and commerce, the raising of money by any mode or system of taxation, the postal service, defence, navigation and shipping, currency and coinage, weights and measures, banking, and the criminal code.

Section 92 contains no general preamble such as that for Section 91, but rather proceeds directly to delineating the exclusive powers of the provinces. They were to be responsible, in the words of Section 92.16, for "Generally all Matters of a merely local or private Nature." Jurisdiction over property and civil rights is set out explicitly, a move that subsequent analysts have seen as an attempt to give control of "culture" to the provinces. Provincial responsibilities of most interest for subsequent economic development are those over direct taxation within the provinces for revenue purposes, the management and sale of public land, hospitals, municipalities, local works and undertakings, and property and civil rights. Section 93 adds education to the list of provincial responsibilities. Agriculture and immigration are listed as concurrent powers in Section 95.

The act contains some other provisions that were important economically at the time, or have become so since. Section 109 states that all lands, mines, minerals, and royalties belonging to the several provinces in 1867 shall continue to belong to them. Section 121 states that all articles of the "growth, produce, or manufacture of any of the provinces shall . . . be admitted free into each of the other provinces." Section 125 states that no lands or properties belonging to one level of government shall be liable for taxation by another. Parliament is given authority over treaties with foreign powers in Section 133. Finally, Section 146 provides for the admission into the union of Newfoundland, Prince Edward Island, British Columbia, and Rupert's Land.

The fiscal arrangements set out in the act deserve special note, given the importance they have played throughout Canadian history. Giving Ottawa unlimited powers to tax, while restricting the provinces to direct levies, meant that the federal government took over customs and excise duties, which contributed 85 percent of total government revenue at that time. Provinces were left with spending responsibilities in excess of their capacity to tax. This fiscal gap was covered by Ottawa's agreeing to make annual per-capita grants to the provinces, to provide a cash subsidy in support of government and legislatures, and to assume all provincial debts. New Brunswick received a special ten-year grant in recognition of its special financial needs, and the same provision was extended retroactively to Nova Scotia in 1869.

Three features of these fiscal arrangements should be noted, less for their immediate relevance than for their role in political and constitutional debates many decades later. First, the clear intent was to make an economic union out of the British North American colonies. The prohibition on indirect taxation by provinces complemented Section 121 of the act in preventing the erection of tariff-like barriers to interprovincial trade. Second, there was a clear commitment to offset fiscal gaps so that each level of government could carry out its constitutionally assigned functions effectively. Statutory payments were set to balance taxation powers and expenditure responsibilities. Finally, there was a commitment to rough fiscal equity across provinces, and a recognition that responsibility for achieving it rested with the federal government. Equal per-capita grants were implicitly equalizing, while special payments to the two poorer provinces were explicitly so.

Conclusion

With Confederation, one era in Canadian economic history ends and another begins. No longer is it possible to cast the story in terms of several distinct and isolated colonies tied (however loosely) to British mercantile policy and to the fortunes of their main staple products. Now, there is a national economy to deal with, and a national focus to bring to bear on economic and political issues. Regional differences did not disappear by an act of the British Parliament, however, so the national perspective must always be complemented by the regional ones. Nor is reference to staples activities sufficient to explain economic development, if indeed it ever was. The industrial revolution is an important new theme. As with the political change, though, it adds to an existing one rather than supplanting it.

Notes

1. Vernon C. Fowke, "The National Policy — Old and New," in *Approaches to Economic History*, edited by W.T. Easterbrook and H.G.J. Aiken (Toronto: McClelland and Stewart, 1967), 239.
2. T.W. Acheson, "The National Policy and the Industrialization of the Maritimes, 1880 1910," in *Atlantic Canada After Confederation*, The Acadiensis Reader, Vol. 2 (Fredericton: Acadiensis Press, 1985), 176.
3. W.L. Morton, *Canada 1857-1873: The Critical Years* (Toronto: McClelland and Stewart, 1964), 21.
4. Fowke, "The National Policy."

Further Reading

Morton, W.L. *Canada 1857–1873: The Critical Years*. Toronto: McClelland and Stewart, 1964.

Creighton, D.G. "Economic Nationalism and Confederation." In *Towards the Discovery of Canada*, edited by D.G. Creighton. Toronto: Macmillan, 1972.

IV

A Modern Economy Established, 1867–1914

IV

The general theme for Canada's economic history in the years between Confederation and the onset of World War I follows directly from the developments outlined in Part III. This theme can be phrased in the form of a question: How would development proceed now that the industrial revolution had spread beyond the United Kingdom to the Continent and to North America, and now that several disparate regional economies in British North America were joined into one economic and political union?

More specific themes follow from this general one. There were to be not one but two industrial revolutions in these years, and each affected the Canadian economy in quite different and complex ways. Old staples industries faced dislocation and adjustment, and new ones appeared. The manufacturing and service sectors grew, partly in response to the country's natural advantages and partly as a result of deliberate government policies. Government policies, in turn, were alternately praised and condemned: praised because, at times and to some, they appeared to promote growth or national unity, and condemned because, at other times and to others, they appeared to be wasteful or regionally disciminatory.

International Background

The first half-dozen years after 1867 were prosperous ones for the international economy. Around 1873, circumstances changed, however. The period 1873–96 used to be known as the Great Depression, with that term understood to imply an actual contraction of real output or, at least, a dramatic reduction in the rate of increase relative to that of preceding decades. However, this view has been considerably modified recently. We now know that the period was less a depression than a deflation. Wholesale prices in the United Kingdom, for example, fell every year but one between 1873 and 1896, after remaining roughly constant or even rising slightly from 1850 to 1873.[1] Some have seen this trend as a monetary phenomenon. The supply of money failed to keep pace with the expansion of economic activity, and prices necessarily fell. Others have viewed it as a reflection of falling costs in important sectors, such as steel, grains, and ocean and rail transportation, that were passed on to consumers. Whatever the cause or causes, the point is that, since there is no necessary, or at least no obvious, connection between deflation and economic growth, it is misleading to refer to the period as a depression.

Aggregate economic performance might have been stronger in these decades than was previously believed, but this period was, nonetheless, one of much disruption and dislocation. This was particularly true in manufacturing, as a result of the growing might of Germany, France, and the United States, and in agriculture, as a result of the appearance of offshore grains in European markets. The predictable result was a return to protectionism, reversing the progress toward freer trade that had been under way since mid-century. An alliance between "rye and iron" in Germany led to the imposition of duties on industrial and agricultural products in 1879, with the rates raised considerably in the 1880s. The French raised agricultural tariffs in 1885 and 1887, and moved to a comprehensive system of duties in 1892. Similar strategies were adopted in most other European nations. Britain resisted these pressures for a time, even though, in relative terms, at least, it was losing the most ground.

An important change occurred in the 1890s, as the world entered into what has been termed the second industrial revolution. The origins lay in a series of technological developments — or improvements, really, since, like most changes of this sort, the steps that actually led to commercial application were merely the final ones in a process of invention and innovation that had begun much earlier. The Bessemer process and the Siemens-Martin furnace increased the quality and uniformity of steel and reduced fuel requirements. Further developments increased the scale of furnaces and mechanized the loading and handling processes. The real cost of steel fell as a result, and it began to be substituted for other materials in everything from construction (the completion of the Eiffel Tower in 1889 being the most dramatic demonstration of this potential) to bridges and shipbuilding.

Parallel advances in the measurement and working of steel had even more dramatic impact. The initial developments were in response to growing demand for high-velocity firearms, sewing machines, cash registers, typewriters, complex farm machinery, bicycles, motors, and other such goods. As the techniques developed, the basis was laid for the internal-combustion engine, the motor car, and the aeroplane. There were French, German, and British automobiles on the road by the turn of the new century, but these developments paled when compared with what was about to happen to the auto industry in the United States. Airplanes, by contrast, developed rather more quickly in Europe than in North America up to the start of World War I. The economic impacts of both inventions were just beginning to be felt at the turn of the century. Their effects were enormous, and, indeed, are still being felt.

Developments in the chemical industry were of great importance as well. A shift to a new production process for soda brought down the costs of dyes and other products, benefiting the textile industry in particular. The range of medicines available to doctors increased. The rise in automobile use prompted advances in petroleum refining and distillation. Plastics was an established branch of the chemical industry by 1900, and the use of cellulose nitrate in photographic film in the 1890s laid the basis for the motion-picture industry. Other cellulose products were the main constituents in synthetic fibres.

Developments in electricity were at least as spectacular and far-reaching in their ultimate economic and social impacts. The properties of electricity were known much earlier, but it was only toward the end of the nineteenth century that knowledge had advanced to the point where electricity could be produced, transmitted, and utilized cheaply and effectively. Distant rivers could now be used to turn turbines, with the output transmitted to urban and industrial areas. Large-scale production from cheap hydro sources meant taking advantage of economies of scale, which, in turn, meant that electricity prices could fall significantly. The stage was thus set for the wide-scale use of electricity in industry and in the home. Like those of autos and airplanes, the economic spinoffs of this advance are still being felt.

Technological advances figure on the supply side of the story of the second industrial revolution. That these advances were put into production when they were, on the scale they were, is explained by changes on the demand side. Prices turned up after nearly two decades of more or less continuous decline. Gold supplies were augmented by discoveries in South Africa, Australia, and the Klondike, and this increase in the world's money supply led to general inflation. Agricultural prices increased relative to manufactured ones as the booming U.S. economy absorbed more and more of its own grain production. Real interest rates were at historic low levels in the 1890s as well, adding to the incentive to invest in new capital equipment.

From Canada's perspective, the major development over the entire period from 1867 to 1914 was the rapid economic growth and industrialization of the American economy. On the eve of the Civil War, half of American commodity output originated in agriculture, and only one-third in manufacturing; by 1900, the positions were exactly reversed.[2] New industries, such as steel, electricity, paper, and chemicals, led the way, but the older, established sectors, such as clothing and textiles, progressed as well. Nor was progress restricted to manufacturing. Total output and, more importantly, output per capita rose significantly in all major sectors. By the beginning of World War I, the United States possessed what was undisputably the world's leading economy.

Canada's Aggregate Economic Performance

The traditional account of Canada's aggregate economic performance after Confederation breaks the era into three periods. The first few years were prosperous ones for the new Dominion. The international economy was buoyant, markets for the main staple products were strong, and capital for investment was available. All that ended with the onset of the Great Depression that began in 1873. Since Canada depended so extensively on exports, foreign capital, and immigration for growth, the international slowdown had especially severe repercussions in this country. The Rowell-Sirois Commission described the period to 1896 as one of "trial, discouragement and even failure.''[3] It was, in Easterbrook and Aitken's words, "one of periodic and prolonged slumps interrupted by brief periods of recovery.''[4]

The contrast between this account of the first 30 years and the story of the decade and a half thereafter could scarcely be sharper. A "fortuitous conjuncture of world circumstances brought with a rush the fulfilment of hopes long deferred," as Rowell-Sirois put it. "A vast and sudden transformation was wrought.''[5] Easterbrook and Aitken note that "it [the boom decade of the early twentieth century] marks one of the major turning points in the evolution of the Canadian economy.''[6] The wheat boom is significant in both accounts, although each source acknowledges the role of the other developments.

The Rowell-Sirois Commission and Easterbrook and Aitken wrote without the benefit of much aggregate economic data, and they were influenced by a view of the international economy that has now been modified. Fortunately, it is now possible to be somewhat more precise about what exactly did transpire in the Canadian economy in this period. A group of academics based at Queen's University, headed by M.C. Urquhart, have recently released the results of a decade of research on historical national-income statistics. Researchers now have available an annual series from 1870 for gross national product in current and constant dollars, along with detail on the individual components of the aggregate series (see Table IV.1). While the task of reconstructing historical data can never be error-free, as the authors readily acknowledge, it is certainly safe to say that this effort by Urquhart and colleagues will inform research in this area for many years.

Table IV.1, derived from the Urquhart data, shows compound growth rates for population, real GNP, and real GNP per capita, by decade, from 1870 to 1910, and for the two periods 1870–96 and 1897–1913. Real GNP grew by 2.3 percent in the first full decade after Confederation and by 3.6 percent in the 1880s, dropped slightly to 3.3 percent in the 1890s, and then accelerated to 6.2 percent for a decade after 1900. The contrast between the earlier and the later years is especially striking if 1896 is taken as the dividing point; real growth was more than 2.5 times greater in the latter period. To put these numbers into perspective, growth over the entire period from 1870 to 1926 averaged 3.6 percent, and between 1870 and 1985 it averaged 3.7 percent. Thus, the economy grew substantially

TABLE IV.1
Percentage Rates of Growth of Population, GNP and GNP Per Capita, Various Periods, 1870–1913

	Population	*GNP*		*GNP Per Capita*
		Current $	*Constant $*	*Current $*
1870–1880	1.61	2.34	2.26	0.67
1880–1890	1.17	3.58	3.59	2.39
1890–1900	1.04	2.85	3.28	2.17
1900–1910	2.80	8.35	6.19	3.32
1870–1896	1.30	2.00	2.38	1.06
1897–1913	2.52	8.52	6.19	3.56

Source: Calculated from M.C. Urquhart, "New Estimates of Gross National Product, Canada, 1870–1926: Some Implications for Canadian Economic Development," in *Long-Term Factors in American Economic Growth*, NBER Studies in Income and Wealth, Vol. 51, edited by Stanley L. Engerman and Robert E. Gallman (Chicago: University of Chicago Press, 1986), 30–31.

below its long-term average in the 1870s, at the average in the 1880s, slightly below it in the 1890s, and well above it in the seventeen years after 1896.

The picture is more mixed yet if per-capita output figures are considered. Population growth over the 1870s was just barely short of real GNP increases, annual per-capita output rising only 0.7 percent on average in that decade. Population growth slowed in the 1880s, and output growth increased, the per-capita figure jumping to 2.4 percent. It remained just below this figure in the 1890s, before jumping to over 3.3 percent after 1900. Looking again at the pre- and post-1896 periods, the difference is again striking. Real output per capita rose by more than three times as much after the break as before it; even population growth was accelerating.

Putting economic data into perspective is always a problem, and never more so than when it comes to talking about economic-growth rates. What is the line between rapid and slow? The exercise of attaching labels implies comparison, and here two perspectives are possible. The first, already done above, is to ask how the economy did in any given period relative to some other time frame. From this perspective, the evidence clearly points to a structural break of some type around the mid-1890s. In Urquhart's words, "The Canadian economy developed in a fundamentally different way after 1900 than it had before."[7]

The other tack is to look at how the economy did in a given time period relative to other, comparable economies. In Canada's case, one obvious comparison is to the American economy. American population increased substantially faster than Canada's before 1900 — almost twice as fast in the 1880s and 1890s, in fact. The pattern reversed after 1900, when Canadian population increase was well above that to the south. The pattern for GNP growth was slightly different from that for population. Real output in the United States grew substantially faster than did Canada's in the 1870s, but only slightly faster the following two decades. After 1900, the Canadian growth rate was nearly double the American one. Data on real per-capita GNP suggest that Americans were increasing their standard of living faster than were Canadians in the 1870s, but that the opposite situation held for the other three decades, with the greatest difference coming between 1900 and 1910.

Direct comparisons of Canada's record with those of other "new" countries of settlement are more difficult since data are not as readily available, but indirect evidence on relative performances *is* available. Rich and growing economies attract international supplies of capital and labour, while poor and slowly growing ones lose them, or at least do not attract their share. By this measure, Canada did poorly, in a relative sense, prior to the turn of the century, and very well for a time thereafter. One estimate[8] is that seven "receiving" countries in total attracted 2.9 million immigrants between 1870 and 1880, 6 million in the 1880s, 4.1 million in the 1890s, and 7.9 million in the first decade of the twentieth century. The United States received the bulk of these migrants — nearly 80 percent in the 1870s, 75 percent in the 1880s, and about 66 percent for the next two decades. Australia, New Zealand, Argentina, and Brazil were, at various times, significant destinations, both before and after 1900.

Canada was a net loser of population in the three decades before 1900, the only new country to be so, but was a significant receiving country in the decade following. Net emigration was 85 000 in the 1870s and jumped to over 200 000 in the 1880s, before falling to just under 200 000 in the 1890s. Between 1900 and 1910, however, net population inflow exceeded 700 000. This amount was still small in relative terms, it must be recognized. Canada received fewer than 10 percent of the total international migrants in this decade, about one-seventh of what the United States did. Canada was not even the second most popular destination after 1900: Argentina was, with about 50 percent more migrants; it was followed by Canada and then closely by Brazil. Still, the net outmigration to 1900, followed by the net inmigration in the next decade, is consistent with the conclusion reached above: that Canada's relative economic position changed at the turn of the century.

Three general conclusions emerge from this overview of Canadian aggregate economic performance in the first half-century following Confederation. First, growth was respectable, if not spectacular, prior to 1900. Certainly, performance appears to have been better, in aggregate and in per-capita terms, than the purely qualitative account of the Rowell-Sirois Commission would suggest. If this impression holds, it means the reasons given by the commission for what it saw as unhappy performance must be deemed suspect as well. There are two possibilities here: if the staples industries truly were fundamental to economic performance, they must have fared better after 1870 than believed. Alternatively, the growth was coming from elsewhere — industrialization, perhaps — in which case the emphasis traditionally placed on staples as leading sectors is misleading. Both explanations could be true, of course, in which case the solution lies in a combination of the two.

The second conclusion is that, however much better performance was than previously believed, it was still not strong enough for Canada to hold its own in the world economy of the time. Other "new" countries, and not just the United States, were experiencing economic booms of the type that Canadian leaders could only dream of. Living standards in this country were not increasing rapidly enough to keep all of our own population growth, much less attract immigrants. It is probably this implication more than any other that accounts for the tendency to think of the years from 1870 to 1900 as ones of "trial, discouragement and even failure."

Finally, it seems clear that some sort of break in Canadian economic growth occurred around the middle of the 1890s. By any measure, the economy performed substantially better after 1896 than it did in the decades before. This development has to be explained, and it has to be squared with the explanation attached to the pattern of growth before 1900. What role did staples industries

— old one and new ones — play in promoting the higher rates of growth of population, GNP, and GNP per capita after 1896, and what role must be ascribed to other factors? What role did government policies play in either case?

Notes

1. S.B. Saul, *The Myth of the Great Depression 1873–1896*, 2nd ed. (London: Macmillan, 1985), 12.
2. Gerald Gunderson, *A New Economic History of America* (New York: McGraw-Hill, 1967), 305.
3. Royal Commission on Dominion-Provincial Relations, *Report*, Book I: *Canada, 1867–1939* (Ottawa: King's Printer, 1940), 65.
4. W.T. Easterbrook and H.G.J. Aitken, *Canadian Economic History* (Toronto: Macmillan, 1965), 392.
5. Royal Commission on Dominion-Provincial Relations, *Report*, 67.
6. Easterbrook and Aitken, *Canadian Economic History*, 482.
7. M.C. Urquhart, "New Estimates of Gross National Product, Canada, 1870–1926: Some Implications for Canadian Economic Development," in *Long-Term Factors in American Economic Growth*, NBER Studies in Income and Wealth, Vol. 51, edited by Stanley L. Engerman and Robert E. Gallman (Chicago: University of Chicago Press, 1986).
8. Alan Green and M.C. Urquhart, "Factor and Commodity Flows in the International Economy of 1870–1914: A Multi-Country View," *Journal of Economic History* 36, no. 1 (March 1976): 217–56.

Further Reading

Gunderson, Gerald. *A New Economic History of America*. New York: McGraw-Hill, 1967.

Royal Commission on Dominion-Provincial Relations. *Report*, Book I: *Canada, 1867–1939*. Ottawa: King's Printer, 1940.

Saul, S.B. *The Myth of the Great Depression 1873–1896*. 2nd ed. London: Macmillan, 1985.

Urquhart, M.C. "New Estimates of Gross National Product, Canada, 1870–1926: Some Implications for Canadian Economic Development." In *Long-Term Factors in American Economic Growth*, NBER Studies in Income and Wealth, Vol. 51, edited by Stanley L. Engerman and Robert E. Gallman. Chicago: University of Chicago Press, 1986.

CHAPTER

11

National Policies

Canadian governments set about immediately to consummate economically the political union of 1867. The new central government faced three specific tasks over and above the act of consolidating its authority in those areas, such as banking and currency, assigned to it by the BNA Act. First, it had to make good on pre-Confederation promises to link the central provinces and the Maritimes by railway. Second, it wanted to bring about, or at least hasten, the opening of the western plains to agricultural settlement under its auspices. Finally, it had to develop a trade policy that would increase access to the United States for primary products and somehow reconcile the demand for increased protection of domestic manufactures with the strong opposition within the country to such a move.

The Intercolonial Railway

The first task facing the new central government was completion of the Intercolonial Railway. Plans to construct a rail line between Canada and the Maritimes had been under way well before Confederation, although, by 1862, they were stalled. The project soon became part of the Confederation negotiations. As Glazebrook expressed it, the majority in Canada probably favoured union without railway, while the majority in the Maritimes probably favoured railway without union.[1] The compromise was union with railway, and the promise to build the Intercolonial was incorporated in the British North America Act.

With the decision to proceed given, what remained to be decided were the route and the method of financing. The line would have to be entirely on Canadian soil, ruling out the short route through Maine favoured by some. A report prepared by Sandford Fleming in 1865 laid out three possible routes — a northern one, by Chaleur Bay; a frontier one, along the St. John River valley; and a central route between the two. The longer, northern line won out, for defence reasons as much as anything, and the route for the Intercolonial — from Rivière du Loup in Quebec through Moncton and Truro to Halifax — was set. A through line was completed by 1876, mostly from new construction but also by making use of sections already completed by the Maritime governments. Three years later, a section from Rivière du Loup to Quebec City was purchased, and the project was completed in 1898 with connections to Montreal.

Financing was an issue throughout. The Intercolonial never attracted private investors, although, as late as 1870, Prime Minister John A. Macdonald still held out hope that it would be operated by the Grand Trunk Railway. This hope was never realized, and, in 1874, the Dominion government placed the line under the control of the Department of Public Works. Construction costs were met by placing a loan of £4 million, with the imperial government guaranteeing the interest on three-quarters of it. Costs exceeded estimates substantially, with the difference met out of general revenue.

The issue of the profitability of the Intercolonial is often raised. The railway never generated enough revenue to cover costs. Its length, high quality of construction, and the lack of a resource hinterland to draw on put it at a permanent disadvantage. The more interesting question is whether it was ever expected to pay its way, whatever the consequences for the users, or whether it was slated from the outset to be a tool of regional development. As we shall see below, different perceptions on this question inside and outside the Maritimes were to cause much resentment and regional alienation decades later.

Opening the Prairies

A major goal of Confederation was to bring about the settlement of the Canadian prairies, and here the task was huge. The land still belonged to the Hudson's Bay Company under the terms of its 1670 charter, although pressure had existed for some time to transfer these rights. Assuming the territory could be obtained, native claims had to be dealt with, the land surveyed, a transportation link established, and settlers attracted. Further, provision had to be made for shaping the settlement process so that the established areas of the country derived the spinoff economic benefits.

The federal government's response to these challenges was a set of economic strategies known, after the fact, as the national policy. This term is generally understood to refer to the land, immigration, railway, and tariff measures implemented in a series of steps between 1867 and 1930, when prairie agriculture settlement was complete. There is considerable dispute today as to whether the national policy is best seen as a systematic and visionary nation-building plan, or as an *ex post facto* construct by scholars wanting to impose some unity of action on the period and some prescience to a group of nineteenth-century politicians. Whatever the motivation, the details are fascinating, and it is to these we now turn.

Land Policy

Formal control over the plains area came in 1868, when Canada literally bought its western frontier. The Hudson's Bay Company gave up its claim to the region, contained in the 1670 charter, in exchange for a lump-sum payment of £300 000, land in the vicinity of its trading posts not to exceed a total of 50 000 acres, and one-twentieth of the fertile belt. The term "fertile belt" was understood to be that area bounded "on the south side by the United States boundary, on the west side by the Rocky Mountains; on the north by the northern branch of the Saskatchewan River; on the east by Lake Winnipeg, Lake of the Woods, and the waters connecting them."[2] The transfer was delayed by the Red River resistance until 1870, when, under the Manitoba Act, a further 1.4 million acres were set aside for "half-breed residents." The remainder of the land was retained by the Government of Canada (meaning that the newly created province of Manitoba would not have the same constitutional status as the four original provinces), to be administered "for the purposes of the Dominion."

There were considerable variations within that fertile belt. Aside from local differences in quality of soil, and availability of water and wood, major geographical features distinguished the region. The northern portion was "parkland," a treed and relatively well-watered region with mixtures of flat and rolling terrain. To the south was the true prairie grasslands, flat and open, although often traversed by sharp coulees and similar features. These features af-

MAP 11.1
The New West

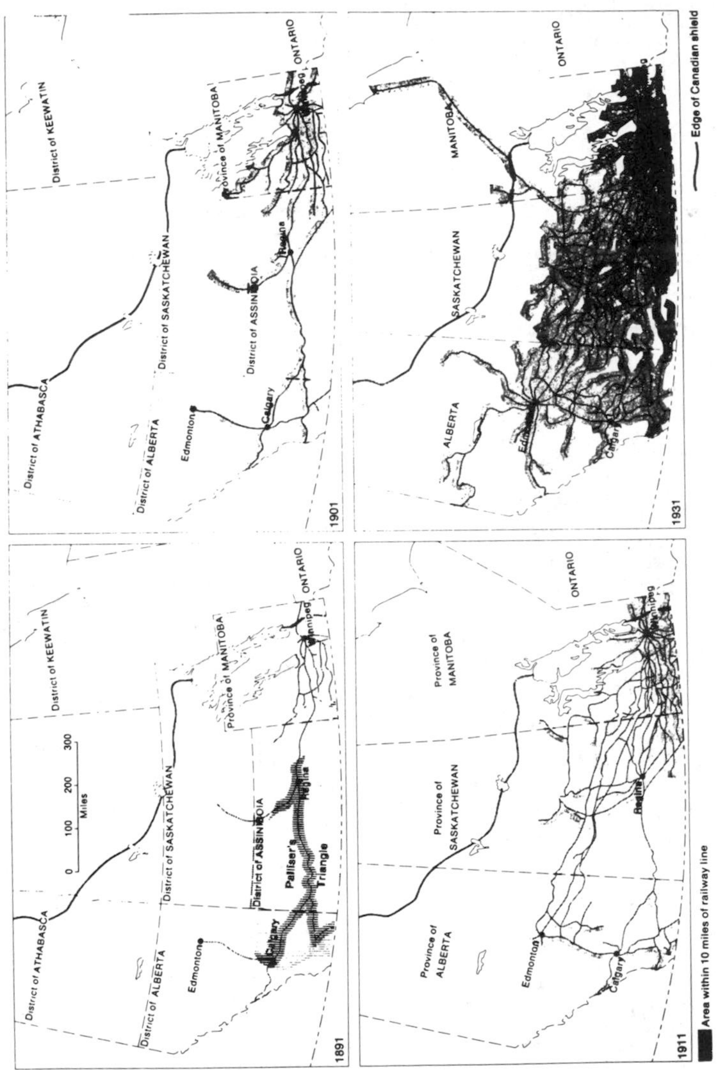

Source: John Warkentin, *Canada: A Geographical Interpretation* (Toronto: Methuen, 1970), 412.

fected contemporary views, and there was a belief in the 1870s that not all of the fertile belt was really suitable for settlement. Specifically, the most likely pattern of settlement was thought to extend from Red River in a northwesterly direction, through the Touchwood Hills to the area of what is now Saskatoon and Battleford. From there, it extended westward, to Fort Edmonton, and southward along the east side of the Rockies. In contrast, the southern region, known as Palliser's Triangle, was seen as marginal land that would be settled only gradually. Before long, promoters would drop such qualifications, but events would prove that the initial analysis was a reasonably accurate one.

Still, what really mattered was that Canada now had a continuous agricultural frontier to replace the one that had been filled in Ontario. Settlement could spread westward from the small core that existed in the Red River–Winnipeg region to the vast prairie beyond. Moreover, the open nature of the landscape and the relative absence of trees assisted in the opening of the region. The slow process of clearing, which, as we have seen, affected pioneer operations in the Canadas, was a minimal problem throughout much of the prairies.

The prerequisite to settlement was the surveying of the land, and, in this process, the open nature of the terrain also assisted rapid progress. A system was formally approved in 1869. The fertile belt was carved into townships running north from the international boundary, and east and west from the Fort Garry meridian. Each township was divided into 36 sections (see Figure 11.1) and each section into 640 acres, like those in the United States and unlike the 800-acre lots in central Canada. Two sections of each township were designated as school lands, to be sold by auction by the Department of the Interior, with the proceeds going to the province or territory for education spending. Another portion went to the Hudson's Bay Company as part of the purchase arrangement. The remaining even-numbered sections were left for free homesteads, each divided into units of 160 acres. Vacant odd-numbered sections were available for railway land grants, and otherwise reverted to the government for sale or special grants. Halfbreed claims, as they were called at the time, were handled through a special system of grants and script. There were also provisions for road allowances, correction lines, and areas set aside for colonization companies.

There were, as a consequence of this system, a variety of ways

FIGURE 11.1

The Prairie Land Survey

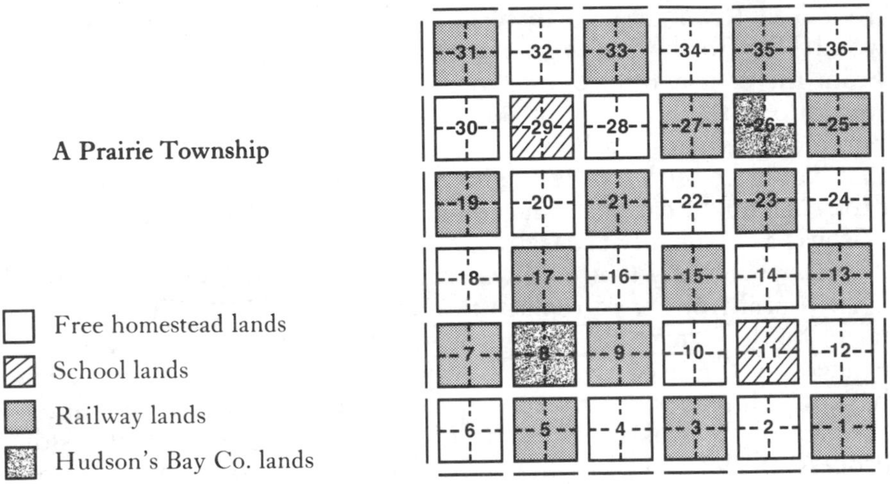

A Prairie Township

31	32	33	34	35	36
30	29	28	27	26	25
19	20	21	22	23	24
18	17	16	15	14	13
7	8	9	10	11	12
6	5	4	3	2	1

Free homestead lands

School lands

Railway lands

Hudson's Bay Co. lands

Source: D.G. Kerr, ed., *Historical Atlas of Canada* (Don Mills: Nelson, 1981), 62.

prospective immigrants could obtain land in the Canadian prairies. The most important type of land acquisition was that of free homesteads. The first Dominion Lands Act, in 1872, provided for homesteads of one-quarter section for a fee of $10 and a minimum of three years' residence, but only outside a belt of twenty miles on either side of a proposed transcontinental rail line. Government land within the block was to sell for $2.50 per acre. Since no farmer could haul grain by wagon twenty miles, this measure put all free land at an uneconomic distance from any transport facility, but since, at the time, there were no rail lines in any case, the effects of such distances were negligible.

Free-homestead policy changed as the prospect of a transcontinental rail line came nearer. An order-in-council in 1879 narrowed the restricted belt to ten miles (but raised the price of government lands therein to $6 per acre). Even-numbered sections outside this belt were available for free homestead, and a price structure was devised for odd-numbered sections. The most important change came in 1882, when all even-numbered sections were thrown open for free homestead, even those within the CPR belt. Thereafter, the main changes related to the possibility of taking out a second homestead (allowed in 1883 and abandoned three years later) and to tightening the definitions of the residence requirement and improvements necessary for patenting.

Next to free homesteads, the railway land grant was the pillar of Dominion land policy. The idea, borrowed from the United States, was simple. As part of its subsidy, a company was given title to blocks of land in the areas through which its line would pass. Railways were, thus, in the land as well as the freight business. The hope was that, with land to sell, the companies would set freight rates to encourage settlement; or, conversely, with freight to haul, they would price the land and promote it for quick settlement. In short, the railway land grant was seen as an incentive system that made the railways' interests identical with those of the government.

The railway land grant idea was part of Canadian land policy from the beginning. Every proposal for a Pacific railway included grants of land as part of the subsidy; only the amounts varied. The grant actually made to the CPR amounted to 25 million acres (details are provided below). Dozens of rival projects — colonization railways — then sprang up, most of which received land as part of their charter as well. Closely related were the colonization companies proper, who received land in exchange not for building rail lines but for promising to bring settlers to the prairies.

For the remainder of the land, essentially the odd-numbered sections the railways passed over, the government experimented with a variety of sales techniques. Provision was made in the 1872 Dominion Lands Act for homesteaders to purchase up to 640 additional acres, but it was withdrawn in 1881. Beginning in 1874, a homesteader could "pre-empt" an unclaimed adjoining quarter at the government price, once patent to the homestead was issued. There was much concern, however, that pre-emption led to speculation, and it was withdrawn in 1890.

Pre-emptions and purchased homesteads were reintroduced in 1908, partly out of concern that 160-acre farms were too small, but mainly because the government wanted the revenue to finance railway grants. Homesteaders located next to odd-numbered sections not taken by railways could purchase a quarter-section from the government for $3.00 per acre. Those having no contiguous quarter-section available could purchase one elsewhere, again for $3.00 per acre. Both provisions were in effect until 1918, when they were withdrawn to make land available to returning veterans of World War I. Overall, nearly 118 million acres of prairie land were granted under Dominion administration, in the proportions shown in Figure 11.2.

Land policy came under considerable scrutiny at the time, and has attracted the attention of researchers more recently. The administration of school lands is almost universally praised. Martin speaks of it as "Dominion policy at its best."[3] The Hudson's Bay Company is almost as universally condemned for doing much the same thing as did the Department of the Interior — speculating on timing and using a reservation price in an attempt to maximize sales revenue. The beneficiaries of the revenue were different, but the effects on the rate of settlement must have been quite similar. Who benefited is thus one criterion that has been used to judge the worth of the system.

Railway land grants have been both criticized and praised. Homesteaders did not like them, seeing them as part of what they termed "land-lock." More generally, however, they have been heralded as a wise and essential part of settlement policy, although a distinction is sometimes drawn between the CPR and the other companies. Tying the railways' interests to those of the government — ensuring that both would be interested in rapid and extensive settlement of the prairies — made the companies important agents of the national policy. They assisted in advertising the region, subsidizing immigrants, and disseminating agricultural techniques. Having railway sections next to free-homestead ones meant that farmers generally had an empty contiguous quarter-section they could purchase when they wished to expand their operation to 360 acres. Even the selection process is sometimes seen as a virtue. Tying up land until railway selections were made allowed settlement of the poorer and drier areas to be at least postponed.

The traditional view on free homesteads is that there were some undeniable waste and inequities associated with them, but that, by promoting rapid and extensive settlement, they served the purposes of the Dominion well. More recent research has tended to argue that it was not necessary to give away land to attract settlers, and that the waste and inefficiency involved in doing so was probably much greater than is realized. Free land did not attract many settlers before 1900; after that date, sales were consistently as robust as

FIGURE 11.2
The Disposal of Prairie Lands, 1870–1930

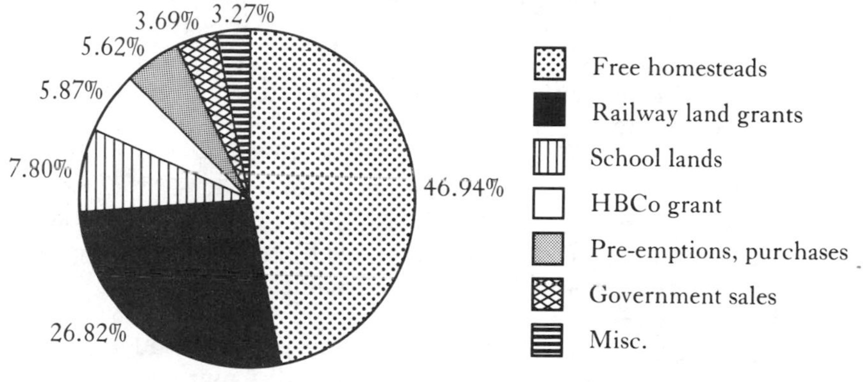

Source: Calculated from Chester Martin, *Dominion Lands Policy* (Toronto: McClelland and Stewart, 1973), 228–29.

free-homestead entries. The waste referred to came from premature settlement. Since homesteads were allocated on a first-come, first-served basis, settlers were forced to claim them before they were economically viable. They had to work them to retain the claim, so capital and labour were committed prematurely. The concept of premature settlement is elegant, but, since no rigorous empirical research has yet been done to test it, the overall efficacy of the free-homestead policy is still an open question.

Transcontinental Railways

Some sort of rail connection was obviously necessary if the agricultural potential of the prairies was to be developed. The distances were vast, and there was no artery transportation equivalent to the one that the St. Lawrence–Great Lakes system had provided for eastern settlement. Construction of the Northern Pacific in the United States in the late 1860s meant that Canada had to start soon if the entire area was not to become part of the American frontier. A final impetus to construction came from the fact that British Columbia had been promised such a line within ten years of its entrance into Confederation in 1871.

The account of the Canadian Pacific Railway has become one

of the better-known stories of Canadian history. Well-known engineer Sandford Fleming was commissioned to survey the route in 1871, a task he completed over the next several years. The Grand Trunk, the obvious candidate to build the line, insisted on linking western sections with existing U.S. lines, and was thus ruled out from the beginning. A charter was drawn up in 1873 authorizing the Canadian Pacific Railway Company — an amalgam of two earlier contenders — to construct a line from Lake Nipissing to some point on the Pacific Ocean. In return, the company was to receive a grant of $30 million and 50 million acres of land, with additional land for branch lines. That plan broke down with the resignation of the Macdonald government in 1873 over a scandal involving political contributions from the railway's backers.

The Liberal government of Alexander Mackenzie (1873–78) was unable to interest another company in the project, and ended up constructing pieces between waterways and American lines. By 1880, more than 700 miles of lines were either completed or under contract.

Macdonald resumed the search for a company to build the line, and in 1880 an agreement was reached with the Canadian Pacific Railway Company, controlled by George Stephen, James Hill, and Donald Smith. In exchange for constructing a line of Union Pacific quality from Montreal to the Pacific Ocean via the Yellowhead Pass, the CPR received numerous incentives from the government. The most important were $25 million and 25 million acres of land. The land was to be in alternate sections of 640 acres each (the odd-numbered ones) in a belt 24 miles deep, on either side of the railway between Winnipeg and Jasper. The land had to be "fairly fit for settlement," meaning that acreage in the railway belt deemed unfit could be exchanged for better land elsewhere. In addition, there were less-valuable concessions, including exemption from taxation for the railway and its grounds and buildings, and similar exemption for the land grants for twenty years. No company could build a line south of the main line for twenty years, existing government lines in the west were handed over to the company, and lines currently under construction were to be completed by the government, and then handed over.

Construction of the line began almost immediately, and was completed in 1885, with the last spike being driven in by the Honourable Donald Smith at Craigellachie, B.C., on the morning of November

7. The main line did not follow that laid out by Sandford Fleming, as specified in the contract, but rather took a more southerly route through Winnipeg, Regina, Moose Jaw, Calgary, and Kicking Horse and Rogers passes, en route to Vancouver. Branch lines were built quickly, though not quickly enough to satisfy the settlers who depended on them. Before the century was out, track ran south from Winnipeg to the American border; north from the main line to Saskatoon, Prince Albert, and Edmonton; and south from Calgary to Macleod. In the east, the CPR, through purchase and construction, extended the line to Toronto and Montreal and established connections through American railways to Portland, Maine. Shortly thereafter, a "short line" was built through Maine to Saint John, giving the company access to Atlantic Canada.

The CPR would be a tremendously successful company, and its founders would be lionized in the business journals of the day as the epitome of business acumen. There is a certain irony in this, for two reasons. First, these businessmen were successful in part because of the vast government subsidies that underwrote the railway. Second, at the time of construction, and for a while after, few thought much of the railway's prospects. As the well-known British magazine *The Economist* said on February 19, 1881, the CPR could expect "a long and dreary season of unprofitableness."

The contrast between the low expectations and the rapid success of the company has led to considerable discussion about the large subsidy that it was given at the time. Was it necessary to subsidize the company at all, or would a railway have been built anyway as the prospects for settlement improved? If a subsidy *was* necessary — to pre-empt American expansion northwards, if for no other reason — was the amount excessive, reflecting the close links between the government and the railway promoters rather than economic necessity? Recent research suggests that some subsidy was indeed necessary if a railway were to be built much before the turn of the century. The actual rate of return earned by the CPR between 1886 and 1895 was below that available on other investments. But the same calculation suggests that the subsidy was substantially in excess of what was needed to make up the difference.

Transcontinental railway development did not stop with the CPR. William Mackenzie and Donald Mann had been involved in railway construction since 1886. By the 1890s, they had begun to buy up railway charters, often with land grants attached to them. In 1896, they purchased the charter for the Lake Manitoba Railway and Canal Company and built a link to the CPR main line. By 1900, they had extended the track into Saskatchewan. Other charters from the federal, Manitoba, and Ontario governments allowed them to begin to build from Winnipeg to Port Arthur, on Lake Superior. Over the next few years, encouraged by the economic boom on the prairies, the company began in earnest to complete a transcontinental line through construction and purchase. By 1905, the only gaps remaining were Ottawa to Port Arthur, in eastern Canada, and Edmonton to the Pacific. Both sections were completed by 1915, with the western section following Sandford Fleming's route from Edmonton through the Yellowhead Pass to Vancouver.

The boom also attracted a railway that, 30 years earlier, had refused to participate in the transcontinental scheme. In 1902, the Grand Trunk Railway put forward a proposal to build west to the Pacific. The attraction of merging the Canadian Northern with the Grand Trunk was not lost on the government. Negotiations failed, however, and construction proceeded on both. The government agreed to build a line from Winnipeg through the northern clay belts of Ontario to the Maritimes. This it did, completing the project in late 1913. Named the National Transcontinental, the line was to be leased to the Grand Trunk rent-free for three years and then at 3 percent of the cost of construction for the next 47 years. The Grand Trunk Pacific, a subsidiary company created expressly for the purpose, built a line from Winnipeg through Edmonton and the Yellowhead to Prince Rupert on the Pacific, opening in September 1914. The Grand Trunk refused to lease the National Transcontinental upon its completion, so Canada's third line operated as a hybrid private-public venture.

Each company built branch lines in addition to their trunk lines. Total mileage on the prairies doubled, from around 2000 miles in the mid-1880s to 4000 in 1899. Construction continued until, by 1913, there were more than 11 000 miles of track in the three provinces. Most homesteaders could thus be assured that their farm either was already served by a railway spur or soon would be.

The actual presence of rail lines in an area was important, but so were the rates charged on grain exports and on materials shipped in. Farmers complained early on of monopoly pricing by the CPR, and their cause was taken up by western politicians, particularly the Manitoba government. Investigations at the time showed that rates in Canada compared favourably to those available on U.S. lines, the next most likely alternative. Nonetheless, political pressure led to the monopoly clause being rescinded in 1888, in exchange for a federal government guarantee of the interest on a $15 million CPR loan. Now, there were no restrictions on other companies' building lines in competition with the CPR.

The famous Crow's Nest Pass Agreement of 1897 is another manifestation of the pressure for lower freight rates. Ottawa agreed, by the terms of that contract, to provide a subsidy of $11 000 per mile, up to a maximum of $3.6 million, to allow the CPR to build a line from Lethbridge through the Crow's Nest Pass to Nelson, B.C., to tap the rich mineral resources of that area. The company, in turn, agreed to reduce "in perpetuity" its rates on grain destined for export and on incoming settlers' effects, such as agricultural implements and construction materials. Known as the Crow's Nest Pass rates, the cuts were made in stages, coming into effect fully in 1899. The rates were suspended during World War I and then reimposed by statute in 1925 at the level agreed to in 1897, where they stayed until the 1980s.

Much has been made of the impact of the Crow rates on the development of the prairie grain economy. There is a general belief that, by lowering the cost of getting prairie wheat to port, the agreement speeded up the rate of settlement and extended it into areas it would not otherwise have reached. This probably overstates the case, however. Freight rates were falling anyway, and, in fact, an agreement between the Manitoba government and the Canadian Northern led the CPR to reduce its rates below the Crow's Nest levels in 1902, and they remained below this ceiling until well into World War I, when the agreement was temporarily suspended. Others have argued that the level of rates was less important than the promise contained in the "in perpetuity" clause. The binding of the rate-setting behaviour of the CPR in this manner, it is hypothesized, assured would-be settlers that the railway would not resume monopoly behaviour once they were established on the land.

Immigration Policy

The third component of the strategy to settle the west was to attract immigrants. The Dominion had assumed control of its own immigration policy in 1867, and the first Immigration Act was passed two years later. Generally, the policy throughout the remainder of the nineteenth century was one of "laissez faire."[4] The overriding objective was to attract population, especially to the farmlands of the west. Only paupers and indigents were unwelcome, as regulations of 1879–80 and 1891 made clear, although colour loomed large unofficially. Otherwise, the government joined with the CPR and other companies in mounting promotional campaigns in Europe and the United States. There were some successes, such as the arrival of Icelandic settlers in Manitoba in 1873. In general, however, results were disappointing. As noted above, Canada had more people leave (mainly to go to the United States) than arrive in every decade of the nineteenth century.

Settlement policy was clearly administered more energetically after 1896, with Clifford Sifton in charge of the Department of the Interior. Expenditures on advertising and promotion rose significantly, and particular efforts were made to attract American farmers. Sifton also removed several of the obstacles to settlement. Administration of the Homestead Act was improved, and railways were pressured to patent land owed to them in order to free up the remainder for homesteading. Efforts were also made to develop the irrigation potential of the drier areas, and to promote ranching and forestry operations. It is difficult to judge how much impact these efforts had in promoting settlement, relative to all the other changes under way at the time. But like the Crow rates, Clifford Sifton is firmly associated with the wheat boom, whatever the evidence.

Tariffs

Commercial policy was the final component of the national policy. At first, the stance of the new Dominion was quite liberal, with tariff rates set as much for revenue purposes as for protection. The first Tariff Act, in 1867, adopted the tariffs of Upper and Lower Canada as they had been in 1866. Duties were raised for revenue purposes in 1870, but the hike was rescinded the next year. The basic duty was raised by 2.5 percentage points in 1874, bringing the average tariff to about 20 percent. Rates then remained virtually unaltered for the next four years.

Canada retained this relatively liberal policy for the first years of Confederation for a number of reasons. The Maritime provinces opposed tariffs strongly, and duties were kept low and even lowered in some cases to placate them. There was also considerable philosophical support for freer trade in Canada. Also, the Dominion was doing quite well on the trade front, given reconstruction and post–Civil War inflation in the United States, so pressure for protection was not strong. Finally, often forgotten is the fact that Canadians never really gave up on the idea of securing a new reciprocity arrangement with the United States and hoped to signal this interest by keeping existing rates down.

Sentiment changed over the 1870s, however. In part, Canada followed the rising tide of protectionism worldwide, and in part the motivation was more local. Demand for manufactured goods grew more slowly in the 1870s than it had in the first few post-Confederation years, and certainly more slowly than had been anticipated. Local firms faced increasing competition as technological change and declining transport costs made imports cheaper. Manufacturing interests began to organize to lobby for increased protection, and found politicians open to their demands. Established interests in the Maritimes and the west opposed tariffs, but the political influence of the former was waning, and that of the latter was negligible as yet. The opposition Conservatives recognized a winning electoral strategy, and based their successful 1878 campaign on a promise to introduce a National Policy of wide-ranging protectionism.

The tariff increases put in place by the Macdonald government in 1879 were avowedly protectionist. The general rate was raised from 17.5 percent to 20 percent. Duties were restored on a range of agricultural products, such as oats, wheat, and barley, presumably to give farmers the impression that protection was intended for them as well. Coal and coke, iron and steel, machinery, hardware, and textiles were given special protection, either through higher rates or the imposition of specific (a flat rate per unit of the product imported) as opposed to ad valorem (a percentage of the landed price of the import) duties. The apogee of protectionism came later, in 1887, after duties were raised even further, especially on iron and steel, farm machinery, and textiles.

Even in the midst of imposing these new and higher duties, the government did not give up hopes of securing some type of reciprocal free-trade arrangement with the United States. The 1879 schedule, for example, listed certain articles that would be admitted duty-free from the United States, should they reciprocate. Efforts to negotiate an arrangement continued throughout the 1880s and into the 1890s, but the two countries were never able to draw up a mutually agreeable list of commodities to be covered. Also, in a flashback to the 1840s and 1850s, American access to the Atlantic fisheries became part of the package, adding yet another complication.

Election of a Liberal government headed by Wilfrid Laurier in 1896 did not spell the end of industrial protectionism, whatever campaign rhetoric might have led voters to believe. Some changes were made on individual items in 1897, but the overall level of protection was altered very little. O.J. McDiarmid notes in his classic study of Canadian commercial policy[5] that the average duty was 23 percent in 1879; 32 percent in 1891; 30 percent in 1896, on the eve of the Liberals' election; and still 27 percent in 1903, after seven years of their administration. In 1879, 70 percent of items were free of duty, whereas only 61 percent were in 1896, and 60 percent in 1903. The Liberals extended the use of bounties and of drawbacks on duty paid on imported components and, in 1904, introduced what has been called the first anti-dumping clause in tariff history.[6]

One of the more notable moves of the Laurier government was the re-establishment of a broad British preferential system in 1897, after nearly a half-century absence. Effective in 1898, products from Britain and British colonies faced duties 25 percent lower than those on imports from all other nations. In 1900, the preference was raised to one-third. No reciprocal advantage was secured, however, much to the chagrin of some Canadian exporters. A third "column" was added to the tariff structure in 1907 as a basis for negotiating special arrangements with other countries, but it remained effectively dormant until 1935.

The final stage in the development of Canadian commercial policy prior to World War I began in 1910, when the idea of a reciprocal trading arrangement with the United States was broached yet again. This time, however, negotiators were able to draw up a list of items and duties satisfactory to both countries. Most natural products were to trade freely between the two countries. Duties on processed agricultural products and farm machinery were lowered, and there were special provisions to cover a range of other products. The agreement passed both the House and the Senate in the United States after short but lively debate. Opposition to it was much greater in Canada, however. In the September 1911 election, the Liberals were defeated soundly by the Conservatives, who appealed to protectionist interests and imperial sentiment under the slogan "No truck nor trade with the Yankees." Reciprocity was dead until, in one of those ironies that makes history so interesting, 78 years later, when a Conservative government introduced a comprehensive free-trade agreement with the United States over the strenuous objections of a Liberal opposition.

Fiscal Arrangements

Another set of policies that deserve some mention here, given their importance later in the narrative, are those dealing with intergovernmental fiscal arrangements. In 1867, as seen above, the federal government was given unlimited power to tax, while the provinces were restricted to direct taxation. Tariffs and excise duties were, by far, the greatest government revenue source at this time and, as indirect levies, were the exclusive preserve of Ottawa. Thus, the BNA Act had to devise a system of payments from the central government to the provinces, setting the stage for the transfers that continue to the present day.

In 1867, Ottawa agreed to remit to each province annually an amount equal to 80 cents for each member of the population of the province, up to a maximum amount, plus a cash subsidy in support of government and legislatures. In addition, the federal government assumed responsibility for all provincial debts. New Brunswick received a special grant of $63 000 per year, to run for ten years, and Nova Scotia received the same in 1869. Separate agreements were made with Manitoba in 1870, British Columbia in 1871, and Prince Edward Island in 1873. The payments were adjusted on occasion until 1907, when an amendment to the BNA Act revised the original fiscal terms. The basic formula was retained, although it was updated to increase the grants going to the provinces.

Provinces supplemented these grants with revenue from a variety of taxes they levied themselves, four of which will be of special interest later. Succession duties were first levied in 1892; by 1903, they had been imposed in all provinces. British Columbia levied the first personal income tax in 1876, followed by Prince Edward Island in 1894, although it was the 1930s before the other provinces followed suit. Quebec imposed taxes on corporations in 1882; by 1907, the practice was general. Prince Edward Island introduced a corporate income tax in 1894, and British Columbia did so in 1901, but, as they had on the tax on personal incomes, the other provinces held off until the 1930s. There were no federal income taxes at this time.

Conclusion

These were the main framework policies within which Canadian economic growth took place between 1867 and 1913. There were many other federal measures not mentioned here, and the provinces and municipalities were active as well. We shall touch on these others, as necessary, below. We have also had occasion to discuss some of the impacts of the main policies in this chapter, and we return to this theme in the chapters that follow. No full evaluation can be given, however, as none is yet available. For all the interest in policy in this period, no synthesis has yet been achieved.

Notes

1. G.P. de T. Glazebrook, *A History of Transportation in Canada*, Vol. 2, Carleton Library #11 (Toronto: McClelland and Stewart, 1967), 111–15.
2. Chester Martin, *Dominion Lands Policy*, edited and with an introduction by Lewis H. Thomas, Carleton Library #69 (Toronto: McClelland and Stewart, 1973), 24.
3. Martin, *Dominion Lands Policy*, 100.
4. Alan G. Green, *Immigration and the Canadian Economy* (Toronto: Macmillan, 1976), 14.
5. O.J. McDiarmid, *Commercial Policy in the Canadian Economy* (Cambridge, MA: Harvard University Press, 1946), 205.
6. McDiarmid, *Commercial Policy*, 217.

Further Reading

Glazebrook, G.P. de T. *A History of Transportation in Canada*, Vol. 3. Carleton Library #11. Toronto: McClelland and Stewart, 1967.

Green, Alan G. *Immigration and the Canadian Economy*. Toronto: Macmillan, 1976.

Martin, Chester. *Dominion Lands Policy*. Edited and with an introduction by Lewis H. Thomas. Carleton Library #69. Toronto: McClelland and Stewart, 1973.

McDiarmid, O.J. *Commercial Policy in the Canadian Economy*. Cambridge, MA: Harvard University Press, 1946.

CHAPTER

12

Agriculture

Agriculture was, by far, the largest sector of the economy in 1870, accounting for more than 40 percent of gross domestic product. By way of comparison, it should be noted that manufacturing made up 22 percent of GDP in that year and the service industries together (excluding construction) another 31 percent.[1] Farm output rose dramatically, if unevenly, in the ensuing decades. As Figure 12.1 clearly shows, gross value added grew rapidly in real terms from 1870 to 1883, rose but at a much slower pace to 1897, and then accelerated to the beginning of World War I and after. Real value added in the 1896–97 crop year was 1.6 times greater than in 1870–71; in 1913–14, it was 3.6 times greater. Both its absolute size and its growth record give agriculture acknowledged pride of place in this period of Canada's economic history.

Two features of the record deserve special mention. First, this impressive growth notwithstanding, agriculture's relative position in the economy declined continuously after 1870. The farm sector's share of GDP fell slightly, to 36 percent in 1880, 28 percent in 1890, 25 percent in 1900, and 22 percent in 1910.[2] However dynamic agriculture was in these years, then, other activities were apparently even more so. Second, the aggregate data mask two quite distinct developments between 1867 and 1913. The great boom in production after 1896 reflects the opening up of the western plains to wheat production, while the changes in output and composition before that date represent growth and structural change in agriculture in the rest of the country, Quebec and Ontario in particular. The dramatic story of the western wheat boom is well known. That agriculture changed so much between 1870 and 1900 is less well known, and it is with these developments that we begin.

FIGURE 12.1
Gross Value Added, Canadian Agriculture, 1870–71 to 1926–27

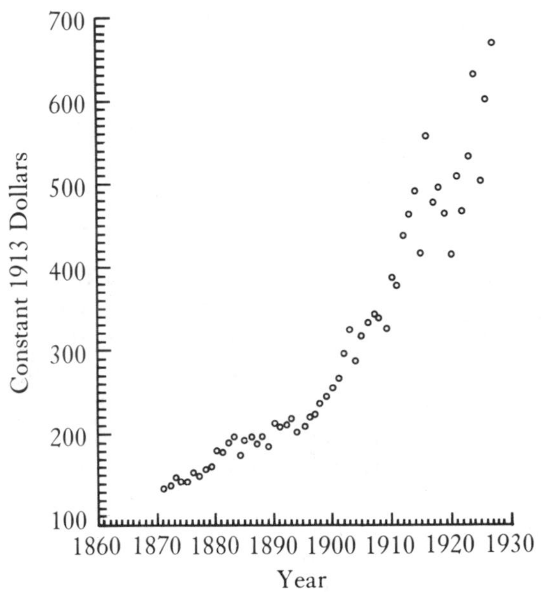

Source: R.M. McInnis, "Output and Productivity in Canadian Agriculture, 1870–71 to 1926–27," in *Long-Term Factors in American Economic Growth*, NBER Studies in Income and Wealth, Vol. 51, edited by Stanley L. Engerman and Robert E. Gallman (Chicago: University of Chicago Press, 1986), 746.

Central Canadian Agriculture

Two features of central Canadian agriculture in the decades following Confederation stand out. First, the region continued the shift out of wheat and into mixed farming that was already evident in the 1850s and 1860s. Second, this restructuring did not proceed without interruption. The eventual transformation reflects the long-run comparative advantage of agriculture in this region. The temporary deviations demonstrate a flexibility in the sector that has only recently been appreciated.

As noted in Chapter 7, Canada was a net wheat importer by 1869. The change in status had both supply- and demand-side elements.

Ontario farmers experienced some of the same problems on the supply side in the 1850s and 1860s that their Quebec counterparts had had earlier in the century. With the growing demand for animals and products, farmers gradually shifted their focus more to mixed farming. A large post–Civil War demand for young cattle in the United States gave impetus to the shift. Wheat acreage in Ontario dropped in the 1860s, and output fell even more. Wheat accounted for less than 16 percent of final agriculture output in that province in 1870–71. Animal products made up over 60 percent, one-third of which was dairy, and two-thirds other products. Since this shift had largely occurred by the time of Confederation, the oft-heard theory that eastern farmers were squeezed out of wheat production by the opening of the prairies is clearly erroneous.

This transformation to mixed farming was reversed temporarily in the middle to late 1870s, as Ontario underwent what McInnis has termed a "mini" wheat boom.[3] Low-cost cattle from the American South and Southwest began appearing after 1870, driving down prices in eastern U.S. markets and, as a result, returns to Canadian farmers. Some turned to the U.K. market, although this trade was not very substantial until the next decade. Others apparently shifted back into wheat production; in the seven years between 1875 and 1882, the value of wheat output nearly doubled. Supply outstripped local demand, and Canada was again a net wheat exporter by 1879.

The long-term trend was re-established in the 1880s. Wheat prices fell as low-cost supplies from the American Midwest appeared on the world market. Wheat acreage and production fell back to pre-1871 levels, and animals and products again became the leading agricultural output. There is some question as to whether the decline of wheat production in the 1880s was a straightforward reallocation of acreage in response to changing relative prices, or whether farmers came to view wheat production as equally profitable but inherently more risky, and withdrew from it in favour of more secure products. The consensus of those who have studied the issue appears to favour the former explanation.

Farmers found markets for their animal products at home and abroad. Beef exports to the United Kingdom climbed in the 1880s, with eastern supplies augmented by shipments from western ranches. Butter and cheese, in particular, grew in importance. Cheese was the fastest-growing agricultural output after 1880, with the U.K. market the primary outlet. Two-thirds of the cheese produced in 1881 was exported, and, by the mid-1890s, this figure had risen to 80 percent. Some writers have referred to cheese as a new staple, although its absolute output was never really large enough to warrant such a leading role. Butter output was consistently much larger in volume terms, for example, but was produced mainly for the domestic market.

The other development of note after 1890 in central Canadian agriculture was the growth of hog production. Canada lacked a cheap food source for pigs before 1890, and production was mainly for on-farm and local use. The situation changed after 1890 as a U.S. tariff on barley drove feed-grain prices down, and as whey, a by-product of cheese production, became available as feed. Canadians also adapted their product to the leaner breed of animal preferred in the British market. Bacon transported relatively well, and Ontario produce began to appear on breakfast tables in Europe.

The agricultural changes taking place in central Canada had important social implications, especially when viewed in conjunction with the simultaneous rise of factories. One of the most important of these concerned the role of women in agriculture. For as long as farming had taken place, women had had an active role in supporting the farm business. Sometimes, as in the pioneer economies, this had meant working alongside their husbands on a daily basis. In other situations, as in large-scale wheat farming, women had left the major commercial crop to the men and had concentrated, instead, on vegetable gardens, on animal care, and on other operations designed to increase farm income and to provide food directly for the farm table.

As Quebec and Ontario farmers moved to a concentration on commercially oriented mixed farming, the place of women in the operation was inevitably altered. In a dramatic example, women found themselves displaced from their traditional roles as milkers and producers of cheese and butter. In other areas of production, the trends were not always so dramatic but, as Marjorie Cohen has shown, the ability of women to earn direct income and to participate equally in the farm business probably declined relative to the pre-Confederation era.[4]

This changing role of women on the farm reflected a more general trend. A high percentage of farm operations in central Canada were now efficient operations with specialized functions, albeit in a mixed-farming economy and with considerable mechanization.

This tendency would continue over the next two generations, and each improvement in crop technique, each additional piece of machinery, meant that more food could be produced with less labour. This changing technology reduced the need for farm labour, male and female. Both the sons and daughters of farmers or farm labourers moved on, seeking opportunity on the frontier or in the rising factory and service sectors of the cities. Between 1891 and 1901, the number of males involved in agriculture declined in both Ontario and Quebec. The data on women are less readily available, but every indication is that their numbers in this sector declined as well. The drop would continue at an accelerated rate in the first decade of the twentieth century, giving rise to a great deal of concern about the undermining of a way of life. From an economic point of view, however, what took place was a natural response to an increasingly efficient industry.

The Prairie Wheat Boom

Of all the economic developments in Canada's first half-century, the prairie wheat boom is perhaps the most dramatic. Certainly, it is the most studied. There are at least three reasons for its central role. First, as seen above, plans to develop the plains for agricultural settlement were a large part of the motive behind Confederation itself, and were basically the entire focus of the national policy. Thus, prairie settlement became the most visible barometer of the success of the new federation — the basis for the doubt and pessimism to 1896 and the exuberance and confidence thereafter.

Second, when settlement did come, it did so with dramatic effect. There were fewer than 75 000 people living in Manitoba and the Northwest Territories in 1871. By 1891, this figure had risen to around 250 000, two-thirds of whom were in Manitoba. By 1911, the three prairie provinces had a combined population of 1.3 million, and Saskatchewan was the largest. Railways criss-crossed the prairies, with two more transcontinental lines in the process of completion. Most of the arable land was at least thinly settled as settlers queued up to purchase land that could not be given away fifteen years earlier. From being a minor factor in world markets, Canada had grown to be a major presence; in 1909, Winnipeg handled more wheat than any other centre in the world.[5]

Third, settlement of the prairies affected more than just that region, as indeed was the hope of Canadian politicians and business leaders from the outset. Wheat was a national staple, and it transformed more than just the prairies and more than just the economy. Canadians far removed from the region earned their livelihood by preparing the region for settlement, supplying the equipment needed to produce the grain, transporting the grain to its markets, and providing for the needs of the farm families. Wheat also created two new provinces, and underlay a regional identity and a regional political perspective that has continued to the present.

There are three main issues to be discussed with respect to the prairie wheat boom. Why did it come when it did? What was its impact on the prairie economy and prairie society? What was its impact on the national economy? We take up these questions in turn.

Establishment of the Wheat Economy

Prairie settlement began slowly and then literally boomed. Homestead entries rose briefly in the early 1880s, with the construction of the CPR, but fell off for the next decade. In some of these years, cancellations exceeded entries, and the stock of homesteads actually declined. After 1897, however, the trend turned sharply upwards. Net entries rose from near zero in 1897 to more than 25 000 in 1903 and 30 000 in 1906. Figure 12.2 shows the same. Of the total net stock of homesteads taken out to 1930, only 8.8 percent were recorded by 1885 and only 20 percent by 1900. Yet, this proportion had reached over 50 percent just six years later, and nearly 90 percent by the outbreak of World War I.

What had changed? Why had nearly three decades of efforts to populate the Canadian west achieved so little when, after 1897, they seemed so spectacularly successful? The quick answer is that Canada was able to capture an increasing share of a secularly rising world wheat trade. Why the international trade in grain increased steadily after the mid-nineteenth century is well understood. Why Canada suddenly entered it so effectively after 1896 when it could not before is still a source of some disagreement.

The main markets for export grains in the nineteenth century were in Europe, particularly Britain. Although Europe was in a position of virtual self-sufficiency in the 1840s, imports grew by the outbreak of World War I to account for nearly 30 percent of total supplies for Europe as a whole and for nearly 75 percent of consumption in the United Kingdom. Demand grew in these

FIGURE 12.2

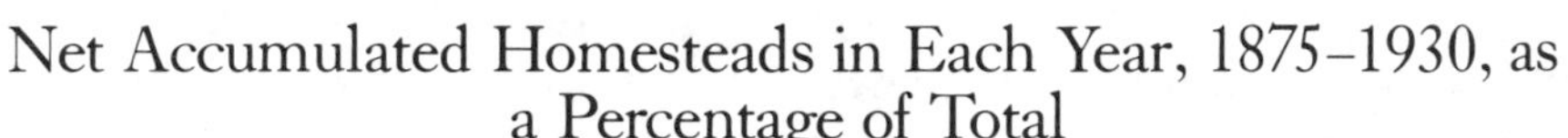

Net Accumulated Homesteads in Each Year, 1875–1930, as a Percentage of Total

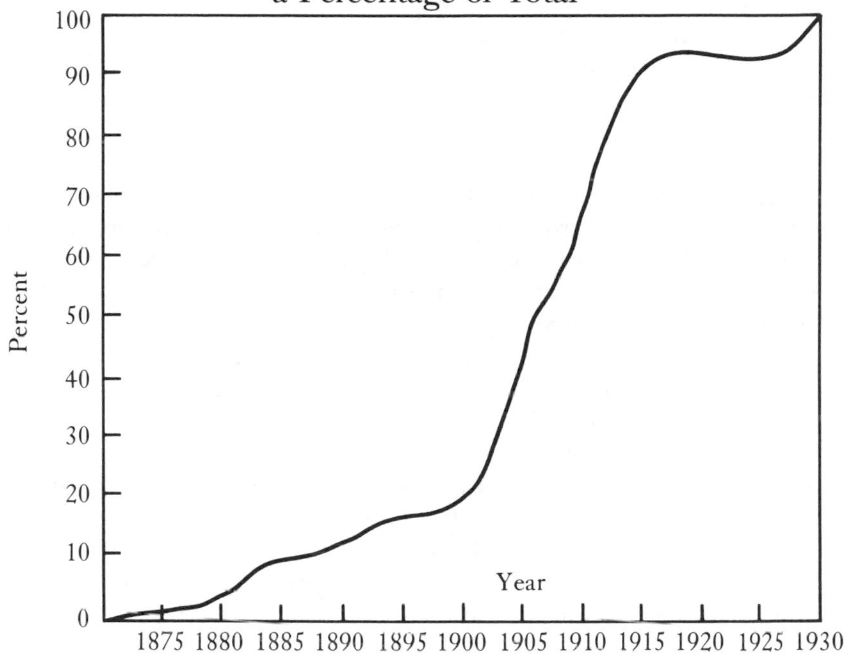

Source: Calculated from M.C. Urquhart and K.A.H. Buckley, eds., *Historical Statistics of Canada* (Toronto: Macmillan, 1965), Series K34–41.

countries, but the main factor behind the shift to international specialization was a dramatic decline in the costs of getting grain from the farm gate to Liverpool. Ocean rates fell, as steel replaced iron and wood in ships, as the vessels became larger, as marine engines improved in efficiency, and as associated port costs fell. Inland rates declined as steel rails were introduced and as engines and rolling stock were improved. With the gap between export and import prices reduced in this manner, Liverpool prices could fall in nominal terms from the 1850s to the 1890s. This fact, together with rising incomes and populations, accounts for the rise in British demand, while prices at the export points could rise more or less continuously, which accounts for the increase in supply from frontier regions.

Canada was a relative latecomer to this growing international wheat trade. The Black Sea area and the United States together effectively accounted for the entire export trade in wheat in 1865–69, and for more than 80 percent as late as 1895–99. Canada supplied only 4 percent of the trade at the turn of the century, about the same as India and about one-half of what Australia did. Yet, this share had quadrupled to 16 percent just fifteen years later, ranking Canada with the United States and Argentina and well ahead of India and Australia.[6]

Canada's lag in entering this trade is puzzling. The Rowell-Sirois Commission (1940) wrote of a favourable conjuncture of circumstances after 1896 that suddenly made wheat production in Canada profitable, and this interpretation quickly became the standard account. Prairie agricultural land was now attractive because transport costs had declined, cereal prices had risen, the costs of inputs to agriculture had fallen relatively, interest rates were at their lowest level in recorded history, international capital and labour flows were increasing, the technology to farm the prairies and to store and transport the product to market was now available, and last, but for the commission certainly not least, Dominion land, transportation, and immigration policies were supportive.

The problem for the commission's explanation is that, while these factors certainly explain why there was settlement on the Canadian prairies at all, they cannot explain why the bulk of it took place in the fifteen years after 1897. Transport costs and prices of farm inputs had been falling for some time, wheat prices were higher in the late 1870s and early 1880s than they were after 1897, and the technology needed on the Canadian plains was basically the same as that associated with the Dakota Boom of the 1870s and 1880s. Capital and labour were invested around the world prior to 1900; they just were not attracted to Canada. Finally, the provisions of the national policy were the same in 1896 as they had been a decade or more earlier.

There is another reason for believing that the bulk of prairie land was beyond the feasible margin of cultivation before the mid-1890s, even with the other factors in line. Except for the small region in southern Manitoba that was already settled by the mid-1880s, either the land was too dry or the growing season too short. The solution to the moisture problem came in the late 1880s with the development of cultivation techniques suitable for semi-arid land. Problems with frost were overcome by the development of Marquis wheat, in widespread use in the region by 1909. With these advances, the Canadian prairies were brought within the feasible region of cultivation, and large-scale settlement began.

Wheat and the Prairies

Settlement followed a crescent-shaped pattern at first, spreading from Winnipeg northwest to Saskatoon, and then on to Edmonton. The wedge thickened gradually as homesteaders took up land in the colder northern fringes and in the drier Palliser's Triangle region of southwestern Saskatchewan and southeastern Alberta. By 1913, less than two decades after migration began in earnest, the entire prairie region was at least thinly settled.

This rapid geographical spread of settlement is reflected in the statistics. In 1901, there were 55 000 farms on the prairies, occupying 15.4 million acres. About one third of this acreage (5.6 million acres) was improved, and 3.6 million acres of it were under field crops. By 1911, the number of farms and the area occupied had increased more than 3.5 times, to 200 000 and 58 million acres. Improved acreage was four times greater, at 23 million acres, and the area under field crops nearly five times as great, at 17.7 million acres.[7]

Wheat was the dominant field crop from the beginning. It accounted for more than 70 percent of the acreage in 1901, with oats making up the bulk of the remainder. Wheat's share fell slightly, to 63 percent, in 1906, and to 59 percent by 1911, although its total acreage increased, from 2.5 million acres in 1901 to 10 million in 1911. Total production in 1911 was 208 million bushels, which represented 91 percent of total Canadian output for that year.[8] Oats took up 28 percent of the acreage in 1911 and flaxseed, at 7 percent, had overtaken barley. Manitoba and Saskatchewan were the most specialized in wheat; Alberta, the least.

Not all who came west came to farm, however. Of the prairie population, 18 percent were classed as urban in 1891, with the term "urban" defined to include incorporated villages and towns as well as cities. This figure rose to 25 percent by 1901 and to 35 percent by 1911. Put differently, the rural population rose by 2.7 times between 1901 and 1911, from 316 000 to 859 000, which is the popular image of the prairies at this time, but the urban one rose by 4.6 times, from 103 000 to nearly 500 000.[9]

The pattern of urban development was a classic hierarchial one, based on the needs of the wheat economy. The main determinant of location on an otherwise essentially flat, featureless plain was the railway. Farmers located as close to it as possible to minimize transportation costs, drawing, in turn, the entire range of distribution and service activities. First in line were the villages and small towns that sprouted at regular intervals along the line to gather the grain and to meet the most immediate needs of the settlers. More than 600 centres with population greater than 100 sprang up after 1900, with hundreds of smaller centres scattered in between.

These smaller centres, in turn, were serviced by larger rural centres such as Brandon, North Battleford, and Red Deer. They were distinguished by their larger populations and greater range of service industries. Above them came the five big prairie cities of Winnipeg, Regina, Saskatoon, Calgary, and Edmonton, spread roughly equidistantly across the prairies. They were service centres to the service centres, so to speak. In addition, they featured some small-scale manufacturing, and were the sites of provincial capitals and universities. Rivalry among them was intense, as each used whatever means available to promote population growth and economic development.

Winnipeg was the undisputed apex of the prairie urban hierarchy in the years before 1914.[10] Its 1891 population of just over 27 000 had grown to nearly 45 000 by 1901, and to nearly 150 000 by 1911, making it, at that time, Canada's third largest city. Geography dictated that all east-west lines be funnelled through one point in southern Manitoba, while local politics determined that this point would be Winnipeg rather than Selkirk or some other centre. It was also the first centre established, which gave it a head start on the other four big cities. In addition to its status as Manitoba's urban centre, Winnipeg was the location of much of the manufacturing and service activity attracted to the prairies. A grain and produce exchange was established in 1887, and a wheat-futures market ten years later. Banks, brokerage houses, shippers, insurance agents, consultants, and wholesalers located in the city to serve the regional and occasionally the national markets. Manufacturing output increased fivefold between 1881 and 1901, and nearly quadrupled in the next decade. Grain-processing, meat-packing, and the production of construction materials dominated.

While Winnipeg experienced some economic diversification, the region as a whole did so only very little. Well into the wheat boom (and, indeed, for a long time thereafter), the prairies were a classic staple economy. Agriculture dominated, although the mix varied somewhat across provinces. Saskatchewan quickly became the quintessential wheat producer. Other grains, animals, and animal products were relatively more important in Manitoba and Alberta. Manufacturing development was small-scale and specialized — some milling, some packing, some production of farm tools and equipment, some production of building supplies. The limited manufacturing development meant that, in a relative sense at least, services — banking, insurance, wholesale and retail trade, personal services, education, and government — were important employers outside of agriculture.

Wheat fostered more than a regional economy, as noted earlier. It also created distinct regional identification and a regional political outlook. In part, this outcome was the result of being a one-product (or, at most, a few) economy, and in part it flowed from the fact that this region's staple economy developed within the structures of the national policy. Agrarian protests against railways, tariffs, banks, and distant governments were not unique to Canada, as a quick look at U.S. plains history reveals. But the litany of grievances was specific. Railways, the CPR in particular, charged exorbitant rates to haul grain to market or supplies to the prairies, and tariffs increased the costs of farm supplies beyond what they could be obtained for south of the border and made local manufacturing development less likely. Interest rates were usurious, and banks would foreclose at the slightest provocation. The political system was structured so that the interests of the more populous central provinces, where the bulk of the manufacturing and service activities were located, would always dominate.

There has been some attempt to assess these claims of regional economic discrimination. It seems clear, for example, that rail freight rates in the development phase of the wheat economy were at least as low as they would have been under the next most likely alternative to the national policy. Similarly, the point was made long ago that the tariffs were in place before there was much settlement; that, to the extent that they raised farm costs, this would be offset by lower purchase prices for land; and that, as the tariffs were lowered over time, farmers would benefit by an appreciation in land

Provincial Archives of Manitoba/N11730

Main Street, Winnipeg, 1876 and 1905. *Winnipeg was the major prairie urban centre in the years before 1914. In 1891, its population was just over 2700; by 1901, it had grown to nearly 45 000; and by 1911, to 150 000 — making it, at that time, Canada's third-largest city.*

Provincial Archives of Manitoba/N7968

values. There is even some attempt to show that the settlement made in exchange for retaining provincial lands under Dominion control until 1930 was fair, at least *ex parte*.

Legitimate or not, however, the perception remains that the prairie provinces were disadvantaged by virtue of developing under the national policy, and that these handicaps have persisted through to today. (We shall have occasion, below, to indicate other examples of the sentiment.)

The Wheat Boom and the National Economy

The wheat boom affected more than just the prairie economy, as the framers of the national policy had foreseen decades earlier. B.C. lumber came across the mountains for use in building the homes, businesses, and grain elevators of the prairies. Ontario and Quebec manufacturers were able to use the protection provided by the national-policy tariffs and the facilities of the transcontinental railways to ship their manufactured products to the region. Backward linkages from the wheat economy included production of steel rails, railway rolling stock, and agricultural implements and supplies. A flour-milling industry developed at transshipment points such as Port Arthur and Montreal to process that grain not directly exported. Producers in all sectors profited from being able to supply the many consumer demands of the new population, from household items and clothing to financial and insurance needs.

While the wheat boom clearly played a significant role in Canadian economic development after 1896, the exact contribution it made is the subject of considerable uncertainty. One common view is that wheat was a perfect staple, in both an economic and a political sense. The dramatic rise in wheat exports pulled Canada out of a recession, if not a depression, and it vindicated the dreams and plans of the framers of Confederation after three decades of frustration.

The most vivid version of this account is, again, that of the Rowell-Sirois Commission. To them, settlement of the west in such short order after 1896 brought "prosperity and rapid economic expansion to the rest of Canada," and, in this atmosphere, "Canadians began to believe themselves to be a great people. Their work in creating the West gave them that sense of common achievement which marks a nation."[11] Easterbrook and Aitken echo this theme when they write that "Canada's whole economic development hinged on this wave of prairie settlement" and that "the east-west economic and political alignment of the country, the linking together of its various regions, was greatly strengthened by the growth of industry in the central provinces."[12]

The logic of this received view is pure staples theory, tempered by a healthy respect for the role of the national policy. Farmers needed machinery and equipment and other inputs to grow the grain, elevators and other terminal facilities to grade and store it, rail lines and lake freighters to transport it, mills to process some of it, and ports to ship it to markets abroad. They required food, clothing, furniture, utensils, and other consumer goods for their own consumption. They needed the services of lawyers, bankers, realtors, teachers, and clergy.

Some of these ancillary industries located near the farms, accounting for the growth of prairie villages, towns, and cities noted above. But the prairie market by itself was too small, and resource endowments too limited, to support the larger-scale, more sophisticated operations. These items had to be imported, which is where the national policy comes in. Federal railway policy ensured that grain would move east, through Canadian handling and distribution facilities, and on Canadian rail lines, rather than south, to join American supplies. Tariffs ensured that Canadian manufactured goods could compete with imported ones, providing not just revenue to central Canadian businesses but also return traffic for the railways. In the words of Rowell-Sirois, "the resolute application of these policies directed the growing demands for capital equipment, for manufactured goods, for distributive and commercial services into Canadian channels, thus bringing expansion in other parts of the Dominion."[13]

As seen above, aggregate or extensive economic growth, as measured by population and GNP, was definitely greater after 1896 than in the preceding three decades, and it is the close association of this growth with the opening of the prairies that suggests the Rowell-Sirois view. Correlation does not imply causality, however, so it is still legitimate to ask what role the wheat boom played in this acceleration. Two points, in particular, suggest that some modification of the more simplistic staples interpretation is needed. The first is the simple observation that there were several other developments of importance under way in other resource industries and in manufacturing and services (discussed below), and they must have had some role in the overall record.

The second qualification comes from the realization that the expansion was not linked directly to wheat exports. Wheat shipments abroad really did not become significant until well into the new century. Net exports were 24 million bushels in 1897 and were still at this level in 1905. They jumped to 47 million bushels in 1905 and rose by another 30 percent, to 62 million bushels, in 1911. By 1914, the figure was 135 million bushels.

Closer inspection reveals that investment rather than exports led the boom. As Figure 12.3 shows, the ratio of investment to GNP rose from around 15 percent on average in the 1890s to over 20 percent after 1902, and to over 30 percent by 1911. Total exports of goods and services, however, hovered around 18 percent of GNP in the 1890s, fell to 15 to 16 percent after 1902, and did not reach their 1890s share again until 1914. The link to the wheat boom is clear, however. Much of the net capital formation witnessed in the late nineteenth and early twentieth centuries was in anticipation of the eventual appearance of wheat exports. With this modification, the association of Canadian prosperity after 1896 with the wheat boom remains credible. As Urquhart concludes, "the evidence of our data supports most strongly the presumption that the growth and many of the changes in the Canadian economy were a consequence of the settlement of the prairies."[14]

The boom after 1896 was not restricted to population and GNP, it will be remembered; per-capita output increased at a faster rate as well. If the wheat boom is associated with the extensive growth, it is natural to ask what its connection was to this apparent increase in average living standards. Specifically, how much better off was the average Canadian on the eve of World War I as a consequence of the wheat boom? Chambers and Gordon took up the issue in 1966 in an article that is justly regarded as heralding the introduction of "new" economic-history techniques in Canada.[15] Their method was appropriately counterfactual. The wheat boom's contribution to living standards, by definition, is equal to real per-capita income in Canada as it actually was in 1911, minus what it would have been in that same year if the development had never taken place. Knowing what actual income was in 1911 poses no conceptual problems, although the task of getting satisfactory estimates is subject to all the uncertainties of working with historical data. Obtaining

FIGURE 12.3

Investment and Exports, 1890–1914, as a Percentage of GNP

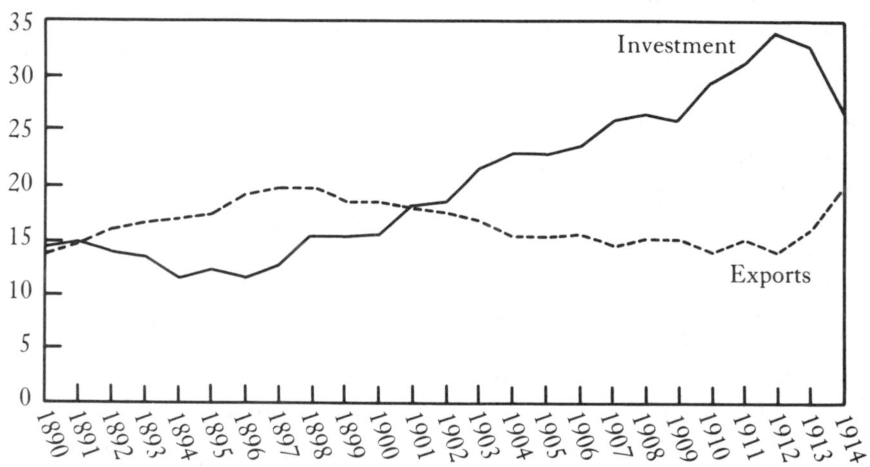

Source: Derived from M.C. Urquhart, "Canadian Economic Growth, 1870–1970," Department of Economics, Queen's University, Discussion Paper No. 734, Table 4.

estimates of its hypothetical value — that is, what real per-capita income would have been in some state of the world that never actually existed — is more problematic. This is precisely the type of challenge that illustrates both the power and the limitations of the new economic history.

Chambers and Gordon estimate that the wheat boom added 1.94 percentage points of the observed 23.6 percent growth in real per-capita incomes between 1901 and 1911. At most, then, by their model, the wheat boom accounted for just under one-twelfth, or 8.4 percent, of the observed rise in the standard of living. More than 90 percent came from increases in the value of manufactured goods, gadgets, and technological change in manufacturing and from other exogenous factors.

These conclusions, running counter, as they did, to the popular perception of the wheat boom as the engine of Canadian economic growth in this period, not unexpectedly attracted considerable attention. An early exchange highlighted the tendency of staples theorists to think in extensive- rather than intensive-growth terms, but added little else beyond pointing out that Chambers and Gordon failed to include some tariff revenue in their estimate. Another contribution disputed their estimate of one of the important pieces of data, arguing that, even by their own model, the wheat boom contributed more to growth. Other authors questioned the very structure of the model, and provided revisions that doubled the contribution, moving it from the status of minor to major contributor to real income growth in this period.

Conclusion

The consensus on the wheat boom and Canadian economic growth might be summarized as follows. It definitely contributed to the extensive growth of the economy between 1896 and 1913, although probably less so than some of the more enthusiastic accounts suggest. There was considerable strength elsewhere in the economy in this period, providing an impetus that is often overlooked by focussing on the more dramatic filling up of the prairies. Its contribution to living standards likely lies somewhere between the estimates of Chambers and Gordon and those of their more enthusiastic revisionists. It had a substantial impact, but so did mining, hydro-electricity, pulp and paper, and general manufacturing- and service-sector expansion. It is to these latter developments that we now turn.

Notes

1. M.C. Urquhart, "New Estimates of Gross National Product, Canada, 1870–1926: Some Implications for Canadian Economic Development," in *Long-Term Factors in American Economic Growth*, NBER Studies in Income and Wealth, Vol. 51, edited by Stanley L. Engerman and Robert E. Gallman (Chicago: University of Chicago Press, 1986), Table 2.13 (p. 42).
2. Urquhart, "New Estimates," Table 2.13.
3. Marvin McInnis, "The Changing Structure of Canadian Agriculture, 1867–1897," *Journal of Economic History* 42, no. 1 (March 1982): 195. Much of the discussion in these pages is based on McInnis's research.
4. Marjorie G. Cohen, *Women's Work, Markets, and Economic Development in Nineteenth-Century Ontario* (Toronto: University of Toronto Press, 1988).
5. Paul Voisey, "The Urbanization of the Canadian Prairies, 1871–1916," *Histoire Sociale/Social History* 8 (May 1975): 77–101.

6. See C. Knick Harley, "Transportation, the World Wheat Trade, and the Kuznets Cycle, 1850–1913," *Explorations in Economic History* 17, no. 3 (July 1980): 218–50.
7. V.C. Fowke, *The National Policy and the Wheat Economy* (Toronto: University of Toronto Press, 1957), 73.
8. Fowke, *The National Policy*, 75.
9. Voisey, "Urbanization of the Canadian Prairies."
10. Alan F. Artibise, "An Urban Economy: Patterns of Economic Change in Winnipeg, 1879–1971," *Prairie Forum* 1, no. 2 (November 1976): 163–88.
11. Royal Commission on Dominion-Provincial Relations, *Report*, Book I: *Canada, 1867–1939* (Ottawa: King's Printer, 1940), 68, 79.
12. W.T. Easterbrook and H.G.J. Aitken, *Canadian Economic History* (Toronto: Macmillan, 1965), 484, 485.
13. Royal Commission on Dominion-Provincial Relations, *Report*, 68.
14. Urquhart, "New Estimates," 64.
15. E.J. Chambers and Donald F. Gordon, "Primary Products and Economic Growth: An Empirical Measurement," *Journal of Political Economy* 74 (August 1966): 315–22.

Further Reading

Chambers, E.J., and Donald F. Gordon. "Primary Products and Economic Growth: An Empirical Measurement." *Journal of Political Economy* 74 (August 1966): 315–22.

Cohen, Marjorie G. *Women's Work, Markets, and Economic Development in Nineteenth-Century Ontario*. Toronto: University of Toronto Press, 1988.

McInnis, Marvin. "The Changing Structure of Canadian Agriculture, 1867–1897." *Journal of Economic History* 42, no. 1 (March 1982): 191–98.

CHAPTER

13

New Industrial Staples

Agriculture was not the only sector to be affected by international events and domestic policies in the decades after Confederation, nor was prairie wheat the only new resource to emerge. Forestry, long a mainstay of the economy, underwent yet another series of adjustments in product mix and in markets for its output, and contributed several new products — wood pulp, newsprint, and paper — to the economy. Mining had long involved mainly a search for precious metals, but, by the beginning of World War I, Canada's portfolio included, in addition to these, a wide array of metallic and nonmetallic minerals and even some petroleum fuels. Rivers that once carried fur traders' canoes and rafts of squared timber now were harnessed to produce electricity for homes and factories.

The developments in these three sectors, diverse as the products may seem, actually have much in common. And while similar in some respects to the parallel development of the prairie wheat economy, these areas also differed in some important ways from that staple. The most obvious example of this difference is in the technologies of the activities. In spite of its relatively late appearance, prairie wheat was essentially a product of the first industrial revolution. The movement onto the prairies in Canada was the last stage of a series of developments in international grain markets that (as seen earlier) date back to 1850. Only vast distances and marginal agricultural lands prevented the appearance of Canadian prairie wheat in world markets in the 1870s and 1880s along with that of other countries of "new" settlement.

The new industrial staples, in contrast, were undisputably the products of the second industrial revolution. Like wheat, they emerged after 1896, partly as a response to an upturn in demand for resource products in the industrial nations. Unlike wheat, however, they required the application of new basic technologies and new techniques. They relied on recent scientific advances that had shown how paper could be made from wood fibre; how metals could be used to great advantage in manufacturing and construction and, then, how they could be freed from the rocks that held them; and how cascading water could light up homes or drive motors in factories hundreds of miles distant.

A second similarity among the new products, and a difference from wheat, lies in their economic impact. At first glance, the products seem inconsequential in terms of the economy.[1] Value added in primary forestry in 1900 was only 1.4 percent of the total for the economy; in 1910, this figure had slipped to 1.1 percent. Wood products and paper products, together, added another 4.3 percent in 1900 and were down to 3.8 percent a decade later. Mining stood at 5 percent of GDP in 1900, and only 2.9 percent in 1910. Electric light and power represented a mere 0.2 percent of GDP in 1900, and 0.6 percent in 1910. Compared to agriculture's 25 percent and 22 percent in 1900 and 1910, respectively, these activities seem insignificant.

Yet, the contribution is best described as indirect, longer-term, and, in a political-economy sense, at least, of fundamental significance. Hydro-electricity is the best example of a product with a major indirect impact; relatively few people were involved in producing electricity directly, yet the implications of cheap power for the rest of the economy were enormous. The contribution of the new staples was longer-term in the sense that, while the developments began in these years, their real impacts came only during and after World War I, and have continued to be important to the present day.

These developments were equally felt in a political-economy sense, and again there are both similarities to and differences from prairie wheat. Like wheat, they opened up new and geographically remote areas to economic activity. Unlike wheat, they attracted much capital to those areas but relatively little labour. There was to be no great flow of immigrants to work in the forests and mines as there was to take up homesteads. Like wheat, the new resources found their principal markets abroad. Unlike wheat, they found these markets in the United States rather than in the United Kingdom, a fact that was to give the economy a north-south orientation along with its east-west one. Like wheat, they were the object of much government attention and planning. Unlike wheat, they received attention from provincial and local, not federal, governments. If prairie wheat was the basis of a great nation-building impulse, the new industrial staples ushered in what, in the 1970s, came to be called "province-building."

Hydro-electricity

Of the new products, hydro-electricity almost certainly affected Canadian economic and political life most profoundly. Economically, hydro has come to symbolize the transition from the "old" industrialism of the nineteenth century, wherein Canada was at a distinct disadvantage internationally, to the "new" industrialism of the twentieth, with its great promise for this nation. Politically, the campaign for public power and the intention to use it to promote economic diversification at the provincial level set a pattern that has continued to today.

The properties of electricity were understood early on, but not until nearly the end of the nineteenth century had that knowledge advanced to the point where electricity could be produced, transmitted, and utilized cheaply and effectively. The first development was the electric generator. By 1880, after a series of prototypes, technology in generation was sufficiently advanced to allow electricity to be produced cheaply and in great quantities. The next major step in the process was the development by Thomas Edison of the central electric system. With this innovation, electricity could be produced at one central site, for use by different consumers at different places, and for different purposes. Transmission was the next hurdle. Electricity could be transmitted long distances only at high voltages, yet safe domestic use required low voltages, such as the 110 volts Edison eventually settled on. The solution came with the development of the transformer. With it, electricity could be stepped up to high voltage for transmission and reduced again for distribution.

The net impact of these developments was that electricity generation could take place in a few large plants, far removed from consumption sites. Specifically, distant rivers could now be used to turn turbines, with the output transmitted to urban and industrial areas. Large-scale production from cheap hydro sources meant taking advantage of economies of scale, which, in turn, meant that electricity prices fell significantly. Canada was well endowed with water power, so the stage was set for a major new industry producing cheap power for a range of new products.

With the capacity to supply electricity improved, the only remaining requirement was to develop ways of using it efficiently. Developments were under way that would make electricity competitive with gas in the lucrative commercial and domestic lighting markets. The perfection of alternating current and the development of an alternating-current motor by the early 1890s opened the way for the use of electricity in providing motive power to industry and the home. Finally, developments in metallurgy at this time spawned the close association between refining and cheap electricity.

The initial developments in hydro-electricity generation were not made in Canada, however, but rather in Niagara Falls, New York. A plant was opened there in the summer of 1895, supplying power first to Buffalo and then to a host of electrochemical industries that were quickly drawn to the power site. This demonstration of the potential of hydro-electricity to promote industrial development, together with the obvious potential for such production in Canada, led to pressure to begin development of the resources north of the border.

Quebec, Ontario, Manitoba, and British Columbia led the way in hydro-electricity development.[2] Five major producers came to dominate the Quebec scene, although only two were in operation as World War I began. Shawinigan Water and Power was the first off the mark. The entrepreneurial initiative for the venture came from a group of Boston financiers, with some Canadian representation added as the company got started. Construction began at Shawinigan Falls, on the St. Maurice River, in 1899, and the first power was delivered in 1903. Financing was an early problem, but, with the initial delivery contracts honoured, the company found it much easier to peddle its bonds in American and British markets.

The progress of the Shawinigan company is especially interesting in that it is instructive of the type of economic activity that came to surround hydro-electricity. Its first contract for hydraulic power was in 1899, with the Northern Aluminum Company, which proposed to locate in the area to use electricity for bauxite reduction and aluminum fabrication. By 1906, this operation was one of the largest aluminum producers in the world. A second contract for hydraulic power, this time with Belgian capitalists looking for a location for a pulp mill, followed one year later. A newsprint mill was added in 1904, and capacity expanded in 1906. The first big contract for electricity came in 1902, in an arrangement with the Montreal Light, Heat and Power Company. The Shawinigan Carbide Company began production in 1904, becoming the second major consumer of electricity. By 1908, this enterprise was controlled by the Shawinigan company, and, by 1909, was a wholly owned subsidiary of it. Further Montreal sales of electricity were negotiated in 1907 with Montreal Street Railway and with Vulcan Portland Cement, indicating the range of linkages to hydro.

Demand for electricity was growing so rapidly by this time that, after 1908, the Shawinigan company declined to make further contracts for hydraulic power, and earlier contracts were bought back. A second powerhouse was completed in 1911, and a second transmission line to Montreal was put into service. The Wabasso Cotton Company of Three Rivers located a thread mill in Shawinigan in 1909, shipping the output to the parent company for weaving into cloth. Two transmission lines to Three Rivers served firms producing iron, bags for cement, and pulp and paper, along with other smaller concerns. Power was also sent via submarine cable to the asbestos and manufacturing industries south of the St. Lawrence. The company also looked to the retail market and, by 1907, was distributing power to 40 communities.

The other significant electricity operation in prewar Quebec was the Montreal Light, Heat and Power Company. Formed out of a series of mergers of small gas and electric companies, Montreal Light, Heat and Power was in complete control of the Montreal market by 1903. Steam provided a significant portion of the generating capacity early on, but hydro gradually replaced it, especially after 1909 when a new plant at the Soulanges rapids was opened, by which time the company was operating three stations. Its output was sold entirely in the city, for residential, urban-transportation, and general-manufacturing purposes.

The pattern of development in Ontario took quite a different turn from that in Quebec. There was some early interest in the Welland River, but the real prize was Niagara Falls. After it was declared a provincial park in 1887 to prevent its spoliation by the overly eager tourist industry, supplicants began almost immediately to negotiate with the Queen Victoria Niagara Falls Park Commission.

In 1892, the Canadian Niagara Power Company, a wholly owned subsidiary of the parent across the river, obtained an exclusive lease to produce power on the Canadian side of the falls. Failure of the company to meet the terms of the lease, and the mounting public concern this neglect was causing, led the Ontario government to renegotiate in 1899, removing the monopoly provision. A second lease was granted to a group of Buffalo industrialists, organized as the Ontario Power Company, in 1900. A third concession — the first to Canadians — was granted in 1903 to the Electric Development Company. The first two firms began construction in 1902; the third, in 1904.

Ontario's shift to public-sector development began in 1902 with the expression of the idea that the smaller towns and cities of the southern part of the province should band together to secure for themselves cheap and reliable supplies of hydro-electric power to enhance their manufacturing bases. The idea quickly took root among the business interests of the region. Some proponents of public power urged the provincial government to get involved, while others pushed for permission for a consortium of municipalities to construct and operate their own system. Premier Ross resisted provincial involvement, but did establish the Ontario Power Commission in 1903 and had it undertake to study the feasibility of a municipal consortium taking charge. The refusal of the existing companies to guarantee a supply of electricity quickly turned the movement into one for public power.

Political pressure led the government to establish the Hydro Electric Commission of Enquiry in 1905, with Adam Beck as its chairman. Its 1906 report recommended the establishment of a publicly owned distribution network. The government responded by creating a permanent hydro-electric power commission, charged with regulating the private utilities and determining the means for distributing electricity to the municipalities.

Opposition to the plan for a provincial role, and to the alternative one for a joint municipal venture (floated by the Snider Commission at the same time), came, predictably, from private companies and other business interests. A furious political battle was waged, with public-power proponents emerging victorious in the municipal elections of 1907 when ratepayers authorized their administrations to enter into contracts with the Hydro-Electric Power Commission to deliver electricity to the towns at specified prices. Hydro then

Ontario Hydro Archives/HP1243

Hydro-electric power station, Niagara Falls, Ontario, 1907. *Niagara Falls was the first source in North America to generate hydro-electric power on a large scale. This new source of light and power had an impact on the economy and politics of Ontario comparable to that of the coming of the railway 50 years earlier.*

moved to sign a contract with the Ontario Power Company for delivery of power at Niagara, and the municipalities, in turn, signed their final contracts with the commission. In 1908, a contract was let by the commission to construct a transmission line connecting Niagara with these municipalities. Ontario Hydro, as the commission was now known, was finally in business; its first "switching on" occurred in October 1910.

Developments in the other two provinces were smaller-scale, understandably, given their smaller populations and economies. By 1900, the Winnipeg Electric Street Railway Company, headed by William Mackenzie of railway fame, had effective monopoly of gas, electric, and public-transit facilities in Winnipeg. In 1902, the company entered into an arrangement with the Ogilvie Milling Company (a large user of power) to develop a hydro-electric site on the Winnipeg River. As that project neared completion, in 1906, Winnipeg ratepayers approved construction of a $3.25 million plant, also on the Winnipeg River. Construction began in 1909, and Winnipeg Hydro, as the second company was known, began delivering electricity in competition with the Winnipeg Electric Street Railway Company in 1911.

Developments in British Columbia began much the same way. The British-owned British Columbia Electric Railway (BCER) dominated utilities in the major centres. Vancouver Power, organized in 1898 to develop a waterpower site, soon came under the control of the BCER. The potential of the province was quickly acknowledged, and the first delivery of hydro-electricity was made in 1903. Unlike what had occurred in Ontario and Manitoba, interest in a municipal venture went nowhere, and BCER retained its monopoly position into World War I and beyond.

Hydro capacity in Canada grew quickly, once development began. Unfortunately, it is difficult to be very precise about the early progress of the industry, as comprehensive statistics are available only from 1917 on. Figure 13.1 shows the record for hydraulic-turbine installation from 1890 to 1914. Because hydraulic power used directly in the pulp-and-paper and other industries is included in the data, hydro-electricity generation is overstated somewhat in this figure. Nevertheless, the growth is impressive. From 72 000 horsepower of hydraulic-turbine installation in 1890, capacity increased 2.5 times by 1900; increased by that amount again by 1905; doubled once more, to 977 000 horsepower, by 1910; and stood at nearly 2 million horsepower in 1914. Ontario and Quebec accounted for the bulk of this capacity — 80 percent in 1900, about that figure in 1914.[3] Ontario lagged behind Quebec in terms of installed capacity until 1905, but retained the level thereafter. In 1914, Ontario had 44 percent of Canada's installed-turbine capacity, and Quebec had 34 percent. British Columbia was a distant third, at around 10 percent; Manitoba next, at less than 5 percent; and the others inconsequential.

It is difficult to know even approximately the impact the development of "white coal" had on Canada's economic fortunes. Hydro developments were important economic events, in and of themselves. Building the dams, installing the turbines, and constructing the transmission lines absorbed a significant amount of the young nation's capital resources and provided employment to many workers. Cheap electricity also attracted a host of power-intensive in-

FIGURE 13.1
Hydraulic Turbine Installations, 1890–1914

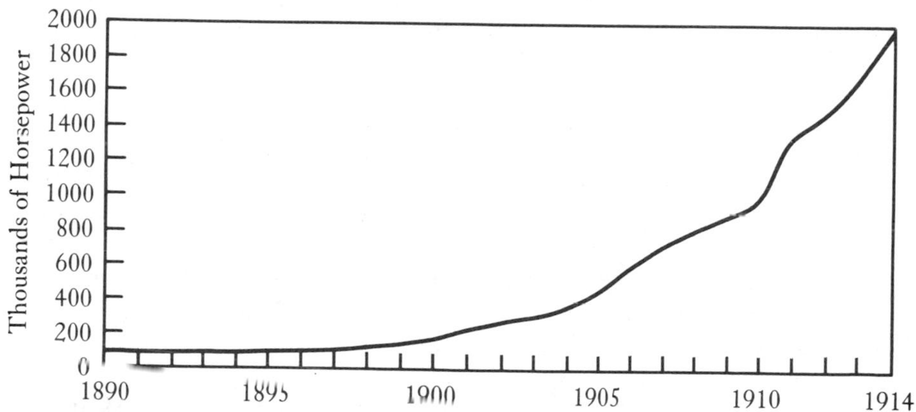

Source: M.C. Urquhart and K.A.H. Buckley, eds., *Historical Statistics of Canada* (Toronto: Macmillan, 1965), Series P75 (p. 454).

dustries to these regions and gave Canada a comparative advantage in a range of industries it has retained to the present day. Some activities used the power directly in the production process, while others used it to drive machinery. (Examples of links to aluminum, carbide, and pulp and paper were given above, and more will be encountered below.)

A further effect, more difficult to quantify but potentially among the most important of all, is the impact the availability of a cheap and reliable power source had on secondary industry more generally. Canada was disadvantaged in terms of a nineteenth-century industrialism based on coal. The only deposits of this fuel were in Nova Scotia and the prairies, far removed from the country's natural centres of manufacturing. Hydro could not compete with coal in terms of supplying heat, but it could in terms of motive power. As the potential of Niagara Falls and the St. Lawrence and its tributaries was developed after 1900, Canadian industry could locate near both cheap power and its main markets. The old disadvantage had disappeared. As an early and influential study of the industry concluded, "hydroelectricity has been a prerequisite to Central Canada's industrial growth."[4]

One further impact of hydro on Canadian society is more difficult to quantify. Cheap electricity transformed the lives of ordinary Canadians in untold ways, many of which had ultimate economic impacts. Electric tramways were among the first users of the new resource. With commuting costs reduced, people could live farther away from their jobs, meaning that the shapes of cities began to change. Electrical gadgets reduced the drudgery of everyday chores in the home. Stoves, refrigerators, vacuum cleaners, and, most of all, reliable methods of lighting began to penetrate at least the middle-class environment by World War I. As Figure 13.2 shows, a whole new consumer industry was born in the process.

The final point to stress is that politicians and business leaders were quick to note the connection between cheap power and industrial development. Control of the resources thus came to be seen as an essential part of what Nelles has termed "the manufacturing condition,"[5] and what in another current terminology would be called "province-building." Thus, throughout its history, hydro has always been more than just another sector. The really mythical role sometimes ascribed today to Ontario Hydro and, especially, Hydro-Quebec in the economic development of their respective provincial economies in fact goes far back in time.

Minerals

Interest in Canada's mineral wealth dates back to 1604, when an engineer accompanying Champlain reported the presence of iron, silver, and copper at St. Mary's Bay in Nova Scotia.[6] For nearly three centuries thereafter, though, the only deposits to attract much attention were those containing gold and silver, coal seams, iron ore, fuel peat, and construction materials such as gypsum and cement. Gold and silver were valuable as precious metals, and could be uncovered and extracted with relatively simple techniques. Coal was used as a fuel for heating purposes, and as an input, along with iron ore, into the production of iron and products. Structural materials were relatively ubiquitous, and again could be extracted and processed simply. Other materials were known to exist, but either there was no significant demand for them or they could not be extracted with the techniques of the time.

This situation changed after the mid-1880s. Figure 13.3 shows the annual value of total mineral output from 1886, when consistent statistics become available, to the eve of World War I. Figure 13.4

FIGURE 13.2

Electrical Products Industry, 1880–1920: Number of Employees and Gross Value of Production

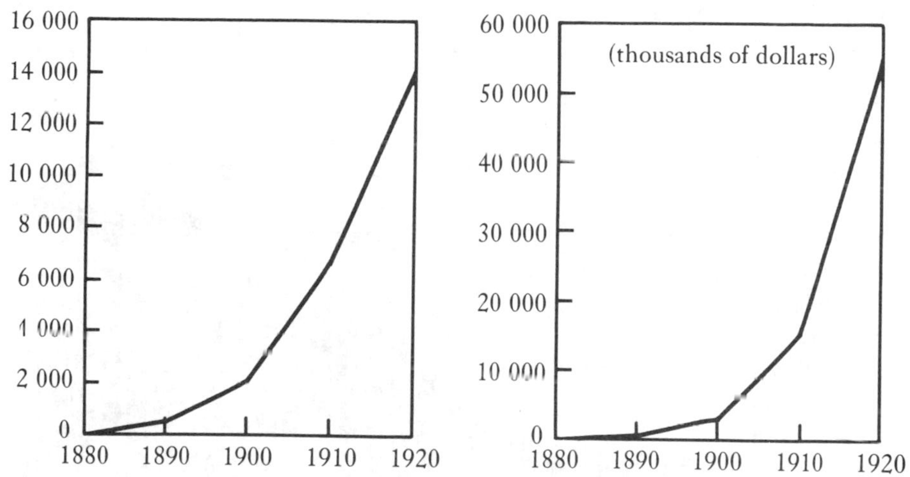

Source: Statistics Canada, *Historical Statistics of Canada*, 2nd ed. (Ottawa: Supply and Services, 1983), R417 and R419.

shows the relative importance of the broad categories of minerals over the same period. Total output doubled, from $10 million to $20 million, between 1886 and 1895, trebled again in the next five years, and then doubled again by 1913. Structural materials consistently accounted for about one-fifth of the total value of output throughout these years. This category includes such items as clay products, cement, sand and gravel, and sandstone. The economics of these cases is relatively uncomplicated. Deposits are located relatively ubiquitously across the country, and are exploited for the local market in step with construction activity. Thus, while structural materials were obviously important as a source of local income and employment, there is little national drama to be found in the figures.

Nonmetallic minerals were the least-important category in 1886, at 12.3 percent of the total output, and declined to about 5 percent of the total by the outbreak of World War I. Absolute value of output rose, nevertheless, from $1.3 million to $7.4 million. With the exception of asbestos, these are the least well-known of the

FIGURE 13.3
Value of Total Mineral Output, 1886–1913

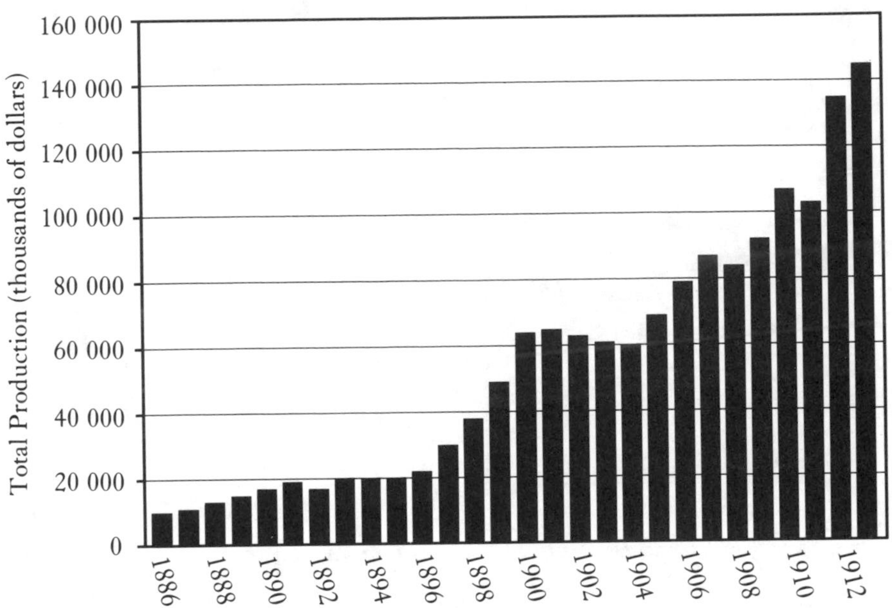

Source: Canada, Dominion Bureau of Statistics, *Canadian Mineral Statistics, 1886–1956* (Ottawa: Dominion Bureau of Statistics, 1957), 48.

minerals. Phosphate was the leading material in this category in 1886, at about 25 percent of the total, with salt, sulphur, asbestos, and gypsum being other important commodities. There was little change in these patterns over the period.

Fuels are a more important and more familiar category. Total output was $4.4 million in 1886 and, by 1913, had risen to more than $41 million. They accounted for more than 40 percent of total mining activity until the turn of the century, when their share slipped below 30 percent, where it remained roughly until 1913. Coal was the dominant commodity throughout in this category, of course, ranging from 82 percent of fuel output in 1895 to nearly 95 percent in 1913. Nova Scotia was the dominant producer. Production and exports from that province grew until the 1920s. A new export activity opened up in the 1880s, and especially after 1900, as coal from Vancouver Island began to go to the San Fran-

FIGURE 13.4

Share of Mineral Output by Main Category, 1886–1913

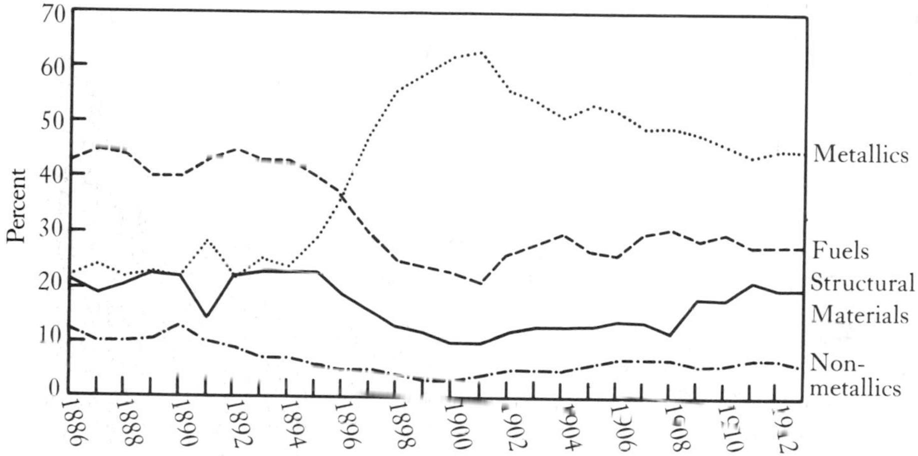

Source: Canada, Dominion Bureau of Statistics, *Canadian Mineral Statistics, 1886–1956* (Ottawa: Dominion Bureau of Statistics, 1957), 48.

cisco and district market. Petroleum from Ontario captured 12 percent of the fuels market in 1886, but fell to near oblivion in the twentieth century as the oilfields ran down. Natural gas grew in importance, by contrast, as the plentiful reserves of Alberta began to develop.

Metallic minerals are the main story of this period, in terms of economic importance as well as of political excitement. Gold is far and away the most spectacular of the lot. This precious metal comes in three forms, and each was important in what was a succession of gold booms. Alluvial gold, that found by panning rivers and lakes, is the most familiar. Canada's first gold rush began in 1858, when deposits were discovered in the Fraser River in British Columbia. Hordes of prospectors arrived immediately, many from the overcrowded California fields. They followed the rivers into the interior, eventually entering the Cariboo District and bringing to this vast wilderness a short-lived but frantic boom.

The next phase of the gold industry was more spectacular yet. News that gold of immense value had been found on the Klondike River brought miners from around the world to this isolated and inhospitable area. Success was immediate, for some at least, and gold production soared. Dawson City grew from a small outpost to a city of over 30 000 in just a few years. The boom could not last, and it did not. By 1910, Yukon gold production virtually ceased, and Dawson City reverted to an outpost.

Gold is also found in ore bodies, either as the principal component or secondary to other minerals. The economics, in either case, is very different from that for alluvial gold. The ore must be mined, and the gold extracted through smelting and refining. Thus, large companies with access to capital and metallurgical expertise replaced solitary prospectors with mules and gold pans. In this respect, at least, gold was a mineral very much like the other metals. Deposits became viable only as chemical methods were developed to separate the ores into their constituent parts, and as cheap power sources became available.

Gold production of this third type began in the Rossland area of British Columbia in the 1890s, with the ore initially being shipped to the United States for smelting. More important developments took place in Ontario, as the vast deposits of the Porcupine and Kirkland Lake areas were opened up. Production from these areas in one year, 1913, exceeded that for all previous years together, and output doubled, then doubled again, after that.

Silver was the metal most sought after, next to gold. Some relatively small production had occurred in the Lake Superior region around the time of Confederation, but the major phase began twenty years later, when important silver deposits were discovered in British Columbia. The ore was so rich that it paid to pack it out by horse and ship it by water or rail to the United States for reduction. Activity spread and grew more diversified as metallurgical advances opened up more deposits, and the development of cheap power drew smelting activities north of the border. British Columbia dominated the sector for twenty years, until the silver deposits near Cobalt were opened up and Ontario became an important producer as well.

Unlike precious metals, there was little use for base metals before the late nineteenth century. Only as industrialization in Europe and the United States proceeded did such metals as copper, zinc, and lead take on any real value. The discovery that steel could be made much stronger by adding nickel alloy was a key development. Reinforced steel was in great demand by the building trades and armament manufacturers. With the prospects of a market established, Canada's vast resources of zinc, copper, nickel, cobalt, and other base metals were of considerable value. Early metallurgical techniques were imported, but Canadian-based companies such as COMINCO were quick to extend them to overcome their own problems and to expand the range of feasible deposits.

The early progress of Canada's base-metals industry was impressive. Copper production increased slowly but steadily from the mid-1880s. Output in value terms was 8 times its 1886 level in 1900, and 30 times that amount in 1913. Lead production rose from a value of a few thousand dollars in the late 1880s to $2.8 million by the turn of the century. Production fell off slightly for a couple of years, and then remained roughly constant until a new flotation process developed by COMINCO during World War I laid the basis for a strong postwar expansion. The first reported zinc production was 788 000 pounds in 1898, for a value of $36 000, and even this had virtually disappeared until World War I demands led to a spectacular recovery.

Nickel is perhaps the most interesting case-study of mineral development in this period. Early on, production from a small mine in the Eastern Townships of Quebec was used locally for costume jewellery and tableware. The rich deposits of the Sudbury area were discovered in the course of constructing the CPR, but at first the nickel was considered an impurity to be removed to get at the more valuable copper and other metals. As demand for nickel grew, a consequence of its use in hardening steel, companies began to experiment with techniques for recovering the metal. The Orford Copper Company obtained a U.S. naval contract to work with the Sudbury ores, and production began. A smelting operation was constructed in Copper Cliff to produce nickel matte. The matte was then sent to a refinery in New Jersey for upgrading into nickel, whence it went to U.S. steel companies. Its main competitor, the Canadian Copper Company, sold its ore to Orford for smelting. In 1902, the two companies joined together to form the International Nickel Company of Canada (Inco Ltd.). Production of nickel rose from practically nothing in 1886 to 7 million pounds by 1900, and to 37 million pounds by 1910. By the eve of World War I, production had reached nearly 50 million pounds.

Pressure soon developed for a refinery to be built in Canada to upgrade the nickel matte prior to export. In part, this was self-serving pleading by a rival nickel company, Nickel Steel of Canada, in conjunction with a consortium of Hamilton businessmen. But the request fit with Ontario's "manufacturing condition,"[7] so provincial, and even federal, politicians were interested in the idea. One apparent obstacle was the graduated U.S. tariff, wherein imports of refined nickel and nickel products faced steep surcharges (directed primarily at French competition initially), but nickel ore and matte entered duty-free. As important, though, was the fact that the New Jersey location was close to the chemical inputs used in the Orford refining process, and to the steel industry that used the output.

Canadian interests argued for an export tax on ore and matte to offset the distortion caused by the U.S. tariff. They were constantly opposed in this objective by Orford (later Inco), who threatened to shut down Canadian production altogether in favour of an operation in New Caledonia. Prime Minister Laurier was dissuaded from imposing an export tax by this pressure, whereupon lobbying efforts turned to the Ontario government. A bill was passed in the legislature in 1900, imposing a fee of $60 per ton on nickel matte, refundable in full if refined in Canada. The measure raised a storm of controversy, resulting ultimately in the federal minister of justice's serving notice of intent to recommend disallowance of the legislation on the grounds that it applied to ore from private lands and was thus *ultra vires* the provincial legislature. The Ontario government gave in to the pressure, and the bill was never proclaimed, although it remained on the books until 1907.

The idea of forcing the refinery operation to shift to Canada resurfaced as a result of two factors. The economics of the industry were slowly changing. Developments in the application of electricity to refining, coupled with Ontario's cheap supplies of hydro power, were gradually making that province the least costly location for a refinery. The real pressure, though, came during World War I from first the suspicion, and then the certainty, that Canadian nickel ore refined in New Jersey was making its way to Germany. The idea that Canadian resources were being used to kill Canadian soldiers was too much of an affront for even the most cautious of Canadian politicians, and the resultant political pressure led Inco to announce a refinery for Port Colborne, and to complete it in 1917. Through economics or politics, or perhaps both, Canada gained an important industry, one that has remained a mainstay of that region of the country until today.

These developments in mining to 1913 are more important for

what they presaged for the economy than for what they actually contributed. The real expansion was to come during and after World War I. Nevertheless, they are important in several respects. They drew attention to geographical regions of the country that had largely been bypassed up to that time; they created a tradition of applying science to resource extraction; they created several Canadian mining companies that are with us today; they provided a spur to hydro-electric development; they were a focus of provincial-government economic-development planning at a time when Ottawa was preoccupied with filling up the provinces with farmers; and they drew Canada increasingly into the U.S. economic orbit.

Forest Products

As seen in Part III, the forest-products sector was in a state of flux at Confederation. Exports of squared timber were still growing absolutely, but were falling in relative importance to those of more processed products — primarily deals, planks, and boards — which represented 70 percent of exports in 1867. Markets were changing as well, largely but not entirely reflecting the shift in the composition of output. Exports to Great Britain were substantially higher in absolute terms in 1867 than they had been in 1850; yet in the latter year, they represented about 50 percent of total exports, while in the former, they had been more than 80 percent.

These trends continued in the immediate post-Confederation period.[8] Exports of forest products were exceptionally strong in the first half-dozen years after. Total shipments in 1873 were up nearly 80 percent over what they had been six years earlier, with the U.S. market being particularly strong. Then came the international slowdown in 1873. Wood exports were especially hard hit by the downturn, most notably those going to the United States. The U.K. market remained reasonably firm, falling only in the late 1870s, and then only for a brief time. The U.S. market collapsed, however. Exports fell from $12.5 million in 1873 to $4.3 million in 1879, when recovery began. For four years, 1875–79, Britain took between 65 and 73 percent of total exports, compared to the 47 percent it had taken in 1873. By 1881, Canadian wood exports had regained their very high levels of the early 1870s, as recovery proceeded in both major markets. Thereafter, though, the trend was flat through to 1897.

The gradual loss of the British market is easiest to explain. There

New Brunswick Museum

West Head Mills, Saint John, N.B. *Although New Brunswick's early timber trade was predominantly in squared timber, eventually lumber, the product of sawmills, increased in importance. It included deals, planks, and boards, and was mainly pine and spruce.*

was a general decline of demand for wood products in Britain as construction slowed and as shipbuilding in wood wound down. What demand remained shifted increasingly to Baltic suppliers. The sluggishness of the U.S. market is more problematic. McInnis finds no obvious explanation in his reconstruction of the data for the period. Dwindling supplies do not appear to have been the problem that some earlier accounts have suggested, and McInnis posits that growing domestic demand may have been an important factor.[9] Urbanization and industrial growth in Canada took an increasing share of the output.

The trend toward processing timber in Canada prior to export began to be reversed in the 1890s. The explanation for the reversal was partly geographical and partly political. The gradual shift of the trade to the upper Great Lakes region made it cheap to cut logs in Canada and float them across the lakes to sawmills in the United States. Exports of logs, which had averaged around $250 000 in the early 1880s, jumped tenfold by 1895. The political component came, as with nickel, in the form of a graduated U.S. tariff. Logs entered freely, while processed lumber products faced duties. The federal government had attempted, in the 1880s, to encourage processing in Canada by imposing export duties on unprocessed logs, but these had been removed in 1890 in exchange for a lowering of the U.S. tariff on sawn lumber. American policy became more protectionist in 1897, when the Dingley Tariff imposed a duty on sawn lumber but left the import of unprocessed logs free. The duty was constructed in such a way as to rise automatically if Canada reinstituted the export tax on logs.

With the export tax rendered useless as a countermeasure, Canadian lumber companies turned their attention to the provincial governments. There was a precedent: British Columbia had instituted an embargo on the export of unprocessed logs from crown lands in 1891. Ontario now adopted a similar measure. Effective April 30, 1898, all pine timber from crown land had to be made into sawn lumber in Ontario. The restriction to timber from crown lands skirted the constitutional issue nicely, since the policy came under the power of the province to manage its natural resources.

On the surface, at least, the export embargo appeared to be effective. The export of logs fell off, and that of lumber continued to grow — $33 million in lumber exports were recorded in 1913, compared to $25 million in 1897.[10] It is not clear, however, how much the success was attributable to the policy per se, and how much it was simply the result of the natural advantage Canada had in sawmilling. Plentiful stands of cheap timber, together with inexpensive hydro-electric power, gave the industry a base in Canada that could not be matched in the United States. It has often been remarked that provincial governments found the political will to implement these measures and to make them stick in the face of lobbying efforts only because economics was on their side. The difficulty in legislating the identical measure for refined nickel, where Canada's locational advantage was less clear, early on, is instructive.

The most significant developments in the forest-products sector, though, came in the form of an entirely new set of uses for wood. Until well into the nineteenth century, paper production, in Canada and elsewhere, was based on inputs of rags, grasses, and straw. Operations were small and oriented to the local market, and the product was relatively expensive. Technology was to change all that. The important breakthrough was the isolation of the cellulose component of wood, and its substitution for rags and grasses. There were two main stages to this operation. Wood was first either ground or treated with chemicals to produce wood pulp. The pulp was then further processed into paper of various kinds. Ground pulpwood, being relatively coarse, was ideal for further working into newsprint, while chemical pulps were required for the production of the finer grades of paper.

Canada possessed vast tracts of spruce that were ideal for processing into wood pulp. This endowment was reinforced by the fact that pulp production, mechanical or chemical, along with some of the further processing, required vast amounts of power. The simultaneous development of the hydro-electric capacity of central Canada provided this very advantage. North American demand was growing rapidly as well, for newsprint in particular. U.S. newspaper circulation rose by more than 80 percent between 1870 and 1909, as a result of growing populations and relatively falling prices.

Firms responded to the possibilities early on.[11] Canada's first groundwood pulp mill opened in Valleyfield, Quebec, in 1866. The first mill to use hydro-electric power appeared in Georgetown, Ontario, in 1888, beginning the close association of those industries that has lasted through to today. The Canadian market was too small to absorb much output, so producers naturally turned to the much larger American one. At first, American producers had adequate supplies of pulpwood close to the major consuming centres, and imports were minuscule. As supplies were used up, wood prices rose, and Canadian resources became competitive. As producers turned to this market, they found a familiar obstacle — a cascading system of duties that allowed pulpwood to enter free, but put increasing levies on wood pulp, newsprint, and processed paper. As it had with the timber provisions, the American tariff increased in the presence of a Canadian export tax on pulpwood.

Canada's cost advantage in wood-pulp production was apparent, given cheap hydro power and vast spruce forests, so lobbying efforts to overturn the American barriers were successful. The main actors, again, were the provincial governments. Ontario passed an order-in-council in 1900, this time without even much fanfare, extending the "manufacturing condition" to pulpwood. Henceforth, all spruce cordwood taken from crown lands had to be manufactured into mechanical or chemical pulp in Canada. The measure was not immediately effective, because U.S. companies could still draw on their own resources and because Quebec refused to follow suit. Eventually, however, Quebec followed Ontario's lead (in 1909), and the two provinces' superior resource endowments prevailed.

As Burley notes,[12] data for the early years of the pulp industry are scattered and unreliable. There were 2.1 million cords of pulpwood cut in Canada in 1913, half of which was exported. This figure declines constantly thereafter, as none of the product is processed domestically prior to export. Wood-pulp output, the next stage of the process, stood at 363 000 tons in 1908, the earliest year for which data are available, and had grown to 855 000 in 1913. One-half to two-thirds of production was exported in these years.

With wood pulp attended to, Canadian attention turned to shifting the newsprint industry north of the border as well. Here, the support of an important ally was key. Newsprint costs in the United States were rising steadily, making access to cheaper Canadian supplies ever more attractive to large U.S. newspapers. Their lobbying efforts were successful, representing one of the few instances in which an interest group was able to have tariffs removed. President Taft lowered the rates on newsprint in 1911, and, in the Underwood schedule of 1913, those on mechanical pulp and newsprint were removed entirely. The stage was set for the development of a major Canadian industry, one that remains important today.

Conclusion

What contribution did these new resource developments make to the acceleration in extensive and intensive economic growth observed after 1896? Given that most of these activities were really only getting under way as World War I approached, the answer in each case must be very little. Some investment in infrastructure was taking place at this time and would, therefore, have contributed to the investment boom noted earlier. Lumber exports were significant, of course, and hydro-electricity had already had an effect on the manufacturing and service sectors. Local imports were always substantial, as the economic progress of a Sudbury or a Trail attested to. Generally, though, it seems safe to conclude that the main contributions of these new staples to the economy overall came during and after World War I.

Notes

1. The figures are from M.C. Urquhart, "New Estimates of Gross National Product, Canada, 1870–1926: Some Implications for Canadian Development," in *Long-Term Factors in American Economic Growth*, NBER Studies in Income and Wealth, Vol. 51, edited by Stanley L. Engerman and Robert E. Gallman (Chicago: University of Chicago Press, 1986), Table 2.13 (p. 42).
2. The following material is drawn from J.H. Dales, *Hydroelectricity and Industrial Development in Quebec, 1898–1940* (Cambridge, MA: Harvard University Press, 1957); H.V. Nelles, *The Politics of Development: Forests, Mines and Hydroelectric Power in Ontario, 1849–1941* (Toronto: Macmillan, 1974); and Christopher Armstrong and H.V. Nelles, *Monopoly's Moment: The Organization and Regulation of Canadian Utilities 1830–1930* (Philadelphia: Temple University Press, 1986).
3. Dales, *Hydroelectricity*, 35.
4. Dales, *Hydroelectricity*, 180.
5. Nelles, *Politics of Development*, Chapter 2.
6. See Canada, Dominion Bureau of Statistics, *Canadian Mineral Statistics, 1886–1956* (Ottawa: Queen's Printer, 1957); and Kevin Burley, ed., *The Development of Canada's Staples, 1867–1939*, Carleton Library #56 (Toronto: McClelland and Stewart, 1970).
7. R.M. McInnis, "Canada in the World Market for Forest Products, 1850–1895," unpublished ms., Queen's University, 1988.
8. The following material is derived from R.M. McInnis, "From Hewn Timber to Sawn Timber: The Canadian Forest Industry in the Latter Half of the Nineteenth Century," unpublished ms., Queen's University, 1988.
9. R.M. McInnis, "Canada in the World Market for Forest Products," unpublished ms., Queen's University, 1988.
10. M.C. Urquhart and K.A.H. Buckley, eds., *Historical Statistics of Canada* (Toronto: Macmillan, 1965), Series K176–183 (p. 337).
11. See Trevor J.O. Dick, "Canadian Newsprint, 1913–1930: National Policies and the North American Economy," *Journal of Economic History* 42, no. 3 (September 1982): 659–87; and Kevin Burley, "Introduction," in *The Development of Canada's Staples*, Part Four, 332–40.
12. Burley, "Introduction," 333.

Further Reading

Dick, Trevor J.O. "Canadian Newsprint, 1913–1930: National Policies and the North American Economy." *Journal of Economic History* 42, no. 3 (September 1982): 659–87.

Nelles, H.V. *The Politics of Development: Forests, Mines and Hydroelectric Power in Ontario, 1849–1941*. Toronto: Macmillan, 1974.

Nelles, H.V., and C. Armstrong. *Monopoly's Moment: The Organization and Regulation of Canadian Utilities 1830–1930*. Philadelphia: Temple University Press, 1986.

C H A P T E R

14

Manufacturing and Services

If the attention given to staples products in the years from Confederation to the outbreak of World War I occasionally seems out of proportion to their underlying importance to the economic and social life of the nation, the opposite situation holds in the case of the manufacturing and service sectors. Manufacturing consistently contributed about one-quarter of GDP between 1870 and 1910. Services were even more important, in an absolute sense. Even omitting construction, the service sector's share of GDP was more than 30 percent in 1870 and rose to 43 percent in 1910. Yet, unlike the wheat boom, or even the new resource staples, we know relatively little about these activities and their growth. There are no general histories, and precious few industry or company studies.

This relative ignorance is, at least in part, an unfortunate legacy of the traditional focus in Canadian economic history on the staples theory. Manufacturing and service activities tend to be cast as derivative to the staples sectors, with government policy being more or less important in fashioning these links, depending on the product in question. Manufacturing consists of processing resource products prior to export, producing inputs needed in the resource sector, or seeing to the needs of the resident population. Service activities arise to collect the staples and transport them to market, to distribute manufactured products to consumers, and to provide nontradable products in local markets.

This relative lack of knowledge about these sectors is unfortunate, for at least two reasons. First, and most obviously, together they constituted more than half the economy in terms of output in 1870, and nearly two-thirds of it in 1910. Their sheer presence, if nothing else, makes them deserving of more attention. Second, as the preceding chapters have shown, developments in the staples sectors alone cannot account fully for the trends in extensive and intensive growth recorded in Canada after Confederation. It thus remains to ask what role manufacturing and services played.

Manufacturing

Growth and Development

The manufacturing sector, by its very diversity, defies easy summary analysis. Included in turn-of-the-century Canadian manufacturing, for instance, were everything from small flour mills employing a few individuals, through intermediate machinery operations, to huge steel complexes. In some cases, technology was simple; in others, exceedingly complex. Some types of manufacturing involved the processing of resource products, while other types turned out more finished producer and consumer goods. Some production was for the local market, protected naturally by distance. In some other types, the market was national, protected by tariffs and other trade impediments. In a few instances at least, production was for customers abroad.

By traditional accounts, the development of manufacturing prior to the outbreak of World War I conformed closely to progress in the economy more generally. The three decades after Confederation were disappointing to those who wished to see Canada emulate the industrial success of its neighbour to the south. Explanations for the relatively slow progress were easy to find. The established staples sectors were on the decline, and no new exports had arisen to take their place. Thus, these critical linkages were missing. Domestic manufacturers were also faced with increasing competition as industrialization in the United States and abroad, coupled with falling transport costs, brought down the prices of imported manufactured goods. The national-policy tariffs helped, but not enough.

After 1896, the account goes, manufacturing growth was both substantial and diversified. In an era when the highly visible developments were in the wheat fields, mines, rivers, and forests, it was noted, urban and industrial areas grew commensurately. This link was taken as evidence both of the staples base of manufacturing and of the success of the national-policy tariffs and transport policies in fostering these spinoff developments.

The first serious attempt to quantify aggregate manufacturing development after 1870 challenged this traditional view somewhat. Gordon Bertram's estimates of the gross value of manufacturing output, shown in the first two rows of Table 14.1, seemed to indicate that development was more continuous than the traditional account implied. Output in current-dollar terms increased at an average annual rate of 3.3 percent in the 1870s and 4.1 percent in the 1880s, before falling back to below 2 percent in the 1890s, then rising at an impressive 8.4 percent in the first decade of the new century. The boom decade is still there, as are the relatively depressed 1890s, but the first twenty years after Confederation look more prosperous. When allowance is made for price changes (Row 2), the pattern is more uniform yet. Real output grew at, or slightly above, the 40-year average to 1890, slowed considerably for a decade, and then rose at a rate somewhat above the average for another 10 years.

From this work, supplemented by some of more recent vintage on manufactured-commodity ouput and on estimates of capital formation between 1870 and 1900, there arose a "revisionist" view of Canadian manufacturing development. The thesis of a boom after 1900, based on the opening of western wheat lands, survived. But the notion that the events of this decade represented a structural break from the past was replaced by the idea that development was more or less continuous from 1870 on, with perhaps a cyclical break in the 1890s. Bertram expressed this point in presenting his original estimates: "In fact, it would appear that a new interpretation of the three decades preceding the Western wheat boom emphasizing growth, rather than secular depression, should be considered."[1]

This conclusion raised some interesting issues for the interpretation of Canadian economic history in the decades after Confederation. If manufacturing growth before 1900, or at least before 1890, truly was more robust than previously believed, one of two conclusions followed. Either the staples sectors that were thought to support manufacturing activity were more robust before 1900 than believed, or manufacturing growth was not as closely tied to these activities as traditional accounts had it. Accepting the first explanation meant re-examining the course of staples development between 1870 and 1900 (something that was done, as previous chapters have shown). Accepting the second explanation meant moving

TABLE 14.1

Compound Annual Rates of Growth of Manufacturing Output and Value Added by Decade, 1870–1910

	1870–1880	*1880–1890*	*1890–1900*	*1900–1910*	*1870–1910*
Gross Value of Output					
Current dollars[1]	3.3	4.1	1.7	8.4	4.3
Constant dollars[2]					
Bertram index[1]	4.5	4.8	2.4	5.5	4.3
Altman index[2]	3.2	3.1	2.1	6.0	3.6
(both 1913 = 100)					
Value Added					
Current dollars[3]	3.0	5.2	1.5	8.5	4.5
Constant dollars					
Altman 1	2.6	2.6	0.6	7.7	3.3
Altman 2	3.1	3.8	1.0	7.6	3.8
(both 1913 = 100)					

Sources: 1. Gordon W. Bertram, "Historical Statistics on Growth and Structure of Manufacturing in Canada, 1870–1957," in *Conference on Statistics, 1962 and 1963*, edited by J. Henripin and A. Asimakopulos (Toronto: University of Toronto Press, 1964).

2. Morris Altman, "A Revision of Canadian Economic Growth: 1870–1910 (A Challenge to the Gradualist Interpretation)," *Canadian Journal of Economics* 20, no. 1 (February 1987): 88.

3. Calculated from M.C. Urquhart, "New Estimates of Gross National Product, Canada, 1870–1926: Some Implications for Canadian Economic Development," in *Long-Term Factors in American Economic Growth*, NBER Studies in Income and Wealth, Vol. 51, edited by Stanley L. Engerman and Robert E. Gallman (Chicago: University of Chicago Press, 1986), Table 2.1.

beyond the naïve staples interpretation of Canadian economic development (something that was done, as well). Few challenged the view that manufacturing boomed after 1900, and that it was associated in some way with the emergence of prairie wheat and other new staples. The only question was how to fit this correlation into a framework that was consistent with the pre-1900 experience.

A second set of estimates of manufacturing activity became available as part of the historical GNP project. These growth rates, presented in Row 4 of Table 14.1, are for value added in manufacturing rather than for gross value of output, and thus avoid problems of double counting. According to these numbers, value added in manufacturing in current-dollar terms grew by 3 percent per annum on average in the 1870s, by 5.2 percent in the 1880s, and by only 1.5 percent in the 1890s, but by an impressive 8.5 percent in the first decade of this century. The general picture is consistent with Bertram's interpretation. Manufacturing grew quite respectably in the two decades after Confederation, before slowing notably in the 1890s. Growth after 1900 was especially strong when contrasted with that of the previous decade, but was so even when measured against the record between 1870 and 1890.

This revisionist interpretation of manufacturing development has come under scrutiny recently. While the debate is technical, and as yet unresolved, it is important enough to mention here. The problem is an old and familiar one: how to deflate current-dollar estimates of aggregate output or value added to strip them of price influences, leaving only changes in real magnitudes. Prices for the individual components that make up the series change at different rates, sometimes in opposite directions, and the relative importance of the sectors alters over time, as some industries expand and others contract. A good price index will allow for these changes. Especially in economic history, though, the appropriate data do not always exist, and series end up being deflated by some more or less adequate proxy for an ideal index.

Bertram's constant-dollar estimates in Row 2 are deflated by a price index constructed long ago by the Dominion Bureau of Statistics (DBS) and, therefore, are reliable only in so far as this is a reasonably accurate indication of the price of the "basket" of manufactured goods represented by the aggregate data. Morris Altman has recently argued that this DBS deflator is, in fact, seriously flawed, and that data exist to construct better ones. His preferred estimates of constant-dollar gross value of output are given in Row 3 of Table 14.1, and of constant-dollar value added in rows 5 and 6. His numbers show a lower growth rate for manufacturing output in the period 1870–1900 than do Bertram's, and a higher one for the decade thereafter. This finding supports the older notion of an abrupt break around the turn of the century, and argues against the gradualist interpretation. The conclusion remains unchanged if value added rather than gross value is used as a measure of manufacturing output, and is made even more dramatic if the data are expressed in per-capita or per-employee terms.

Altman advances these numbers as a "challenge to the gradualist interpretation" of manufacturing development over the period 1870–1910. In his view, there was a radical break with the past around 1900, associated in some unspecified manner with the wheat boom. He phrases the conclusion this way: "Bertram's optimistic view of Canadian manufacturing growth in its first years should be rejected, while the more pessimistic view put forth by the old economic history should, once again, be given serious analytical consideration."[2]

Unfortunately, there is as yet no consensus on what actually did happen to aggregate manufacturing output between 1870 and 1913. Resolution of this question will have to await further vetting of these empirical issues. In the meantime, though, it is important not to exaggerate the differences of opinion. All accounts agree that there was a dramatic boom in manufacturing output in the period 1900–1910, and a smaller one in the 1880s. Growth was slower in the 1870s, but still well above that of the 1890s, a decade that consistently emerges as the most disappointing by far of the entire period.

The aggregate picture gives one essential perspective on manufacturing development in these years, but it obscures a number of others. Table 14.2 shows the composition of GDP in manufacturing for the main industrial subdivisions for the census years 1870 through 1910. Looking first at the year 1870, a clear hierarchy of activity is apparent. Wood products (mainly planks and boards) are at the top, accounting for over one-fifth of total manufacturing value added. Next in the hierarchy is a group of three activities — iron and steel products (agricultural implements, foundry and machine-shop products, boilers and engines, cutting and edging tools, pumps and windmills, sewing machines, wire), leather products (footwear and harness), and foods and beverages (flour and grist mills; butter, cheese, and meat products; breweries and distilleries) — each contributing around another 15 percent of value added. Transportation equipment (wooden ships and carriages) and clothing make up a third tier, with their shares of 7 percent being one-half the level

TABLE 14.2

Percentage Distribution of Gross Domestic Product, Manufacturing, Census Years, 1870–1910

	1870	*1880*	*1890*	*1900*	*1910*
Food and beverage	14.6	13.9	15.3	16.6	14.3
Tobacco and products	1.3	1.2	1.6	2.0	1.9
Rubber products	0.2	0.2	0.3	0.8	1.0
Leather products	15.2	12.4	8.6	7.9	5.9
Textiles (excl. clothing)	3.5	4.9	5.5	6.4	4.0
Clothing	7.0	9.1	11.2	10.8	11.2
Wood products	21.0	21.4	20.4	17.0	16.0
Paper products	0.9	1.0	1.4	2.4	2.7
Printing and publishing	3.0	3.5	3.4	4.5	3.5
Iron and steel products	16.6	14.9	15.8	14.5	16.8
Transport equipment	7.7	6.9	6.9	5.4	6.9
Nonferrous-metal products	1.0	1.8	1.9	3.1	5.4
Electric apparatus and supplies	—	—	0.2	0.8	1.6
Nonmetallic minerals	3.1	3.4	3.0	3.2	3.8
Petroleum and coal products	1.5	1.3	0.6	0.5	0.5
Chemical products	2.0	2.3	2.1	2.3	2.9
Miscellaneous industries	1.4	1.9	1.8	1.9	1.7

Source: M.C. Urquhart, "New Estimates of Gross National Product, Canada, 1870–1926: Some Implications for Canadian Economic Growth," in *Long-Term Factors in American Economic Growth*, NBER Studies in Income and Wealth, Vol. 51, edited by Stanley L. Engerman and Robert E. Gallman (Chicago: University of Chicago Press, 1986), Table 2.18.

of those activities in the second tier and one-third that of wood products. A fourth tier comprises textiles, nonmetallic minerals, and printing and publishing, with about 3 percent each. The remaining activities, grouped at the bottom, account for 2 percent or less.

Table 14.3 shows how the manufacturing sector changed after 1870. The industries are ranked in order of their contribution to GDP in manufacturing in 1870. The first column gives the compound annual rate of growth for each sector between 1870 and 1900, and the second reports the rank of the sector in 1900. Columns

TABLE 14.3

Changes in the Structure of Manufacturing, 1870–1910

Rank in 1870	*Compound Annual Rate of Growth 1870–1900*	*Rank in 1900*	*Compound Annual Rate of Growth 1900–1910*	*Rank in 1910*
Wood	2.5	1	7.8	2
Iron and steel	2.8	3	10.1	1
Leather	1.0	5	5.4	6
Food and beverage	3.7	2	6.9	3
Transport equipment	2.0	7	11.3	5
Clothing	4.7	4	8.9	4
Textiles	5.3	6	3.4	8
Nonmetallic minerals	3.3	9	10.4	9
Printing and publishing	4.7	8	5.8	10
Chemical products	3.6	12	11.0	11
Petroleum and coal	-0.1	17	8.2	17
Miscellaneous	4.2	14	7.8	14
Tobacco	4.7	13	7.9	13
Nonferrous metal	7.2	10	14.5	7
Paper	6.7	11	10.1	12
Rubber	8.7	15, 16	11.5	16
Electrical apparatus and supplies	—	15, 16	16.2	15
Total manufacturing	3.2		8.4	

Source: Calculated from M.C. Urquhart, "New Estimates of Gross National Product, Canada, 1870–1926: Some Implications for Canadian Economic Development," in *Long-Term Factors in American Economic Growth*, NBER Studies in Income and Wealth, Vol. 51, edited by Stanley L. Engerman and Robert E. Gallman (Chicago: University of Chicago Press, 1986), Table 2.17.

3 and 4 do the same for the period 1900–1910. A growth rate above the average of that for all manufacturing will raise that industry's share, while a rate below the average will reduce it, even if the

sector has grown in absolute terms. Whether the rank alters from period to period depends on the relative sizes of the changes.

The most striking development to 1900 is the fact that the three largest industries in 1870, and four of the top six, had growth rates below the average for manufacturing as a whole. Leather was particularly sluggish, growing by only 1.0 percent per annum in comparison to the 3.2 percent growth overall, and falling from the third-largest activity in 1870 to the fifth-largest in 1900. Transportation equipment, wood, and iron and steel products did only slightly better. Foods and beverages and clothing were the only industries of the top six in 1870 to grow faster than average to 1900, moving from fourth to second and from sixth to fourth in ranking, respectively, as a result. All fourth-tier activities grew at above-average rates, and all but one (petroleum and coal products, whose output actually declined in current-dollar terms) of the group of smallest activities did as well.

The result of these changes was that, by 1900, the hierarchy seen in 1870 had broken down somewhat. Wood products no longer stood alone in importance, but rather ranked about equally in terms of share of manufacturing GDP with foods and beverages and iron and steel products. There is a drop of some four percentage points from these three to the next-most-important activity, clothing, but thereafter the decline in percentage share is more or less continuous. Leather's relative decline (from 15.2 percent of manufacturing GDP in 1870 to 7.9 percent in 1900) is particularly noteworthy.

The industries that grew relatively in the 1870–1900 period are of two basic types. First, there are those linked to the emerging new resource products. Nonferrous metals, paper, chemicals, and nonmetallic minerals are examples. Electrical apparatus and supplies is perhaps another, to the extent it was associated with hydroelectricity developments. Some components of the food-and-beverage sector should also be included here — cheese and meat products, in particular, as a previous chapter has shown. Success in these sectors reflects the nation's comparative advantage in resource production and processing.

The other type of growth activity before 1900 occurred among those industries producing more finished goods for the domestic market in competition with imports. Rubber products, textiles, printing and publishing, tobacco, clothing, miscellaneous industries, and some food-and-beverage activities (bakeries, canneries, confectioneries, and brewers and distillers) fit into this category. Demand for these products rises as population and incomes do, and demand is deflected toward Canadian products and away from imports to the extent that domestic firms can compete with imports, depending on relative costs of production (which, in turn, resolves into relative factor prices and relative efficiencies of production) and tariff protection. Population and income were rising in Canada in these years, so it was natural that demand for the products would grow. How important tariffs were in reserving this burgeoning market for Canadian suppliers has never been adequately tested.

Sectors below the line, so to speak, were there for a diverse set of reasons. The lumber industry's difficulties with shifting markets and foreign tariffs were discussed in Chapter 13. The slow growth in transportation equipment reflects, in part, the decline of the wooden shipbuilding industry. The fall in the relative importance of leather products is less obviously explainable, given the apparent success of some of the other consumer-goods industries. Part of the drop may come from mechanization of agriculture, with the associated fall in demand for harnesses.

The pattern of industrial expansion between 1900 and 1910 is different in several respects from that of the earlier period. Most notably, iron and steel products and transportation equipment, two large sectors that were sluggish performers to 1900, fared relatively well in the next decade. Conversely, two other large sectors — textiles, and foods and beverages — slipped from above-average to below-average performance. There are some similarities between the two periods as well. Industries associated with the resource sectors (such as electrical apparatus and supplies, nonferrous metals, chemical products, nonmetallic minerals, and paper) remained relatively expanding sectors. Wood and leather continued their relative decline, although both continued to grow absolutely.

By 1910, as a consequence of these changes, the hierarchy of manufacturing activity had flattened out even more. Now, a group of four industries shared top spot in terms of share of manufacturing GDP — iron and steel products, wood products, foods and beverages, and clothing. The drop in percentage points of share to the next-most-important category (transportation equipment) is quite marked, but thereafter the rankings fall off more or less continuously.

The two sets of stimuli to manufacturing development identified for the period 1870–1900 are evident in this decade as well. Resource-related industries continued to perform relatively well. Canada had a natural comparative advantage in the production of these products, and often in their initial processing or in the provision of inputs to them. Occasionally government policies such as those discussed in Chapter 13 aided in attracting the linked activities. Consumer goods expanded as well, as population and income rose and as tariffs continued to provide protection from imports. The relative growth of these activities is smaller than it was in the earlier period, mainly because of the especially strong performances of some of the other activities.

The new element in the decade after 1900 was the performances of those activities linked most obviously to the opening of the western plains to wheat production. Iron and steel products is perhaps the most obvious example, and the development of this industry is most instructive of the process of industrialization in Canada after Confederation.[3] Output of ferrous metals in 1870 was almost entirely secondary products, using scrap or imported iron as inputs. There had been a number of attempts to produce primary iron in Canada earlier, with little success. Even the St. Maurice forge, in operation since 1730, ceased production in 1883. Nowhere did there seem to be the right combination of resources (iron ore and coal, mainly), skilled labour, and markets.

The introduction of tariffs on iron and steel in 1879 helped matters somewhat. Nova Scotia had ample deposits of coal and reasonably accessible supplies of iron ore, so it was in that province, not unexpectedly, that a primary iron-and-steel industry was first established. Beginning in the 1870s as an operation to manufacture iron products from scrap material, Nova Scotia Steel cast Canada's first steel ingots at Trenton in 1883. Shortages of inputs and the encouragement given by the "iron tariff" of 1887 led to the establishment of a blast furnace at Ferrona and another at Londonderry. The capital for these early ventures came from local merchant families, although control of the Londonderry ironworks soon passed to Montreal. Expansion continued, as Nova Scotia Steel acquired ore deposits on Bell Island, Newfoundland, and collieries on Cape Breton, and erected a new steel plant in Sydney Mines. It was, by then, a fully integrated operation, owning blast and open-hearth furnaces, rolling mills, forges, foundries, and machine shops.

A second venture in Nova Scotia was larger yet. Boston and

Montreal investors formed the Dominion Coal Company in 1893 to refinance several Cape Breton collieries. In 1899, the Dominion Iron and Steel Company erected a steel works at Sydney, and soon the company was the largest in Canada. Its most important product, by far, was steel rails, with its own rail plant taking most of the output.

Iron and steel production in central Canada followed shortly, helped by the fact that technological changes had gradually reduced the amount of raw-material inputs needed per unit of output, freeing the sector from the need to remain at resource sites and allowing it to draw closer to markets. Quebec had numerous secondary operations, but no significant primary production. A group of Hamilton capitalists founded the Hamilton Blast Furnace Company in 1895, the first modern iron-making plant in Ontario. Ore was shipped in from Minnesota and coal from Pennsylvania via Lake Erie and the Welland Canal. In 1899, the company merged with Ontario Rolling Mills to form the Hamilton Steel and Iron Company. The first steel output was in 1900. Another blast furnace was added in 1907. In 1910, the Steel Company of Canada, eventually to be the nation's premier steel-maker, was formed when the primary iron-and-steel plant at Hamilton was merged with most of the rolling and finishing companies in Ontario and Quebec.

The final operation came in 1901, at Sault Ste Marie, under the initiative of the American promoter Francis Hector Clergue. Algoma Steel was formed at the turn of the century as one of a number of ambitious projects by Clergue in the Sault Ste Marie region. The location was chosen to be near the Helen Mines ore deposits of Northern Ontario and with a view toward being advantageously situated to supply western Canada's demand for steel rails. The project was encouraged by a contract from the Laurier government for steel rails, the first given to a Canadian firm. Production began in 1902, and the first rails were rolled, but work on the iron furnaces lagged behind. The company collapsed in 1903, mainly because of mismanagement, but was resuscitated that same year as the Lake Superior Corporation. Coal was imported from West Virginia and, for a time, ore from Minnesota. Problems were gradually overcome, and the company prospered, as the demand for steel rails in the west grew.

The agricultural-implement industry is another interesting case-study of Canadian industrialization.[4] Prior to Confederation, and

National Archives of Canada/PA-17696

Wire mill of the Dominion Iron and Steel Company, Sydney, N.S. *The steel works at Sydney were built by the Dominion Iron and Steel Company in 1899; soon, the company was the largest in Canada. Its most important product, by far, was steel rails, with its own rail plant taking the bulk of the output.*

for a considerable time thereafter, the sector was characterized by numerous small-scale operations, producing a wide variety of tools and implements for local farmers. The more enterprising of the group, notably the Massey Company and the Harris Company, made regular trips to the United States, often returning with the rights to manufacture the new machines in Canada. There was little or no independent innovation.

The industry began to change in the 1880s. The tariff on agricultural implements was raised from 17 to 25 percent in 1879, and to 35 percent in 1883, in an apparent attempt to promote a Canadian industry. Output did increase significantly in the ensuing decades, and production became more concentrated. There were 221 firms in 1891, producing \$7.5 million. In 1901, 114 firms produced \$9.6 million, and 88 firms produced \$20.7 million in 1910. Employment nearly doubled over the period, and the value of capital increased more than fivefold. The main concentration took place in Ontario. That province hosted only 55 of the total of 88 Canadian plants in 1906, but together they produced 92 percent of the value of output.

The domestic market soon became constraining. Both Massey and Harris began to sell farm equipment overseas in the late 1880s, giving Canada one of its few secondary-manufactured-goods exports of the time. The two first merged in 1891 to form the Massey-Harris Company and, in the same year, absorbed the newly merged Patterson-Wisner complex. In 1910, Massey-Harris opened a plant in the United States, giving Canada one of its early multinational companies. The American giant International Harvester established a subsidiary in Canada in 1902. International Harvester, together with Massey-Harris and the smaller Canadian company Cockshutt, dominated the Canadian scene for decades.

The iron and steel industry developed behind tariff protection, largely on Canadian initiative. Agricultural-implement production developed behind tariffs, as a mix of Canadian and American firms. A third example, that of the automobile industry, completes the spectrum, for it developed behind tariffs, almost completely as a foreign-dominated operation. It was not that Canadians did not try. One source lists 500 Canadian-owned automobile manufacturers in Ontario between 1897 and 1933, 32 of them coming prior to World War I.[5] They could not survive independent of American connections, mainly because the Canadian market was too small to allow for the scale of operation required to compete in this uncertain, capital-intensive, and high-technology industry.

American motor companies were interested in establishing branch operations in Canada to skirt the 35 percent tariff and to get access to the British Empire markets. Ford entered into an agreement with the Ontario carriage-maker Gordon McGregor in 1904, establishing Ford of Canada. Another carriage-maker, Sam McLaughlin of Oshawa, entered into an arrangement with Buick in 1907 to use its engine in a McLaughlin-designed and -produced chassis. The company survived for a time, producing high-quality but costly vehicles, before selling out to General Motors in 1918.

Spatial Distribution

Manufacturing did not develop evenly across the nation. In 1870, Ontario hosted 52 percent of manufacturing activity, measured by value of output; Quebec did another 35 percent; and the remainder was in the Maritimes. By 1900, when the western provinces appear in the data, Ontario's share was still above 50 percent, while Quebec's had fallen to 32 percent, and the Maritimes' to 10 percent. Ontario's relative position held firm through the boom after 1900, while those for Quebec and the Maritimes slipped further. The west's share went from essentially nothing in 1870 to about 13 percent in 1910.[6]

The trends are more revealing yet if primary (essentially resource-processing) and secondary activities are distinguished. Ontario's constant overall share was the result of a significant decline in its relative position as a primary producer, offset by a notable increase in its share of secondary activities. Quebec lost, in a relative sense, on both counts, and about evenly so. The Maritimes slipped in both categories as well, although, in their case, the decline was proportionately greater in secondary products. The relative decline in primary products in all three established regions reflects the fact that most manufacturing activity in the western provinces centred on processing resources.

These aggregate data illustrate the development over this period of an industrial heartland in Canada, centred in Ontario and, to a lesser extent, in Quebec. It was not that manufacturing output in total grew more rapidly in central Canada than elsewhere. Indeed, over the period 1870–1910, Ontario actually lost a little of its lead as the western economies developed, and Quebec lost a lot. It was, instead, the specialization that arose across regions in the type of manufacturing that gave rise to an industrial heartland. The outlying regions of the country concentrated on primary manufacturing activities, usually simple processing of resources. These activities were oriented to resource sites because there was significant weight loss in the initial stages of production or because electricity was a key input. One exception was clothing, a labour-intensive industry that was drawn to the Maritimes by the relatively low wages there. Atlantic Canada, the prairies, and British Columbia hosted, as well, small-scale secondary activities, serving the local market and protected naturally by distance.

Ontario and Quebec, by contrast, attracted a disproportionate share of secondary activities — in some cases (such as machinery and autos), representing virtually the entire national production. In essence, the central provinces were the natural location within Canada to host these industries. Population was larger and more geographically concentrated, and incomes were generally higher. The region was just across the Great Lakes from one of the most advanced and rapidly industrializing regions of the world. As well, in these matters, growth begets growth. The more industrial activity there is in an area, at least up to a point well beyond Ontario and Quebec in these years, the more likely other sectors are to locate there to take advantage of interindustry linkages, pools of skilled labour, and specialized business services.

One obvious, but often overlooked, point should be made here: it is misleading to refer to Ontario and Quebec as the emerging industrial heartland. In fact, most of the two provinces was, and indeed remains, more like the periphery of the country in terms of economic structure, depending on lumber, pulp mills, mines, and hydro-electric projects for its livelihood. The real heartland was a group of industrial cities stretching from Windsor in Southern Ontario, along the Great Lakes, to Montreal in Quebec. There were even important differences between the industrial areas of Ontario and Quebec. The former province specialized much more obviously in producer goods, while Quebec drew more consumer goods such as clothing and textiles.

Tariffs and Industrialization

The way in which manufacturing developed after 1870 had many implications for future generations of Canadians and for future political debates. Three issues, in particular, stand out, all relating to the fact that industrialization occurred behind the protection of the national-policy tariffs. The first concerns the efficiency of at least some of the manufacturing ventures that emerged in this period. Tariffs, it is alleged, created not just a secondary manufacturing sector in Canada but a high-cost, inefficient one. The broad protection offered by the tariffs meant that industry in Canada developed as a "miniature replica" of that in the United States. There were too many firms, producing too many product lines, given the small size of the market. All could operate only because of protection, which guaranteed that tariffs would be a long-time feature of the Canadian industrial scene. Canadians would pay the price for this inefficiency in the form of real incomes that were lower than they otherwise could be, and by being saddled with a manufacturing sector that remained sluggish and conservative compared to those in other Western industrial nations.

Foreign ownership is the second issue. It is often alleged that tariffs are responsible for the very high levels of foreign control of Canadian industry, in that they created trade barriers sufficiently high that foreign firms, primarily American ones, were induced to establish branch plants in lieu of exporting. As Michael Bliss has noted, however, to the extent the claim is true, it does not rank as one of the bitter ironies of the national policy. Businessmen and politicians of the day anticipated this development; indeed, they sought it. American branch plants, located behind the tariff to provide for the Canadian market, would provide industry and employment in a nation hungry for industrial development.[7]

The final legacy is the tremendous regional strife that has accompanied tariffs and industrialization from the very beginning. The tendency for much of the protected industry to locate in Southern Ontario and Quebec has already been noted. Sometimes this concentration is itself ascribed to tariffs, but this claim is incorrect. Tariffs may have induced industry to locate in Canada rather than export over the tariff, but, once this decision was taken, the choice of where to situate in Canada was strictly a business one. The heartland, with its relative natural advantages, inevitably won out.

More legitimately, the tariff was seen by many as a means of redistributing income from the periphery to the centre. The farmers of the prairies, the loggers of British Columbia, and the fishers of the Maritimes received little or no protection. Indeed, they needed none, as their industries were internationally competitive. Yet, they paid tariff-inflated prices for the tools and implements of their trades, and for the clothing, furniture, and comforts they provided for their families. The benefits went to central Canadians, in the form of jobs and higher profits in the protected industries. However correct these claims are, and analysis of them is very complex, they have remained a prominent feature of political debate to today.

Service Industries

At the time of Confederation, the service sector contained both the largest and most sophisticated of Canadian businesses and the smallest and most rudimentary (railways and banks come to mind in the first category, country stores and taverns in the latter). In some cases, the market was the village; in others, it was the nation, and occasionally the world. Much of the sector, such as education and government services, was not even profit-oriented. An additional problem in describing this sector, one that continues to today, is the difficulty of measuring output. For these reasons, it is impossible to give anything like a comprehensive overview of service-sector development in a few pages. We therefore first focus on what the aggregate patterns of development were, and then look in a little more detail at a few of the more important activities.

The general pattern of development in the service sector is shown in Table 14.4. In 1870, about 30 percent of GDP originated in these activities. The largest group, at one-quarter of the total, was community, business, and personal services. Four others (residential rents, transportation, real estate, and wholesale and retail trade) made up most of the remainder. What is striking to the contemporary reader is the unimportance then of activities so familiar today Banking and finance contributed only 2 percent to GDP, and utilities and communication were not even represented. Most interesting, perhaps, is that governments, together, constituted less than 3 percent of GDP, and municipalities were more prominent than provinces.

Over time, the dominant impression is the steady increase in the relative importance of service activities. From 30 percent of GDP in 1870, the share for these industries rose to 37 percent by 1890, and to 43 percent by 1910. The increase is partly statistical. As the economy grew in size and sophistication, firms purchased more and more of their services externally. Thus, as M.C. Urquhart notes, growth here comes at the expense (in a statistical or accounting sense only) of growth in recorded primary and manufacturing output. Consumers, too, relied on the market more for services they had previously provided for themselves, or had acquired through barter.

Part of the shift to services reflects new activity, though. Communications and utilities appear, from 1890 on, as the new technologies developed. The demand for transportation services grew as the economy expanded, particularly as the western wheat economy opened up, and the increase in that sector's share reflects that trend. Residential rents became more important as rising population and income increased the demand for housing. The increase in the share of wholesale and retail trade is particularly striking, going from 6 percent of GDP in 1870 to well over 10 percent by 1910. In part, this represents an absolute growth in trade; in part, it reflects increasing specialization in the sector. There was more

TABLE 14.4

Percentage Distribution of Gross Domestic Product at Factor Cost, Average of Three Years, Centred on Census Years

	1870	*1880*	*1890*	*1900*	*1910*
Agriculture	37.1	36.2	27.8	24.8	21.6
Forestry, hunting, trapping, and fishing	2.7	3.0	3.1	3.0	2.1
Mining	1.3	1.1	1.9	5.0	2.9
Manufacturing	22.4	21.9	25.3	22.2	22.5
Manufactured gas	0.1	0.2	0.3	0.1	0.1
Construction	5.7	4.2	4.8	3.9	7.8
Transportation	5.5	5.2	5.9	6.9	7.8
Electric light and power	—	—	0.1	0.2	0.6
Communications	—	—	0.1	0.2	0.5
Banking and finance	2.1	2.2	2.9	4.3	4.1
Residential rents	5.9	5.8	5.7	6.8	6.7
Federal government services	1.3	1.7	1.8	1.8	1.6
Provincial government services	0.5	0.6	0.6	0.6	0.8
Municipal government services	0.9	1.2	1.3	1.3	1.4
Education	1.0	1.4	1.2	1.2	1.1
Wholesale and retail trade	5.9	7.0	7.5	7.5	10.4
Community, business, and personal services	7.4	8.1	9.6	9.6	7.6
Public-resource royalties	0.3	0.3	0.5	0.5	0.4

Source: Calculated from M.C. Urquhart, "New Estimates of Gross National Product, Canada, 1870–1926: Some Implications for Canadian Economic Development," in *Long-Term Factors in American Economic Growth*, NBER Studies in Income and Wealth, Vol. 51, edited by Stanley L. Engerman and Robert E. Gallman (Chicago: University of Chicago Press, 1986), Table 2.13.

handling of goods between the manufacturer and the eventual consumer. Governments' share of GDP rose slightly, and the ranking of federal-municipal-provincial remained intact.

Banking and finance nearly doubled in relative importance between 1870 and 1910 — from 2 percent of GDP to 4 percent. Even the latter figure understates the central role of this sector, however, for, in a very real sense, the development of Canada's capital market from Confederation to World War I is the best available barometer of the maturation of the economy more generally. The leading text on the subject defines a capital market as "being comprised of institutions and individuals engaged in transferring funds from those in surplus to those in deficit and in facilitating changes in ownership of financial claims that process inevitably creates."[8] The first function is that of financial intermediation, the second that of financial brokerage.

The financial sector in any economy is both a contributor to and a reflection of economic growth and development. It is a contributor in that it brings about a more effective marshalling of savings for use by those wishing to invest in capital equipment or for consumers purchasing "big-ticket items" such as houses and automobiles. It reflects growth and development because, as an economy matures, its need for specialized financial services grows. Pioneer economies need only some broadly acceptable medium of exchange to facilitate the limited trade of goods and services that takes place. Trading economies need banks to accept deposits, make loans, discount notes, and trade in foreign currencies. Modern economies need all these, plus specialized activities and facilities such as real-estate transactions, life insurance, fire and casualty insurance, trust funds, savings banks, and mutual funds.

E.P. Neufeld divides the Canadian financial sector into four broad groups — chartered banks, private banks, private nonbanks, and public-sector institutions. We discussed chartered banks in Chapter 6. Private banks — that is, individuals or firms operating as banks — did not have the right of note issue. Private nonbanks constitute a range of institutions offering specialized financial services, such as savings banks, life-insurance companies, fire- and casualty-insurance companies, building and mortgage companies, and trust companies. Public institutions historically were Dominion-note-issue and post office and government savings banks.

The main development in the financial sector prior to Confederation was that of chartered banks. The Bank of Montreal operated continuously from 1817, although it did not receive its charter until 1821. The Bank of New Brunswick was actually the first bank chartered in British North America, in 1820. Other banks followed, until, by 1867, there were 33 chartered banks with some 133 branches. Together they accounted for 78 percent of all of the assets of the financial sector at this time. Some operated under royal charter, others under colonial charter, and a few under the Free Banking Act passed by the Province of Canada in 1850. The intent of this legislation, modelled after similar provisions in the United States, was to encourage the development of unit banking by tying the issue of bank notes to government securities. It was largely unsuccessful, however, and the provision was withdrawn in 1880.

Private nonbank institutions developed more slowly. There were six savings banks in 1867, with about 3 percent of total financial-sector assets. There were 28 building societies, existing to provide financing for real-estate development. They accounted for 9 percent of recorded assets. There was one Canadian life-insurance company, the Canada Life Assurance Company, which began operations in Hamilton in 1847, and, in 1867, held about 1 percent of the assets. About 30 fire-insurance companies — some British, some American, and some Canadian — held another 3 percent. Government note issue accounted for 4 percent, and the Federal Government Post Office Savings and Savings Bank (taken over from the Maritime provinces in 1867) for about 3 percent.

Under the BNA Act of 1867, the Dominion government assumed responsibility for currency and coinage, and for banking. There was some pressure to structure the financial system along the free-bank lines of the United States and of the 1850 act noted above, but the proposal was opposed by the banks (other than the Bank of Montreal) and the idea died. The Dominion Notes Act of 1870 restricted the chartered banks to issuing notes of a minimum denomination of $5, giving the government monopoly control over $1 and $2 bills. The Uniform Currency Act of 1871 extended decimal currency throughout the Dominion and defined the British sovereign as the standard coin. The first formal legislation governing banking came with the Bank Act of 1871, which largely restated existing provisions with respect to the chartering of banks, the minimum subscribed capital, the conditions for note issue, and other regulations.

The Canadian financial system developed dramatically between Confederation and World War I. Total assets in current-dollar terms rose from $171 million in 1870 to $290 million in 1880, to $499 million in 1890, to $832 million in 1900, and to $2.4 billion in 1913. The average annual growth rate between 1870 and 1910, in current-dollar terms, was 6.5 percent, and, in constant-dollar terms, 6.1 percent (which, as earlier chapters indicated, was substantially faster than those for the output of goods and services). Financial assets stood at 31 percent of GNP in 1870, 50 percent in 1880, 62 percent in 1890, 79 percent in 1900, and 80 percent in 1910.

Table 14.5 shows the composition of the financial sector in this period. Chartered banks dominated the sector in 1870, with 73 percent of total assets. Private nonbanks, together, held another 19 percent, with building societies and mortgage-loan companies being the most prominent of these. The situation changed markedly after 1870. Chartered banks grew more slowly than the sector as a whole to the mid-1890s, when they controlled less than half of the total assets. They recovered their share slightly thereafter, rising to nearly 60 percent by the outbreak of World War I. They retained this level to 1920, but then declined again.

Canada's banking sector took on its modern form in this period. The total number of banks rose to a peak of 51 in 1874 before falling to 44 in 1880, 41 in 1890, 35 in 1900, and 28 in 1910. The number of branches multiplied, rising from 123 in 1868 to nearly 2400 by 1910. Some familiar names emerged in this period as well. The Bank of Montreal has already been mentioned. The Bank of Nova Scotia was chartered in Halifax in 1832, moved to Toronto in 1900, and absorbed the Bank of New Brunswick in 1910. The Bank of Commerce began operations in Toronto in 1867. In 1900, it took over the Bank of British Columbia, in operation in that province since 1862. The Merchants' Bank of Halifax was founded in 1869, becoming the Royal Bank of Canada in 1901 and moving to Montreal five years later. The Bank of Toronto opened in 1853; the Dominion Bank, in the late 1860s.

The real story of the period, though, was the growth of the private nonbank activities. Together, they doubled their share of financial assets between 1870 and 1913. Nearly all the growth came from building societies and mortgage-loan companies and from life-insurance companies. Banks were restricted in the real estate they could take as collateral for loans, which left a niche in the market for firms willing to take on these longer-term commitments. Life-insurance companies grew dramatically, as sales representatives

TABLE 14.5

Share of Total Financial Assets by Sector, 1870–1913

(percentage of total)

	1870	*1880*	*1890*	*1900*	*1913*
Chartered banks	72.6	55.4	49.5	52.6	57.4
Private nonbanks	18.9	34.2	39.5	37.2	34.4
Quebec Savings Banks	3.7	3.1	2.6	2.5	1.9
Life insurance companies	2.4	3.4	8.6	13.1	14.1
Fraternal benefit societies	—	—	0.3	1.0	1.9
Fire and casualty insurance companies	3.2	3.1	3.5	3.3	3.3
Building societies and mortgage-loan companies	9.6	24.6	24.5	16.2	10.6
Trust companies	—	—	—	1.2	2.6
Public	8.4	10.3	11.0	10.2	8.3
Dominion notes	5.2	4.9	3.1	3.4	5.7
Post office and government savings	3.2	5.4	7.9	6.7	2.4
Federal annuity, insurance and pension account	—	—	—	—	0.2

Source: Calculated from E.P. Neufeld, *The Financial System of Canada: Its Growth and Development* (Toronto: Macmillan, 1972), Appendix Table B, 612–32.

from Canadian companies spread across the country and eventually around the world. New companies sprang up, many to become household names — Ontario Mutual (1871), Sun Life (1871), London Life (1874), and Manufacturers Life (1887), among others. Canadian companies wrote 50 percent of the business in 1870, and 65 percent in 1900.

Financial brokers began to appear, as the supply of government debt, chartered-bank stock, railway bonds, and stocks and other financial instruments grew. A board of brokers was formed in Montreal in 1863. In 1872, it began calling itself the Montreal Stock

London Life Archives

London Life Headquarters, 1905. *Life-insurance companies and other private nonbank activities grew dramatically between 1870 and 1913, doubling their share of financial assets. Canadian life-insurance companies wrote 50 percent of the business in 1879, and 65 percent in 1900.*

Exchange; in 1874, it received a charter under Quebec law. The Toronto Stock Exchange went through a number of guises before becoming officially incorporated in 1878. This activity was not limited to central Canada, though. The Winnipeg Stock Exchange was established in 1903, the Vancouver Stock Exchange in 1907, and the Calgary Stock Exchange in 1914.

Competition Policy and Labour Unions

The trend to business concentration noted in both manufacturing and services not unnaturally attracted the attention of some in the economy — small businesses, farmers, and consumer groups, in particular. There were allegations of price-fixing, predatory pricing, price discrimination, and misleading advertising. A spate of publicity in the 1880s led to the establishment of a select House of Commons committee on combines, and Canada's first Anti-combines Act in 1889. There was little support for interference into what were generally seen as necessary and justifiable actions by businesses to ensure a fair return. Michael Bliss concludes that "the 1889 law was pious anti-monopoly posturing that had no effect on anything."[9]

Labour Unions

As was the case for many other institutions, this period was crucial to the development of labour unions in Canada. These years brought the first powerful union movements and associations in Canadian history. They also saw the emergence of what was to be the dominant form of twentieth-century unionism in Canada — the American-affiliated craft union.

Early examples of union activity can be traced to the first decades of the nineteenth century. These were isolated and usually transient examples, however, and significant unionization was, to a large degree, a product of industrialism. Specifically, the period from 1850 through the 1870s saw the rise of many individual unions and a series of "associations," in which various unions in a city or region developed an umbrella organization to co-ordinate affairs and provide mutual support, among other activities. The Toronto Trades Assembly, which was established in 1871, included some fourteen area unions and typified the efforts to link union activities. In 1873, a national organization, the Canadian Labour Union, was formed. Though national in design, it cannot be said to have represented anything like all of the unions that existed at that time.

In these early years there was no fixed pattern of union organization. Some unions, such as the British Amalgamated Society of Carpenters and Joiners, were affiliated with British unions. Others, such as the Railway Conductors, were associated with American unions. Still others, such as the Nova Scotia coal miners' Provincial Workmen's Association, were purely local responses to the needs of workers and had no international affiliations. Most, but not all, were craft unions (tied to a particular skill, such as carpentry). The one thing they did have in common was the difficult task of asserting the power of workers in an era that glorified the myth of individualism and looked with suspicion on associations of workers as antithetical to the spirit of individual initiative.

Perhaps the most interesting, and certainly the most powerful, example of union organization in the years before 1900 is the Knights of Labor. This American-based union (formed 1869) spread to Canada in the mid-1870s and was, by the later 1880s, the most powerful union organization in Canada.

The Knights were an unusual organization, combining trade union activity with much of the ritual and social life of fraternal lodges, such as the Masons. It was also a completely open union, interested in representing all workers, regardless of skill or gender. Its open policy on membership and its tremendous success also meant that it was little loved by traditional craft union organizations. These craft unions, increasingly dominated by American internationals, grew relatively stronger by the end of the century, in part because of the strong support they received from their American headquarters and from the American Federation of Labor.

By the early twentieth century, the internationals were sufficiently strong to assert their control over the Canadian national association, the Trades and Labor Congress (TLC). In Berlin (now Kitchener), Ontario, in 1902, the internationals supported a series of resolutions at the annual TLC convention that banned dual unionism and gave AFL-affiliated unions primacy in any dual-union controversy. The net effect was to destroy the already declining Knights of Labor and to make many Canadian unions into miniature replicas of their American counterparts. The continental integration that was taking place in business was thus paralleled, even exceeded, by that emerging in unionism.

The rise of unions caused much controversy. Blood was shed in bitter strikes, panicky politicians vied to condemn this threat to the established order, and union leaders reciprocated with militant rhetoric drawn from the more radical politics of European socialism that often belied their own weakness and moderate goals. Businessmen, the most vociferous of all, condemned the restraint of trade that unionism represented, while conveniently forgetting their own associations and price-fixing arrangements. In fact, however, the rhetoric did not reflect reality. The union movement in the early twentieth century was hardly a threat to the social order, nor does it appear to have altered in any significant way the economic structure of Canadian industry. Indeed, unionism in the decade and a half before the war was declining in numbers and power, and whatever assistance it may have been able to give individual workers, it cannot be said, in these years, to have altered the course of Canadian economic development, however much Canadian businessmen might have lamented.

Conclusion

Several summary impressions emerge from this overview of manufacturing growth between Confederation and World War I. First, much activity depended directly on key resource industries. Two categories, wood and food-and-beverage products, together accounted for over one-third of total output in 1870, a figure that was only slightly lower 40 years later. Adding in other activities — such as pulp and paper, nonferrous-metal products, nonmetallic minerals, and petroleum and coal products — that were just coming onto the scene in 1910 brings the total of this category of manufacturing even higher. Their prominence and longevity are not difficult to explain. Favourable resource endowments, access to the appropriate technology, and gradually expanding domestic and international markets tell the story. The link to resources meant they often located in peripheral areas of the country.

The second point to make is that a considerable amount of other manufacturing growth was linked, at least indirectly, to resource sectors. That in agricultural implements and farm supplies, such as wire and tools, clearly was, as was production of rails and railway rolling stock for the prairie wheat economy. So, too, was the production of machinery for the pulp-and-paper mills, the hydro plants and transmission lines, and the mines and quarries that were opening up. Success in this second type of manufacturing activity is more complex to explain. Certainly proximity to and familiarity with the resource sectors played some role in allowing Canadian suppliers to compete with imports. Tariffs were undoubtedly important in other instances (the examples of iron and steel, agricultural implements, and machinery come to mind). Despite the tie to resources, however, location was mainly in the heartland region.

The third general point to note is that there was a significant amount of industrial development that was essentially independent of resources, except in so far as they provided residents and immigrants with income to spend. Food-and-beverage activities, such as breweries and distilleries, fall into this category, as do those in tobacco, leather, clothing and textiles, printing and publishing, electrical appliances, furniture, musical instruments, clocks, bicycles, carriages, automobiles, and so forth. The determinants of growth in this category of manufactured products are least understood. Demand for such products is generally a function of population and income levels, so the fact that Canadians would be purchasing more and more of them between 1870 and 1913 is hardly surprising. The responses of Canadian suppliers to the incentives, including such things as location decisions and the role of the tariff, are yet to be studied carefully.

The final point about manufacturing growth is that industrialization behind tariffs left the country with a range of policy issues that remain contentious nearly a century later. Debate over how to restructure Canadian industry, over Canadianization, and over the regional effects of commercial policy has recurred throughout the twentieth century.

Canadian service industries showed impressive growth and development in the period from 1867 to 1913. The economy was well served by its wholesale and retail trade networks, business and personal services, transportation and communication facilities, and sophisticated capital market. Canadian firms dominated these sectors, in contrast to the situation in some of the resource and manufacturing activities. Some — notably those in banking, life insurance, and railway-engineering consulting — had moved beyond Canada to the world market. The big companies operating in national and international markets were concentrated in Toronto and Montreal, just as similar facilities in other countries were drawn to the larger centres. But shops, branch banks, lawyers and accountants, and post offices were found in every town and hamlet.

The success of the service industries does not lack its share of interesting unresolved issues. Some have seen in this very success the reasons for the relative truncation of domestically owned goods industries, although this argument is taken less seriously now than it was at one time. Why, and with what effects, did Canadian banking evolve differently from its American counterpart, given that so much else in the economy followed trends set south of the border? Why was foreign ownership not a factor in this sector, as it was in most goods industries? Were there regional or sectoral biases in the provision of credit, as is often alleged? What were the factors behind the development of the not-for-profit activities? Clearly this is a sector of the economy that needs considerably more attention than it has received to date.

Notes

1. Gordon W. Bertram, "Historical Statistics on Growth and Structure of Manufacturing in Canada, 1870–1957," in *Conference on Statistics, 1962 and 1963*, edited by J. Henripin and A. Asimakopulos (Toronto: University of Toronto Press, 1964), 93.
2. Morris Altman, "A Revision of Canadian Economic Growth: 1870–1910 (A Challenge to the Gradualist Interpretation)," *Canadian Journal of Economics* 20, no. 1 (February 1987): 88.
3. These paragraphs are drawn from W.J.A. Donald, *The Canadian Iron and Steel Industry* (Boston: Houghton-Mifflin, 1915); William Kilbourn, *The Elements Combined: A History of the Steel Company of Canada* (Toronto; Clark, Irwin, 1960); Kris E. Inwood, *The Canadian Charcoal Iron Industry, 1870–1914* (New York and London: Garland, 1986); and Michael Bliss, *Northern Enterprise: Five Centuries of Canadian Business* (Toronto: McClelland and Stewart, 1987).
4. See W.G. Phillips, *The Agricultural Implement Industry in Canada* (Toronto: University of Toronto Press, 1956); and Bliss, *Northern Enterprise.*
5. Ian M. Drummond, *Progress Without Planning: The Economic History of Ontario from Confederation to the Second World War* (Toronto: University of Toronto Press, 1987), Table 12.2 (p. 419).
6. Bertram, "Historical Statistics."
7. Bliss, *Northern Enterprise.*
8. E.P. Neufeld, *The Financial System of Canada: Its Growth and Development* (Toronto: Macmillan, 1972), 2–3. Much of what follows is from this source. See also Bliss, *Northern Enterprise*; and R. Craig McIvor, *Canadian Monetary, Banking and Fiscal Development* (Toronto: Macmillan, 1961).
9. Bliss, *Northern Enterprise*, 362.

Further Reading

Bertram, Gordon. "Economic Growth in Canadian Industry, 1870–1914: The Staple Model and the Take-off Hypothesis." *Canadian Journal of Economics and Political Science* 29, no. 2 (May 1963): 159–84.

Bliss, Michael. *Northern Enterprise: Five Centuries of Canadian Business.* Toronto: McClelland and Stewart, 1987.

Brown, R.C., and G.R. Cook. *Canada, 1896–1921: A Nation Transformed.* Toronto: McClelland and Stewart, 1974.

Neufeld, E.P. *The Financial System of Canada: Its Growth and Development.* Toronto: Macmillan, 1972.

CHAPTER

15

Regional Growth and Welfare

The regional dimension always figures in discussions of Canadian economic growth and welfare. We want to know not just how the national economy progressed but also how each of its constituent regions did. In part, the motivation comes from history. Canadian economic history before 1867 consists of the separate stories of several distinct territories that had relatively little to do with each other, until political union brought them together. It is natural, then, to want to follow their subsequent progress as well, if only to see how it was affected by the union. In part, as well, the interest stems from the fact that Canada was established as a federation from the outset. Provincial loyalties and interests were recognized and ratified by this decision, meaning that regionalism would forever be a part of the Canadian political and economic scene. Finally, the interest reflects the modern realities of notable regional differences in growth rates, unemployment, standard of living, and other areas in Canada. History, it is hoped, might give some clues as to the origins of these differences. The interesting point is that, as this chapter will show, there is a surprisingly long history of regional differentiation.

Population is often used as a summary measure of economic performance, on the grounds that, as we have seen throughout this volume, migration flows are broadly responsive to relative economic incentives. As Table 15.1 shows, the most obvious shift in Canada in the 40 years following Confederation is the rise in the importance of the western provinces. There were about 110 000 people living west of the Ontario-Manitoba border in 1871 — only slightly more, in other words, than the population of Prince Edward Island at the time. By 1895, this figure had jumped to 350 000, pushing the region past New Brunswick but not yet Nova Scotia. By 1911, population was over 1.7 million, nearly double that of the three Maritime provinces together and only just short of that of Quebec. Put differently, at Confederation, the western region accounted for just 3 percent of Canadian population, one-third of which was in British Columbia. By 1911, the share had risen to nearly a quarter (24 percent), one-fifth of which was in British Columbia.

The west's relative gain is obviously reflected in a relative loss somewhere. Interestingly, the largest drop in share of population between 1871 and 1911 was Ontario's decline of nearly 9 percentage points, from 44 to 35 percent of the total. Quebec's share fell by 4.5 percentage points, to below 28 percent, and that of the three Maritime provinces by 7.3 percentage points, or from 20 percent of the Canadian total in 1871 to 13 percent of it by 1911. Prince Edward Island actually lost population, it should be noted; in all other provinces, the natural increase was larger than the net migration.

The westward shift is evident in the regional distribution of output as well. Estimates of gross value added (GVA) by province for 1890 and 1910 are reproduced in Table 15.2. The three Prairie provinces accounted for only 5 percent of national output in 1890 but more than 17 percent in 1911. British Columbia's share rose from 3.3 to over 8 percent, meaning that the western provinces, together, produced over 25 percent of national GVA in 1911, compared to only 8 percent in 1890. Again the relative loss is spread over all other provinces, and again the largest relative drop is in Ontario — from nearly 50 percent of national output in 1890 to 41 percent in 1911. Quebec fell from 26 to 23 percent, and the Maritimes from 16 to 10 percent.

The relative sizes of provincial economies, as measured by population or gross value added, provide one perspective on the regional makeup of the nation. Another, in many respects a more interesting one, is relative economic well-being. How well off was the average Maritimer in 1890 compared to his or her central Canadian counterpart? What effect did two decades of technological changes, new staples, the opening of the west, and industrialization have on this statistic? Column 1 of Table 15.3 shows, for each province, the value

TABLE 15.1

Share of Population by Province, Census Years 1871–1911

(percentage of total)

	1871	*1881*	*1891*	*1901*	*1911*
Maritimes	20.7	20.1	18.2	16.7	13.0
P.E.I.	2.5	2.5	2.3	1.9	1.3
Nova Scotia	10.5	10.2	9.3	8.6	6.8
New Brunswick	7.7	7.4	6.6	6.2	4.9
Quebec	32.3	31.4	30.8	30.7	27.8
Ontario	43.9	44.6	43.7	40.6	35.1
Prairie provinces	0.7	1.4	3.2	7.9	18.4
Manitoba	0.7	1.4	3.2	4.8	6.4
Saskatchewan	—	—	—*	1.7	6.8
Alberta	—	—	—*	1.4	5.2
B.C.	1.0	1.1	2.0	3.3	5.4
Yukon	—	—	—	0.5	0.1
N.W.T.	1.3	1.3	2.0	0.4	0.1

*Included with N.W.T.

Source: Calculated from M.C. Urquhart and K.A.H. Buckley, eds., *Historical Statistics of Canada* (Toronto: Macmillan, 1965), Series A2-14.

of its share of national output in 1890 minus its share of population for that year. If a region had exactly the national average income, this figure would be zero. A negative number means that that province's per-capita GVA is below the national average (its share of population exceeds its share of output), while a positive one implies the reverse (its share of output is greater than its share of population). As the table indicates, for the Maritimes, Quebec, and Saskatchewan, population shares were below those for output. Quebec was relatively the worst situated, followed by Nova Scotia, Saskatch-

TABLE 15.2

Gross Value Added by Province, 1890 and 1910

	1890		*1910*	
	$ million	*% of Canada*	*$ million*	*% of Canada*
P.E.I.	14.1	1.8	16.0	0.8
Nova Scotia	64.1	8.1	114.2	5.6
New Brunswick	49.1	6.2	75.7	3.7
Quebec	208.7	26.3	474.8	23.2
Ontario	391.2	49.3	845.5	41.4
Manitoba	30.3	3.8	113.1	6.5
Saskatchewan	9.7	1.2	121.4	5.9
Alberta	*	*	98.7	4.8
B.C.	26.1	3.3	165.6	8.1
Canada	793.3	100.0	2,045.0	

*Included with Saskatchewan

Source: Alan Green, *Regional Aspects of Canada's Economic Growth* (Toronto: University of Toronto Press, 1971), Tables B-1, B-2 (pp. 85-86).

ewan, Prince Edward Island, and New Brunswick. For (in order) Ontario, British Columbia, and Manitoba, however, per-capita output exceeded the national average. In Ontario, the difference was substantial; in British Columbia, it was less so; and Manitoba was only slightly above the national average. Even at this early date in Canadian economic history, apparently, the easternmost provinces were the poorest region of Canada; Ontario and British Columbia were the most productive; and the Prairie provinces fell somewhere in between. While figures for one year are always suspect, the finding does suggest to contemporary observers that today's regional disparity patterns have a long history.

Column 2 of Table 15.3 shows the same figures for 1910, and Column 3 gives the difference between Column 2 and Column 1. A negative number in Column 3 means that that province's per-capita output fell relative to the national average between 1890 and 1910; that is, its relative economic status fell. A positive entry means it rose; output rose faster than population over the period. Inter-

TABLE 15.3

Share of National Output Minus Share of National Population and Minus Share of National Labour Force by Province, 1890 and 1910

	Share of Output Minus Share of National Population		*Change in Shares,*	*Share of Output Minus Share of National Labour Force*		*Change in Shares,*
	1890	*1910*	*1890–1910*	*1890*	*1910*	*1890–1910*
P.E.I.	–0.5	–0.5	0	–0.4	–0.4	0.0
Nova Scotia	–1.2	–1.3	–0.1	–1.7	–0.8	0.9
New Brunswick	–0.4	–1.2	–0.8	–0.5	–0.7	–0.2
Quebec	–4.5	–4.7	–0.2	–1.9	–0.8	1.1
Ontario	–5.6	6.2	0.6	3.9	5.0	1.1
Manitoba	0.6	0.1	–0.5	0.4	0.0	–0.4
Saskatchewan	–0.8	–0.9	–0.1	–0.1	–1.8	–1.7
Alberta	— *	–0.4	—	— *	–1.1	—
British Columbia	1.3	2.7	1.4	0.3	0.5	0.2

*Included with Saskatchewan

Source: Alan Green, *Regional Aspects of Canada's Economic Growth* (Toronto: University of Toronto Press, 1971), Table II-9 (p. 43).

estingly, of the five provinces with below-average output per capita in 1890, four saw their relative position fall further by 1910, while that of the fifth (Prince Edward Island) remained unchanged. The largest relative deterioration was in New Brunswick, and the smallest were in Nova Scotia and Saskatchewan. Conversely, British Columbia and Ontario increased their lead further, with the former province showing the greatest relative gain. The only apparent case of convergence to the national average was Manitoba, whose positive standing in 1890 was almost completely eroded by 1910. The two decades between 1890 and 1910, one of relative recession and one of clear boom, appear to have exacerbated rather than narrowed relative economic inequalities.

What lay behind these regional disparities? Why were the Maritimes and Quebec relatively poorer in 1890 and 1910? Why were Ontario and British Columbia richer, and why the Prairie provinces in between? In a purely statistical sense, aggregate output per capita can be different across regions for one of two reasons. Output per person will be lower in a region, all else being equal, if the ratio of those working to the total population is lower — that is, if the dependency rate is higher. This circumstance arises when age structures (more very young or very old), labour-force participation rates (less participation by women, for example), or unemployment rates are different.

Second, per-capita output will vary if output per worker does, even if employment rates are constant. There are two reasons why output per worker might be different across regions. The first is what is termed an industry-mix effect. If output per worker is higher in some sectors than in others (manufacturing compared to fishing, for example), and if industrial structures differ across regions (fishing is more pertinent in one region, and manufacturing in the other), measured aggregate output per worker will differ. The Maritimes are poorer, on average, because there are more fishermen in the labour force, and fishermen are poorer. The other possible explanation is a productivity effect. Industrial structures may be similar, but output per worker in any given sector is higher in one region than in another. Fishermen and factory workers both earn more in Ontario than in the Maritimes because, for whatever reasons, both are more productive. Both situations can be true, in which case disparities are even greater. Or they can be offsetting, in which case measured disparities will be less.

Green's regional data can be used to examine each of these explanations of the pattern of regional disparities in 1890 and 1910. The details are complex, but the picture that emerges from his analysis can be summarized as follows. First, differences in employment rates explain some of the overall disparity in output per capita in both 1890 and 1910, though they do not do so in a way that reveals much about underlying mechanisms. Computing output per member of the labour force rather than per person, as is done in Columns 4 and 5 of Table 15.3, brings most provinces closer to the national average, but it moves some further away (Nova Scotia and New Brunswick in 1890; Saskatchewan and Alberta in 1910). Furthermore, the direction of the effect reverses between 1890 and 1910 in these instances.

The second conclusion is that industrial structure accounts for part of the disparity as well. Ouput per employed worker did vary significantly across sectors in both 1890 and 1910, being highest in forestry and manufacturing, and lowest in agriculture. Likewise, there was some diversity in industrial structure across provinces in both years. Prince Edward Island and the Prairie provinces were disproportionately agricultural, the Maritimes and British Columbia were more heavily dependent on fishing, and Ontario and Quebec were the most industrialized. Still, there was less variation at this time as a result of industrial structure than a contemporary observer might expect. The share of manufacturing in provincial output in Nova Scotia, New Brunswick, and British Columbia was only slightly below those of Ontario and Quebec, and Ontario was the most agriculturally dependent economy in 1890 after Prince Edward Island, Manitoba, and Saskatchewan. Thus, while structure matters some in explaining disparity at this time, it cannot matter much.

If participation rates and industrial structure do not explain much of the regional variation in GVA per capita, productivity per worker within given activities must. This factor is both significant and consistent, as it turns out. Per-capita output in Ontario is consistently among the highest in the country in all sectors, for example, while the corresponding figures for the Maritimes are consistently among the lowest. Part of the variation might still be an industry-mix effect, as the industry categories used are still quite broad. But the impression remains that the main cause of regional income disparities, even at this early stage of Canadian economic history, was differences in labour productivity. For whatever reasons — differences in scale of output, in capital per employee, in education and skills, in access to technology — the value of output per worker apparently varied systematically and significantly in 1890, and grew worse to 1910. As we shall see below, this finding can be duplicated using data for the post–World War II period, which makes the conclusion more plausible, but also more depressing.

An explanation must be sought in the particulars of the regional economies themselves. The position of Atlantic Canada is particularly interesting in this respect, and has received the most attention. Therefore, it will be looked at in detail as an example of regional differentiation.

The Relative Economic Decline of Atlantic Canada

Newfoundland

While not part of Canada in this period, Newfoundland was an important component of the account to 1867, and becomes so again after 1949. Thus, it would be remiss not to fill in the intervening years, at least briefly.

The inshore salt cod industry continued to dominate Newfoundland's economy throughout the nineteenth century. During the period from the granting of responsible government in 1855 to the mid-1880s, the industry "flourished."[1] Prices for fish were above long-term trend in every quinquennia, as were volumes in four of the six. A crisis set in thereafter, lasting for nearly two decades. Prices fell and volume declined. The male labour force employed in catching and curing fish declined from a historic high of 60 000 in 1884 to under 37 000 just seven years later. As Alexander notes, the traditional economy had reached a limit to its extensive growth.

The reaction of the Newfoundland government to the downturn after the mid-1880s was much like that of its Canadian counterpart. Employment had to be found in other sectors of the economy, which meant government had to introduce policies to promote development. Homestead laws and bounty systems were established to speed up land clearing and cultivation in an attempt to establish an agricultural frontier. Provision was even made, in 1884, to partition land into townships, sections, and quarter-sections, as had been done in the Canadian west. Subsidies were offered to manufacturing industries, and expositions organized. Railway construction was promoted, as was construction of dry-docks and roads.

Most of these efforts had little success, however. The land was acidic and expensive to clear. Improved acreage did increase somewhat, and there was a modest growth in livestock numbers and products, but the island still imported most of its food requirements. A small local market precluded the emergence of manufacturing enterprises of any scale, and the lack of industrial experience made it unlikely that export ventures would develop. Emigration was inevitable, and, between 1884 and 1901, an estimated 1500 to 2500 individuals left the island each year. Thus, Newfoundland entered the twentieth century still looking for ways to employ new entrants to the labour force along with those being displaced from the fishing sector.

As Alexander phrases it, the solution after 1900 consisted of "a search for foreign direct investment firms to develop modern resource industries through a package of advanced management and technology."[2] The development of the Bell Island ore mines by Nova Scotia steel interests was noted in Chapter 13. Pulp and paper, mining, smelting, and food-processing were other ventures sought and occasionally obtained. The hope was that the new technologies opening up the Canadian Shield and the interior of British Columbia could do the same for the island.

There was some progress in these other sectors, although, like all such trends, it is not clear what part government attitudes and policies played exactly. Agricultural output increased 2.7 times, in current-dollar terms, between 1884 and 1901, and increased another 80 percent to 1921, when it accounted for more than 25 percent of the value of gross output. Forestry developed very slowly to the 1920s, but jumped in relative importance thereafter. Mining never exceeded 7.5 percent of the gross value of output until the 1930s. The value of fishing output rose in absolute terms to 1911, although, as a share of total output, it fell from two-thirds in 1884, to one-half. Manufacturing rose slowly but steadily, and roughly retained its relative position in the economy.

Overall, though, Newfoundland's economy neither diversified nor developed rapidly enough to overcome its long-run structural problems. Emigration averaged between 1000 and 1500 persons per annum between 1901 and 1945. The economy remained highly dependent on the earnings from a few exports and a few markets to finance the importation of a broad range of imported consumer and capital goods. As trade opportunities declined in the 1930s, Newfoundland would be especially vulnerable. Coupled with the onerous debt accumulated by the government from railway construction and other development expenditures, the burden became too great. The government surrendered independence and Dominion status in early 1934, and reverted to British control.

The Maritimes

The facts on Maritime economic development after 1867 are indisputable. As Table 15.1 indicated, population grew more slowly than in the rest of Canada. This rate is perhaps not surprising, given the opening of the prairie frontier to settlement. It also grew more slowly than regions other than the Prairies, however, as Figure 15.1 indicates for Ontario. Indeed, the population of Prince Edward Island actually declined from 1891 to 1911. Aggregate output grew more slowly as well, at least after 1890, when estimates are first available. Thus, by either measure, the region played a smaller role in the Canadian economy in 1910 than it had at the time of Confederation. Its share of manufacturing declined, especially the production of the more processed goods. Living standards, as measured by output per capita or per worker, were the lowest in the nation in 1890, and they continued to decline, in a relative sense, until the outbreak of World War I.

If the facts are not in dispute, the explanations certainly are. Interestingly, writing on the topic has gone through at least three separate phases. A very old view linked Maritime economic difficulties to Confederation. The region prospered in the 1850s and 1860s, the account would have it, but began to lag thereafter. Tariffs and railway policies were the particular villains. Tariffs diverted the region's attention from its traditional trading partners to the central Canadian provinces; the completion of the transcontinental rail system brought Canadian manufactured goods into the region rather than taking Maritimes ones west, as had been hoped; and the expectation that Atlantic cities would serve as ice-free ports for exports to Europe never materialized. Thus was born the legacy of Maritime dissatisfaction with Confederation that fuelled seccessionist movements at the time, and resentment that has lingered to today.

This view was challenged in an influential study prepared for the Rowell-Sirois Commission by Maritime economic historian S.A. Saunders.[3] He linked the problems of the region to the unfortunate fates of its staples products, and to its natural disadvan-

FIGURE 15.1

Maritime Population as a Percentage of Ontario's, 1851–1911

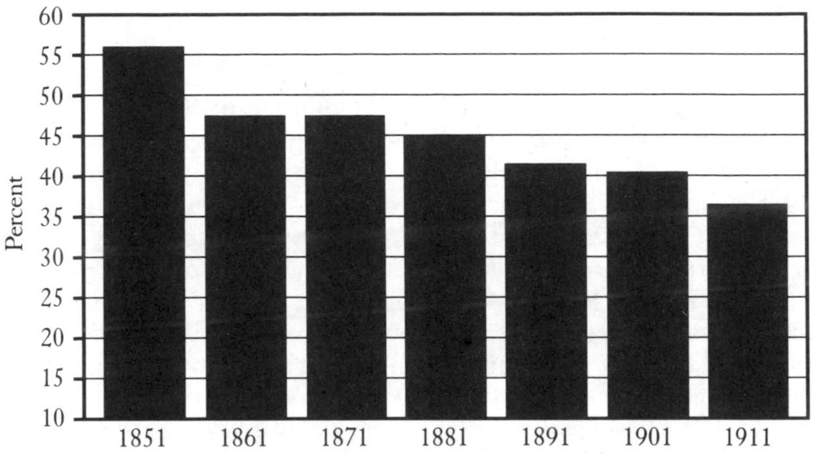

Source: Calculated from M.C. Urquhart and K.A.H. Buckley, eds., *Historical Statistics of Canada* (Toronto: Macmillan, 1965), Series A2–14.

tages with respect to the new industries. The region's relative decline set in when demand for its main exports fell off. The British market for timber and ships fell off completely in the 1880s. The West Indies trade slowed as well, and, with it, the profitable carrying trade. Finally, the appearance of steam and steel ships on world trade routes spelled the end of the successful North Atlantic carrying trade.

The decline persisted because of an inability to compete in new ventures. The failure of the region to switch from wood and sails to steel and steam doomed shipbuilding and shipping. Geography and a relatively poor resource endowment put the region at a disadvantage with respect to manufacturing development. As the natural barriers of transportation costs fell away, it was inevitable that central Canadian concerns would dominate the national market. Distance meant, as well, that hopes for being the eastern terminus for the trade of the continent were unrealistic. Boston and New York in the United States and Montreal in Canada were much better positioned for that role.

The obvious place to begin an assessment of Maritime development after Confederation is with the shipbuilding and shipping industries of the region. These were demonstrably successful activities at mid-century. Maritime-built vessels found ready markets in the United Kingdom, and the region's ships and sailors could be found in all the major ports of the world. If any sector had the demonstrated entrepreneurial talent and experience to capitalize on the opportunities in the new industrialism, this was surely the one. Since it clearly did not make the transition to the new technology, understanding why might provide some insight into the more general problems the region faced.

The Atlantic Canada Shipping Project at Memorial University has made available a more complete picture of this important sector. Shipping and shipbuilding were two quite separate activities, as it turns out, and the incentives to invest in one or the other varied substantially across the region. In Saint John and along the Bay of Fundy, the traditional picture of the industry remains largely intact. The timber trade was the primary stimulus to shipbuilding and ship operation, and the U.K. market was the primary destination for both timber and vessels. The timber trade was less important in most Nova Scotia ports, though, and totally absent in Prince Edward Island and Newfoundland. Coastal and fishing vessels were important product outputs in these ports, and the market was the local fisheries, the coastal trade, and the West Indies carrying trade.

Out of this research have come two important points regarding the secular decline of the region after Confederation. The first conclusion is more in the nature of confirmation that an earlier revision to the economic history of the region was probably accurate. The role of shipbuilding and shipping in the local economies was never as great as traditional accounts, particularly that of Harold Innis, made out. The linkages of these activities to the rest of the economy were too limited for them to have played the propulsive role in regional economic development usually attributed to them. But, if there was never a golden age based on wood and sail, the appearance of steel and steam cannot be responsible for the stagnation in the region. The cause must lie elsewhere.

The research has also strived to refute the thesis of entrepreneurial failure, through a reinterpretation of the factors behind the great surge in shipowning in the 1860s and 1870s. Earlier accounts had pictured the increased activity in ship registration within the region as something forced on it by the decline in demand in Britain for wooden ships. Left with the vessels, shipbuilders were forced to operate them to cut losses. This adherence to a technology and an industry that was so obviously in decline was often cited as evidence of the economic difficulties of the region.

The account that emerges, instead, is that the surge in registrations was a continuation of a trend that had begun much earlier, and that parallels a similar one in the United Kingdom. Investment in shipping was not an unpropitious gamble, but rather a "finely judged attempt to seize expanding opportunities, and then to maintain rates of return as demand for sailing ship services fell."[4] It was a rational act, since rates of return to shipping at that time were likely at least equal to those available in other sectors. Owners went to great lengths to improve the productivity and performance of their vessels to maintain profits. Thus, it was a noble and enterprising group that faced the end when it came, and not the myopic builders-cum-inadvertent-owners of "floating coffins" that is sometimes supposed.

The mystery of the failure to adjust to new technologies is not solved, but one prime candidate is apparently banished. If shipbuilders and shipowners were as calculating and entrepreneurial as this research pictures, the fault cannot have been with lack of local expertise in the industry. Individuals and firms capable of maintaining a profitable living out of a declining wooden-ship industry certainly must have been capable of operating in the new environment, given a fair chance.

Where, then, does the explanation lie? One explanation is offered by T.W. Acheson in an influential essay on Maritime industrialization between 1880 and 1910.[5] He finds that Maritime entrepreneurs responded initially to the opportunities the national-policy tariffs of 1879–87 offered. Iron and steel and textiles were the main focuses, with attention given as well to sugar-refining and a range of miscellaneous manufacturing. For a time, progress was marked: Nova Scotia's industrial growth rate in the 1880s was the highest in Canada, for example. The ventures were indigenous, put in place by individuals or groups of individuals with long-time attachments to the region, and were scattered throughout the region rather than being concentrated in one or two larger centres.

These enterprises were unable to weather the long depression of the 1880s and 1890s, however, and eventually went out of business or were taken over by outside interests. Valiant efforts at adapting to change notwithstanding, the adjustment was simply too momentous. The problem was that the age of wood and sail had not created the proper conditions for a transition to industrial development. The new transportation routes and the new industrialism required a regional metropolis, a concept that was entirely foreign to the region. The early industrialization attempts failed because they had taken place in scattered communities that, however natural they were for Atlantic markets, were unsuited for continental ones. Communities that might have assumed this leadership role — Halifax, for example — failed the region because their merchants preferred to invest in banks and stocks rather than in industry.

The challenge in this interpretation to Saunders's position (outlined above) is important. For Saunders, there never could have been much diversification in the region beyond the original staples base. Natural disadvantages were just too great. No amount of tinkering with tariff or freight rates would have made much difference, and no group of merchants, however astute, could have held off the inevitable decline for long. For Acheson, there could have been sustained industrial growth, and there very nearly was. The essentials were there; the failure was human. The blame, if there is to be any, lies with regional merchants, who did not, or could not, make the transition to the new age.

Another explanation turns, inevitably it seems, back to Confederation and the national policy. There is a difference, though. The argument is not so much that the arrangements of 1867 worked *against* the interests of the region as that they did not work actively enough *for* it. Why, it is asked, did the Dominion government not choose to subsidize its Maritime transport the way it did its inland rail lines, and thereby ensure that Atlantic ports would serve the transcontinental trade? Why were even more favourable freight rates (the rate structure was biassed in favour of shipments west from the Maritimes already) not extended on the Intercolonial Railway, to allow Maritime coal and manufactured goods to compete in central Canadian markets?

Like the Acheson interpretation, posing these questions presumes that Maritime industrialization and economic diversification were real possibilities in the late nineteenth century — missed opportunities, as it were. To find the argument credible, one would need to believe that fairly small changes in transportation rates or in Dominion subsidies could have had enormous effects on industrial prospects. Simply putting the issue in that manner suggests the probable answer. Looking at regional entrepreneurship seems a more promising alternative for those not content with the economic and geographic determinism of S.A. Saunders. The likelihood even here, though, is that one will uncover more cases like the "nationalization" of the Bank of Nova Scotia outlined by James Frost. In his words, "the virtual disappearance of regional banking in the Maritimes suggests that in order to survive and prosper it was necessary for the Bank of Nova Scotia to expand beyond its native region."[6]

In sum, regional disparities were present in Canada as early as 1890. Rapid national economic growth, between 1897 and 1910, only increased these disparities, and the pattern evident across regions at that time is almost identical to that which exists today. The disparities can be broken down into differences in regional labour-force participation rates, industrial structures, and worker productivities, but they cannot be explained thereby. Any of the factors cited above is as much a consequence as a cause of relative underdevelopment.

Notes

1. David Alexander, "Newfoundland's Traditional Economy and Development to 1934," in *Atlantic Canada After Confederation*, The Acadiensis Reader, Vol. 2, edited by P.A. Buckner and David Frank (Fredericton: Acadiensis Press, 1985), 15.
2. David Alexander, "Newfoundland's Traditional Economy and Development to 1934," in *Newfoundland in the Nineteenth and Twentieth Centuries*, edited by James Hiller and Peter Neary (Toronto: University of Toronto Press, 1980), 20.
3. S.A. Saunders, *The Economic History of the Maritime Provinces*, edited and with an introduction by T.W. Acheson (Fredericton: Acadiensis Press, 1984).
4. Eric W. Sager and Lewis R. Fischer, "Atlantic Canada and the Age of Sail Revisited," in *Perspectives on Canadian Economic History*, edited by D. McCalla (Toronto: Copp Clark, 1987), 107.
5. T.W. Acheson, "The National Policy and the Industrialization of the Maritimes, 1880–1910," in *Atlantic Canada After Confederation*, 176–201.
6. James D. Frost, "The 'Nationalization' of the Bank of Nova Scotia, 1880–1910," in *Industrialization and Underdevelopment in the Maritimes, 1880–1930*, edited by T.W. Acheson, David Frank, and James D. Frost (Toronto: Garamond Press, 1985), 54.

Further Reading

Acheson, T.W., David Frank, and James D. Frost, eds. *Industrialization and Underdevelopment in the Maritimes, 1880–1930*. Toronto: Garamond Press, 1985.

Buckner, P.A., and David Frank, eds. *Atlantic Canada After Confederation*. The Acadiensis Reader, Vol. 2. Fredericton: Acadiensis Press, 1985.

Green, Alan. *Regional Reports of Canada's Economic Growth*. Toronto: University of Toronto Press, 1971.

Hiller, James, and Peter Neary, eds. *Newfoundland in the Nineteenth and Twentieth Centuries*. Toronto: University of Toronto Press, 1980.

V

The Turbulent Years, 1914–1945

V

The dominant feature of the period from 1914 to 1945 is unprecedented volatility in the business cycles of the international community and, therefore, of Canada. The era is defined by several short, sharply delineated periods: World War I (1914–18), postwar inflation and recession (1918–21), a return to growth and temporary prosperity (1922–29), massive depression (1929–33), halting recovery (1933–39), and wartime prosperity (1939–45). Along the way, institutions were transformed, economic structures changed, and human psychology altered. These three decades were among the most turbulent in modern history.

This turbulence contrasts with the preceding period, for the years from 1897 to 1912 possessed a degree of continuity in economic terms. They were years of more or less ongoing prosperity, continuous rises in the general Canadian standard of living, and steady increases in Western production and immigrant arrivals. Canadians had come to regard as normal extensive growth, ever-increasing wheat exports, and British investment. In other words, even growth, if reasonably uninterrupted, provides a sense of stability.

The unity was apparent internationally as well. Though Britain was under challenge by Germany and the United States for industrial and financial supremacy, Canadians, before World War I, had little doubt about the power and importance of their own Empire. It was, as the cliché went, the Empire on which the sun never set, and it was as well the home of some of the largest industrial concerns, most powerful concentrations of capital, and most renowned (or infamous) businessmen. Canada thus possessed an optimism that came not only from its own growth but from its participation as a member of the Empire of nations of the world's greatest industrial power.

This anglocentric view of the economic universe was reinforced by certain realities. London was the centre of the world's money markets, and the pound sterling was the international currency of choice. Even more important, however, was the fact that the major international powers of the world all used gold to back their currencies. It was not a perfect medium and, as we have seen throughout this book, shortages or increases in the gold supply of the world could have a significant effect on international economic cycles. At the same time, it had the advantage (when combined with the dominance of the British pound) of creating a common set of rules by which the expansion of commerce and finance could take place. Throughout the half-century before World War I, international currency markets were extremely stable as a result of the gold-based monetary system.

These, then, were the elements of unity that ended in 1914. For World War I shattered the old order and ushered in a troubled and turbulent era in which the world sought to redefine its economic institutions and its monetary arrangements. It can also be argued that World War I had the most profound long-term impact of any of the distinct phases that were to follow. It destroyed the existing balance of power, bringing England's long reign of economic supremacy to an end. Equally, the defeat of the German Empire interrupted its economic growth and left that former industrial power under massive obligations of foreign debt and war reparations. Imperial Russia had never been a major industrial nation, but its size, natural resources, and large population had made it important economically before the war. The war, however, brought massive losses to Russia and, in 1917, culminated in the Russian revolution. For years thereafter, the nation was torn apart by civil strife and its economy was a shambles. By contrast, the United States, a rising industrial power from the Civil War on, emerged from World War I in a dominant position economically. It not only was the greatest industrial power on earth but had gone internationally from being a net debtor to being a net creditor. The American dollar was fast replacing the British pound as the international currency of the day, though the transition would not be complete until after World War II.

The emergence of the U.S. dollar could not, however, provide the stability internationally that had existed in the prewar period. For one thing, the dollar did not yet have the prestige or convertibility that the pound sterling had possessed. For another, America came to the role of international lender and financial player slowly. Most importantly, however, the gold standard had fallen apart during World War I. The massive expenditures of wartime had forced nation after nation to abandon the standard. There were attempts to put the old order back in place in the 1920s. These efforts were largely directed at the resurrection of the old era of the gold standard, often in unrealistic ways. The attempts failed, and, thus, one of the features that contributed to this era of turbulence was the absence of a stable international monetary system.

Canada was affected by these changes more than most countries. As an export-oriented nation, Canada was especially affected by the disruption in the international economic environment. Inevitably, these changes created new difficulties and instabilities in selling goods on the world market. More particularly, the rapidly shifting economic strength of the traditional major trading partner (Great Britain) and the rising challenger (the United States) had a profound effect on Canadian market orientation, investment patterns, and political relationships. The growth sectors of the postwar years were those that served the tremendously wealthy American market. By the end of the 1920s, Canada was still highly dependent on the economy of the North Atlantic triangle, but now it was the United States that was the most important part of that relationship, whether one looks at the source of investments or imports, or the destination of exports.

The next turn of events brought what has become known as the Great Depression. In part, this unprecedented downturn of the world economy was the result of too many goods chasing too few customers. Or, to put it another way, the ability of modern technology to produce goods appeared, for a time, to have outstripped the ability of people to consume them. This decline in consumer spending, and other factors, brought investment to a standstill. Moreover, these were persistent problems that would resist solution until the rearmament of World War II finally created the necessary demand to overcome the slump.

Why this depression hit is a complex and contested issue. Why was it that the vast, complicated, and intricate international systems of production and trade should go so completely awry that it would take a major war to restore the system? Some have argued in terms of cyclical theory, suggesting that a peculiar conjuncture of cyclical events occurred in the 1930s. It may have been, for example, that a number of medium- and short-term cycles turned downward at the same time. Or, as was a popular theory among critics of capitalism at the time, there might have been a giant industrialist-capitalist cycle, rising with the first industrial revolution of the eighteenth century and ending with the collapse of the second industrial revolution in the 1930s. Others saw technological change, currency fluctuations, monetary contraction in the United States, and trade wars, among other issues, as central to this unprecedented event.

Once again, however, it is hard to ignore World War I in the coming of the Depression. Many of the problems in the international trading and financial systems that were later singled out date from the war. Currency instability, for example, had become a significant problem in the later 1920s, when the United Kingdom overvalued the pound, France undervalued the franc, and the United States tremendously undervalued the dollar.

Instability in international currency was mirrored by excess production in key areas. This trend, also, was a part of the volatility of the international economy caused by the Great War. The war increased new manufacturing and agricultural capacity. By the later 1920s, as war-ravaged territories regained their ability to produce, the world faced a glut of commodities. Nations responded by building protective barriers around their own goods. As the 1920s ended, the problem became worse rather than better, and nations were forced to stockpile an ever-larger percentage of production. It could not go on forever, and, in the latter part of 1929, the gradual decline in commodity prices turned into a freefall.

Once the Depression hit, it fed upon itself. Collapsing expectations, financial crises, shrinking international trade, and increasingly restrictive trade barriers sent the international economy into the most drastic collapse of the industrial era. By 1933, the bottom of the Depression, international trade had declined to one-third of what it had been at the beginning of 1929. Unemployment skyrocketed, nations were destabilized, and an industrial world used to economic progress settled into an era of stagnation. In Canada, and in much of the Western world, governments, business, labour, and other groups proved equally incapable of finding a sure road out of the quagmire. Only in Germany, where the Nazis embarked on a massive rearmament program, was there anything like a successful attack on the Depression. It was an example that most nations were loath to follow.

In an ironic and tragic way, however, the Nazis were responsible for ending the Depression not just in Germany but internationally. Their aggressive foreign policy eventually forced a response from other European nations, and led, of course, to World War II. With the coming of war, the final great shift of these years took place. As had been the case in 1914–18, modern industrial war demanded that the full productive capacity of the engaged nations be utilized. The Depression ended, and Western economies underwent tremendous growth. Equally important, World War II also brought an end to the tremendous volatility ushered in by World War I. For out of this war came a new concern with the stability of international trade. Better currency and trade systems were established, while the United States adopted a series of policies calculated to encourage stability in international trade. The short, sharp fluctuations of the past quarter-century would be replaced by longer-term cycles of prosperity and growth.

CHAPTER

16

World War I and the Canadian Economy, 1912–1921

People in the midst of boom do not like to think about its end. So it was with the boom that began in the late 1890s. In Canada, there was especially great optimism. The Dominion went from strength to strength. The years from 1910 to 1912 made the earlier periods of strong growth look pale. In January 1913, officials of the Dominion Department of Finance could say proudly that "the year just closed has been phenomenal as to increase [in economic activity], the amount being almost double that of last. The bank clearings show an increase of almost 35% while the total value of building permits issued practically 100%. . . . The outlook for 1913 is even better."[1]

They were wrong. The year 1913 brought with it a sharp recession that marked the end of the long cycle of international prosperity that had begun in the late 1890s, a cycle with which Canada was closely associated. Observers at the time and economists after the fact have attributed the arrival of the 1913 recession in Canada to a tightening of credit on the London money market. Money became more expensive to borrow, and speculative capital — including speculative capital for Canada — became harder to find.

There *was* a tightening of the London money market in 1913, and undoubtedly it triggered the 1913 recession. That is not the whole story, however, for, even in 1913, Canada continued to receive a generous flow of British funds, equal to that of any year except the previous two.[2] The severity of the recession was determined, instead, by the nature of the growth cycle in its final phase. The long-term boom had rested on a healthy international economy and on the development of Canadian staples exports, particularly in agriculture. It was sustained by large numbers of immigrants and by capital inflows that made it possible to build the infrastructure necessary for continued growth.

Sometime after recovery from a mild recession in 1907, the nature of the boom in Canada changed. An ever-larger influx of foreign investment increasingly provided the main driving force in the Canadian economy. As one economist has noted, the level "of outlay on fixed capital formation" in the final years before the war "must have few counterparts" in the world.[3] Investment, particularly British investment, was sent west to feed urban prairie development. "Booming" of towns, as the phrase of the day went, brought large amounts of investment that seemed to go indiscriminately into a wide range of serious, frivolous, and even fraudulent development schemes. By 1913, as the recession loomed, capital imports amounted to one-sixth of GNP, compared to one-twentieth only a decade earlier.[4] Canada's standard of living and rate of growth were thus tremendously dependent on the continued interest of foreign investors. Foreign investors, in turn, focussed their attention on speculative areas, such as real estate and construction, that were extremely vulnerable to any downturn in the economy.

The pattern can be seen statistically by looking at Canada's external trade relationships. As Table 16.1 indicates, Canada had had a deficit on current account since 1901. In other words, Canadians bought more goods and services abroad in these years than they sold. As explained in the introduction to this book, this imbalance meant that Canadians were using, in aggregate, more goods and services than they were themselves producing. Foreign supplies made up the differences, and foreigners advanced them in exchange for financial claims on the economy. Thus, the current-account deficit was offset by a net capital-account inflow, coming mainly from Britain.[5]

From 1910 on, the deficit on the current account increased dramatically. Merchandise exports rose from $201 million in 1903 to $269 million in 1909, and reached $443 million by 1913. Imports rose much more spectacularly, from $251 million in 1903 to $429

TABLE 16.1

Balance of Payments on Current Account

(millions of dollars)

1901	–23.1	1910	–251.3
1902	–32.0	1911	–363.7
1903	–74.1	1912	–421.3
1904	–97.5	1913	–408.2
1905	–87.3	1914	–288.2
1906	–102.0	1915	–57.3
1907	–166.9	1916	+22.9
1908	–134.4	1917	–81.8
1909	–158.3	1918	+50.3

Source: Statistics Canada, *Historical Statistics of Canada*, 2nd ed. (Ottawa: Supply and Services, 1983), G34–46.

million in 1910, and to an amazing $655 million by 1913. Exports were now less than two-thirds of imports, and Canada had a current-account deficit of more than $400 million — a figure greater than total imports only four years earlier! The problem was that a deficit on current account this large was unstable. Canadians were, in effect, living beyond their means, and only the optimism of the British investor made it possible to do so. If financial capital inflows were to fall off, there would have to be a parallel and offsetting adjustment on the real side of the ledger.

The tremor that went through the London money markets in the winter of 1912–13 thus caused an earthquake in a highly vulnerable Canadian economy. The results were instantaneous and showed most dramatically in the volatile housing market. Over the next year, building permits declined nearly one-third compared to numbers in the previous year. Especially hard hit were the western cities, where speculative activity in real estate had led to overconstruction. The number of permits issued for Winnipeg, Regina, Calgary, and Vancouver fell 85 percent and more between 1913 and 1915. Edmonton, which had issued more than $9.2 million in building permits in 1913, issued only $300 000 worth, or 3 percent of the former figure, in 1915.

Related industries were immediately affected. The lumber and brickmaking industries, which had supplied the construction boom, produced less and employed fewer people than before. The collapse of construction in 1913–14 rippled through the rest of the economy in a manner that indicates the vulnerabilities of the Canadian economy. In spite of continuing strength in the export area and in spite of a record number of immigrants and homestead entries that year, Canada plunged into a recession. Unemployment rose across the country. Land prices tumbled — especially in the west — and bankruptcies skyrocketed. Companies with assets worth some $8.7 million failed in 1913; the next year saw $13.7 million in failures.

The collapse soon exposed other vulnerabilities. Most dramatically, it began to bring into serious doubt Canada's reckless railway expansion of recent years. By 1914, as the Grand Trunk Pacific and Canadian Northern extended their track toward transcontinental status, it began to appear as if a reckoning was soon due on the accounts. Railway mileage in Canada had more than doubled between 1895 and 1915, while total capital liabilities of railways had doubled in the ten years after 1904, to a staggering $1.8 billion. It was very likely that, as had been the case in the 1850s, Canada had built too much for the traffic available. By 1915, as Michael Bliss points out, Canada "had more railways per capita than any country in the world."[6] The railways were appearing cap in hand with greater regularity at the doorstep of the Canadian government. The trouble was that the end of such visits seemed nowhere in sight.

Another problem was, paradoxically, a factor that had been part of Canada's success story over the previous fifteen years — large-scale immigration. Immigrants had been crucial to the development of the prairie frontier, the new staples trades, and the manufacturing- and service-sector development that had characterized the Canadian economy in the boom years. Large-scale immigration, however, was desirable only if there was sufficient growth to employ the newcomers. By 1913–14, the economy was stagnant overall and declining in such labour-intensive areas as construction. Yet, that same year, apparently as yet unaware of the change in the economy, a record 402 000 immigrants arrived in Canada.

The economy's inability to absorb the immigrants was most obvious in the west. That region had for years been the great destination of choice. By 1913–14, however, the west was in an even more difficult position than was the rest of the country. It was there that construction had slowed most dramatically and that the faltering transcontinental railway lines were located. Moreover, 1914 was a bad year for crops in many parts of the region, and the average yield declined in all principal field crops. The heart of the great boom of earlier years was, thus, the region that felt the recession most acutely. Unemployment increased and, although statistics are incomplete, wages appear to have headed downward across a wide range of occupations.

In summary, then, the final years of the "wheat boom" had been fuelled by high expectations for continued growth. Real-estate speculation and construction, as well as the free-spending railways, had drawn ever-greater amounts of foreign investment to Canada. Those investments supported ever-higher levels of Canadian imports and made possible the successful absorption of increasing numbers of immigrants. When investment faltered in 1913, everything fell into disarray: construction collapsed, bankruptcies soared, unemployment rose. Railways found private investment harder and harder to come by and increased their pressures on government. The great boom was over.

The Impact of the War

In August 1914, after years of rising tension, the great nations of Europe went to war. The British Empire, allied with the French and the Russians, was to be pitted in conflict with the German and Austro-Hungarian empires for the next four years. This massive conflict, known to contemporaries simply as the Great War, profoundly affected the Canadian economy. Over the next seven years, the economy of war, and, then, of postwar adjustment, shaped the nation's economic activity. The recession ended by 1915. Inflation then became a problem, as an overheated economy struggled to meet both the overseas demand for war-related goods and domestic needs. Current-account deficits turned to surpluses, and unemployment largely disappeared. Peace, however, would bring another readjustment and a great deal of hardship. Not until well into the 1920s did even a façade of normalcy return to the Canadian economy. The international economy remained unstable, and the

Canadian economy remained vulnerable to events abroad.

None of this was known in 1914. Canadians were, as were so many elsewhere, initially naïve about the war. They were sure it would be short, glorious, and sensationally victorious. Given such assumptions, they had no comprehension of the stress it would place on industrial economies. The economy of full production and inflation was still eighteen months to two years away. At the beginning, therefore, Canadian politicians saw nothing on the immediate horizon that indicated an impending end to the recession.

Indeed, the initial effect of the war was to make the recession worse. Capital imports, such an important part of the economy before the war, all but collapsed by 1915, to only 2.5 percent of GNP. The already shaky industries that depended so much on heavy investment were hit immediately. Construction continued its collapse from the previous year, hitting bottom in 1915. Railways, already overextended and in trouble, were forced to cut back operations. Workers were let go in large numbers. By 1915, there were 50 000 fewer employees in railway or related activities than there had been only two years earlier. The Canadian government continually pleaded with its British allies to send more war orders of all sorts to Canada. The depressed state of the economy, the government argued, made such trade absolutely essential to the economic health of the nation.

As the war continued, things turned around. Victory in the Great War would rest as much on the efficient application of technology and on mass production as on military strategy. The two sides had to pit their two economies, as well as their two armies, against each other. If the former could not produce, the latter would not be able to stay in the field. Food, clothing, transportation, and, most of all, the instruments of destruction were required in such quantities as the war went on that the Canadian recession became a boom. Canada became a major supplier of food and materiel to the Anglo-French war effort. Canadian wheat and Canadian bacon fed the soldiers at the front, while Canadian-made uniforms clothed them. Canadian ammunition would, after a while, be used to kill the enemy.

The turnaround can be seen, in a most general way, in some overall facts and figures. Merchandise exports trebled, from $442 million in 1913 to $1.2 billion by 1918.[7] Imports, which stood at $632.6 million in 1913, fell to $521.6 million in 1914, and to $516.4

million in 1915, before rising again to reach $953.4 million in the final year of the war. Overall, the current account went from a deficit of $408 million in 1913 to a surplus of more than $50 million in 1918. The situation was exactly the reverse of what had prevailed earlier. Now, Canadians were producing more goods and services than they themselves were using, with the difference being reflected in a net capital outflow.

The absolute, and then relative, decline in imports during the war was not the result of self-denial on the part of Canadian consumers. Canadians, it would seem, were extremely reluctant to give up the luxury goods that they had become accustomed to in the final years of the boom. In spite of a range of higher tariffs, many luxury items remained in high demand. Instead, the drop in imports was the result of three things. The first two were by-products of the continuing recession: lumber and timber imports dropped off considerably as construction collapsed, while the second area of sharp decline came in railway-related equipment — rails, cars, ties, and other materials. The final area was more general and more important: Britain could no longer export large amounts of goods to Canada, as too much of its production was taken up with the domestic war effort. Thus, British exports to Canada dropped by one-third between 1913 and 1915 (see Table 16.2). For the most part, Canadians appear to have replaced these items with domestic products.

The tremendous growth in exports was paralleled by events in the labour market. Demand for workers increased, while supply available to local industry diminished. The increased demand for labour was the result of war-fuelled production increases throughout the economy. On the supply side, the army took tens of thousands of individuals out of the labour force. Also, the long-standing inflow of immigration into Canada slowed to a trickle as the war disrupted the normal patterns of resettlement. The number of immigrants to Canada declined from a high of more than 402 000 in 1913 to fewer than 145 000 by 1915, and only a little more than 48 000 in 1916. Unemployment effectively ended by 1915; in much of the country, there was a serious shortage of workers by midwar.

The end of the recession was a mixed blessing. The overheated war economy, accommodated by the expansion of the money supply authorized at the beginning of the war, meant that inflation soon set it. Estimates indicate that significant inflation existed by 1916

TABLE 16.2
Imports from Britain, 1911–1918

($ millions)

1911	109.9	1915	90.2
1912	116.9	1916	77.4
1913	138.7	1917	107.1
1914	132.0	1918	81.3

Source: Canada Year Book, 1918, 290.

and that, between 1914 and 1920, prices almost doubled (see Figure 16.1). Canadians were not used to such rapid changes in prices, and this inflation would cause considerable unrest in the later years of the decade, and into the 1920s.

Manufacturing, Agriculture, and the War

These changes had a profound impact on various parts of the economy — not the least interesting of which may be found in the manufacturing sector. Until 1914, Canadian manufacturing had been the protected "infant" of the Canadian economy. While wheat, timber, and other resources were traded internationally, most Canadian manufacturing business was done within the highly protected domestic economy. As late as 1913, only about 7 percent of Canadian secondary manufactured goods were sold overseas.[8] Moreover, manufacturing, as was the case in other areas of the economy, was in a slump at the beginning of the war. The question for contemporaries, then, was whether Canadian manufacturers could improve their position in the international marketplace in wartime.

Manufacturing faced serious problems early in the war. While Canadian workers remained unemployed and Canadian factories operated at low capacity, the British sent war orders to the neutral United States. Canadian businesses complained that they were not getting their fair share of war orders. The British were not just being perverse, however. The simple fact was that Canadian industry in 1914–15 was often incapable of meeting the high technical standards required by military purchasers, especially in munitions. Rumours of corrupt dealings on the part of those politically con-

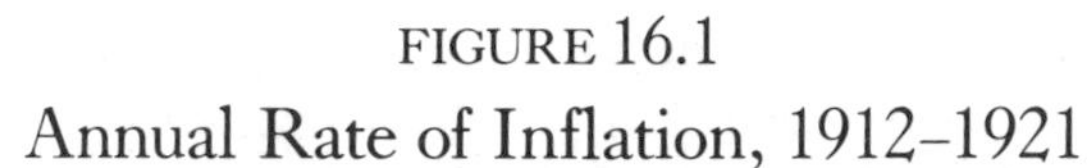
FIGURE 16.1
Annual Rate of Inflation, 1912–1921

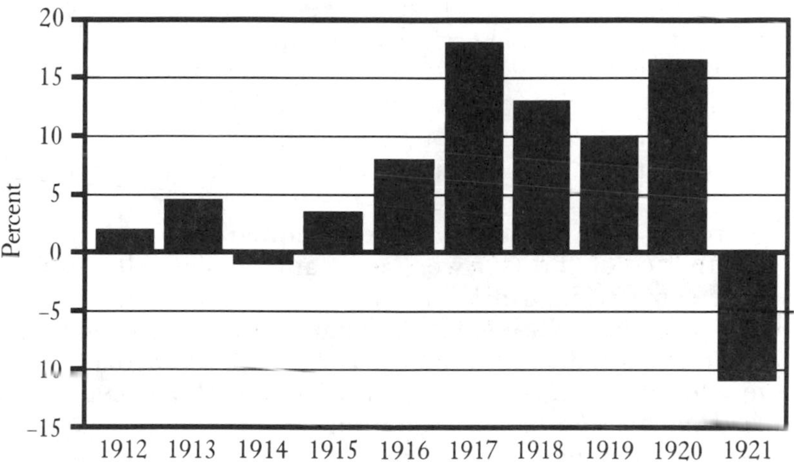

Source: M.C. Urquhart, "New Estimates of Gross National Product in Canada, 1970–1926," in *Long-Term Factors in American Economic Growth*, NBER Studies in Income and Wealth, Vol. 51, edited by Stanley L. Engerman and Robert E. Gallman (Chicago: University of Chicago Press, 1986), Table 2.9.

nected to the Minister of Militia, Sam Hughes, only added to the tainted image. All in all, it was a shabby beginning for Canadian wartime manufacturing. By May 1915, some $170 million in orders had been received for various Canadian munitions. Only $5.5 million had been delivered.[9]

By the latter part of 1915, things began to change. Canadian companies were learning the necessary skills and adopting the techniques required by meticulous military purchasers. The British, their own capacity now stretched to the limit, were willing to look to the capable Canadian firms.

The most significant single British decision affecting Canadian manufacturing came in November 1915. The British government asked Canadian packing-house magnate Joseph Flavelle to head a purchasing agency known as the Imperial Munitions Board (IMB). Responsible to the British government, this board was headed by a Canadian, and most of its staff were located in Canada. Within weeks, hundreds of new contracts were pouring out to Canadian companies to supply the shells, casings, fuses, and other instruments needed to continue the war of attrition in France.

The activities of the IMB were massive. As early as February 1916, the IMB was spending $5 million a week. The British orders for the first half of 1917 alone were $250 million, and the IMB was the nation's largest employer. New companies had to be created by Flavelle when existing ones either could not meet specialized requirements or could not keep up with demand. By 1917, the board was so successful that "something between one-quarter and one-third of all the ammunition used by the British artillery in France, [and] more than one-half the shrapnel," came from Canada.

The activities of the IMB were dramatic, but similar trends, if not of the same scale, can be shown in all manufacturing sectors affected by the war. Estimates of Ontario production by 1915 indicate that war production accounted for at least a quarter of all trade in activities as diverse as tent- and sail-making, manufacture of boilers and engines, and production of automobiles, explosives, steel and iron, plumbing equipment, and woollen goods and yarns.[10] Perhaps two figures most clearly sum it up: first, total wages and salaries in manufacturing increased by more than $300 million between 1915 and 1918; second, while 7 percent of Canadian manufactured goods were sold overseas in 1913, the figure rose to 40 percent by 1918.[11]

The other key sector of the economy during the war was agriculture. Central to agricultural exports in recent years, of course, had been the west. At the beginning of the war, however, the west was in desperate economic shape. Construction had collapsed, building companies folded across the region, and investment in urban centres was withdrawn by overextended eastern and British investors. Unemployment rose dramatically, with the building trades leading the way. In Winnipeg, unemployment among some building trades has been estimated to have been as high as 90 percent by the winter of 1914–15.[12]

The farmers were only marginally better off. For varied reasons, they, too, were extremely vulnerable to any economic downturn. From about 1910 on, there had been a movement, urged on by the Dominion government, into the marginal wheat lands of Palliser's Triangle. Thousands of new farms had been established in areas of southeastern Alberta and southwestern Saskatchewan on lands that, only a few years earlier, had been dismissed as unsuited

Vancouver Public Library no. 910

Women munitions workers at Vancouver Engineering Works Ltd., 1917. *Within weeks of the appointment of Canadian packing-house magnate Joseph Flavelle to head the Imperial Munitions Board, hundreds of new contracts were pouring out to Canadian companies to supply ammunition used by the British artillery in France. By 1917, between a quarter and a third of all ammunition, and half of the shrapnel, came from Canada.*

for settlement. As was true of the marginal Laurentian lands in Quebec or the Shield in Ontario, such regions were capable of supporting a farm family only in the best of times. It was not one of those times in 1914. Further, the rapid growth of the west and the buoyant optimism of the era had encouraged farmers to take on more and more debt to establish themselves quickly. They were, thus, not in a position to survive any extended weakness in agricultural markets. Finally, the farmers found that they had to face all of these circumstances and a mediocre harvest as well. The 1914 crop year was one of the poorest in recent history. Average wheat yields plunged to fewer than sixteen bushels an acre after having been at twenty per acre in 1913. Nor did price compensate, as there were only two slight upward movements.

The recovery of agriculture during World War I showed parallels to that in manufacturing. The turnaround came in late 1915. Good weather created a record crop — a phenomenal 360 million bushels of wheat — that year. Moreover, there was a demand for it. The war was disrupting shipment of supplies from Russia and other parts of Europe, and the large armies in France had to be fed. Thus, prices held in spite of the large crop, and the agricultural sector produced a greater value of products than ever before.[13] Farmers found themselves on the road to recovery.

For the duration of the war, wheat reigned supreme. Any doubts about marginal farm lands or overextended credit disappeared as wheat prices continued to rise. In 1917, when the British said they would take all the wheat Canada could deliver, wheat rose to $2.21 a bushel. Acreage sown to wheat increased by 50 percent from 1914 to 1917, and new farmsteads continued to be created in spite of the choking off of immigration. Others expanded existing holdings. It was a joke among agricultural students at the University of Saskatchewan that their classes were full of former real-estate agents, caught in the crash of 1913, who now sought to make their fortunes in the new area of fast money — wheat.[14]

The extraordinary circumstances of war had two results. First, the farmers who had been in such dire straits in 1913–14 were, by 1917, riding the crest of a wheat bonanza. The good price they were getting for their wheat not only brought in immediate income but led to rapid increases in the value of their property. Land prices for prime wheat acreage rose as high as $90 an acre by the end of the war. For those unfortunate enough to buy at the height of the land boom, it would be the end of another world war before values returned to their 1918–19 levels.[15] Many took advantage of the increased value of their land and sold out to others who wished to operate on a larger scale. Thus, farm size increased steadily throughout the latter part of the year.

Among those who resisted the temptation to sell, the tendency was to put the profits of these years not into debt retirement or savings but into further increases in the size or capital of their operations. Tractors were not yet common, but trucks and automobiles made their appearance in ever-larger numbers through the war and immediate postwar years. Standing gasoline engines, a variety of mechanized aids to production, and, of course, improvements to house and barn were common in these prosperous years. In hindsight, many would rue the failure of the farmer to hunker down, eliminate debt, and prepare for the storm that was to come. Given the record of prairie prosperity, 1913–14 notwithstanding, prairie farmers were reacting in a rational manner, seeking to maximize both capital assets and operating profits. Nothing in the past generation of prairie development suggested they should do anything else.

The abnormal conditions of war changed the role of the government in the marketing of grain. Since 1899 and the Manitoba Grain Act, government had been involved in questions of grading, transportation, and storage of grain. Until the war, however, the involvement had been at arm's length, with the Dominion acting to try to ensure that the various parties involved — elevator companies, grain exchanges, farmers, and overseas customers — operated according to understood rules of behaviour. The grain business was still essentially a free-market operation in 1914, albeit one hedged in by rules.

During the war, the free market no longer operated in agriculture. As early as 1915, the Canadian government commandeered 13 million bushels of wheat for war purposes. As time went on, the demands of war increasingly meant that Canadian farmers were selling their wheat not to British wholesalers but to the British government. By 1917, as mentioned above, the British government asked for every surplus bushel that Canada could produce. In response, the Canadian government stepped in to ensure that the marketing of grain was orderly. In June of that year, the government established the Board of Grain Supervisors, giving it the right to fix prices and to handle all bulk overseas sales. In 1919, this body was replaced by the Canadian Wheat Board, which took over responsibility for the marketing of grain. Though the government saw this as a temporary wartime measure and abandoned the experiment in 1920, farmers saw it as the long-sought response to their demands for direct government involvement in the grain business. The political and economic pressure to resume that involvement would ultimately prove irresistible.

Agriculture was not just a western activity. Indeed, as Ian Drummond reminds us, Ontario produced a greater value of agricultural produce than any other province, and agriculture was Ontario's most important industry.[16] Quebec, it might be added, was also a major producer, ranking just behind Ontario and Saskatchewan in field-crop production in 1914. In the central and Maritime provinces, as in the west, there was a response to the opportunities of the war.

For Ontario, Quebec, and the Maritimes, things were quite different from what they were in the west, however. The west was a region oriented toward the production of export staples, especially wheat. In the eastern provinces, the agricultural activities were more mixed, and the picture during World War I was more complex. This is especially true of central Canada, where, as seen in Chapter 12, farming had for a long time been largely directed at domestic markets. Garden produce, cattle, dairy products, hogs, and sheep were all important in the region. Central Canada had ceased to be an important supplier of wheat in the previous century, though there was a temporary revival of wheat production in Quebec as farmers sought to cash in on wartime demand. In general, however, local markets remained an important destination for eastern agricultural produce throughout the war. Overseas demand thus affected eastern farmers less dramatically than it did those in the west.

This emphasis on domestic markets does not mean that the export market was irrelevant. Butter, beef, and, most of all, hog production responded to wartime demands. Bacon was especially easily preserved and was, therefore, an important part of every soldier's rations throughout the war. The average hog price rose from $6.62 in 1911 to nearly $20.00 by 1919. Canadian pork exports multiplied ninefold between 1913 and 1919. Those Canadian farmers lucky enough to have large herds at the outbreak of the war stood to make windfall profits. Over the next four years, herds increased, especially in Quebec and Alberta, as farmers sought to profit from wartime demand.

The wartime prosperity and the longer-range trends inherent in modern agriculture were bringing about changes on central Canadian farms, as they were on western ones. Though eastern farms were small by western standards, they, too, were getting larger, on average. The smallest farmers, those with fewer than ten acres, were disappearing. There was no real place for the subsistence farmer in a business that was increasingly efficient in operation. This efficiency was aided by the introduction of machinery. As in the west, tractors were still scarce. Only one farm in 30 possessed a tractor, even in prosperous Ontario, by 1921. In Quebec and the Maritimes, they were even more scarce. Automobiles and trucks

Provincial Archives of Alberta/B270

The Gearneau Bros. threshing outfit, Edmonton. *Because such machines as this steam-driven thresher were so expensive, threshing crews of fifteen to twenty men moved with the machinery from farm to farm at harvest time, several farms thus sharing the expense.*

were becoming common, however. More than eight times as many farmers in Ontario had trucks as had tractors by 1921.[17] As trucks became more numerous, the numbers of horses began to decline. The Ontario horse population reached its peak in 1916 and then began a permanent decline. In the east, as in the west, land values appreciated, though more so in Ontario than in the Maritimes or Quebec.

There is still much detailed research to be done on eastern agriculture in the war years. The information that does exist, however, leads to the tentative conclusion that the war was less important to the shape of agriculture in Ontario than to that in any agricultural province and that, overall, the east (and British Columbia's small agricultural sector) was less affected by the war than were the prairies. Longer-term trends dominate the changes taking place, while, in spite of the buoyant overseas market, local markets remain central to farm prosperity. Regional and interprovincial disparities do not seem to have been significantly altered, though the abandonment of marginal farms may have been delayed by wartime demand.

The War and the Economic Structure of the Nation

What was the effect of all this wartime activity — in agriculture, manufacturing, and elsewhere — on Canada's overall economic structure? There have been four common conclusions about wartime activity. One has emphasized the importance of the war to Canada's industrial and mining development. The second has stressed the regional inequities of this industrialization, particularly in western Canada. The third has concentrated on western agriculture and has seen various destructive tendencies resulting from the war. The final one has pointed to the changing role of government during the war and the longer-term effects of that change. Each of these conclusions requires comment.

The first — on the significance of manufacturing during the war — has been optimistic. "By the end of the war Canada was launched as a significant industrial nation," concluded historian Donald Creighton in the 1960s.[18] Others have echoed similar sentiments. Canada, the argument went, surprised itself with its ability to produce highly sophisticated manufactured materials in the pursuit of the war effort. Employees responded to the demand for war products and moved to the new industries. Plants opened and exports increased. The recession at the end of war, it was true, was an inevitable consequence of the end of war production, but the war was nevertheless important to the development of a modern industrial economy.

In general terms, this argument holds, though there are some important qualifiers that must be added. Of course, there is little doubt that the war spurred manufacturing. What is more important, however, is whether there were long-term effects coming about as a result of the changes of these years. If the period from 1910 to the mid-1920s is looked at, rather than 1914–18, it is possible to distinguish, in at least the most general way, between the short-term demands of the wartime economy and the longer-term effects of the war experience on the Canadian economy.

In the manufacturing sector, the use of a longer cycle does have an effect. As Figure 16.2 indicates, the constant-dollar value of manufacturing did increase significantly, whether shorter- or longer-term figures are used. The relative position of manufacturing, however, increased considerably during the war years, only to recede after the war. The recession of 1921 did much to wipe out the gains

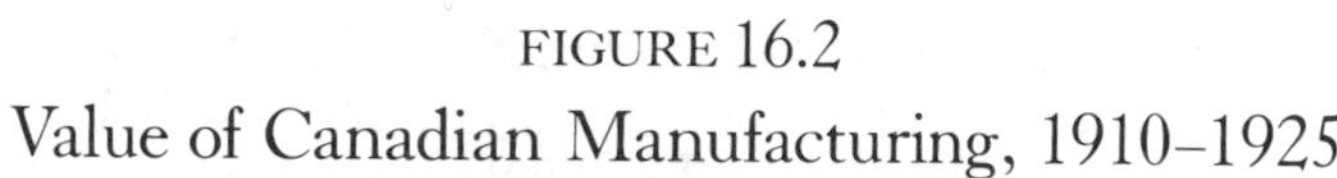

FIGURE 16.2
Value of Canadian Manufacturing, 1910–1925

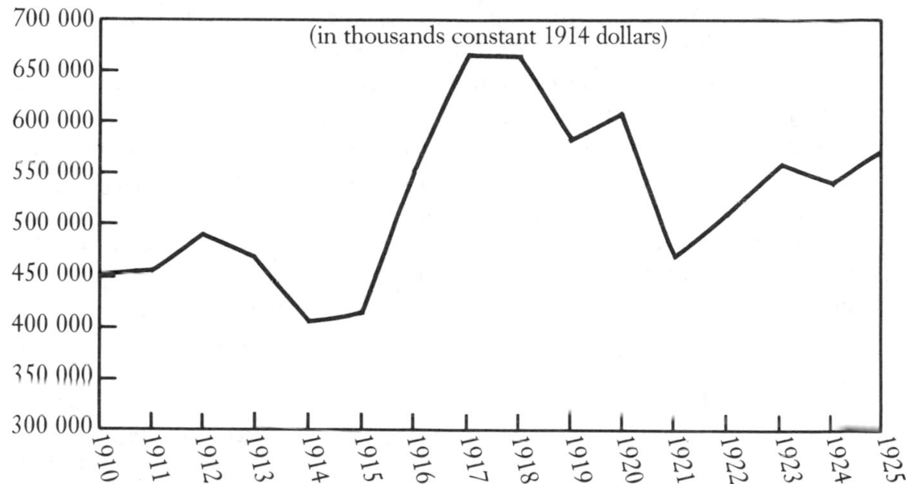

Source: M.C. Urquhart, "New Estimates of Gross National Product in Canada, 1970–1926," in *Long-Term Factors in American Economic Growth*, NBER Studies in Income and Wealth, Vol. 51, edited by Stanley L. Engerman and Robert E. Gallman (Chicago: University of Chicago Press, 1986), Tables 2.1 and 2.9.

of recent years, revealing the temporary nature of many wartime effects. Similarly, the relative place of manufacturing increased during the war, from 22.5 percent of GDP (1910) to 25.1 percent (1920). By 1926, however, it had dropped to 21.1 percent.

The impact of the war and subsequent recession is shown particularly dramatically in the area of employment. Employment in manufacturing in 1921 was nearly 70 000 fewer than in 1910. The two recessions (1913 and 1921), in other words, had a more powerful effect than the war. Even by 1923, the work force had increased only marginally. This employment trend shows up in industry after industry. Those that saw tremendous increases in size as a result of the war saw equally dramatic slippage in the postwar recession. Thus, for example, employment in steel rose from 66 000 in 1910 to a high of 90 000 by 1918. By 1921, it was back to 61 000. The rise and fall of employment in the chemical industries were even more dramatic. From having slightly fewer than 11 000 employees in 1910, the industry expanded to a high of 55 000 by 1917. By 1921, it was back down to 12 000. The trend is apparent whether one looks at employees, production levels, or number of plants.

In the manufacturing sector, the only exception to this trend was in the automobile industry, where employment rose dramatically through the war but did not slide back in the postwar recession. It is likely, however, that this overall growth would have taken place with or without the war, though the precise timing of it might have been altered. The automobile was a revolutionary new technology and, as will be discussed in Chapter 17, a natural growth sector. This does not alter the basic fact that whatever increases in employment were brought about by the war were lost in the postwar recession. It would be 1928 before employment in manufacturing surpassed the wartime figure.

If the work force in manufacturing was not growing, it was changing. As Table 16.3 indicates, there was an actual decline in what might be termed loosely "production workers" between 1910 and 1923, with decline occurring even before the onset of the postwar recession. Conversely, numbers of supervisory and office employees increased by a phenomenal 70 percent in the same period. By 1923, this group accounted for one in six manufacturing employees, compared to the one in twelve in 1910. Finally, and perhaps, in part, because of this structural shift, real wages increased significantly between 1910 and the early 1920s, though of course such increases varied tremendously from sector to sector and region to region.

Overall, then, the war did increase the importance of manufacturing in Canada, but it actually decreased the opportunities for a "blue-collar" worker to find employment in this sector. Conversely, the white-collar component was growing, though there are indications that this development was the result of trends in the business world that predated the war.

The growth, stresses, and structural changes of manufacturing had significant consequences for the Canadian economic and social makeup. The war, and the boom economy it engendered, especially in manufacturing, also raised serious questions concerning the regional distribution of economic growth. Thus, any discussion of the impact of manufacturing must look at both the social and the regional consequences.

In social terms, the economics and politics of the war did much

TABLE 16.3

Manufacturing Employment, 1914–1923

Year	*Production Workers*	*Supervisory and Office Employees*	*Ratio*
1910	465 029	42 948	0.091
1917	523 491	62 454	0.119
1920	499 063	75 558	0.151
1923	437 259	73 849	0.168

Source: Statistics Canada, *Historical Statistics of Canada*, 2nd ed. (Ottawa: Supply and Services, 1983), R1–22

to change the role of women. Partly, this change was occasioned by the longer-term rise of the nonproduction sectors mentioned above. As is discussed in Chapter 17, the new clerical and secretarial jobs that were developing in the office very quickly became female-dominated.[19] Even in more traditional areas of manufacturing, however, women found at least temporary opportunities as a result of the war. The rapid development of manufacturing in the war years, coupled with the labour shortage discussed earlier, expanded the role of women in industry beyond the traditional needle trades, though not as extensively as would be the case during World War II.

Perhaps most importantly, the war brought an increasing number of women into the public sphere as the organizers and operators of the numerous volunteer agencies that sought to assist in the war effort. Such bodies as the Patriotic Fund, the YWCA, and the Imperial Order Daughters of the Empire operated on both the local and the national levels and were organizations of considerable size and scope. This was important for the services the organizations provided, which filled a crucial gap in an era when government did not fully comprehend or accept the social burdens imposed by war. It was also important because the success of women, both in industry and in patriotic activities, did much to undermine Victorian stereotypes of women as weak and frail creatures.

None of this is to say that World War I revolutionized the role of women. At war's end, most industrial jobs would once again be reserved for men. Yet, change was occurring. The structural revolution in head offices meant than an increasing number of relatively well-educated women would be a growing presenee in the world of paid work. Second, the activities of women in the war, in wartime politics, and in longer-standing reform movements had won women the right to vote in national elections by 1918. The twentieth century was already eroding the rigid stereotypes that placed men in the "public sphere" and women in the "private" one.

The war also had significant effects upon labour. In the early years of the war, workers, glad for a job and imbued with patriotic fervour, had put aside long-standing grievances. By 1916–17, however, the rise of significant inflation, as well as the obvious wealth being acquired by some employers, brought considerable tension to labour-management relations. The government, determined to maintain production, showed little sympathy for workers' demands, while intemperate rhetoric on both sides inflamed matters.

This growing tension was most dramatic in the west. Western unionism had traditionally been somewhat more militant than its eastern counterpart and, by the end of World War I, it was considerably more so. Radical union leaders and social reformers saw the war as a critical juncture in history. Would the rhetoric of freedom and democracy apply to the home front or not? Such beliefs led to new experiments in unionism, including such syndicalist notions as the One Big Union that flourished briefly in the west in the postwar years. In a series of escalating clashes, unions across the region, and in the nation as a whole, confronted management. In 1919, in a number of general strikes, of which the one in Winnipeg was the most famous, they sought to demonstrate that they had the power to change the direction of Canadian society. They did not have that power, as it turned out, and most of the strikes were lost at great cost to the workers involved. In the wake of these events, the national mood of militancy declined, though individual pockets remained.

Related to this debate about the impact of war on class and sex roles is one about the impact of wartime manufacturing on regional economic activity in Canada. One school of thought argues that the government deliberately favoured the development of industrialization in the central provinces, especially at the expense of the west, which was supposed to grow wheat.[20] This view requires qualification. The vast war contracts of such bodies as the Imperial Munitions Board did go largely to Ontario and Quebec. Such firms as the Steel Company of Canada in Hamilton, the T.A. Russell Automobile Company of Toronto, the Dominion Bridge Company of Montreal, and branch plants such as Canadian Westinghouse, received the lion's share of contracts.[21] There is no evidence of any deliberate intent here. Cost-effective war production, not regional equity, was the goal of policy makers in this period. Thus, production tended to go to existing industries, and, as nearly eight out of ten prewar jobs in Canadian manufacturing were located in Ontario and Quebec, it is not surprising that these provinces got the great majority of the contracts. Indeed, there were times when deliberate searches were undertaken, on political grounds, for a western firm with which to do business.

Moreover, while the period from 1910 to 1921 did increase central Canada's share of total national manufacturing, it is hard to pinpoint the exact cause. It is impossible to say with any certainty that this was the result of the war itself, and even more difficult to claim it was the result of IMB war orders. Just as important was Ontario's ability to weather the postwar Depression. Moreover, the west saw an increase in manufacturing, as did central Canada. While not a great number of war contracts went to the west, manufacturing centres such as Winnipeg gained tremendously from the prosperous agricultural sector. Winnipeg was the third-largest city in the nation, and its population grew by more than 40 000 between 1911 and 1921. Overall, therefore, Manitoba in particular, and the west in general, saw its share of Canadian manufacturing employment grow in spite of the failure of the IMB to give the region what it felt to be its fair share of contracts.

The gains of the west and the centre were not shared by the Maritime provinces. Though the Maritimes saw an increase in the absolute gross value of production during the war, that growth was slight in absolute terms and did not prevent further erosion of the relative position of the region.[22] It is revealing, for example, that the region's share of national manufacturing employment dropped from 11 percent in 1910 to just over 6 percent by 1921. The absolute number of employees in this sector of the economy dropped by approximately 45 percent in ten years! This is especially important because the Maritimes' resource industries were mature, and significant new growth was not to be expected from them. Only manufacturing could provide the necessary growth, and it was not doing so.

Even this dramatic decline, however, cannot be attributed to the war with any certainty. As has already been discussed, the problems of Maritime manufacturing had already begun to show up during the previous boom. From 1880 to 1910, the real output of Maritime manufacturing had grown at only about 60 percent of the national rate.[23] Moreover, the worst was yet to come. Indeed, wartime activity may have slowed the decline, at least in some parts of the region. It is most likely that the deindustrialization of the Maritimes that was taking place was part of a longer-term trend and not specifically as a result of the war.

This leaves one other question: Was agriculture in the west led into destructive practices as a result of the temptations of the war? Specifically, three charges have been laid. The first is that wartime demands led the farmer to a dangerous reliance on wheat. The second is that the rise in debt that accompanied the farmers' search for short-term gains hurt them in the long run. The third is that the high prices in the later part of the decade meant that farmsteads were extended onto marginal lands that should never have been opened.

Of these, the first charge seems the least relevant. Western farmers had always been grain growers and, in spite of pleas from agricultural officials that they should turn to mixed farming, would have remained grain farmers, with or without the war. The increase in wheat during the war was, therefore, not a major step and could easily be reversed. Given that, the increase in wheat production was a rational response to high prices. The second point is true but not directly attributable to the war. Farmers were, indeed, heavily in debt at the end of the war but, as argued above, this response on their part would likely have taken place in any boom, given the experience of recent years.

The third point does have some merit, though it, too, is only partly attributable to the war. Western farms continued to increase in number through the war, and many farmers moved to areas that were marginal at best. Thousands of new homesteads were established, for example, in parts of the infamous Palliser's Triangle stretching through southeastern Alberta and southwestern Saskatchewan. The results were disastrous. From 1918 through 1921, the region experienced drought. Poor crops in the last year of the war only foreshadowed the disasters that were to come. In 1919, many areas in this region saw the entire crop wiped out. Through the early 1920s, farm abandonment replaced homesteading, foreshadowing the population exodus that would come in the Great Depression of the 1930s. In all of this, the war was to blame, but only in part. So, too, was the Canadian government, which, even before the war, had encouraged settlement of a region that should never have been settled.[24] With this important exception, however, the evidence that exists indicates that many long-standing assumptions about the impact of the war are, at best, only partly correct and often quite wrong.

The Role of Government

Perhaps the most dramatic impact of the war came in the fiscal arrangements of government. In the prewar era, the budgets of the Dominion government had certain striking characteristics. First, by any modern standard, they were minuscule. In 1913, the Dominion spent approximately $185 million, up sharply from the $136 million spent in 1911. Second, in spite of the grumbles that occasionally issued forth from British investors, overall Canadian debt was small. From 1900 on, the Dominion government regularly ran surpluses on operating accounts and, in spite of the heavy commitments to railways in recent years, the per-capita debt in Canada was lower in 1913 than it had been in the 1880s.[25]

Finally, government financing in the years before the war depended on very different taxation policies than those of governments of recent decades. The Dominion, in 1913, did not have, nor had it ever had, any corporate or personal income tax. What people or companies earned they kept. Instead, revenue came from indirect taxation — customs duties, and excise taxes or non-tax receipts, such as those of the post office. Of these, by far the most important were customs duties, which, as Figure 16.3 indicates, accounted for just a little less than two-thirds of all revenue. The heated debates that raged over tariff policy in the earlier years of the nation's history are more understandable, given this figure. Tariffs were the tax that most directly affected the average Canadian in the years before World War I.

The war began a revolution in government taxation. Initially, the Canadian government assumed that the war would be a short one, and it began its war effort with a modest $50 million appropriation, to be financed by some tariffs on luxury goods, some bor-

FIGURE 16.3

Sources of Dominion Government Revenue, 1912

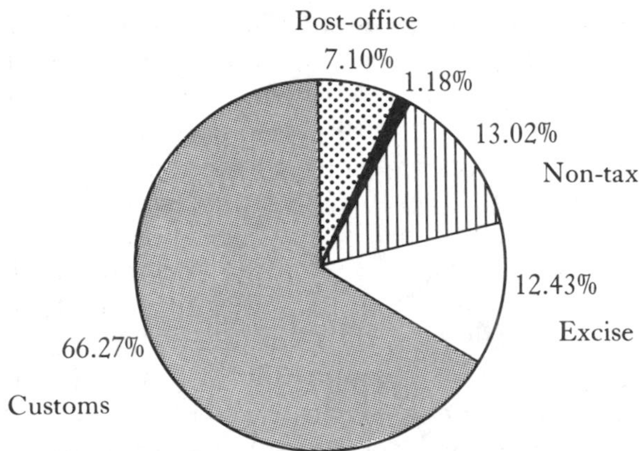

Source: M.C. Urquhart and K.A.H. Buckley, eds., *Historical Statistics of Canada* (Toronto: Macmillan, 1965), Series G1–25.

rowing in the British market, and an expansion of the money supply of the Dominion. The war was not short, however, and the $50 million did not fuel government defence expenditures even to the end of 1914. Soon, the government found itself spending on a completely unprecedented scale. Even in 1914, expenditures rose to $246 million. By 1917, they would be $574 million and, by their peak in 1919, $740 million. In just five years, the expenditures of the Dominion had quadrupled!

During much of the war, the government's position was that this additional expenditure should be financed largely through debt. This view was partly pragmatic, given the limited experiences with different types of taxation and the fear that the recession-mired economy of 1914–15 could not handle additional taxation. It was also partly philosophical. Finance minister Thomas White had this to say about it in 1916: "We are justified in placing upon posterity the greater portion of the financial burden of this war, waged as it is in the interests of human freedom, and in their benefit in equal if not in greater degree than our own."[26] Thus, government allowed the national debt to rise in order to handle war costs. By 1918, the net debt would nearly quadruple from its prewar figure, to $1.2 billion.

Debt has to be financed, however.[27] Traditionally, Canadians had looked abroad to wealthier and more developed pools of capital to handle their debt requirements. The railways and many of the other great projects of the Dominion had drawn their funds from the seemingly limitless British investment markets. Thus, in 1914, the Canadian government turned there once more, raising some $60 million soon after the war began. Inevitably, however, the British market was a limited source of war funding. It was not long before the British war effort absorbed all domestic capital. The Canadian government then looked to the second great capital market of the world — New York. A war loan for $45 million was first floated there in August 1915, and further loans would be floated throughout the duration of the war.

The greatest portion of borrowed funds came from a surprise source — Canada. No one had suspected that the savings of Canadians were sufficient to finance government borrowing needs on any great scale. After all, Canadian governments and Canadian entrepreneurs had looked abroad for funds ever since William Merritt had found that there was insufficient savings in Upper Canada to finance the Welland Canal. This idea had never really been challenged over the years. Indeed, Canadian governments had never tried to raise significant funds domestically. No bond issue in the history of the Dominion had been for more than $5 million.[28]

When war came, therefore, domestic loans were not seen as a meaningful source of funds. "The gross amount would be quite small," concluded White, in 1915, of any possible bond issue in Canada.[29] He was wrong. When the government did turn to the domestic bond market in 1915, White called for $50 million from the Canadian public — and subscribed $100 million! This set the pattern for the rest of the war, as issue after issue was floated and the Canadian public responded. By the time the war was over, Canadians had funded the vast war effort out of their own savings to the amount of $2 billion, ten times what had been secured abroad.

Though the majority of war costs were handled through borrowing, the government found itself under increased pressure, as time went on, to implement new taxes. In part, this was the result of the feeling that at least a portion of the costs should be borne out of current revenue. More important, however, were the building political forces. Many corporations and individuals had made considerable profits during the course of the war. As the sacrifices of the general public mounted, there was a growing cry to ensure that the burden of the war was distributed among all classes in society. New taxes aimed at the well-off could ensure at least a symbolic redistribution.

In response to growing fiscal and political demands, the government moved into direct taxation. In 1916, a business profits tax was introduced, with revisions the next year. Most important to the future fiscal management of the government and to future Canadian citizens was the imposition in 1917 of the Dominion Income War Tax. To say it was an important wartime measure makes sense only with the advantage of hindsight. At the time, it was seen neither as an important revenue-gatherer nor as a very onerous tax. Even by 1919, after the rates had been twice revised upwards, a married man making $2500 (a quite comfortable salary at the time) paid only $20 in income tax. The vast bulk of the population paid no tax at all (see Table 16.4). Finally, the government promised that this precedent of the income tax had been introduced only because of the dire necessities of war. Once the war was over the tax would be repealed.

Income tax was never repealed. The responsibilities and costs of the government could not be returned to prewar days. First of all, as the war had been financed largely through the use of debt, the government had to increase its revenue, at least to the point where it could handle the service charges on that new debt. By 1920, those debt charges had risen to $164 million. Second, there were other long-term costs associated with the war. The most important of these was the commitment to veterans in disability allowances, pensions, and other payments. Before the war, such payments had not even existed. By 1920, they had reached $76 million. Thus, debt service and pensions alone were greater than all government expenditures in 1913. The clock would never be turned back, though to do so remained a heartfelt yearning among certain politicians and civil servants of the 1920s and later.

There was one additional charge on the government that arose during the war years, though not directly from the war. The long-emerging crisis with the new railways came to a head by midwar and forced both a restructuring of much of Canada's railway system and a new commitment of government. Underlying this was the imminent collapse of the sprawling, debt-ridden Canadian Northern railway system and the increasing difficulties of its rival, the Grand

TABLE 16.4

Dominion Income War Tax Payable, 1917 and 1919

Income ($)	*1917* *Single*	*Married*	*1919* *Single*	*Married*
1 500	—	—	20	—
2 000	20	—	40	—
2 500	40	—	60	20
3 000	60	—	80	40
5 000	140	80	160	120
10 000	420	360	662	620
20 000	2520	2460	4127	4085

Source: R.C. Brown and G.R. Cook, *Canada, 1896–1921: A Nation Transformed* (Toronto: McClelland and Stewart, 1974), 232.

Trunk Pacific. In their bid for transcontinental status, both had spent recklessly and then had looked to governments, federal and provincial, to bail them out. The war only made matters worse as private money markets dried up. By 1916, the government grants, given with increasing reluctance, were the only things that prevented the railways from collapsing. In that same year, a royal commission was appointed to investigate the problem and, before long, the government was moving toward ownership of the railways.

Between the initial move and the final result, there was much agonized political discussion and much expenditure of money. How much should be paid in compensation to shareholders? Should the relatively healthy parent company of the Grand Trunk Pacific, the Grand Trunk, be taken over? (It was.) Were alternatives to outright government ownership possible? (They weren't.) In the end, there was no choice. The government simply could not allow these private companies to continue to return endlessly for more handouts. However, neither could the government allow them to collapse. Nationalization was the only answer and, in 1922, the new Canadian National Railway system was created.

The absence of any real freedom of choice is apparent in the basic numbers involved. For example, the Canadian Northern had, by 1916, amassed an amazing $104 million in loan guarantees from the Dominion government. Had it collapsed, the Dominion would have had to make good on that amount. Even more seriously, Ontario and the western provinces had also given guarantees. The largest amounts were from Manitoba and British Columbia, which had guaranteed $25.5 million and $40 million, respectively.[30] To put these numbers in perspective, either figure represented three to four years' current revenue for the province in question. To have let the Northern collapse would have endangered the solvency of at least two, and perhaps more, Canadian provinces; would have seriously hurt the finances of the Canadian government; and would likely have taken a national bank along for good measure. Small and medium-sized companies may be allowed to collapse with impunity. Those who are the biggest, and especially those who have the biggest debts, seem, throughout Canadian history, to have been rescued in one form or another. Thus, by the time the dust had settled, the Canadian government found itself the reluctant owner of more than 20 000 miles of railway lines.

Conclusion

The war brought important changes in the Canadian economy, changes that would last long beyond the war itself. The size and role of government had changed. Agriculture and manufacturing were both profoundly affected by the war and by postwar recessions. Regional shifts were taking place, and the long-term movement of the economy toward urbanization and industrialization continued. Yet, all this was but a small part of the effect of the war. The conflict had also killed 60 000 Canadians, and millions of combatants overall. It had also left the international financial and economic structure in a state of chaos. The question for the future was whether the international community would have the resiliency and the wisdom to reassert some long-term stability. For, as some at the time recognized, the war had unravelled the old economic system, but there was, as of 1920, no certainty as to what was being built on its ruins. What emerged would determine the economic future of Canada, as it would that of other nations.

Notes

1. Cited in R.C. Brown and G.R. Cook, *Canada, 1896–1921: A Nation Transformed* (Toronto: McClelland and Stewart, 1974), 198.
2. Donald G. Paterson, *British Direct Investment in Canada, 1890–1914* (Toronto: University of Toronto Press, 1976), 26.
3. M.C. Urquhart, "Canadian Economic Growth 1870–1980," Queen's University, Department of Economics, Discussion Paper No. 734, 28.
4. M.C. Urquhart, "New Estimates of Gross National Product, Canada, 1870–1926: Some Implications for Canadian Economic Development," *Factors in American Economic Growth*, edited by Stanley L. Engerman and Robert E. Gallman (Chicago: University of Chicago Press, 1987), Table 2.11.
5. The process by which a financial inflow such as that experienced by Canada in this period is transformed into a new inflow of real goods and services is known as "the transfer problem." Keynes addressed it in his study of German separation payments, and Jacob Viner's study of the process in Canada between 1900 and 1913 is one of the most famous early works by a Canadian economist. See Jacob Viner, *Canada's Balance of International Indebtedness, 1900–1913* (Cambridge, MA. Harvard University Press, 1924).
6. Michael Bliss, *Northern Enterprise: Five Centuries of Canadian Business* (Toronto: McClelland and Stewart, 1987), 328.
7. Statistics Canada, *Historical Statistics of Canada*, 2nd ed. (Ottawa, Supply and Services, 1983), Tables G34–46.
8. Cited in Brown and Cook, *Canada, 1896–1921*, 234.
9. The following paragraphs on the IMB are drawn from Michael Bliss, *The Life and Times of Sir Joseph Flavelle* (Toronto: Macmillan, 1979).
10. Ian Drummond, *Progress Without Planning: The Economic History of Ontario from Confederation to the Second World War* (Toronto: University of Toronto Press, 1987), Appendix, Table 9.1.
11. Brown and Cook, *Canada, 1896–1921*, 240.
12. David J. Bercuson, *Confrontation at Winnipeg* (Montreal and Kingston, McGill-Queen's University Press, 1974), 26.
13. Urquhart, "New Estimates," Table 21.
14. John Thompson, *The Harvests of War: The Prairie West, 1914–1918* (Toronto: McClelland and Stewart, 1978), 61.
15. P. Voisey, *Vulcan: The Making of a Prairie Community* (Toronto: University of Toronto Press, 1988), 40.
16. Drummond, *Progress Without Planning*, 291.
17. These figures from Drummond, *Progress Without Planning*, 41.
18. Donald Creighton, *Canada's First Century* (Toronto: Macmillan, 1970), 136.
19. Graham Lowe, *Women in the Administrative Revolution* (Toronto: University of Toronto Press, 1987).
20. Thompson, *Harvests of War*, 59–72.
21. Bliss, *Flavelle*, 259–83.
22. David Alexander, "Economic Growth in the Atlantic Region, 1880–1940," in *Atlantic Canada After Confederation*, The Acadiensis Reader, Vol. 2, edited

by P.A Buckner and David Frank (Fredericton: Acadiensis Press, 1985), 146–75.

23. David Alexander, "Economic Growth in the Atlantic Region," Tables 6 and 7.
24. See David Jones, *Empire of Dust: Settling and Abandoning the Prairie Dry Belt* (Edmonton: University of Alberta Press, 1987).
25. The provinces and municipalities were accumulating greater debt loads, however. See Royal Commission on Dominion-Provincial Relations, *Report*, Book I: *Canada, 1867–1939*, 81–82.
26. Brown and Cook, *Canada, 1896–1921*, 230.
27. The material on war finance is drawn from Brown and Cook, *Canada, 1896–1921*, Chapter 11; R. Bothwell, I. Drummond, and J. English, *Canada, 1900–1945* (Toronto: University of Toronto Press, 1989); J. Deutsch, "War Finance and the Canadian Economy," *Canadian Journal of Economics and Political Science* 6, no. 4 (1940): 525–42; and F.A. Knox, "Canadian War Finance and the Balance of Payments," *Canadian Journal of Economics and Political Science* 6, no. 4 (1940).
28. Deutsch, "War Finance and the Canadian Economy," 527.
29. Brown and Cook, *Canada, 1896–1921*, 231.
30. These figures are taken from John Eagle, "Sir Robert Borden and the Railway Problem 1911–1920," Ph.D. thesis, University of Toronto, 1972, p. 9.

Further Reading

Alexander, David. "Economic Growth in the Atlantic Region, 1880–1940." In *Atlantic Canada After Confederation*, The Acadiensis Reader, Vol 2, edited by P.A. Buckner and David Frank. Fredericton: Acadiensis Press, 1985.

Brown, R.C.; and G.R. Cook. *Canada, 1896–1921: A Nation Transformed.* Toronto: McClelland and Stewart, 1974.

Deutsch, J. "War Finance and the Canadian Economy." *Canadian Journal of Economics and Political Science* 6, no. 4 (1940): 525–42.

Drummond, Ian. *Progress Without Planning: An Economic History of Ontario from Confederation to the Second World War*. Toronto: University of Toronto Press, 1987.

Lowe, Graham. *Women in the Administrative Revolution*. Toronto: University of Toronto Press, 1987.

Thompson, J. *The Harvests of War: The Prairie West, 1914–1918*. Toronto: McClelland and Stewart, 1978.

CHAPTER

17

Uneven Growth, 1922–1929

The decade of the 1920s has always posed a problem to those seeking to describe it historically. Until recently, there has been no clear overall picture of these years. They remained a sort of no-man's-land, sandwiched between the much-studied World War I and the equally interesting Great Depression. The result was a series of contradictory popular images. On the one hand, there was the model of gaiety summed up in the phrase "The Roaring Twenties." Images appropriated from American popular culture were easily transferred to the Canadian landscape — flappers, model-T Fords, and prohibition moderated by bathtub gin. On the other hand, there were contradictory images of a nation torn apart by regional, political, and class grievances. New political parties formed and faded. Economic prosperity seemed uneven and uncertain. Moreover, the regional and other divisions made it difficult to talk of a "Canadian experience" through these years. The image of the 1920s remained obscure and confusing.

In part, this confusion mirrored reality. The 1920s were a fragmented decade, confusing in its complexity and denying easy categorization. For one thing, it was sharply divided chronologically. Canada began these years with the sharp recession of 1921, and growth remained slow throughout much of the country until mid-decade. Then, all seemed to change, as confidence returned and Canadians embarked on an investment and consumption spree that echoed, at least faintly, the heady days of the prewar boom. The boom came faster to some areas than to others; in some parts of the country, it never came at all. Some industries, such as coal mining, were in trouble throughout the period, wherever located, while others, such as automobile manufacturing, grew at an amazing rate. Some, such as the steel industry, seemed divided within themselves; Stelco recovered well from the 1921 recession, while such firms as the British Empire Steel Company (BESCO) and Algoma struggled.

The confusing image may also be the result of changes in patterns of growth in the economy that were not fully understood at the time. Agriculture, and the related theme of western settlement, had been the underlying forces shaping the economy for a generation. In absolute terms, agriculture would continue to be important in the 1920s, but the great infilling of the prairies was largely complete; as a result, the growth of the agricultural sector as a whole slowed.

The question was what would replace it as an "engine of growth," and there were various possible answers. Other primary sources and primary-resource industries grew rapidly in the decade. So, too, did manufacturing, which continued the rise to the prominence that had been a feature of previous decades. Finally, there was the relatively new and still-emerging importance of the tertiary sector, which would be the fastest-growing one during the decade. Employment in such areas as transportation and trade increased by some 250 percent from 1901 to 1931.[1] Related to this development was continued urbanization. In this decade, Canada became more urban than rural; it was also a time when the larger urban centres took a more prominent role than ever in directing the economy of the nation as a whole.

All of these things meant that the nineteenth-century strategy that had emphasized an east-west flow of manufactures from the centre to a resource-based hinterland seemed, to the degree it had ever been fully accepted, increasingly outmoded. National economies seemed to have broken down into regional ones, just as national political parties were increasingly challenged by regionally based movements.

Sectoral, regional, and chronological fragmentation thus marked the decade and explains much of the confused imagery that surrounds it. Yet, it is possible to delineate certain crucial elements that shaped these events and give at least a modicum of unity to any discussion of the decade. In particular, this was an era of international instability, American economic power, and new technologies, particularly in consumer goods. These three forces, in turn, provide a means by which this complex decade can be comprehended.

International Instability

As we indicated in the introduction to Part V, the challenge that faced the world after 1918 was simple in conception, if tremendously complex in implementation. The international system required that the United States employ its tremendous economic might to restore some sort of stability to the international trading and financial systems. In particular, it was crucial that the economies of Europe be restored as quickly as possible and that American international investment replace the declining presence of British capital. Distinct from but related to this issue was the necessity of establishing international monetary stability, either by a return to the gold standard or by some other method.[2]

The challenge was not met. The American economy, with a large and wealthy internal market, had less need for the world than the world had for the Americans, at least in the short run. The United States felt free to pursue what it saw as national self-interest without fully accepting the burden that came with being the richest nation in the world. Nor were Europeans immune from short-sightedness, as they, too, sought quick solutions to dangerous problems. As a result, political decisions intervened to make matters more rather than less difficult. First, there was the question of reparations; second, there was the problem of interallied war debts.

Reparations were a plan to make Germany pay for at least a portion of Allied war costs. They followed from the position taken by the Allies at the peace conference that Germany was morally responsible for the war. The plan was based on appealing but ultimately simplistic logic. The guilty should be punished, and the punishment could assist war-shattered economies, while enabling Allied governments to avoid implementing excessively high taxes. Moreover, and especially important to war-ravaged France, the continual drain on Germany's financial strength would hinder any attempts by the country to regain great-power status. In pursuit of these aims, the Allies had demanded and received a £1 billion interim payment during the initial peace negotiations. Then, in 1921, the Allies presented a bill to Germany for £6.5 billion worth of goods and services, to be paid in regular instalments over the next decades.

Not only the losers would have to pay, however. Britain and France had borrowed massively in order to finance their own war effort. The U.S. treasury alone had lent the two countries some $7.7 billion. Now, as the United States recoiled from its involvement in European affairs, it was politically popular in that country to take a hard line and demand repayment. The Allies protested that such repayments should be forgiven as another American contribution to the war effort, since the United States had joined so late, and pointed out, further, that such a drain on Western Europe would only hinder the restoration of economic stability. The Americans were not impressed and continued to push for repayment.

The issues of reparations and war debts were related. The American insistence on Allied repayment made German reparation payments crucial to the Allies. In effect, Allied debtors hoped to avoid undue strain on their own economies by using a portion of German reparation payments to mollify the Americans. German payments would flow to France and Britain, and then to the United States. Americans would then, presumably, invest overseas to strengthen the international community.

There were several flaws in this scheme. For one thing, the German economy and economic will were not up to bearing the burden of reparations in the immediate postwar period. The entire German monetary system collapsed soon after reparations were begun. Hyperinflation in 1921–22 made the Deutschmark worthless and forced the Allies, led by the Americans, to slow down reparation payments to something approaching a bearable rate. Second, American investment did not flow abroad, in either the direction or the amount that would have allowed it to assume the role taken by British capital before the war. Thus, throughout the first part of the decade, the international financial community remained in considerable turmoil. Financial systems that should have contributed to the recovery of international trade served only to disrupt it further.

By the mid-1920s, there was some stabilization. The American Dawes plan, which combined rescheduled reparation payments with American loans to Germany, helped. Moreover, Britain and other nations began to return to the gold standard through the middle of the decade. Finally, European nations were recovering a degree of equilibrium and were thus able to resume international trade on a greater scale than before.

For all these improvements, international finance was in a precarious state. There were too many points of instability. The British resumption of the gold standard, for example, had been at prewar values. Yet, relative to the prewar world, Britain was in a weaker economic position. A highly priced currency (against gold) did not reflect the reality of demand for the British pound. Conversely, the American dollar remained undervalued, and American investment abroad never matched the huge current-account surplus in that nation's international accounts, a surplus made worse by American protectionism. America's foreign-exchange reserves piled up, and the international monetary system became more imbalanced.

Volatility thus marked the international financial system in these years. Canada was not immune. It had, more than most, depended on British capital and on the stability of British financial institutions. It, too, experienced a series of shocks to its financial system, including the movement off the gold standard in 1914, inflation in the period from 1916 to 1920, and then massive recession. The decade thus began with a severe challenge to the strength of the Canadian monetary and financial structures.

Banking and monetary policy in Canada at the end of the war were fairly straightforward. There was no central bank and, until 1914, Canada had operated under the gold standard. This, along with the strength of the British pound, had provided a stable climate for monetary operations, and the government had had little to do with banking except to regulate the rules under which the chartered banks operated by means of the Bank Act, which was revised every decade. Banks were largely self-policing, however. There was, for example, no equivalent of the modern superintendent of financial institutions. Though the war had forced Canada off the gold standard, the banks had continued to operate with a significant degree of independence. Both banks and the Dominion could issue notes and, with the war over, the banks were largely left alone to handle the provision of credit in the nation.[3]

The shocks of the war and postwar years revealed some of the weaknesses of the traditional system. Some of Canada's financial institutions, it turned out, were not as sound as had been thought. Most serious was the 1923 failure of the Home Bank. Unexpectedly, 71 branches closed their doors and announced to shocked customers that they would not be able to get their money out. In addition, the Bank of Hamilton, the Bank of Ottawa, and the Merchants Bank, among others, sought mergers to avoid collapse or were taken over by larger institutions to restore confidence in institutions that were no longer able to compete. The public became increasingly nervous with each merger, revelation, and news story. More and more deposits concentrated in the hands of the largest banks — the ones thought safest. By 1928, as Michael Bliss notes, the "Montreal, the Commerce, and the Royal [banks], controlled 70 per cent of the banking assets in one country."[4]

The banking system is but one example — if a high-profile one — of the way in which the decade's volatile international and domestic circumstances affected the business and financial community in Canada. New technologies, shifting demand in resources, rapidly changing world conditions, and the shift from wartime to postwar demand — all brought change. Old and familiar firms disappeared, while brash newcomers assumed importance. Old sectors of the economy remained stagnant or collapsed, while new industries multiplied. To understand the course that these events took it is necessary to look at the other major forces shaping the Canadian economy.

The New Resources and the American Market

Of all the international circumstances that affected Canada, perhaps the most important was the economic power of the United States. For Canadian businessmen and investors, this was the overriding reality of the decade. The vast, prosperous, and growing American market was essential to any country that depended on exports; it was especially crucial to Canada, which had long depended on trade with the international community, in general, and with its American neighbour, in particular. Moreover, given the relative decline in availability of British capital flows, Canadian development would need alternate sources of investment. Now, the Americans had the vast savings, and it was, thus, American inflows of capital that would shape economic development. American markets and American investment would have a significant effect in determining what sectors of the Canadian economy prospered over the coming years.

The importance of the United States to Canadian economic development can be seen even in the most general figures. Britain's declining role in the Canadian economy is equally apparent. In terms of imports into Canada, for example, Britain had been undergoing long-term decline. The war accelerated that decline, and imports from Britain dropped to a low of 8 percent of the Canadian total by 1919. That figure was artificially low, of course, and the British did regain some of the market. Never again, however, would it account for even 20 percent of Canadian imports. In contrast, by the 1920s, approximately two-thirds of all imports came from south of the border (see Figure 17.1).

Canada's orientation toward American imports has always been balanced by its orientation toward Britain as an export market. By the 1920s, however, the Americans were also becoming Canada's most important destination for exports. In 1923, for the first time in history, Canada exported more to the United States than to Great Britain. The two would alternate positions as export receivers over the next few years, but the trend was clear. After declining to a low of $292.6 million in 1922, Canadian exports to the United States rose, until, by 1928, they reached $478 million and accounted for nearly 40 percent of all Canadian exports (see Figure 17.2). The United States was by far Canada's most important trading partner by the end of the decade.

Patterns of international investment in Canada are even more revealing. As Table 17.1 indicates, as late as 1914 British investment accounted for more than 70 percent of total foreign funds coming into the country. The war changed all that. Britain fell into debt, while the United States found its international financial position strengthened. In just nine years, British investment fell to less than 46 percent of the total, while American capital imports went to 51 percent. Never again would the mother country come close to the United States in its investment in Canada.

This American investment was different in character than that from Britain. The British had favoured bonds that gave them a relatively stable rate of return but conferred no direct control of the company. American investors were interested in equity investment — that is, in common shares — and with American money, therefore, often came American control. Indeed, much of the American investment in the years after the war was involved in the setting up of branch plants. The Canadian tariff made it attractive for American companies to establish in Canada in order to avoid the tariff.

Over the longer term, the branch-plant phenomenon would become a contentious political issue in Canada. There is a danger, however, of projecting post–World War II concerns with American

FIGURE 17.1

Imports from the United States and Britain, 1891–1929, as a Percentage of Total Imports

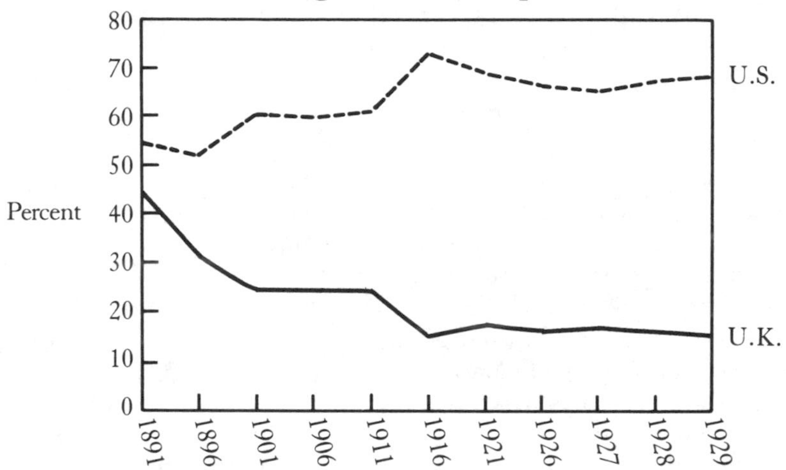

Source: Derived from Statistics Canada, *Historical Statistics of Canada*, 2nd ed. (Ottawa: Supply and Services, 1983), Series F342–47.

investment into this earlier era. All American investment, whether in bonds or shares, or in the establishment of new branch plants, was considered desirable. Canada's primary concern, as in earlier years, was to ensure that jobs were created in Canada rather than in the United States for the processing of Canada's exports. Moreover, given the inability of British capital to continue its role as Canada's main banker, the American funds were a much-needed replacement. Without them, Canada's rate of growth would have been much slower in the postwar decade.

Certain sectors of the Canadian economy were more favoured than others by American customers and capitalists who found goods or opportunities in Canada that could not be matched south of the border. By examining those areas that did or did not appeal to Americans in these years, it becomes easier to comprehend the mixed pattern of growth and stagnation that characterized the 1920s.

What Americans seemed to want from Canada more than anything else in this period was pulp and paper. As was shown in Part

FIGURE 17.2

Exports from Canada to the United States and Britain, 1891–1929, as a Percentage of Total Exports

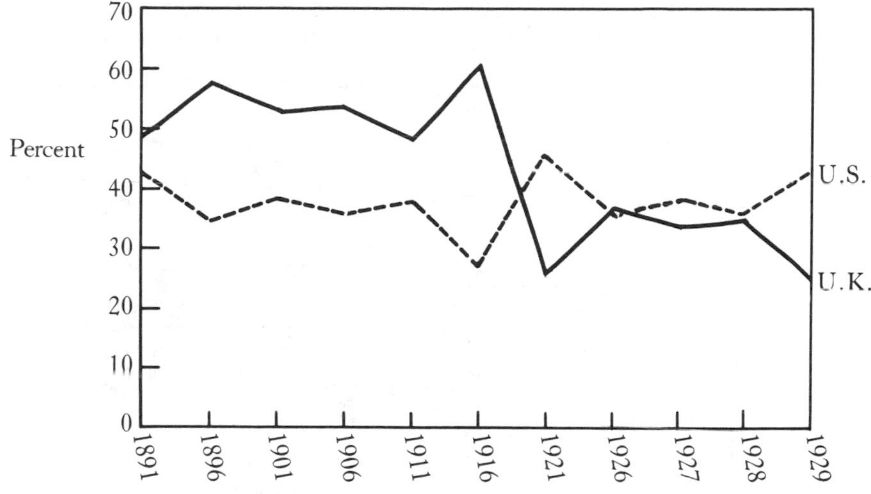

Source: Derived from Statistics Canada, *Historical Statistics of Canada*, 2nd ed. (Ottawa: Supply and Services, 1983), Series F334–41.

IV, the increase in the size and readership of newspapers helped expand the demand for pulp and paper. Canada, it was also shown, was well situated to take advantage of the demand because of its large supply and because the American Underwood tariff lowered duties on Canadian paper exports to the United States. The results were dramatic. American newsprint production remained more or less constant between 1913 and 1919, while Canadian production more than doubled, to more than 840 million tons.

The recession of 1921 slowed growth only temporarily, for the American demand for newsprint seemed insatiable. By 1929, the 61 million newspapers read at the end of the war had increased to 93 million.[5] Canada supplied the demand. Through the 1920s, some $356 million was invested in the industry — the largest investment in any of the primary-resource industries. Jobs increased to more than 30 000, and Canadian output of newsprint tripled between 1920 and 1929. That was a sixfold increase from 1914. Can-

TABLE 17.1

British and American Investment in Canada, 1910–1930

Year	*($ millions)*		*(% of total investment)*	
	U.S.	*U.K.*	*U.S.*	*U.K.*
1910	487	1958	19	77
1911	563	2203	20	77
1912	645	2417	20	76
1913	780	2793	21	75
1914	881	2778	23	72
1915	1070	2772	27	69
1916	1307	2840	30	66
1917	1577	2739	35	61
1918	1630	2729	36	60
1919	1818	2645	39	57
1920	2128	2577	44	53
1921	2260	2494	46	51
1922	2593	2464	50	47
1923	2794	2471	52	46
1924	3094	2372	55	42
1925	3219	2346	56	41
1926	3465	2355	58	40
1930	4660	2637	61	36

Source: Statistics Canada, *Historical Statistics of Canada*, 2nd ed. (Ottawa: Supply and Services, 1983), Series G188–202.

ada produced more than twice as much newsprint as the United States and was the world's largest papermaker (see Table 17.2). The importance of the American market can be seen in the fact that 80 percent of this massive production went south of the border.

Not surprisingly, an industry of this much interest to the United States was, in a significant degree, developed with the aid of American capital. Entrepreneurs south of the border were quick to recognize the rising demand for newsprint in their own country and the possibilities of Canadian stands of timber. Thus, for example, the Brooks-Scanlon Company, based in Minnesota, established the

TABLE 17.2
Newsprint Production, 1913–1930

(millions of tons)

Year	*Canada*	*United States*
1913	402	1305
1914	470	1313
1915	549	1239
1916	662	1315
1917	726	1359
1918	770	1260
1919	841	1324
1920	938	1512
1921	849	1225
1922	1142	1448
1923	1315	1485
1924	1453	1481
1925	1633	1530
1926	2075	1684
1927	2286	1485
1928	2645	1417
1929	2981	1392
1930	2985	1282

Source: Trevor Dick. "Canadian Newsprint, 1913–1930: National Policies and the North American Economy," *Journal of Economic History* 42, no. 3 (1982): 678.

first successful paper mill in British Columbia. In Ontario, Quebec, and New Brunswick, Canadian mills already existed, but American funds flowed north into the expansion or reorganization of existing ventures or in the creation of new ones.

Another area dependent on American demand and American investment was mining, especially of such nonferrous products as gold, nickel, asbestos, and copper. New consumer products, such as the automobile, and new technologies, such as electricity, were all growth industries, and so too were the products that they contained. In this way, asbestos in brake linings, nickel and zinc in automobiles, and copper wiring in the new electrical devices on the market fuelled the mining industry.

As was the case for pulp and paper, the major part of this growth was the result of international demand, especially from the United States. In some cases, such as asbestos, practically all the product went south. In others, there was a greater demand in Canada; in all cases where strong growth occurred, the international market was crucial. In some cases, the growth in this international market was spectacular. Thus, for example, the value of zinc exports more than quintupled. Those of nickel also quintupled, in spite of the absence of armament production. Gypsum exports tripled between 1918 and 1929 and were practically unaffected by the recession of the early 1920s. Of course, not all minerals exhibited such dramatic increases, but the overall impact was a sharp increase in the exports of a crucial sector of the economy.

At the same time, it is important to note that the growth of the 1920s, whatever its peculiar characteristics, was part of a longer cycle in mining. The boom had begun in 1900 and had continued until 1930. Before that time, only gold and coal had been of importance in Canadian mineral production. By the end of the 1920s, things had changed. Coal was still important, but was not growing in value. Gold was experiencing such growth, however, and had been joined, in descending order of importance, by copper, nickel, lead, silver, asbestos, and zinc. The mining industry, which had been centred in the Yukon and British Columbia, was now important in several provinces, foremost in Ontario. Total mineral production of $64.4 million in 1900 had grown to $307.1 million by 1929.

Domestic Demand: Consumers and the New Technologies

In some instances, dramatic growth was fuelled by domestic demand. The 1920s were an era in which technologies developed in the prewar years became more practical in design and more widespread in use. This application, both in industry and in consumer durables, revolutionized the way of life of Canadians and provided the decade with some of its most important growth.

Looking back at the postwar period, Canada's senior political economist, Harold Innis, would characterize this era as one in which, above all else, new sources of power replaced old. Specifically, it was during this period, he argued, that coal and steam, which had powered the industrial revolution, were being replaced by electricity. Certainly, if one is looking at the new technologies of the postwar period, electricity is the place to begin.

Of course, as has been indicated, electricity had been around for some time; by World War I, considerable progress had been made in the development of practical applications of electricity in street lighting and industry. Important though the prewar period was in terms of the application of electricity, in the 1920s electricity became a common source of power, both in the home and in the factory. For the urban, middle-class consumer, electricity provided new comforts, ranging from reliable evening light to refrigerators, radios, and electric stoves. These comforts spawned new industries, some sizable and some quite small. The important point, however, is that all of them were new technologies and, therefore, their development represented the growth of new opportunities. The shipment of radios, for example, grew from 18 531 in 1925 (the first year for which statistics are available) to more than 170 000 by 1930.

Moreover, the production of electricity was itself a major source of capital development. The prewar period brought about a significant rationalization of the earlier combinations of private and municipal generating companies. The growth in demand that had permitted those steps, however, was nothing compared to that in the twelve years after World War I. Between 1919 and 1930, the amount of electricity generated by Canadian utilities rose from 5.5 million to 19.5 million kilowatt hours. Such growth required a tremendous increase in generating capacity and, thus, the construction of electricity-generation facilities became a major source of economic growth in the decade. The development of electric-power stations created capital investment of some $690 million, an amount greater than that invested in the entire primary sector during the same period.[6]

For all its importance, electricity and its products were overshadowed by another technology — the automobile. Before the war, the automobile had been a curiosity, its market confined to the adventurous and the very wealthy. In 1911, for example, there was one automobile in Canada for every 335 people. In the 1920s, however, the automobile became part of Canadian life. Increasingly efficient production systems and basic designs pioneered by such firms as Ford began to make the automobile affordable to larger

National Archives of Canada/PA-55051

Traffic jam, 1923. *In the 1920s, the automobile became a part of Canadian life, necessitating many changes to the traffic laws. In 1918, some 275 000 automobiles were registered in Canada; by 1923, that number had more than doubled, in spite of recession; by 1929, it had risen to nearly 1.9 million.*

segments of the public. The Canadian public responded with enthusiasm. In a large nation with a thinly spread population and a cold climate, efficient transportation had always been in demand. The automobile was the latest in a line of advances that went back to canals, steamboats, and primitive pioneer roads. In 1918, some 275 000 automobiles were registered in Canada. By 1923, that number had more than doubled, in spite of recession; by 1929, it had risen to nearly 1.9 million (see Table 17.3).[7]

This sort of increase made automobiles one of Canada's major growth industries through the 1920s. Of course, some automobiles were imported, but, generally, the Canadian automotive business was competitive internationally, with 30 percent of production going overseas by 1928.[8] To meet domestic and foreign demand, more than a quarter-million automobiles a year were made in Canada

TABLE 17.3

Automobile Production and Registrations, 1917–1929

Year	*Production*	*Registrations*
1917	93 810	197 799
1918	82 408	275 746
1919	87 835	341 316
1920	94 144	407 064
1921	66 246	465 378
1922	101 007	513 821
1923	147 202	585 050
1924	132 580	652 121
1925	161 970	728 005
1926	204 727	836 794
1927	179 054	945 672
1928	242 054	1 010 664
1929	262 265	1 888 929

Source: T. Traves, *The State and Enterprise: Canadian Manufacturers and the Federal Government, 1917–1931* (Toronto: University of Toronto Press, 1979), 102.

by the latter part of the decade. Automobile assembly was only a part of the story. Auto parts and services, gas stations, and the improvement of roads to accommodate the automobiles provided jobs. The capital expenditure on highways alone was greater than that in mining. Nearly 15 000 men and women were employed by auto or auto-parts producers by the end of the decade. As one business magazine said at the time, "If the production value of the plants producing automobile supplies, tires and refined petroleum be added to that of the automobile industry proper, the total considerably exceeds that of any other industry."[9]

The automobile revolutionized individual travel and living habits. It provided people with a new, convenient, and rapid form of transportation from door to door. Though its effects were not fully apparent until after World War II, the automobile would forever change the layout of cities, separating home from work to a greater degree than the street railway ever could. It would allow the farmer to by-pass the local corner store for the larger centre and give the salesman from the city quicker access to the byways of the country. Already, in the 1920s, commercial trucks were becoming important to deliveries and transport, challenging both the horse-drawn carriage and the railway. By 1928, there were more than 130 000 commercial vehicles registered in Canada.[10] Like the railway in the nineteenth century, the automobile would eventually become an essential part of the lives of Canadians. Even in the 1920s, the love affair was apparent. Canada had a greater number of passenger cars per capita than any country in the world, except the United States.

The impact of the automobile was, however, uneven. Regional inequities existed as a result of income disparities, need, and the availability of roads. Ontario was, by far, the most motorized province by the end of the decade, with nearly 47 percent of all automobile registrations. It was also the province with the greatest hard-surface road mileage, outside of major cities. The first intercity concrete highway had been completed between Toronto and Hamilton in 1915; by 1928, there were some 5374 miles of concrete or macadamized roads in the province. Of the other provinces, only Quebec, with 1822 miles, and British Columbia, with 347, had any significant hard-surface roads at all. Cars and trucks were popular on the prairies, however. Level terrain made gravel or dirt roads relatively easy to build and maintain, and the vast distances made efficient transportation essential. Motorized vehicles were also quickly incorporated into farming to make transportation more efficient. Saskatchewan had just as many motor vehicles per capita as Ontario and 50 percent more than the Canadian average.

The automobile industry grew as a result of domestic demand, which would seem to make it distinct from those resource industries that depended on the United States. Yet, even in this industry, the United States was important. The automobile was, after all, a technology that first became a mass-market phenomenon in the United States. That combination of technology and marketing was, to a large degree, what shaped the automobile industry in Canada after World War I. During that decade, the independent Canadian automobile industry disappeared, to be replaced by branch plants of the giant American corporations.

As with many other new technologies, the automobile was initially made by a variety of small firms in both Canada and the United States. New businesses, former carriage-makers, and others got involved in turning out this new transportation novelty in the

Courtesy of Ford of Canada Archives

Mechanized assembly line, 1914. *The Ford Motor Company was the first to adapt the assembly line to the auto industry. Ford entered the Canadian auto market by taking over the MacGregor Company, and, in 1913, was turning out more cars than any other factory in the British Empire. The Brooks Automobile Company produced the last distinctively Canadian automobile in the mid-1920s, but, in 1927, it ceased production.*

prewar years. Not-so-famous lines such as the Fossmobile, the London Six, the Redpath, the Russell, and the Everitt were all produced in Canada by Canadian manufacturers in the early years. As the automobile moved from novelty to mass market, however, low costs of production were essential. That could be accomplished only with a good design and with a large-scale plant. Mass advertising by larger companies ensured that people gravitated toward better-known names while forsaking the lesser-known ones.

By the end of World War I, the process of consolidation was well underway. Smaller firms fell by the wayside or were taken over by larger ones. This was a process common both to Canada and to the United States, but the harsh reality in Canada was that the smaller firms tended to be Canadian, the larger ones American. Successful U.S. firms such as Ford had both the money and the technology to out-perform smaller Canadian firms. Ford took over the MacGregor Company and was, by 1913, producing more cars than any other factory in the British Empire.[11] General Motors took over McLaughlin of Oshawa, while other companies folded. By the mid-1920s, the Brooks Automobile Company produced the last distinctive Canadian automobile. Both its method of locomotion — it was steam-powered — and its price — nearly eight times the price of a Model T — indicated its limited future. It ceased production in 1927 and, henceforth, the Canadian automobile industry would be a branch-plant operation.

Regional Characteristics

The key sectors of growth that have been discussed, whether fuelled by domestic demand and American capital or by American demand and American capital, whether primary-resource or advanced technologies, had one common characteristic — they were unevenly distributed around Canada. Practically every automobile produced in Canada in 1927, for example, was produced in Ontario. Ninety-eight percent of pulp-and-paper production occurred in New Brunswick, Quebec, Ontario, and British Columbia — 94 percent in just Quebec and Ontario. Eighty percent of sawmills, an industry feeding the construction boom on both sides of the border, were located in Quebec, Ontario, and British Columbia. Nearly 75 percent of all electric stations were located in Ontario and Quebec; and 83 percent of all mineral production was located in Quebec, Ontario, and British Columbia.

What of the other regions — the Prairies and the Maritimes? For both, the decade was one of frustrated expectations and of resulting political protest. In the west, the story was not one of absolute decline but of a volatile economy and slower rates of growth than had been experienced in past decades.

There were several reasons for this. For years, the western wheat boom had driven the Canadian export economy. Wheat exports had grown from a little under 10 million bushels in 1901 to just short of 46 million bushels by 1911, and to an amazing 157 million bushels by 1916. Wheat and flour were Canada's most important exports, and Canada accounted for nearly 20 percent of all international exports in wheat by World War I; wheat and wheat products, in turn, accounted for a third of all Canadian exports. Further, as has been discussed, the booming wheat economy created other areas of growth, as capital development in the region sought to keep up with the growth of agriculture.

What the war had masked, however, was the fact that the 1913 recession had marked the end of the feverish period of prairie agricultural growth and, with it, large-scale investment in the region. During the war and postwar periods, the west had gone through boom and slump, and it would again. Nevertheless, the period of rapid frontier growth was coming to an end, and the expansion of the prairie wheat economy was no longer the central dynamic of Canadian economic growth.

In fact, the 1920s were not particularly good years for agriculture. As was noted in Chapter 16, the prairies were severely hit by the 1921 recession. For the next few years, low prices or low yields slowed recovery. It would be the middle of the decade before the value of wheat production returned to 1920 levels. The same was true of all other principal field crops in the region. For the Prairie west, the difficulties of this sector were all important. Only in Manitoba did agriculture account for less than an absolute majority of the provincial net value of production and, even there, at 49.5 percent, it was by far the largest sector of the economy. In Alberta (69.8%) and Saskatchewan (85.2%), nothing else was even significant.[12]

Also important is the fact that changing world conditions and more restrictive Canadian immigration policies meant that the inflow of immigrants was much slower than it had been before the war. In 1913, Canada had taken in a record 402 000 immigrants. In contrast, in no year in the 1920s did the country take in even 40 percent of that number. In the ten years before the Great War, Canada had taken in more than 1.9 million people. In contrast, between 1919 and 1928, inclusive, some 1.1 million arrived, and a much smaller percentage of those went west than had before the war.

The result was regional stagnation in the early years of the decade. Gross agricultural wealth in all three Prairie provinces remained below 1920 figures well into the decade. There was an increase in population — this was still an area with open land available — but, between 1921 and 1926, the Prairie provinces experienced no relative population growth. Manitoba actually saw its share of

Canadian population decrease marginally, as it did its share of gross value of production. This was a dramatic downturn for a region that, since the late 1890s, had been the fastest-growing part of the country in terms of both population and output.

None of this was easily accepted in the west. The region felt increasingly estranged from a political system that, westerners believed, spent too much time catering to tariff-protected central Canadian manufacturers. The resentment exploded, and the Prairie provinces formed the core support for a new third-party movement known as the Progressives. Electing 55 MPs in 1921, the Progressives were a clear reflection of the west's unwillingness to accept readily the end of the great era of agriculture in Canadian economic development.

The party did not last and, by 1926, it was much weakened as voters returned to traditional parties in large numbers. There were many reasons for the decline of the Progressives but one of them had to do with changing economic circumstances in the west. In 1925, the average price of wheat had gone over $1 a bushel for the first time since 1920 while the total crop had been a respectable 395 million bushels. The next year, prices slid somewhat, though remaining above $1 a bushel, but yields were up, so that total value of the crop increased.

The middle of the decade thus marked a return to prosperity in much of the Prairie west, although it would be short-lived. Total net farm income on the prairies increased from a decent $317 million in 1926, to $363 million by 1928. Farm acreage, which had remained more or less stagnant from 1921 to 1926, and had actually decreased in Manitoba and Alberta, began to increase again. Between 1926 and 1931, nearly 20 million acres of new farm holdings were established on the prairies. As agricultural returns improved, so too did other activities in the region, from immigration to investment, to construction. One estimate indicates that construction contracts on the prairies increased from a rather poor $19 million as late as 1924 to more than $101 million by 1929 — a 500 percent increase in five years!

Such prosperity gave many in the west the idea that their region was now back in a long-term growth cycle such as had existed before the war. That was not the case, for the west did not resume the role it had had before 1914. Even during the relatively prosperous period after 1926, prairie farm investment contributed less than 8 percent to domestic capital formation. In the period immediately before the war, its contribution had been approximately twice as great.[13] Immigration, farm investment, and other figures told the same story — the great era of growth of the "Last Best West," as Laurier had termed it, had passed.

Westerners may have been frustrated while awaiting a return to growth and prosperity but, at least for them, the years after 1925 did bring recovery. In contrast, the Maritimers found themselves continuing to experience the dismal pattern that had been noticeable in past decades. In every sector, the Maritime economy experienced stagnation or decline. There was no such thing as a prosperous 1920s for that region. Net value of production reached a peak in 1920, at $325 million. The next year, as in the other parts of Canada, the recession took its toll, and that net value declined by $90 million. While the rest of Canada began a recovery — whether slow or fast — from the collapse, the Maritimes found themselves in the grips of a deep recession. Figures continued to decline through 1924 and, even when recovery began, it was not enough. As Table 17.4 indicates, the Maritimes never did reach 1920 values again in the decade. Nor would they in the next.

The recession in the region was widespread. In manufacturing, the steel industry suffered throughout the decade. The British Empire Steel Corporation, on Cape Breton Island, had been set up after the war in the hope that reconstruction demands would create a strong demand for steel. That was not to be. There was overcapacity in world steel construction and BESCO was not capable of competing effectively internationally for a variety of reasons. Within Canada, the decline of railway construction removed one of the major areas of demand for steel, as rails were no longer being laid in great numbers. As the steel industry faltered, so, too, did the coal industry, which had provided the fuel for the smelters. At no time in the 1920s was Maritime coal production equal to levels reached during World War I.

Things were not much better for the region's traditional primary-source exports, such as fishing and lumber. Both were affected by the new higher rates of the American Fordney tariff. Nova Scotia apples were hurt by a competitive British market. The value of fruit exports declined steadily through the latter half of the decade. Fish-

TABLE 17.4
Net Value of Production in the Maritimes, 1920–1929

Year	*($ millions)*	*(% of Canadian total)*
1920	325.0	8.8
1921	235.2	8.3
1922	219.2	7.5
1923	211.5	6.9
1924	192.5	6.4
1925	205.0	6.2
1926	241.5	6.6
1927	230.1	5.9
1928	252.8	6.1
1929	240.3	6.1

Source: Canada Year Book, 1920–1930.

ery production fluctuated during the decade, showing some modest growth but never reaching the values of World War I. Only in pulp and paper, in New Brunswick, was there steady growth, but that did little more than offset decline in other sectors of the forest-products industry.

Problems in these key sectors rippled through the rest of the Maritime economy. Population declined relative to the rest of the country, with Prince Edward Island actually suffering years of absolute loss. A declining economic base meant that provincial governments had less revenue and were thus less able to develop the infrastructure of the region, such as highways, to the same extent as were other provinces. Overall, the plight of the Maritimes was neatly summarized by economic historian S.A. Saunders:

> The decade of the 1920s started out badly for the Maritime Provinces, as it did for most other parts of the world, with all major branches of industry severely depressed. Elsewhere in North America and, more significantly, in Canada, there soon came a fair amount of recovery; and, before the end of the decade, a period of exceptional prosperity. In the Maritime Provinces, recovery

> from the acute post-war depression was long deferred, and the period of prosperity experienced in most other parts of the Dominion has not yet arrived.[14]

Historians and economists have debated the reasons why the Maritimes continued to have such a dismal economic record. In effect, their discussions have generally echoed the arguments already discussed for the prewar era. One school of thought has been that the region was simply too peripherally placed to take advantage of industrialization. Nor did the Maritimes have primary resources with sufficient potential to compensate for this handicap. Fish and lumber were important, of course, but they were no longer growth industries, and thus could not provide the region with sustained economic development.

Another view takes a less deterministic position and argues that governmental decisions — especially in Ottawa — did much to hamper the region at a time when it needed help. Most often pointed to are the changes that took place in the Intercolonial Railway (which connected the region to the rest of the country) when it was incorporated into the new national system that would become the CNR. Until the 1920s, rates on the Intercolonial had been 20 to 50 percent lower than comparable ones in Ontario. Such rates, it was argued, allowed Maritime manufacturers to break into central Canadian markets. After 1920, the rate structures turned against the Maritimes, and local manufacturers found themselves unable to compete in central Canada.[15]

Certainly, at the time, there was a strong sense of regional grievance throughout the Maritimes. Just as the west turned to the regionally based Progressive party in 1921, so the Maritimes took to the Maritimes Rights Movement, and politicians of all kinds found it useful to focus on the injustices handed out to the region. There *were* injustices. Federal government indifference, reversals on railway rates, and maintenance of the tariff structure — all hurt the region. To say that there were stupidities and injustices, however, is quite different from blaming such things for the decline of the region's economy. The economy had been in decline for a long time. The fact that the Dominion seemed indifferent to this plight naturally led to political protest. The underlying forces, however, rested on much more than freight rates. In the 1920s, the most significant feature of the Maritime economy was its inability to compete either in the American market (in some cases, because of American tariffs) or in the new consumer technologies of the decade.

Urbanization

The economic developments of the 1920s helped reshape the urban centres of the nation. Those that could take advantage of the sectors of growth increased their own prosperity and importance, while others sank in standing. In part, this was a continuation of general, longer-term trends toward urbanization. Indeed, the 1920s can be seen as the first decade in which urban concerns and urban life were as important to the economy as were rural ones. By the end of the decade, more Canadians were classified as urban than rural. More significant than this was what was happening among "urban centres." The smallest towns and villages were not growing nearly as quickly as were the larger ones. As transportation facilities improved and as manufacturing was concentrated, local services and small-scale business disappeared. Larger metropolitan centres took over. The trend toward urbanization is, thus, if anything, understated. Anyone who moved from an incorporated village of 1500 people to a city of 100 000 was not judged by the census to have contributed to the rural-urban shift. Yet, there is no doubt that, in terms of the nature of employment, consuming habits, and leisure activities, the person who had made the move had become urbanized.

There were winners and losers, even among the larger centres, during the decade. The most spectacular winner was Vancouver, which more than doubled in population between 1911 and 1931, becoming Canada's third-largest city. Vancouver had had the potential for rapid growth from the time that the Canadian Pacific Railway decided to make that city its western terminus. Until World War I, however, it had never really been able to extend its hinterland eastward, over the Rocky Mountains. The growing timber and pulp-and-paper industries in British Columbia and the increased importance of shipments to the Far East contributed to the city's growth before and during the war. With the opening of the Panama Canal in 1914, Vancouver became a major port for goods headed, not just across the Pacific, but to the eastern United States and Europe. Moreover, goods flowing in from those points could now come via Vancouver rather than Winnipeg. Even grain bound for Europe from the western prairies became more economical to

City of Vancouver Archives/STR.P.1 N22

Vancouver, B.C., 1897 and 1931. *Vancouver had had the potential for rapid growth from the time that the Canadian Pacific Railway decided to make the city its western terminus. But it was not until 1911 that its dramatic development began: it more than doubled in population between 1911 and 1931, and became Canada's third-largest city.*

City of Vancouver Archives/AIR.P.53 N.28

ship west rather than east. The Alberta-Saskatchewan border can be taken as a rough dividing line for grain shipments and, by 1928, some 79 million bushels were exported via Vancouver. By the end of the decade, Vancouver had more than 6 million tons of shipping clearing through its harbour, by far the largest amount in Canada.

The other major gains, made from the early 1900s through to 1930, were Toronto's. From the mid-nineteenth century onward, Toronto had been contending with Montreal for dominance in Canada. It had always been contending from a position of second place, however, and had never really threatened Montreal's dominance as the population and business centre of Canada. It would be a while yet before Montreal's position was surpassed, but it is plausible to argue that Toronto became sufficiently powerful in this period that it could seriously challenge Montreal for economic supremacy in Canada, though the challenge would not be resolved until well after World War II.

There were several reasons for this. Perhaps most importantly, Toronto's immediate hinterland continued to see rapid growth and the Oshawa-Toronto-Hamilton "golden horseshoe" was the most industrialized area of Canada. By 1929, nearly 40 percent of all of Ontario's manufactures came from Toronto and Hamilton alone.[16] Crucial new industries, such as automobile manufacturing, were centred in this area. Toronto's aspirations were also nicely matched by those of the provincial government located in that city. Also important to Toronto's economy was the role played, after 1900, by the Ontario government and Toronto-based financiers in the mining activities of the Shield. In the 1920s, as the mining boom continued, Toronto financial operations dominated Canadian-owned activities, and Toronto financial intermediaries handled American investments in the Shield or American mergers with Canadian firms. Toronto had become the mining centre of Canada; when operations expanded into northern Quebec and Manitoba, they continued to be centred in Toronto rather than in Montreal or Winnipeg.

The result of all this was dramatic growth for the city. Population increased from 381 000, in 1911, to 631 000, by 1931, in the city itself and would be much larger if surrounding communities were taken into account. Towns such as Mimico, Forest Hill, Eastview, Thornhill, and Oshawa had, among them, a population greater than that of Halifax or Edmonton, yet all were satellite communities

Toronto railyards, 1926*. The extent and bustle of the railyards demonstrate Toronto's rapid growth into a major city, centre of the Oshawa-Toronto-Hamilton "golden horseshoe" — the most industrialized area of Canada. By 1929, nearly 40 percent of Ontario's manufactures came from Toronto and Hamilton alone.*

to Toronto. By the latter part of the decade, building permits in Toronto alone were greater than those issued in Montreal, Quebec City and Three Rivers put together, or — to use another comparison — greater than all the building permits of the three Prairie provinces.[17]

In contrast, Winnipeg underwent a relative decline. It was still the most important prairie city, but its aspirations to become the "Chicago of the North" faded rapidly. Vancouver cut into its hinterland from the west, while other western centres, such as Edmonton, Calgary, Regina, and Saskatoon, grew larger and more able to handle local distributing and wholesaling functions. The removal of wheat trading from the activities of the Winnipeg Grain Exchange with the creation of the Canadian Wheat Board lessened that city's hold over the prairies' major crop. Population growth in Manitoba was slower than in the more westerly (and increasingly Vancouver-oriented) areas of Alberta.

TABLE 17.5

Urban Populations of Major Centres, 1901–1931

	1901	*1911*	*1921*	*1931*	*1931 as percentage of 1901*
Montreal	328 172	490 504	618 506	818 577	249
Toronto	209 892	381 833	521 893	631 207	300
Vancouver	29 432	120 847	163 220	246 593	839
Winnipeg	42 340	136 035	179 087	218 785	517
Hamilton	52 634	81 969	114 151	155 547	295
Quebec	68 840	78 710	95 193	130 594	189
Ottawa	59 928	87 062	107 843	126 872	211
Calgary	4 392	43 704	63 305	83 761	1900
Edmonton	4 176	31 064	58 821	79 197	1885
London	37 796	46 300	60 959	71 148	188
Windsor	12 153	17 829	38 591	63 108	517
Verdun	1 898	11 629	25 001	60 745	3197
Halifax	40 832	46 619	58 372	59 275	145
Saint John	40 711	42 511	47 166	47 154	116

Source: Derived from *Canada Year Book*, 1932.

Though some cities gained more than others, all the major cities of Canada increased in population during the decade (see Table 17.5). The population of the nation was growing, and a larger and larger percentage of it was living in the cities. Further, for those employed in manufacturing, real wages increased during the decade.[18] The combination of people flowing into the cities and of rising incomes in many areas of the country created a considerable boom in housing construction once the recession of 1921 had passed. Streetcars and automobiles made the separation of home and work more and more possible. In all but the smallest cities, new residential neighbourhoods began to spread outward from industrial areas, as the "respectable working class" and the white-collar "middle class" sought to escape the social and physical ills that they associated with the heterogeneous mix of the inner city.

By the later 1920s, the contribution of this residential construction to capital formation was considerable. Between 1924 (a year of relatively slow construction) and 1929, building construction of all types more than doubled, to $572 million. Residential construction accounted for about $230 million of that. The process of urbanization was not only a response to economic conditions but a significant economic force in its own right.

All of this domestic capital expenditure, in housing and elsewhere, raises a question about the nature of the prosperity of the latter half of the decade. This chapter has argued that the relationship with the United States was central to Canadian prosperity in the 1920s, whether in terms of sale or investment. Yet, the building construction boom, as well as the amounts spent on, say, road construction and the expansion of paper mills, has led to the argument that, after 1925, "it was domestic capital formation, not export growth, which was propelling Canada's economy upward.[19]

The point about the importance of domestic capital formation is relevant, as Figure 17.3 indicates. In the latter part of the decade, the ratio of gross capital formation to GNP did increase significantly, even approaching something akin to the heady days of the prewar wheat boom. Yet, it would seem impossible to separate capital formation from external relationships — in terms of both exports of

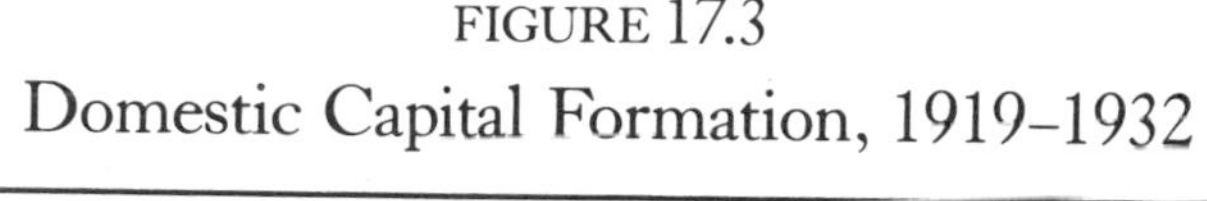

FIGURE 17.3

Domestic Capital Formation, 1919–1932

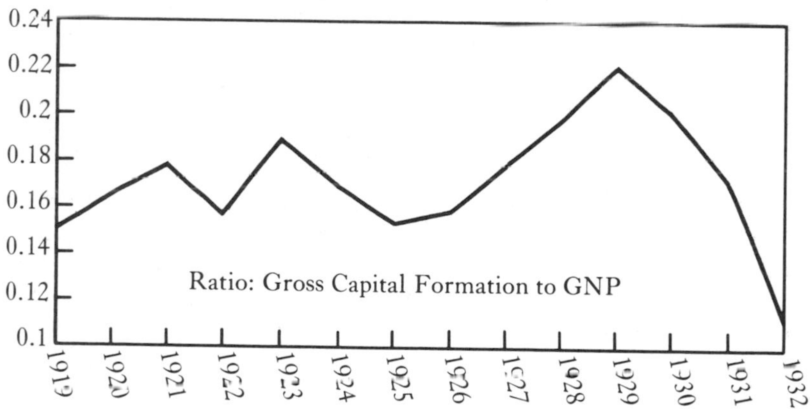

Source: M.C. Urquhart, "Canadian Economic Growth, 1870–1980," Queen's University, Department of Economics, Discussion Paper 734, Table 4.

merchandise and the inflow of investment. Canada was a small economy, very much dependent on exports. Wheat, pulp and paper, minerals, and other such exports were crucial to expectations for the Canadian economy, to employment in the country, and thus to the sale of such new technologies as automobiles. Moreover, export/GNP ratios remained high in the latter part of the decade, higher than comparable figures in the prewar years.[20] Capital formation, whether in industry or housing, occurred in good measure simply because Canadians and foreign investors continued to be optimistic about Canadian prospects and because increased exports, among other things, had allowed the Canadian standard of living to rise, at least in some regions of the country. When the prospects for external trade fell, as it was about to, domestic capital formation would also fall.

Conclusion

What then can be said about the 1920s as a whole? First, Canada was a very different nation economically than it had been even twenty years before. World War I and the subsequent decade had changed many things. Of these, perhaps two general themes stand out. First, manufacturing — whether primary or secondary — was now an important part of the Canadian economy, accounting for a greater percentage of total Canadian production than did agriculture by 1927. By the same year, manufacturing and construction, together, made up an absolute majority of that production. Agriculture was still very valuable, of course, and primary production (which included some processing) was greater than secondary. Still, the trends were apparent. The rural-agricultural nation of the late nineteenth century was now becoming an urban and industrial one.

The second, and obviously related, structural change came in the composition of the work force. Two things were happening. First, as might be expected, a smaller and smaller percentage of people worked in agriculture. Whereas, in 1901, more than 40 percent of Canadians were classified as following "agricultural pursuits," by 1931, that figure had fallen to less than 29 percent. Even more interesting was the rapid growth of new areas in the nonagricultural sector. The first half of the twentieth century was the great era for the rise of the white-collar occupations: first, as front-office staff for corporations, then in "white-collar" corporations and activities such as finance, and finally (and still largely in the future in 1929) in government. For example, employment in finance, insurance, and real estate was among the fastest growing of any in Canada between 1911 and 1931, rising from just under 37 000 to more than 92 000.

Along with the white-collar revolution, which, it must be emphasized, was still underway at the end of the 1920s, a revolution in office procedures occurred, which, as was discussed earlier, created the clerical and secretarial role, as it is known in the modern world. It also provided an entry point (and a ghetto) for women in a whole new range of occupations. To continue the example of finance: female employment went from 3500 in 1911 to nearly 25 000 by 1931. Contemporaries in both world wars paid a great deal of attention to the woman who left the home to work in industry as a part of the war effort. This emphasis, though useful for war morale, tended to underplay the longer-term forces of industrialization and bureaucratization that were changing and increasing women's role in the work force in more fundamental ways. It is not surprising to say that many women did not work in the 1920s. That is generally known. What is surprising, perhaps, is the number who did. When these new clerical and secretarial employees are added to such "traditional" female occupations as teaching (71 000 women by 1931), health (nearly 53 000) and the harsher working-class world of textiles (61 737), it becomes clear that women's role in the economy was of much greater importance than was acknowledged at the time, or for long afterwards. By 1931, some 750 000 women worked and accounted for one job in five in the country.[21]

What, then, of the material position of Canadians, whether male or female, in the years after World War I? Overall, the standard of living in Canada does appear to have gone up significantly. Only the period 1900–1910 saw a greater growth in real GNP per capita. It is difficult to translate this statement on overall wealth to one that gives some estimate of the distribution of that wealth. Recent estimates, however, have concluded that real wages did increase for the period 1913 to 1926 and that, on average, the employed worker was in better economic circumstances by the later 1920s than he or she had been at the end of the war.[22]

It is also clear, however, that not all people experienced this rise in the standard of living or enhanced opportunities for work. For

General office, Canadian Aeroplanes Ltd., Toronto, 1918. *The "white-collar revolution," which began around the turn of the century and was still under way at the end of the 1920s, brought with it a revolution in office procedures that created the secretarial and clerical role, as it is known in the modern world. In creating a whole new range of occupations, it provided an entry point (and a ghetto) for women in the work force.*

those living through the decade, the nature of the 1920s depended on the region in which one lived and the sector of the economy in which one worked. In the larger cities, especially in central Canada and on the west coast, job opportunities expanded, at least after 1921. New areas opened up and many more people worked in either manufacturing or the burgeoning tertiary sector. Employment as clerks, truck drivers, nurses, and teachers, was much more common by the end of the decade than before, as were factory workers. In the Prairie west, and in parts of central Canada, that prosperity was felt only toward the end of the decade. The first half was spent simply recovering from the postwar recession. In contrast, those in the Maritimes or in marginal agricultural areas did not have a good decade. Unemployment and management-union confrontations in depressed areas, such as Cape Breton, revealed dramatically that prosperity was far from universal.

Uneven though this prosperity was, it would soon be looked back upon with nostalgia. For, by the end of the decade, the entire international trading and monetary systems were on the verge of collapse. Canada, as a small nation that depended on massive exports for prosperity, was to be affected more than most. The nation was on the eve of the Great Depression.

Notes

1. Kenneth Buckley, *Capital Formation in Canada* (Toronto: McClelland and Stewart, 1974), 11.
2. This summary of events is based on William Ashworth, *A Short History of the International Economy, 1850–1950* (London: Longmans, Green, 1952).
3. Irving Brecher, "Canadian Monetary Thought and Policy in the 1920s," *Canadian Journal of Economics and Political Science* 21, no. 2 (1955): 154–73.
4. Michael Bliss, *Northern Enterprise: Five Centuries of Canadian Business* (Toronto: McClelland and Stewart, 1987), 387. On banking reorganization in the 1920s generally, see Bliss, *Northern Enterprise*, 385–88.
5. John Thompson and A. Seager, *Canada, 1922–1939: Decades of Discord* (Toronto: McClelland and Stewart, 1985), 79.
6. Royal Commission on Dominion-Provincial Relations, *Report*, Book I: *Canada, 1867–1939*, 116.
7. T. Traves, *The State and Enterprise: Canadian Manufacturers and the Federal Government, 1917–1931* (Toronto: University of Toronto Press, 1979), 102.
8. Ian Drummond, *Progress Without Planning: The Economic History of Ontario from Confederation to the Second World War* (Toronto: University of Toronto Press, 1987), 152.
9. Cited in Traves, *The State and Enterprise*, 103.
10. *Canada Year Book*, 1930, 653.
11. Bliss, *Northern Enterprise*, 396–97.
12. D. Owram, "Economic Development of Western Canada: An Historical Overview," Economic Council of Canada Discussion Paper No. 219, p. 22.
13. Figures from Buckley, *Capital Formation in Canada*, 9, 28.
14. S.A. Saunders, *The Economic History of the Maritime Provinces*, edited and with an introduction by T.W. Acheson (Fredericton: Acadiensis Press, 1984; originally published 1939), 43.
15. E.R. Forbes, "The Origins of the Maritime Rights Movement," in *Canada After Confederation*, The Acadiensis Reader, Vol. 2, edited by P.A. Buckner and David Frank (Fredericton: Acadiensis Press, 1985), 286–98.
16. Drummond, *Progress Without Planning*, 182.
17. *Canada Year Book*, 1930, 451–52.
18. Gordon W. Bertram and Michael B. Percy, "Real Wage Trends in Canada, 1900–1926: Some Provisional Estimates," *Canadian Journal of Economics* 12, no. 2 (May 1979): 299–311.

19. R. Bothwell, I. Drummond, and J. English, *Canada, 1900–1945* (Toronto: University of Toronto Press, 1987), 219.
20. M.C. Urquhart, "Canadian Economic Growth, 1870–1980," Department of Economics, Queen's University, Discussion Paper No. 734, Table 4a.
21. Statistics Canada, *Historical Statistics of Canada*, 2nd ed. (Ottawa: Supply and Services, 1983), 107–23. These figures probably underestimate the female labour force because they would likely miss many temporary and part-time workers who drifted in and out of the labour force as family and economic circumstances demanded.
22 Royal Commission on Dominion-Provincial Relations, *Report*, Book I: *Canada, 1867–1939*, 116; Bertram and Percy, "Real Wage Trends"; Elizabeth Bartlett, "Real Wages and the Standard of Living in Vancouver, 1901–1929," *B.C. Studies* 51 (Autumn 1981): 3–62.

Further Reading

Bothwell, R., I. Drummond, and J. English, *Canada, 1900–1945*. Toronto: University of Toronto Press, 1987.

Dick, Trevor J. "Canadian Newsprint, 1913–1930: National Policies and the North American Economy." In *Perspectives on Canadian Economic History*, edited by Douglas McCalla. Toronto: Copp Clark, 1987.

Drummond, I. *Progress Without Planning: The Economic History of Ontario from Confederation to the Second World War*. Toronto: University of Toronto Press, 1987.

Thompson, J., and A. Seager. *Canada, 1922–1939: Decades of Discord*. Toronto: McClelland and Stewart 1985.

Traves, T. *The State and Enterprise: Canadian Manufacturers and the Federal Government, 1917–1931*. Toronto: University of Toronto Press, 1979.

CHAPTER

18

The Great Depression, 1929–1939

In 1929, the business cycle turned downward, bringing the boom of the previous four years to an end. This in itself was not unusual, for, as we have seen, the Canadian economy was often characterized by short and sharp fluctuations in economic activity. This time, however, the pattern was different. What initially appeared to be a regionally based agricultural slump proved to be a major international economic collapse. Its effects were soon felt across the nation, and, over the next months and years, the economy not only failed to recover but slid inexorably downward in what seemed an endless decline. By the time the bottom was reached, in 1933, more than one in four Canadians was out of work, many municipalities and provinces hovered on the edge of bankruptcy, and thousands of individuals had been forced to shut down their businesses or farms.[1]

Even at the bottom, there was no end in sight. Haltingly, the economy did begin to recover. First one sector and then another would show modest improvement, and newspapers and politicians would trumpet the beginning of good times. Yet the good times proved to be elusive, and promising recoveries were checked by renewed problems. Thus, in 1937, after the best year of the decade, a recession occurred, wiping out much of the gain that had been made. Even a decade after the slide began, more than one in ten Canadians was out of work, and farm income was still less than half of what it had been at its peak, in 1928. As Table 18.1 indicates, only in 1939 did gross national expenditure in constant dollars fi-

TABLE 18.1
Gross National Expenditure

(1971 dollars)

Year	*Value* *($ millions)*	*Index* *(1928 = 100)*
1928	16 831	100.0
1929	16 894	100.4
1930	16 174	96.1
1931	14 118	83.9
1932	12 654	75.2
1933	11 811	70.2
1934	13 245	78.7
1935	14 279	84.8
1936	14 912	88.6
1937	16 410	97.5
1938	16 545	98.3
1939	17 774	105.6

Source: Statistics Canada, *Historical Statistics of Canada*, 2nd ed. (Ottawa: Supply and Services, 1983), Series F47–55.

nally surpass that of 1929. Never in its history had Canada faced such an extensive period without growth.

This was the decade of the Great Depression, and it was unique. No other industrial downturn in history was so massive or so persistent. It affected all areas of Canadian life. A people and a nation used to growth and new opportunities had to face decline and stagnation. Tremendous psychological, social, and political tensions resulted. New attitudes were born, as were new political parties. Regional balances and regional outlooks shifted. The beliefs held about the industrial system also shifted, as did the demands for action by the state. Years, even decades, after the Depression ended, people would point back to it and its lessons as a dire warning against smug comfort in the midst of prosperity. It is no exaggeration to say that this economic cataclysm altered some of the most basic assumptions of Canadians and shaped much of later political, social, and economic history in this country, as it did elsewhere.

The International Impact of the Depression

The Great Depression was not a phenomenon peculiar to Canada, though there were aspects unique to this country. Rather, Canada was caught up in a vast international collapse, over which it had little control. The Canadian economy had weaknesses of its own, of course, but, as discussed in the introduction to Part V, the underlying problems of the 1930s were international in scope.

These international forces created a depression much as a series of waves batters away at a shoreline. No single event could have caused the catastrophic collapse that occurred, but repeated shocks sent the economy spiralling downward. The commodity glut that developed late in the 1920s began the downturn. The weakened economy was pushed into depression by the unstable state of international currency relationships. The collapse of stock-market prices in the fall of 1929, especially in New York, after months of speculative buying, created a sense of panic. Excess capacity in other areas prevented recovery in any reasonable time frame. In other words, problems in the primary-resource sector alone would have forced an economic readjustment around the end of the 1920s. The other areas of weakness turned that readjustment into a disastrous worldwide depression that hit all the industrialized nations of the world and was particularly disastrous to North America. Government reactions around the world did as much to prolong the crisis as to resolve it.

The collapse, when it came, contained elements of the fantastic and the absurd, but there was, all in all, a relentless logic about it. By 1929, increasing weaknesses internationally were masked by a tremendous speculative boom in U.S. stock prices. Heady profits for the middle classes and for the large-scale investor meant that the world's richest economy was, whatever else might happen, at the centre of the world's stage. Indeed, in spite of a number of weakening sectors, U.S. nominal gross national expenditure rose by a very strong 7 percent in 1929. The nature of the growth, however, only exacerbated the growing problems of the international economy. Offshore savings were increasingly drawn to the last place in the world they were needed — American stock exchanges —

and away from international investments. Then came the incident that many would see, mistakenly, as the primary cause of the Depression: the stock-market crash of October 1929. The bubble burst in New York, and, over the next few months, prices headed inexorably downward on stock exchanges around the world.

The collapse of the stock market brought the problems of the international economy sharply to the fore. Investor confidence was lost, and decisions to purchase or build were postponed. Companies cut back production and allowed overly large inventories to deplete. Orders ceased, and trade began to decline with greater and greater rapidity. In the last three months of 1929, American imports alone declined almost 20 percent. That was only the beginning of a slide that would last nearly four years.[2]

The rapid shift in market fortunes and declining trade soon affected the already weak international financial system. International banking and trading institutions, not to mention nations, found themselves with a growing number of bad debts and with an increasingly unstable foreign-currency market to deal with. Currencies began to fluctuate wildly, as many nations experienced difficulties with their balance of payments. Under such pressures the gold standard, which had been so tenuously patched back together in recent years, began to unravel. In 1931, the gold standard was given a major blow when Britain abandoned it. It went into nearly total eclipse two years later, when the United States did the same.

As markets shrank, nations sought to cushion themselves against the worst effects. In their efforts to do so, they often made things worse. In particular, there was a general move to high levels of protectionism. The theory was that at least the domestic market could be preserved for local producers. Instead, the rise of tariff walls around the world only hastened the shrinkage of international trade and put barriers in the way of any easy recovery. By the beginning of 1931, the value of international trade had declined to less than two-thirds of what it had been at the beginning of 1929. As mentioned earlier, by 1933 it would be one-third.[3]

As the national income figures in Table 18.2 indicate, the severity and exact shape of the Depression varied from nation to nation. In France, for example, the government had for some time been following policies that encouraged the inflow of gold. When the Depression hit, therefore, the French were in an unusually strong position in terms of international currency movements. Likewise,

TABLE 18.2

The International Impact of the Depression

(1932 as a percentage of 1929)

Nation	*Industrial Production*	*National Income*
Austria	61	83
Canada	58	55
France	77	84
Germany	58	59
Japan	98	84
United Kingdom	83	85
United States	53	48

Source: A.E. Safarian, *The Canadian Economy in the Great Depression* (Toronto: University of Toronto Press, 1970), 98.

they had long paid high consumer prices in order to preserve their inefficient domestic agriculture and were, therefore, little affected by the commodity glut on the world markets. In the United Kingdom, the 1920s had never been that prosperous and, as a result, there had been less overcapacity developed in certain key sectors. There was a severe financial crisis, however, and British investments overseas declined still further, as that once-dominant industrial nation abandoned both the gold standard and free trade by 1932. Nevertheless, the English depression was not as severe as that in many countries; by 1936, the economy had reached the point where it had actually grown when compared to its 1929 level.

For Germany and Austria, things were much worse. Both were debtor nations, with credit balances, currencies, and economic psychology still very much affected by the war and immediate postwar economic distress. As the decline accelerated in 1930, overseas investment by such major financial powers as the United States and Great Britain shrank. Those with debts, therefore, faced severe problems in providing ongoing funding and in maintaining foreign exchange rates. For both countries, the rumblings reached a crisis with the collapse, in May 1931, of the Credit-Anstalt, Austria's largest bank. This only hastened the loss of investor confidence and caused further funds to flee. Regimes were destabilized, as the public lost whatever tenuous faith it had had in the democracies imposed after World War I.

Amid all the variations in the depth and characteristics of the Depression, it is striking to see just how hard hit Canada was in relative terms. Britain, France, and Japan experienced a much smaller decline in their economic performance. Even unstable Germany, defeated in war, destabilized by reparations, and in considerable economic and political turmoil, maintained its national income to a higher degree than Canada's and its industrial output to the same degree.

Why was Canada so vulnerable to these international events? There are several reasons. First, and most obviously, Canada was dependent on exports. At the end of the 1920s, Canada was one of the most export-oriented industrial nations in the world, with some 22 percent of gross national expenditure attributable to merchandise exports, compared to less than 5 percent in the United States. In some sectors, the export market was the only meaningful market. Some 80 percent of Canadian produce from forests, farms, and mines was exported. Its largest export, wheat, accounted for an incredible 40 percent of all world exports and thus, if that international market collapsed, Canada would be harder hit than most.[4]

Moreover, Canada's huge dependence on exports rested on relatively few products. As Table 18.3 indicates, wheat and wheat flour together accounted for more than 36 percent of all exports. When forest products, such as paper and boards, were added, the figure amounted to more than half. Automobiles provided the only exception among leading exports to Canada's reliance on primary resources or their direct manufactured products. To state the figures in a slightly different way, exports from farm products, animal products, and forest products between them accounted for nearly 80 percent of all Canadian exports. Lack of diversification in Canadian export goods therefore made the country vulnerable. A decrease in demand for relatively few goods could cripple Canadian foreign trade.

This vulnerability was made worse because such a large percentage of Canadian exports depended on just one market — that of the United States. In 1929, well over one-third of all Canadian exports went to the United States, and products headed south of the

TABLE 18.3
Major Canadian Exports, 1929

	($ millions)	*(% of total Canadian exports)*
Wheat	428.5	31.5
Paper	142.3	10.5
Flour	65.1	4.8
Boards	47.7	3.5
Autos	43.1	3.2
Fish	34.9	2.6
Copper	26.9	2.0
Barley	25.7	1.9

Source: Canada Year Book, 1930, 477.

border were concentrated in a few key areas. Wood and paper, animal products, and nonferrous metals (for example, copper, nickel, and gold) accounted for more than three-quarters of all Canadian exports to the United States. As was shown in Chapter 17, two of the largest growth areas of the 1920s, mining, and pulp and paper, had grown in response to the demands of the American market. Further, in a general sense, trade with the United States had been one of the most important factors in shaping development in the decade after the war.

Just how dependent Canada was on the United States quickly became apparent with the economic collapse in 1929. The U.S. economy fell farther than that of any other industrialized nation in the world (see Table 18.2). American domestic investment and output rapidly declined through 1930 and 1931 and, with them, American purchases abroad. To make matters worse, the U.S. government reacted to the sliding economy by retreating even further behind tariff barriers. The Hawley-Smoot tariff of 1930 raised tariffs on both agricultural and manufactured goods with devastating effect on Canadian trade. By 1932, Canadian exports to the United States in such important areas as meats and agricultural products were worth less than they had been at the beginning of World War I. Metals were not much better off. The combination of the decline in U.S. activity and the protectionism that it wrought meant that by 1932 the total level of Canadian exports to the United States was less than half of what it had been in 1929. Indeed, that 1932 total of just over $235 million was less than exports in wood and paper alone had been just three years earlier.

The decline of exports to the United States is not the whole story. Canada's largest single export, after all, was wheat, and that was marketed not in the United States but in Europe, especially in the United Kingdom. Nearly $277 million in Canadian wheat and wheat flour was sent to the United Kingdom in 1929 — a figure that was of greater value than any single item exported to the United States. Agricultural produce of all sorts accounted for more than $325 million of the total of $433.9 million. In other words, the British were only slightly less important than the Americans as a market for Canadian exports, and the British dependence on Canadian wheat meant that Canadian exports to Britain were even more concentrated on a single commodity than were exports to the United States.

Britain's economy did not decline as severely as that of the United States and might have served, therefore, to restrain the fall in Canadian exports. Unfortunately for Canada, however, the worldwide glut of agricultural goods forced prices rapidly downward. By 1932, the value of Canadian agricultural exports to Britain had been reduced by two-thirds. The impact of this drastic decline of exports was reflected in a disastrous domestic situation. The Depression was hardest on those who farmed or depended on the farmer for a livelihood. The Depression in Canada began on the prairies, and it was there that its effects were felt most fully.

In fact, the problems of the international wheat market meant that the downturn in Canada began early, leading rather than following that in the United States. For some time, international wheat prices had been weakening, but for Canada, this had been masked, to a large degree, by two things. First, the wheat pools and the government had been increasing the amounts of wheat held rather than selling in poor international markets. Second, Canadians had been growing more wheat. In 1928, for example, the Canadian wheat crop was a record 566 million bushels, and this meant that the total value of wheat production was only a little lower than the previous year, in spite of a sharp decline in prices.

A boom crop that allowed farmers merely to maintain their standard of living was an ominous sign; the next year, things began to fall apart. Average yield on the prairies declined almost 40 percent, and the crop was cut by nearly 100 million bushels. International exports declined even more sharply, by some 200 million bushels, while national income in agriculture declined from $856 million in 1928 to $608 million in 1929.[5] The farmer could no longer compensate for falling prices with increased volume, and the entire economy of the prairies headed into a decline that began to undermine the whole wheat-marketing system and, soon after, the political and economic infrastructure of the Prairie provinces.

The declining prices that set in toward the end of 1929 created havoc in the wheat pools. It was pool practice to give out an initial (and conservative) payment to farmers when they brought their grain to the elevators in the fall or winter. Once the grain was sold and the yearly returns had been determined, "bonus" payments would be made. The better the price, the larger the bonus. In the fall and winter of 1928–29, the wheat pools gave out an initial payment of $1 a bushel. This was, as usual, below the existing price and below the expected price for wheat. Before long, however, wheat prices had declined below the $1 prepayment. In response, the pools held back wheat, hoping that the decline was a temporary one. As a result, Canadian wheat exports declined by nearly 200 million bushels (see Table 18.4).

The collapse in wheat prices created an immediate crisis for farmers. Many had expanded their acreage under production after the bumper crop of 1928, and many had accumulated additional debt to do so. Now, not only were there to be no bonus payments, but the full elevators indicated that prices next year were to be low. Further, the pools were in serious financial trouble because of their failure to foresee the collapse of wheat prices, and only loans from the provinces allowed them to continue. Even so, the existing debts would have to be recovered out of next year's profits. The best a farmer could hope for was a mediocre year in 1930, and that would happen only if crops were good and prices remained more or less steady.

Instead, what they got was an average harvest and a continued decline in prices. Yield was up somewhat, but it was apparent, even before the crops were harvested, that the international wheat market was becoming a major disaster. The wheat pools had been cautious in their initial payments, being determined not to repeat the previous year's performance. Their caution was insufficient and, as

TABLE 18.4
Wheat Prices and Production, 1927–1933

	Price (cents/bu)	*Production (000 bushels)*
1927	146.3	479 665
1928	124.0	466 726
1929	124.2	302 192
1930	64.2	420 672
1931	59.8	321 325
1932	54.3	443 061
1933	68.1	281 892

Source: Statistics Canada, *Historical Statistics of Canada*, 2nd ed. (Ottawa: Supply and Services, 1983), Series M228–238 and M249–300.

the months of late 1929 and early 1930 went by, the international price just kept falling. In the end, wholesale prices were barely half what they had been the previous year, and the total value of the wheat crop was only 45 percent of what it had been in 1928. The next year was worse, and the year after that worse still, as the vast unused stocks of wheat were dumped on the world and prices continued downward. By 1932, the total value of Canadian wheat was less than one-third of the 1928 figure. The wheat pools were collapsing under the debt they had assumed, and the farmers of the prairies were being forced out of operation by the thousands. Net farm income for the three Prairie provinces together in 1932 was minus $3.1 million. Only four years before, it had been $363 million![6]

The disaster to the prairies was to have profound effects throughout the 1930s (more will be said about this below). The important point to note here, however, is that the collapse in wheat alone would have created serious economic problems for Canada. Since the 1890s, grain farming had been central to Canadian economic welfare in general, and to Canadian exports. Even had there not been a general collapse, Canada would have had to cope with significant adjustments in its trade prospects and with a region that was plunging into greater poverty than the country had ever known.

Overall, then, the collapse of Canadian exports explains, to a large degree, why our economy suffered so much more than many. Our American markets failed because the United States was devastated, and our largest single export, wheat, was devastated by a general fall in the international value of that product. This collapse in prices was exacerbated over the next few years by bad weather and irregular crops throughout much of the prairies. As a result, overall Canadian merchandise exports declined from a high of $1.27 billion in 1929 to $396 million by 1932.[7]

The collapse of exports, and of the earnings of those who depended on exports for their livelihood, cannot fully explain the Depression, however. This is true for several reasons but, most obviously, there is the simple fact that exports would undergo considerable recovery by the second half of the 1930s. The Canadian economy as a whole would not keep pace. As A.E. Safarian noted, in his classic study of the Canadian economy in the Depression, "investment in durable assets by 1937 was less than half the 1929 level, while exports of goods and services had almost attained the 1929 level."[8] Things had not returned to normal, nor was the spectre of depression banished. Unemployment remained at least four times as high as it had been in the late 1920s, and prices and wages remained low in a number of industries. Exports may be central to understanding the beginning of the Depression, but to look at them alone would make it difficult to understand the depth and persistence of what followed.

The lagging of economic recovery behind the recovery in exports was linked to the nature of investment in Canada. In the later 1920s, there was a tremendous amount of investment in Canada. As was argued at some length in Chapter 17, it was capital formation that provided a major engine of growth in these years. There were new hydro-electric plants, new automobile factories, and new pulp-and-paper mills. The problem, as Safarian concluded, was not only that good investment opportunities were used up but that such investment could continue only if there was ongoing expansion in the Canadian economy. Canada, in sum, went on a building binge that was reminiscent of that undertaken by railways before World War I. The fastest-growing part of national income was investment in durable assets.

Such levels of investment were exceedingly optimistic, even for the heady days of the later 1920s. The newsprint industry, for example, had been such a growth area that investors began to pour money into new facilities to satisfy the seemingly insatiable appetite of American newspapers. Nearly $200 million was invested in pulp and paper from 1926 to 1929. By the end of the decade, Canadians had made investments that could be recouped only if the market expanded at a very healthy rate. The declining price of newsprint, and the fact that market growth was not increasing as fast as Canadian capacity, indicated, even before the crash, that such growth was unlikely. With the Depression, of course, newsprint markets collapsed, and Canada was burdened with a great deal of excess capacity. By 1932, according to one industry estimate, only 51 percent of newsprint capacity was being utilized.[9]

The automobile industry, like that of pulp and paper, had seen heavy capital investment in the latter part of the decade, and automobiles too were vulnerable to the Depression. For one thing, nearly one-third of automobiles manufactured were exported. For another, many people saw automobiles as a relative luxury and would quickly postpone the decision to purchase one (or replace an old one) in hard times. Between 1929 and 1933, consumption fell from more than 262 000, to 61 000 — a figure lower than in any year since the war. At the low point, automobile production was employing only about one-tenth of existing capacity.

One could go on to cite equally dramatic incidents of decline in other industries. In the years 1929 to 1933, no sector of the economy showed any meaningful growth, and most showed tremendous decline.[10] Even at the industry level, the exceptions are so few as to illustrate in a stark way the widespread nature of the Depression. Only electric refrigerators and gold, two rather different products, resisted the tendency to decline.

The heavy investment of the 1920s and the resultant excess supply of the 1930s caused an almost total collapse in domestic investment. Exports may have fallen to less than half of what they had been, but gross domestic investment fell to an incredible 11 percent of what it had been in the heady days of the later 1920s. From being one-fifth of GNP, it declined by 1933 to approximately one-twelfth, and this at a time when overall GNP was falling. Construction workers were, with farmers, the hardest hit of all groups of workers in Canada. Further, simple recovery of production to 1929 levels would not guarantee renewed investment. Even before the Depression, most sectors had adequate plant and machinery in place to meet demand. Recovery would soak up excess capacity rather than generate new investment. Only significant new growth or the longer-term effects of obsolescence would generate domestic investment, and, even then, only if business saw improved prospects for the future. Lack of domestic investment would thus prove a crucial factor retarding the recovery of the economy once the bottom of the Depression was reached in 1932–33. It would be 1945 before business investment recovered to the absolute level of the 1920s, and 1949 before it reached the same percentage of GNP![11]

Related to the heavy capital investment of the 1920s was the growth of debt. Businesses, farmers, and governments took on increased liabilities to meet the opportunities and demands that faced them, especially in the years after 1925. Those new paper mills, houses, apartment buildings, roads, and auto-parts factories had been built on the assumption that debts would be retired easily over a few years. Thus, not only was there excess capacity in the system because of past expansion but that useless capacity also drained wealth to meet interest payments. High fixed debts, largely owed to foreign borrowers, thus exacerbated the burdens of declining revenue. Further, the Depression meant that debt levels were, in real terms, not only fixed but increasing. As prices declined from 1929 through 1932, the real value of debt increased accordingly. The real value of a debt contracted in 1929 would increase almost 30 percent by 1933.

Nowhere were past expansion and high debt to haunt Canadians more than in the case of railways. As has been indicated in earlier chapters, the drive to establish new transcontinentals in the years after 1900 had led Canadian railways to a point where they were overexpanded by 1915. The result had been both the creation of the new nationally owned CN system and the end of massive railway construction. In the 1920s, for example, railway mileage barely increased at all, going from 38 000 miles in 1920 to just over 41 000 by 1928.

This lack of growth does not mean that the railways were putting their houses in order and building up surpluses against a rainy day. Both CN and CP indulged in considerable expansion through the 1920s in such areas as hotels and steamships. The debt of both companies increased, even during this prosperous decade.[12] To make matters worse, CN was saddled with an existing large debt left over from the earlier consolidation process. The charges on this debt, as well as the new debt acquired through the decade, meant that, even in the good times of the later 1920s, CN was unable to cover operating expenses and debt charges. Losses between 1923 and 1931 were a staggering $546 million, and, even during the bumper crop year of 1928, annual losses for the government system were nearly $48 million.[13] It was a burden on the public accounts in the best of times. The worst of times were about to come.

As the Rowell-Sirois Commission would note a few years later, the collapse of western agriculture that came about in the Depression "struck at the heart of the Canadian railway structure."[14] The Canadian railways had been developed in the image of the national policy's vision of an east-west exchange of primary resources and manufactured goods. Hauling the millions of bushels of wheat off the prairies and carrying the consumer goods, the farm implements, and the immigrants to the west had dictated railway construction in Canada during the previous half-century. Suddenly, there was less grain to be hauled, and the people in the west could not afford all of those manufactured goods from the east. In addition, the huge quantities of logs and newsprint that had been brought by rail out of Ontario, New Brunswick, and British Columbia were less in demand. Between 1928 and 1931, the annual total tonnage of forest products hauled by Canadian railways had decreased by half. Total railway freight in Canada declined from a record 141 million tons in 1928 to 75 million tons by 1936.

Such a decline in traffic meant disaster for the debt-laden railways. Even the formerly profitable Canadian Pacific went into the red and suspended dividend payments for several years. It looked healthy compared to Canadian National, however. Annual losses on that line rose to an incredible $112 million a year, an amount equivalent to more than one-third of the annual revenue of the Dominion government! By 1935, the funded debt level of the railway system had climbed to more than $3 billion, in spite of severe cost-cutting measures.

The debts of the railways were so massive that they affected the public accounts, but the problems of rigid and high debts applied to many factories, farms, and governments in the country. Indeed, many individual farmers faced parallel circumstances, albeit on a smaller scale, to those of railways. Mortgages of $5000 or $10 000 that seemed a reasonable investment back in 1925 or 1926 became a crushing burden as wheat prices collapsed. In many cases, debt levels exceeded the newly depressed total values of the whole farming operation. The payment of interest often exceeded the annual income in farming operations. And banks were a lot less willing to wait upon a farmer's future than they were a railway's.

Each of the circumstances described above was harmful enough individually; however, their total effect and the relationship among them created the sequence leading to the Great Depression. To recapitulate: by the later 1920s, international commodity gluts posed a serious problem for world trade. Canada, as a nation dependent on that trade, was bound to suffer from the increasingly inevitable adjustments that would be needed to rid the world of excess inventories. Already by 1929 the Prairie west was suffering from the effects of such adjustments and a bad crop year. There had been other such adjustments, such as those in 1913 and 1921. In 1929, it was different, however. The international trading and currency systems were unstable, and the beginning of recession, exacerbated by the collapse of the New York markets, triggered a series of crises that led to protectionism and to a progressive shrinkage of world trade. For the next three or four years, the world lurched from crisis to crisis, as the international economy continued to shrink and as international financial and monetary systems proved incapable of handling the drastic downturn. All of this was bad enough, but Canada was also hampered by two additional circumstances. First, the massive capital investment of the later 1920s meant that the economic recovery would have to be considerable before there was a significant demand for new investment. Second, and worst of all, since Canada's was an export-dependent economy with only a small domestic market, there was little that could be done. Exports would recover only when the international community decided it needed Canadian products again. Domestic investment and, eventually, expansion, would come only some time after that.

Social Cost and Social Response

There is a danger in presenting all these trends and numbers. While they illuminate the causes of the Depression, they tend to understate its effects. The Depression was more than an economic curiosity; it was an event that engulfed the lives of most Canadians. It is at the level of the individual and the family that the bloodless figures of economics turn into a very human story of hardship. Beginning in 1929, with the farmers and those small-town tradesmen dependent on farmers, people began to see their livelihoods slip away. The local hardware or feed store that had prospered during the 1920s suddenly found its clients delinquent in their accounts, or simply absent altogether. From the farms and the local suppliers, it spread to the larger western centres and to companies dependent on farmers — implement firms, the railways, and others. Then, by the fall and winter of 1929–30, industrial centres began to be affected. Layoffs occurred, and then plant closings. Declining auto sales meant that the industrial heartland of Ontario began to experience serious unemployment. In three years, the number of employees in manufacturing decreased by nearly 200 000; more than half of this decline was in Ontario.[15] With each layoff, of course, local stores suffered a loss in business. There was no unemployment insurance to cushion the blow, and labour unions rarely had the strength to prevent wages from being lowered or benefits trimmed in those companies that still operated.

Shrinking markets and declining expectations meant that businesses avoided new investment. New machinery was not ordered, the new factory was not built, and production was cut to allow time to get rid of the suddenly stagnant inventory. More factory workers, more construction workers, more suppliers found themselves without work. Thus, the interdependent nature of the Canadian economy became apparent, as the troubled economy of 1929 turned into the recession-laden one of 1930 and the collapsing one of 1931 and 1932. By 1933, one in four Canadians was out of a job, and there was absolutely nothing on the horizon that gave hope for better prospects in the near future.

Initially, Canadians reacted to these new circumstances by doing two things. First, they postponed the purchase of "consumer durables," or what might, in modern parlance, be termed the "big-ticket items." This was why automobile consumption fell so sharply, as did the price of housing. However, Canadians tried to maintain their standard of living in other ways. Consumer spending decreased by only 4 percent in 1930, as Canadians dipped into their savings in the desperate hope that better times would return before the funds ran out.[16] Such expenditures helped to slow the onslaught of the Depression, but were far from sufficient to stem the tide and, of course, savings did not last forever. By 1932 and 1933, as unemployment brought more and more families into poverty, people were avoiding not only the major expenditures but also the minor and normal ones. People were driving not only older cars but fewer of them. In 1932, for the first time since the invention of the automobile, the number of automobiles registered in Canada decreased.[17] Clothes that had been patched in 1930 became shabby and threadbare by 1932. Children often went without shoes in summer, especially in the hard-hit prairies, and the housing stock began to deteriorate, as little new construction was undertaken and as needed renovations went undone for lack of funds. Health deteriorated, as people avoided trips to doctors and dentists. Each year, the Depression exacted a little more from the people.

All of this took a severe psychological toll as well. The rhythms of the seasons and the boom-and-bust cycle inherent in many primary-resource industries mean that Canadians were used to periodic unemployment. The 1930s were different, however, for two reasons. First, unemployment now had a longer duration. People were not out of work for a month, or for six months, but often for years. For those graduating from school, the prospects of getting a job, any job, were daunting at best. For men who lost their jobs after years with a company, for farm families who lost years of work, or for the young person unable to find work, the most discouraging thing was the sheer length of time before prospects eventually improved.

The Depression was also different from other recessions because it was so widespread. Certain professions — logging, fishing, and construction among them — routinely experienced fluctuating employment. The Depression hit everywhere, however, and unemployment struck whole groups of occupations and classes of citizens that had previously been assumed to be free of such cyclical variations. The middle classes, who had previously looked with a certain disdain and suspicion upon those out of work, now found themselves just as vulnerable to unemployment as the working classes. A good many prejudices had to be discarded as the newly unemployed learned what it was like to be without work for prolonged periods.

What they found out was that it was not very pleasant. The support systems that existed for those out of work were minimal. Much of the reason behind this was historical. The unemployed and indigent are in a different position in an urban-industrial society than in a rural and agriculturally based one. In the latter, lack of mobility preserves family networks, which can be turned to in times of difficulty. Further, the line between "employment" and "unemployment" is less well-defined in a system resting upon agriculture. The mobility that came from urbanization and the dependence on wage employment that went with industrialization, however, made for a very different world and demanded a different series of support systems. In Canada, however, industrialization and urbanization were very recent phenomena. Only in the fifteen years or so before the Depression had Canadians even begun to grapple with the implications of industrial unemployment.[18] Some measures had been introduced, such as Workmen's Compensation and Dominion-sponsored labour-referral services. Overall, however, progress had been limited.

One of the reasons for the slow progress had been resistance of Canadians themselves to such new programs. Many (including some who found themselves out of work in the 1930s) had opposed such measures in the name of a "rugged individualism" that had built the country. Further, in the 1920s, both the public and the governments they elected had been more concerned with reducing the national debt than with increasing social services. There was thus no unemployment-insurance system, no health care for the poor, except charity wards, no family allowance, and only the most rudimentary of old-age pensions.

There were systems in place to prevent starvation for the indigent. Aside from private charities and churches, there was a complex and uneven public-relief system to provide for those with no other means of support. The character of this relief system was shaped by constitutional law and by public prejudice. Constitutionally, under the British North America Act, welfare was a provincial responsibility and, in fact, relief had always been seen as a local responsibility, rooted in the municipality or county and usually dependent on the local property-tax base. Second, there was a widespread feeling that relief systems would only encourage indigence unless they were made as basic and rudimentary as possible. Under what was known as the doctrine of "less eligibility," this was often translated into the maxim that relief should always guarantee a standard of living lower than that attainable through the worst job available, lest people be tempted out of the productive work force.[19]

When the Depression hit, two problems quickly became apparent. First, the demeaning aspects that had been built into the system

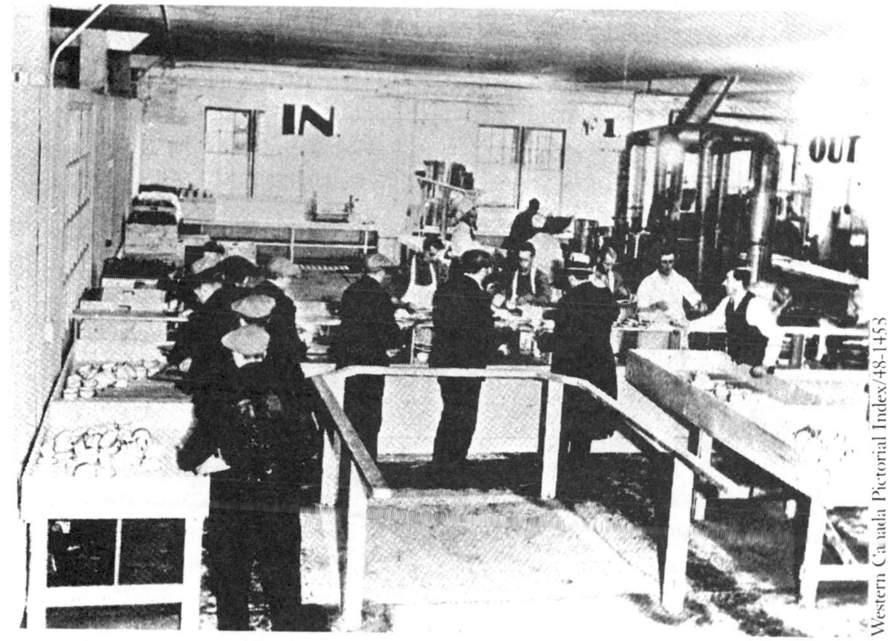

Western Canada Pictorial Index/48-1453

Soup kitchen, Edmonton, 1933. *During the Depression, many homeless and unemployed people depended on soup kitchens for their one meal of the day. Private charities and churches often sponsored soup kitchens, depending on volunteers (sometimes matrons from the most wealthy areas of the town) to staff them.*

made it all that much harder for those faced for the first time in their lives with the need to ask for assistance. Regulations varied from community to community (in itself, a problem of inequity) but the doctrine of "less eligibility" meant that, with few exceptions, for people on relief, life was encumbered by rules that made little sense. Rules against drinking and against the possession of a telephone, for example, were often argued to be measures to ensure the public charge did not become too extravagant. They were also, however, often indications of petty bureaucratic suspicion that the person on welfare was prone to dishonesty and lazy indulgence. What, for example, can one make of the regulation in Saskatchewan, that a person on relief not only not own a car (which might make some sense) but not possess a driver's licence? Likewise, it is possible to understand the concept of "make-work projects" if the work being done provided a useful service to the community supporting those on relief. When, as James Gray relates of his own experience in Winnipeg, that project involved digging a hole, putting rocks into it, and refilling it, then the only purpose seemed to be to punish the unemployed. Those dependent on this sort of system knew exactly what such rules and activities implied about them, and they often found it one of the most humiliating things about being out of work.

Aside from being inhumane and inequitable, the system was financially fragile. The municipally based relief system could function only so long as a small minority of citizens depended on relief at any given time. With the deepening of the Depression, however, more and more people flooded on to relief rolls, and they were staying there for longer periods of time than had previously been the case. Indeed, many would be dependent on public support for years. As a result, as Table 18.5 shows, the relief burden increased enormously. By 1931, three provinces were each spending more than all together had the year before. The relief burden had increased sixfold in one year and, by 1934, it would be up eightfold. And 1930 had been a bad year by previous standards![20]

The problems in the relief system increased because of the tendency of many people to leave their homes and set out for new areas. Single males were especially transient, using some of Canada's overbuilt freight capacity to move around the country. It was not just single males, however; whole families moved as well. On the prairies, people moved from the drought-ridden south, northward to the relatively favoured parkland. In Ontario and Quebec, people drifted in from the lumber communities to the larger cities. The long-term depopulation of the Maritimes continued, though there were few prospects anywhere else. In some cases, the moves were rational attempts at material betterment. In many instances, however, the very process of movement was sufficient rationale in an age that was otherwise so confining.

Such movement made the already overburdened relief system even more ineffective. Municipalities were not prepared for the influx of thousands of new unemployed into their already hard-hit centres. Cities such as Vancouver, which attracted so many of the unemployed, would quickly have gone bankrupt had they tried to fund them all. Other cities, less affected by unemployment, nevertheless wanted to keep tax rolls down, and, finally, many citizens just wanted to keep these "undesirables" away. The result was a

TABLE 18.5

The Relief Burden by Province

(millions of dollars)

	1930	*1931*	*1932*	*1933*	*1934*	*1935*	*1936*	*1937*
P.E.I.	0.03	0.32	0.24	0.06	0.41	0.94	0.62	0.58
Nova Scotia	0.10	2.60	3.80	3.20	2.40	3.00	2.70	2.60
New Brunswick	0.30	2.60	0.50	1.90	1.30	2.40	2.50	1.50
Quebec	2.00	17.30	18.80	22.20	31.80	26.50	35.40	30.80
Ontario	2.40	21.30	33.40	32.40	60.70	54.50	38.50	28.20
Manitoba	1.60	8.60	7.40	7.10	7.50	9.80	12.20	9.80
Saskatchewan	5.90	24.00	13.20	10.30	21.10	18.60	22.70	62.30
Alberta	2.40	6.70	5.90	4.90	6.00	7.00	9.20	7.60
B.C.	2.20	8.40	8.90	8.10	9.90	11.30	10.00	9.00
TOTAL	16.93	91.80	92.10	90.20	141.10	134.00	133.80	152.40

Source: Canada, Royal Commission to Dominion–Provincial Relations. *Report*, Book I, Tables 59–68.

Glenbow Archives/NC6-12955B

A transient hitches a ride on a freight train, c. *1934. During the Depression, single males were especially transient, hopping freight trains ("riding the rods") to move around the country. Sometimes whole families moved: on the prairies, from the drought-ridden south to the north; in Ontario and Quebec, from the lumber communities to the larger cities.*

series of residency requirements for relief that prevented new arrivals from getting assistance locally. In this way, too, the local nature of relief systems did not reflect the reality of Canada.

Table 18.5 also indicates how unevenly the burden of relief in Canada was distributed. The western provinces, in general, and Saskatchewan, in particular, were hit much harder than were eastern provinces. Relief costs rose more quickly and remained higher for longer periods of time. Overall relief expenditures in the 1930–37 period stood at an average of 3.6 percent of provincial incomes. The burden ranged tremendously, however. Ontario, for example, had an average burden of 2.7 percent; New Brunswick, 2.4 percent.

In contrast, Saskatchewan's was a staggering 13.3 percent. At the local level, the burdens could often become even more dramatic. Small rural municipalities in southern Saskatchewan might have 50 percent of the population on relief, with the other 50 percent behind in their taxes! Obviously, the municipal-based system of funding could not survive under such circumstances. Equally obvious, however, was the fact that with burdens like these, several provinces were bound to prove as incapable of bearing this burden as were the municipalities.

In sum, then, the impact of the Depression was made worse by the absence of any meaningful social-security system. The system that did exist was rudimentary both in the services it was intended to deliver and in the tax base upon which it rested. Municipalities, and then provinces, were driven to the edge of bankruptcy as relief costs spiralled. The whole system would have collapsed had it been left unaided. Necessity made it very quickly apparent, therefore, that unemployment, and the human misery that went with it, were a national rather than a local crisis. To understand how this basic human and financial dilemma was responded to, it is necessary to look at the range of government activity during the Depression.

The Government Response to the Depression

In the face of an economic whirlwind such as that encountered between 1930 and 1933, governments proved inadequate. They did not have the theory, the means, or the will to handle the Depression. They were constrained by the constitution, by the open nature of Canada's economy, and by their own fiscal capabilities. Many ideas were proposed, and various schemes were tried, but the record of government action during the Depression is one of uncertainty and, with a few exceptions, lack of success.

The response of government to the Depression was shaped, above all, by one basic fact. The responsibilities and demands on the government had changed dramatically in recent years, but constitutional rigidities and other factors had prevented a smooth adjustment of financial resources to respond to these new demands. Specifically, the twentieth century had made certain responsibilities of the province much more important and, consequently, much more expensive. Children were staying in school much longer and were attending school, when they were enrolled, on a much more regular basis. Thus, education costs rose dramatically. With the development of the automobile, roads and bridges became a much more expensive proposition as well. Finally, the demands of new technologies, such as electricity and telephones, often fell to the municipalities or provinces. As a result, provincial expenditures soared in the years after World War I. In 1913, total current expenditures for all provinces had been only $48.9 million. By 1929, the total was $163 million.

Such a rapid rise in expenditures was inevitably accompanied by an increase in debt. While the Dominion government was actually reducing its debt level through the 1920s (and trying, therefore, to repay some of the costs of the war), the provinces and municipalities found debt a convenient way to defray some of the immediate burdens imposed by public demand. Thus, total provincial-municipal debt charges increased from just over $51 million in 1921 to more than $85 million by 1930. Like the farmer's mortgage or the businessman's bank loan, these were fixed charges that would become an increasing burden as revenues declined and relief burdens mounted.

Clearly, then, most of the provinces were in no shape to undertake major new initiatives during the Depression. The majority were scrambling simply to survive, and realized very quickly that they would be able to do so only if the Dominion government assumed some of their financial burden. As for the Dominion government, it ultimately had no choice. If the provinces began to go bankrupt, the responsibilities would inevitably fall to the Dominion anyway, and there was, with each passing year, an ever-better chance that some bankruptcies would, indeed, occur. By 1935, outgoing prime minister R.B. Bennett warned his successor, Mackenzie King, that several provinces, especially in the west, were effectively bankrupt.[21]

Initially, the Dominion government took an active if somewhat unimaginative role in facing the Depression. Mackenzie King's Liberals were unceremoniously tossed out by the electorate in 1930, and R.B. Bennett's Conservatives came into office pledged to quick action. This they took, not only by raising the tariff but by initiating a series of public-works programs to provide employment in hard-hit spots of the nation. Also, they undertook a series of ad hoc grants to the provinces to assist in relief payments and brought in such measures as the Unemployment and Farm Relief Act of 1931. Dominion welfare payments alone rose from a negligible $2 million in 1929 to $48 million by 1932. Overall, Dominion expenditures increased by $132 million between 1929 and 1932. In the meantime, revenues had decreased by $140 million, as tax revenues dried up. The net effect of this was that government expenditures did work in a countercyclical fashion during the initial years of the Depression. The Dominion actually increased expenditures but, even if the struggling provinces and municipalities are included, the expenditures were the component of national income most resistant to decreases.[22]

This situation did not last. The tremendous rise in costs necessitated by municipal and provincial relief and by Dominion assistance programs caused deficits to rise inexorably. By 1933, provincial debt levels had risen to more than $1.5 billion, and the Dominion balance changed from a budgetary surplus of $68 million on the 1928 year, to a deficit of $160 million on that of 1935. Accumulated federal government debt increased from $3.2 billion in 1929 to $4.1 billion by 1933, and $4.5 billion by 1935.

The rising deficits soon paralyzed government. In 1931, with international financial collapse well underway, Bennett became nervous about the level of Dominion expenditures. "We must now talk in thousands where we previously spoke in millions," he wrote, "or we will be bankrupt."[23] Saving dollars became the major theme of government administration. Thousands of civil servants were let go, while those who retained their jobs in government service had their salaries cut. Public-works expenditures were slashed, as building construction and even repairs were postponed. Contracts for new construction were lower than at any time since the early 1890s. Thus, even the most standard and traditional of government unemployment measures — public works — was abandoned by 1932–33 as a means of dealing with the Great Depression. The collapse was thought too massive and the government deficit too large.

As Figure 18.1 shows, cutbacks after 1933 meant that the government no longer acted as a countercyclical force (albeit an ineffective one) and may actually have slowed potential recovery in the subsequent years. For this it has received much criticism. If only the Dominion government had accepted the new currents of Keynesianism, the argument runs, it would have seen the advantage of massive deficits and have undertaken greater initiatives.

Yet such criticism is really beside the point, for several reasons.

FIGURE 18.1

Dominion Government Expenditure, 1929–1939, as a Percentage of GNP

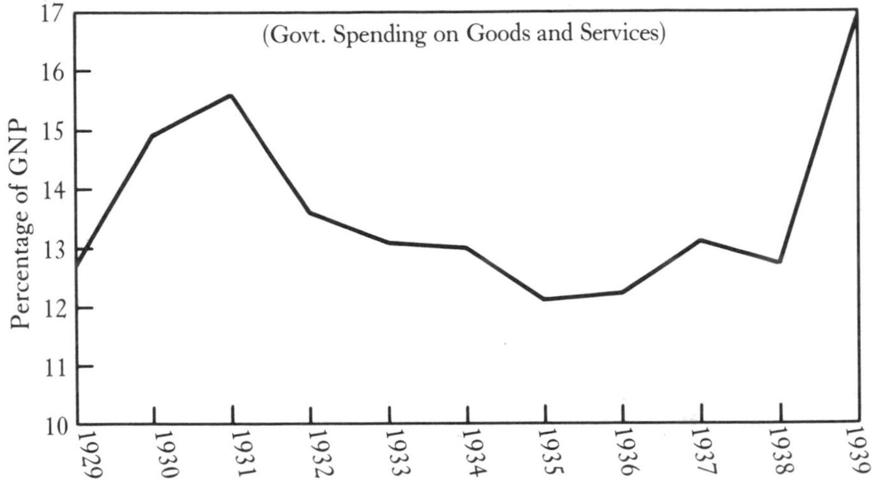

Source: Derived from Statistics Canada, *Historical Statistics of Canada*, 2nd ed. (Ottawa: Supply and Services, 1983), Series H1–51, F1–152.

First, the deficit was a real problem. Annual debt charges had before World War I amounted to less than 9 percent of annual revenue. The war had changed all that, of course, and the debt carried out of the war drained 26 percent of current revenue by 1928. By 1935, it would consume an amazing 43 percent of annual revenues. Almost one dollar in two in the Dominion budget was going just to handle the national debt. Both the level of the debt and the dramatic change in that level were bound to affect politicians. Even in a post-Keynesian world, it would have taken considerable faith in economic theory to have maintained spending in such a fiscal position.

Second, the government was simply not yet a large enough institution that people thought of it as being able to affect the direction of the whole economy. Public works and such measures might provide short-term relief, but the fiscal power of government was not as great as it would be in the post-1945 period. At the beginning of the Depression, for example, Dominion government expenditure was about 6.5 percent of GNP. In 1975, it was more than 20 percent. For the government to have had an effect on the Canadian economy, it would have had to adopt a level of spending and a deficit completely out of accord with Canadian history and existing wisdom. It is hardly surprising that such a course was not followed.

The third problem was constitutional. Under the British North America Act, and subsequent court decisions, the powers of the Dominion government were severely limited in areas that became crucial during the Depression. In particular, Section 92 gave responsibility for welfare and unemployment to the provinces. As has been discussed, the provincial control of welfare created difficulties for recipients in terms of residency and equity, both in the capacity of the provinces and in the treatment of Canadians. From the governmental point of view, however, the most serious problem was one of divided jurisdiction. Those that had the constitutional jurisdiction (the provinces) could not, with a couple of exceptions, pay for it. However, the only body in the nation that might be able to co-ordinate some sort of national response to the Depression, and had the fiscal power to develop necessary welfare schemes, was seriously hampered by constitutional barriers — barriers it often used to avoid responsibility.

The result was an unsatisfactory series of compromises and ad hoc programs. Once R.B. Bennett gave up on his initial public-works schemes, he increasingly funnelled funds to the provinces to handle the growing relief problems. By 1934, with provincial and municipal credit exhausted throughout much of the nation, the Dominion was funding more than 30 percent of all relief expenditures. On the prairies, the Dominion government had, by this time, assumed the vast proportion of relief costs. The provinces simply had no money. At the same time, constitutional rigidities meant that the government paying the funds had little or no say as to where much of the money was going. Dominion politicians and civil servants mumbled darkly of inefficient and corrupt provincial governments. More imaginative proposals for Dominion action — on the occasions when they did come — always faced the constitutional barrier, and as a result the most unimaginative expenditure of all — relief, or the dole, as it was known — became, almost by default, the only serious fiscal outlay of the government in the face of the Depression.

As Figure 18.1 indicates, this was true of both the Bennett administration, which lasted until 1935, and the revived King administration, which was returned in that year. The funds continued to flow outward to the provinces because there was practically no way to stem the tide. In other areas, both the Liberals and the Conservatives were much more cautious. Budgetary expenditure by the Dominion actually decreased relative to gross national expenditure in the latter half of the Depression. This shift was intentional, as the Liberals, seeing an opportunity in the modest recovery that was taking place by 1935, moved to try to balance the budget. "I believe," said Liberal finance minister Charles Dunning, "that no country can go on indefinitely with heavily unbalanced budgets."[24] Thus, while government expenditures may have been a positive force in slowing the decline from 1929 to 1933, they were, if anything, a force working as a modest brake on growth during the period of recovery. Only in 1939, as defence expenditures began in preparation for war, did Dominion expenditures as a percentage of GNE recover to 1935 levels.

Such restricted expenditures meant, of course, that it was practically impossible for government to undertake meaningful new social or economic programs. It was very difficult, for example, to create a systematic "safety net" for those caught in the downturns of modern economic cycles. It was simply too expensive. A decade of depression, therefore, failed to bring about any significant improvements in social security; those would come later.

There was one exception to this tendency, but it, too, proved how unprepared the Canadian governmental structure was for a crisis such as the Depression. This exception came in 1935, when R.B. Bennett announced a wide-ranging series of reforms patterned on the American New Deal. Speeches urging a minimum wage, unemployment insurance, and other far-reaching measures were, after some delay, brought to Parliament. There was a great deal of debate at the time about Bennett's motivation and whether this was a sincere effort to reform capitalism or a cynical election ploy. In terms of results, however, the debate is largely irrelevant, for two things occurred that prevented Bennett's New Deal from being implemented. First, Bennett was defeated by King's Liberals, and, second, the New Deal ran into a constitutional problem. In 1937, the Judicial Committee of the Privy Council of the United Kingdom, then the final court of appeal, declared key elements of Bennett's program *ultra vires*. Even when the will did exist, the federal structures of Canada imposed serious barriers to economic reform.

By and large, therefore, constitutional and economic restraints meant that government policy under Bennett and King would concentrate on less far-reaching (and less expensive) reforms. In general, these reforms took two directions. One was toward regulation in the marketplace in the name of economic order. Excess production, fierce competition, and unregulated capitalism were seen by the pundits of the day as central to the Depression. It is not surprising, therefore, that this tendency toward regulation emerged. Many of the agricultural quota systems that exist today have their roots in such Depression legislation as the Natural Products Marketing Act (1934). The Bank of Canada was established the same year, in response to growing demands that some order be brought to the financial marketplace. These were Conservative measures, and Mackenzie King was more reluctant to enter into the regulation of economic activity. Even he found, however, that many of the measures he inherited, including the Wheat Board, were sufficiently popular to justify his expanding their activities.[25]

The other major direction of government policy during the Depression was the manipulation of trade with the outside world through the use of tariffs and negotiated agreements. Initially, as has been shown, the tendency was toward massive protectionism. Bennett's first action on assuming office was to raise tariffs on a number of goods. In so doing, he was following the general international tendency and retaliating, in particular, against the extreme protectionism of the United States. It was conventional wisdom and completely standard policy; however, it was of dubious benefit.

The problem for Canada in such a measure was twofold. First, it only exacerbated the international trend toward restrictions on international trade, when such trade was vitally important for Canada. Second, in Canada, protectionism had significant regional implications. Domestic manufacturing and a few specialty crops were protected — largely in Quebec and Southern Ontario. Resource production, dependent on exports and largely free from serious import competition, gained nothing. Those who worked in those sectors thus bore the burden that the tariff imposed in terms of higher costs. In regional terms, this meant, in effect, that Southern Ontario and the industrial portions of Quebec gained, while the vast hinterland — east and west — suffered.[26] Much of the effect of Dominion money funnelled into the devastated west in the Depression was probably offset by the high tariff policy pursued, at least in the early years of the Depression.

Yet high tariffs were never, in themselves, a primary goal of Canadian trade policy. Bennett came into office promising to "blast" his way into the markets of the world. That is, with high tariffs in place, he could approach Canadian trading partners for specific arrangements. For reasons of patriotism and because the Americans showed no inclination to deal, Bennett's first approach was to the British. Ottawa convinced the Commonwealth that Canada should host a 1932 imperial economic conference to discuss ways and means of combatting the Depression. After much rhetoric and some hard negotiating, that conference gave Canada preference in the British market for such key products as wheat, apples, and lumber. In return, Britain got concessions in the Canadian market, largely at the expense of the United States. Over the next months and years Canada and Britain negotiated further arrangements within the Commonwealth so that a freer, though hardly free, trade zone did emerge within the Commonwealth.

King and the Liberals pursued this policy of bilateral trade arrangements with enthusiasm when they were elected in 1935. Liberals traditionally believed in free trade, but the active pursuit of free trade was also an inexpensive policy to bear. Following a failed Bennett initiative, King moved, soon after his election, to negotiate a trade deal with the United States. In 1938, his government further reduced duties in a trilateral arrangement with Britain and the United States.

These agreements did not end the Depression in Canada. The reality was that international protectionism might have impeded recovery but the forces underlying the Depression were so deep that trade agreements by themselves could not have a significant effect on the general course of the Canadian economy. The agreements undoubtedly did help certain sectors, at least to a degree. More dramatic, perhaps, was the fact that they rechannelled existing trade. By the end of the 1930s, more trading was done in economic blocs such as the Commonwealth,[27] and in the wake of the 1932 agreement Canadian exports to Britain surpassed those to the United States. Conversely, by 1939, with subsequent agreements in place, the Americans had again become our primary export market (see Table 18.6), though long-term trends as well as specific agreements accounted for this fact.

TABLE 18.6

Destination of Canadian Merchandise Exports

(millions of dollars)

	United States	*United Kingdom*	*Total*
1929	488	290	1178
1930	369	235	880
1931	237	170	601
1932	157	178	495
1933	166	210	532
1934	217	270	648
1935	260	303	732
1936	333	395	954
1937	359	402	1041
1938	270	339	844
1939	380	328	906

Source: Statistics Canada, *Historical Statistics of Canada*, 2d ed. (Ottawa: Supply and Services, 1983), Series G389–400, G381–5.

Overall, then, government response to the Depression was a mixture of the old and new. There were significant new interventions in the marketplace in the regulatory bodies that were established, and there was the potential inherent in such bodies as the Bank of Canada for a much more interventionist approach than was taken during the 1930s. Yet these innovations were limited in scope, and their full potential would often not be realized until later. The most important government instrument for manipulating the economy was the same one it had always been — the tariff structure — and fiscal practices, though evolving, remained fundamentally the same as before.

While governments stumbled along — trying what they could and what they dared — new parties promised recovery through nationalism and central planning, through unorthodox monetary measures, and a host of other schemes. At the provincial level, the public turned increasingly to varying degrees of economic and political unorthodoxy. Premiers Duff Pattullo in British Columbia, Mitch Hepburn in Ontario, Maurice Duplessis in Quebec, and, most unorthodox of them all, William Aberhart, who was elected in Alberta in 1935, promised solutions to the Depression. Whatever else they may or may not have accomplished, however, none of them ended the Depression. The fact was that government, as it was known in Canada, could have, at best, a marginal effect on the course of the Depression.

Conclusion

Recovery, like the Depression itself, began with international events. Beginning in late 1932, and through 1933, the economies of several European nations, and, most importantly for Canada, that of the United Kingdom, began to improve. The 1932 Imperial Economic Conference meant that Canada was in a particularly good position to take advantage of this improvement, and Canadian trade with Britain increased considerably between 1932 and 1937, reaching 90 percent of the 1928 figure. This helped Canada's overall level of exports, which began their long climb back toward the levels of the 1920s. For the next three years, recovery continued. Central to this recovery was the fact that by 1934–35 exports to the United States were also recovering. Between 1932 and 1937, total exports more than doubled and were once again approaching the levels of the later 1920s. Though led by exports, this recovery was reflected as well in a gradual increase in consumer purchases and in employment. Current-account balances remained strong, largely because Canadians were purchasing much less abroad than they had been in the 1920s. The one area that lagged was domestic investment because the improvement that was taking place had not yet removed the depression psychology that made businessmen hesitant to invest, nor had it utilized the excess capacity still existing in many industries.[28]

There was one final setback. In 1937, the United States economy slumped badly, wiping out many of the gains made in the previous few years. Canada was directly affected, as American purchases of Canadian goods decreased by almost one-quarter between 1937 and 1938. In Canada, this decrease directly affected numerous jobs and indirectly affected the psychology of recovery. Practically all major indicators slumped.[29] By the end of 1938, the slump was over, and there was modest improvement once again in the overall Canadian economy. Still, the 1937–38 recession showed the fragile nature of the recovery that had been taking place and, most importantly, reinforced the psychology of depression. Only the most extreme external events could overcome such a psychology and bring the international economy fully out of the Depression within the foreseeable future. Unfortunately, those events did indeed come as Europe moved toward war. Modern industrial warfare, as World War I had clearly shown, placed tremendous demands on both agricultural and industrial economies. As war neared, the psychology of depression began to lift and, with war itself, the greatest depression in history was over. The world traded in one catastrophe for another, and more horrendous, one.

Notes

1 Precise unemployment figures are impossible to come by for the 1930s. See Udo Sautter, "Measuring Unemployment in Canada: Federal Efforts Before World War 2," *Social History* 15 (November 1982): 475–87.
2. Charles P. Kindleberger, *The World in Depression, 1929–1939* (Los Angeles: University of California Press, 1975), 125.
3. William Ashworth, *A Short History of the International Economy, 1850–1950* (London: Longmans, Green, 1952), 203; Kindleberger, *The World in Depression*, 172.
4. J.H. Thompson and A. Seager, *Canada, 1922–1939: Decades of Discord* (Toronto: McClelland and Stewart, 1985), 195; A.E. Safarian, *The Canadian Economy in the Great Depression* (Toronto: McClelland and Stewart, 1970), 42.
5. Safarian, *The Canadian Economy*, Table 50.
6. The figures in the previous few paragraphs generally come from the Canada Year Book for 1930 and 1933. The net-income figures come from Statistics Canada, *Historical Statistics of Canada*, 2nd ed. (Ottawa: Supply and Services, 1983).
7. Statistics Canada, *Historical Statistics*, G57–83.
8. Safarian, *The Canadian Economy in the Great Depression*, 2.
9. Safarian, *The Canadian Economy in the Great Depression*, 131.
10. Edward J. Chambers, "Canadian Business Cycles and Merchandise Exports," *Canadian Journal of Economics and Political Science* 24 (1958): 166–89.
11. Statistics Canada, *Historical Statistics*, F14–32, column under "Business Gross Fixed Capital Formation"; M.C. Urquhart, "Canadian Economic Growth 1870-1980," Queen's University, Department of Economics, Discussion Paper No. 734, Table 4a.
12. Thompson and Seager, *Canada, 1922–1939*, 94.
13. Figures are drawn from Safarian, *The Canadian Economy in the Great Depression*, 50; and Royal Commission on Dominion-Provincial Relations (hereinafter cited as R-S), *Report*, Book I, *Canada, 1867–1939*, 161.
14. R-S, *Report*, Book I 161.

15. Statistics Canada, *Historical Statistics*, R1–22.
16. The 4 percent figure comes from Safarian, *The Canadian Economy in the Great Depression*, 76.
17. Canada Year Book, 1933, 686.
18. See, for example, Province of Ontario, "Report of the Commission on Unemployment," Ontario Sessional Paper No. 55, 1916. See also D. Owram, *The Government Generation: Canadian Intellectuals and the State, 1900–1945* (Toronto: University of Toronto Press, 1986), 50–79, 23.
19. James Struthers, *No Fault of Their Own: Unemployment and the Canadian Welfare State 1914–1941* (Toronto: University of Toronto Press), 57.
20. R-S, *Report*, Book I, 163.
21. D. Owram, *Government Generation*, 228.
22. Safarian, *The Canadian Economy in the Great Depression*, 77.
23. Cited in James Struthers, *No Fault of Their Own*, 57.
24. Cited in J.H. Perry, *Taxes, Tariffs and Subsidies*, Vol. 1 (Toronto: University of Toronto Press, 1955), 294.
25. On King and the wheat board, see H.B. Neatby, *William Lyon Mackenzie King*, Vol. 3: *1932–1939: The Prism of Unity* (Toronto: University of Toronto Press, 1976), 305–8.
26. See W.A. Mackintosh, *The Economic Background of Dominion-Provincial Relations* (Toronto: McClelland and Stewart, 1964), Chapter 7.
27. Safarian, *The Canadian Economy in the Great Depression*, 140.
28. Edward J. Chambers, "The 1937–38 Recession in Canada," *Canadian Journal of Economics and Political Science* 21 (1955): 293–308.
29. Chambers, "The 1937–38 Recession."

Further Reading

Kindleberger, Charles P. *The World in Depression, 1929–1939.* Los Angeles: University of California Press, 1975.

Owram, Doug. "Economic Thought in the 1930s: The Prelude to Keynesianism." *Canadian Historical Review* 66, no. 3 (September 1985): 344–77.

Safarian, A.E. *The Canadian Economy in the Great Depression*. Toronto: McClelland and Stewart, 1970.

Struthers, James. *No Fault of Their Own: Unemployment and the Canadian Welfare State, 1914–1941.* Toronto: University of Toronto Press, 1983.

Thompson, J.H., and A. Seager. *Canada, 1922–1939: Decades of Discord.* Toronto: McClelland and Stewart, 1985.

CHAPTER

19

World War II, 1939–1945

When World War II began in September 1939, it marked the final of the three great external cataclysms (along with World War I and the Depression) that rocked the Canadian economy in the first half of the twentieth century. It also helped bring the Depression to an end. For that reason, the war can be seen as a part of the turbulent era that began in 1914, and it is so treated in this book. Yet, it should be noted that the postwar world that would follow is understandable only in the light of what happened during the war. For the war provided the economic impetus, nationally and internationally, that ushered in a long-term cycle quite different from the short, sharp fluctuations that had characterized the earlier decades.

First, the war saw the beginning of a long-term cycle of prosperity, marked by only short interruptions. By the time that cycle drew to a close in the early 1970s, the Canadian standard of living had increased to a level unimaginable during the pessimistic years of the 1930s. Second, the war and postwar years brought dramatic sectoral shifts within the economy. For much of the twentieth century, industry had been challenging agriculture's dominance. It was only during and immediately after World War II, however, that the shift from farm to factory was completed. As we shall see, the war gave a tremendous impetus to large-scale industry and heavy manufacturing. Hundreds of thousands of new jobs were created during the war, and most of these were maintained after the war. In contrast, though farming prospered considerably from the war, it would not be a source of new jobs. Increased technology on the farm and the lure of the manufacturing sector meant that people would continue to leave the farm in significant numbers. Another aspect of these sectoral shifts was not fully apparent in the early 1940s but would be central in the longer term. The tertiary sector of the economy had grown fairly rapidly in the interwar years but had never been a crucial part of the Canadian economy. Between 1939 and 1971, however, that changed. The tertiary sector would become the fastest-growing area of the economy and would transform the social and economic structure of the nation.

Finally, there was government. Over the course of this book, we have seen occasional appearances of government's active developmental role through Canadian history. The canals of the 1840s, the Canadian Pacific Railway, the Grand Trunk Pacific, and other ventures have revealed that Canada always had a government willing to participate in economic matters. Yet, the slump of 1919, and especially the Great Depression, also indicated just how limited governments were in the face of major economic forces. Governments might act as developers, but, whatever the voters may think, only rarely did politicians dare to think governments had the resources to shape the economy.

Part of the reason was the size of Canadian governments, which, in the nineteenth and early twentieth centuries, were puny affairs. World War I aside, governments had neither the revenues nor the willingness to take on the management of a whole economy. In 1939, Dominion-government revenue amounted to only $562 million, or $49.73 for every man, woman, and child in the nation. Even had the modern theories of interventionism been accepted in Ottawa, such paltry revenues meant that governments could have had little effect on the nation's economic direction. For such reasons, government policy has, thus far in this book, emerged into the foreground only rarely. That will change in the next several chapters, however, for the role and power of government was about to expand dramatically.

In the latter half of 1939, of course, these longer-range shifts were not foreseeable. Indeed, for those in government and business who had to try to plan, the evident pattern was one, not of stability and growth, but of chaos. Only twenty years after the "war to end all wars" had itself ended, Europe was again plunging toward conflict. By spring of 1939, both Britain and France had ended their policy of appeasement toward Germany. Further aggression by Hitler and the Nazis would mean resistance. Thus, when Hitler invaded Poland at the beginning of September, war seemed inevitable. Canadians knew, moreover, that, if it came, they would be participants. The pull of Empire and the sense of concern for Britain were still strong. When Britain and France declared war on Germany, Canada soon followed suit.

Though Canadians went to war, they did so without the optimism of 1914. The memories of World War I were too fresh in their minds. The human slaughter seemed about to be repeated. Moreover, the fear of national disunity hung over the people and the government. Finally, the mentality of the Depression was very much present as well, as people wondered how the fragile recovery of the last few years would be affected by war. Revenues remained sluggish, and deficit reduction, so long a goal of governments, seemed unlikely with the tremendous new demands of war.

For all these reasons, the first months of war were characterized, not by total effort but by concerns about overcommitment and by a strong interest in ensuring that the war benefited the Canadian economy. The cynical might even argue that the domestic economy was paramount in government thinking. In fact, Under-Secretary of State for External Affairs O.D. Skelton argued in a 1939 brief to the prime minister, "it is in the economic field that we can give aid that will be most effective to our allies and most consistent with Canadian interests."[1]

This policy of what one historian has called the "reign of the dollar" came to an end in the disastrous spring and summer of 1940.[2] With German military victory in Denmark, Holland, Belgium, and France, Canadian policy makers finally realized that any doctrine of limited war made no sense. Henceforth, the Canadian economy moved toward total war. Peacetime calculations of budget-balancing or appropriate taxation levels disappeared, to be replaced by the much grander concept of the nation's total economic capacity.

Even before this policy of total effort had completely taken hold, the war brought about immediate changes in the economy. War orders flowed to manufacturers, who began to gear up idle capacity for the work that was beginning to come their way. Not all would immediately get what they wanted, but the effect overall was dramatic. The number of employees in manufacturing increased by 300 000, or some 50 percent, between 1939 and 1941. In the meantime, ever-larger numbers of men and women were begin taken into the armed forces. The persistent unemployment of the Great Depression was but a memory by 1941. The problem was now shortages of labour, especially skilled labour, which brought the difficulties of supplying the tremendous demands of a modern industrial war to the fore. From the economics of overcapacity, Canada quickly came to experience the complex changes of rapid growth and structural transformation.

The same rapid transformation affected the international economy, on which Canada was so dependent. Trade patterns shifted dramatically as Britain ceased to export goods, while looking to Canada to supply both the traditional primary resources and, before long, manufactured materials. Exports to the United Kingdom increased 50 percent from 1939 to 1940, and, by 1944, had increased 300 percent, to $1.194 billion.[3] Such rapid shifts would, before long, create serious concerns over the balance-of-payments situation and long-term currency relationships. In other words: who was going to pay for the British orders?

Domestic or international, however, the situation was complicated by the necessity of ensuring maximum effectiveness for the war machine. The economy could not be left to work out its future through some sort of invisible hand. The demands of government, not the open marketplace, would determine the direction in which production, employment, export trade, and many other things moved. In understanding the complex patterns of World War II, it is thus with government that we must begin, for government, more than ever before, was truly central to the direction of the Canadian economy.

The Government

On the surface, the Canadian government seemed little prepared for war. A decade of depression had taken its toll here, as elsewhere. In spite of the cutbacks, debt had continued to climb for all levels of government. By 1939, it was more than $5 billion for the Dominion government alone, and politicians maintained their steady warnings of disaster if this burden was not diminished. Moreover, though more diverse than in 1914, the sources of revenues (see Figure 19.1) still rested mainly on customs duties (23 percent), excise

FIGURE 19.1

Sources of Federal Government Revenue, 1937

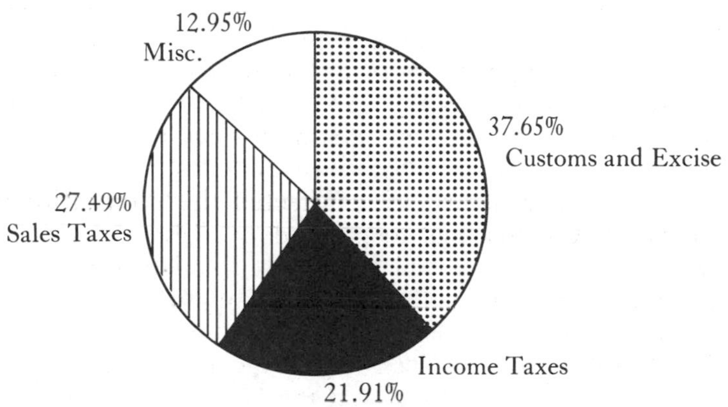

Source: Derived from Statistics Canada, *Historical Statistics of Canada*, 2nd ed. (Ottawa: Supply and Services, 1983), Series G1–25.

tax (15 percent), and sales taxes (27 percent). All of these depended, to a degree, on consumption of goods and, as Borden found in 1914, wartime stringency demanded a reduction in such consumption.

The financial limitations were compounded by the relatively restricted role of the Dominion government. The civil service consisted of only 45 000 people, of whom nearly 12 000 were involved in delivering the mail. Aside from the obvious need for growth in the armed forces (it had fewer than 10 000 permanent members in 1939, even after four years of modest rearmament), the government would need to increase its capacity tremendously if it was to oversee a modern industrial war.

In spite of these problems, the government managed the transition from peace to war, and the subsequent management of the war, extremely well. In the process, government expenditures would increase some 800 percent; the armed forces would reach 4.3 million; and the civil service would mushroom into dozens of new agencies employing some 115 000 men and women. The national debt, which seemed so horrific at a little over $5 billion in 1939, would be more than $18 billion by the end of the war. There were numerous crises and many mistakes along the way, but the amazing thing was that, relatively speaking, it went as well as it did.

As such success implies, the government was better prepared for the crisis than its size in 1939 would indicate. Many individuals inside and outside of government had, in the interwar years, been discussing the role of government planning and intervention in the modern state. The shocks of World War I, and of the postwar slump, had created severe criticisms of laissez-faire economics. More and more government officials, politicians, and those members of the public who were concerned with government called for an interventionist state that would help regulate, or at least ameliorate, the swings of the economic cycle. This new attitude was paralleled, and reinforced, by the growing presence in the civil service of a coterie of individuals trained in modern social-science theory. The old generalist was being replaced by the new expert. Such people as former Queen's University professors O.D. Skelton and Clifford Clark, under-secretary of state in the Department of External Affairs (appointed in 1925) and deputy-minister of the Department of Finance (appointed in 1932), were creating an activist civil service that believed in the possibilities of economic and social planning.

In the 1920s, such changes had been slow. Public desire for a more efficient response to an urban-industrial society was muted by memories of the huge interventionist government of World War I and by fear of high taxation. In the 1930s, the Depression had provided a powerful impetus for discussions of change. The new experts had gained in influence, and such key interventionist measures as the Bank of Canada Act were passed. Economic theory also encouraged an activist government. The famous British economist John Maynard Keynes was, by the middle 1930s, advocating the use of massive countercyclical fiscal and monetary measures to help dampen the effects of economic cycles. Moreover, an increasing number of Canadian economists, and even a few politicians, were beginning to listen to what he said.

At the same time, the Depression limited what could be done. As Chapter 18 indicated, concern with deficits was ever-present and limited any expensive new measures. Constitutional barriers also blocked interventionist action in the key areas of welfare and social security. Moreover, the whole debate over intervention became highly charged ideologically. Advocates of socialism or of regulated capitalism mixed with social-welfare measures had not gained sufficient support to allow any drastic departure from existing structures and practices.

The war changed that. For one thing, it gave the government an authority it had not had during the crises of the Depression years. The War Measures Act, passed in 1914, was still on the books and was proclaimed even before the war began. This act allowed for a central direction of the economy in a way not possible in peacetime situations. The normal legislative processes could be set aside and orders-in-council used for a series of sweeping measures that would not have even been dared in peacetime. In effect, a command economy became possible, in theory, and was utilized, to at least a limited degree. Before long, wages and prices, essential industries, strikes, employment, and a host of other things usually mediated by the marketplace were brought under strict government control.

One of the most important assertions of Dominion power came at the expense of the provinces. As we have seen, constitutional divisions had limited the abilities of governments to respond to the Depression. The Dominion government had even set up a royal commission in 1937 (the Rowell-Sirois Commission) to look at the whole problem of such divided jurisdictions. Royal commissions would never resolve the problem, but the war would set it aside, at least temporarily. When several provinces failed to accept the provisions of the Rowell-Sirois report, Mackenzie King moved to take over all taxation for the duration of the war. Grants to the provinces would keep them afloat and, indeed, the grants were relatively generous, given an improving economy. Nevertheless, the fiscal direction of the economy was in Dominion control, to an unprecedented degree.

Revenue was another area where things had changed drastically after the Depression. Now that the Dominion had control of fiscal planning, it was able to innovate a series of new measures. Those measures, moreover, were possible and successful because the economy was buoyant. A nation of full employment and production was able to generate taxes for government activity in a way that the depression-ridden 1930s could not. Finally, war made high taxation acceptable. Canadians who normally would have balked at rapid increases in taxation accepted increase after increase in the name of the war.

With constitutional power and public tolerance, the government thus set out to finance a war. As had been the case during World War I, that financing would come from a mixture of higher revenue and increased debt. The latter was largely accomplished domestically, as war-bond drives began almost immediately and continued for the duration. Eventually, some $9 billion would be raised from the Canadian public.[4] Much more than in World War I, however, the government recognized from the outset the necessity of increased taxation. The minister of finance said in 1939, "we shall follow as far as may be practicable a pay-as-you-go policy."[5] There was a desire to keep long-term debt down, and a recognition, moreover, that taxation served a dual purpose. First, it provided the government with revenue for the war. Second, in a time when the government was placing tremendous demands on the economy, it had the effect of forcing a reduction in private consumer demands that might compete with war needs. As a contemporary economist noted, such competition could only lead to inflation, and this, "uncertain in its course and uneven in its effects, makes impossible the equitable allocation of the burden of war."[6]

Government taxation thus followed a definite course. In contrast to World War I, the government relied primarily on income taxes — personal and corporate — rather than on the inelastic excise and customs duties. Indeed, the customs duties were used primarily as devices to control international flows of currency rather than as revenue-gatherers. As for income taxes, the first step in 1939 saw an immediate 20 percent increase in tax rates, followed by further increases in 1941 and 1942. Some adjustments were made thereafter in process and structure, but the major changes had taken place during the first three years of the war. The results were crucial to the government's war effort. Income-tax revenues rose from $142 million in 1939 to a high of more than $1 billion by 1944. These changes also made it a tax that affected the average Canadian and not just the wealthy. In 1938–39, a little more than 250 000 Canadians, just over 2 percent of the population, paid income tax. By 1941, the figure had risen to 871 000 and, by 1945, to 2.25 million, or between 18 and 19 percent of the population.[7] The other major innovation in taxation was excess-profits taxes (something argued about for a long time during World War I). These were brought in in 1941 and yielded more than $400 million by the middle of the war. Succession duties, adjustments to sales taxes, and other less significant changes also brought increased revenue. Even the post office saw its revenue increase by some $15 million during the course of the conflict![8]

The results of such increases in taxation in a healthy economy were dramatic. As Figure 19.2 indicates, revenue rose dramatically each year, from just over $500 million in 1939 to a peak six times as great by the end of the war. Expenditures were, naturally, much greater, increasing nearly eightfold, to more than $5 billion. In 1939, government expenditure had amounted to less than 4 percent of gross national expenditure. By 1945, it was nearly 18 percent, a figure higher than it had ever reached, even in World War I when the GNP was much smaller. It was really only in the 1940s that Canadians experienced Big Government for the first time.

Not only did the revenue-gathering capabilities of government change, but so, too, did the sources of that revenue. Indeed, World War II marked the culmination of a long-term shift in Canadian taxation policy. Until World War I, as was shown earlier, government revenue depended almost completely on customs and excise duties. In 1914, these two categories accounted for more than 77 percent of all government revenues. World War I introduced the new income and corporate taxes that began the shift from indirect to direct taxation. Even in 1937, however, as Figure 19.2 indicates, these sources were central to government financing.

World War II completed the process begun by the Great War. The new taxes supplanted the old as the primary source of government revenue and, therefore, as the central features of any fiscal management of the economy. By 1947 (allowing for the winding down of the war), customs and excise taxes accounted for only 14.5 percent of total revenue, while income taxes had risen to almost a third. When excess-profits taxes are added to this figure, the result is 45 percent (see Figure 19.3).

The revolution in fiscal matters alone would have marked a major change in the nature and scope of government in Canada. Taxation and borrowing, however, were only the most basic parts of the complex government system that evolved to fight the war. Getting the money was only the first step, for, as has already been stated,

FIGURE 19.2

Federal Government Revenue and Expenditures, 1938–1945

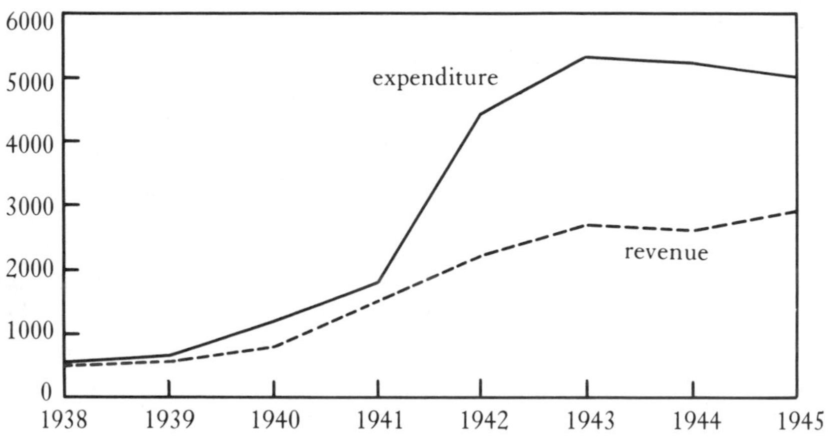

Source: Statistics Canada, *Historical Statistics of Canada*, 2nd ed. (Ottawa: Supply and Services, 1983), Series G1–25.

modern total warfare demanded a sweeping series of innovations to allow the government to use its new revenues and powers with maximum efficiency.

What developed in World War II was a complex series of arrangements between various government circles and between government and the private sector. In order to make the chaotic structures of these years comprehensible, it is worth dividing the situation into two categories — economic management (of which the fiscal measures discussed earlier were a component) and industrial production. At the same time, the complex overlaps between these two areas must be kept in mind.

Economic Management

Though many early steps had been taken in the prewar years, in 1939 the government was groping its way toward some sort of comprehensive approach to economic management. Keynesian theory,

FIGURE 19.3

Sources of Federal Government Revenue, 1947

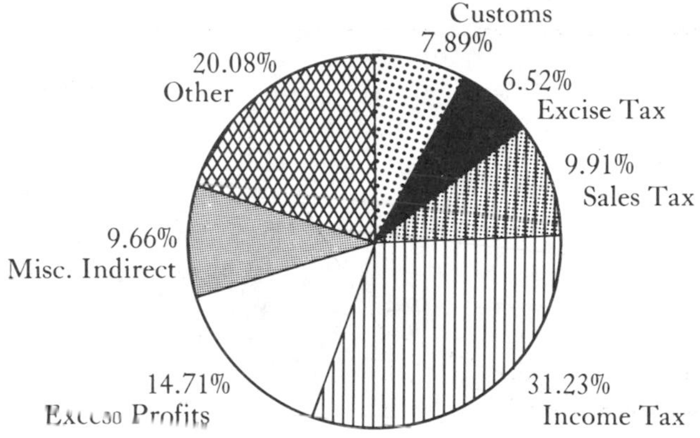

Source: Statistics Canada, *Historical Statistics of Canada*, 2nd ed. (Ottawa: Supply and Services, 1983), Series G1–25.

with its concept of managing aggregate demand, contained within it the potential for a wide-ranging approach to economic planning. It is a long way from theory to practice, however, and, though Keynesian theory was known to many civil servants in 1939, they had not had the time, the mandate, or the knowledge to institute some sort of grand master plan. Rather, much of what they did in the first couple of years of the war would be defined in modern terminology as "crisis management." Hundreds of issues pressed upon an overworked civil service, and they responded as best they could.

While no master plan was instituted at the beginning, there did evolve, over time, a fairly comprehensive economic system. The planners at the Bank of Canada, the finance department, and the Privy Council had a clear sense that economic stability was crucial to the successful prosecution of the war. Whereas in World War I the government had hoped to run "business as usual," no such illusions existed in World War II. Crises led to responses. Key goods were rationed to ensure supplies for the army and for war industry. Taxation policy, as we have already noted, ensured that consumer demands were restrained. Credit arrangements with Britain ensured a continual flow of production for the sake of the war effort. Two examples, however, will serve to indicate the structure and range of government economic intervention during the war years.

The first of these, and the most important for the average Canadian, was the institution, in 1941, of strict wage and price controls. By that time, the slack in the economy had been absorbed, and prices were beginning to rise. Government officials recognized that inflation could lead to labour instability and production uncertainties. Thus, in spite of the concerns of Prime Minister Mackenzie King that the marketplace could not be ignored, finance officials persuaded the government to institute a tremendously complex bureaucracy known as the Wartime Prices and Trade Board to control prices across the nation. This was reinforced by a monetary policy that recognized, as the governor of the Bank of Canada put it in 1940, that printing large additional quantities of money would be highly inflationary and a "grossly inefficient and unfair method of distributing the real burdens of war."[9] In spite of occasional problems, both with workers and with manufacturers, the system worked. Inflation remained modest, averaging between 5 and 6 percent per annum over the whole war, compared to more than 20 percent in World War I.

The second example comes in the area of international trade. With the war, demand for Canadian goods — both agricultural and manufactured — increased dramatically as the United Kingdom and other Allies equipped themselves, using Canadian minerals or manufactures, and fed themselves with Canadian agricultural produce. Canadian exports to the United Kingdom doubled between 1939 and 1942 and almost doubled again between 1942 and 1944. At the same time, imports also increased — these from the United States — at almost as great a rate. Overall, however, the balance of commodity exports remained favourable and, thus, in normal times, the increases could have been seen as the result of a revival of foreign trade.

Things did not work out quite so easily. Serious imbalances soon developed because Britain had turned its productive capacity inward. It was thus no longer exporting and, therefore, was unable to earn foreign currency. Until about 1941, Britain was able to pay Canada by depleting its reserves. Even then, however, there were problems caused by British restrictions on the pound's convertability. By 1941, the British supply of foreign-currency reserves was seriously depleted. In terms of international currency flows, the country was broke. Canada, of course, had no intention of cutting off a war ally from valuable supplies and, thus, undertook a series of credit arrangements and outright gifts to ensure the continued flow of supplies across the Atlantic.

This situation meant that the traditional balance between British surpluses and American deficits was disrupted. Purchases from the neutral United States between 1939 and 1941 had to be paid for in American dollars. Canadian reserves of American dollars and gold were, thus, under pressure from our mounting trade deficit with the United States. In 1940, that deficit was $269 million; in 1941, $313 million.

The government recognized the potential of currency problems from the beginning of the war and, in response, had established a body known as the Foreign Exchange Control Board. Over the first two years, it progressively stepped up measures to discourage the expenditure of American dollars for nonwar purposes. Regulators met on a weekly basis in Ottawa to use the vast powers that existed in wartime to reshape Canadian consumption. Certain imports were restricted or abolished. Tourist travel was curtailed, and a number of imported goods rationed.

In this case, though, even the most ardent efforts of the civil service seemed insufficient. The outflow of currency and gold increased and was stemmed, not because of Canadian regulations but because the United States acted. In spring 1941, in what is known as the Hyde Park Agreement, the Americans agreed to undertake a series of defence-related purchases in Canada. Thereafter, the pressures eased, though controls were maintained by Ottawa for the duration to ensure that the war effort, not the Canadian consumer, benefited by this agreement.

These two measures indicate something of the degree to which the normal marketplace system of the Canadian economy was altered by government intervention during the war. The war was being fought as much on the home front as it was on the battlefield. Moreover, unlike what had occurred during World War I, politicians, the public, and, especially, the civil service saw control of the economy, in the broad sense, as an inherent part of that war effort. Issues that had been the subject of hot debate for decades were suddenly resolved as the government moved to intervene directly in the managing of the economy. By the end of the war, thousands of orders-in-council and approximately 115 000 civil servants testified to the changes that had been wrought. Emergency powers would eventually lapse and the budgets would be trimmed, but there was no returning to the prewar concept of government. Economic management was now seen by the public, by enthusiastic civil servants, and by many politicians as the responsibility of government. For better or worse, the efforts to succeed at this enormous task have shaped much of Canadian government history since the war.

Production

The other and closely related aspect of the war effort was the production of resources for military use, not only by Canadian forces but by the British and the other Allies. The term "resources," as opposed to "equipment," is used to indicate just how sweeping the production effort for the war was. There were military items, such as tanks, airplanes, ammunition, mechanical parts, uniforms, boots, shelter, and on and on. There were also the components and materials required to manufacture such items — steel, lumber, mine output. Energy was also necessary, and, thus, oil and electric production were items of concern throughout the war. Food had to be delivered to feed the troops, the workers who supplied the troops, and the population generally. Finally, efficient transportation, especially across the Atlantic, demanded a rapid increase in merchant-marine capacity and in escort vessels. In other words, just as the financial planning of modern warfare encompassed the whole economy, so, too, did the supply of modern warfare draw in most sectors of production.

At the centre of Canadian war production was the newly created (April 1940) Department of Munitions and Supply and its energetic minister C.D. Howe.[10] Howe was extremely competent and not at all unwilling to assume command. Indeed, given the powers of the War Measures Act, Howe was, through much of the war, effectively a dictator of Canadian war production. At his command, key resources could be allocated, plants taken over for war production, vast orders let without tender, new lines of production ceased or begun.

Howe did not do everything himself. Rather, much of the

success of the operation rested on his decision to use what became known as the "dollar-a-year" men. These were senior businessmen who were willing to work for Howe for the famous "dollar a year" retainer in order to help war production. Because they were experienced at production and because they most often already knew the particular sector they were assigned to, they could take up their tasks relatively quickly and pursue them effectively. Howe also trusted them to make decisions and gave them considerable power. There were problems and there were scandals, but by and large the crisis atmosphere of the war led to co-operation, while the tremendous power of these men made them able to do things that would never have been possible or desirable in peacetime.

One of the most striking legacies of Howe's munitions and supply department was the crown corporation. These government-owned businesses became a favourite technique of Howe and his officials for filling gaps within the private sector. To coax a new company into life (even with promises of government contracts) would take time — too much time. However, a stroke of the pen could create a crown corporation, and necessity caused Howe to use his pen often. During the war the government created some 28 crown corporations, including such major presences on the postwar scene as Eldorado Mining, Polymer Corporation, and much of the Canadian aircraft industry.[11] Overall, the government built some 98 war plants and had acquired, by the end of the conflict, hundreds of millions of dollars in assets. As with the changing patterns of taxation and economic management, the presence of the crown corporations and these assets helped transform the nature of Canadian government, not just during the war but after.

By the time Munitions and Supply was fully in operation at mid-war, it was a vast government agency that was rivalled only by the defence department itself in terms of importance. More than 5000 were employed by it directly, and as many as 25 000 worked for crown corporations set up to handle war production. More than 800 000 worked in war production overall, and, in one way or another, most of their jobs were connected to the activities of Munitions and Supply.[12] Overall, it produced some $9.5 billions' worth of war material for the Canadian and Allied armed forces. Through this department flowed the great bulk of wartime contracts from the government, an amount reaching some $797 million by the peak of the war.[13] It alone was spending considerably more than the entire prewar budget and did so, historians have generally concluded, with a fair degree of efficiency.

Within a short period of time, Munitions and Supply greatly expanded the capacity and expertise of new industries and, indeed, whole sectors of the economy. Thus, for example, such a high-technology industry as aircraft production started from practically nothing in 1939–40 but increased dramatically so that, by midwar, Canada was producing more than 4000 aircraft a year. Likewise, Canada was able to develop both the large merchant marine and the necessary naval escort vessels, even though, after years of depression, shipbuilding had been practically extinct. Finally, in this list of examples, the excess-steel capacity that had plagued that industry during the 1930s was suddenly insufficient, and Munitions and Supply moved forcefully to expand the industry to meet the needs of war production.

The activities of Munitions and Supply provide the link between the war-related activities of the government and the broader question of the impact of the war on the economic activity of Canada as a whole. They also give us an idea of the different aspects of that impact. On the one side, there was the actual effect of the war on day-to-day activity — in business, labour, and other areas. As the legacy of the crown corporations reveals, however, the war also had a longer-term impact. Considerable structural change was wrought by such a massive infusion of war-related activity. We will look at the impact of the war on the broader economy and then, at the structural legacy of the war itself.

The Impact on the Economy, 1939–1945

When the war began in autumn 1939, the Canadian economy, though far improved from the dark days of 1932–33, was still mired in depression. The net value of production for industry was still below 1929 levels, as was GNP. Further, this was a national trend. No province had a greater personal-income level in 1939 than in 1929.

The story was the same when it came to investment. The excess capacity that had plagued industries at the beginning of the Depression had effectively halted capital investment. Even after a decade, this had not been reversed. Gross capital formation at the end of the 1930s was only half what it had been in 1929.[14] By 1939, however, a new problem had developed. Much of Canada's machinery and plant was aging. Many factories, mills, and mines desperately needed an infusion of capital in order to make them efficient producers. Yet, a depression psychology still plagued many businessmen, and, without some guarantee of increased business, they were unlikely to take the necessary risks.

All of this showed up in unemployment and the general standard of living across the country. The stock of residential housing was run down, and building permits remained well below 1920s levels. Instead, many, especially young people, remained at home or resided in boarding houses. Marriages were postponed, as were families. Marriage ages were higher, and overall fertility rates lower, in 1939 than they had been in the 1920s. The most persistent reminder that the economy had not recovered was the continuing unemployment. A survey in June 1939 indicated that more than 11 percent of unionized employees in Canada were without work.[15]

The war finally ended the Depression, and did so very quickly. The twin demands of the army and war production quickly soaked up unemployment: by 1941, the 11 percent figure had dropped to 4 percent. Similarly, the war provided the incentive for businessmen to overcome their reservations about the economy and invest in new plant and equipment. Those who continued to have reservations would be cajoled by Howe and his officials; failing that, the investment would be made directly by the government. The result was an investment upswing that took capital formation over $1 billion in 1941 for the first time since the boom days of the later 1920s.

More revealing, however, is what happened to capital investment in manufacturing. It would quadruple between 1939 and 1941 and, over the first four years of the war, accounted for nearly one-third of all capital formation in the country. The dominance of the manufacturing sector in capital formation was reflected in other areas as well. Thus, while the overall labour force increased by 14 percent, manufacturing employment increased from 627 000 in 1939 to more than 1.25 million by 1943, or by 100 percent. Gross value of production more than doubled during the war, while total wages paid more than tripled![16]

Thus, while practically all sectors were affected by the war, it was manufacturing that changed the most. In effect, the war was leading — much more than World War I had done — to a restructuring of the Canadian economy. World War II ushered in the age of heavy manufacturing in Canada. Steel making, transportation manufacturing, refining of minerals, aircraft production, and a dozen other areas received such a boost from the war that they became newly important and vibrant industries for the postwar world. By 1943, when the Dominion Bureau of Statistics analyzed Canadian production by sectors, "manufactures" accounted for more than 70 percent of the total. In contrast, during the 1920s, the comparable figure had been 57 percent.[17] Once mighty agriculture had slipped from 29 to 12 percent in the same years.

Such differences in growth between sectors raised all sorts of questions at the time, and after. First, and most importantly, if manufacturing was the key to economic growth in this new era, was that growth going to be distributed evenly across the country? Ontario and Quebec had always dominated manufacturing in Canada, and therefore, as we saw in World War I as well, the fear was expressed that the rapid growth of the war would primarily benefit those provinces. Politicians from the west and the Maritimes called loudly on Howe and others to ensure that they got their "fair share" of the new production bonanza.

This did not happen. The government and Howe, though they made occasional efforts to look for regional contracts, did not see the role of Munitions and Supply as one of redistributor of the wealth. War production was the primary concern and, thus, speed was of the essence. Existing capacity (whether in terms of plant or work force) made it easier to get an operation going, and, thus, the great bulk of Munitions and Supply activity was centred in Ontario and Quebec. More than half of all wartime industrial employment was located in Toronto and Montreal.[18] British Columbia also did relatively well because of its important primary-manufacturing sector.

It is important to keep these events in perspective. There was no grand conspiracy between the central provinces and the Dominion government to deprive the rest of the nation of wartime prosperity. Rather, as mentioned above, the focus of the government was on the war, rather than on regional balance. Second, all regions did well by the war. Agriculture rebounded in the west; in the Maritimes, both the lumber industry and the large presence of the navy and merchant marine brought considerable growth. It is thus in relative, not absolute, growth that regional differences become apparent, and, even there, as Figure 19.4 shows, it is not a case of

FIGURE 19.4

Percentage Change in Provincial Share of Gross Value of Production, 1938–1944

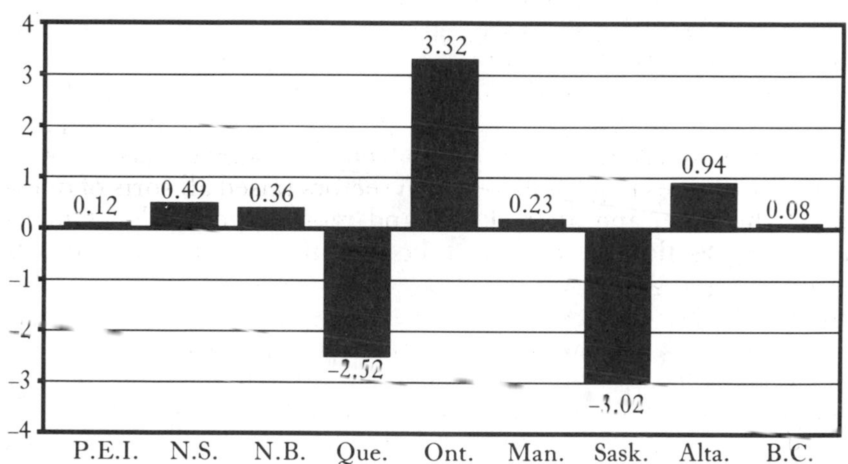

Source: Canada Year Book, 1939–45.

central Canada gaining at the expense of the regions. Indeed, though Ontario grew at the fastest relative rate, Quebec, outside of Montreal, lost considerable ground, and several other provinces gained. In terms of per-capita income, Ontario and British Columbia were the only two provinces above the national average.[19]

That said, the continued concentration of manufacturing in central Canada had important implications. Some of the best-paying and steadiest employment was in the manufacturing sector, and that sector was less susceptible to the boom-and-bust syndrome of natural-resource economies — partly because it was more easily protected by tariff barriers. Also, though this was not known at the time, certain key industries centred in Ontario and Quebec would experience considerable growth in the postwar years. Finally, one of the most dramatic areas of postwar growth would not be manufacturing but related financial services. These would tend to cluster in the largest cities of the nation — Toronto, Montreal, and Vancouver — where the manufacturing capacity was already centred.

Because that manufacturing capacity was concentrated in central

Canada, with new plant, machinery, and expertise, the war had a long-term regional effect. Coupled with the decline of agriculture and with the disastrous regional implications of the Depression, the dynamics of growth for the Canadian economy would rest for some years in a narrow corridor running from Windsor to Montreal. In contrast, the Maritimes and the Prairie west, though better off than during the Depression, lagged behind central Canada in terms of economic growth after the war. Only the discovery of large oil fields in Alberta in 1947 and 1948 prevented the prairies, as a whole, from returning to long-term relative decline in terms of value of production, population, and personal wealth. To sum up, then: in regional terms the war reinforced the existing wealth and economic power of the industrial centre of Canada, though the whole nation benefited from overall rapid growth.

Changes in labour reflected both the structural changes that were taking place and the rising level of wealth in the country. The dramatic nature of that doubling in the number of manufacturing workers that was mentioned earlier can be seen when compared to other sectors. Mining actually decreased in numbers, transportation remained steady, and trade increased by 20 percent. Farming also seemed to be a declining source of employment, with the farm population decreasing. Thus, the profile of the Canadian work force was changing. By 1945, more than half of the nonfarm portion of it was employed in some form of manufacturing, and that manufacturing activity was both more likely to be secondary and increasingly located in or around a few major urban centres. Nearly 85 percent of manufacturing employment was in the provinces of Ontario, Quebec, and British Columbia.

The prosperity of the war years and the rise of urban manufacturing also encouraged the growth of labour unionism. These unions were now largely, but not completely, within the internationalist framework of pragmatic, or "bread and butter," unionism and were represented by the two competing national labour organizations, the Trades and Labor Congress and the Canadian Congress of Labour. There were, in addition, the Canadian and Catholic Confederation of Labour, as well as smaller umbrella organizations. Unionism, though not united, thus entered the war with a series of national organizations and with much greater clout than it had had on the eve of World War I.

Organized unions found the war a contradictory period. In one sense, the war years were frustrating ones. Wage and price controls, Defence of Canada regulations, and public opinion hemmed in union activity and restricted meaningful collective bargaining. Yet, the war also gave organized labour unions tremendous benefits. The King government, determined to avoid the mistakes of World War I, carefully sought out union opinion and acted sympathetically to union organizers, at least the moderate variety. Thus, between 1939 and 1944, union membership in the country more than doubled, to some 750 000 workers.

Another, and a potentially even more significant, result of the war was the tremendous increase in the numbers of women in the work force and the range of occupations in which they were active.[20] Behind this, of course, is the simple reality of economic necessity. Military recruitment of males, plus the general demand for workers made recruitment of labour from new sources essential. Women, traditionally excluded from most areas of industrial work, suddenly found themselves able to gain entry. Two further factors were present that attracted women into the work place. First, there was economic necessity. Many families were still recovering from the Depression, and the opportunity to gain income was not to be passed over lightly, especially when the husband was often in a low-paying armed-forces position. Second, the social stigma attached to middle-class women entering the work force was reversed. To work in, say, an aircraft plant or a truck factory was suddenly a patriotic duty. By 1942, the need was so great that the Women's Division of the Selective Service Agency was established to register women between the ages of 20 and 24. The intention was to recruit them into war work.

The changes were dramatic. Tens of thousands of women who would never otherwise have considered work headed off to the factories. By the middle of 1943, more than 200 000 women were engaged in war work directly, and more than a million were in the labour force. Some 50 000 served in the armed forces. By this time, as well, the government was actively recruiting married women into the war industry, in spite of the strong social belief that women with children should remain in the home. Indeed, so great was the demand for female labour that the government even made provisions for Dominion-provincial day-care funding.

At the end of the war, the forces that brought women into the labour market were reversed. It having been their patriotic duty

National Archives of Canada/C-467

Women factory workers, World War II. *During the wartime labour shortage, many women who otherwise would not have been working took jobs in plants and factories as a patriotic duty. By the middle of 1943, more than 200 000 women were engaged in war work directly, and more than a million were in the labour force.*

to go to work, it was now considered their motherly or wifely duty to leave the work place and free up jobs for men. Women, it was argued in endless fashion, as the end of war approached, should return to their nurturing roles within the family and allow men to return to their areas of expertise. Thousands of women did leave the work force, as marriage and birth rates soared. For most of these women, and for society as a whole, the idea of working and raising a family at the same time was unacceptable. Personal choice, social pressure, and economic circumstance thus meant that participation rates dropped from a high of 33 percent to a postwar level of 25 percent. Still, the effort of women in war and their success at their jobs were one more blow struck at sex-role stereotypes. Since many women, moreover, enjoyed the taste of independence that a job and a paycheque created, the participation rate remained higher after the war than before. By 1956, the *number* of women working had surpassed the high point of the war (see Table 19.1).

TABLE 19.1

Number of Women with Jobs, 1937–1956

(thousands)

1937	688	1947	898
1938	677	1948	914
1939	686	1949	967
1940	733	1950	1019
1941	800	1951	1063
1942	874	1952	1094
1943	1184	1953	1124
1944	1199	1954	1146
1945	1193	1955	1191
1946	889	1956	1259

Source: Statistics Canada, *Historical Statistics of Canada*, 2nd ed. (Ottawa: Supply and Services, 1983), Table D–261.

It was not until 1967, though, that the *percentage* of adult women in the work force surpassed that of World War II.

Looking to Reconstruction, 1943–1945

By 1943, with rearmament accomplished and with the war beginning to turn in the Allies' favour, citizens and officials increasingly looked beyond the immediate pressures of the war to the sort of life that would face them once the conflict ceased. The memories of the Depression were vivid, and many expressed the concern that the prosperity of the war was an exception that would fade away once peace returned. Such thoughts were reinforced by the experience of World War I, which had ended in victory only to see mass unemployment and economic instability. The public, recorded one government agency, faced the postwar world with a "feeling akin to dread." This was reflected in the polls, where the social-democratic Co-operative Commonwealth Federation (CCF) was, by 1943, at its highest standing ever. The message was clear. The war effort was all very fine, but those who could provide some economic security — some plan to hold on to what had been gained — would receive a favourable hearing from the electorate.

By this time, however, the government was seriously beginning to turn its attention to plans for the postwar period. The officials of the Bank of Canada and the departments of Finance and Munitions and Supply were increasingly concerned with how the eventual transition from war to peace could be managed without severe shock to the economy. As a result, the last half of the war saw an increasing number of committees, task forces, and parliamentary hearings called to address what became known as the period of "reconstruction." Though there were differing ideas of what reconstruction should emphasize, it had two general elements. First, it involved the idea that a considerable degree of planning and of intervention by government would be necessary to ensure that the demobilization of the military and of war industry went smoothly. It also had broader connotations, involving the idea of a reshaping of social and economic structures to usher Canada into a new era and thereby prevent it from slipping into the malaise that had characterized the Depression years.

Reconstruction had different emphases, depending on the part of the government from which the plans emanated. Some of the most enthusiastic and far-reaching schemes came from those who felt that the war had to be used as an opportunity to restructure the capitalist system. Memories of the Depression, as well as inspiration drawn from social-planning documents in Britain and the United States, led them to advocate a widespread system of social security. Giving the public a sense of security, they argued, was crucial to preventing the return of a depression psychology. Further, it was a matter of social justice to ensure that the newfound prosperity of the war led to a redistribution of wealth within the population.

Such themes had been a general part of political and intellectual discussion in Canada for some years. They became a serious part of discussion for reconstruction when the Report on Social Security was released by Leonard Marsh in 1943. Marsh was director of research for a committee formed by Ian Mackenzie, the minister of labour; and Marsh's report ranged freely across the whole panoply of social-security measures. A comprehensive rather than piecemeal approach must be devised, he warned, and accordingly he advocated an immediate move toward such measures as public health care, children's allowances, improved old-age pensions, and unemployment benefits. Even funeral benefits were advocated.

Marsh's report received a great deal of publicity. Ultimately, however, reconstruction did not take the path advocated in that report, or by Ian Mackenzie. Others in government, though also concerned with reconstruction, felt that much of Marsh's work was hasty and ill-conceived. They, too, had memories of the Depression, but those memories centred on the large budget deficits, the constriction in trade, and other factors that had prevented recovery. To them, social security, though worth considering, would be idle dreaming unless the economy was healthy enough to support such expensive measures. The business cycle, not the welfare state, was their primary focus.

The military and C.D. Howe's people were especially concerned with the short-term impact that the end of war would bring. Close to 2 million troops and war-industry workers would have to find new occupations once the war ended. This vast movement would be happening at the time that government production was winding down and thus, presumably, in a climate of economic downturn. In order to prevent the sharp economic dislocation that had characterized the end of World War I, a complex series of plans and programs was developed. A new department, Veterans' Affairs, implemented a whole range of benefits for returning soldiers, including subsidized mortgages, health- and hospital-care benefits. job training, and education allowances. For industry, Howe's department, which would formally change roles in 1944 when it became the Department of Reconstruction, introduced a number of programs designed to ensure that industry continued a high level of production once war contracts ended. Typical were a series of beneficial depreciation allowances brought in for industries buying new equipment to shift from wartime to peacetime production. Quick write-offs of new equipment against current high profit levels made the new investment attractive to companies. To the government, the immediate cost in tax revenues was worth it to encourage companies' continued investment at war's end.

In the Department of Finance and Bank of Canada, the concern was to take the Howe plans, Veterans' Affairs measures, Marsh proposals, and the myriad other schemes floating around, and try to package them so that they made some sort of sense in terms of macro-economic planning. Indeed, the belief that macro-economic planning was possible and that government could influence the direction of the economy was perhaps one of the most significant factors influencing the planning for the postwar world. By the 1940s, experience and theory were coming together. The theory was that of Keynes, and the experience was the success of the civil service in harnessing the economy of the nation, particularly in such measures as wage and price controls. Now, they felt the time had come to take what they had learned and put it to use in the postwar era. Only such confidence allowed a government White Paper on reconstruction to commit itself in 1945 to "a high and stable level of employment."

The belief in economic planning and the theory behind it are complex and cannot be described fully here. There are a couple of dominant themes, however, that typify the changes that were taking place. The first was the belief in the importance of maintaining aggregate demand. If people and businesses could be kept purchasing, then their demands would create the jobs and profits to allow continued consumption. Success, in other words, was self-fulfilling. The trick was to provide consumers with the incentive, material and psychological, to go out and spend. Once again, various measures were eventually put in place. Taxes were lowered, war bonds were cashed, compulsory savings plans (used by government during the war) were ended. Most dramatically, the planners borrowed from the social-security side of things by supporting the implementation of the family allowance in 1945. This scheme was unique because it handed out government money, not on the basis of direct need but on the basis of the presence of children in a family. This vast giveaway of a $250 million a year was calculated to put spending dollars in the hands of Canadians so that they would consume. It was also designed to assist in the re-election of the hard-pressed Liberal government. It succeeded on both counts.

The other thing the planners had learned from the prewar period was the essential reality that Canada could not succeed without international prosperity. Given the nation's orientation to exports, all those schemes to encourage Canadian business and consumers would eventually crumble if international customers weren't found for our products once the war ended. W.A. Mackintosh of the Department of Finance summed it up very well: "The kind of world which will emerge after the war, will have more effect on Canada's destiny than any changes which are taking place in Canada during the war."[21] As a result, Canadian politicians and civil servants were generally very internationalist at the end of the war. They were as active as possible in supporting the establishment of international monetary relations at such conferences as the one held at Bretton Woods in 1944, which founded the International Monetary Fund.[22] They were enthusiastic in their support for the lessening or removal of barriers to international trade, and in their support of U.N. agencies seeking to rationalize trade.

In general, this internationalism accorded with the general mood of the age. For, while it is true that the Canadians involved were effective and competent, they were also fortunate. What really mattered more than anything else was that the United States had also learned something from history. It had withdrawn into its shell after World War I, and for many, this was a basic cause of the Great Depression. At the end of World War II, the Americans moved aggressively onto the world stage. It was, by 1945, by far the most powerful nation in the world. Had its tremendous wealth not been circulated widely in the world, the same instabilities that had marked the 1920s and had ultimately so hurt the United States would have all too probably recurred. The Americans recognized this danger; thus, they, too, came down in favour of an international monetary order (now resting largely on their dollar) and, through such schemes as the Marshall Plan, moved to rebuild Europe as far as possible. As the largest trading partner of the United States, Canada could only benefit from such openness and vast wealth.

Conclusion

Both domestically and internationally, Canada moved into the postwar world with relative ease economically. GNE did drop a little in 1945 and 1946, but had rebounded by 1947, and would increase consistently through the postwar years. Likewise, unemployment increased only temporarily and, even at that, never approached the levels of the 1930s. Indeed, levels of less than 4 percent were standard through the postwar years. Finally, real gross national expenditure dropped only marginally at the end of the war, and then moved upward again. There was no significant drop, even in per-capita GNE, in spite of the end of war production (see Figure 19.5). Given the shift from war materiel to consumer goods, this meant that the standard of living of Canadians improved substantially in the immediate postwar years.

FIGURE 19.5

Index of Gross National Expenditure, 1939–1949

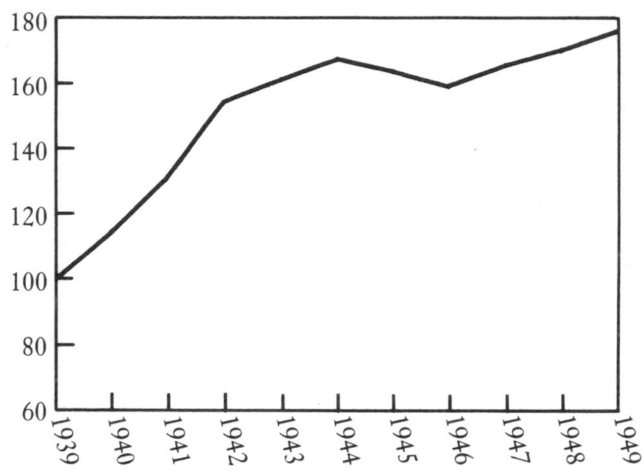

Source: Derived from Statistics Canada, *Historical Statistics of Canada*, 2nd ed. (Ottawa: Supply and Services, 1983), Series H1–151.

International trade was also a success story for Canada. True, there was a drop of more than a quarter in exports from 1945 to 1946. This was hardly surprising, given the end of the vast industrial war machine. Thereafter, exports recovered, however, with the United States (39 percent) and the United Kingdom (25 percent) as, by far, our most important purchasers. Conversely, the United States was, for at least a while after the war, practically our only source of foreign goods, accounting for more than 70 percent of all imports to Canada through the rest of the 1940s.

Prosperity and the ever-greater importance of the United States were two legacies of the war. A third was the much larger government that has been the subject of so much discussion in this chapter. Budgets and civil servants also declined only temporarily at the end of the war. New taxes, coupled with postwar prosperity, gave governments the opportunity to continue the sort of wide-ranging planning that had characterized the war years. Often, the plans were more grandiose than the practice, and the ability to control the economy was often overstated, but the reality was that World War II brought Canada into an era when government had a much more profound impact on the economy than it had had in the past.

Yet, there is a danger in placing too much emphasis on the successes. The postwar prosperity had not ended regional disparity and regional tension. One of the major failures of bureaucratic planning at the end of the war came at the hands of provinces insistent on retaining or regaining their rights. In the postwar years, federal-provincial relations would grow increasingly acerbic, and the concern for regional equity would become a major issue in politics. Likewise, whatever social-security measures were brought in by 1945, a whole host of them had been set aside for want of money, jurisdiction, or will. The next twenty years would see an ongoing debate as to how much social welfare was possible and desirable. Finally, the great prosperity of the United States and Canada's dependence on that prosperity would create new concerns in the postwar decades. American trade and American investment would be central to Canadian hopes and fears in the postwar world.

Notes

1. Cited in C.P. Stacey, *Arms, Men and Governments: The War Policies of Canada, 1939–1945* (Ottawa: Supply and Services, 1970), 9.
2. Stacey, *Arms, Men and Governments*, 6.
3. Statistics Canada, *Historical Statistics of Canada*, 2nd ed. (Ottawa: Supply and Services, 1983), G389.
4. Robert Bothwell, Ian Drummond, and John English, *Canada, 1900–1945* (Toronto: University of Toronto Press, 1987), 363.
5. Cited in J.H. Perry, *Taxes, Tariffs and Subsidies*, Vol. 2 (Toronto: University of Toronto Press, 1955), 335.
6. A.F.W. Plumptre, *Mobilizing Canada's Resources for War* (Toronto: Macmillan, 1941), 113.
7. Perry, *Taxes, Tariffs and Subsidies*, 697.
8. This summary of changing taxation from Perry, *Taxes, Tariffs and Subsidies*, Vol. 2.
9. Cited in Thomas Courchene, "The Interaction Between Economic Theory and the Bank of Canada Policy," in *Economic Policy Advising in Canada: Essays in Honour of John Deutsch*, edited by David C. Smith (Montreal and Kingston: McGill-Queen's University Press, 1981), 163.
10. The following paragraphs rely on R. Bothwell and W. Kilbourn, *C.D. Howe: A Biography* (Toronto: McClelland and Stewart, 1979).
11. On crown corporations, see J. de N. Kennedy, *A History of the Department of Munitions and Supply*, 2 vols. (Ottawa: King's Printer, 1950).
12. Kennedy, *Department of Munitions and Supply*, Vol. 2, viii.

13. Kennedy, *Department of Munitions and Supply*, Vol. 2, 298. Note that this includes only the "Canadian account." If amounts handled through the Department for British and other purchasers were included, the figure would be much higher.
14. Statistics Canada, *Historical Statistics of Canada*, 2nd ed. (Ottawa: Supply and Services, 1983), F135–52.
15. This is from *Canada Year Book*, 1946, 751.
16. Statistics Canada, *Historical Statistics of Canada*, D318–28; D124–33. M.C. Urquhart, "Canadian Economic Growth 1870–1980," Queen's University, Department of Economics, Discussion Paper 734, Table 6.
17. These figures are from *Canada Year Book*, 1946, 191; and 1930, 185. They may not be directly comparable with other figures and that is why they are introduced as they are. Also note that these figures include primary manufacturing.
18. R. Bothwell, "'Who's Paying for Anything These Days?': War Production in Canada, 1939–1945," in *Mobilization for Total War*, edited by N.F. Dreizeger (Waterloo: Wilfrid Laurier University Press, 1981); on employment figures, see Kennedy, *Department of Munitions and Supply*, Vol. 2, 503.
19. Robert Bothwell, Ian Drummond, and John English, *Canada Since 1945*, 1st ed. (Toronto: University of Toronto Press, 1981), 24.
20. For a detailed study of women in World War II, see Ruth Roach Pierson, *They're Still Women After All: The Second World War and Canadian Womanhood* (Toronto: University of Toronto Press, 1986).
21. Cited in Doug Owram, *The Government Generation: Canadian Intellectuals and the State, 1900–1945* (Toronto: University of Toronto Press, 1986), 301.
22. One of the nicest summaries of these events is in A.F.W. Plumptre, *Three Decades of Decision: Canada and the World Monetary System, 1944–1975* (Toronto: McClelland and Stewart, 1977), chapters 1–2.

Further Reading

Bothwell, R. "'Who's Paying for Anything These Days?': War Production in Canada, 1939–1945." In *Mobilization for Total War*, edited by N.F. Dreizeger. Waterloo: Wilfrid Laurier University Press, 1981.

Bothwell, R., and W. Kilbourn. *C.D. Howe: A Biography*. Toronto: McClelland and Stewart, 1979.

Granatstein, J.L. *Canada's War: The Politics of the Mackenzie King Government*. Toronto: Oxford University Press, 1975.

Pierson, Ruth Roach. *They're Still Women After All: The Second World War and Canadian Womanhood*. Toronto: University of Toronto Press, 1986.

Plumptre, A.F.W. *Three Decades of Decision: Canada and the World Monetary System, 1944–1975*. Toronto: McClelland and Stewart, 1977.

Stacey, C.P. *Arms, Men and Governments: The War Policies of Canada 1939–1945*. Ottawa: Supply and Services, 1970.

VI

The Modern Era: Since 1945

VI

The decades after World War II are among the most difficult of our economic history to summarize, partly because the economy was more complex and partly because we know more about it. Data are more plentiful; records are more complete; and, for some readers more than others, and for some events more than others, memories are still relatively fresh. Nonetheless, recognizing the considerable risk of oversimplifiction, four features stand out when looking back on these years.

The first impression is that of significant growth and structural change. Today's economy, when compared to that of 1945, is larger, richer, and much altered. Technology has made it possible to produce ever-greater quantities of grain, lumber, ore, steel, and automobiles with less labour. Workers have found employment, instead, as retail clerks, data-processors, teachers, nurses, and research scientists. These new jobs are mostly in cities and, relative to the past, are increasingly taken by women and by visible minorities. Much more economic activity now originates directly in the public sector, and that which is still private is almost certainly touched by a plethora of government regulations. The typical Canadian now lives in the suburbs; commutes to his or her service-sector job; has a spouse that is employed, at least part time; and consumes a quantity and range of products that would have been unimaginable to his or her grandparents.

The second impression qualifies the first one. Even in the midst of all this structural change, much in the economy is unchanged. We remain a small, open society, be it with respect to international commerce or to ideas and ideologies. Natural-resource products, raw and partially refined, are key exports. Foreign capital, technology, and labour still contribute to economic growth. The United States remains the dominant influence in most respects, perhaps more so even than in 1945. Ontario and Quebec continue as the industrial and service heartland of the nation, with the west and the Atlantic regions specializing in staples products. The pattern of regional economic disparities is virtually unchanged: provinces at the bottom in 1945 (or in 1890, for that matter) are still there today.

The third observation is that, in terms of overall macro-economic performance, the years between 1945 and the early 1980s divide naturally into two distinct periods. The first ran from the end of the war to the early 1970s, and the dominant characteristics were growth and prosperity. An initial period of uncertainty as postwar reconstruction was underway was followed by more than twenty years of sustained, albeit uneven, economic expansion. Inflation was generally but not always under control, and unemployment was normally, though again, not always, at acceptable levels. Performance altered dramatically after 1973. Economic growth fell off sharply, inflation and unemployment rates rose, and government deficits soared. Inflation was brought under control in 1981–82, but at the cost of some of the highest unemployment rates seen in Canada since the 1930s.

The fourth point is that the turnaround in economic performance in the 1970s was accompanied by a distinct shift in attitudes to economic management. Much had been expected of government in 1946. The success in restructuring the economy to meet wartime needs seemed to indicate that it could be similarly engineered to meet peacetime challenges. New Keynesian techniques promised to even out business fluctuations. Ambitious plans for health, education and income-security measures were planned to ensure that some of the fruits of the growth and prosperity flowed to the less fortunate in society.

The economic difficulties after 1973 seriously challenged this faith in economic management. Economic theorists had to rethink notions of inflation and unemployment, while policy makers sought remedies for them in everything from monetary and fiscal measures to wage and price controls. Attempts to direct the economy came to be viewed increasingly as policies that acted instead to distort it. Fine-tuning at the micro level went the way of the stabilization-policy counterpart. No major social programs were introduced after the late 1960s. Instead, efforts turned to cutting back existing ones to make them fit tighter government budgets, and to reforming them to remove what were considered to be their perverse incentives.

Many of these developments Canada shared with other Western industrial nations. The technology that raised Canadian living standards and that moved workers off farms and out of the mines and forests and into the cities did so in other nations as well. Women are more active in labour markets everywhere now, and increasing numbers of ethnic minorities can be found in many Western countries, tempted by economic opportunity. Even new social values such as feminism and ecological awareness reflect broader international trends. Thus, much as we like to take the credit for our accomplishments, or to focus the blame, as the case may be, in many respects Canada remains what it has always been, a small part of a very large world.

Some developments were specific to Canada, however. Technology and trade liberalization proceeded world wide after 1945, to be sure; yet, the particular impact these developments had on Canada was a function of our resource endowments, our human skills, and even our policies. No other nation quite mixed economic and constitutional issues the way Canada did, be it with respect to the implementation of the welfare state, energy policy, the sovereignty-association referendum in Quebec, or the debate over the internal economic union. In at least a few respects, then, in the postwar period, as in earlier times, the story is uniquely Canadian.

International Background

The immediate economic concern in North America in 1945 was the prospect of stagnation. Those responsible for economic policy remembered that it had taken a world war to wrench the economies out of their decade-long slump of the 1930s, and they wondered whether the end of hostilities meant a return to depression conditions. All countries had significant numbers of men and women in their armed forces who would somehow have to be reabsorbed into the civilian labour force. Machinery and equipment diverted earlier to wartime use likewise would have to be reconverted to peacetime employment. With governments cutting back on spending, concern arose in each nation as to where the demand would come from to absorb the peacetime output of goods and services.

For the nations of Europe, the problem was exactly the reverse.

Their economies were too badly damaged to meet even the immediate needs for food and shelter, much less the longer-term one of reconstruction. North America had the capacity to meet these needs, but Europe did not have the dollars, earned from export sales, to pay for them. Even without this "dollar gap," as it came to be called, resurrecting international exchange would be no easy task. Depression and war had left in their wake a great number of restrictions on the international flow of goods, services, capital, and labour. Nearly every country had imposed high tariffs and quotas on imports, and had made it difficult or impossible for immigrants to enter. Most, as well, had instituted exchange controls during the war, and had left them in place in the uncertainties of the immediate postwar period.

As it turned out, the problems in North America never emerged, and the European ones were quickly solved. Aggregate demand was unexpectedly high in North America in the postwar years. Consumers drew upon assets accumulated during the war to make postponed purchases, and businesses responded by investing in plant and equipment to turn out these products. The dollar shortage was solved by a series of loans and export credits. The first was the Anglo-American Loan of 1946, but the most famous were those under the Marshall Plan. Between 1947 and 1950, a total of $9.4 billion went from the United States to the neediest countries of Europe. The Organization for European Economic Cooperation (OEEC) was formed in 1948 as a framework for this aid, eventually becoming the Organization for Economic Cooperation and Development (OECD), as we know it today.

More important for the longer term was the manner in which the world's leaders turned to the task of resurrecting international exchange. A meeting at Bretton Woods, New Hampshire, in 1944 set out the basis of the postwar international system of exchange. Signatories agreed to remove, in stages, all exchange controls. They further committed themselves to a system of fixed exchange rates. In effect, currencies henceforth were to be fixed relative to the U.S. dollar, which, in turn, was tied to gold. Exchange-rate adjustments were allowed if balance-of-payments conditions warranted, but only within a small range, without prior consultation and approval. Credit was available to countries experiencing temporary difficulties. A permanent agency, the International Monetary Fund (IMF), was established to police the Bretton Woods Agreement and to provide loans to members. IMF membership was 44 in 1947, but grew to 107 twenty years later.

The main progress in liberalizing trade in goods and services came under the General Agreement on Tariffs and Trade (GATT). The GATT came into existence at a conference held in Geneva in 1947. Originally, it was intended to be an interim arrangement until the Havana Charter of the International Trade Organization (ITO) was ratified. The ITO died in 1950, but GATT survived to play a leading role in postwar trade liberalization. It set out a code of conduct that member nations were expected to follow with respect to their exports and imports, and it provided a forum for on-going negotiations aimed at reducing trade barriers. The 1947 session managed to reduce or bind more than 45 000 tariff rates. A subsequent session in France, in 1949, continued this process and set the stage for the more significant liberalization to come.

The results of these initiatives on the trade and monetary fronts were impressive. There were some initial economic difficulties in the immediate postwar period as the new institutions and arrangements were introduced and as reconstruction began. Conditions in Europe improved in 1945 and 1946, before suffering a setback in 1947. But, by 1948, the level of production in this region exceeded that of 1939, and growth continued thereafter. Trade increased faster than production, a result of the liberalization and a foreshadowing of a trend that was to continue well into the future. Most of this trade was among the industrial nations, and most of it was in manufactured goods.

The formation of the OEEC was but a start to economic integration in Europe. The European Payments Union was established in 1950 to facilitate capital movements within Europe, to be replaced by the European Monetary Agreement of 1958. Most importantly, an initiative for a French-German coal-and-steel pool led, in 1953, to the establishment of the six-nation Common Coal and Steel Market. The success of this venture helped to overcome opposition on the continent to further economic integration, and, on June 1, 1958, the Treaty of Rome was signed, establishing the European Economic Community (EEC).

International trade continued to benefit from liberalization measures initiated under the IMF and GATT. Negotiating sessions were held in England in 1951, in Geneva in 1956, at the Dillon Round in 1960, and at the Kennedy Round between 1964 and 1967. Significant tariff reductions were achieved at these sessions, and progress was made on regulating the use of non-tariff barriers (NTBs). The Kennedy Round was particularly successful. Duties on 60 000 tradable industrial products were reduced an average of 35 percent. Major industrial nations went even farther. Sectoral arrangements were initiated for certain products, and less-developed countries participated on a less than fully reciprocal basis.

Partly as a consequence of these initiatives, world trade grew sixfold between the years 1948 and 1973, or at an annual rate of about 7 percent. This increase was faster than that for production, meaning that the ratio of trade to output grew in all OECD nations. Most of the trade was among Western nations, and it was concentrated in manufactured products. Between 1963 and 1973, for example, total world trade grew by 6 percent per year, while that in manufactured goods rose by nearly double that, at 11 percent.[1] The phenomenon came to be known as "intra-industry trade," with products from the same broad industrial grouping appearing as both exports and imports in each country's balance-of-payments accounts.

Complementing this growth in trade was one in capital movements. Portfolio investments were common prior to the Great Depression, and they continued as restrictions were removed and exchange convertibility was re-established. The major development, though, was the dramatic increase in direct investment, mainly by multinational corporations (MNCs). These took all kinds of forms. Some MNCs integrated vertically backwards to raw-material sources or transportation and distribution facilities, or forward to processing facilities. Others set up subsidiary operations in other nations, to duplicate parent-company operations in some cases, and as part of intra-industry specialization in others. Direct investment was a way of transferring technology and managerial expertise in addition to capital, so the contribution to world economic growth was accentuated. American MNCs were the most prominent by far, but companies based in Japan, Britain, Holland, Germany, and even Canada were important.

Sometime in the early 1970s (1973, for convenience), circumstances changed markedly. The next ten years were marked by serious, widespread, and sustained deterioration in the macro-economic performance of the Western industrial nations. Prices had been gradually increasing in the late 1960s, but this phenomenon seemed easily explainable as classic demand-pull inflation. The surprise came after 1972, as economic growth slowed and unemployment rates began to climb. Inflation did not recede as the (then) orthodox Phillips Curve analysis predicted, but remained steady or rose even further.

Table VI.1 shows the extent of the change in the economic performances of the main Western industrial nations. Real gross domestic product per capita rose an average of 2.6 percent in the United States between 1962 and 1973, but only 0.6 percent between 1973 and 1982. Prices increased by 3.4 percent on average over the earlier period, and 8.4 percent in the later. The average unemployment rate changed from 4.9 to 7 percent. The deterioration was not as marked in Europe or Japan, but it was significant nonetheless. Real growth rates fell by a factor of 3.6 in the United Kingdom between the two periods, by nearly three times in Japan, and by more than twice on the Continent. Unemployment and inflation rates climbed commensurately.

Economists are still trying to explain the appearance and persistence of this bout of stagflation, as the phenomenon of simultaneously rising inflation and unemployment came to be called. Inflation received a major push in 1971 and 1972 in the face of the robust and widespread economic boom of those years. The magnitude and breadth of the expansion were largely unanticipated, which meant that producers of a broad range of primary products were caught unawares as demand grew faster than available supplies. Crude-oil prices had been creeping up gradually under these pressures, but jumped precipitately in 1973 with the outbreak of the Arab-Israeli War and the consequent embargo on international oil shipments. The failure of the Peruvian anchovy harvest and of crops around the world added to the upward pressure on commodity prices.

These were the supply-side implications, but there were aggregate-demand ones as well. The rise in raw-material prices meant a terms of trade movement in favour of primary-product producers and against those nations importing them on a net basis. Since the OECD countries are mainly in the latter category, the commodity-prices boom meant a reduction in aggregate real incomes and a consequent fall in spending, adding to the economic slowdown. Some Western governments resisted the cuts in real in-

TABLE VI.1
Measures of Stagflation in the Major OECD Countries

	Average Growth of Real GDP Per Capita (%)	*Average Growth of Value-added Price (%)*	*Average Unemployment Rate (%)*
United States			
1962–73	2.64	3.18	4.90
1973–82	0.55	8.13	6.99
Japan			
1962–73	7.31	5.13	1.13
1973–82	2.64	6.34	1.94
Germany			
1962–73	3.31	3.30	0.74
1973–82	1.66	4.66	3.65
France			
1962–73	4.11	3.93	1.51
1973–82	1.94	11.09	4.50
United Kingdom			
1962–73	2.43	4.72	1.98
1973–82	0.68	14.93	5.61
Italy			
1962–73	3.59	4.35	4.73
1973–82	1.74	17.72	7.07
Canada			
1962–73	3.80	3.27	4.44
1973–82	0.84	10.24	7.48

Source: John F. Helliwell, "Comparative Macro-Economics of Stagflation," *Journal of Economic Literature* 26, no. 1 (March 1988): 2.

comes, initially by attempting to maintain aggregate demand through expansionary monetary and fiscal policies. These moves postponed the eventual adjustment, but added to the inflationary impetus, so the record was not much improved.

Real incomes did eventually fall everywhere, as adjustment to the terms of trade effect set in. Unemployment rates rose as expected, but so did inflation rates. The notion of a stable trade-off between these two variables (the Phillips Curve) that had dominated economic thinking for a decade or more had to be abandoned as economic theorists sought explanations for the stagflation phenomenon. Now, another decade and a half later, macro-economics distinguishes between long- and short-run trade-offs, emphasizes the role of expectations in decision making, and concentrates on wage and price flexibility over the business cycle.

As stagflation continued, the view gradually arose that these difficult economic times were more than a macro downturn. Analysts began to speak of a productivity slowdown that was more structural in nature. Several explanations of why this might be so appeared. The rise in oil prices induced a shift away from energy and capital and toward labour in most production processes. The gradual shift of the economy from high-productivity primary and manufacturing pursuits to lower-productivity services would drag down aggregate-growth rates. Some saw the explanation as being the greater emphasis on environmental control that resulted in lower measured output increases. Others attributed it to the fact that the actual pace of technological change was slowing, perhaps inevitably so, as nations matured economically. But some economists, such as UBC's John Helliwell, maintained that the excess capacity accompanying the downturn was the main explanation; a resumption of robust economic growth would return productivity to its former levels.

The policy responses to the economic record from 1973 to 1982 were varied and often confused as a result of the uncertainty as to the underlying problems. Macro-economic policies toward the oil-price shock varied significantly. Some nations attempted to phase in the adjustment, while others dealt with it "cold turkey." Hostility to the OPEC nations rose, and threats were made to retaliate with food and other blockades. Debate raged as to which nations were most responsible for spreading inflation and unemployment or, conversely, which needed most to act to fight it. Demands to protect domestic groups from foreign competition increased and fears of renewed protectionism arose. The world's political leaders met, and met again, as did their bureaucrats and central bankers.

Growth and Structural Change in Canada: 1947–1982 at a Glance

In most respects, development in Canada mirrored that in the international economy. The economy grew larger, it grew richer, and it underwent a significant change in structure. The record was not smooth, though, nor was it uniform. The years from the end of World War II to sometime in the early 1970s were ones of unparalleled growth and prosperity, and of generally satisfactory macro-economic performance. The decade thereafter, by contrast, was one of slower, consistently higher rates of unemployment, and occasional double-digit inflation.

As seen throughout this book, the most useful summary measures of the size of the economy are gross national product and population.[2] In current-dollar terms GNP in Canada increased from $13.9 billion in 1947 to $374.4 billion in 1982, or by nearly 27 times. Much of this increase is simply price inflation. In real terms (1981 dollars), GNP rose from $74.1 billion in 1947 to $344.5 billion in 1982, or by 4.6 times. Population approximately doubled over the same period, rising from 12.5 million in 1947 to 24.5 million in 1982. On a per-capita basis, then, real GNP rose about 2.4 times. Expressed differently: the average Canadian was more than twice as well off in 1982 as he or she was at the end of the war.

Performance was not uniform, however, as Figure VI.1 shows. After a slow start in the immediate postwar period, growth in real GNP was robust (except in 1954) through to 1956. It then slowed notably for the next five years, before the economy entered a long period of expansion, from 1962 to 1973. The deterioration since 1973 is striking. As Table VI.1 shows, real GDP per capita in Canada rose an average 3.8 percent per annum between 1962 and 1973, but by only 0.8 percent between 1973 and 1982. Only in the United States was the difference in performance between the two periods more marked. Growth was at 1960s levels in 1976 and was a respectable 4.6 percent in 1978, but was disappointing in every other year.

FIGURE VI.1

Percentage Change in Gross Domestic Product, 1948–1988

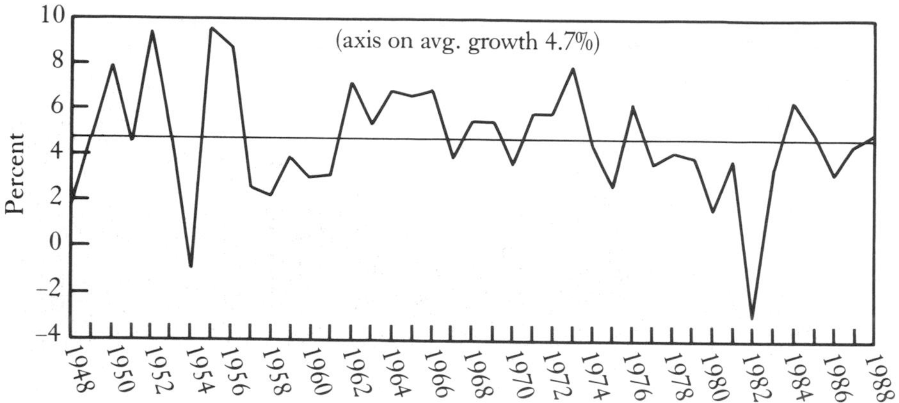

Source: Canada, Department of Finance, *Quarterly Economic Review*, June 1989: 8.

Macro-economic performance differed markedly between the two periods as well. As Figure VI.2 shows, unemployment rates have fluctuated from year to year, but the trend is strongly upwards. One way to summarize the trend is to note that unemployment rates of around 2 percent signified full employment in the early 1950s. In the mid-1960s, rates of less than 4 percent were considered inflationary, while today, economists speak of natural rates of unemployment of 6 percent and even higher. To put the point even more starkly, Prime Minister Diefenbaker was in political trouble in the early 1960s for unemployment rates that Prime Minister Trudeau, near the end of his term, or Prime Minister Mulroney today, would be delighted with.

The postwar record on inflation is more volatile yet (see Figure VI.3). A bout of inflation accompanied the lifting of wartime controls in 1948 but quickly subsided. Prices rose again dramatically during the Korean War, before falling to an annual rate of increase in the 1 to 2 percent range to the mid-1960s. Inflation began to rise thereafter, reaching nearly 5 percent by decade's end, dropped slightly in 1970 and 1971, and then accelerated to above 10 percent in 1974 and 1975. The rate fell slightly for four years thereafter, and rose to double-digit levels again in 1980, before dropping to about 4 percent today. As with unemployment, the trend is as in-

FIGURE VI.2
Unemployment Rate, 1947–1988

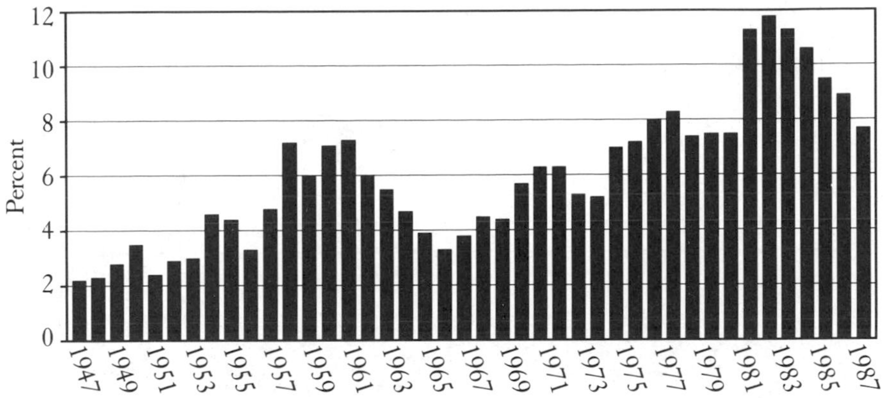

Source: Derived from Canada, Department of Finance, *Quarterly Economic Review*, June 1989: annual reference tables.

teresting as the annual fluctuations. A rate of 4 to 5 percent today is normal; yet in the late 1960s, those rates were viewed as a significant policy problem.

Table VI.2 provides three summary measures of structural changes in the economy. The impression given depends on the statistic used. Goods industries, including construction and utilities, accounted for over 39 percent of gross domestic product in 1947. Their share rose slightly, to 41 percent, by 1963, before dropping back to 37 percent by 1981. By this measure, they held their own in the economy, contrary to what is often believed. In terms of employment, though, they did not. Nearly 60 percent of the labour force produced goods in 1947, but only 32 percent did in 1981. Measured in terms of shares of capital stock, the record is in-between. Goods activities accounted for 39 percent of the nation's capital stock in 1947, and 31 percent in 1981. The difference in the two measures reflects the fact that productivity, particularly labour productivity, increased faster in these activities than it did in the economy as a whole.

The record varies notably within the goods-producing sector. Agriculture, forestry, and fishing and trapping declined in relative importance in the economy overall, no matter how the shift is measured. The fall in agriculture's share of total employment from over

FIGURE VI.3
Rate of Inflation, 1947–1988

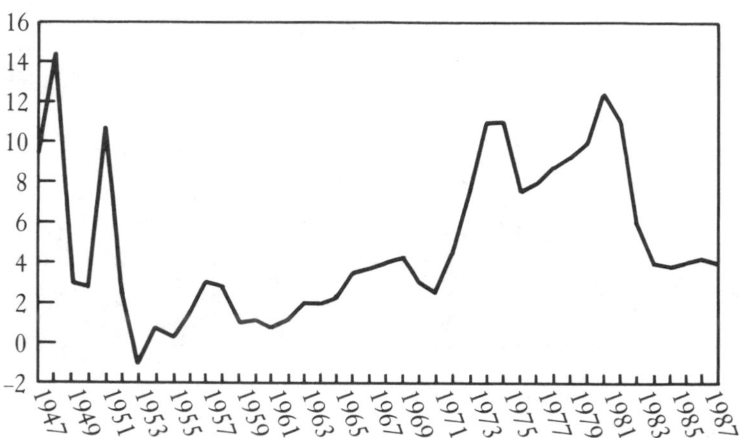

Source: Derived from Canada, Department of Finance, *Quarterly Economic Review*, June 1989: annual reference tables.

23 percent in 1947 to less than 5 percent in 1981 is, by far, the most dramatic number in the table. The exodus from farms, which had been progressing for decades before World War II, accelerated in these years. Manufacturing maintained its share of GDP, but lost in terms of labour and capital employed. Mines, construction, and utilities increased in importance by each measure.

These trends in goods industries are mirrored by those in services. Services produced 61 percent of GDP in 1947 and 63 percent in 1981, accounting for four out of every ten workers in 1947 and six out of every ten in 1981; and holding 60 percent of the capital stock in 1947, and 70 percent in 1981. Like that for the goods industries, the pattern is quite mixed within the group. Three sectors — trade; finance, insurance, and real estate; and business and personal services — rose in relative importance by each measure, although their shares of employment rose, by far, the most rapidly. Transportation, storage, and communication increased its share of output, but lost in terms of inputs, indicating above-average productivity gains, as in some of the goods industries. Public administration slipped in terms of output and capital stock shares, but almost exactly doubled its share of the work force.

TABLE VI.2

Share Distribution of Real GDP, Employment, and Net Capital Stock, Twelve Sectors, Canada, 1947, 1963, and 1981

(percentage of total)

	GDP			*Employment*			*Capital Stock*		
	1947	*1963*	*1981*	*1947*	*1963*	*1981*	*1947*	*1963*	*1981*
Agriculture	6.4	4.7	2.5	23.3	10.3	4.7	8.7	6.9	5.4
Forestry	1.4	0.9	0.6	3.3	1.3	0.7	0.5	0.6	0.4
Fishing and trapping	0.4	0.3	0.2	0.5	0.4	0.4	0.3	0.2	0.2
Mines	1.9	3.7	2.9	1.6	1.7	1.7	2.4	2.5	8.9
Manufacturing	21.8	22.2	21.6	24.3	22.8	17.8	18.2	16.8	15.3
Construction	5.8	7.3	6.2	4.7	5.7	5.5	0.9	1.0	1.0
Utilities	1.1	2.2	3.2	0.3	1.1	1.1	7.7	12.8	15.5
Transportation, storage, and communications	8.5	8.3	10.5	9.3	8.7	7.7	22.2	16.4	13.0
Trade	12.1	11.5	12.5	12.5	15.6	17.8	4.0	5.0	3.6
Finance, insurance, and real estate	11.9	12.3	13.2	2.4	3.7	5.3	1.4	2.7	5.8
Services	19.4	18.2	19.7	5.9	9.0	15.8	7.3	10.1	12.6
Public administration	8.9	8.9	6.7	10.9	19.6	21.7	26.4	21.8	18.3

Source: Michael F. Charette, Robert P. Henry, and Barry Kaufmann, "The Evolution of the Canadian Industrial Structure," in *Canadian Industry in Toronto*, Royal Commision on the Economic Union and Development Prospects for Canada, Research Study No. 2, edited by Donald G. McFetridge (Ottawa: Supply and Services, 1986), 67.

TABLE VI.3

Employment Change in Selected Industries, Canada, 1961–1979

Industries in Which Employment Declined	*Absolute Decline in Employment*	*Change in Industry Employment (%)*
Agriculture	16 378	–25.3
Forestry	9 850	–13.1
Gold Mines	10 884	–70.6
Uranium Mines	714	–13.5
Coal Mines	2 874	–27.8
Dairy Factories	7 999	–23.4
Flour and Breakfast Cereals	700	–11.9
Biscuit Manufacturers	107	– 1.6
Bakeries	7 335	–21.2
Confectionary Manufacturers	1 397	–13.5
Sugar Refineries	352	–11.4
Tobacco Products	1 645	–16.0
Rubber-Footwear Manufacturers	1 816	–43.8
Leather Tanneries	1 385	–39.0
Shoe Factories	5 655	–25.9
Leather-Glove Factories	696	–40.0
Cotton Yarn and Cloth Mills	8 144	–46.6
Wool-Yarn and Cloth Mills	3 435	–40.8
Fibre-Preparation Mills	299	–34.1
Thread Mills	150	–15.1
Cardage and Twine	389	–40.0
Narrow-Fabrics Mills	415	–16.9
Cotton and Jute	273	–26.8
Hosiery Mills	4 242	–47.4
Coffin and Casket	655	–45.7
Asphalt and Related Products	405	–21.6
Radio and TV Receivers	4 191	–58.8
Clay Products	383	– 7.1
Manufacturers of Mixed Fertilizers	553	–34.0
Paint and Varnish Manufacturers	793	–10.0

Industries in Which Employment Declined	*Absolute Decline in Employment*	*Change in Industry Employment (%)*
Broom, Brush, and Mop	486	–19.4
Repair Construction	9 990	– 7.0
Water Transportation	2 508	– 7.0
Railway Transportation	30 288	–24.5
Highway and Bridge Maintenance	416	–21.3
Final Demand Categories		
Domestic Defence	12 872	–11.5
Defence	40 500	–33.4

Industries with High Employment Growth	*Increase in Employment*	*Change in Industry Employment (%)*
Petroleum and Gas Well	18 401	201.1
Other Nonmetal Mines	3 988	164.3
Services Incidental to Mining	23 108	271.1
Vegetable-Oil Mills	762	136.1
Wineries	696	112.4
Plastic Fabrication, Nes.	24 554	304.0
Carpet Mat. and Rug Ind.	5 162	290.1
Miscellaneous Textiles	11 359	145.1
Office Furniture	3 409	107.8
Metal Casting and Extruding	3 585	132.6
Hardware Toll and Cutlery	11 919	129.3
Miscellaneous Machinery and Equipment	37 998	124.8
Commercial Refrigeration and Air Conditioning	3 132	191.9
Motor Vehicles	26 878	107.5
Truck Body and Trailers	12 891	354.6
Motor-Vehicle Parts and Access	34 452	168.8
Railroad Rolling Stock	6 054	144.9
Miscellaneous Transportation Equip.	4 256	199.1
Ready-Mix Concrete	5 016	116.1
Refractories	803	100.1
Manufacturers of Toilet Preparations	3 729	111.3

Industries with High Employment Growth	*Increase in Employment*	*Change in Industry Employment (%)*
Other Engineering Construction	31 991	125.9
Air Transportation	26 232	164.7
Services Incidental to Transportation	32 215	382.6
Pipeline Transportation	2 390	102.2
Electric Power	40 018	111.3
Water and Other Utilities	3 152	449.0
Banks and Credit Unions	118 631	156.0
Other Finance, Insurance, and Real Estate	169 126	224.2
Education and Related Services	9 817	102.5
Health Services	47 934	136.5
Motion-Picture Theatres	11 198	129.5
Other Recreational Services	43 082	315.6
Professional Services to Business	228 290	343.9
Advertising Services	14 308	186.5
Accommodation and Food Services	260 161	131.6
Other Personal Services	77 628	179.1
Photography	6 856	145.7
Miscellaneous Repair and Maintenance	58 517	414.6
Miscellaneous Services to Business and Personal	131 642	320.5
Final Demand Categories		
Education and Related Services	93 530	233.3
Miscellaneous Services to Business and Personal	14 270	280.4
Recreational Services	3 224	148.6
Non-Profit Organizations	122 524	120.1
Education and Related Services, Government	317 621	145.9
Other Government Services	402 392	102.0

Source: Michael F. Charette, Robert P. Henry, and Barry Kaufmann, "The Evolution of the Canadian Industrial Structure," in *Canadian Industry in Toronto*, Royal Commission on the Economic Union and Development Prospects for Canada, Study No. 2, edited by Donald G. McFetridge (Ottawa: Supply and Services, 1986), 87–91

The categories shown in Table VI.2 are sufficiently aggregated that, with a couple of exceptions, they are difficult to relate to. Table VI.3 thus provides a more detailed industry listing, grouped according to industries experiencing actual declines in employment between 1961 and 1979 and those gaining. Interestingly, the more than 16 000 jobs lost in agriculture did not represent the largest decline. That distinction went to defence, at over 40 000, followed by railway transport at 30 000. Other notable absolute declines were in domestic defence, gold mines, repair construction, forestry, and cotton yarn and cloth mills. The largest absolute gain in employment was in government services, followed by education and related services (also mainly government), banks and other financial services, accommodation and food services, and services to businesses.

These tables and charts record the three prominent developments in the economy in the postwar period, but they tell us nothing about why the economy grew in size, why it became richer, and why the structural changes took place. There is an easy, almost simplistic answer to each of these questions. Aggregate output grew because demand for goods and services was high and rising and because Canadians were able to marshal the capital, labour, and technology needed to meet the demands. The economy grew richer because, for a variety of reasons, ranging from increases in efficiency to technological progress, it was able to extract more output for each input of factors. The structure changed because the demand increases were not uniform across products and because the productivity gains were not uniform across industries. The task in the remainder of Part VI is to look at each of these points in more detail.

Notes

1. Jock A. Finlayson, "Canadian International Economic Policy: Context, Issues and a Review of Some Recent Literature," in *Canada and the International Political/Economic Environment*, Royal Commission on the Economic Union and Development Prospects for Canada, Research Study No. 28, edited by Denis Stairs and Gilbert R. Winham (Ottawa: Supply and Services, 1985), 13.
2. The data are from Canada, Department of Finance, *Quarterly Economic Review: Annual Reference Tables*, June 1989.

Further Reading

Bothwell, Robert, John English, and Ian Drummond. *Canada Since 1945: Power, Politics, and Provincialism*. Rev. ed. Toronto: University of Toronto Press, 1989.

Canada. Royal Commission on the Economic Union and Development Prospects for Canada. *Report*, Vols. 1–3. Ottawa: Supply and Services, 1985. The commission also published 72 volumes of research grouped into four areas — economics, political science, law, and the interdisciplinary area of federalism and the economic union. These studies are an obvious starting point for anyone interested in postwar Canadian economic, political, and constitutional development.

C H A P T E R

20

Growth and Prosperity, 1946–1973

The period from the end of the war to the early 1970s ranks, in retrospect, as one of the most prosperous in Canada's economic history. The nation was well placed to benefit from the economic changes sweeping the world. The liberalization of trade opened markets for Canadian goods and services and provided lower-cost imports. The resumption of international capital and labour flows expanded the capacity to meet the demands for the products. Added to these stimuli were other more internal factors, such as growing population and income, rising labour-force participation rates, new infrastructure developments, more education and training, reallocation of activity from slow-growth to rapid-growth sectors, and new resource discoveries.

The period was not without its problems and setbacks, of course. Postwar stagnation was feared in Canada as much as anywhere else. Inflation was a problem in the early 1950s, and sluggish growth was in the latter half of the decade when politicians and central bankers clashed over the appropriate policy stance. Already in the late 1960s there were signs of the stagflation that was to preoccupy policy makers in the next decade. Concern was growing about the capacity of the economy to continue absorbing immigrants at the same rate, and discussion of costs of reliance on foreign investment were becoming common. But these items were minor compared to what Canadians had just been through and, still unbeknownst to them, what they were about to encounter.

Conversion to a Peacetime Economy, 1945–1950

The transition to a peacetime economy took a different turn than expected. Economic growth in the immediate postwar period was far more robust than most had dared predict. Real GNP declined in 1946 but rose consistently thereafter. Increases in aggregate demand were strong and widely based. Ottawa cut back its expenditures on military supplies in 1946–48, but these reductions were partially offset by new projects, such as the Trans-Canada Highway cost-sharing venture, signed with the provinces in 1948. Difficulties reaching international markets were reflected in early postwar export figures, but, again, not as badly as feared. Beginning in 1948, European nations could use American credit under the Marshall Plan to buy Canadian goods, and that provision, together with our own export credits, meant that sales abroad fell less than might otherwise have been the case.

Other components of aggregate demand picked up the early slack left by the government's demilitarization.[1] Consumer spending had been curtailed during the war by rationing and the absence of key goods such as new automobiles, so there was considerable pent-up demand and a large stock of liquid assets in the hands of the public to finance it. Consumption rose by over 11 percent in real terms in 1946, and 7 percent in 1947; fell off in 1948; and then rose by over 6 percent in 1949 and 1950. Business investment was particularly strong, as firms set about retooling to meet peacetime demands, stimulated, at least in part, by federal tax provisions. Spending on new plant and equipment rose by over 30 percent in 1946 and nearly the same amount in 1947, and remained strong for the next three years.

Much of the growth in investment spending represents the switch of manufacturing capacity from military to civilian use. But the numbers also reflect a significant recovery of the major resource industries from the lull they found themselves in in the latter stages of the war. Pulp and paper, lumber, asbestos, gypsum, primary aluminum, and other minerals were able to expand production, in part in response to U.S. demands, until, by 1948, they had regained their prewar position in our export trade.

One notable example of this early resource development was the discovery of significant oil and gas reserves in western Canada, Alberta in particular. Leduc #1 came in in February 1947, followed

Imperial Oil

***Imperial Oil's Leduc #1 "blows in."** The first Leduc (Alberta) oil discovery was made in February 1947 and was followed by a number of other large discoveries of oil and gas reserves in western Canada. A pipeline was built to take oil eastwards, reaching Regina by June 1949, and the Manitoba/North Dakota border soon after. From there, it crossed U.S. territory to a terminus at Superior, Wisconsin, and thence was transported by steamer to Sarnia, Ontario.*

in quick order by a number of other large discoveries. Regional demand for petroleum was quickly met, and surplus supplies became available. The Interprovincial Pipeline Corporation was incorporated under federal legislation to take oil eastward. The line reached Regina by June 1949 and the Manitoba–North Dakota border by the fall of that year. From there, it proceeded through U.S. territory to a terminus at Superior, Wisconsin, where lake tankers picked up supplies for Sarnia. Plans were under way at this time to take crude oil west and to transport natural gas, but approval had not yet been given.

Stabilization Policy, 1945–1950

With the unexpected strong aggregate demand, inflation rather than stagnation was the main policy problem in the immediate postwar period. The consumer price index, which had moved very little during the war, leapt up in 1947 and 1948, as wartime controls were removed. Little use was made of active stabilization measures, however, bows to the new Keynesian demand management theory notwithstanding. Budgets were consistently set, not to regulate aggregate demand but to reduce the share of government in the economy. Taxes were reduced in every budget from 1945 to 1949, and they remained unchanged in 1950. Monetary policy was concerned mainly with supporting government bond prices, meaning that interest rates were kept low, so there was little monetary restraint on inflation from this quarter.

Exchange-rate policy in the immediate postwar years was erratic, to say the least. As a signatory to Bretton Woods, Canada was committed to maintaining a fixed exchange rate and to removing restrictions on exchange convertibility. There was considerable difficulty finding the correct price for the dollar. It was appreciated to par with the U.S. dollar in 1946, largely as an anti-inflationary measure. The jump was too large, as it turned out, contributing to a balance-of-payments crisis in 1947 that was countered by increasing the severity of exchange controls. The British pound was devalued in 1949, and Canada responded with a 10 percent cut of its own. Now, the rate was too low, resulting in a speculative capital inflow. Thus, in 1950, international commitments notwithstanding, a decision was made to float the dollar. One year later, the last of the wartime exchange restrictions were removed.

The net impact of reconstruction in Europe and rapid growth in the United States was to alter Canadian trading patterns in a fundamental and, as it turned out, permanent fashion. Canada had, for a very long time, imported more from the United States than it exported, and exported more to Europe than it imported. A trade deficit with America was offset by a surplus with Europe. The pattern of imports changed little after the war, but that for exports shifted dramatically. The United States took 38 percent of our exports in 1946, and Britain and Western Europe 47 percent. These proportions had shifted to 50 percent and 33 percent, respectively, just two years later and to 65 percent and 21 percent by 1950. Henceforth, the United States was to be Canada's dominant market, as well as supplier, meaning that our economic fortunes would be intertwined to an even greater extent than before.

War and the Resource Boom, 1951–1956

Economic growth was very rapid between 1951 and 1956. Except in 1954, when real GNP actually declined, growth rates were above 4.5 percent in two years, above 8 percent in two others, and at a postwar high of 9.5 percent in 1955. Unemployment, which had been at 3.6 percent in 1950, dropped to 2.4 percent the next year and rested at the 3 percent level until 1953. The recession in 1954 drove the rate up to 4.6 percent, but it fell below 4 percent again by 1956. The boom was also reflected in inflation rates. The consumer price index jumped nearly 11 percent in 1951, before dropping to 2.5 percent in 1952, then below 1 percent until 1956.

The origins of this growth were war, resource development, and demographic change. The outbreak of the Korean War in June 1950 provided an immediate stimulus to the economy. Government expenditures increased by over 30 percent in real terms in 1951, and 23 percent in 1952, as Canada contributed to the war effort. Exports boomed, as the war created a demand for Canadian resource products, in particular. Both components of spending fell off in 1953, accounting for the lower growth rates of that year, and both declined in real terms in 1954, contributing to the fall in real GNP. Spending on consumer and investment goods was weak in 1954 as well. The upswing in 1955 and 1956 was centred in resource exports and the investment needed to bring these projects into being. Strong consumer spending added fuel to the boom.

Several high-profile resource and investment projects dominated the headlines. The petroleum industry expanded greatly in these years. As demand in Ontario markets grew, the Interprovincial Pipeline was extended to Sarnia, reaching that city in 1953. Transmountain's plans to take oil west, through the Yellowhead Pass to Vancouver and Seattle, received considerable impetus from the Korean War emergency. Crude-oil production rose significantly, from 47.6 million barrels in 1951 to 181 million in 1956, at the height of the Suez crisis. Exports increased even more dramatically, going from a mere 342 000 barrels in 1951 to 55.7 million in 1957.

Natural-gas projects had a tougher time with regulatory authorities. Already in 1949, Alberta had moved to control the export gas from the province, and had created Alberta Gas Trunk Lines (AGTL) to prevent outside control of gas collection. Federal authorities were concerned with ensuring that any gas exports were surplus to domestic needs, and were insistent that pipelines to eastern and western markets pass through Canadian territory. This stance contrasted sharply with that adopted for crude oil, where there had been virtually no debate over ownership of the pipeline companies or routing of the lines.

Permission was given in 1951, in the midst of the Korean War, to build a line from southeastern Alberta to Montana, to fuel the Anaconda Copper smelter. Another permit was given to Westcoast Transmission to ship gas from its northern fields to Vancouver and to the U.S. Pacific Northwest. Exports were approved, in this instance, because Vancouver demand was insufficient to support a pipeline by itself, and because the northern supplies were judged to be surplus to Canadian needs.

The most controversial project, by far, concerned transporting natural gas to markets in Ontario and Quebec. Unlike oil pipelines that had taken the most direct route to eastern markets, natural-gas pipelines, it was generally agreed, should run entirely through Canadian territory, whatever the transportation economics. There was also concern over foreign ownership of this utility, so much so that Minister of Munitions and Supply C.D. Howe merged one American company with a Canadian one to form Trans-Canada PipeLines Limited before a permit was issued to begin construction. A bill to provide government financial assistance to the project required closure before it was passed by Parliament in 1956, a move that is widely cited as being the issue John Diefenbaker used to bring down the Liberals the following year. Assistance was given, the line was constructed on Canadian territory, the loan was repaid, natural gas flowed to Toronto and Montreal in 1958, and the company ended up Canadian-controlled. Natural-gas production, which had been 67.8 million cubic feet in 1950, jumped to 320 million by 1957.

Other projects were equally high-profile. The idea of improving the St. Lawrence Seaway to allow ocean-going vessels to sail into the heart of the continent goes far back in Canadian history, as the earlier discussion of the nineteenth-century canal system indicated. The St. Lawrence Seaway Authority was established in 1951 as a crown corporation, authorized to construct a deep waterway between Montreal and Lake Erie, in conjunction with the United States if possible, but otherwise alone. American interest in the project had never been great, but it was stimulated at this time by two developments. The hydro-electric potential of the system was realized at a time when both central Canada and New York State anticipated shortages of electric power. Negotiations on this aspect had produced a joint proposal to the International Joint Commission in 1952. Interest in the Seaway came with the knowledge that Mesabi iron-ore desposits, soon to be exhausted, could be replaced by supplies from Quebec-Labrador shipped up the system.

The U.S. Congress finally approved the plan, and a treaty was signed in 1954, providing for joint construction and ownership of the works. The Seaway was opened in 1959, and various initial operating difficulties overcome by 1962. The completion of the Seaway had important benefits for Canada. It lowered the cost of shipping prairie grain to export markets, thereby raising farm incomes. By allowing Quebec-Labrador iron ore to reach steel centres in central Canada and the United States, it opened up a new and important staple. These two products dominated Seaway shipping from the beginning. Finally, it added to the hydro-electric capacity of the two central provinces.

As noted, U.S. interest in the Seaway stemmed, in part, from the access this route gave the Great Lakes steel towns to Labrador iron-ore resources. By 1947, it had become clear that the Mesabi range in Minnesota would not be able to meet U.S. requirements for much longer. The Iron Ore Company of Canada was formed as a consortium of Canadian and American firms in 1949, and began a massive development of the Schefferville deposits the following year. U.S. Steel began development at Lac Jeannine a few years later, with the first rail shipment coming in 1961. Other, smaller developments followed, with some sales being made in Japan and Europe in addition to the United States. The result was that Canadian iron-ore production, which had been at about 2 million gross tons in 1945, jumped to 14.5 million by 1955 and over 21 million before the decade ended. One-third of production was exported to the United States in 1945, and over 60 percent by 1959.

The uranium industry grew dramatically for a time as well. The U.S. and the U.K. goverments were the main buyers of the ore in the immediate postwar period. The U.S. government subsidized production via the Atomic Energy Commission through an elaborate system of contracts and price supports. The Atoms for Peace initiative by President Eisenhower in 1953 opened up civilian access to uranium, giving spur to the nuclear-power industry. The combination of military and civilian demand in the United States generated an export boom in Canada, with sales jumping from $1.6 billion in 1956 to $13.5 billion by 1959. Canada set up the Atomic Energy Control Board in 1946 to conduct research and to regulate all aspects of the nuclear industry. Atomic Energy of Canada Limited (AECL) was created as a crown corporation in 1952 to develop a capacity in nuclear power. AECL had the first CANDU reactor in operation by 1962.

The other resource industries benefited from growing international demand. The U.S. government used stockpiling practices to increase world nickel production and to reduce Inco's monopoly of the metal. Falconbridge was the main Canadian beneficiary of this practice. Inco expanded into northern Manitoba toward the end of the decade, opening a mine at Thompson in 1960. Quebec's asbestos industry grew, although it is probably most famous for its 1949 strike and the catapulting into politics of Pierre Trudeau and other Quebec intellectuals. Canada's cheap hydro resources continued to draw metal-refining activities, the Canadian Reynolds smelter at Baie-Comeau, built in 1955, being one of the more notable projects.

As important to the daily lives of Canadians as these big projects, though, was the way in which their own activities shaped consumption and investment. Canada, along with the United States and Australia, underwent a major demographic shift in the period after World War II. This was the famous baby boom, which, as Figure

20.1 shows, involved a reversal in a long-term decline in the birth rate at a time when infant-mortality rates were declining sharply as a result of improvements in nutrition and medical techniques. Through the 1950s, the marriage rate soared, family formation followed, and with it came a lifestyle that dictated consumption at a high level.

Houses had to be bought to accommodate all these new families. As the houses were often suburban, automobiles had to be bought to take the breadwinner to work and to move the rest of the family to school and to shopping or recreation areas. Radios, and then television sets, were bought in record numbers to entertain the young families. By the early 1950s, school construction reached record levels as governments sought to provide places for these new children to be educated. Likewise, in an era of affluence, business soon learned that children themselves were a consumer market. New products were spawned, from Davey Crockett hats to hula-hoops. Unprecedented affluence marked the rise of this new and large generation of children. Materialism became a deeply imbued social ethic that was tied into the provision of security. This was, after all, only fifteen years after the Depression.

FIGURE 20.1

Crude Birthrate per Thousand of Population, 1926–1970

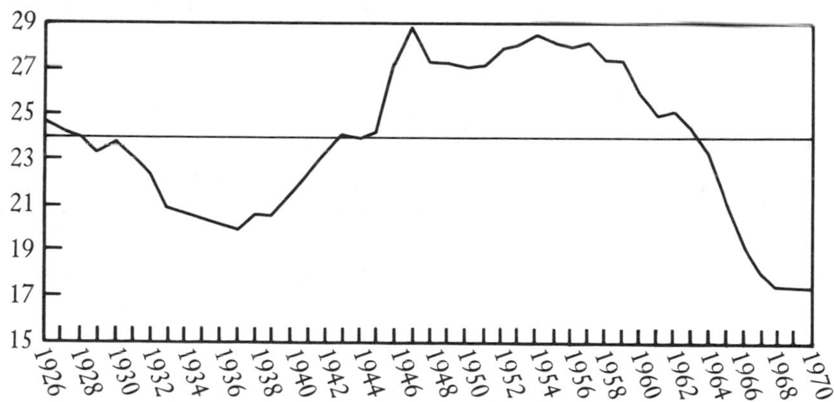

Source: Statistics Canada, *Historical Statistics of Canada*, 2nd ed. (Ottawa: Supply and Services, 1983), Table B4.

Canada Mortgage and Housing Corporation/9411-8

***A typical suburb built just after World War II.** The end of the war brought with it the baby boom, which resulted in a greatly increased demand for family housing. In 1947 alone, 76 000 homes were built, many of them in new suburbs without access to public transportation. Every family needed a car to get to work, and to shopping or recreation, causing an explosion in the new- and used-car markets. By the 1950s, building and car manufacture had become major industries in Canada.*

Stabilization Policy, 1951–1956

Fiscal policy continued to be neglected in favour of other government-spending and taxation objectives, as it had been in the immediate postwar period. Financing the Korean War effort obviously dominated objectives in 1951 and 1952, and cutting back on the government sector did in 1953. There was little change in either spending or taxation in 1954, even as the economy slipped into recession. The 1955 budget has been described as the first truly "Keynesian" one in the postwar period, aimed, as it was, at stimulating the economy in the face of the slack evident in the 1954 data. It is widely acknowledged to have come too late, however, as the economy was already into the 1955–56 resource and investment boom by then.

Monetary policy was used more actively beginning in 1950. The first increase in the bank rate in the postwar period took place in October of that year as an anti-inflationary measure. Under the then governor of the Bank of Canada, Graham Towers, monetary policy relied less on controlling the overall growth of the money supply and more on restricting credit through selective controls and moral suasion directed at the banking sector. James Coyne replaced Towers as governor in 1954, and monetary policy was eased as the Korean War pressures ended. It was tightened again in 1955, and more so in 1956, in the face of the boom of those years. A notable parallel development was the steps taken in 1953 and 1954 to broaden the Canadian financial market by introducing government Treasury Bills and by giving dealers in them access to Bank of Canada credit lines.

The Canadian dollar was floated in October 1950, as noted above; all restrictions on foreign-exchange transactions were removed the following year. The dollar appreciated, gradually reaching par with the U.S. dollar, and then traded at a premium from 1952 on. This appreciation served as an effective anti-inflationary tool, as the rise in the dollar reduced the demand for Canadian exports and increased the demand for, and reduced the price of, imports.

Recession, 1957–1961

Economic growth slowed appreciably toward the end of 1956 and remained at relatively low levels for the next five years. Consumption spending grew at half the rate in 1957 and 1958, as it had done in 1956, rose slightly in 1959, and then slowed again for two more years. Investment was especially weak, dropping, in real terms, to a 6 percent increase in 1957 from 18 percent the previous year, and then declining in three of the next four years. Exports stagnated in 1957 and 1958, and rose at only a fraction of their mid-1950s rate through to 1961. The consequence of this weak growth in aggregate demand was that unemployment rates rose from 3.4 percent in 1956 to over 7 percent in 1960 and 1961. As if this development were not perplexing enough, inflation jumped in 1957, and was higher in 1958–60 than it had been in 1955, at the height of the boom.

In part, the Canadian economy was following the American one into this downturn. Another factor accounting for the severity of the recession in Canada is that the major investments associated with resource exploitation were nearly completed. With no new major projects in the wings, investment spending would naturally fall off. Further, many of the market opportunities for Canadian products had been the consequence of unusual circumstances — the Korean War, the Suez crisis — and these would inevitably reverse as normal conditions returned. The U.S. government had announced, in 1956, the end of price supports and subsidies for uranium production to take effect in 1962, for example, and Canadian sales fell dramatically from 1959 on.

The performance of the petroleum sector provides a good example of the difficulties facing the economy in these years. High-cost oil from Saskatchewan and Alberta had been unable to penetrate markets east of the Ottawa River. Refiners in Quebec and the Atlantic provinces were supplied, instead, by imports from the Middle East and Venezuela. The U.S. market had not grown as much as had been hoped, either, as a result of these same cheap offshore supplies. The American government instituted a system of voluntary import limitations in 1957, and made them mandatory two years later. Canada was exempted from the quotas on security grounds, but sales of western crude oil and natural gas into the United States rose only slowly, and, except in the Suez-crisis years, the industry operated well below capacity.

Western provincial governments and the smaller independent producers lobbied hard for guaranteed access to the large Montreal market in the face of this excess capacity. The response of the Diefenbaker government was to appoint the Royal Commission on Energy (the Borden Commission) in 1957 to look at petroleum production and marketing. The report resulted in the creation of the National Energy Board in 1959 and what became known as the National Oil Policy (NOP) in 1961. Known as the deal with something for everyone, the NOP essentially ratified the continental marketing pattern that had operated since 1947. The Atlantic provinces and Quebec continued to import cheaper offshore oil. Ontario and the western provinces received western Canadian crude. Ontario paid slightly more for its oil as a result, but a prohibition on refinery shipments from Montreal allowed it to develop its own petrochemical industry. The United States agreed to import more Canadian crude, thereby providing compensation to the independents for their "loss" of Quebec. Guaranteed access to Ontario and expanded markets in the United States provided increased employment and economic activity for the western provinces.

The Diefenbaker government did try to develop new areas of production in the economy in this period. It came into office in 1957, trumpeting the idea of a northern vision, including a "Roads to Resources" proposal. This idea essentially involved overseeing the construction of expensive infrastructure to open up the supposed vast economic potential of the Canadian North. Some facilities were built, and some new resource projects were begun, but, generally, the scheme came to little, given the economic realities of the time. There were other projects, such as the South Saskatchewan River Dam, price supports for agricultural products, winter-works grants, and an attempt to develop European and Commonwealth trade.

Stabilization Policy, 1957–1961

The period from 1957 to 1961 ranks as one of the most interesting in the postwar period in terms of stabilization policy. It was the first evidence of what was to become known later as stagflation — a simultaneous rise in both inflation and unemployment. The government, and some economists, interpreted this phenomenon as implying that the problems were structural rather than cyclical in nature. Labour demand and labour supply were becoming increasingly mismatched, as a result of technical change and other such factors. The solution, accordingly, was seen to lie in manpower policies, such as those for winter works mentioned above, and in retraining and education. Partly as a result of this view, fiscal policy was not used expressly in a countercyclical fashion. Finance minister Donald Fleming attempted consistently to run a balanced budget, although the poor economic conditions meant this goal was never achieved. Only in 1961 and 1962 did he propose to use spending and taxation to create jobs and reduce unemployment, but by that time both the recession and the Conservatives' political time were coming to an end.

Monetary policy dominated professional and even public discussion. Monetary policy was restrictive for the first three-quarters of 1957, before becoming appropriately expansionary for the last quarter and for most of 1958. Difficulties soon arose, however. A massive amount of wartime debt was coming due in 1958. The government opted to refinance the entire amount through the issuing of new debt — the so-called conversion loan of 1958. The refinancing was carried out, but only by increasing the average maturity of the debt significantly, driving up interest rates and offsetting attempts to expand the economy.

This problem was compounded in the next two years by the decision by Governor Coyne to adopt an extremely restrictive monetary stance. Money-supply growth virtually ceased, and interest rates rose from 1959 through to mid-1961. High interest rates, in turn, attracted short-term capital inflows, driving up the Canadian dollar and further dampening economic growth. A very public dispute arose between the governor and the government over the appropriateness of this policy and over who had ultimate responsibility for the conduct of monetary policy. The confrontation ended with Coyne's forced resignation in July 1961, but only after considerable uncertainty in Canadian financial markets and untold political embarrassment to the government.

An Extended Boom, 1962–1973

The economy took a significant turn for the better after 1961. Real GNP grew at 7.1 percent in 1962, compared to the average of 2.9 percent from 1957 to 1961. Except in 1967 and 1970, when growth slowed momentarily, GNP expanded by between 5.2 and 7.7 percent every year until 1973, creating the longest sustained boom in modern times. Unemployment, which had been over 7 percent in 1961, fell to below 4 percent in 1966, before creeping up to over 6 percent by the early 1970s. The move to full employment was reflected in the inflation rate. Consumer prices were rising at less than 1 percent in 1961, but increased to over 4 percent by the end of the 1960s, and were at 7.7 percent in 1973, after slowing somewhat in 1970 and 1971.

All components of aggregate demand contributed to this boom. Consumption demand was strong in every year except 1970. Investment grew rapidly to 1966, slowed to the end of 1970, and then rose again to 1973. Exports were especially robust, compared to earlier years. After a slow start in 1962, they rose by over 9 percent in real terms in 1963, and by over 13 percent the next year. A slight weakening in 1965 was followed by five buoyant years, a slackening in 1971, and two expansions thereafter.

Mild bouts of inflation notwithstanding, the 1960s and early 1970s were prosperous years, and this prosperity was reflected in the rising levels of consumption. Between 1963 and 1973, retail sales increased more than $20 billion, and automobile registrations by 40 percent. Dwelling starts went from an already healthy 150 000 in 1962 to an amazing 268 000 a decade later. Affluence and a changing job market also meant that more Canadians could proceed to higher education than ever before. Undergraduate enrolment at universities more than doubled, to nearly 285 000 students — more than quadruple the number at the beginning of the 1950s. Very real poverty still existed, but Canadians, as a group, were enjoying a level of prosperity that was unparalleled in our history.

Several factors contributed to the strength and duration of this economic expansion. Some of the economic prosperity evident in Europe spilled over into Canada. The most obvious explanation, though, is the vigorous, sustained, and broadly based boom that was under way in the United States, aided in the early years by tax cuts and other stimulative policies, and, in later ones, by spending on the Vietnam War. The devaluation of the Canadian dollar to 92.5 cents (U.S.) in 1962 and its pegging at that level gave Canadian products, manufactured ones in particular, a competitive edge in U.S. markets. Large wheat sales to China and the Soviet Union brought the agricultural sector out of the generally flat state it had been in since 1952. Large public-sector spending on educational facilities to deal with the children of the baby boom continued. There was also considerable work in preparation for the Montreal World's Fair in 1967.

Another new staple developed at this time as well. Saskatchewan potash reserves had been known for some time, but technical difficulties had interfered with all attempts to exploit them. A solution to the flooding problem allowed the first mine to open at Esterhazy in 1962. Nine others followed, the last being completed in 1970. Production rose from nothing in 1961 to 3.6 million tons in 1970. Output was mainly (about 95 percent) for export to the United States for use in fertilizer production, although some sales to Ontario and Quebec and to Pacific Rim nations were made as well. Production capacity increased much faster than demand, and the industry operated well below its potential throughout the decade.

The petroleum sector grew steadily in these years, buoyed by the generally prosperous times and the support of the NOP. Output of crude oil rose from 189.5 million barrels in 1960, to 350 million in 1967, and to 654.3 million in 1973. Exports rose consistently as well, from only 42.2 million barrels in 1960 to 414.4 million in 1973. Natural-gas production and exports grew apace. Permission had been granted in 1962 to build a 31 500-barrel-per-day oil-sands plant in Fort McMurray. It began operation in 1967 as the world's first "oil mine," but was plagued by a host of technical problems and showed continued losses until 1974, when oil prices improved.

The most notable development in the manufacturing sector in this period undoubtedly was the Auto Pact. In the early 1960s, the Canadian auto industry was a high-cost miniature replica of its U.S. counterpart. Branch plants of the Big Three American companies assembled the full range of automobiles in Canada behind a tariff wall of 17.5 percent. Auto-parts imports faced a duty of the same level as well unless certain Canadian content rules were met, in which case the parts came in duty-free. The American duty was lower, at 6.5 to 8.5 percent, but was still high enough to shut out assembly in Canada for export. Prices for automobiles were about 10 percent higher in Canada than in the United States, and Canadian wages were around 30 percent lower.

A royal commission (the Bladen Commission), charged in 1961 with looking into the industry, recommended an extension of the Canadian-content definition as a means of promoting production for export. The government opted, instead, for an extended-duty remission plan, whereby duties paid by the firms were returned according to the increase in parts exports reported. U.S. authorities responded by initiating a countervail hearing, charging unfair export subsidies. A frenzy of political negotiations followed, resulting in a agreement signed by Prime Minister Pearson and President Johnson in January 1965.

The agreement brought about duty-free trade in new vehicles and parts between Canada and the United States, but, at Canadian insistence, only for vehicle manufacturers. There was a 50 percent North American content provision in the agreement, and some safeguards to Canadian parts producers. More significant, though, were letters of agreement that the Canadian government managed to obtain from the Big Three auto producers, guaranteeing minimum levels of production in this country.

The agreement had an immediate and dramatic impact on automobile and parts production in Canada. In 1965, motor vehicles and parts surpassed pulp and paper in terms of value of shipments, to become Canada's most important industry.[2] The increase took the form of an integration of the North American market. Imports of vehicles from the United States accounted for 40 percent of the Canadian market in 1968, compared to just 3 percent in 1964. Of vehicles produced in Canada in 1968, 60 percent were exported to the United States, compared to 7 percent four years earlier. The number of lines produced here decreased, but production of those retained jumped sharply to take advantage of scale economies. Autos and parts became the leading item in our trade accounts and made up the bulk of the increase in finished manufactured products. Auto prices became more nearly even between the two countries, and wages of Canadian auto workers rose to equal those of their American counterparts.

Stabilization Policy, 1961–1973

Fiscal and monetary policies operated more consistently after James Coyne was replaced as governor by Louis Rasminsky. The first Liberal budget in June 1963, by finance minister Walter Gordon, aimed at reducing the deficit, and was, thus, mildly contractionary. It is better known, though, for its attempts to limit the flow of foreign capital into Canada by imposing special taxes on foreign takeovers and on foreign firms operating here. The measures were so widely condemned that they were withdrawn shortly afterwards. The next three budgets were neutral, or slightly expansionary, reflecting the buoyant economic times. Inflation was a problem by 1966 (the government had already asked the Economic Council of Canada to look at inflation in the economy, in 1965), so the budget of that year was mildly contractionary. A brief slowdown in 1967 prompted a more expansionary budget, but this was quickly corrected as the temporary nature of the slowdown was recognized.

Inflation was the explicit concern of the budgets of 1968 and 1969. A ceiling was placed on expenditure increases, civil-service hiring was frozen, and a tax surcharge was imposed. Further measures were adopted in 1969, as the government announced that it "really meant business." The stance was eased slightly in March 1970 in the face of the apparent slowdown in economic activity, and was reversed in December of that year, as concern shifted to rising unemployment. Additional funds were poured into high-unemployment areas, unemployment-insurance benefits were increased, and incentives were offered to encourage business investment.

Concern with unemployment continued in the next three budgets, as the government interpreted record levels of unemployment as indicating substantial excess capacity in the economy. The 1971 budget was substantially more expansionary than that of the preceding year, the most notable provision being the substantial extension and broadening of unemployment-insurance benefits. Job creation was recognized as the most urgent priority in May 1972, as additional tax and expenditure measures were introduced. This period ends with a budget in February 1973 that was described by finance minister John Turner as "strongly expansionary." Taxes were cut, expenditures were increased, and a number of tariff and excise taxes were reduced to ease inflationary pressures.

Monetary policy was expansionary in the early years of the expansion as well. This stance was changing by the spring of 1965, as inflationary pressures became evident. Policy became restrictive for the remainder of the decade, except during a brief period from mid-1966 to early 1967, and again in mid-1968, as the economy softened temporarily.

Two factors prevented the bank from exercising the degree of restraint it wished in these years, however. As is well understood now, but was only imperfectly so at the time, a small open economy such as Canada's cannot maintain both a fixed exchange rate and an inflation rate different from that of its major trading partners. To understand this dilemma, consider the situation facing the bank as it attempted to deal with inflationary pressures in the late 1960s. Tighter credit conditions led to higher interest rates, which meant short-term foreign capital was attracted to Canada. As the demand for Canadian dollars grew, the central bank had to intervene to keep the dollar fixed, which meant that the initial attempt to restrict the growth of the money supply was offset.

To exacerbate this problem, Canada had agreed, in 1962, to a ceiling on its holdings of foreign-exchange reserves in return for exemption from the U.S. Interest Equalization Tax. This provision meant that Canadian interest rates could not rise above those in the United States since the bank was constrained in the volume of U.S. dollars it could purchase to keep the dollar pegged. The result of these two factors was that the money supply grew much faster in the late 1960s than was warranted by the inflationary pressures, and in spite of the declared intentions of the bank to restrain inflation.

Pressure built up on the Canadian dollar to the point that the authorities decided to unpeg it in May 1970. It appreciated immediately, reaching par with the U.S, dollar in 1971, and rising to a premium for the next few years. This decision was anti-inflationary in two respects. Appreciation reduces pressures of aggregate demand on supply, and it lowers the price of imported goods and service that figure prominently in the Canadian consumer price index. It also makes monetary policy an especially effective policy tool. The capital flows induced by monetary tightening put further pressure on the dollar, which complements the anti-inflationary effects of the higher interest rates.

Unfortunately, Canadian authorities did not avail themselves of this opportunity to reduce inflationary pressures. Inflation did come down in 1970, a direct reflection of the appreciation. But the money supply grew very rapidly, from the float through to 1975, in the range of 10 to 15 percent. There are two explanations for this seemingly perverse behaviour. Like the fiscal authorities, the bank was misled into thinking that the unemployment statistics indicated excess slack in the economy when they really were showing a change in the nature of declared unemployment. There is also some indication that the bank was under pressure to prevent too much appreciation of the dollar, meaning that interest rates could not be allowed to rise as much as purely anti-inflationary objectives demanded. Whatever the reason, most analysts now believe that this excessive growth in the money supply fuelled the inflationary pressures that mark the beginning of the next period of our chronology.

Conclusion

Overall, economic conditions were prosperous in the first 25 years following World War II. The years were not problem-free, though, and many of these difficulties were to resurface in more serious form later. Business fluctuations remained, atttempts at Keynesian stabilization techniques notwithstanding. Fine-tuning turned out to be more difficult, technically and politically, than anticipated, so there were few periods when one can say that active and concerted countercyclical policies were pursued. Budgets and monetary policies were directed at other goals more often than they were at inflation or unemployemnt. Yet when this era is compared to what preceded it — the Great Depression and World War II — Canadians can be excused for thinking that, on the whole, the economy and their governments had performed rather well. Compared to what was to come, they can even be forgiven a little nostalgia.

Notes

1. The data are from Canada, Department of Finance, *Quarterly Economic Review: Annual Reference Tables*, June 1989.
2. *Canada Year Book*, 1968, 694.

Further Reading

Campbell, Robert M. *Grand Illusions: The Politics of the Keynesian Experience in Canada, 1945–1975*. Peterborough: Broadview Press, 1987.

Canada. Royal Commission on the Economic Union and Development Prospects for Canada. *Report*. Vols. 1–3. Ottawa: Supply and Services, 1985. See also the 72 research volumes published in conjunction with the commission's report.

CHAPTER 21

Policy Innovation, 1946–1973

Canadians responded well to the opportunities available in the 25 years after World War II. They were able to marshal the requisite supplies of capital, labour, and technology and to allocate them to meet the growing demand for their goods and services. For the most part, this supply response was market-driven. In some instances, however, government policies were used to facilitate the growth or to shape it in particular ways. Some measures were aimed at increasing the supply of factors, with a view to promoting extensive growth. (Immigration and foreign-investment policies are examples here.) Others were aimed more at increasing the efficiency with which capital and labour, domestic or foreign, were allocated within the economy. (Commercial or transportation policies come to mind.)

Still other policies introduced after 1946 were less attempts to promote economic growth than they were moves to take advantage of it. There was a determination to use the apparatus of the state to provide for the health, education, and income-security needs of individual Canadians, coming out of the experiences of the Great Depression and World War II. Regional economic disparities, long a feature of the federation and occasionally the target of isolated and ad hoc policy responses, became a major policy concern. This new, or at least intensified, commitment to seeking equity, reflected the prosperity of the time and the growing fiscal resources of the state. Redistribution is more palatable politically in an expanding economy than in a stagnant or shrinking one, as experience after 1973 would show.

Aggregate Supply Policies

Canada, it will be recalled, was a net exporter of capital from the outbreak of World War I through to the end of World War II. This trend was reversed after 1950. Canadian savings grew, as population and incomes did, but they were not sufficient to finance the high rates of investment taking place. Net capital inflow was highest during the 1950s. It fell off, in relative terms, thereafter, even becoming negative (Canada was again a net capital exporter) for a couple of years in the early 1970s, and again in 1982. Even at its highest point, though, foreign capital's relative position fell far short of the levels it reached in the first fifteen years of the twentieth century.

This foreign investment was different from that received earlier in our history in two important senses. First, it was predominantly American in origin. Second, and related to the first observation, it was predominantly direct (equity) as opposed to portfolio (bonds and other financial instruments), meaning that control usually resided with the foreign investor. The great surge in investment came in the 1950s; by 1960, the basic patterns were set — 80 percent of the capital was held by Americans; 60 percent of Canadian manufacturing was foreign-controlled, including 75 percent of oil and gas and 60 percent of mining, but a minuscule amount of railways and utilities. Within manufacturing, foreign control ranged from almost none in some sectors to nearly all the assets in others. Investment continued after 1960 but more or less in step with the growth in the economy. Canadians invested abroad at the same time as foreign savings were entering the country; the capital flow was not all one way.

Foreign capital entered Canada to take advantage of the earnings opportunities available, but that entry was facilitated by a relatively liberal policy. With a few notable exceptions, such as financial institutions and utilities, foreign capital was welcomed in the 1950s, indeed eagerly sought. This open stance came under considerable scrutiny in the late 1960s and early 1970s. The Watkins Report in 1968 and the Gray Report in 1972 focussed on what they saw as the costs (economic and political-cultural) of reliance on foreign investment. These concerns, and the political support they generated, led to the creation of the Canada Development Corporation (CDC) in 1971 and the Foreign Investment Review Agency (FIRA) of 1973. The CDC was intended to promote investments by Canadians in Canadian companies. FIRA's mandate was to screen new foreign investment to determine whether it was of significant benefit to the Canadian economy, with "benefit" defined by five specific critera. FIRA was criticized from the outset, both by those who saw it as unnecessarily constraining necessary foreign investment and by those who saw it as an ineffective guardian of Canadian interests.

The supply of labour to the economy grew over time in three separate ways — in domestic population, in immigration, and in increases in participation rates. As mentioned earlier, Canada experienced a baby boom in the immediate postwar years, with births running at 27 to 28 per 1000 population (see Figure 20.1). These began to decline by the late 1950s, falling to the 15-per-1000 level of the 1980s. Death rates declined slowly but continuously throughout. These trends in birth and death rates altered the age structure of the population notably. The proportion of the population aged 0–14 grew rapidly between 1941 and 1961, but fell off thereafter and, in 1981, was below its 1941 level. Not surprisingly, those aged 15–24 increased in relative importance after 1961, and those 25–64 after 1971. Persons aged 65 and over rose in relative importance throughout.

The second source of the requisite labour skills was immigration. Mainly, immigrants respond to economic incentives in this country relative to those in their own country. Canada was growing rapidly in these years, creating both high and rising wages and employment opportunities, and was thus an attractive destination. Its political stability and generally high quality of life merely added to its attractive powers.

Canada's policy facilitated this immigration, but only after it adjusted to take account of changing conditions in the world supply of immigrants. As seen earlier, the policy to 1930 was aimed at populating the farms, mines, and woods of the nation with workers that were as white and as British as possible. Restrictions on immigration had been tightened in the Great Depression and in wartime, but these were gradually loosened after 1946, as the demand for labour grew faster than did internal supplies. Sponsorship privileges were widened, preference was extended to unskilled and general labourers (though ethnic-group restrictions still applied), and most-preferred status was accorded to citizens of France in 1948, and Germany and Italy in 1950.

Regulations were further loosened in the early 1950s. The inflow of displaced persons had largely ceased by 1953, although an estimated 32 000 Hungarians were admitted in 1957, following an unsuccessful attempt at revolution in their country. The overall immigration stance was definitely expansionary in the mid-1950s, reflecting the economic boom that was under way. An interesting debate went on at this time over the correct posture to take with respect to immigration. One view, associated since with the Department of Labour, was that flows should be tuned to reflect the short-term requirements of the labour market. The other perspective, held by Citizenship and Immigration, was that the policy must be longer-term and structural in nature, ignoring temporary shortages or surpluses of labour.

A major shift in the orientation of Canadian immigration policy came after 1956. The expansionary stance began to change as unemployment rates crept up. Now there was an abundance of unskilled workers but a continuing shortage of skilled ones, professionals, and entrepreneurs with capital. Numbers needed to be regulated, and the skill composition changed. The ethnic composition had to change as well. Whatever genuine embarrassment there was with Canada's overtly racist policy at this time, there was also a practical consideration. Supplies from traditional sending areas were drying up, as economic expansion in Europe continued. There was no choice but to move to other areas of the world for the type of immigrant needed.

The new policy came by order-in-council in 1962. Emphasis was put on immigration of professionals and other highly skilled immigrants. Unskilled ones were discouraged. National preferences were also abolished; entrance, in principle at least, was open to anyone meeting the skill qualifications. A new department was created in 1965, and a formal credits system introduced in 1967. Candidates could earn points up to some maximum in each of several categories. The criteria were a blend of the two perspectives mentioned above. Some were identifiably short-term in outlook, intended to adjust supplies to current labour-market conditions. Others were longer-term in nature, with the emphasis on skills.

The third component of the increase in labour supply was a rise in the overall participation rate, almost entirely the result of the

Officials of the Canadian Embassy process visa applications from Hungarian refugees after the Hungarian Revolution. *In 1957, an estimated 32 000 Hungarians were admitted to Canada, reflecting the expansionary immigration policy of the mid-1950s — a result of the economic boom that was then under way. However, this policy began to change after 1956, when unemployment rates crept up.*

entrance of large numbers of women and youths into the labour force. Figure 21.1 shows the trends. The participation rate for men aged 25–54 remained roughly constant, at around 95 percent. Those for youths aged 15–24 and for women 25–54 rose dramatically, from 55 percent to nearly 70 percent for the former and from less than 40 percent to nearly 70 percent for the latter. Put differently: males held more than three-quarters of the jobs in the economy in 1956, about two-thirds of them in 1973, and fewer than 60 percent in 1983.[1]

These shifts in participation rates were partly an economic phenomenon, as women and youths responded to the new types of jobs available and to the higher wages they offered. Nearly half the jobs held by females in 1983 were in personal and business services, and another 18 percent were in wholesale and retail trade. Only in finance, insurance, and real estate and in personal and

FIGURE 21.1
Participation Rates among Certain Demographic Groups, 1966–1983

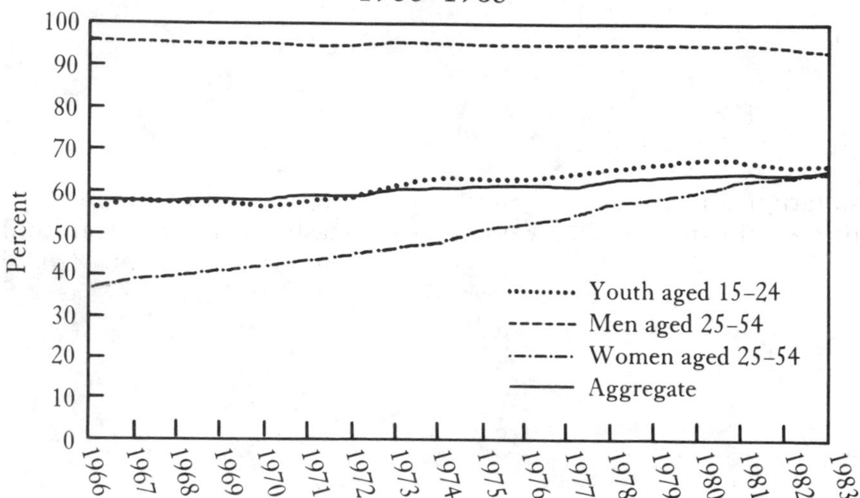

Source: Royal Commission on the Economic Union and Development Prospects for Canada, *Report*, Vol. II (Ottawa: Supply and Services, 1985), 16.

business services were women the majority of workers. The changes in female participation rates were partly social in origin as well, reflecting changing attitudes of women toward the home and the work place. By increasing the total labour supply and by altering its age and skill mix, these changes in participation rates are as much a contributor to the postwar economic record as a reflection of it.

The efficiency of the economy was enhanced to an uncertain extent by a series of policy initiatives designed to affect the allocation of resources in the economy. Commercial policy is a prime example. Canada was well situated to prosper from the liberalization of the international economic environment taking place after 1945, which explains, in part, why this nation was so active and visible in the reconstruction efforts. The last of the wartime foreign-exchange restrictions were gone by the early 1950s, as noted above. That left tariffs and other trade barriers, and here the process was both slower and more complicated than for exchange restrictions.

Canada signed the GATT agreement in October 1947. Interestingly, however, the first substantive move to liberalize trade came, not in a multilateral but rather in a bilateral framework. In one of the lesser-known stories of the immediate postwar period, Canadian negotiators, with the explicit blessings of Prime Minister Mackenzie King and his important advisers, obtained a general trade agreement with their American counterparts. All duties between the two countries were to be removed immediately, quantitative restrictions on imports were to go over a five-year period (with important exceptions on both sides), and there was to be joint consultation on agricultural marketing. But, at the last moment, the prime minister, fearing a political backlash on the political implications of turning to the Americans and away from the British, vetoed the proposal. Forty years later it would be taken up again, and this time it would go through.

Canada participated in the early GATT rounds, although not much progress was made. The Kennedy Round, beginning in Geneva in 1964, was more successful. Canada objected to the concept of linear tariff reductions (50 percent across the board) introduced at that time, on the grounds that the system worked against countries dependent on raw-material exports and manufactured imports. Canada preferred to negotiate, instead, on a product-by-product basis, a position reluctantly agreed to by the other participants. The end result was that Canada made concessions on some $2.5 billion of imports, about $2 billion of which were from the United States, in exchange for concessions of a similar amount by the Americans.[2]

As a result of Canada's participation in these GATT rounds, its tariff levels came down significantly. The ratio of duty collected to total imports stood at 11.1 percent in 1945, at 9.7 percent in 1960, and at 6.4 percent in 1970. This large drop in average protection came about, in part, from a reduction in tariff levels on dutiable imports and, in part, from an extension of the range of items admitted duty free. Duty collected as a percentage of dutiable imports was 21.1 percent in 1945, 17.7 percent in 1960, and 15.2 percent in 1970. At war's end, 40 percent of imports entered duty free. In 1960, 44 percent did and, in 1970, nearly 60 percent.[3]

Transportation issues have always loomed large in Canadian policy debates, and the postwar period was no exception. A major change in policy toward the railways came in 1967 with the passage of the National Transportation Act. Believing that developments in trucking had introduced competition where there had been little or none before, the government gave the railways considerably more freedom to set rates according to market considerations. There were exceptions, the most notable of which were the retention of the statutory grain rates and the controls on the abandonment of prairie branch lines. All provinces but Alberta regulated the entry and operation of trucking within their jurisdictions, and Ottawa set out the terms for interprovincial hauls. Airlines were tightly regulated, through control over fare schedules and routes.

Two policy areas of much smoke but no fire were tax reform and competition policy. The Royal Commission on Taxation (the Carter Commission) recommended a fundamental restructuring of the Canadian tax system in its report, published in 1967. The reforms did not survive the lobbying pressures they encountered, though, and little change was made. Similarly, studies of competition policy and proposals for reform met stiff opposition and were abandoned, with little or no legislative changes.

Provinces were active in promoting economic development as well. Like the national government, they intervened with tax incentives, subsidies, and regulations to increase the amount of economic activity within the province. Some, notably the smaller ones, were as intent on affecting the mix of activity, to diversify away from what they saw as excessive dependence on a few cyclically unstable resource industries. These efforts attracted little attention in the 1960s and early 1970s but, as Chapter 22 will show, became the focus of a major policy debate a decade later.

Seeking Equity

The period from 1945 to 1973 was exceptional in one way, if in no other. Most of the social policies and regional-development commitments we now take for granted as an essential part of the Canadian fabric had their beginnings in these years. Federal and provincial governments played a relatively small role in these areas prior to the Great Depression. Welfare was a private responsibility, assisted by churches and other charitable institutions, and, as a last resort, by municipalities. Attitudes changed significantly during the Great Depression, as Chapter 18 has indicated. The state was forced to take a more active role in managing the economy and in providing relief to the unfortunate; these tasks increasingly fell to the federal government.

There were some joint federal-provincial education and retraining programs after World War I, a variety of workers' compensation schemes, and mothers' pensions in some of the provinces. The most notable achievement, perhaps, was the introduction of old-age pensions in 1927; Ottawa and the provinces shared the costs of providing pensions to those over age 70 who met certain residence requirements and income restrictions. The federal share of old-age pensions was raised to 75 percent in 1931 as an inducement to provinces not yet in the scheme, and assistance was extended to blind persons in 1939. Further progress was stalled by constitutional challenges, and then by the emergencies of war, but was not completely halted. A constitutional amendment was secured in 1940 to allow the federal government to implement contributory unemployment insurance, and a national scheme was introduced the following year. Family-allowance payments were begun in 1944, introducing the country's first universal welfare-payment program.

Enthusiasm for social-policy reform was high coming out of the war, but political and constitutional realities soon resurfaced. The Veterans' Rehabilitation Act was passed in 1945 to provide educational benefits to returning veterans. Federal civil servants had drawn up a blueprint for a postwar social-policy system in a document known as the Green Book proposals, and the Conference on Reconstruction was convened in Ottawa in 1945 to discuss them. The provinces, or at least the larger and wealthier ones, immediately rejected these proposals, as they did those put forward in 1946 at a reconvened session. Hopes for any type of comprehensive national social policy were emphatically quashed. Henceforth, social-policy formation was to be as much an exercise in federal-provincial relations as it was in program design.

The next 25 years or so saw a bewildering series of proposals, negotiations, counterproposals, more negotiations, program implementations, and program redesigns. To make some sense of the sequence, it helps to keep a few general points in mind. It is useful to know, first, that, while there are a great many programs, each with its own acronym, they fall broadly into three types — education and occupational training, health and hospitalization insurance, and income security. The "income security" category can be futher subdivided into four types of policies, each with its own objectives.[4] Some programs (demogrants) apply to all Canadians who fall into certain classes, such as those based on age, irrespective of income or anything else. Family allowances and old-age security are examples. Another type, such as Guaranteed Income Supplements, provide income assistance to those meeting means tests. A third type of program is aimed at particular groups in society, such as the blind and disabled. The final type is social insurance, which provides benefits in times of need, based on contributions during working years. The Canada and Quebec pension plans and unemployment insurance are examples.

The second essential point is to understand the challenge policy makers faced. Everyone's objective was to provide health, education, and income security to individual Canadians. The only question was how to do it. Secondary motives, such as political and bureaucratic rivalry — which were certainly present — aside, both Ottawa and at least some provincial governments felt they should have the paramount role. Ottawa was interested in national standards and transferability among provinces. The provinces claimed the constitutional right that was certainly theirs, but also wanted the freedom to tailor policies to meet their own particular needs. Premier Stuart Garson commented in 1946, "a very substantial part of this increase [in expenditure] must come under provincial jurisdiction, namely in education, health and public welfare, natural resource development, road building, provincial public works."[5] Such a shopping list made provincial claims on the public purse a central part of postwar development of social programs.

The need to compromise brings up the third, and final, point. Social-policy formation in Canada was inextricably bound up with federal-provincial fiscal arrangements. To understand the sequence of development, then, one must have some notion of developments in this most complex and arcane area.

As pointed out in Chapter 19, the federal government took over exclusive authority for personal and corporate income taxes and succession duties during World War II, providing compensation to the provinces in the form of unconditional transfers. The first postwar arrangements, in 1947, continued this format. Ottawa offered to "rent" exclusive access to personal and corporate income taxes and succession duties. Provincial governments that agreed not to exercise their constitutional rights to tax in these areas received transfers from Ottawa. Provinces could remain outside the scheme, in which case the federal government offered tax credits to their residents. Seven provinces signed up for the scheme in 1947, while

Ontario and Quebec opted to impose their own corporate tax. The same basic system was implemented again in 1952, with Ontario joining in this time but Quebec remaining outside.

Tax rentals were replaced in 1957 by tax sharing. Ottawa still collected all the personal and corporate income taxes and succession duties for provinces participating in the scheme. The new feature was that payments to each province in lieu of levying their own taxes were geared to the revenue Ottawa actually collected in that province. Transfers were set at 10 percent of the personal income tax collected in the province, 9 percent of the taxable income of corporations, and 50 percent of the succession duties collected. As before, provinces not agreeing to the scheme received tax abatements of the same amount, providing them with the room to levy their own charges. Eight provinces took up the complete offer; Ontario agreed to the guidelines for personal income taxes, but levied its own corporate income tax and succession duties; Quebec levied all three taxes itself.

This change in the basis of the tax-rental payment opened up a new issue in federal-provincial fiscal relations — that of differential tax-revenue capacities among provincial governments. As long as rental payments were made on a per-capita basis, the fact that some provinces were wealthier than others, and thus had richer tax bases than others, made little difference. Once payments were expressed as a share of revenue actually collected in the province, though, the rough equity disappeared; for example, 10 percent of personal income tax collected in British Columbia was worth more on a per-capita basis than 10 percent of it collected in Newfoundland. The B.C. government would be in a better position to provide public services to its residents than would Newfoundland, and the principle of general equity among Canadians, regardless of where they lived, would be compromised. Since provinces played a key role in funding social programs, the problem was potentially serious.

The solution was to introduce a formal system of equalization payments, modelled along the lines of the National Adjustment Grants proposed by the Rowell-Sirois Commission nearly twenty years earlier. Very briefly, the formula worked as follows: officials first calculated the per-capita transfers due to the two wealthiest provinces (Ontario and British Columbia, at this time) under the tax-sharing formula, and took a weighted average of the two. Each province was then entitled to receive an unconditional transfer in an amount necessary to bring its payment, calculated on its own base over these three tax sources, up to that weighted average. Nine provinces received transfers (only Ontario did not). In this way, the principle that each province should be able to provide services equal to the average Canadian standard without having to resort to taxes of greater-than-average severity was preserved.

A major change in federal-provincial fiscal arrangments came in 1962 when tax-sharing was replaced by tax-collection agreements, instituting the system still in place today. Provinces were required to pass legislation setting their own personal and corporate income-tax rates. In return, Ottawa lowered its rates to give the provinces the "tax room" they needed. The federal government agreed to collect the provincial taxes free of charge if certain conditions were met, the most important being that provincial rates were expressed as a percentage of basic federal tax. Eight provinces agreed to the system for both personal and corporate taxes. Ontario agreed for personal income taxes, but levied and collected its own corporate income tax. Quebec stayed out of the system entirely. Much the same arrangements were set in 1967 and again in 1972.

The basis of equalization was changed in 1962 from that of the two wealthiest provinces to the average of all provinces, and 50 percent of provincial natural-resource revenues were included as part of the tax base. These changes had the effect of removing the two westernmost provinces from the recipient category. The system was further extended in 1967, when equalization entitlements were calculated on the basis of sixteen separate provincial tax sources. A further four categories were added in 1972 and one more in 1973 for a total of 21. Fiscal capacities were calculated for each province for each tax source, and a payment was made only if the sum over all sources was negative. Since the base was intended to be broadly representative of taxes open to provinces, the principle of equalization was more securely met.

With these backgrounds in mind, the sequence of social-policy innovation can be briefly outlined. The first, and perhaps most important, area to be discussed is that of health care. For constitutional reasons, the early efforts came from the provinces. For reasons that are less apparent, but no less fascinating, these were almost entirely in the west.

The first major government initiative came in 1947, when Saskatchewan introduced its Hospital Services Plan. Residents paid a compulsory monthly premium and received, in return, free hospital care. British Columbia followed with a similar scheme in 1948, although it was financed by an increase in the provincial sales tax. The federal government became involved the same year. National health grants were introduced to provide funds to the provinces for health surveys, hospital construction, tuberculosis control, professional training, mental health, cancer control, medical rehabilitation, and crippled children. All grants were closed-ended. Some required matching contributions by the provinces; others did not. This program is of special note in that the federal-provincial cost-sharing aspect serves as an early indication of the form that social policies were to take over the next two decades. The national health grants were extended in 1953 to cover child- and maternal-health programs.

A major advance in health care came in 1957, with the Hospital Insurance and Diagnostics Services Act. Provinces making in-patient hospital services available upon specified terms and conditions were eligible to receive federal transfers of approximately 50 percent of total outlays. Only five provinces entered the program as it began, although by 1961 all were participating.

Progress toward a comprehensive national health-insurance scheme continued in the 1960s. Once more, Saskatchewan was the pioneer. The CCF government of that province introduced a comprehensive medical-insurance scheme, to come into effect in July 1961. Financing came from increases in provincial sales taxes and personal and corporate income taxes, and from annual premiums. It is, unfortunately, equally famous for the political furor it caused, including a virtually unheard-of event, a doctors' strike. As fondly as the move is now looked upon in the history of Canadian social policy, it is sometimes forgotten that the CCF lost the next election, largely because of the fall-out from the medicare issue.

The next step was the appointment of the justly famous Royal Commission on Health Services (the Hall Commission, after Justice Emmett Hall). Its report, issued in 1964, called for a full-scale government-sponsored health-insurance program. The Medical Care Act was passed in 1966, establishing a health-insurance system to come into effect in 1968. It, too, was a shared-cost program. Provinces had to tailor medical-insurance plans to meet federal definitions of universality of coverage, portability of benefits, accessibility without user fees, and administration by a nonprofit agency.

In return, they were entitled to claim approximately 50 percent of their total expenditures on medical care over the year (the formula was devised in such a way that an individual province could get slightly more or slightly less than 50 percent, depending on its costs relative to the national average).

The net result of these changes was a revolution in government expenditures. Medical care was taken on as a social responsibility, rather than as an individual one. A generation or more of Canadians have since grown up assuming they have a right to free, accessible health care. At the same time, the costs to the public purse have been enormous. Health is now the largest single item in provincial-government expenditures, and fears have been expressed as to whether current levels of health care will be affordable in the face of an aging population.

Education was the next category to receive attention. In 1951, Ottawa began to pay a grant of $0.50 per capita to universities and colleges. Quebec did not allow its institutions to accept the grants, although eventually (in 1960) it did receive a tax abatement as compensation. The next initiative was the Technical and Vocational Training Assistance Act of 1960, which committed federal funds to capital construction and to a wide variety of educational programs. The Canada Student Loans Act was passed in 1964. Under this legislation, the federal government agreed to guarantee loans taken out by students and to pay interest on them while the student was attending school. Quebec did not participate in the plan, but received grants instead.

One other change came as a provision of the 1967 Fiscal Arrangements Act and, in retrospect, can be seen as a forerunner to an important restructuring of the system a decade later. Ottawa ended its system of per-capita grants to colleges and universities. In its place, it agreed to pay 50 percent of eligible operating costs of post-secondary institutions, financed in part by a further transfer of tax room to the provinces and in part by cash grants.

There were some important changes in the area of income security. Since the British North America Act excluded the federal government from participating in contributory pension schemes, the 1927 legislation was designed as a shared-cost, non-contributory plan. The constraint was removed by a constitutional amendment in 1950; in 1951, the Old Age Security Act was passed. Under this legislation, Ottawa took over sole responsibility for pensions for persons over age 70. The next year, the Old Age Assistance Act was passed, wherein the federal government agreed to pay 50 percent of old-age assistance for those aged 65–69, with a means test. A companion act extended pensions to blind persons, continuing a feature of the former Old Age Pensions Act. The eligibility age was reduced to 65 years in 1965, to be fully in effect by 1970. Finally, the Guaranteed Income Supplement was introduced in 1967, to add to the incomes of low-income pensioners.

These pensions were all non-contributory. Moves to establish a national contributory plan began with a proposal by Prime Minister Diefenbaker to the provinces in 1962. Negotiations were continued the following year by the new Liberal government, running into opposition from Quebec, which had its own scheme in mind, and Ontario, which favoured reform of private schemes. A series of compromises and modifications followed that overcame Ontario's objections and allowed integration of the Canada and Quebec plans. The Canada and Quebec pension plans came into effect in January 1967. Pensions were to be paid from a fund supported by contributions from employers and employees. The fund was to be self-supporting, with early surpluses lent to the provinces (a factor in their decisions to go along with the scheme, no doubt).

There were numerous federal-provincial shared-cost programs based on tests of needs or means in existence by the 1960s. The Canada Assistance Plan was introduced in 1966 to bring separate programs for old-age assistance, blind persons' allowances, allowances to the disabled, and unemployment assistance into one comprehensive package. Ottawa shared the cost of these programs equally, subject only to a few conditions on terms and operations. Analysts ever since have pointed to this plan as one of the more successful of the co-operative social-policy efforts.

The final item to be discussed is that of unemployment insurance. The 1940 plan remained in existence after 1945, and coverage was gradually broadened to include more occupations. A major, and as it turned out, controversial, reform was introduced in 1971: coverage was extended to nearly every worker in the labour force, and the plan was made significantly more generous. The qualifying period for benefits was reduced, benefits were raised, regional and extended benefits were recognized, and sickness and pregnancy were included. The intent was to ease the plight of the unemployed. It did this, but at the cost, subsequent analysis seemed to show, of raising the average unemployment rate.

As this period of our history ended, Canada had in place a comprehensive social-security system. Hospital and medical costs were covered, post-secondary and technical education were being funded, contributory and non-contributory pension plans were in place, special benefits were available to particular groups, and a fairly generous unemployment-insurance scheme was in place. All had been introduced in a uniquely Canadian fashion, through what one influential text termed "federal-provincial diplomacy."[6]

Regional Development and Policy

Social policy is aimed at individuals grouped by categories, such as age or particular need, irrespective of where they may live. It took on a federal-provincial perspective in Canada only for constitutional reasons. Regional-development policy has precisely the opposite perspective: it is aimed at disadvantaged regions, as defined by measures such as average income or unemployment rates, irrespective of the individual incomes within them. As is the case for social policy, though, serious interest in it is a postwar phenomenon.

Figure 21.2 shows the trend in relative personal incomes per capita for the provinces. Two observations are obvious. First, there is a considerable difference between the average income of the richest province and that of the poorest. Personal income per capita in Newfoundland in 1949 was 51 percent of the national average, while in Ontario it was 120 percent, more than twice as great. Second, while the disparities have narrowed somewhat in the postwar period, they remain substantial. Newfoundland had risen to 68 percent of the national average by 1982, while the richest province, now Alberta, stood at 113 percent. If earned income rather than total personal income is taken as a measure, thereby excluding transfer payments, most of the narrowing disappears. Such convergence as there is apparently is mainly a result of transfer programs; underlying relative economic strengths and weaknesses have not altered perceptibly.

These figures raise two interesting questions: How can the disparity at any time be explained? How can one explain the pattern over time, the remarkable constancy of relative positions, in particular? Unfortunately, there are no clear answers to either of these questions. The factors associated with disparities are well known. Low-income regions tend to have a smaller proportion of their population in the 16–64 age category, lower labour-force participation rates, higher unemployment rates, lower wages for given occupations, lower capital-labour ratios, and a slower rate of adopting technical change. However, these are as much symptoms as they are causes of underdevelopment, and, to date, analysts have not made much progress in explaining the spread of earnings disparities.

The constancy in relative positions in the postwar period is surprising, given the type and magnitude of economic change that has taken place. The resource boom of the early 1950s, the stubborn recession that followed, and the boom of the 1960s altered the trend lines only a little, and only temporarily. Aggregate growth rates did differ markedly among provinces. But interregional trade and capital and labour flows were sufficiently responsive to offset these differences in economic opportunity. Ontario, Alberta, and British Columbia grew faster in these years, but they did not noticeably get relatively richer. Atlantic Canada grew more slowly, but managed to retain its relative living standard.

While concern over the economic fate of lagging regions is as old as Confederation, recognition of the issue reached a new stage with the publication of the Gordon Commission report in 1957. At first, the policy emphasis was on rural poverty. The Agriculture Rehabilitation and Development Act of 1961, which dealt mainly with utilization of marginal farmland, was superseded in 1964 by the Agriculture and Rural Development Act, which was more explicitly developmental in nature. The Fund for Rural Economic Development carried this orientation even farther, designing economic-development strategies for areas deemed to be "promising" and providing for adjustment assistance for those not so designated.

The scope of regional-development policy soon expanded to focus on particular regions and to include industrial development. The Atlantic region, comprising Canada's poorest provinces, first received explicit attention in 1962 with the establishment of the Atlantic Development Board. It was converted, the next year, from a research and advisory body to one with some program responsibilities and funds to disburse, most of which went to social-

FIGURE 21.2

Provincial Per-Capita Incomes Relative to the National Average, 1949–1987

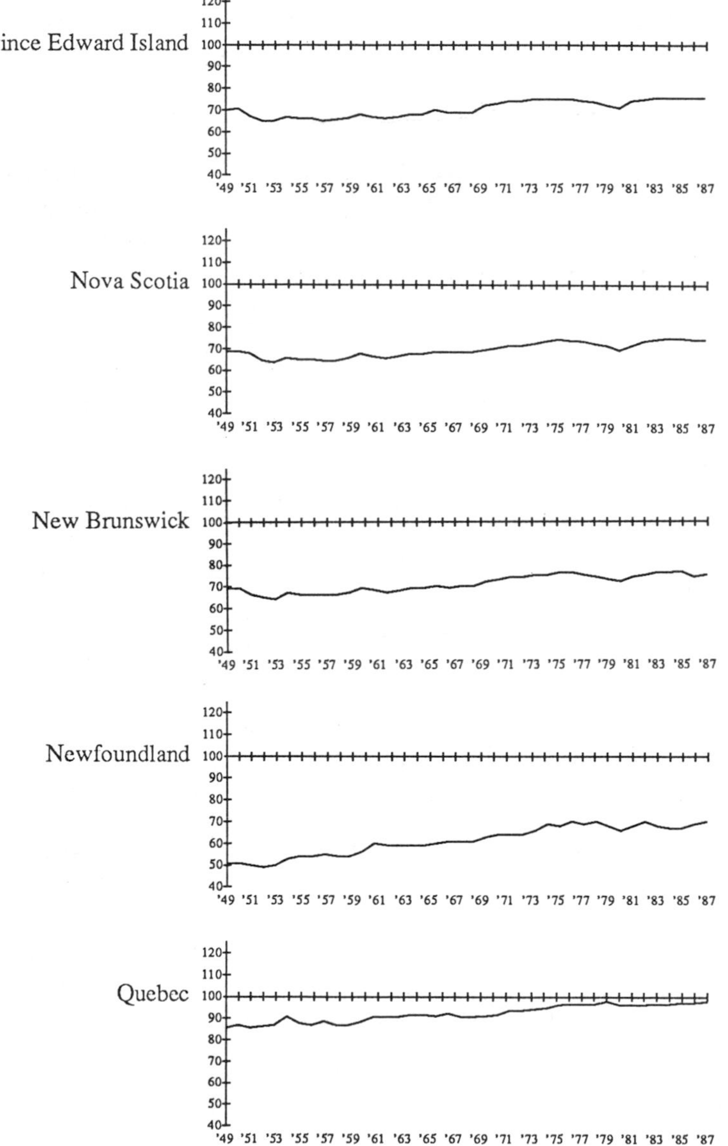

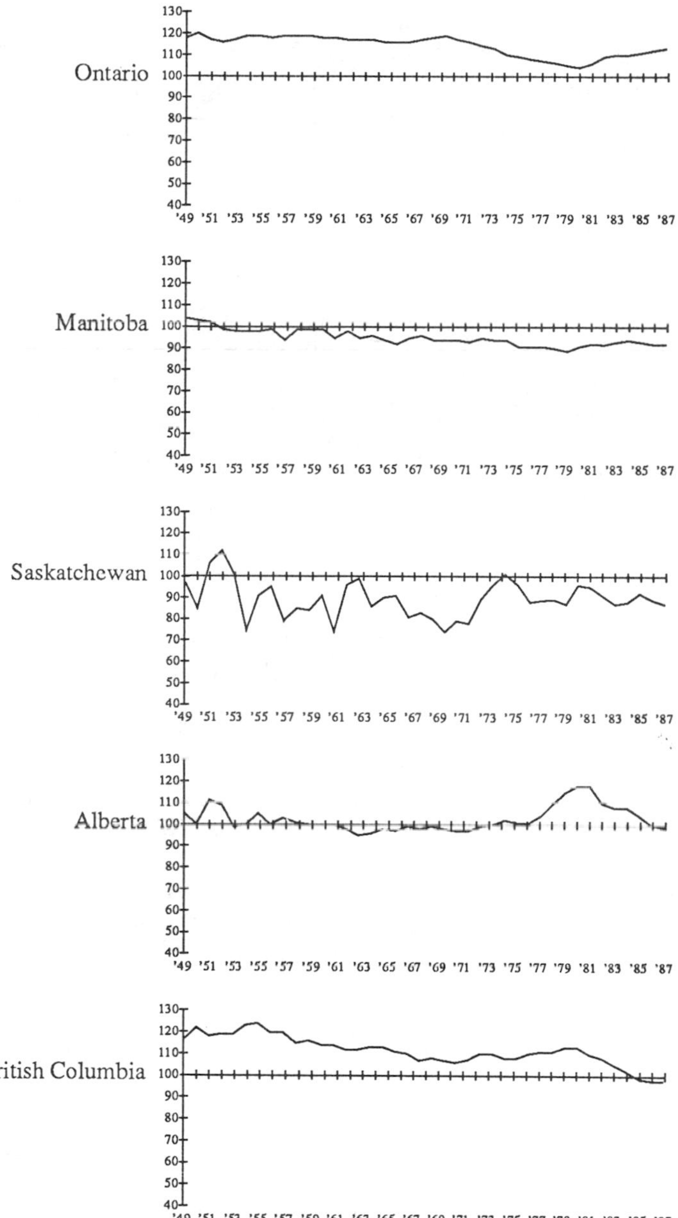

Source: Derived from Canada, Department of Finance, *Quarterly Economic Review*, June 1989: annual reference tables.

infrastructure projects. The Area Development Agency was established in 1963 to promote industrial development in poorer regions. Firms locating in specified areas were eligible for tax benefits and, after the introduction of the Area Development Incentives Act in 1965, for cash grants.

Regional development was given a more focussed orientation and a higher profile with the formation of the Department of Regional Economic Expansion (DREE) in 1969 and the appointment of a powerful minister. Certain urban areas in poorer provinces were designated as special areas, qualifying for funds to support the provision of social infrastructure and intended to act as nodes or growth poles around which other developments would cluster. The earlier industrial-subsidy practice was continued under the Regional Development Incentives Act (RDIA), again providing grants and other concessions to firms willing to locate in designated areas of the country.

Conclusion

DREE did not live up to its early expectations, however. It gained a reputation for spending vast sums of money with little appreciable effect on regional disparities. RDIA grants were particularly suspect. Critics claimed that only rarely did they actually influence a location decision; that, when they did, it was to draw a firm from one poor region to another; and that they seriously distorted the allocation of resources. There were also criticisms of its administrative procedures. The provinces found it too centralized and inflexible. Other federal departments with sectoral responsibilities resented DREE's economic-development mandate. What seemed to be good regional-development policy was not always good transportation or agriculture or industrial policy. A change of direction was imminent as the 1970s began.

Notes

1. Royal Commission on the Economic Union and Development Prospects for Canada, *Report*, Vol. 2 (Ottawa: Supply and Services, 1985), Table 7-10, 20.
2. J.L. Granatstein, "Free Trade Between Canada and the United States: The Issue That Will Not Go Away," in *The Politics of Canada's Economic Relationship*

with the United States, Royal Commission on the Economic Union and Development Prospects for Canada, Research Study No. 29, edited by Denis Stairs and Gilbert R. Winham (Ottawa: Supply and Services, 1985), 45.
3. J. Harvey Perry, *A Fiscal History of Canada: The Postwar Years* (Toronto: Canadian Tax Foundation, 1989), 837.
4. See Keith G. Banting, *The Welfare State and Canadian Federalism* (Montreal and Kingston: McGill-Queen's University Press, 1982).
5. Douglas Owram, *The Government Generation: Canadian Intellectuals and the State, 1900–1945* (Toronto: University of Toronto Press, 1986), 324
6. Richard Simeon, *Federal-Provincial Diplomacy* (Toronto: University of Toronto Press, 1972).

Further Reading

Banting, Keith G. *The Welfare State and Canadian Federalism*. Montreal and Kingston: McGill-Queen's University Press, 1982.

Guest, Dennis. *The Emergence of Social Security in Canada*. Vancouver: University of British Columbia Press, 1980.

Perry, J. Harvey. *A Fiscal History of Canada: The Postwar Years*. Toronto: Canadian Tax Foundation, 1989.

Savoie, Donald. *Regional Economic Development: Canada's Search for Solutions*. Toronto: University of Toronto Press, 1986.

Simeon, Richard. *Federal-Provincial Diplomacy*. Toronto: University of Toronto Press, 1972.

CHAPTER

22

Economic Challenge and Policy Frustration, 1973–1982

The decade after 1973 was one of the most turbulent in Canada's political and economic history. Macro-economic performance deteriorated markedly and in ways that seemed to contradict what we thought we knew about the operation of a modern industrial economy. Growth slowed, leading some to look beyond cyclical factors to fundamental weaknesses in the economy. Policies that were once thought to promote growth or equity were now often thought to do just the opposite. The federal-provincial consensus, which had seemed (more to some than others, admittedly) to facilitate innovative policy formation, disintegrated into regional strife.

Canada was affected by international developments after 1973 in a number of ways. As a trading nation, and a small one at that, we could not avoid dealing with world inflation. The prices of everything we bought and sold internationally were rising. These influences could be offset by letting the exchange rate appreciate — a possibility, given the floating of the rate in 1970. But this action would reduce aggregate demand and, hence, raise unemployment further, so the choice was a cruel one.

As a net exporter of primary products, including energy, Canada stood to benefit in aggregate in real-income terms from the terms-of-trade shift that was part of this international inflation. Each unit of grain, ore, timber, or oil we produced bought more units of autos and computers than it did before 1973. While this development was undoubtedly positive, it did carry with it a major problem. A terms-of-trade shift of the magnitude experienced by the world in 1973 and after required considerable adjustment. For reasons that are more political than economic, this adjustment was a particularly difficult one for Canada to make. The pressures to adjust, and the resistance against doing so, provide one of the major themes of the political economy of the nation in this period.

Finally, as a nation with a generally uncompetitive manufacturing sector, especially in the high-technology end of the spectrum, Canada was especially fearful of the growing competition from Japan and the newly industrializing economies, of growing instability in international trade and finance, and of threats of increased protectionism in the United States.

Economic Performance

The macro-economic record in this period illustrates the extent of the difficulties. Real GDP growth fell to 4.4 percent in 1974, from 7.7 percent the year earlier, and to 2.6 percent in 1975. It rose to a respectable 6.2 percent in 1975, but declined thereafter, before actually falling for only the second time since the war, in 1982. The slow growth was reflected in unemployment rates. The proportion of the labour force unemployed jumped from 5.3 percent in 1974, to 6.9 percent the next year, then rose to over 8 percent and finally to 11 percent in 1982. The origin of the term "stagflation" is indicated by the fact that consumer prices did not fall, even in the face of this great slack in the economy. The inflation rate jumped to over 10 percent in 1974 and 1975, came down a couple of percentage points to 1979, and then rose again to double-digit levels through to 1982.

The slowdown was accounted for initially by a slowing of export and investment demand. The former actually declined in real terms in 1974, and especially in 1975, while the latter saw its growth rate halved, and then cut again. Export demand recovered somewhat by 1976, but, by this time, investment demand had become even weaker, and consumer spending was off as well. During the poorest years from 1980 on, all components of aggregate demand were relatively weak. Consumption, investment, and export spending declined in real terms in 1982, for example.

Stabilization Policy

Canadian policy makers were as uncertain of how to deal with these new macro-economic challenges as were their counterparts elsewhere. Allowing the exchange rate to float in 1970 created the opportunity to isolate Canadian price increases from those abroad, which did happen in the first year, as the currency jumped to par with the U.S. dollar. The money supply grew very rapidly for a period thereafter, though, as officials were concerned with preventing a further appreciation of the exchange rate. This fact, combined with generally expansionary fiscal policy, meant that Canadian inflation rates hit double-digit figures by 1975.

Stabilization efforts in this period faced, not just slower economic growth but also changes in the underlying structure of the labour market. The natural rate of unemployment (or, in more modern terminology, NAIRU — nonaccelerating inflation rate of unemployment) had risen significantly, although this shift was not recognized at first. Changes in the composition of industry and, hence, in required labour skills, the entrance of women and younger workers into the labour force, and more generous unemployment-insurance benefits added to the numbers of workers reporting spells of unemployment in any period. Attempts to reduce unemployment below this new higher NAIRU through expansionary monetary and fiscal policy in 1973 and 1974 merely exacerbated the inflation rate.

Stabilization policy took two dramatic turns in 1975. The Bank of Canada abandoned its practice of monitoring credit conditions and adopted, in its place, an avowed monetarist approach to monetary policy. In a speech that had been dubbed the "Saskatoon Monetary Manifesto," Governor Gerald Bouey acknowledged that control of inflation required control of the money supply and, in particular, that the rate of growth of money had to be slowed if inflation were to be lowered. Applying the monetary brakes too rapidly would be disruptive, however, so a policy of monetary gradualism was introduced. Money-supply growth-rate targets were announced, initially in the range of 10 to 15 percent, to fall to 8 to 12 percent in 1976 and eventually to 4 to 8 percent.

A few weeks after the governor's speech, the government announced a comprehensive system of wage and price controls, and established the Anti-Inflation Board (AIB) as a monitoring and research agency. Ceilings were imposed on prices and wages for larger firms and in the government sector. The AIB had the power to review wage settlements in larger companies and to roll them back if they were deemed excessive. The board could also monitor price increases and profit margins of the companies, and roll these back if warranted. There was a large number of exceptions to this latter provision, however, notably food products and imports.

These anti-inflation policies were only partially successful. The money-supply targets proved notoriously difficult to achieve, partly because the bank continued to pay attention to the value of the exchange rate, and partly because of the instability of demand for the money-supply variable (M1) chosen. High interest rates encouraged financial innovation by the banks to the point where the traditional correlation between interest rates and the demand for money, as represented in M1, broke down completely. Subsequent research has shown that the AIB likely had some success in bringing down the rate of increase of money wages and, thus, of inflation. It created considerable social tension in the process, however, as it was opposed throughout by the labour movement, and eventually ended up being challenged in the Supreme Court.

It took an international slowdown and the drastic monetary stringency of 1981 to bring inflation really under control. In mid-1981, the Bank of Canada jammed on the monetary brakes. The nominal stock of money actually fell in the last half of the year, at an annual rate of 14 percent. Interest rates shot up as a direct consequence. The 90-day Treasury Bill rate reached 21 percent, creating a large wedge between Canadian and U.S. rates. The depreciation of the dollar was reversed as a result, but at the expense of a significant decline in real economic activity. Inflation declined, and unemployment rose above 12 percent. The Canadian economy entered into what has since been dubbed "the Great Recession."

Another prominent and closely related feature of this period was the secular deterioration of government-budget balances, that of the federal government, in particular. Prior to 1974 federal revenues and expenditures were in approximate balance. After that date, however, rising expenditures coupled with the introduction of deindexation and tax credits turned the balance consistently negative. The recession of the early 1980s made the situation much worse. The federal deficit in 1985 was in excess of $35 billion, and the deficit-to-GNP and the debt-to-GNP ratios were growing rapidly. Economic views of government deficits slowly altered as a result. Where once it was common to teach that debts governments owed to their own citizens did not matter, now it became fashionable to worry about the distortionary implications of large public-sector borrowing requirements.

Rethinking Framework Policies

As stagflation continued, Canadians, too, began to debate whether the difficulties went beyond a macro-economic slowdown to reflect a more fundamental productivity decline. To some observers at least, Canada's long-term economic prospects were particularly unfavourable. At issue was our ability to compete successfully in what was widely acknowledged to be an increasingly difficult international economic environment. Those expressing concern saw the difficulties as partly external and partly internal. The obvious external factor was the dramatic success of Japan in making inroads into Western markets and, even more ominously perhaps, the appearance of a whole set of Japan imitators known as newly industrializing countries. Japan appeared to have cornered the high-technology end of the market, while the other countries were taking over production of the standard-technology items. Canada was able to secure contracts for some resource products with these nations, but those sales fell far short of the mounting import bill for manufactured products.

The internal factors were related to perceived difficulties with the structure of the Canadian economy. Many felt that our historical advantage in natural-resource industries was ending as we cut the last of the virgin timber, mined the last of the high-quality ore, moved to the Arctic and offshore for our petroleum, and witnessed the salinization of our soils. Other analysts continued to point out that secondary manufacturing was less efficient than that of our trading partners as a result, depending on the writer, of our tariff policies and those of our trading partners, of government sponsorship, of foreign ownership, or even of the conservatism and myopia of the Canadian business class.

Still others saw the problem as being in the rigidity and inflexibility that decades of well-intentioned but misguided policy interventions had imparted to the economy. Unemployment insurance was the most-often cited of these examples. The increase in benefits and the liberalization in terms introduced in 1971 were held by many to have added one to two points to the unemployment rate by encouraging longer job searches and less interregional and intersectoral mobility. Inappropriately high minimum wages, rent controls, regional-development incentive grants, bailouts of troubled firms, agricultural price supports, trucking regulations, and so forth — all were cited at one time or another as examples of the factors behind the increased rigidity of the economy.

There was considerable debate at this time about the need for a coherent strategy for economic development to overcome these internal and external obstacles. Two main views developed, each associated with a federal-government research agency. The Economic Council saw trade liberalization as the best way to bring about the necessary reorganization of industry, with a bilateral Canada–United States free-trade arrangement as the most promising vehicle. Access to the large U.S. market would allow industries in which Canada had a comparative advantage to exploit economies of scale in production and distribution. Those that could not compete after a suitable adjustment period would be phased out of existence.

The Science Council advocated trade liberalization too, although not of the bilateral variety. Unlike the Economic Council, it wished to develop Canadian industrial expertise through some sort of industrial strategy prior to entering into such arrangements, rather than relying on the liberalization to achieve it. A wide variety of industrial strategies were proposed, although most contained some element of selecting particular sectors for promotion ("picking winners"), based on assumed comparative advantage, degree of Canadian ownership, or level of technological sophistication. Promotion was to take the form of relaxing anti-combines regulations to allow larger operations, research and development grants, special tax incentives for modernization or Canadianization, and occasionally even public-sector equity and management participation.

Neither proposal attracted Ottawa at this time, or rather both did. Trade liberalization proceeded with Canada's participation in the Tokyo Round of GATT. Negotiations began in 1973, but stalled soon thereafter as a result of political difficulties in the United States and the European Economic Community. When meetings finally resumed, they proceeded quickly, resulting in significant tariff concessions and some progress on nontariff issues. Reductions commenced in 1980, to be spread over eight years. Once these concessions were in place, a Canadian-government study estimated that tariffs on most manufactured goods in Europe and Japan would be around 5 to 7 percent and those for the United States about 4 percent, and that about 90 percent of current Canadian exports would be entering their markets duty free.[1] The world had come a long way from the prohibitive protection of the 1930s.

The Tokyo Round also paid considerable attention to nontariff barriers. There was concern that progress made in eliminating duties could be more than offset by nations protecting domestic industries through technical regulations, quotas, customs procedures, and the like. A list prepared by the GATT staff at the time listed 600 separate measures. Progress was sought, and some was achieved, on ways to adjudicate disputes as they arose, so as to avoid retaliatory action. Considerable problems remained, however.

Industrial strategies proved more elusive. The minister of Industry, Trade and Commerce announced intentions of developing a coherent policy in 1972, but nothing specific emerged from this initiative. The Foreign Investment Review Agency (FIRA) was established in 1974 in response to a recommendation of the reports on foreign investment mentioned above. It was empowered to screen takeover proposals above a certain size and to recommend rejection if it felt there were not sufficient demonstrable benefits for Canada. It was also to negotiate to increase these benefits whenever possible. A related initiative was the Canada Development Corporation, established in 1971 to provide a mixed public-private presence in key sectors of the economy.

Pursuit of a comprehensive industrial strategy continued later in the decade with the establishment of 23 sectoral task forces, charged with making recommendations for 21 manufacturing industries, plus construction and tourism. These tier-1 committees were followed by tier-2 ones that concentrated on more broadly based economic strategies rather than on specific sectoral issues. Both measures fell victim to government austerity before they could have any significant legislative impact.

An interesting initiative came at the very end of this period, in November 1981, with the economic statement released as part of the budget of that year. It was based on the view that Canada's economic future lay in its rich natural-resource base. These sectors would be the leading ones around which manufacturing and services would evolve to serve them. Numerous resource mega-projects such as oil-sands plants, offshore exploration and development, pipelines, and hydro-electric developments were envisioned. No sooner was it out, however, than energy prices began to fall and, with them, the notion that resources could be a permanent leading edge to growth.

Immigration policy underwent a fundamental review in the 1970s as well. A Green Paper was issued in 1975 that led, after public debate, to the new Immigration Act in 1978. Compared to previous Canadian immigration policies, this one was relatively restrictive, reflecting, among other things, the much higher unemployment levels of the period. Canadian officials were required, for the first time, to announce target levels, or quotas, for total immigration. The act also linked the volume and compositon of the flow of independent or "economic" immigrants to narrowly defined labour market conditions. Separate provisions applied to family reunification and refugee flows. The point system was retained, and the goal of removing the racial and other discrimination that had dominated early Canadian policies was reaffirmed. With finetuning, this system prevails today.

Rethinking Equity

Framework policies were not the only ones to come under scrutiny in the 1970s. Just as a buoyant economy and growing government revenues had facilitated the introduction of a broad range of social and regional-development measures, so, too, did a slowly growing economy and mounting government deficits lead to pressure for reform and retrenchment. The oil crisis, the Quebec sovereignty-association debate, and other developments so poisoned federal-provincial relations that whatever reform was needed was doubly difficult to achieve.

Social Policy

With fiscal dividends replaced by large and growing budget deficits, it is not surprising that one of the distinguishing features of the period after 1973 was a retrenchment on the social-policy front. A sweeping social-security review early in the decade proposed the introduction of a guaranteed annual income, for example, but the idea was never acted upon. Family allowances were made more generous in 1973, and the provinces were given more control over the structure of benefits. Refundable child tax credits were introduced in 1979, providing welcome relief to low-income Canadians. Generally, though, it was no longer possible in the climate of the 1970s to attack a problem by throwing public-sector money at it.

The focus in the social-policy area shifted from providing new programs to deciding how existing ones should be funded. The main concern lay with the federal-provincial shared-cost formulae. While, arguably, it had been necessary to circumvent the constitutional roadblock that existed in 1946, neither level of government was happy with this technique in the 1970s. Without the extra revenue from robust economic growth, Ottawa became concerned with the open-ended commitment it had for funding provincially administered programs. Federal officials began to speak of the programs as "established," meaning that more direct responsibility for them could be turned over to the provinces. The provinces, for their part, long had had difficulty with conditional grants, arguing that they forced the federal social-policy agenda upon them and restricted their administrative freedom, once in place.

Ottawa had proposed several times in the 1960s to pull back in the social-policy field, and had even done so, in part, for postsecondary education in 1967. It made good on these proposals in a major way in the 1977 Federal-Provincial Fiscal Arrangements and Established Programs Financing Act. The federal share of the costs of postsecondary education, hospital insurance, and medicare was now to be paid half by cash grants and half by a transfer of tax points to the provinces. This technique made the federal grant a lump-sum one, with the provinces free to allocate these funds among those programs or any others as they wished. The grants were still broadly conditional, but much less so than they had been in their original formulation.

As it turned out, however, it was far from clear what the federal government had in mind in 1977. They continued to keep track of established program transfers by major category, even though the grant was lump-sum. As provinces began to reallocate monies among programs, as the terms of the arrangements seemed to allow, they opened themselves up to charges that they were diverting funds to uses for which they were not intended. The extra-billing dispute is another example of this confusion. The Canada Health Act (1984) punished provinces that allowed doctors to bill patients beyond medicare rates by reducing transfers dollar for dollar. Provinces eventually had to comply with the act, given the stakes involved, but not without considerable resentment over what they saw as federal-government interference in the operation of the plans.

Regional Development and Policy

Regional-development policy received a change of emphasis in the 1970s in much the same direction as did social policy. The centralized system established under DREE was discarded in favour of one that placed more emphasis on provincial-government participation. Beginning in 1974, each province signed a General Development Agreement (GDA) with the federal government. The agreements established the goals of regional development in that jurisdiction, and broad guidelines as to how the programs were to be implemented. Specific projects were then drawn up by a committee of officials from the two governments, and administered by the province. Ottawa contributed 50 percent of the project costs in the wealthier jurisdictions to 90 percent in the poorest ones.

Predictably, General Development Agreements soon came under fire. Federal officials felt they were losing control over regional-development projects, and politicians saw all the credit going to their provincial counterparts. The scheme was abandoned in 1982. Responsibility for regional development was spread more widely throughout the federal bureaucracy. DREE, and Industry, Trade, and Commerce, were combined into one department — Regional and Industrial Expansion. Economic and Regional Development Agreements were signed with each province, and the federal role in planning and administration was made more explicit. The cycle of regional-development policies was complete. In fifteen years, a highly centralized system (DREE) had given way to the highly decentralized one (GDAs), which had, in turn, been abandoned for something in between.

Efficiency and Equity in the Economic Union

A related set of regional issues in this period stemmed from the regional makeup of the economy and the political system. There was a growing perception that the Canadian economy was becoming increasingly fragmented along regional lines, and that this development, together with frequent and serious federal-provincial disputes, was reducing the efficiency of the national economy and compromising our ability to manage economic and social policy effectively. Just as the need to be competitive and to plan effectively was greater than ever, it seemed to many, the domestic market was becoming increasingly fragmented, and our institutional ability to carry them out was diminishing.

The debate on regional fragmentation and policy co-ordination came to be expressed in a language developed for the European Economic Community. Canada was viewed as an economic union, with ten (or more, if the North was included) members. Analysts looking at the national economy from this perspective found numerous examples of barriers to the interprovincial flow of goods, services, capital, and labour. Agriculture marketing boards were organized along provincial lines, liquor regulations protected local suppliers, provincial-government procurement policies discriminated against non-residents, professional associations restricted out-of-province firms, the trucking industry faced ten sets of regulations, and so forth. Tax harmonization, or rather the lack of it, became an issue, as provinces increasingly used this tool to achieve their own economic and social goals. Further, the fact that the equalization scheme did not fully offset the fiscal disadvantages of the poorer provinces in the federation was held to cause socially inefficient interprovincial migration. Early work on each of these topics seemed to indicate that the efficiency losses were small — in the order of 1 percent of GNP at most — but there was always the nagging doubt that these findings were a product of the methodology used and that they understated the true costs.

The concern with economic management stemmed from the recognition that provinces had considerable economic powers under the constitution, and that they would be led to use them in ways that were consistent with their own economic objectives, even if these conflicted with central-government objectives. Any number of examples were cited. Federal-government counter-cyclical stabilization efforts could be thwarted by pro-cyclical provincial ones, especially given the increase in the share of spending and taxation accounted for by the provinces by this date. Federal trade negotiators constantly had to worry whether provinces would implement provisions of international treaties that came under Section 92 responsibilities. Environmental regulations often stopped at provincial borders, even if the water or ducks or polluted air did not.

Perhaps the most dramatic issue of this type in these times, though, was that of regional fairness, long a salient factor in

Canada. Notions that the federation operated consistently to the advantage of some regions and to the disadvantage of others were rife in the 1970s. Interestingly, all regions felt aggrieved at some time or other and to varying degrees. Atlantic Canadians chafed at the failure of national economic growth and decades of regional-development policy to pull their region out of its long-term relative economic decline. Federal policies on fisheries, energy, tariffs, and transportation were cited as factors contributing to this decline.

The development of an Ontario view on national-policy issues was a relatively new phenomenon. Ontario's interests had always been equated, fairly or not, with those of the national government. Energy issues, in particular, altered this perception somewhat, as the province began to press more openly for policies that reflected its status as the major consuming province. The design of the equalization scheme meant that firms and persons resident in Ontario were carrying the major tax burden for the payments that western resource revenue windfalls were generating, so there was pressure to alter the scheme.

The most dramatic developments took place in Quebec and the west, though. Quebec nationalists have long argued that the Canadian federation is biased against that province's long-term economic and social development. This debate took on an urgent form after 1976 with the election of the separatist Parti Québécois government, and the debate thereafter about its plans for sovereignty-association with Canada. This was the time of the famous "battle of the balance sheets," with the Quebec government publishing one set of accounts showing that Confederation was a net financial drain to Quebec and the federal government publishing figures that showed exactly the opposite. The defeat of the referendum in 1980 somewhat reduced the fervour of this dispute. The promise of a renewed federalism made during the debate set the stage for the patriation of the constitution and the Charter of Rights in 1982 and, given Quebec's refusal to sign at that time, ultimately the Meech Lake Accord.

Economic alienation in the west in this era found its most formal expression at the Western Economic Opportunities Conference in 1973. Convened by the federal government, it gave vent to a series of grievances on the alleged adverse effects on the west of federal policies on freight rates and transportation generally, government purchasing practices, banking and monetary policy, and tariffs. It

Young people celebrate the* P.Q.*'s victory at the polls, November 1976. *Quebec nationalists have long argued that the Canadian federation is biassed against Quebec's long-term economic and social development. This debate grew dramatically in urgency after the 1976 election of the separatist Parti Québécois government.*

was energy, though, that gave the sentiment its most dramatic expression. The OPEC price increases of 1973–74 and 1979–80 put the federal government in the position of having to reconcile the directly competing interests of the producing and consuming regions. While Ontario, at times, may have thought its interests were being sacrificed, as noted above, western governments had no doubts that theirs certainly were.

The first steps taken by Ottawa, in September 1973, in response to rising world oil prices were to freeze the domestic price and to impose an export tax on shipments to the United States. The producing provinces responded by increasing their royalty charges for the use of crown reserves; Ottawa retaliated by declaring royalty payments not eligible as deductions for purposes of calculating federal corporate income tax. Western premiers expressed a sense of outrage at federal policy, the like of which had not been seen in decades. There followed a long series of federal-provincial negotiations in which tax loads were shifted and oil and gas prices brought more into line with those prevailing internationally.

This relatively harmonious state of affairs was shattered by the doubling of oil prices in 1979–80, following the outbreak of the Iran-Iraq War. The federal government reacted to this development with the National Energy Policy (NEP). Among its various measures were ones to maintain Canadian oil and natural-gas prices well below projected international values, to tax a significant portion of the economic rent through a variety of measures, to redirect exploration and development to the north and east coasts, and to increase the degree of Canadian ownership in the sector. The producing provinces reacted very bitterly to this announcement, resorting in the end to reducing shipments of oil to the east, withholding permission to begin construction of a proposed oil-sands plant, and launching a court challenge to some features of the act.

A truce of sorts was reached in 1981, as the producing provinces agreed to a revised set of pricing and taxation arrangements. Unfortunately for the planners, agreement was reached just as international oil prices began to decline. Now the policy problem was reversed. At issue was how to back out of the taxation imposed on the industry so as to keep it viable. The producing provinces cut back on royalty charges, and the federal government suspended some NEP taxes and reduced the incidence of others. Difficulties remained, however, and demands came from both the industry and the producing provinces that all remaining petroleum taxes and all regulations on pricing and sales be removed.

The equalization scheme came under great pressure after 1973 as a result of these energy developments. The problem lay in the fact that the resource revenues were concentrated in a few small western provinces. The mechanics of the equalization formula meant that Ottawa had to compensate all other provinces, including populous Ontario and Quebec, for their lack of such revenues. Escalating payments threatened to bankrupt the federal government, a problem made worse by the fact that it had no direct access to the energy revenues. To make matters even worse, Ontario eventually became a "have not" province under the formula, entitled to receive equalization payments.

The solution was sought, first, in a series of ad hoc adjustments to the existing formula (including a provision that effectively excluded Ontario) and then in a change in the formula itself. Beginning in 1982, the base on which entitlements were calculated was changed from an average of all provinces to an average of five only. Alberta and the four Atlantic provinces were excluded. By omitting Alberta's revenues from the calculation, the problem of equalizing oil and gas revenues was avoided. Leaving the Atlantic provinces out as well, with their lower average tax bases, was a way of reducing the impact of the loss of energy revenues.

Conclusion

Canada faced some considerable challenges in 1982. Inflation had just been brought down from its recent near-record levels, but at a huge cost in terms of unemployment. Federal deficits were large and growing, reducing the government's ability to react to economic challenges, as well as creating problems of its own. The international economic environment appeared to threaten in ways it had not since the Great Depression. Talk of renewed protectionism, especially in the United States, was common. The success of the "new Japans" in capturing market shares for everything from textiles to automobiles was evident. Our economy seemed poorly situated to deal with these challenges, given the continued poor record in the high-technology areas and renewed fears about the long-run viability of many of our major resource sectors. The impacts that the brand-new charter would have on our political and economic life were unknown. The economic union was still fragmented, and memories of separatism and of acrimonious disputes over energy pricing and taxation were still fresh.

As if the number and seriousness of the threats were not enough, there was also a sense that our ability to deal with them was eroding. At times, the problems themselves seemed to elude conventional understanding and analysis. Stagflation and persistent regional disparities are good examples. In other instances, the solution seemed clear, but our institutions did not seem up to the challenge. Governments, federal and provincial, seemed unable or unwilling to undertake fundamental reform. They appeared at times to be paralyzed by the complexity of the issues: mounting debt, jurisdictional disputes, and regional alienation. Policies had swung from centralizing to decentralizing, and then back to centralizing, in less than a decade. They embraced elements of reliance on the market (multilateral trade liberalization) and elements of interventionism (the NEP). Policies were primarily traditional (tight monetary and fiscal policy) and partly experimental (wage and price controls). This sense of uncertainty and indecision, of being genuinely stumped as to how to proceed, was particularly evident in the early 1980s.

Notes

1. J. Harvey Perry, *A Fiscal History of Canada: The Postwar Years* (Toronto: Canadian Tax Foundation, 1989), 835.

Further Reading

Norrie, Kenneth, Richard Simeon, and Mark Krasnick. *Federalism and the Economic Union in Canada*. Royal Commission on the Economic Union and Development Prospects for Canada, Research Study No. 59. Ottawa: Supply and Services, 1985.

Perry, J. Harvey. *A Fiscal History of Canada: The Postwar Years*. Toronto: Canadian Tax Foundation, 1989.

CHAPTER

23

Conclusion: 1982 and Beyond

More years will have to pass before developments after 1982 can be put in proper perspective. For a time, it looked as though 1981 or 1982 would come to be seen as a turning point in Canadian economic and political development. In part, this observation is based on the fact that the seriousness of some of the country's problems, and the policy paralysis that accompanied them, came to be recognized and acknowledged at that time. In part, as well, it comes from noting what seemed like a significant change from earlier periods in the type of policy solutions intended to address them. The qualification comes because the rhetoric has not always been followed up consistently.

Evidence that these problems were recognized comes from noting the mandate — indeed, even the title — of the Royal Commission on the Economic Union and Development Prospects for Canada (the Macdonald Commission), established in the fall of 1982. The commission was to investigate and report on "the long term economic potential, prospects and challenges facing the Canadian federation and its respective regions, as well as the implications that such prospects and challenges have for Canada's economic and governmental institutions, and for the management of Canada's economic affairs." Further, the commission was to recommend "the appropriate national goals and policies for economic development" and "the appropriate institutional and constitutional arrangements to promote the liberty and well-being of individual Canadians and the maintenance of a strong competitive economy."[1]

For a time, there appeared to be a logic or underlying unity, intentional or otherwise, to the policy agenda brought to bear on the problems with the change in government in 1984. The key features of the approach were a hesitant and partial, but nonetheless clear, tendency to reject economic planning in favour of market solutions, and an effort to take the regional character of the country more into account when formulating economic and social strategies. This orientation reflected, in about equal measure, the legacies of the sequence of economic and social policies followed prior to 1984, and the underlying global challenges of the 1980s.

The policy steps taken by the Mulroney government since its election in September 1984 fitted into a general pattern. The energy sector received almost immediate attention. Accords were signed with the western and Atlantic provinces after extensive negotiations. The main objectives were to deregulate the petroleum sector and to remove the special taxes that had been imposed on the industry in the previous decade. Henceforth, oil prices were to be established in the international marketplace. Natural-gas prices were to follow, but more slowly, since deregulating this product was more difficult. Most of the taxes were removed at this time, as well. The Petroleum and Gas Revenue Tax (PGRT) was to be phased out gradually, but was ended prematurely in October 1986, in response to worsening economic conditions in the industry.

Another immediate priority of the government was to reduce the size of the federal deficit. Finance minister Michael Wilson released an economic and financial statement in November 1984, just two months after assuming office. That document outlined the government's concern about the size of the deficit and the mounting debt, and outlined plans for bringing it down to a more appropriate level. The significant point for the theme of this paper is that the stance was supply side-oriented and geared to restoring confidence in the economy. There was no talk of using taxes and expenditures to stimulate demand in the traditional Keynesian sense, even though the economy was obviously seriously underemployed.

Deficit reduction remained a major concern of the finance minister, although his success was mixed. Revenue did not rise as fast as hoped, nor did expenditures fall as far. The premature end to the PGRT cut into revenues. Economic growth has been slower than expected as well, so the narrowing of a deficit that automatically accompanies an upswing has not been strong. Unforseen expenditures on aid to the agriculture and energy sectors, together with an unsuccessful attempt to deindex old-age pensions, kept expenditures high. So did the 1988 election, which saw the government make a number of expensive spending commitments. Concern with the deficit remains.

Deregulation is another observable facet of current policy. The energy measures discussed above fall into this category. Initiatives begun by the previous government to deregulate the airlines have been continued, and extended to include trucking and rail transport. Discussions with the provinces, not without some testiness, resulted in steps to relax restrictions on the operations of the banking and securities industries.

Other components of government policy are longer-term in nature. A prime example is the Canada–United States free-trade agreement. The genesis of this effort lies in the so-called Shamrock Summit, held in Quebec City on March 17–18, 1985. Prime Minister Mulroney and President Reagan agreed on that occasion to give the highest priority to finding ways to reduce trade barriers between the two countries. Six months later, letters were exchanged between the two leaders, pledging to negotiate a bilateral trade arrangement. Negotiating teams were established and immediately began a long and intensive series of negotiations. Talks threatened to collapse on several occasions, including literally in the very last hour. An accord was signed on October 4, 1987, containing the elements of a comprehensive bilateral free-trade arrangement. After some legal drafting, it was tabled in the House of Commons in December and signed by the two leaders in January 1988.

The agreement still needed formal approval by both parties. As noted earlier in this book, twice before in this century, agreements in principle on reciprocal free trade had been reached between negotiators of the two countries, only to have the deal scuttled at the last minute by Canadians. Such was not to be the case this time, however. The Americans ratified the agreement after only perfunctory debate. The Canadians, however, did so only after an election that concentrated almost entirely on the free-trade issue and reached levels of passion and emotion that had rarely been seen. In a delicious historical reversal of the situation in 1911, the Conservatives were the party of free trade, and the Liberals the guardians of Canadian identity and independence. The free-traders won: the agree-

Les grands Ballets Canadiens/Andrew Oxenham

Les grands Ballets Canadiens perform* Carmina Burana, *choreographed by Fernand Nault. *Such "cultural industries" as the ballet are notable exceptions to the free-trade agreement, which will remove nearly all barriers to the free exchange of goods and services between Canada and the United States over a ten-year period.*

ment was passed by the House, and Canada–United States free trade came into effect January 1, 1989.

The details of the agreement need not detain us here. Suffice it to say that it will remove nearly all existing barriers to the free exchange of goods and services between the two countries over a ten-year period. There are exceptions, notably in agriculture and in cultural industries. A resolution mechanism is to be established to cover disputes emanating from the treaty or from future countervailing decisions of either country. The agreement also contains a provision relating to bilateral trade in energy products, and another to capital flows.

Tax reform is another facet of the economic program. Specific plans were announced after much study and consultation. Reform was to proceed in two distinct steps. The first, already in place, dealt with personal and corporate income taxes. The objects were to enhance horizontal equity (treatment across equals); modify vertical equity by increasing the degree of progressivity, particularly toward low-income groups; and enhance neutrality vis-à-vis the tax systems of other countries, particularly the United States.[2] The second step is to be a federal Goods and Services Tax (GST), to come into effect in January 1991.

The Meech Lake Constitutional Accord is not usually thought of as an economic document; yet, should the accord — or a facsimile of it — come into effect, it would have some important implications in this direction. The provisions with respect to the federal spending power and the right of the provinces to opt out of national programs with compensation, subject to certain broad conditions being met, would inevitably affect economic- and social-policy formation. An annual First Ministers' conference on the economy would be formalized as well, guaranteeing provincial input into important economic decisions.

Other measures can be mentioned very briefly. A flurry of interest for an expanded national role in forestry seems to have waned in the face of opposition from the provinces. Regional-development efforts have taken the form of establishing development and diversification funds for the Atlantic and western provinces, but otherwise have stuck to traditional techniques. Established social programs are reputed to be under review with regard to their long-term financial implications, with some major reform proposals expected. The only major new social-policy initiative to date is a proposal for a national day-care system, advanced prior to the 1988 election but apparently abandoned in the 1989 budget.

Taken as a package, these measures constitute a consistent policy agenda, with the twin themes of an increasing reliance on market signals to guide the allocation of resources and a desire to accommodate the diverse regional nature of the Canadian economy and society more formally in the formulation of economic and social policy. Meech Lake is the best example of the latter objective, while all the other measures are representative of the former one. Some initiatives represent explicit attempts to correct for previous policy failures, while others are more obviously geared to meet the challenges of the coming decades. The question is whether the will to reform will overcome the temptation to seek short-term political gain.

Notes

1. Canada, Royal Commission on the Economic Union and Development Prospects for Canada, *Report*, Vol. 3, S61–65.
2. Thomas J. Courchene, "Tax Reform: The Impact on Individuals," in *Tax Reform: Perspectives on the White Paper*, edited by Edward A. Carmichael (Toronto: C.D. Howe Institute, 1988).

Index

Index

To the owner of this book:

We are interested in your reaction to *A History of the Canadian Economy* by Kenneth Norrie and Douglas Owram.

1. What was your reason for using this book?

   ☐ university course
   ☐ college course
   ☐ continuing education course
   ☐ personal interest
   ☐ other (specify)

2. In which school are you enrolled? ______________________

3. Approximately how much of the book did you use?

   ☐ ¼ ☐ ½ ☐ ¾ ☐ all

4. What is the best aspect of the book?

5. Have you any suggestions for improvement?

6. Is there anything that should be added?

Fold here

Business Reply Mail

No Postage Stamp
Necessary if Mailed
in Canada

POSTAGE WILL BE PAID BY
Acquisitions Editor
College Editorial Department
Harcourt Brace Jovanovich, Canada
55 Horner Avenue
Toronto, Ontario
M8Z 9Z9

Tape shut

717042